Information Communication Technologies and the Virtual Public Sphere:

Impacts of Network Structures on Civil Society

Robert Cropf
Saint Louis University, USA

William S. Krummenacher
Saint Louis University, USA

Information Science
REFERENCE

An Imprint of IGI Global

Senior Editorial Director:	Kristin Klinger
Director of Book Publications:	Julia Mosemann
Editorial Director:	Lindsay Johnston
Acquisitions Editor:	Erika Carter
Development Editor:	Michael Killian
Production Coordinator:	Jamie Snavely
Typesetters:	Keith Glazewski, Julia Mosemann, Natalie Pronio, Milan Vracarich, Jr.
Cover Design:	Nick Newcomer

Published in the United States of America by
Information Science Reference (an imprint of IGI Global)
701 E. Chocolate Avenue
Hershey PA 17033
Tel: 717-533-8845
Fax: 717-533-8661
E-mail: cust@igi-global.com
Web site: http://www.igi-global.com/reference

Library of Congress Cataloging-in-Publication Data

Library of Congress Cataloging-in-Publication Data

Information communication technologies and the virtual public sphere :
impact of network structures on civil society / Robert Cropf and William S.
Krummenacher, editors.
      p. cm.
  Includes bibliographical references and index.
  Summary: "This book demonstrates how the virtual public sphere uses
information communications technology to empower ordinary citizens to engage
in effective public discourse and provide the technological means to effect
political change"--Provided by publisher.
  ISBN 978-1-60960-159-1 (hardcover) -- ISBN 978-1-60960-161-4 (ebook)
  1. Internet in public administration. 2. Political
participation--Technological innovations. 3. Information
technology--Political aspects. I. Cropf, Robert A. II. Krummenacher,
William S., 1975-
  JF1525.A8I4675 2011
  303.48'33--dc22
                          2010040834

British Cataloguing in Publication Data
A Cataloguing in Publication record for this book is available from the British Library.

Table of Contents

Preface xii

Acknowledgment xiv

Chapter 1
Introduction 1
Robert Cropf, Saint Louis University, USA
William S. Krummenacher, Saint Louis University, USA

Chapter 2
Deliberative Machines in Techno-Political Arrangements: A Theoretical Discussion 35
Laurence Monnoyer-Smith, University of Technology of Compiègne, France

Chapter 3
Communicative Mechanisms of Governance: E-Democracy and the Architecture of the
Public Sphere 52
Lori Anderson, Radford University, USA
Patrick Bishop, Lancaster University, UK

Chapter 4
Habermas, Networks and Virtual Public Spheres: A Blended Deliberative Model from
Developing Countries 72
Veena V. Raman, Pennsylvania State University, USA

Chapter 5
Issues of Digital Disempowerment and New Media Networking (NMN) in Relation to
E-Government 92
Kenneth L. Hacker, New Mexico State University, USA
Eric L. Morgan, New Mexico State University, USA

Chapter 6

'Videoblogging' Human Rights on YouTube: An Ethical Dilemma 116

    Jacques DM Gimeno, University of Asia and the Pacific, Philippines

    Bradley C. Freeman, Nanyang Technical University, Singapore

Chapter 7

Conceptualizing E-Participation in the Public Sphere 141

    Jenny Backhouse, University of New South Wales, Australia

Chapter 8

An Investigation of the Use of Computer Supported Arguments Visualization for Improving
Public Participation in Legislation Formation 156

    Euripidis Loukis, University of the Aegean, Greece

    Alexander Xenakis, Panteion University, Greece

    Nektaria Tseperli, Kapodistrian University of Athens, Greece

Chapter 9

The Role of Trust in the Global Acceptance of E-Government 173

    John J. Burbridge Jr., Elon University, USA

    Jayoti Das, Elon University, USA

    Cassandra E. DiRienzo, Elon University, USA

Chapter 10

Perspectives on E-Government in Europe 195

    Sylvia Archmann, EIPA – European Institute for Public Administration, The Netherlands

    Just Castillo Iglesias, EIPA – European Institute for Public Administration, The Netherlands

Chapter 11

Exploring the ICT Capabilities of Civil Society in Sub-Saharan Africa: The Zambian Case 207

    Joshua C. Nyirenda, Saint Louis University, USA

Chapter 12

Setting the Foundation for E-Democracy in Botswana: An Exploratory Study of Interventions 229

    Kelvin Joseph Bwalya, University of Johannesburg, South Africa

    Tanya Du Plessis, University of Johannesburg, South Africa

    Chris Rensleigh, University of Johannesburg, South Africa

Chapter 13

Challenges of E-Disclosure in Romanian Public Authorities 242

    Adriana Tiron Tudor, Babes-Bolyai University, Romania

    Adina Simona Popa, University "Eftimie Murgu" of Reşiţa, Romania

    Rodica Gabriela Blidişel, West University from Timisoara, Romania

Chapter 14

Making Room for E-Government through Succession Planning 276

Kim Loutzenhiser, Troy University, USA

Afterword 287

Compilation of References 294

About the Contributors 327

Index 333

Detailed Table of Contents

Preface xii

Acknowledgment xiv

Chapter 1

Introduction 1

Robert Cropf, Saint Louis University, USA

William S. Krummenacher, Saint Louis University, USA

This chapter traces the development of virtual public spheres from civil society to e-Democracy. In this book, we bring together international scholars to analyze the impact of ICT on civil society, in particular, the transition from e-Government to e-Democracy that is facilitated by virtual public spheres. Contributions to this book address several important issues ranging from the conceptual development of virtual public spheres to the challenges facing e-Participation and e-Government efforts. Several contributors to this book touch upon the conditions needed to faciliate e-Democracy and the challenges confronting e-Democracy efforts in developing countries. A little explored area of e-Government, e-Administration, is correctly identified by several chapters as potentially making contributions to e-Democracy and virtual public spheres.

Chapter 2

Deliberative Machines in Techno-political Arrangements: A Theoretical Discussion 35

Laurence Monnoyer-Smith, University of Technology of Compiègne, France

This chapter explores the theoretical consequences of a conception of deliberative devices as a technical mediation, and more specifically how it helps to redraw the frontiers of grassroots participation. To understand the position of technology in deliberation, we must appreciate how the device itself structures the distribution of opportunities for citizens to speak up. The existence of "deliberative machines" gives them a tribunal and a space for interaction that would be difficult to find in real world arenas of public debate. Our theoretical frame is inspired by the French philosophers Foucault and Deleuze and will drive us to question the nature of these "deliberative machines": I will propose to consider them as symptoms of transition between two types of setups, in a context of conflict between conceptions of representation and participation in reflexive democracies.

Chapter 3

Communicative Mechanisms of Governance: E-Democracy and the Architecture of the
Public Sphere 52

    Lori Anderson, Radford University, USA
    Patrick Bishop, Lancaster University, UK

Significant claims have been made that developments in Information Communication Technology (ICT) can lead to e-democracy. This chapter starts with a review of some of these studies of e-government and e-democracy trials. Finding these studies largely unsatisfactory for determining advances in democracy, we then look at the kinds of communication that are needed to facilitate the political conversation of deliberative democracy. In particular, we introduce a communication typology, based on the work of David Bohm, to see how the new technology might be used to shape the architecture of the public sphere to create political conversation.

Chapter 4

Habermas, Networks and Virtual Public Spheres: A Blended Deliberative Model from
Developing Countries 72

    Veena V. Raman, Pennsylvania State University, USA

This chapter examines Habermas' conceptualization of the public sphere as it applies to a non-Western context, in Bangalore City, India. It provides examples of how information and communication technologies are being used to empower ordinary citizens to participate in local governance, though deep digital divides persist. The chapter highlights problematic aspects of using technologies to promote better governance in the face of pervasive asymmetries in access to resources, power to leverage networks, and in levels of civic competencies. Drawing on the capabilities approach, it argues that there is need for a blended model of deliberative 'e-democracy' that does not privilege online venues and interactions, but employs technologies in strategic combinations with existing civic networks to improve governance in developing countries.

Chapter 5

Issues of Digital Disempowerment and New Media Networking (NMN) in Relation to
E-Government 92

    Kenneth L. Hacker, New Mexico State University, USA
    Eric L. Morgan, New Mexico State University, USA

Employing a structurational perspective, this chapter addresses the relationship between political participation, emerging media, new media networking, and e-democracy. While new media networking increases the potential for political participation, depending on various factors such as access, usage and skills, the potential exists for increasing disempowerment as well. The chapter concludes with recommendations for the use of new media networking in ways that enhance e-democracy

Chapter 6
'Videoblogging' Human Rights on YouTube: An Ethical Dilemma.. 116
Jacques DM Gimeno, University of Asia and the Pacific, Philippines
Bradley C. Freeman, Nanyang Technical University, Singapore

This chapter discusses what happens when, instead of co-existing, our online and offline worlds clash. This chapter discusses a fundamental theme of modern human communication that involves a shift from traditional face-to-face interaction to one that is heavily mediated. Specifically, this chapter focuses on the role of different websites in providing a virtual public sphere, one exemplified by YouTube, where anonymity and immediacy greatly influence human communication in ways that may result in either fomenting greater divisions among societies and propagating a culture of carelessness and disregard for human rights or one where human rights abuses are exposed but victims' identities are concealed and carefully protected.

Chapter 7
Conceptualizing E-Participation in the Public Sphere... 141
Jenny Backhouse, University of New South Wales, Australia

This chapter reviews the current understanding of the role of e-participation in democratic processes, in particular emphasizing the deliberative aspects of participatory democracy and the factors that impinge on successful participation initiatives. The chapter concludes that e-participation has a role to play in a modern society where the Internet is increasingly the medium of choice for social communications. However e-participation projects need to be appropriately developed so that they truly engage the citizenry and encourage meaningful participation in deliberative facets of democracy.

Chapter 8
An Investigation of the Use of Computer Supported Arguments Visualization for Supporting
Public Participation in Legislation Formation 156
Euripidis Loukis, University of the Aegean, Greece
Alexander Xenakis, Panteion University, Greece
Nektaria Tseperli, Kapodistrian University of Athens, Greece

Argument Visualization' (CSAV) methods for addressing problems and supporting and enhancing public participation in the legislation formation process. Based on an analysis of this process and its main documents a comprehensive approach to the use of CSAV in the legislation formation process is designed, which covers all its fundamental stages and documents, and assists citizens and civil society groups to participate in it in a meaningful and effective manner with a reasonable amount of effort. It is based on the issue-based information systems (IBIS) framework. Based on the conclusions of this evaluation an enrichment of the IBIS framework has been developed for improving the visualization of the main content (articles) of bills and laws.

Chapter 9

The Role of Trust in the Global Acceptance of E-Government.. 173
John J. Burbridge Jr., Elon University, USA
Jayoti Das, Elon University, USA
Cassandra E. DiRienzo, Elon University, USA

Using cross-country data from 140 countries, this empirical study extends past research by examining the impact of trust on the level of e-government where national diversity is used as a proxy of trust within a nation. The major empirical finding of this research shows that, even after controlling for the level of economic development and other socio-economic factors, trust as measured by ethnic and religious diversity, was a significant factor affecting e-government usage.

Chapter 10

Perspectives on E-Government in Europe 195
Sylvia Archmann, EIPA – European Institute for Public Administration, The Netherlands
Just Castillo Iglesias, EIPA – European Institute for Public Administration, The Netherlands

The e-government scene in the EU is undergoing profound changes. The gradual increase in online availability of services has now reached a point where new challenges are appearing, such as trust-building, increasing citizens' confidence and the use of existing services, as well as the need for new more efficient e-inclusion policies. Citizens of today have new demands which require new responses, also in terms of enhancing the participatory process. ICT and e-government have an important role to play in this respect.

Chapter 11

Exploring the ICT Capabilities of Civil Society in Sub-Saharan Africa: The Zambian Case 207
Joshua C. Nyirenda, Saint Louis University, USA

Civil society is argued to have been the most significant force of many forces that eradicated entrenched authoritarianism in Africa, in the early 1990s, ushering most of these countries to multi-party democracies. With weak economies, civil society faces many challenges in resource mobilization and in mobilizing the masses for national causes. Information communication technologies are increasingly being seen as an aid to the mobilization and organization challenges of civil society. Using eGovernance as a proxy measure for ICT capabilities for civil society, this chapter conducts an exploratory study using secondary baseline data collected by international institutions on Sub Saharan Countries. The relationship between ICT capabilities and the several civil society development indicators (press freedom, civil liberties, and various other variables) is investigated. Later the Nation of Zambia (a country with moderate ICT capabilities in the region) is used for a qualitative case study to explore how ICT capabilities and various contextual issues influence ICT applications by civil society organizations to enhance operational capabilities such as collaboration and mobilization efforts.

Chapter 12

Setting the Foundation for E-Democracy in Botswana: an Exploratory Study of Interventions........ 229

Kelvin Joseph Bwalya, University of Johannesburg, South Africa
Tanya Du Plessis, University of Johannesburg, South Africa
Chris Rensleigh, University of Johannesburg, South Africa

Botswana has started building its e-Democracy institutions as it accords citizens the opportunity to participate in the democratic process using appropriate ICT platforms out of the realization that participatory democracy is crucial in placing a country at a competitive edge in the contemporary global socio-economic value chains. This chapter presents an exploratory study that aims to discuss the different interventions that are being put in place by the Botswana government and its co-operating partners as setting the foundation for implementing full-scale e-Democracy applications such as e-Forums and e-Voting. The chapter also presents obstacles and challenges that have not been met insofar as building virtual public spheres in the realm of participatory e-Democracy in Botswana is concerned. Attention is given to how virtual public spheres should be used as collaboration and networking platforms both in the private and public sectors of Botswana.

Chapter 13

Challenges of E-Disclosure in Romanian Public Authorities 242

Adriana Tiron Tudor, Babes-Bolyai University, Romania
Adina Simona Popa, University "Eftimie Murgu" of Reşiţa, Romania
Rodica Gabriela Blidişel, West University from Timisoara, Romania

There is a growing pressure on governments to broaden the scope of their financial responsibilities from accounting to accountability. Starting from the international context of good corporate governance characteristics, we examine the implication level of the internet in Romanian Local Public Authorities as a tool of transparency improvement for the citizen's use. Due to the pivotal role played by citizens in participatory governance, we analyzed the information disclosed by LPA websites focusing mainly on the financial information, as the financial resources have a special role in the local development and represent the base for a prompt reply to the citizen's needs. The final part proposes a Romanian LPA good e-governance model as well as e-disclosure improvements for citizen's trust in LPA information.

Chapter 14

Making Room for E-Government through Succession Planning 276

Kim Loutzenhiser, Troy University, USA

The rush to have needed technologies has outpaced recruitment and training strategies to manage the technology infrastructure that makes e-Government work. The infrastructure of e-Government includes concepts tied to the provision of a seamless flow of services, logical one-stop-shops, efficiency and an ability to do more with less. These concepts, however, will not support e-Government indefinitely without adequate succession planning. The succession planning for this year and beyond must include training, maintaining and transitioning employees in a world where technical competencies need to be addressed and citizens clamor for more direct involvement. Succession planning, more than any other tool, can tap into the diversity pipeline, something that could narrow the digital divide. Succession planning can address the benchmark strength in human resource capacity tied to e-Government. The thrust of e-Government requires a closer look at employees and the kind of talent needed to communicate through technology in a way that is usable, helpful and easy.

Afterword 287

Compilation of References 294

About the Contributors 327

Index 333

Preface

The chief objective of this book is to assist the lay reader in understanding the phenomenon of digital democracy that is occurring around the world. Information and communication technology (ICT) has the tremendous potential to alter in significant ways how we govern ourselves and engage in political activities. Facilitating citizen access and participation in governance and policy making has been part of the appeal of ICT to forward-thinking people, both inside and outside governments, ever since the very first personal computers were introduced publicly. Many governments, however, use e-government—in some cases quite heavily—to pursue a "services first, democracy later" approach (Clift 2003, para. 21). Indeed, the democratic aspects tend to be ignored or downplayed by governments, which more frequently focus on technology as a means to facilitate the efficient delivery of services. However, as e-government has taken root all over, more and more societies clamor for the next stage—the transition to e-democracy.

Another important objective of the book is to introduce the reader to a useful framework for understanding the diverse patterns of e-democracy development around the world. In this regard, we draw on the public sphere theory of Jurgen Habermas in order to make sense of the plethora of virtual public fora that have been making vital contributions to e-democracy. In the course of this exploration we ask questions such as: What is different about ICT-mediated political discourse? How can government and civil society work together to develop effective virtual town halls? What are some of the possible pitfalls one is likely to encounter along the way to e-democracy, and how might these be best avoided? Is e-democracy possible in developing countries and under what conditions? These are some of the questions that are raised and answered in the book.

Finally, the book's last objective is to provide examples of effective virtual public spheres based on such efforts throughout the world. In many chapters, the authors provide cases of successful deliberative democracy online experiments, which they analyze for their efficacy, and which will provide models of online public spheres that should prove useful to students and activists.

Simply stated, the book's mission is to provide the most up-to-date information on an important development in the use of ICT in politics by government and civil society: The widespread proliferation of virtual public spheres. Although its focus is largely on developed countries, it should also prove valuable to users in developing countries as well. Indeed, a few of the chapters have been written about the experience of developing countries in moving towards e-government and e-democracy. The book strives to be exhaustive in its coverage, but at the same time, readable. As much as possible, the use of specialized jargon has been avoided or defined within the text. In short, the editors' objective is nothing short of making this the most up-to-date and readable book on virtual public spheres currently available to readers. Furthermore, we attempt to bridge the gap that currently exists between the more theoretical discussions of deliberative democracy online that is found, mostly in scholarly books and journals, and the practical reports, mostly on the World Wide Web, of state-civil society net experiments.

Up to now, there has been very little written exclusively on the role of deliberative forums in e-democracy and few attempts to summarize, interpret, and understand international examples of virtual public spheres. This book fills the gap with both theoretical and empirical treatments of the subject. It is our hope that readers will find this book a useful guide to an important political development on the Internet.

Robert Cropf
Saint Louis University, USA

William S. Krummenacher
Saint Louis University, USA

Acknowledgment

The editors would like to express their gratitude to numerous individuals without whom this project would never be completed. We thank our chapter authors for their valuable contributions to this book. Next we express our thanks to the Editorial Advisory Board for their invaluable assistance. The reviewers deserve our heartfelt thanks as well. Our development editors at IGI Global proved to be most helpful, and we appreciate their prompt responses to our frequent queries. A special word of thanks also goes to our graduate assistant, Paul Woodruff, who provided us with excellent research at the beginning stages. Last but not least, we especially thank our families—Gail, Jeremy, and Hannah for Bob, and Amie for Scott—for putting up with late nights and weekends working on the book.

Robert Cropf
Saint Louis University, USA

William S. Krummenacher
Saint Louis University, USA

Chapter 1
Introduction

Robert Cropf
Saint Louis University, USA

William S. Krummenacher
Saint Louis University, USA

ABSTRACT

As the second decade of the twenty-first century begins, information and communication technology has brought about significant changes in the way that people participate in political discourse and engage in civil society. This has led to a surge in scholarly interest in virtual public spheres, or the deployment of network structures to advance public discourse with the goal to influence political outcomes. This book brings together international scholars to analyze the impact of ICT on civil society, and in particular, the transition from e-government to e-democracy that is facilitated by virtual public spheres. Contributions to this book address several important issues ranging from the conceptual development of virtual public spheres to the challenges facing e-participation and e-government efforts. Several contributors to this book touch upon the conditions needed to facilitate e-democracy and the challenges confronting e-democracy efforts in developing countries. A little explored area of e-government, e-administration, is correctly identified by several chapters as potentially making contributions to e-democracy and virtual public spheres.

INTRODUCTION

The first decade of the twenty-first century has seen the rapid infiltration of new media applications such as Facebook, Twitter, LinkedIn, MySpace and many others into the mainstream of society. The recent events in the middle east are a powerful indication of the power of social media to effect social and political change. These applications are just the most recent examples of information and communication technologies (ICT) which have been used to connect people on an unprecedented global scale. Connecting on this scale and in this manner, a recent development in human history, allows individuals to send and receive information and communicate any time

DOI: 10.4018/978-1-60960-159-1.ch001

and anywhere. This ability to bring vast numbers of people together and create online communities has led some to believe that ICT and the Internet can be used to revitalize government and politics through the creation of virtual public spheres. The offline public sphere enables discourse that is both critical-rational (see below) and politically influential (Calhoun 1993). The virtual public sphere represents a singular opportunity for the significant empowerment of large numbers of people through the creation of a new type of social space; an environment totally created by interactive technologies where masses of people engage in political, social and economic issues; and one designed to foster greater public deliberation in government and policy-making. These are electronic meeting places where individuals of all races, genders, religions and social classes can come together and deliberate on matters of vital interest to society. Moreover, these virtual townhalls are not physically rooted in specific geographical locations, which characterized previous town halls; they encompass a virtually unlimited physical area; one where anyone taking an interest in a particular issue or policy question can join in the discussion. The virtual public sphere thus has the potential to significantly augment civil society and contribute to building e-democracy in the truest sense.

The Public Sphere from the Polis to E-Democracy

The concept of the public sphere is deeply rooted in the Western political and sociological traditions[1]. The virtual public sphere is simply a "reboot" of an old idea. Furthermore, civil society, which contributes significantly to the public sphere, also has a venerable tradition that requires some explication before we can begin our discussion of digital democracy. Calhoun (1993) argues that "Civil society and public sphere are not precisely equivalent concepts" (p. 269). He sums up the crucial relationship between the two concepts as

one where a successful public sphere "depends on favorable organization of civil society" (p.276). What follows in the rest of this section therefore is a definition of the term and a critical examination of different models of civil society throughout modern times.

The Western conception of civil society has changed dramatically; for example, in ancient times, it was believed that there was no clear-cut distinction between the state and society. However, in modern times there has been a tendency to draw a sharp line between the public and private aspects of society, particularly in the United States and the United Kingdom. Moreover, since the advent of modern industrial capitalism, there has been the view of the social realm as being also separate from the realm of commercial enterprise. Virtual public spheres thus take shape in a context where there is general agreement that an important conceptual distinction can be drawn between the public sphere and the sphere of state authority on the one hand and the sphere of commercial affairs on the other. In addition, until very recently, this domain has been physically constrained; in other words, for each nation there was one and only one civil society. In the boundary-less universe of cyberspace, however, civil society extends, in theory, beyond national borders to create a truly global public sphere.

Civil society has been defined as "the arena of uncoerced, collective action around shared interests, purposes and values. Therefore, as the arena of social life that consists primarily of voluntary relations and encompasses all forms of non-coerced individual participation in public life. Thus consisting of organizations such as charities, non-governmental organizations (NGOs), community groups, women's organizations, faith-based organizations, professional associations, trade unions, self-help groups, social movements, business associations, and political and social advocacy groups" (London School of Economics Centre for Civil Society 2004, Definition of Civil Society section) Due to its voluntary nature, informal bonds hold the public sphere together According to scholars, a key indicator of the strength of civil society is the robust presence of social capital or social connections of richness and depth. Thus, as far back as the Greek city-state, the vitality of the polity depended to a large extent on the strength of the social bonds between its citizens. Social ties and the public sphere remain closely intertwined according to contemporary theorists; these linkages are generally characterized as creating a purposeful community of shared values. According to one author:

It is a coming together of individuals seeking political stability in their search for the Good Life, but also allowing for diversity and tolerance both within the community and in relation to others. It is a modern political ideal (Setianto, 2007).

Technology has been criticized for being disruptive of these close social ties in some accounts (Heim, 1993; Fukuyama, 1999; Nie & Erbring 2000). Nonetheless, technology has its advocates who argue that the many-to-many, decentralized and non-hierarchical social interactions found on the Internet is inherently more democratic than the one-to-many, centralized and hierarchical broadcast technologies; and thus offers a new model for the flow of power in society, that is, e-democracy. New social media, the Web, cell phones, text messaging, blogs, etc., therefore, represent a radical departure from the traditional means of communication within and between the masses and social institutions. E-democracy proponents point to the different ways that the Internet and, more generally, ICT are reshaping our views of government and political participation. To take one recent example, the Obama presidential campaign's adept use of new media, which has re-wrote many of the rules by which modern-day political campaigns are waged.

Despite the changes wrought by new technologies, the virtual public sphere still owes much to earlier conceptions of the public sphere. In our discussion, although we presume that the public sphere depends to a significant extent on civil society, as with Calhoun (1993) we believe that they are not at all synonymous. The public sphere is a space wherein critical-rational dialogue between citizens can occur regarding political issues or governance matters. Civil society, however, makes a necessary contribution to the dialogue within the public sphere, whether traditional, i.e., offline or virtual, and therefore shapes the public sphere in critical ways. Therefore, in the section below we provide an overview of the evolution of thinking regarding civil society and the public sphere beginning with precursors from the Enlightenment and continuing to Jurgen Habermas in the present-day. This discussion, although brief, illustrates significant examples of theories of civil society and sets a context for our examination of e-democracy and the virtual public sphere to follow.

Models of Civil Society

As noted earlier, virtual public spheres are the heirs to an intellectual tradition going back to the ancient Greeks and their polis or city-state, in which citizens tried to harmonize their individual needs with those of the society's. In other words, according to the Greeks, there should be no practical difference between the demands of society and the demands of the political system on the individual. Plato's Good Citizen, for example, is one who participates in political activity and places the Greater Good before his own self-interest (Brown, 2009). Aristotle also viewed the polis as society's chief organizing principle and did not recognize any distinction between the state and rest of society. A natural extension of this view is, "Even if the end is the same for an individual and for a city-state, that of the city-state seems at any rate greater and more complete to attain and preserve. For although it is worthy to attain it for only an individual, it is nobler and more divine to do so for a nation or city-state." (Aristotle in Miller

2010, Political Science in General section). Thus the earliest conceptions of society were strongly state-centric in their orientation.

During the Enlightenment period (roughly the sixteenth through the eighteenth centuries in Western Europe), a view evolved which argued that society came about as the result of a social contract, one which allowed civilization to emerge out of the savagary prevailing in the state of nature. Thus civil society was an organic development that marked the transition from a barbaric state of affairs to one of government and laws. The Englishman, Thomas Hobbes, for example, viewed the state as the creation of civil society and the one institution that can prevent it from falling back into the anarchic conditions of the state of nature(O'Brien, 1999, Age of Reasoning section). For his countryman, John Locke, however, the central concern was less about the anarchy of the struggle of all against all and more about a state that threatened the rights of society (O'Brien, 1999, Age of Reasoning section). According to Locke, legitimate political authority grows out of the freedom to form associations (O'Brien, 1999, Age of Reasoning section). For Locke, civil society is both a precursor to the state (like Hobbes) and an effective counterbalance against overreaching government (unlike Hobbes). For the German, Immaunuel Kant, civil society is the source of laws, which acts as the bulwark that prevents individual rights from being trampled on. Furthermore, Kant regarded civil society as the place in which the private interests can be reconciled with the universal principle which treats individuals as ends in themselves and not merely as means to other ends (Kant in Calabrese 2004, 318).Thus for Enlightenment thinkers, the state and civil society are distinct entities, with the latter jealously guarding its independence from the former.

Modern conceptualizations of civil society mark a further departure with regard to the relationship between the state sphere, the commercial sphere and the private sphere. Whereas the En-lightenment philosophers developed the notion of civil society as independent of the state by the 19th and 20th centuries, there occurs the further division of the public sphere from both the state and the economy. In large part, this split was the intellectual community's response to the rise of modern industrial capitalism and its resulting social changes. As a result of these changes, there was the increasing sense that the democratization of Western society depended on the vitality of civil society.

At the beginning of the modern period, the work of the 19th century Frenchman, Alexis de Tocqueville represented a bridge from the civil society theories of the Enlightenment to the theories of Hegel and Marx. Based on his observations of American life, Tocqueville argued that strong voluntary associations, particularly political ones, helped to buttress democratic government from the more destructive forces of modern society. Civil society, he believed, helps to transmit the core values and norms of democracy to the people by serving as the "great free schools of democracy" (Foley & Edwards 1996, p.44). According to Tocqueville, political association actually form the core of civil society rather than the other way around: "one may think of political associations as great free schools to which all citizens come to be taught the general theory of association" (ibid).

The modern ideal of civil society evolved over the next two centuries, essentially, as a response to the growth of capitalism, which led to the compelling need for society to come to grips with the increasing dominance of the modern economy and industrial system. Thus, a number of significant theories emphasized the central importance of economic or historical forces in shaping society. G.W.F. Hegel distinguished between the state and civil society in his *The Philosophy of Right*. Hegel did not assume, however, that all the interactions in civil society would be peaceful; capitalism breeds conflicts and inequalities which must be dealt with by the state. Hegel, moreover, views the state as representing the highest ethical ideal, and saw in this the unfolding of historical forces, thereby assigning the process an inevitability. Others such as Marx were less optimistic with regard to civil society's capacity to withstand capitalism's onslaught. According to Marx, civil society was the arena where conflicts between capitalist class and the working class took place. In contrast to Hegel, Marx did not think the state represented the highest good in society, rather he believed that the state governed on behalf of the capitalists.

The German political philosopher, Jürgen Habermas (1989, 1996), is credited with introducing the concept of the public sphere as a distinct domain existing outside the social spaces dominated by private family relations, the economic exchange relations of business and commerce, and the bureaucratic relations of the State. In his conceptualization, the public sphere serves as a forum for deliberation about politics and civic affairs. In this regard, the public sphere promotes the core individual rights that lie at the heart of modern liberal democracies, including the freedoms of speech, press, assembly and communication, and 'privacy rights' (Cohen and Arato 1992, 211). These freedoms are needed to ensure society's autonomy from the state. Thus, for Habermas, the public sphere can be succinctly defined as a domain of social relations that exist outside of the roles, duties and constraints established by government, the marketplace, and kinship ties.

Habermas conceived of the public sphere as both descriptive of a specific historical era and also as an ideal type. Historically, what Habermas refers to as the bourgeois public sphere was an outgrowth of the 18th century Enlightenment in Europe, blossoming in the cafes of England and salons of France, which became the centers of enlightened public opinion regarding art and politics. However, the bourgeois public sphere went into decline in the 19th century as a result of the increasing domination of the capitalist economy, which eventually gave rise to the mass broadcasting media that effectively transformed a literate and deliberative public into today's disengaged consumers of politics, art and culture (Keane, 1998, p. 160). As an ideal type, Habermas' public sphere refers to a commons area in which private citizens can engage in open deliberation regarding politics and other civic matters in an environment relatively free of economic and social class distinctions.

In terms of thinking about civil society, there has been an evolution from the polis (small, homogeneous, personal, state- and ethno-centric) to the modern (large, heterogeneous, impersonal, multi-ethnic and non-state-centered). Along the way, civil society has emerged as a separate and distinct entity, one viewed as a counterpart to, and check on, the power of both the state and marketplace. The emergence of global civil society, still in its initial phases, raises some important questions and issues that will increasingly dominate the political discussions of this century, which we will discuss in some detail in the next section. One can conclude from our previous discussion the continuing strength of the idea of civil society; this concept, often regarded as utopian in its aspirations, still has the intellectual authority to motivate people around the world to renew political institutions and create new ones in response to changing historical conditions and social forces. As an enduring ideal it is as old as the Greek polis and as contemporary as e-democracy.

E-Democracy

In the previous section, we examined the idea of the public sphere as it has evolved up to this point in history. We analyze in this section more recent work on the public sphere which seeks to adapt it to twenty-first century political and economic conditions and emerging social realities. As ICT use has become more commonplace throughout the developed and developing world, more researchers and theorists regard it as an effective tool to facilitate the transition to e-democracy. The discussion in this section covers a variety of different perspectives coming from a diverse range of research examining e-democracy developments throughout the world. In this section our attention is focused on two overarching themes: first, theoretical explanations and models of virtual public spheres; second, making the transition from e-government to e-democracy, which focuses primarily on issues revolving around structural opportunities and challenges surrounding participation and engagement in the political and governance processes.

For the first theme, we analyze theoretical models that explain how ICT can contribute to virtual public spheres and ultimately to the improvement of democratic government. While ICT can lead to increases in the amount of information and interactions in society, in general the quality of either one has not always been of a consistently high level to sustain a new vision of online civil society. The models discussed below address the issue of what the best ways are to create virtual public spheres to help effect eventual political change. Next we examine research that focuses on the structural aspects (both institutional and technological) of making the transition from e-government to e-democracy. Current structural challenges which need to be overcome include barriers to access (that is, the digital divide), inadequate resources, citizen satisfaction with e-government, social characteristics of the country, and others described in detail below. Finally, we conclude this introductory essay with two brief case studies of current examples of virtual public spheres.

Theoretical Models of Virtual Public Spheres

As noted above, researchers and theorists have begun incorporating the scholarship on ICT into broader notions of civil society. They draw from a well-developed philosophical articulation of the traditional public sphere to address ICT's many transformative effects. ICT scholars have developed a number of ways to conceptualize and characterize virtual public spheres and their overall contribution to democracy.

The literature dealing with ICT-mediated public spheres has grown rapidly in the past decade. In early theoretical work on the virtual public sphere, many recognized the seemingly endless potential of ICT. Some believed ICT-mediated discourse was a way to remedy the problems with the traditional public sphere. This group of scholars set out to frame an ideal type for virtual public spheres and their research offered practical examples that approximated the ideal. Others noted ICT's darker side. They pointed to ICT's inability to improve public discourse and challenged the notion that ICT was inherently democratic. More recent scholarship has begun to incorporate elements of both views, highlighting ICT's possible contribution to democracy while recognizing the hazards associated with the virtual world.

Scholars who believe that ICT has the potential to revitalize the public sphere make a crucial contribution to the literature. This work is both normative in its attempt to create a vision for ICT's contribution to democracy and empirical in its assessment of progress toward that goal. Moreover, this line of scholarship demonstrates the way ICT contributes to a transformation of the traditional public sphere. Many of these theorists approach their work by drawing upon the philosophical writings of Jurgen Habermas mentioned in the previous section. Poor (2004), for example, uses Habermas to create a framework for analyzing virtual public spheres that meet the following criteria:

"1. Public spheres are spaces of discourse, often mediated.
2. Public spheres often allow for new, previously excluded, discussants.
3. Issues discussed are often political in nature.
4. Ideas are judged by their merit, not by the standing of the speaker."

Others have used one or more elements of Habermas' work to identify and assess the quality of discursive spaces online (Dahlberg, 2001; Papacharissi, 2002). Indeed, the "new space" offered by ICT mediation has prompted intense speculation about whether or not a new type of public sphere has truly emerged with the use of ICT. A number of scholars point out that the new spaces for dialogue provided by ICT are not equal to the development of a new public sphere because there is no guarantee of rational deliberation. As Papacharissi (2002, p. 11) puts it, "a virtual space enhances discussion; a virtual sphere enhances democracy." Indeed, some critics argue that the ICT-mediated environment produces the wrong set of conditions for incubating a genuine public sphere, a point which we return to later.

Those optimistic about the potential of ICT-mediated discourse see advanced technology as democratizing speech in itself. They see ICT as creating a organic, evolving public square that spans geographic boundaries and paves the way for the creation of a global public sphere. In this conception, ICT provides citizens with a means to access a vast array of information, opinions and ideas. Information is decentralized and accessible to a broad range of individuals. In contrast to the broadcast mass media, the Internet makes accessible more information to a greater number of people with no centralized control dictating the source. This wider array of sources produces an instrument of information and communication heretofore unknown in history. The shift away from elite control over information dissemination is viewed as both empowering and potentially transformative. ICT enables new forms of self-expression and engagement. As Froomkin (2004) notes, "they begin to form new communities of discourse," which "can grow into forces capable of influencing the public sphere". New technologies such as blogs and wikis help foster these new communities of discourse and offer the possibility of meeting some of the stringent demands of discourse set forth by Habermas.

Similarly, others (e.g., Dahlberg 2001; Katz, 1997) find that online discourse involves encounters with multiple opinions and ideas. They point out the way online discourse meets the more stringent demands of critical-reflexive debate. Those who argue that one or many public spheres exist in the virtual world have begun to develop a set of criteria which these new deliberative spaces must meet in order to be considered in some ways equivalent to their offline counterparts. Their work shows that, to a greater or lesser extent, public spheres can indeed make up part of the virtual world. Dahlberg (2001, 2004), for one, uses Habermas' original conception of the public sphere to develop six criteria for online public spheres (see Table 1). These criteria include: autonomy from state and economic power; exchange and critique of moral-practical validity claims; reflexivity; ideal role-taking; sincerity; and discursive inclusion and equality. Poor (2004), identifies four essential elements that distinguish virtual public spheres from other ICT-mediated spaces. Such spaces must be spaces of discourse; allow for new, previously excluded, discussants; include discussion of political topics and judge ideas by their merit, not by the standing of the speaker.

The requirements are designed to foster an environment in which authentic discourse regarding public issues can occur, whether online or offline. A cursory glance of the list, however, indicates that the criteria might be difficult to achieve under normal conditions. For example, the sincerity requirement demands that participants refrain from engaging in strategic behavior during discourse. Acting strategically, however, might affect the outcome of an issue in a manner that materially benefits one side over the other. In other words, the requirement stipulates that the parties involved make every effort at full disclosure even though that might not be in the best interest of one or the other party. Additionally, the criteria are normative in nature and are not practicably enforceable. The requirements are expectations of behavior which if carried out

7

Table 1. Ideal Requirements of Public Sphere Discourse

Speech Requirement	Key Characteristics
Deliberation of reasoned moral-practical Validity claims	Reciprocal critique of value positions backed by reasoned arguments and not simply asserted
Reflexivity	Critical self-examination of participants' cultural values, assumptions and interests; scrutiny of larger social context
Ideal role taking	Understanding an argument from the other's perspective; commitment to discourse; respectful listening
Sincerity	Obligation to total information disclosure relevant to issue under consideration; participants must disclose their intentions, interests, needs and desires regarding issue at hand
Discursive inclusion and equality	All participants have the equal right to make or challenge any assertion related to any issue under consideration
Autonomy from state and economic power	Discourse should be free of commercial or governmental influence

Source: Adapted from Dahlberg (2001)

would result in the ideal speech situation that Habermas describes. However, what incentives exist for participants to commit themselves to acts that may not be reciprocated by the other side? These types of questions have no easy answers in either the offline or online worlds.

Dahlberg's (2001) and Poor's (2004) work establishes a set of requirements for the online public sphere. Both authors, drawing from Habermas, focus on the requirements for civic discourse presented by the "new spaces" of the Internet. Admittedly, their criteria constitute a very stringent set of requirements. Dahlberg notes that, based on the research, only the first item, exchange and critique of political claims, can be said to be truly prevalent in online deliberations. Indeed, it is arguable that reasoned critique of opposing value positions is actually the norm in ICT-mediated political discourse. The bulk of political discussion on the Internet is more likely to resemble the echo chamber model of like-minded people talking to each other rather than a reasoned debate involving two sides of an issue (Sunstein 2002; Leadbeater, 2007). Nonetheless, there is a growing body of evidence that ICT mediation provides better overall conditions for achieving these ideal discourse requirements than does the current-day mass media. Dahlberg and others cite

successful examples of democratic deliberation on the Internet, which can serve as benchmarks for the online public spheres we discuss later in this book. Minnesota E-democracy, the creation of political activists in the state, is an example of an online experiment in democratic discourse, which has managed to survive and even prosper from the early days of the World Wide Web[2]. In addition, at the end of this chapter, we have brief case studies of two different types of virtual public spheres. One is the product of a non-profit agency in the UK, the Hansard Society, with a long history of providing political and civic education. The other represents the efforts of a more recent non-profit organization in the US, AmericaSpeaks, which is involved with a similar type of civic engagement promotion over issues of national import.

According to Dahlberg, ICT-mediated discourse can approach the Habermasian ideal public sphere through careful attention to issues such as formal rules and guidelines governing discussion and continuous oversight to enforce those regulations. For example, he makes note of "guidelines imploring participants to present their positions carefully, listen to others, and take time to reply." With respect to sincerity, he points out that the forums on Minnesota E-democracy require all participants to use their real names, e-mail address

Table 2. Comparison of Virtual and Traditional Public Spheres

Versions of the Public Sphere	Advantages	Disadvantages
Traditional	• *Face-to-face interaction* – allows all elements of human expression including verbal and non-verbal cues • *Can build place-based and individual capacity*	• *Distance* – limits participation to specific geographic places of interaction • *Resources* - requires a significant commitment of time and resources
Virtual	• *Geographically unconfined* – participants can interact across anywhere • *Greater information* – ICT can harness large volumes of content quickly • *No timing requirement* – users can engage at different times • *Reduces the costs of communication*	• *Anonymity* – user identities can reduce the potential for authentic online public discourse • *Polarization* – users gather into like-minded groups • *"Flaming"* – users engage in conflict oriented communication

and city of residence on every posting. The forum's rules explicitly prohibit the use of pseudonyms and anonymous postings of any kind[3]. Requiring a respectful attitude on the part of the participants is another effort to reduce or eliminate the amount of flaming that would normally be found on a political discussion website.

Minnesota E-democracy, therefore, explicitly recognizes and has mechanisms in place to overcome the disadvantages identified in Table 2. In fact, according to Dahlberg, the only serious threat to online democratic discourse is the question of guaranteeing freedom from both state and economic power. In the context of non-democratic political regimes such as China the threat from the government is obvious. However, in democratic societies the potential for government to impinge on Internet freedom is less of a threat than the gradual crowding-out effect caused by commerce. He observes that online democratic deliberation is in danger of being overwhelmed by commercial interests and privatized forms of user participation, by which he presumably means online gaming and the interaction found in virtual worlds such as Second Life. In the end, in spite of the generally optimistic findings of his research, Dahlberg offers a deeply pessimistic view of the future of online deliberative democracy. He avers that the virtual public sphere is in danger of following Habermas' bourgeois public sphere into

decline and in large part for the same reason: The increasing commercialization and privatization of deliberative space.

Setting aside for a time the issue of requirements for a successful discursive space, another practical issue deals with the question of whether there are multiple spheres emerging online rather than a singular, homogeneous public sphere (Ansen and Brouwer, 2001; Dahlgren, 2001; Fraser, 1992). Indeed, an argument can be made that at least two types of online or virtual public spheres are emerging and that each one contributes to offline democratic culture in specific ways. Before turning to these types, however, it is important to first address the differences between online and offline public spheres and the potential and limits of the online public sphere.

Virtual vs. Traditional Public Spheres

In what ways do the new spaces created by ICT-mediated discourse represent a new form of public sphere? How do they compare to the standard conception of the public sphere? Answering both questions enables us to address the problem of singular versus multiple virtual public spheres. Traditional forms of civic engagement are bound by time, space and resource constraints; while ICT allows for asynchronic, geographically unconfined interaction, which are comparatively lower-cost in terms of material and immaterial resources than previous forms of interaction. Traditionally, a public forum requires an actual physical space within easy travelling distance of the participants who then had to have the means and the motivation to attend. ICT-mediated discursive environments significantly reduce or eliminate the need for a physical location commodious enough to contain all of the participants; there is no travel involved; and therefore there is no need to expend time and money in travelling to and from the public meeting. From at least an economic perspective, lower costs of participation would lead naturally to an increase in demand; the closer costs approach zero the greater the number of individuals who would be likely to engage in online civic deliberation subject to the constraints of time, personal attention and interest levels, etc. To date, however, optimism about the considerable potential of online public spheres has greatly outpaced the empirical findings of actual e-democracy websites (Albrecht, 2006). As technological advances continue to lower costs of participation, the last barriers to full participation will be the constraints mentioned above. Before these final barriers can fall, however, the advantages of online public spheres must be leveraged to their maximum potential. It is only then that a sizable proportion of the citizenry will recognize the benefits of ICT-mediated discourse as a means to strengthen civil society.

Some scholars point to ICT-mediated discourse as a means to fundamentally remake democratic politics at the grassroots level. Shirky (2008), for example, promotes the use of the Internet to aid in grassroots organizing for the renewal of democratic politics. The Internet can be used to revitalize offline political activism as well as provide a means for online engagement. The connection between virtual and traditional public spheres is also underscored by a number of ICT scholars. AmericaSpeaks, discussed later in this book, is just one example of the way traditional public spheres are using ICT to enhance public debate.

As the preceding discussion indicates, both virtual and traditional public spheres offer advantages and disadvantages for civic engagement. Table 2 highlights this comparison between the online and offline public sphere. It is important to note that this characterization offers only a stylized depiction of the overall body of work in this area. As research on the virtual public sphere expands, components of this framework will need to be expanded and refined.

Many of digital deliberation's drawbacks are broadly related to the ability of users to conceal their true identities online and to channel their attention to items of their choosing. Anonymity on the Internet brings to mind the humorous New Yorker cartoon punch line "On the Internet no one knows you're a dog." Users can choose how much or how little of their actual personal identity they wish to reveal. While in itself this poses no problem and, indeed may confer certain real benefits; nevertheless, it raises issues that relate to the requirements of sincerity and respectful dialogue in Table 2. For instance, Dahlberg (2001) asserts that in democratic discourse either online or offline, "Each participant must make a sincere effort to provide all information relevant to the particular problem under consideration, including information regarding intentions, interests, needs and desires." (p.623) Thus the intentional or unintentional concealment of one's true identity, undermines all participants' efforts to engage in sincere discourse, which may lead to the erosion of trust between them. Furthermore, Dahlberg maintains that one of the characteristics of "ideal role taking," another essential component of democratic dialogue, involves "respectful dialogue." The conferral of anonymity online means that there are few consequences for rude or disrespectful behavior towards others, a phenomenon so common on the Internet that it has its own nickname, "flaming." It is not our intent to counter each of these challenges to virtual public spheres; several writers have ably rejected these threats as inevitably detrimental to ICT-mediated discourse (see, for example Dahlberg [2001] and Benkler [2006]). However, it suffices to note here, that these difficulties are not insurmountable but they should be recognized and dealt with.

As a counterpoint to this work, an opposing stream of thought asserts that the technologies mentioned above contribute to the erosion of civil society and lead to greater social fragmentation, both online and offline. ICT-mediated discourse, from this perspective, tends to exacerbate existing social inequalities and serves to further commodify everyday life. Furthermore, marginalized groups are placed at even greater disadvantage as the social hierarchy is reproduced online and the gap (digital divide) between those who have access to ICT and those who do not threatens to harm democratic life online. According to this view, the tendency toward fragmentation leads to the loss of the commonality which is thought to be essential to the public sphere.

That there is a long running debate between those who argue that the online environment is not conducive to public spheres and those who argue that one or many online public sphere(s) exist cannot be denied. Those who argue against an online public sphere base their critiques on several attributes or effects of ICT mediation. For example, some emphasize the tendency toward fragmentation that is characteristic of ICT-mediated discourse. Gitlin (1998), to take one example, argues that the online environment is producing isolated "sphericules" that erode common discourse rather than creating a discursive space which approximates a Habermasian public sphere. Moreover, it is highly unlikely in light of the nature of ICT mediation, that there would be a monolithic online culture which would engender such a common discourse. Nevertheless, the important question is whether the lack of a cohesive Internet culture jeopardizes efforts at creating online spaces that contain a critical mass of the requirements for a Habermasian public sphere.

Polarization is often remarked upon by critics as a glaring example of a downside of ICT-mediated discourse in fostering genuine public engagement and political deliberation. Networked environments allow individuals to manufacture their own virtual worlds, which they can then use to exclude all others who are unlike themselves or do not share common interests. This phenomenon is similar to the "echo chamber" effect that some observers have commented on (e.g., Leadbeater, 2007). The major drawback of insularity and the echo chamber effect for the creation of genuine public spheres is that it hampers authentic dialogue and debate as people tend to surround themselves online with others who are of like-mind. The community of interest so formed is narrow and frequently at odds with the interests of the broader community. Thus unless genuine differences of opinion can occur--indeed, are encouraged to occur--online discussions can quickly become one-sided and the Internet an incubator for social and political conformity and extremism. Instead of an opportunity for creative tension and disagreement which can lead to innovative solutions to social problems, the Web can inculcate a pernicious form of group-think that can further fragment society into narrower and narrower interest groups. A related point raised by Sunstein (2001) is that the very omnipresence of overwhelming amounts of information and the lack of anything like filters on the Internet will bring about a decline in rational public discourse. This criticism has been forcefully rebutted by the work of Benkler (2006) and Anderson (2008) who counter that "the wisdom of crowds" as reflected in recommendations, incoming links on websites and blogs, and playlists serve as effective filters for the vast majority of Internet users.

Yet another perspective, based in part on the growing empirical literature on ICT-mediated discourse and civic engagement, takes a third approach. On the one hand, ICT-mediation may indeed produce a number of negative impacts on online public discourse. On the other hand, ICT also brings into being a number of tools, opportunities and strategies that can be used to address deficiencies in current democratic discursive practices. From this perspective, ICT-mediated discourse is one of a larger set of interactive tools, participatory processes and political institutions that shape the current public debate. This perspective avoids sweeping generalizations concerning ICT use and civil society and instead emphasizes the highly contextual and dependent nature of online public spheres. In other words, online public spheres are embedded in a particular political culture and are therefore bound by a set of social values, political principles and cultural attitudes regarding the efficacy of citizen participation in the governance process. The exact forms that ICT-mediated political discourse will take and its outcomes on the policymaking process ultimately depend more on the national political culture than on technology. At the same time, however, ICT-mediated discourse offers a number of advantages/ disadvantages beyond what is possible with the channels for public discussion provided by the mass broadcast media which has long dominated Western societies. Indeed, many of the chapters in this book (see Monnoyer-Smith, etc) highlight the importance such differences and demonstrate how ICT creates new possibilities and challenges.

In the realm of political theory, the nexus of civil society and ICT has been elucidated by contemporary authors such as Robert Putnam (2000) and Yoshai Benkler (2006). Efforts to link communication technologies, which has the capacity to enhance communication between individuals and groups, and civil society, which provide them with the means to share their experience and create knowledge together, date to the dawn of the personal computer revolution. Putnam believes that ICT is a valuable tool in the struggle to restore civil society to its former vitality although he seriously doubts the claims of some of technology's most fervent supporters (Putnam, 2000, p.166). Moreover, Putnam is more than a little ambivalent when it comes to technology in general. On the one hand, he is critical of the entertainment uses of the Internet because, like television, it effectively

serves to isolate and privatize leisure time. Putnam argues that online entertainment, even more than television, promotes individualized, interactive experiences that occur primarily in private, and therefore hinder social connectedness and eventually may come to replace it. On the other hand, he recognizes the following strengths of ICT: 1) the ability of individuals to find and communicate with others who share their interests; 2) more egalitarian discourse practices than in non-computer mediated interactions; and 3) more cost-effective over long distances. Nonetheless, Putnam sounds a note of caution by asserting that the non-verbal cues that are a normal part of everyday real-world interactions are missing from computer-mediated interactions resulting in a potential degradation of social capital. Putnam's response to proponents of virtual community such as Howard Rheingold (1993) and Nicholas Negroponte (1995) seems to be that no amount of online community-building will serve to replace the decline in civil society that he observes in the real world. Thus, Putnam's position is that ICT can supplement but not replace face-to-face social connections.

Benkler (2006) asserts that the democratic ramifications of computer networks are in many ways more far-reaching than Putnam realizes. He maintains that the Internet offers the promise of achieving the type of deliberative democracy conceived of by theorists including Habermas. However, the current mass-media controlled public sphere where political discourse is sharply limited to political and economic elites would have to be replaced by a discursive environment free of corporate and governmental constraints. Thus, in contrast to the current hierarchical control of intake, in the networked information economy, anyone with a computer and Internet access can make online posts or create a blog on the Web. Moreover, the Internet effectively reduces the costs of communication with a wide audience to virtually zero. This allows individuals to express their political opinions without fear of offending corporate or government sponsors.

His belief that ICT might one day become a major force for global social and political change is predicated on the networked information model. In contrast to mass media which require high levels of capital investment and typically concentrates the media in the hands of a small number of either multinational or state-run corporations, the networked model is characterized by modest capital requirements.

While it is true that early promise of "click on" democracy (see e.g., Davis, Elin and Reeher, 2002) has yet to be fulfilled, Benkler feels that it is far too soon to give up on the Internet's capability to help enhance civil society. The evidence points to experiments that work and can be replicated elsewhere. Building eDemocracy will require more work and take longer than originally expected but the basic premise that underlies the initial optimism remains fundamentally sound. Benkler argues the relative modesty of outlay required for a Web presence, individuals and groups have access to numerous tools that link entities across time and space, allow them to build and participate in communities of their choosing, spread their message to diverse constituencies, and collaborate over a networked environment. These tools include but are not limited to: 1) the Web; 2) wikis, a tool that enables individuals to collaborate on content creation using the Web; 3) blogs, or weblogs, which allows individuals to upload personal content to the Web; 4) social networking sites, which allow individuals to use the Web to form virtual communities; and 5) handheld and other portable computing devices, which can be used to empower individuals and groups to communicate "from the field." This allows, for example, neighborhood organizations to provide and receive information regarding public services from government agencies.

No doubt the "virtualization" of public life presents a number of tremendous practical and theoretical challenges. We can only begin to address some of the most significant questions in this book, however, including: What difference does it make, for example, to transition from the offline to a virtual environment? Do new virtual public spaces offer a singular, overarching public sphere comparable to the traditional public sphere or do multiple public spheres composed of various interests merge and blend when appropriate? How do developed and developing countries differ in making the transition to virtual public spheres? For example, Raman, in this book, discusses the challenges faced by virtual public spheres in developing countries and suggests a workable model. Finally, if we allow for multiple public spheres, how can we sort out the variety of emerging public spaces in the virtual world? These questions address many of the fundamental changes to public life which are being created by the transition to the online environment.

Making the Transition from E-Government to E-Democracy: The International Experience

ICT increases both the convenience and speed with which people can connect with each other and, at the same time, it lowers the costs of communication, especially compared to earlier technologies. Furthermore, the Internet has virtually unlimited capacity to store information, which makes it an invaluable resource for citizens. These advantages give rise to increased opportunities for participation and engagement with the political process. However, as electronic contacts between citizens and government continue to escalate, the quality of those contacts (in particular, those between individuals) has not been of a consistently high level. Most observers agree though that e-government provides one of the best opportunities to help promote increased public engagement. This is only likely to occur, however, if people derive some real satisfaction from their online contacts with government. Thus, the first stage in the transition to e-democracy involves e-government.

E-government refers to government's use of ICT to exchange information with, provide, and receive services with citizens, businesses, the various units of government and levels of government (local, regional and central) in order to improve internal efficiency, the delivery of public services, or processes of democratic governance. E-government emerged during the 1990s, as governments began to adopt many e-business and e-commerce techniques from the private sector.. According to the West (2004), "Electronic government refers to public sector use of the Internet and other digital devices to deliver services and information. Although personal computers have been around for several decades, recent advances in networking, video imaging, and graphics interfacing have allowed governments to develop websites that contain a variety of online materials. "

Facilitating citizen access to and participation in government has always been a large part of technology's appeal to activists.x The ability of citizens to initiate direct contact with government is dramatically enhanced by the Internet, according to e-government proponents. However, this aspect of communication and information technologies tends to be overlooked by governments, which far more frequently view the Internet as a means to improve the efficiency of government operations, rather than as a means to improve government-citizen relations, which is actually a more tangible benefit to citizens (Northrup, et al 1990, 511).

Has e-government brought about an increase in citizen satisfaction? Cohen (2006) examines levels of citizen satisfaction from Internet contacts with US government. The context is the public dissatisfaction with government, which has been on the rise in Western democracies since the 1970s, particularly in the US. One of the appealing aspects of e-government, according to some people, is that it can be used to reverse negative attitude towards government by facilitating more positive citizen contacts with government. The assumption is that as communication grows so will positive feeling on the part of the citizens towards government and government workers. Thus satisfactory contacts may bring about increased citizen feelings of trust

and support toward government and its leaders. However, an unsatisfactory contact experience might produce the opposite effect, that is, lead to a further deterioration of citizen attitudes toward government. He cites the 2003 Pew e-government Survey, which found that Americans who use the Internet to contact government express higher satisfaction levels with their contact experience when controlling for several important variables including citizens' social and economic characteristics and the outcome of the contact.

E-Government and E-Democracy

Cohen's research provides support for the belief that those with the most access and competence in using ICT, that is, men, whites, highly educated, well-off, older people, and the non-disabled, would obtain the most satisfaction from using the Internet to contact government. Meanwhile, barriers continue to exist for citizens not members of the above groups and who experience hardships in using the Internet. Some of the impediments result from technical design issues including poorly designed web pages o were incomplete, difficult to navigate, and/or out of date. Others, however, result from unresponsive government including unanswered emails to public officials. These issues, in conjunction with lengthy time periods waiting for an adequate governmental response, reduced the Internet's advantages as an effective medium for connecting citizens to government. While the high-access, high-competence groups rated using the Internet to connect with government more highly, groups with less access or less technically competent, for example, Hispanics, the disabled, or less well-off groups in general had significantly lower levels of satisfaction. Thus, the Digital Divide (see below) exposed serious fault lines in the ability of different groups in society to achieve satisfaction in their contacts with government. Solutions to structural issues such as those above focus on improving the Internet as a medium for effective citizen contact with government, primarily through creating web sites that are more responsive to meeting citizen needs. This concentration on structural improvements would aid governments in developing better portals which would both help citizens gain access and increase their overall satisfaction with online services. Some authors in this volume, including Anderson & Bishop, Backhouse, Nyirenda, and Bwalya et al, discuss the importance of structural changes in improving the e-government experience.

Distinguishing Between E-Government and E-Democracy

Misuraca (2006) makes an important distinction between government and governance, which can be used to distinguish between e-government and e-democracy. While the two concepts are usually interconnected, Misuraca contends that governance is about more than just government and encompasses the entire political process and not just the ends, while government's primary preoccupation is the foundation and regulation of institutional systems of achieving public administration. His argument, thus, is that governance concerns itself with how governmental institutions relate to citizens and the magnitude of the participation in this relationship (Misuraca, 2006). These differences can be transferred over to the distinction between e-government and e-democracy.

In comparison to previous uses of technology to achieve participation and obtain feedback from the citizenry, through telecommunications such as telephone, television and telefax; e-democracy, or e-Governance as Misuraca refers to it, provides an even more robust participatory process. More significantly, the widely recognized capability of ICT in this regard, as noted earlier, is its ability to foster many-to-many communication, whereas telephone, telefax, radio and television are limited to few –few and few-to-many communication at best. Also noteworthy is the direction in the exchange of communication. Under the old tech-

nology, two-way flow of information only exists in the few-to-few mode of communication (e.g., telephone or telefax), while in the few- to- many mode (e.g., radio or television), the direction of the flow is one way. The Internet, however, provides a multi-way—even simultaneous many-many—communication medium. It also provides the convenience of collaboration of many users without actual physical convergence.

More fundamentally, Misuraca contends that governance is chiefly conceptual in nature, suggesting that while all the technology required for e-democracy may be available, nevertheless, the level of public engagement may still be low. In developing the 'conceptual' notion he argues that e-democracy is using ICT, mainly the Web, to develop a "new conception and attitude of governing and managing where participation and efficiency are required of all the partners linked in a network." At the core of e-democracy, therefore, is the reinvention of government in a manner that encourages civic engagement and full democratic participation at the different levels of government in the agenda setting process. In other words, the key to the successful transition to e-democracy is virtual public spheres. Using ICT to promote public discussion of issues and to encourage civic engagement has so far lagged behind the service-based approach typical of much e-government. As Steven Clift observes, democracy often takes a back seat to efficient service delivery, which stems from the technology offering cost-savings and greater efficiency to government (Clift, 2003).

Many researchers have approached the issue of e-democracy from the perspective of the role that national governments can play in the process. To take just one example, Takao (2004) examines the emergence and importance of the Japanese government's using a framework developed based on an examination of such systems in other countries. Japan's adaptation to ICT varies at different levels of government, with local governments better able to integrate the use of ICT for public input and information dissemination in the policy process than the national government. The UK has been generally out front in efforts to promote political participation and strengthen democratic practices, through the use of the Internet and other ICT-based media. After more than a decade of using such technologies, Wright (2006) analyzes the effects of e-democracy in the UK. Wright views as instructive the beginning of the UK e-democracy movement, which the Blair government began in an effort to forge "a new relationship between the individual and the state." This was described in the "The Green Paper," which was a government document that proposed two policy tracks for ICT development: eVoting and eParticipation. Two notable attempts at creating online public forums came in the form of the Downing Street Speakers Corner and Citizen Space E-democracy Forum websites. Downing Street was designed to allow citizens to interact with government officials and other citizens over policy issues. However, the site came under major criticism for its lack of government involvement and its heavily moderated forum, which was viewed as 'over-censored' (see the discussion below on content moderation). Citizen Space provided a forum for citizens to discuss policy issues with other citizens. However, this site also faced severe criticisms for its use of 'silent' moderation, which led to participants downgrading the content found on the site. Thus, both British government-driven attempts at e-democracy, Citizen Space and Downing Street performed well-below expectations, so much so that the British government has backed away from sponsoring similar e-democracy efforts in recent years. The focus instead has been on smaller-scaled policy forums that can be used to effectively facilitate consultation between the public and government (Wright 2006b).

While citizen satisfaction with online contacts with government is a vital element in any large-scale effort to create e-democracy, another crucial component is the willingness of national governments to provide resources to build the necessary infrastructure for virtual public spheres.

Wright (2006a) points out that government in many countries is the only institution with the authority to command both the types and level of resources necessary to undertake any serious e-democracy effort. Without state intervention, in many cases, online civil society would hardly exist at all. This observation, however, leads to the even more fundamental question of how e-government contributes to e-democracy, for, as several contributors to this work indicate, there can be instances of well-developed e-government services without e-democracy. Thus, effective e-government is a necessary but not a sufficient condition for virtual public spheres. Recognizing this, some researchers have asked, "What explains the development of e-democracy by different types of governments?" Implicit in this is the idea that the type of government is a precondition for e-democracy. Van der Graft and Svensson (2006) assert that the individual country's usage can vary significantly in form and extent. Based on their findings, three types of explanations exist for this variation: 1) ones based on objective rationalization and modernization, 2) ones based on political evaluation and discretion, and 3) ones based on the technology itself as a driving force of institutional change.

Object rationalization and modernization refers to the belief that modern democratic procedures and processes are out-of-date and require updating (Van der Graft & Svensson, 2006). In light of these deficits, investing in e-democracy provides an opportunity to address democratic needs. This perspective is most often applied by governments to justify their investment in e-democracy. The development of e-democracy, according to the second explanation, is framed as an expression of popular political will. Citizens can participate in policy discussions, engage in dialogue with each other and policy makers and, through direct actions like electronic voting or electronic referenda, affect policy outcomes. Finally, the technological force explanation refers to the belief that advances in technology drive change in institutions. So, for example, as governments have implemented the use of ICT to improve their operations, so have citizens and interest groups, too, increased their ICT usage in an effort to be fully engaged in the political process.

In their examination of e-democracy development in Dutch municipalities, van der Graft and Svensson (2006) subject these different explanations to an empirical test. They find the technology-as-driving-force explanation the most compelling. In other words, e-democracy efforts are more likely to occur if the municipalities possess the necessary means of technology, that is, hardware, software and specialized ICT departments. This would seem to indicate that the largest constraint facing the transition from e-government to e-democracy is technological. Can this result be generalized to other countries? Van der Graft and Svensson believe that it can, they point out that: "It is evident that similar forms of pressure to apply more technology in the democratic process can be witnessed elsewhere" (p.133). However, the relationship of technology with e-democracy remains unclear. One could, with equal plausibility, argue that the causal direction is actually the reverse, that political reform serves as precondition for embracing technological innovation. The idea that more advanced ICT is associated with e-democracy fails to explain why the US, one of the most technologically advanced countries, still lags behind other countries, notably Canada and the UK, in certain key indicators of e-democracy. Part of the answer to that question lies in the subject of the next section, which deals with online participation and access issues.

Who Participates? The Question of Access

A robust e-democracy guarantees free and equal access for all participants regardless of social or economic status. Questions of access generally refer to the processes of inclusion and exclusion found in virtual public spheres. Among the earliest

and most prominent inquiries into e-democracy revolved around the question of access, which can be broadly inclusive or severely restricted, depending on the structure and the role of individuals interacting within them.

Access can be viewed a number of ways; from the means to connect to the virtual world to the ability to make one's voice heard through ICT mediation (Dimaggio and Hargittai, 2001; Albrecht, 2006). The technology creates the potential to expand entry to the political process but gaps in access, often referred to as the 'Digital Divide', must be overcome to reach its full democratic potential (Norris, 2001). Internet penetration and use is notoriously asymmetric across place and socioeconomic conditions, with significant variance from one nation to another and across such factors as income, education and race (Ismail & Wu, 2003; Norris, 2001). As Habermas and other scholars point out, free and equal access to the public sphere is paramount to democratic discourse. Access to and use of ICT thus plays a pivotal role in whether or not virtual public spheres can reach their full democratic potential.

The digital divide is well documented and consists of several dimensions. Perhaps its most obvious aspect is the widespread variance in ICT availability, particularly among the developing countries (see chapters by Nyirenda and Bwalya et al). This disconnect is the most basic challenge to e-democracy in many countries. Many communities, especially in the developing world, simply lack the technological infrastructure or the wherewithal to offer ICT that is readily accessible to the vast proportion of the citizenry. This gap between those who have the technology and those without, both within countries and among countries, presents a formidable barrier to full enfranchisement in the virtual public sphere. The driving idea behind this key aspect of the lack of full access is the notion that less resources lead to less participation, which puts at grave risk the notion of e-democracy. Thus, communities in developing nations face far greater difficulties in providing access at rates similar to communities in countries with more wealth and resources. This divide between rich and poor nations is further aggravated by socioeconomic conditions and spatial inequalities. As in traditional public spheres, those with higher socioeconomic status are better equipped to acquire the tools, in this case ICT, and urban areas have infrastructure for providing ICT to a broader community. Thus, the less affluent and rural dwellers are most likely to be without reliable access to ICT even in developed countries.

For these reasons, several initiatives now focus on creating the infrastructure for ICT use or expanding that infrastructure to underserved areas and populations. Several cities and counties in the U.S., for example, are moving toward providing wireless Internet access at no direct cost to users. Such an approach begins to treat ICT access the same as access to public utilities such as owning a telephone. Programs like the Technological Opportunities Program (TOP) provide grants to nonprofit entities to reduce disparities in low-income areas (Kvasny, 2006). Many universities and private organizations are taking similar steps. The $100 laptop is yet another initiative aimed at reducing barriers to access. Currently, many public libraries and schools in the U.S., including the vast majority in urban areas—provide computer facilities with high-speed Internet access.

Additionally, patterns of ICT *use* vary depending on resources and other social characteristics (Dimaggio and Hargittai, 2001). For example, those with disabilities have less access to the Internet and are online less than those who do not have a disability (Dobransky and Hargittai, 2006). Generational gaps exist, as well. Adults may have greater access to ICT, but younger age groups tend to spend more time online (Kraut et. al., 1996). Other characteristics, however, have shown recent improvements in narrowing the digital divide. There is some evidence that the digital divide between genders has narrowed in recent years (Ono and Zavodny, 2003). Evidence of this narrowing of the digital divide comes mainly

from developed countries, however, as many developing countries still face a considerable gap *vis-à-vis* their more developed counterparts and within their boundaries.

Probing the manner in which virtual public spheres provide access to all citizens reveals several serious constraints. Access is a multidimensional concept that can be best understood as a series of gaps or disconnects, rather than as a continuum from none to total access. These gaps currently limit the potential of e-democracy, but they are not surprising given the relative infancy of widespread ICT use. By examining access, we are able to evaluate the characteristics of those who may enter the online public sphere and determine ways to bridge these gaps.

A deeper issue relates to the way online access reproduces inequalities in the existing social structure and the how these inequalities restrict the ability of all to engage in civic matters. Online forums, even those sponsored by government (are often filtered and monitored. Some ICT users are more capable than others in navigating the online environment. Online public spheres vary tremendously in their interfaces with the public, some are very "user-friendly" and others are decidedly less so. These and other elements privilege those in control of ICT-mediated spaces for public discourse and those tech-savvy users who engage the online setting. Therefore, the terms on which online public spheres operate and the ability of users to engage each other and the mediated space become essential to providing a forum that is "free and equal" to all participants.

User restrictions are important elements of ICT-mediated political discourse. Some scholars have focused their attention on the impact of location and individual use of ICT (Bimber, 2000). Location limits autonomous online engagement by applying social, structural and political constraints. Dimaggio and Hargittai (2001) point out that access points at work or in public places may require monitoring and filtering of user activity. ISPs provide their own set of restrictions for users and some nations, notably China, continuously monitor online activity. Beyond these issues, online public spheres have internal characteristics that may also impose limits on users either intentionally or unintentionally. Forms of moderation and policies regulating online inter-actions can affect whose voice is heard. While policies and moderators may indeed be helpful in improving the quality of discourse on online public spheres, careful attention must be paid to the way they can limit expression. Online settings, for example, may privilege abbreviated comments and expression. Though concision is not limited to online behavior and settings, it plays a notable role due to the need to harness and organize the massive amount of information for discussion. However, *who* does the limiting and *how* they do it play key roles in online environments. These constraints, which are typically designed to help manage discourse and to keep abusive behavior at a minimum, have the potential to restrict user autonomy. Thus, there is often a trade-off which must be made between encouraging free expres-sion and assuring a reasonable environment for online deliberation.

Citizens must also have the capacity to make their voices heard in online environments. ICT users vary considerably with regard to their "Internet competence" (Dimaggio Hargittai, 2001). Good language skills and the ability to effectively collect and assimilate online data are two core competencies for Internet users. Users who are fluent in their use of language are better able to articulate their ideas and can make more persuasive cases for their positions. Other users are better able to locate reliable information and draw upon it to support their arguments. While some might struggle to find supporting data when it is readily available or identify dependable sources. Either skill set can have the impact of skewing online discourse. Frequent and skilled users can translate these skills into a form of discursive domination. Some research points out that frequent participants, or 'old hands,' tend

to take control of online debates, though often in positive ways (Albrecht, 2006). To provide a more egalitarian atmosphere, online environments can be designed in ways that are user friendly for those with a variety of ICT abilities. For example, information can be posted on e-democracy web-sites to help new users or those unfamiliar with online discourse become more familiar with the norms of deliberation in virtual settings. In ad-dition, links with informational websites can be included to equalize disparities in data-gathering skills between different users. At the end of this chapter, we present some examples of virtual public spheres that employ tools to improve the level of online debate and information-gathering.

The situations described above make clear that structural issues related to networks are a critical component in the issue of online communication and political deliberation. These structural aspects are dual in nature; they are either an artifact of technological constraints (e.g., the presence of wireless access in an area) or legal-regulatory con-straints. In both cases, they structure the way users interact in ICT-mediated space. Often, whether or not the structure of a virtual public sphere makes it more conducive to the Habermasian ideal is a matter of the particular purpose and population addressed. Policies, moderators and user-friendly applications can help ensure that all voices are heard make e-democracy better able to reach its full democratic potential. E-democracy issues of a structural nature are taken up in the next section.

Major Structural Aspects of E-Democracy

Some suggestions that have been made to improve ICT as a tool for e-democracy include changing structural aspects of networks and encouraging political actors to use the technology. For example, regarding the corporate manipulation of informa-tion, Noveck (2000) recommends that govern-ments mandate the use of value neutral search filtering tools for searching the Web. Additionally,

Web applications need to be developed that more easily link discussion forums with information sources to enhance debate and foster more civil discussion. Another issue is the public's privacy needs have to be better protected as e-democracy continues to expand. However, there has been little demand so far for this protection of user privacy rights. Additionally, Web-based industry should both promote the use of and educate the public on basic privacy measures (e.g., encryption) as a means to keep unwanted invasions of privacy from occurring. Thus, through the implementation of some structural reforms and changes, Noveck argues that the Internet's e-democracy potential can be fulfilled.

In light of the structural challenges, Noveck (2000) states that the following preconditions must be met before there can be democratic deliberation on the Web:

- free and easily accessible Internet
- easy to use applications for all ages and skill levels
- easy to find e-democracy sites
- e-democracy sites that support encryption
- e-democracy sites must facilitate conversation, interaction, deliberation, education, and engagement
- e-democracy sites should encourage people to slow down, read, deliberate, and then engage in dialogue

Finally, citizens must be given forums that demand accountability from participants and forums in which all participants are actively involved. In many respects, these preconditions represent a bare minimum of structural adaptations needed to allow virtual public spheres to thrive and flourish. Several of the chapters, for example, Burbridge et al, Raman, Bwalya et al and others discuss similar prerequisites to online deliberative democracy later in the book.

Another challenge in moving from e-government to virtual public spheres is re-envisioning the role played by intermediaries in the political process. Due to the Web's ability to directly connect users, many direct democracy advocates have hastily predicted the demise of interest groups and political parties, the traditional middle-men of politics. In one of the very few studies to examine the critical position of political parties, legislative representatives, traditional interest groups and journalists play on the Internet, Edwards (2006) develops a conceptual framework for analyzing the ICT strategies of intermediaries and their effects on democratic intermediation. In addition, Edwards argues "the Internet encourages the emergence of various new intermediaries, including voter information websites, moderated online discussion forums and mobilization platforms on specific issues. Increased competition between intermediaries and an ensuing reconfiguration of positions between 'old' and 'new' intermediaries in democracy thus appears a more likely outcome than does the outright disappearance of intermediaries." [p.163]

Intermediaries need to pursue different ICT strategies to develop or strengthen relationships with citizens. These strategies depend on several factors including:

1. Type of democratic practices: representative, direct, pluralist, deliberative, client, or associative
2. Citizen role in the process: pragmatic-conformist, critical-responsible, deferent-dependent and inactive outsiders

The type of intermediaries is also a significant factor and includes the following:

1. Preference Intermediaries: politicians, elected representatives, and interest groups
2. Information Intermediaries: the media and other interpreters/commentators of primary information
3. Interaction Intermediaries: moderators and facilitators of public deliberation

The quality of e-democracy thus represents the complex interplay between different types of democratic practices, citizenship roles, and intermediaries. Edwards elaborates on the strategies used by each of the intermediary groups to link their function with ICT and public needs. ICT exerts its chief influence on both the information and interaction intermediaries. Until recently, all three types of intermediaries have been dominated by institutional political actors and the corporate media. However, as virtual public spheres begin to expand their scope of influence, inroads are made into the powerbase of traditional political actors and the corporate media, which could undermine their monopolistic hold on the public debate. The major element in this framework, nevertheless, remains the preference intermediaries, which are often accorded a unique place in political process by virtue of the fact that they have been institutionalized through laws, traditional customs, the economy, etc.

Edwards and others suggest that re-designing current structures and procedures to empower and encourage citizens to participate is necessary to successful online deliberative environments. However, the focus on how to improve e-democracy by designing new virtual governance arrangements that are successful in soliciting, incorporating, and building public participation is still in its relative infancy. In an examination of online formats used by the Dutch since 1994 to increase public participation and engagement in the policy formation process Bekkers found that three motives are behind these efforts. First, the desire to bridge the gap between politics and administration on one hand and citizens on the other Second, valuing of the input of stakeholders in the policy formation/implementation process. Third, introducing competing policy viewpoints to enrich and stimulate debate on a wide variety of topics.

Overall, governmental efforts have not produced the desired results in these three areas, which leads the author to examine different types of online communities. One community that has shown conspicuous success in fulfilling each of the three criteria is the Linux community, which has evolved into a worldwide network of open source software developers, in an effort to create and disseminate an alternative computer operating system to Microsoft Windows. This community has been successful because it allows for 1) creative competition that allows participants to discuss, critique, and improve on others' ideas, 2) accessibility of all relevant information and 3) embracing trial and error along with feedback on outcomes.

Bekkers concludes that there are certain attributes that increases the viability of a virtual public sphere, besides the above described features; these include ensuring that there is bottom-up creation and that policy issues are narrow and clear, rather than general and vague. In addition, a trial and error process is emphasized that requires participants to be not only diligent, but also critical of themselves and others, and to be willing to suggest alternatives to improve deliberative processes online. Generally, developing an e-democracy that is truly effective cannot be wholly the task of government, no matter how well-intentioned and generous. Ultimately, virtual public spheres must be rooted in the wishes and desires of the citizens who will ultimately participate and shape policy through online deliberation.

Bekkers (2004), Benkler (2006), and Cropf and Casaregola (1998, 2005) point out that ICT-mediation in the form of virtual public spheres creates unique opportunities for the peer-production of civil society. In other words, ICT provides citizens a means for exerting more influence and more direct involvement in the political process through greater and more improved access to large amounts of information, lower costs for the dissemination of knowledge, and by improving inter- and intra- group communication. The enhancement of the democratic process occurs most directly through the deliberative processes that are both facilitated and augmented by ICT.

Figure 1. Content Moderation

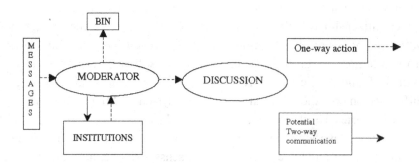

The promise of online public spheres has led many to examine the challenges and opportunities faced by these electronic forums as they look to transform the political process through technology, as Monnoyer-Smith, Hacker & Morgan, Gimeno & Freeman, Backhouse and other chapters herein point out. However, this potential will go untapped if traditional political and institutional interests insist on monopolizing public policymaking as they have in the past. It goes without saying, moreover, that far from voluntarily relinquishing control over the policy deliberations, political parties and the corporate media are likely to resist the encroachment on their power that online public spheres represent.

Political decision-making and policy-making are referred to frequently as two areas that are ripe for improvement by e-democracy. Until recently, information and communication channels have proven to be easily controlled by a powerful few—the political, corporate and media elite. The Internet offers virtually unlimited access by ordinary citizens to the types of information heretofore monopolized by policy elites, allowing knowledge regarding issues to be more widely distributed among the broader population, which can lead to more effective policymaking. Many problems still exist, however, including the role that online moderators play in facilitating citizen discussions and interactions with government. Bekkers refers to this issue as the interaction intermediaries problem. Research exploring two different styles (con-

tent and interactive) of moderation (see Figures 1 and 2) that have been used to facilitate citizen discussion groups in the United Kingdom has raised some significant questions regarding a new policy monopoly (White, 2006). The advantages and disadvantages of each style are compared in an examination of two different sites: Downing Street (operated by the Prime Minister's office) and the e-democracy Forum, a policy discussion site that is hosted on Citizen Space.

One important finding of this research is clearly designed and structured e-democracy forums are more likely to be successful if they are guided by an impartial moderator. Facilitating meaningful debate using virtual public spheres requires first, a transparent rationale and clear rules governing activities on the site and second, ensuring participants that their voices will not be censored for posting content that, while reasonable and respectful, is critical of the government or the forum's sponsors. There are two types of moderation that occurs on deliberative democracy sites. The first, content moderation (see Figure 1), uses a silent moderator who provides no feedback either to participants or to the groups hosting the discussion. Communication is viewed as being one-way in this model. Any posts that are deemed 'unacceptable' or 'controversial' by the moderator can be removed without warning or explanation, creating what some view is a 'conspiratorial atmosphere'. The second, interactive moderation (see Figure 2), supports two-way

Figure 2. Interactive Moderation

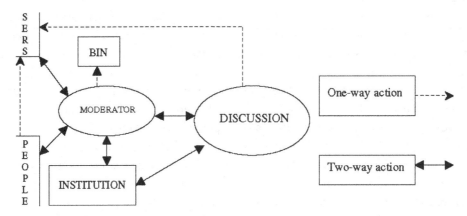

communication in which the moderator works to bring "new citizens and political institutions into the discussion; encourages existing users to respond; moderates the content of messages, attempting to maintain civility, where possible, by persuasion and not censorship; frames the debate and sets sub-topics; provides feedback to the institution; and participates in the debates." (Wright 2006, p.556) E-democracy can be most enhanced by the second type of moderation. In order to do this, however, the forum's sponsors must specifically build-in to their site capacity for this type of moderation. At the present time, the most likely means of accomplishing this is through selection of either paid or voluntary staff who are trained in the requisite skills of interactive moderation. Insofar as virtual public spheres do not automatically have the organizational capacity for interactive moderation their effectiveness as forums for e-democracy is seriously limited.

E-democracy researchers often point to increased access to public, in particular elected, officials as one of the chief assets of the Internet. Research on international communication patterns between citizens and government indicate wide variations on this point. In an analysis of seven European countries by Cardoso, Cunha and Nascimento (2004) the communication patterns of members of parliament are investigated. They show that the legislatures in these countries are still at an early stage of exploiting the full range of ICT to support parliamentary and partisan political activity, and that traditional mass media is still the preferred means for political communication. MPs primarily use ICT for internal communication within the political party or within the institution of parliament; and on a very limited basis for external communication with constituents, journalists, lobbyists, etc. Use of the Internet for political campaigning is seen to be largely dependent on the political party's electoral strategies, limiting individual initiatives by MPs. Furthermore, the MPs seemed disinterested in a more extensive use of ICT (e.g., for e-democracy or e-Governance types of projects). In this respect, there seems to be a marked difference between the European politicians and their American counterparts, especially as represented by the Obama campaign. One of the main reasons for this disinterest include the existence of a significant Digital Divide between the affluent and less well-off, especially in the Southern European countries.

Parvez found that, on the whole, local officials in the UK view ICT as a means to expedite communication and receive documentation rather than developing more participatory means for citizens to influence governance (Signification). Essentially, ICT is viewed as a means for enhancing the current representative democracy rather than fundamentally altering it to strengthen the deliberative process. It was also found that ICT usage was legitimized by the following activities: helping local governments address Central Government's directives, responding to local external and internal pressures, and by realizing cooperative government arrangements, developing strategic partnerships, and improving service delivery. However, the use of ICT for enabling a participatory form of democracy lacked similar legitimization. Current UK e-government plans are the result of top-down planning that cuts lower-level officials and the public out of the development process entirely. Additionally, bureaucrats, rather than elected officials, were the key actors in controlling the flows of information between citizens and other stakeholders in local areas. Thus, ICT was being used by local government to accomplish what had been done in the past except a little better and faster. There was no sense that ICT should be used to facilitate and enhance e-Democratic practices.

Various aspects of online deliberation in politics and policymaking have received close scrutiny in assessing the effectiveness of e-democracy efforts. Various deficiencies of the Internet with regard to e-democracy have been identified including the following: unequal access to political discussion, gives a competitive edge to technologically proficient citizens, discourages people from sharing their real viewpoints, encourages likeminded individuals to form online communities, and is actively used by an elite few. Given these inequities, some critics argue that there isn't much difference between online and traditional politics. In order to test this critique of e-democracy, Albrecht (2006) examines an online debate between citizens of Hamburg, Germany, over city development occurring over a four-week period. Many of the negative characteristics of the Internet were not as prevalent as originally thought; therefore, the quality of the online discussions was not diminished. As a result of the findings, Albrecht proposes a model for explaining participation and representation in e-democracy

deliberations. Overall, Albrecht argues that there are four groups of factors influencing who participates in an online debate and that determines what is communicated. These factors include the political and cultural interests unique to individuals participating in these forums, the rate of internet usage by different groups, the cultural perception that the participants have of the political deliberative process, and finally recognition that online discussions are a form of large-scale communication, where we can observe emergent self-organization of content.

Cardoso, Cunha and Nascimento's case study focuses on problems associated with vertical ICT communication in Portugal. Participation in electronic debates is, by and large, avoided by politicians because few are either capable of, or willing to, use the Internet for political discourse. Other major faults with ICT identified in the study include:

- Limited citizen access to the Internet,
- Limited citizen familiarity with official websites,
- Limited literacy and computer skill proficiency,
- Weak political culture (meaning direction-less dialogue and questions initiated by constituents),
- Disinterest by MPs to participate in forums.

The findings of Cardoso, et al, are of limited utility, particularly with regard to the political use of the Internet in more technologically advanced countries. Nevertheless, they provide a glimpse of the issues that e-democracy faces in parts of the world where ICT has yet to play major role in either government or commerce. Over time, as ICT becomes more available and inexpensive, it can be expected that in those countries, some of the issues identified in the study will become less important.

While e-democracy has been heralded as a tool to revive democratic politics, Nugent (2001) cautions that, "A new technology or communications medium is more likely to reflect and supplement the existing political order than alter it." Communication directed toward political actors has been met with disappointment by many citizens who grow frustrated when their emails or other messages go unanswered. For the most part, citizens fail to grasp the nature of the political system and the overwhelming amount of information that officials must deal with. Though this aspect of communication has not lived up to expectations, other tools such as e-petitions have provided more fulfilling outlets for concerned citizens.

As Nugent (2001) and others point out, our political and social structures play just as, or perhaps a more, significant role as technology in determining the efficacy of e-democracy efforts. Without a clearer understanding of the objectives of e-democracy, as well as institutional and governmental structures that influence the role of ICT in these endeavors, our attempts at e-democracy will be undermined. Parvez (2006) tries to make sense of the role e-democracy plays in light of Structuration theory. Structuration theory, he contends, argues that technology by itself does not constitute social reality. Rather it requires human actors and social practices in order to have social meaning. In this way, the theory avoids technological determinism.

Has the advent of Web-based politics brought about a dramatic improvement in democracy? Not necessarily. Television and radio headlines are typically replicated on internet news sources, emphasizing national politics while leaving out local politics. Furthermore, trust in government and political participation is still relatively low, despite a slight increase in voter turnout during the 2008 presidential race. However, the Internet does show the potential for improvement. As the 2008 election cycle indicates, the Web allows for instantaneous information and communication, better and easier ways for citizens to coordinate political action, and a wider range of information sources.

A central element in e-democracy is the issue of using ICT to foster citizen participation. Fuchs (2003) examines three models of democracy (antique, liberal, and electronic) with the purpose of identifying the best means of enhancing political participation by citizens. Fuchs argues that participation cannot be faciltated by relying on one of the models, but rather that all three are necessary to foster citizen participation in the process.

In Antique Democracy, citizen participation in the political process is direct, lasting and comprehensive. Deliberation occurs among those who are physically present and by subsequent communication in public places (e.g. the agora). This type of deliberation is the authentic expression of the collective will of the demos, i.e., all citizens. [Refer to the discussion of ancient civil society earlier in the chapter.] In contrast, Liberal Democracy consists of indirect participation (i.e., election of representatives), sporadic and limited participation by citizens, advocatory discussion by visually present representatives and journalists, subsequent communication in the primary life-world (family, friends, colleagues), and aggregation of individual interests by means of procedural rules.

Thus, if Antique Democracy is taken as the ideal, by comparison, modern Liberal Democracy might seem a pale imitation of democracy. Under Liberal Democracy, choice of the rulers by the ruled substitutes for genuine self-government; advocatory discussions in the mass media replaces deliberative democracy; and decisions are limited to an elite and involve a limited number of subjects. Furthermore, authentic popular will is replaced by particular group interests. All of these observed differences between Antique and Liberal Democracy demonstrate the difficulties faced in promoting true citizen involvement in modern government. Additionally, growing populations of modern states, the sheer quantity of decisions needing to be made, the complexity of problems and individual citizen preoccupation with personal issues has created a situation where the tenants of Antique Democracy have become impractical.

What can e-democracy do to improve the situation? ICT can assist by providing tools that can enhance citizen participation. Increased participation is the cornerstone of three modern theories of democratic renewal: "strong democracy" put forth by Barber; "discursive democracy" by Habermas; and "directly-deliberative polyarchy" theory by Cohen and Sabel. "Participatory democracy is thus the normatively desirable and the practically necessary form of democracy; it is: "desirable both in itself and as a problem solver." (Cohen & Sabel 1997: 314) Three important aspects of e-democracy include directness of participation (all citizens making political decisions), deliberation (the means by which political discourse is conducted), and institutionalism (the media through which participatory practices are upheld and supported).

Two distinct participatory possibilities thus begin to take shape: (1) the use of ICT-mediated referenda and (2) interactive communication in which a common will of citizens can be formed deliberatively. There are, however, several basic critiques that have been directed at both possibilities. First, there are too many important policy questions to leave to large populations to decide in e-referendums There is also a lack of adequate information to inform citizens of important information surrounding voting referendum issues, low motivation to participate, and lack of accountability for referendum policy. Second, deliberation using online formats is equally troublesome because the Internet is fragmented and doesn't allow for complete interaction between all citizens. Additionally, "partners in communication are neither physically nor visually present; they are mutually anonymous others." Thus, as the anonymous other is not identifiable as a citizen belonging to the same community, it becomes difficult to shape a common will that will serve that community.

The importance of meaningful public policy debate to virtual public spheres cannot be overemphasized (Bennett and Entman, 2001). Online discussions concerning the means and ends of politics are key to sustaining a true e-democracy: the "policy sphere is a subset of the public sphere where ideas and feelings explicitly connect with – are communicated to, from, or about – government officials, parties, or candidates for office who may decide the outcomes of issues and conflicts facing society" (Bennett and Entman 2001, p.4). Virtual public spheres must have some direct connection to real policy-makers to fulfill the promise of e-democracy.

Case Studies of Virtual Public Spheres

In several chapters, important examples of virtual public spheres are highlighted that demonstrate both the potential and limits of ICT and computer-mediated discourse for forming and directing the public's attention toward issues that vitally affect their political interests. These attempts at e-democracy show how online environments can be connected to the political process in a way that seeks to influence policy outcomes. The two case studies below examine the strengths and weaknesses of two ambitious e-democracy projects, which attempted to use ICT to comprehensively contribute to the public's ability to comprehend and influence public policy.

The Hansard Society's E-Democracy Project

The Hansard Society is a non-partisan civic organization located in the United Kingdom, which has had a long-standing commitment to using ICT to further the mission to "strengthen parliamentary democracy and encourage public involvement in politics" (Hansard Society, n.d.). To this end, the Society has sponsored several projects as part of their online democracy program. These online deliberative democracy initiatives are briefly described in the section below, including the outcomes of these efforts and how these projects have contributed to making public policy.

1. *Debate Mapper*

As previously noted, reasoned debate is a key component of both offline and online political deliberation. However, as also noted, online political discussion often shows the tendency to devolve into political mudslinging and destructive partisanship. In order to get beyond this impediment to rational political discourse, one of the tools the Hansard Society had made available to participants on its online forums is the Debate Mapper, the creation of a politician and academic, who designed it to collaboratively model and evaluate debates in politics. It is difficult to say whether this program actually contributes to improving online dialogue as the tool itself lacks an intuitive user-interface. In all fairness, however, the program available to the public in early 2008 was a beta version. As applications like this become more available and easier to use, they have the potential to increase the likelihood that citizen input will contribute to the development and improvement of government policies. As of June 2010, however, the Debate Mapper function appears to be absent from the Hansard Society's Digital Democracy web pages; perhaps as a result of the application's lack of user friendliness.

2. *Digital Dialogues*

The Hansard Society also collaborated with a UK government agency to conduct case studies to recommend ways in which government can encourage and enhance civic engagement through the use of ICT. The major findings of this collaboration include the following:

- ICT can help to realize the public's desire for a mechanism that will facilitate and expand citizen engagement in the public policy-making process
- Online public engagement offers several logistical and transparency advantages in comparison to its offline counterpart
- Both offline and online strategies are necessary; neither one works alone in bringing about a revival of the public sphere
- It is less about the technology and more about "the quality of content, interaction and outcomes." The active involvement and enthusiastic support of public officials is especially important
- Public officials' ability to adapt to ICT is crucial but this adaptability varies greatly
- Efforts to foster public engagement must be "owned" by the highest-ranking officials in all affected government agencies in order to be effective.

Interestingly, some of the findings would seem to contradict Van der Graft and Svensson, (2006) particularly the point about technology being less important that other variables in predicting e-democracy outcomes. The Hansard case studies also found that the total number of participants by itself tells very little about the quality of the virtual public sphere. Of far greater predictive value were indicators such as who participated, why they participated, and what outcomes resulted from their participation. Guidelines for public use and moderation policies must be clearly explained and available on the site. Generally speaking, the web sites lacking submission guidance and policy information resources were limited in their effectiveness.

Regular Internet users were attracted to participate in the experiment; moreover, these were people who had not been previously active in the policy process. Therefore, more people were motivated to take part because of the combination of interest in issues and the opportunity to interact with policy makers. Although many users visited the sites on a regular basis, few of these repeat visitors actually contributed to the online discussion. Reasons for the low rates of participation include skepticism over credibility given to their input, low self-efficacy, and lack of policy knowledge and skills.

3. *Parliament for the Future*

The UK Parliament's Group on Information for the Public commissioned the Hansard Society to examine how Parliament could more creatively use ICT to better serve the British public. The report, *Parliament for the Future,* which resulted from the effort reached a number of conclusions which will be summarized here (Hansard Society, 2007).

The report criticized current British government policies towards ICT as "uncoordinated, hesitant and costly" (p 83). Moreover, due to external pressures related to the public's enthusiastic embrace of the Internet, this approach is no longer tenable. In order to help Parliament reorient its policies to better align itself with public opinion, the report makes several recommendations, the chief focus of which is to make Parliament's use of ICT more transparent and provide for more citizen input. It is not clear, however, whether the Hansard Society endorses meaningful citizen input into Parliament's deliberations using ICT. As this would require a dramatic change in the current Parliament's attitudes toward public participation, it is highly doubtful that the Society would take such a position.

AmericaSpeaks

This organization, founded by Carol Lukensmeyer in 1995, is also the subject of an extensive discussion in chapter seven. America*Speaks* is an organization devoted to civic engagement, dialogue and participation in public issues. The organization draws upon the tradition of the town hall meeting to bring face-to-face, small group interactions together with ICT mediated, large-scale information sharing. Using the 21st Century Town Meeting™, America*Speaks* provides a technologically innovative way to integrate characteristics from both the online and offline public spheres.

Town hall meetings have a long distiguished history in American democracy. De Tocqueville and other early observers of American life noted the frequent use of this form of democratic self-governance. These forums allowed all citizens some form of participation in decision-making at the local level. The town hall meeting has been standard practice in many local governments in New England for centuries. Still, these forums struggle to attract a cross-section of the voting population and tend to privilege the articulate while suppressing differences.

America*Speaks* has updated the town meeting concept and in the process addressed many of its flaws. 21st Century Town Meetings have several components. Meetings are organized around a public issue and an outreach effort is undertaken to register potential participants. Efforts are made to identify the representativeness of participants according to several criteria, including socio-economic status. Efforts are then made to reach out to groups that are underrepresented. ICT is helpful, at this stage, in sorting through data and connecting to community organizers.

Actual town meetings draw several thousand participants and are often held in large auditoriums filled with tables for small group discussion. Participants have wireless devices that they use throughout the day to enter data. This data is transferred to a centralized system that can be projected on a large auditorium screen for display to the entire group. Participants are separated into smaller groups and a trained facilitator moderates the discussion. Volunteers provide folders of background information while experts and public officials are available for questions. Staff members organize the data they receive through a wireless connection to all small group tables. These "theme team" members then categorize the ideas and present them back to all groups for refinement and clarification (Lukensmeyer and

Table 3. Traditional v. 21ˢᵗ Century Town Meetings

Component	Traditional Town Meeting	21ˢᵗ Century Town Meeting™
Access	Open Participation	Organized Participation
Scale	Large scale	Combination of large scale and small group
Facilitation	Elected moderator	Theme teams, trained small group facilitators
Feedback	Voting results	Real-time themes, voting
External Links	No outside connections	Outcomes presented to stakeholders and government officials, websites for participant follow-up

Bingham, 2002). Theme teams are the centralized apparatus of this largely decentralized structure and rely heavily on ICT to manage and disseminate information.

When the meeting ends, citizens vote on the final product using wireless devices and can see the final results. Public officials and other key stakeholders generally agree to take some action based on the outcome of the proceedings. In some cases, the town hall meeting is supplemented with moderated online forums, surveys and websites for post-meeting follow-up. Overall, the America*Speaks* engagement adds a broader set of knowledge and skills to the policy process.

America*Speaks* continues the town meeting traditional, but remedies many of its flaws with ICT and small group methods. The 21ˢᵗ Century Town Meeting is unique in that it uses ICT to enhance the quality of large-scale civic engagement. Various technologies aid in bringing together a representative group of participants, organizing and disseminating information and providing real-time data on decisions (Lukensmeyer and Bringham, 2002). When combined with sophisticated small group dialogues, the 21ˢᵗ Century Town Meeting becomes a model for creating high-quality dialogue among citizens. These characteristics are notably different than the historical town hall meeting. 21ˢᵗ Century Town Meetings organize participation so that underrepresented groups are included in the process. They also provide skilled facilitation and connections to public officials outside of the town meeting environment. Table 3

demonstrates the differences between this model and the traditional town hall meeting.

The findings from the two case studies are helpful in understanding public attitudes toward online civic engagement and shedding some light on the operational arrangements of e-democracy. In many respects, the reports' findings echo those of the research studies we examined earlier in the chapter. Taken all together, the findings of these case studies present a convincing case for the efficacy of ICT to enhance pre-existing means of civic engagement. The findings, however, point to limitations which need to be addressed in order to improve current online discussions regarding politics and policymaking. The strengths of virtual public spheres, according to the Digital Dialogues report, can be grouped into two broad classes: cost-effectiveness and transparency. ICT usage effectively brought down the cost of citizen involvement in both the Hansard and America*Speaks* examples; and social networking allows more people to observe how policymaking actually occurs in a modern western democracy. However, the chief value of the case studies, particularly the Hansard Society one, is in their pointing out some serious limitations in ICT's ability to make good on the promise of enhancing and expanding democracy.

As the studies make abundantly clear, it is unreasonable to expect that e-democracy alone will revive civil society. Efforts to engage the public online must be combined with traditional attempts to strengthen civil society. Online public spheres only complement, and do not replace, offline civic engagement in a healthy democracy. This finding, along with the one on civic organizations having yet to avail themselves of the full potential offered by Web 2.0 applications, indicates that virtual public spheres present only the opportunity to enhance civil society and does not necessarily result in Strong Democracy. This is also something noted in many of the chapters to follow.

The Hansard studies furthermore make plain that government should not attempt to direct online public sphere efforts at engagement but instead must play a role in ensuring that such endeavors succeed. This crucial qualification points to a limitation, one that is not inherent in the medium itself but as one that is related to its use by government bureaucrats. The cost effectiveness of ICT makes it highly attractive to governments seeking to cut expenses and save money. The public sector, faced with escalating demands from citizens, views online engagement as a low-cost means to interface with the public. However, the volume and intensity level of administrative involvement with citizens increases as a result of ICT, and unlike the previous experience of government-citizen interaction, people public expect and demand that this interface include officials at the highest levels. Needless to say, top level government officials will have to do more than make a show of inviting input from the public.

As the above case studies show, virtual public spheres provide citizens with increased opportunity for influence and more direct involvement in the political process through improved access to information, lower costs to disseminating information, and improving inter- and intra- group communications. Several chapters in this volume examine the challenges and opportunities faced by online public spheres as they seek to transform the political process using technological means. What the case studies and many of the authors cited in this chapter suggest is the possibility of technologically-driven social transformation. However, nowhere is this possible future articulated more forcefully than in Williamson (2006), where he explores both the technical and social spheres of influence associated with community information distribution, but also provides a description of a third sphere which he names the transformative praxis. This sphere focuses on the opportunities, processes, and solutions that are created by disruptions in current processes and power structures, which are enabled by the emergence of networks based on ICT. Key to these processes is the change agents that originate within the community and government. New technical systems are often created and implemented by these actors to support community goals. Research findings suggest that advances in the processes and systems within the technical sphere emerge as a result of the disruptions from the social sphere. In other words, these advances lead to the third sphere, the transformative praxis.

According to Williamson:

"Transformative praxis is the link between the human and the technical and provides the space for a reclaiming of [social] power in order to implement new [technical] systems. The significance of these attributes is that changes (new or modified strategies, processes, systems) occur in the technical sphere through a transformative process that originates in the ideas and actions taking place in the social sphere (through awareness building and advocacy). The social sphere is linked to the technical sphere through transformative praxis."

The theme of transformation also occurs in the work of Vedel (2006) who identifies the three ages of the e-democracy. The first age, the 1950s, saw the emergence of cybernetic sciences; the second age, 1970s and 1980s, witnessed the advent of cable TV and personal computers, and the third age, 1990s to the present, is one in which e-democracy truly emerges as a potent social force. As in Williamson, the notion of technology generating a permanent rupture with existing social processes leading to a transformative period is a central theme of Vedel's analysis. He finds that most research centers on embedding ICT in current political systems rather than on the design and implementation of e-democracy projects. Rather than relying on traditional systems, Vedel stresses the importance of information, discussion, and decision-making as the key dimensions of an alternative sequence making up the e-Democratic process. Furthermore, he elucidates the four main assumptions which make up the premise of e-democracy. First, a demanding concept of citizenship; in order to make rational decisions, citizens need to be fully informed. The Internet has provided the information for citizens to be able to find virtually anything they want or need to be rational political actors. However, many do not have the time, inclination or the intellect to collect and analyze all of that information. Instead, Vedel states that "it is more important to determine what kind of political knowledge is practically needed to be a good citizen. " (p.233)

Other issues include transparency and debate on the Web. Transparency issues can be complicated on the Web. While citizens should have access to government information, this can also hinder the operation of government. Citizens, however, could be inundated by information, which could serve as a means to confuse the public. On the question of debate, Vedel notes discussion can now occur easily through the Internet. However, the focus of e-democracy has been to champion discussion while at the same time ignoring decision-making. Additionally, discussion via the Internet is supposed to up hold democratic ideals of inclusion and citizenship. Yet, as some writers noted earlier, this medium can be inherently discriminatory to those who do not have a mastery of written language. Furthermore, virtual public spheres could mark the effective end of intermediary bodies, a point that Edwards (2006) also makes. One of the arguments often made by extreme e-democracy proponents is that large-scale intermediaries like political parties and the mass media would become obsolete with the increasing dominance of online public spheres. However, it may be both

unrealistic and undesirable that the influence of political parties and legislatures subsides, as each still performs vital functions within a democracy.

Thus it is possible to divide e-democracy into several camps according to their vision of the e-Deliberative process. For example, Dahlberg (2001) recognizes three prominent camps: communitarian, liberal individualist, and deliberative. The first two are focused on pre-discursive expression of shared values or private interests respectively; while the deliberative camp contends that a 'strong' model of democracy requires rational-critical discourse by the public. He examines each of these perspectives and explores current efforts throughout the world that have used a deliberative online format to increase public participation in policy making and evaluation.

Finally, in addition to real world examples and case studies, the qualifications for facilitating Habermasian rational-critical discourse need to be identified to provide a better understanding of how to create and maintain effective e-democracy. Dahlberg concludes that online public spheres require not only developing deliberative spaces, but also attracting participation from citizens who have been socialized within a commercialized and individualized culture, which is generally hostile towards public deliberation. Thus virtual public spheres must not only provide opportunities for more participation and civic engagement, they must also function as the schoolhouses of a new type of communitarian culture, one where rational-critical discourse is taught and practiced. It is only then that we will have reached the culmination of the development of civil society from Polis to e-democracy.

REFERENCES

Albrecht, S. (2006). Whose voice is heard in online deliberation? A study of participation and representation in political debates on the Internet. *Information Communication and Society, 9*(1), 62–82. doi:10.1080/13691180500519548

Bekkers, V. (2004). Virtual policy communities and responsive governance: Redesigning online debates. *Information Polity, 9*(3-4), 193–203.

Bennett, W. L., & Entman, R. M. (Eds.). (2001). *Mediated politics: Communication in the future of democracy*. Cambridge, UK: Cambridge University Press.

Bimber, B. (2000). Measuring the gender gap on the Internet. *Social Science Quarterly, 81*(3), 868–876.

Brown, E. (2009). Plato's ethics and politics in The Republic. In. E. N. Zalta (Ed.), *The Stanford encyclopedia of philosophy (Fall 2009 edition)*. Retrieved from http://plato.stanford.edu/archives/fall2009/entries/plato-ethics-politics/

Calabrese, A. (2004). The promise of civil society: A global movement for communication rights. *Continuum: Journal of Media & Cultural Studies, 18*(3), 317–329. doi:10.1080/1030431042000256081

Calhoun, C. (1993). Civil society and the public sphere. *Public Culture, 5*(2), 267–280. doi:10.1215/08992363-5-2-267

Clift, S. (2003). *E-democracy, e-governance, and public net-work*. Retrieved from http://www.publicus.net/articles/edempublicnetwork.html

Cohen, J., & Arato, A. (1992). *Civil society and political theory*. Cambridge, MA: MIT Press.

Cohen, J., & Sabel, C. (1997). Directly-deliberative polyarchy with Charles Sabel. *European Law Journal, 3*(4), 313–342. doi:10.1111/1468-0386.00034

Cohen, J. E. (2006). Citizen satisfaction with contacting government on the Internet. *Information Polity, 11*, 51–65.

Cropf, R., & Casaregola, V. (1998). Virtual town halls: Using computer networks to improve public discourse and facilitate service delivery. *Research and Reflection, 4*(1). Retrieved from http://www.gonzaga.edu/rr/v4n1/cropf.htm

Cropf, R., & Casaregola, V. (2007). Community networks. In Anttiroiko, A. V., & Malkia, M. (Eds.), *Encyclopedia of digital government*. Hershey, PA: IGI Reference.

Dahlberg, L. (2001). The Internet and democratic discourse: Exploring the prospects of online deliberative forums extending the public sphere. *Information Communication and Society, 4*(4), 615–633. doi:10.1080/13691180110097030

Dobransky, K., & Hargittai, E. (2006). The disability divide in Internet access and use. *Information Communication and Society, 9*(3), 313–334. doi:10.1080/13691180600751298

Edwards, A. (2006). ICT strategies of democratic intermediaries: A view on the political system in the digital age. *Information Polity, 11*(2), 163–176.

Fraser, N. (1992). Rethinking the public sphere: A contribution to the critique of actually existing democracy. In Calhoun, C. (Ed.), *Habermas and the public sphere* (pp. 109–142). Cambridge, MA: MIT Press.

Froomkin, A. M. (2004). Technologies for democracy. In Shane, P. (Ed.), *Democracy online: The prospects for political renewal through the Internet* (pp. 3–20). New York: Routledge.

Fuchs, D. (2003). *Models of democracy: Participatory, liberal and electronic democracy*. Presented at the ECPR Joint Sessions of Workshops, Edinburgh, U.K. March 28th-April 2nd, 2003.

Fukuyama, F. (1999). *The great disruption: Human nature and the reconstitution of social order*. New York, NY: The Free Press.

Gitlin, T. (1998). Public sphere or public sphericules? In Liebes, T., & Curran, J. (Eds.), *Media, ritual, identity* (pp. 168–175). London: Routledge.

Hansard Society. (2010). *Digital democracy*. Retrieved from http://hansardsociety.org.uk/blogs/eDemocracy/

Heim, M. (1993). *The metaphysics of virtual reality*. New York, NY: Oxford University Press.

Institute for the Quantitative Study of Society. Stanford University. Retrieved from http://www.stanford.edu/group/siqss/Press_Release/Preliminary_Report-4-21.pdf

Ismail, S., & Wu, I. (2003). *Broadband Internet access in OECD countries: A comparative analysis*. (FCC Office of Strategic Planning and Policy Analysis Working Paper: Washington, DC).

Keane, J. (1998). *Civil society: Old images, new visions*. Stanford, CA: Stanford University Press.

Kraut, R., Patterson, M., Lundmark, V., Kiesler, S., Mukophadhyay, T., & Scherlis, W. (1998). Internet paradox: A social technology that reduces social involvement and psychological well-being? *The American Psychologist, 53*(9), 1017–1031. doi:10.1037/0003-066X.53.9.1017

Kvasny, L. (2006). Cultural (re)production of digital inequality in a US community technology initiative. *Information Communication and Society, 9*(2), 160–181. doi:10.1080/13691180600630740

London School of Economics Centre for Civil Society. (2004). *What is civil society?* Retrieved from http://www.lse.ac.uk/collections/CCS/what_is_civil_society.htm

Lukensmeyer, C., & Brigham, S. (2002). Taking democracy to scale: Creating a town hall meeting for the twenty-first century. *National Civic Review, 91*(4), 351–366. doi:10.1002/ncr.91406

Miller, F. (2010). Aristotle's political theory. In E. N. Zalta (Ed.), *The Stanford encyclopedia of philosophy (Spring 2010 edition)*. Retrieved from http://plato.stanford.edu/archives/spr2010/entries/aristotle-politics/

Misuraca, G. C. (2006). E-governance in Africa: From theory to action: A practical-oriented research and case studies on ICTs for local governance. *ACM International Conference Proceeding Series, 151*, 209-218.

Nie, N., & Lutz, E. (2000). *Internet and society: A preliminary report*. Stanford

Norris, P. (2001). *Digital divide. Civic engagement, information poverty and the Internet in democratic societies*. New York, NY: Cambridge University Press.

Northrup, A., Kraemer, K., Dunkle, D., & King, J. (1990). Payoffs from computerization: Lessons over time. *Public Administration Review, 50*(5), 505–514. doi:10.2307/976781

Noveck, B. S. (2000). Paradoxical partners: Electronic communication and electronic democracy. *Democratization, 7*(1), 18–35.

Nugent, J. (2001). If e-democracy is the answer, what's the question? *National Civic Review, 90*(3), 221–233. doi:10.1002/ncr.90303

O'Brien, R. (1999). *The philosophical history of the idea of civil society*. Retrieved from http://www.web.net/~robrien/papers/civhist.html

OECD. (2003). *Broadband Internet access in OECD countries: A comparative analysis*.

Ono, H., & Zavodny, M. (2003). Gender and the Internet. *Social Science Quarterly, 84*(1), 111–121. doi:10.1111/1540-6237.t01-1-8401007

Papacharissi, Z. (2002). The virtual sphere: The Internet as a public sphere. *New Media & Society, 4*(1), 9–27. doi:10.1177/14614440222226244

Parvez, Z. (2006). Informatization of local democracy: A structuration perspective. *Information Polity*, *11*(2), 67–83.

Poor, N. (2005). Mechanisms of an online public sphere: The website slashdot. *Journal of Computer-Mediated Communication*, *10*(2).

Setianto, B. (2007). Somewhere in between: Conceptualizing civil society. *The International Journal of Non-Profit Law*, *10*(1), 109–118.

Shirky, C. (2008). *Here comes everybody: The power of organizing without organizations*. New York, NY: Penguin Press.

Takao, Y. (2004). Democratic renewal by digital local government in Japan. *Pacific Affairs*, *77*(2), 237–262.

van der Graft, P., & Svensson, J. (2006). Explaining e-democracy development: A quantitative empirical study. *Information Polity*, *11*, 123–134.

Vedel, T. (2006). The idea of electronic democracy: Origins, visions, and questions. *Parliamentary Affairs*, *59*(2), 226–235. doi:10.1093/pa/gsl005

Williamson, A. (2006). *Disruptive spaces and transformative praxis: Reclaiming community voices through electronic democracy*. Paper presented at the Community Informatics Research Network Conference, Prato, Italy.

Wright, S. (2006a). Electrifying democracy? 10 years of policy and practice. *Parliamentary Affairs*, *59*(2), 236–249. doi:10.1093/pa/gsl002

Wright, S. (2006b). Government-run online discussion for: moderation, censorship, and the shadow of control. *British Journal of Politics and International Relations*, *8*(4), 550–568. doi:10.1111/j.1467-856X.2006.00247.x

ENDNOTES

[1] Distinguish between the sociological concept of the public sphere and civil society, which is more of a political perspective.

[2] Minnesota E-democracy was established by Steven Clift and others in 1994 as the "world's first election-oriented website. (http://www.e-democracy.org/). The organization uses the Internet to, in their words, "improve citizen participation and real world governance through online discussions and information and knowledge exchange." Their discussion pages emphasize the value of respectful online political conversations that are based on participants' geographic location.

[3] Dahlberg (2001) pp.625, 626. He also observes that ideal role taking is furthered by the forum's managers' insistence on prohibiting verbal abuse, list self-management, and guidelines for civil communication online. Furthermore, rules that strictly limit users to two messages per day ensure that every participant is accorded the full opportunity to be heard.

Chapter 2
Deliberative Machines in Techno–Political Arrangements:
A Theoretical Discussion

Laurence Monnoyer-Smith
University of Technology of Compiègne, France

ABSTRACT

This chapter explores the theoretical consequences of a conception of deliberative devices as a technical mediation, and more specifically how it helps to redraw the frontiers of grassroots participation. To understand the position of technology in deliberation, it is vital to appreciate how the device itself structures the distribution of opportunities for citizens to speak up. The existence of "deliberative machines" gives them a tribunal and a space for interaction that would be difficult to find in real world arenas of public debate. This chapter's theoretical frame is inspired by the French philosophers Foucault and Deleuze and will question the nature of these "deliberative machines". This chapter will propose to consider them as symptoms of transition between two types of setups, in a context of conflict between conceptions of representation and participation in reflexive democracies.

INTRODUCTION

However, deliberation theorists have only recently been taking into account the substantial layer of technology in their analyses of political discussion and deliberation. Their defense of the delibera-

tive paradigm against elitist polyarchic models of more or less democratic and conservative outlook primarily concentrates on either the normative dimension of deliberation, its limitations and its grounding in language (Schudson, 1997; Manin, 2005; Bächtiger, Pedrini, 2008) or on measuring the quality of debating itself (Steiner *et al.*, 2004; Black *et al.*, in press). Different disciplines are

DOI: 10.4018/978-1-60960-159-1.ch002

helping to structure our understanding: while analysis of devices for public speaking hail from sociology (Bourdieu, 1991 [1982]) and political philosophy, notably the more critical feminist authors (Fraser, 1992; Young 1996, 1999, 2002; Sanders, 1997; Wilhelm, 2000a, b), political communication offers a growing body of research into online devices and attention is now returning to a closer look at the conditions under which that speaking happens.

This is our startpoint for discussion that aims to base analysis of the mechanisms of eParticipation squarely upon the technology. This chapter seeks to question the place of these "deliberative machines" in the broader context where the forms of political mediation are recomposed and to show how they contribute to the rearrangement of power devices embedded in standard mediations. Our theoretical frame is inspired by the French philosophers Foucault and Deleuze and will drive us to question the nature of these *deliberative machines*[1]: I will propose to consider them as symptoms of transition between two types of setups (Deleuze, 2002 [1977]), in a context of conflict between conceptions of representation and participation in reflexive democracies.

SOME BACKGROUND: HOW DO WE MERGE DELIBERATION AND TECHNOLOGY IN OUR THINKING?

The technological sophistication of eParticipation devices and level of browsing skills they require of the average citizen might easily have caused researchers to adopt a theoretical standpoint other than that which eventually prevailed. We might have borrowed from Luhman's theory of autopoiëtic political systems or from Habermas' theory of a systemic colonization of the life world by instrumental rationality. Few set forth a global theory of the development of political devices, like Andrew Barry (2001) who is analyzing the expansion of interactive technologies as charac-

teristic of a new deuleuzian *diagram* of relation between persons and artifacts. Or, in a more sociological perspective, few academics link the digitalization of social and political mediation with a critique of power circulation in the public space (Castells, 2009).

At the outset, online deliberation and consultation devices were primarily envisioned as new ways of deepening democracy within the scope of the deliberative paradigm laid down by philosophy and political science (Macpherson 1977, Barber 1984, Cohen 1986, Dryzek, 2000). From there, researchers took an interest in the impact of technology on political discussion – even to the point where it questioned the validity of the deliberative paradigm (Dahlgren, 2006). Because the enduring deficit of representation of the citizenry in modern society makes the problematization more acute (Coleman, 2005a, b), researchers have leaned towards either cyber-realism or cyber-optimism, with the realists regularly carrying the day: without being entirely "politics as usual", boundaries of the decision making process didn't seem to have deeply evolved (Muhlberger, 2004).

Without reviewing research to date into eParticipation (Price, 2009; Greffet, Wojcik, 2008), it is worth pointing up the underlying relations between the citizen's political experience of eParticipation and the shape of technical devices that inscribe it.

The first issue is the technological context in which deliberation occurs and differences from face to face interaction (Muhlberger, 2005; Witschge, 2002, 2004, 2008):

"Initial research into virtual political debate in the 1990s often exploited Habermas' notions of public sphere and deliberation. Generally, researchers compared its characteristics against those of the ideal public space, only to end up with the disappointing conclusion that information and communication technology (ICT) cannot attain the deliberative ideal." (Greffet, Wojcik, 2008, 25)

As these two colleagues well show, the basic question of their studies is how technology impacts the criteria demanded by deliberative theory, e.g. inclusion, sincerity, dissent and transparency – the total number of criteria varies over time and between authors. (Dahlberg, 2001 ; Stromer-Galley 2005, 2007 ; Janssen, Kies, 2005).[2]

Empirical testing of Habermasian categories poses methodological problems that more of less lead to a reinterrogation of the deliberative framework (Dahlgren, 2006; Dahlberg, 2007; Chaput, 2008; Monnoyer-Smith, 2009) from the standpoint of pragmatic or culturalist critique. Thus it essentially sees technology as a tool of deliberation, not as a specific political setup that remolds the political decision-making process: we shall return to authors who hold this latter view.

That said, there is a second type of research into eDeliberation, which has generated substantial literature that addresses technological devices. These analyses actually attempt to define device configuration factors that shape, constrain or rechannel a citizen's eParticipation although truly comparative analyses are rare because of the limited hybridization of deliberative devices, virtual or real (Wright, 2005 ; Blondiaux, Cardon, 2006, Monnoyer-Smith, 2006a,b).[3] Vincent Price recently reviewed a selection of case studies and summarizes those technical features of eDeliberation systems likeliest to affect the course of discussions and actor attitudes. It emphasizes agenda flexibility, moderating and other device characteristics deemed critical to securing participation (Price, to be published). This focus on the nature and hands-on technical functioning of devices amounts to a shift in the problematic of deliberation. It is as if we had a normative typical ideal model for deliberation and then researchers were to return to the devices themselves (and especially digital ones) in a quest for the contours of an embedded model of deliberation therein – a model that was operative because designed by the actors using it. It is now not so much a matter of measuring the gap between a given device and the

quality criteria, but rather one of interpreting the offset with respect to previously existing devices. This is what Scott Wright and John Street (2007) flatly propose:

"The argument here is that political clients commission websites, and in so doing they make choices about what function the site is to fulfil. At the same time, we suspect that the design of the discussion forum commissioned itself shapes subsequent deliberation...The potential importance of design is not limited to the architecture of the internet itself (...) but to the nature of the interface: how it is designed and constructed. We suggest ...to focus on issues and processes that have been neglected for too long. This article has argued that website design, and the commissioning of that design, may be crucial to appreciating the democratic potential of the web" (p. 864).

This approach has triggered renewed interest in the technological dimension, especially in the French literature, long deeply sceptical of finding anything innovative in the devices of eDeliberation.[4]

This approach specifically targets the effects of transfer from one device to the next and the impact of new technological frameworks on actor relations. In turn, following a pragmatic trend in linguistic, analytical methodology in this field ceased to treat discussion as mere "text" but now also reckoned "production context" into its thinking. As Tamara Witschge writes (2008):

"Critical Discourse Analysis (DCA) considers language to be a social practice, views the context of language use as crucial to the analysis of it and takes particular interest in the relation between language and power ... It takes discourse not merely to refer to an isolated text, but includes the context in which a text is produced and consumed, as well as the wider societal practice in which the text exists" (p.78).

DCA thereby rounds out qualitative interviews with actors who set up devices and with more quantitatively inclined methodologies that try to profile those actors. This approach is indeed trying to grasp the internal setup of devices.

In so doing, it is possible to expand the spectrum of problematics by also including website designers in the discussion-building process, especially when we look at the drafting of topics made available for public debate. It is then unsurprising to wonder about the shift in relations to power induced by deliberative devices: either they compete against preexisting realworld devices and discussion formats – and casts of actors – or they are filling in a mediation deficit between political leaders and the citizenry. As Witschge (*op.cit.*, p. 79) notes: "Online texts are part of broader social practices and reflect, negotiate or resist, and feed back into existing social power relations like any other discourse and thus this aspect of the discourse needs to be examined."

Where mentioned, power is re-embedded in the device and discussed in terms of decision-making capability – what we see is treatment as a unit of the concepts and devices of deliberation. In his study of the forms and formats of youth involvement in politics, Stephen Coleman shows this population has not been appropriating the wide assortment of online devices that political leaders specifically designed to reach youth because the devices project a concept of citizenship that alienates them. Such technically orchestrated "managed e-citizenship" presupposes F2F contact of some sort(s) between youth and elected representatives but youth express any commitment to society through social networking, or "autonomous e-citizenship" (Coleman, 2008). This observation transpires in the variety of platforms for eParticipation that reflect a general trait found in all devices of power and described by Foucault (1975, 1976, 2003, 2004): the devices are embedded in a web of practices, techniques, norms, values, rights and obligations. Neatly described by Lawrence Lessig (1999), the embedding process is about inserting digital de-

vices of social, economic and legal consequence into the architecture (or "code") – devices beyond what Foucault could have included among his disciplinary devices. We shall return to this issue.

One interesting consequence of this research is to produce an important effect of denaturalization on the more traditional procedures of public debate and to raise questions about the role of language therein. Embedding norms and values in the architecture of a device does not happen only in cyberspace discussions but in all forms of mediation generated by our political cultures. We need only look back at traditional debating to see how they are set up to favour specific communicational formats. It is worth looking more deeply into Feminist criticism of Habermasian theory which says that the formalism required to take the floor and assert a validity claim actually sidelines a large share of the population, especially women and underschooled members of ethnic minorities (Young, 1996). More radically, criticism targets the embedded norms and values that help configure the forms of expression. By building procedure from language, Habermas did not see he was condoning a power device that favoured those who mastered its coding (Monnoyer-Smith 2009). In "Language as a symbolic power" (1991), Bourdieu correctly notes:

"This is the essence of the error [committed] by Austin (or Habermas thereafter) when he thought he had found the principle of language efficiency in discourse itself, i.e. in the strictly linguistic substance of the word... Seeking the principle of logic and language efficiency in language amounts to forgetting that power originates outside language. In fact, language usage, as well the manner and matter of discourse, depends on the social status of the speaker and whatever control he has over institutional language which is official, orthodox and legitimated" (emphasis added by Bourdieu)[5].

The damper on Bourdieu is that, if language is indeed legitimated by external factors such as social status –or gender (Graddol, Swann, 1989)- acknowledged by an audience, public debates procedures transcend this phenomenon: in this context, production of the legitimate word is conditioned less by social status in itself than by the device that utters it (Manin, 1987)[6]. Learning the procedural codes of decision-making is part of the upbringing of the children of the elite and it is not surprising for Bourdieu to equate the legitimate word with high social status without examining the production procedures of the format for personal expression. This conceptual shortcut is not neutral however for it ignores the technological element of any device that enables expression before audiences.

In short, while eDeliberation research has not problematized it, perception of the technical element of devices has been evolving over time in discussions on the form and configuration of online personal expression. We are moving from conception of technology as an external constraint on pre-existing expression to analysis of how the norms and practices of power become embedded in the technology. In other words, we have come to consider deliberative devices not only as 'machines' but also as complex political mediations.

THE DEVICES OF POWER, ITS ARCHITECTURE AND DELIBERATIVE MACHINES

The above considerations shed new light on the devices of eParticipation: they constitute both hybrid artifacts that connect technological objects and microworlds of actants into an action process (Latour, 1987, 1993, 1999), and elements of a setup[7] that materializes a form of socio-political organization in time and space (Deleuze, Parnet, 2002 [1977]; Deleuze, 1995 [1990]). We would like to develop now those two dimensions of our "deliberative machines".

Machines as Part of a Network of Actants

Of particular relevance here is Bruno Latour's research, which stresses continuity between scientific and technical production and human and political reality. By rejecting any ontological difference between science and society, Latour's innovation sociology visualizes the technological artifacts in terms of their "pleats" (*plis*) by showing how they embody traces of the society that generated them.[8] He asserts that the distinction between politics and science dates back to Robert Boyle's invention of the vacuum pump in the 17th century and the quarrel it triggered with Thomas Hobbes (Shappin, Shaeffer, 1985; Latour, 1993). This is when the scientific community erected the paradigm of experimentation and rejected any political considerations in the administration of scientific proof. Boyle held that science should rely entirely on experimental protocols recorded in laboratory reports and validated by peers. This was at loggerheads with Hobbes' rhetorical defense for a more holistic approach with no empirical basis.

Latour holds it is inane to divorce science and technology from politics and society because it prevents a proper understanding of the hybrid artifacts (i.e. manmade technologies) that constitute actants on a par with humans in a sociotechnological setup (Latour, 1993).[9] In this context, technology is not neutral but embodies a plan it *translates* into technical language. Like politics, science and technology cannot be confined to their capabilities and actors, but must be conceptualized as "states of existence": ""science" and "politics" do not qualify areas of activity or capabilities but states in the sense of "gaseous" or "liquid" wherein we find controversial objects whose purpose is to compose the world as we know it" (Latour 2008, 24). He further considers that technological artifacts generate mediations among actants. Thus, Boyle's vacuum pump is a hybrid artifact that functions (pretty poorly) in interaction with man while its operating principle undermined the rhetorical foundations of scientific proof for its era and imposed the empirical style in use to this day. The artifact materialized a setup that helped define science as we know it today: its "nature" (or reality of the "vacuum") and "culture" (the specific attitude to science as an organizer and institutionalizer of actors) are indissociably interconnected such that the diffusion of science and its paradigm are in complete overlap.

This also applies to deliberative devices. They are artifacts within a setup that frames the decision-making processes which constitute *pleats* that embody the entire organization behind the setup, i.e. a business operation, distribution of powers, citizen/government relations, concepts of civic duties and more. In the wake of Latour, Steve Woolgar (2001) focuses on the designers of technological artifacts to show how their profiling of end user affects the technical configuration through conscious or semi-conscious projections. We too emphasized this by analyzing online polling, electronic voting, eDeliberation and other types of interactive platforms for what they say about conceptualizations of good citizenship (Monnoyer-Smith, 2006). Given that a technological device is the product of expression among its actants, it embodies traces of their negotiations and its evolutionary potential depends heavily on the lead-time to start-up: "Seen in these terms, techniques and devices can become political…in the sense that technical designs and devices are bound up with the constitution of the human and the social" (Barry, 2001, 9).

Therefore, deliberative devices are politics not only because they are objects falling within the sphere of politics, but also because they embody a given particular notion of what forms of politician/citizen mediation are desirable and not.

Like all technological artifacts, deliberative devices produce mediations (Latour, 2005) and help structure decision-making relations between their human and non-human actants. Andrew Barry develops this further in an analysis of the current forms of political mediation in order to show that modern "technological societies"[10] fit the same "diagrams" (Deleuze, Guattari, 1988, Deleuze,1990) of interactivity and networking (Barry 2001), thereby impregnating all relations between users and technological artifacts. Therefore, deliberative platforms are based on the same model of knowledge and power sharing as MySpace and other Web 2.0-based social networking websites. Similarly, Beth Noveck's notion of "Wiki-government" matches the imperative of interactivity in a bid to create a new relationship with decision-making in politics: "Now…new technology may be changing the relationship between democracy and expertise, affording an opportunity to improve competence by making good information available for better governance" (Noveck, 2008, 32). "We have the know-how to create « civic software » that will help us form groups and communities who, working together, can be more effective at informing decision-making than individuals working alone" (Ibid. 40).

More broadly, Barry holds that, because interactive technologies encourage active user participation in a variety of formats, they will find widespread use for political mediation in a bid to stimulate the most 'active' dimension of citizenship, political rights and participations rights which tend to develop in modern democracies[11] (e.g. television and radio, now affected by technological convergence).

Why Deliberative Setups Do 'Leak'

The concept of "diagram" used by A. Barry is of utmost pertinence in our context because it allows us to embrace in the same time the heterogeneous components of a network of actants, their evolution in a chaotic and complex society, and the constructive relation between the evolution of setups in a society and broader diagrams in which they both take place and contribute to define. In this paragraph, I will have recourse to those concepts to explain how "deliberative machines" challenges actual conception of relation between citizens and the political sphere and the role of technological artifacts in this process.

The concept of diagram was developed by Foucault (1977 [1975]) in "Discipline and Punish" and later used by Deleuze (2002, 1988). Although it is a difficult concept to grasp, we can interpret it as an abstract general model of relations which could be compared to the concept of paradigm in a Kuhnian perspective but without the structural reference that it might induce. Produced by the life world, it enables the emergence of foucaldian microdevices of power across the entire social landscape, and for Deleuze, "setups of desirability". Diagrams embed systems into a sort of global ecology in which setups seen in a variety of social landscapes find their meaning, e.g. panoptism (disciplinary diagram) or what Barry sees as interactivity and networks.[12] They recall "a tactical deployment with different persons in a fixed place who perform a certain number of functions" (Foucault, 1977, [1975, 200]). As such, diagrams formalize local power processes into some schematic form: Deleuze sees diagrams as a "cartographic" representation of relations among individuals, institutions and whatever other form of being who operates in power devices or materialized setups (Deleuze, 1988). Although diagrams largely frame local setups and power devices, their relation is more of a constructivist one: a diagram is not a structure which fully determines the content of a setup; it evolves with it, and is largely framed by it in return. In the following paragraphs, I exploit this fluctuating characteristic of diagrams to stress the role played by our deliberative setups in the emergence of reflexive citizenship.

Power Circulates within Devices and Setups

Setups and devices are notions that enable us to conceive of power as an effect of structure, not as attributes that the device confers upon a person or group of people. Power that has no essence but is simply operative: "you need to know where it goes, how it goes, from who to whom, from which point to which, using what procedures and to what effect" (Foucault, 2008 [2004, 3]). Power arises from the kinds of relations that exist between people and technological artifacts and then diffuses into the maze of relational networks. Relative strength between any two individuals is a product of how the power device is set up: power is not to be found in things such as a tool, object or datum but in the configuration of the device itself. Foucault holds that all devices are power devices because you obtain a power effect in the very instant you establish a relational structure. On the other hand, Deleuze rounds out the notion of device (dispositif) with that of setup (agencement), because he does not qualify all devices as power devices. Setups materialize a desired state, scale of value and set of justifications.[13] Power devices are an element of setup that delimitates power's frontier within a setup, structure the relations between actors and enable power to flow. They suffer neither reduction to a form of repression nor assimilation to any ideology.

The link between power and the configuration of any device yields a finer grasp of the device's constituent elements. It not only "normalizes" by producing a behavioral norm but, at a more fundamental ontological level, it constitutes the way people structure their identity, and therefore act, feel and think. Nevertheless, I want to defend here a more anthropological approach to technology, as with Leroi-Gouhran, who sees technology as "anthropologically constitutive", i.e. it helps structure the normative references of the individual within a given environment. Is this perspective, technology and normative preferences evolve together.

For authors like Agamben, devices have become more and more disciplinary: modern societies typically strategize and only become more repressive insofar as they deploy constrictive devices in greater numbers. Giorgio Agamben reformulates this perspective through a highly instrumental view of devices that "reflect an economy, i.e. a set of practices, knowledge, measurements and institutions that aim to govern, manage, guide and control human behavior, gestures and thinking in a direction deemed useful" (Agamben, 2009, [2007, 28][14]).

Without sharing the repressive, deterministic dimension of devices asserted by Agamben and Foucault largely because we see in it the entire socio-technical network presided over its design and actor's ability to reframe part of its component, we can nonetheless exploit Barry's conceptual framework to view "deliberative machines" as microdevices of power within a vaster setup that lays down the relationship of democracy to decision-making in modern societies. The participation and deliberative devices discussed here do indeed carry out –at least technically- a reterritorialization of power that structures sharing of the decision-making within the deliberation paradigm cited at the start of this paper. These devices enable a different basis for mediation between political leaders and the citizenry, creating new political spaces and hubs of governmentality. In so doing, they encode normative principles by embedding them into the structure of technological artifacts (and literally so with digital technology).

Leaking Setups

The second point is that Deleuze and others see the constrictive, or even repressive, dimension is not the full analytical picture because any setups has *lines of flight*[15] (Deleuze, Guattari, 1988), in other terms, they "leak". Foucault and Deleuze have a different conception of how devices and set ups evolve and change over time. Foucault (1977) describes "resistance" phenomenon's to normalization induced by the restrictive dimension of power devices whereas Deleuze understanding of "set ups" includes in itself the ability to evolve and "move" (although not in a luhmanian autopoïetic fashion but rather by exploiting its

heterogeneous and chaotic internal composition). Because existing setups "leak" - i.e. they are out of reach of actants and drift away from them- they end up challenging the diagram in which they were framed. Contradictions can then emerge from setups which were envisioned within the scope of a specific paradigm. We can therefore understand those 'leaks' for example as De Certeau's (1980) description of reading tactics developed by users under the metaphor of "poaching" (*braconnage*), an anti-disciplinary practice opposing the pedagogic pretension to "*inform* a population, that is to 'give form' to social practice" (1980, 239). Similarly, the sociology of innovation's description of technical mediations (Akrich, 1992) as sociopolitical negotiations around a new technological framework shows how a given technological setup is being reconfigured locally by actants and how these interventions challenge the power sharing inscribed therein. This process of reconfiguration consists of a *deterritorialization* of power, a new geographical repartition of it. Framed in setups which leaks, social space recomposes itself around those leaks into open-ended setups.

In closing this section, we should review a number of deliberative machines characteristics from the standpoint of power devices in the context of a setup (*agencement*) such as deliberation. We have seen that they may be viewed as hybrid artifacts at the heart of a socio-technical network and that they inscribe both (1) normative principles and designer-actants into their structure as well as (2) the power sharing that comes with those principles. Deliberative machines belong to a category of devices such as election systems and institutional organizations which allocate power and distribute it within the political sphere. Our hypothesis here is that they, as actants within a setup, participate in a movement which redefines the nature of citizenship embedded in their structure and proposes a new diagrammatic frame: they are the symptom of the existence of a leak.

Actually, all diagrams are vulnerable to tensions and *lines of flight* or *leaks* that introduce

Figure 1. Schematic diagram of deliberate devices

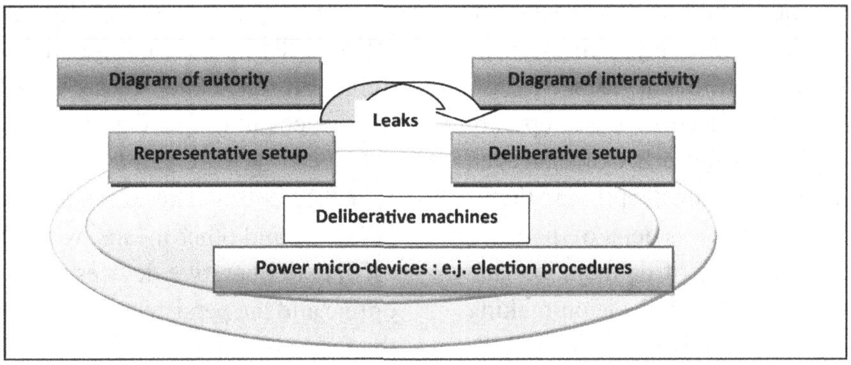

perturbations capable of evading, reinscribing or deviating the justifying principles inscribed in the machines code. Setups "leak" not only because they are not disciplinary devices controlled by a set of institutions, but also because their heterogeneous nature allows actants to redefine themselves within its frame.

Figure 1 summarizes our conceptual frame and clarifies the tensions exerted on the deliberative machines. They can be viewed both as leaks within the context of the representative diagram and power devices in both deliberative and representative diagram as they organize a repartition of power.

EMPIRICAL RESEARCH WITHIN THIS CONCEPTUAL FRAME

It could be interpreted as treason to Deleuze's thought to bring his concept down to the empirical field as he has never really been interested in their operational power. Nevertheless, its heuristic value resides in its ability to enlighten us on the way technologies are appropriated by users.

What could be interpreted as a leaking phenomenon within the context of deliberative setups?

Deliberations devices (on and off-line) can create –at least they sometimes do- spaces of discussion which contradicts the logic of representation which is carried out by modern democracy's

elective system, precisely because they open the decision-making process to a wider variety of actors. Caught between a deliberative setup and a more representative setup (in a shumpeterian sense of the word), these devices are in an awkward position which creates tensions and conflicts between participants. Indeed, they don't exactly fit within their ecology: deliberative machines propose new interactions with politicians and new actions for citizens, and both are following a contradictory logic (Coleman, 2005b). The first ones are often reluctant to give up their prerogatives as representatives (even if they believe in participatory democracy), the last ones are calling for a direct input in the final decision. Academic research has underlined many times how public consultations can present a Janus Face: on one hand, citizens are mobilized to participate, hoping to significantly contribute to the final decision; on the other hand, they often learn *in fine* that their arguments either had a limited impact or couldn't be processed to the appropriate authorities[16] (Coleman, 2004; Talpin, Wojcik, 2009, Talpin, Monnoyer-Smith, 2010).

The normative conflict between deliberation and representation is observable in many contexts: municipal discussion forums (Wojcik, 2008), participatory budgeting (Sintomer & al., 2008, Peixoto, 2008; Talpin, 2007), platforms still wondering and hesitant about how participation should happen (Jankowski, Van Os, 2004) or national public debates (Monnoyer-Smith, 2006,

2007). Citizen response varies from rejection of these procedures and dwindling participation to engaging with a view to moving their message despite the inhospitality of the devices.

Deliberative and representative set ups are obviously perfectly compatible. S. Coleman even argues for an approach of "direct representation", which amounts to a reassessment of political mediation through the lens of deliberation that concerns the first phases of the decision-making process. It thus protects the role of elected officials as representatives along with all the forms of ongoing interaction that can be set up to reach the citizenry, such that representation remains a permanent and constructive activity (Coleman, 2005a, b). In this conceptual frame, deliberative setups do leak in the sense that their presence in a representative political system is always a challenge between participatory - (or) deliberative- and representative conceptions of citizenship. Their appropriation varies according to local context, in a very deleuzien evolving environment.

Deliberative setups offer *lines of flights* for many participants who would not have entered a public discussion otherwise, or would have had difficulties expressing themselves F2F, as the aforementioned feminist literature has shown.

In previous research (Monnoyer-Smith, 2006a,c, 2007), I have shown how on-line deliberative devices have been appropriated by various users in such a way that (1) they have managed to make their opinion heard despite an unfriendly technical design and (2) that it allows women, less informed citizens, and lower income categories to find their way to the deliberative process. However, this does not mean that disparities disappear online: other studies also report a strong presence of those social categories that already dominate offline activity, i.e. educated, politically concerned, male Caucasians. "Not only are there many more men than women posting on the list, but also a masculine, agonistic style of discourse pre-dominates despite the high level of respect fostered." (Dahlberg, 2001, 626) and

this is particularly true in the case of politically-oriented websites (Hill and Hughes, 1998; Davis, 1999; Wilhelm 2000). Beyond the inequality of online presence and access, we also see gender differences in usage, e.g. women are less likely than men to share creative input online (Hargittai, Walejko, 2008). The dominance effect through language and other means, which is written into off-line deliberative devices, does not disappear online and the persistence of the gender divide in the forms of expression provided to citizens only means the borders have shifted, not vanished.

In this sense, one advantage of deliberative "machines" over F2F participation is the potential to diversify access formats into discussion forums, blogs, mailing lists and chats in order to open up expression space to a wider range of populations… or at least to those who actually enter the device.

It is then clear that online debate is a real alternative to speaking in public (Witschge, 2002; Monnoyer-Smith, forthcoming): we have shown that people with a limited argument repertoire do participate more online as expression in public is often monopolized by informed and socially active citizens. At this point, it is not worth wondering whether they will succeed in doing it, but rather, in a very latourian perspective, to point at the technological potentiality of deliberative setups as an indicator of new normative aspirations. The deleuzian concept of *lines of flights* helps us to understand how citizen use a setup in ways which have not been previously conceived by the initiating actors, mainly elected officials.

CONCLUSION

In this contribution, I wanted to point out the extent to which the analysis of deliberative devices helps to redraw the frontiers of grassroots participation. To understand the position of technology in deliberation, we must appreciate how the device itself structures the distribution of opportunities for citizens to speak up. The existence of "deliberative machines" gives them a tribunal and a space for interaction that would be difficult to find in real world arenas of public debate.

Our analyses disagree with Foucault's description of deliberative machines as tools that impose the rules of power and show that they form part of a more global setup for deliberation which reterritorialize power. Therefore they provide a unique platform of argumentation and rhetoric without offline equivalent, to women, the less-informed and the socio-culturally deprived. It is not that technology itself fails to motivate these subpopulations, but simply that citizens with an established presence in other discussion spaces will exploit technology differently. One hypothesis arising from our theoretical frame is that the setup of these discussion spaces provide a reflexive arena for actors who design and promotes these machines because they realize the intrinsic limitations of F2F participation. In this context, Bruno Latour's research suggests that the new forms of mediation, which these machines constitute, reflect a search for reconnecting the citizenry with politics. Technological artifacts can thus not be reduced to their purely mechanical dimension and must be perceived in all their sociological substance. While we can always situate their instrumentalization in the context of a deliberative setup that would reinforce the traditional powers of representation, field observations report that they can also attract actors who rework the traditional forms of political mediation. From that point, any analysis of the appropriation of devices should take account of the gap they generate in the distribution of power among various categories of the population. Indeed, we will be able to evaluate the contribution of online debating in function of the aptitude of these new categories to produce new normative references that differ from those that usually result from traditional offline deliberations.

What we find more interesting than analyzing the "quality" of deliberation is what questions these devices raise for the powers that be. From that standpoint, researchers investigating usage should pay particular attention to the actors involved in the design of the "deliberative machine". In this sense, Deleuze's notions of "setup" and "diagram" enable reassessment of the position of deliberative procedures in a broader sociotechnical context that takes into account the normative positioning of "actants" and its inscription in technical artifacts. The evolution of deliberative setups will eventually allow us to ask whether they will displace the forms of the exercise of traditionally liberal-minded decision-making powers towards something more deeply democratic.

REFERENCES

Agamben, G. (2009). *What is an apparatus? and other essays*. Stanford, CA: Stanford University Press.

Akrich, M. (1992). The description of technical objects. In Bijker, W. E., & Laws, J. (Eds.), *Shaping technology/building society. Studies in sociotechnical change* (pp. 205–224). Cambridge, MA: MIT Press.

Bächtiger, A., & Pedrini, S. (2008). *Dissecting deliberative democracy: A review of theoretical concepts and empirical findings*. Paper presented at the EPOP Conference, Manchester.

Barry, A. (2001). *Political machines. Governing a technological society*. London, UK: Athlone Press.

Benett, L. (2008). Youth and digital democracy: Intersections of practice, policy and the market-place. In W. L. Bennett (Ed.), *Civic life online: Learning how digital media can engage youth*. (pp. 25-50). The John D. and Catherine T. MacArthur Foundation Series on Digital Media and Learning. Cambridge, MA: The MIT Press.

Benhabib, S. (Ed.). (1996). *Democracy and difference: Contesting the boundaries of the political*. Princeton, NJ: Princeton University Press.

Black, L., Burkhalter, S., Gastil, J., & Stromer-Galley, J. (2009). Methods for analyzing and measuring group deliberation. In Bucy, E., & Holbert, R. L. (Eds.), *Sourcebook for political communication research: Methods, measures, and analytical techniques*. Mahwah, NJ: Routledge.

Blondiaux, L., & Cardon, D. (2006). Dispositif participatifs. *Politix, 75*, 3–9. doi:10.3917/pox.075.0003

Bourdieu, P. (1991). *Language and symbolic power*. Cambridge, MA: Harvard University Press.

Cala Carrillo, J., & de la Mata, M. L. (2004). Educational background, modes of discourses and argumentation: Comparing women and men. *Argumentation, 18*, 403–426. doi:10.1007/s10503-004-4906-1

Calenda, D. (2006, November). *Digital encounters with politics. The political use of the Internet by young people in three European countries*. Paper presented at the Open international research and postgraduate seminar Politics on the Internet: New Forms and Media for Political Action, Department of Political Science & International Relations, University of Tampere (Finland).

Cappella, J. N., Price, V., & Nir, L. (2002). Argument repertoire as a reliable and valid measure of opinion quality: Electronic dialogue during campaign 2000. *Political Communication, 19*, 73–93. doi:10.1080/105846002317246498

Castells, M. (2009). *Communication power*. Oxford, UK: Oxford University Press.

Chaput, M. (2008). Analyser la discussion politique en ligne. De l'idéal délibératif à la reconstruction des pratiques argumentatives. *Reseaux, 150*, 83–106.

Coleman, S. (2001). The transformation of citizenship. In Axford, B., & Huggins, R. (Eds.), *New media and politics* (pp. 109–125). London: Sage.

Coleman, S. (2004). Connecting parliament to the public via the Internet: Two case studies of online consultations. *Information Communication and Society, 7*(1), 1–22. doi:10.1080/1369118042000208870

Coleman, S. (2005a). New mediation and direct representation: Reconceptualizing representation in the digital age. *New Media & Society, 7*(2), 177–198. doi:10.1177/1461444805050745

Coleman, S. (2005b). *Direct representation. Towards a conversational democracy*. London: IPPR publication.

Coleman, S. (2008). Doing IT for themselves: Management versus autonomy in youth e-citizenship. In L.W. Bennett (Ed.), *Civic life online: Learning how digital media can engage youth.* (pp. 189-206). The John D. and Catherine T. MacArthur Foundation Series on Digital Media and Learning. Cambridge, MA: The MIT Press.

Coleman, S. & Rowe C. (2005). *Remixing citizenship. Democracy and young people's use of the internet*. Research report, Carnegie Young People Initiative.

Dahlberg, L. (2001). The Internet and democratic discourse. Exploring the prospects of online deliberative forums, extending the public sphere. *Information Communication and Society, 4*(4), 615–633. doi:10.1080/13691180110097030

Dahlberg, L. (2007). Rethinking the fragmentation of the cyberpublic: From consensus to contestation. *New Media & Society, 9*(5), 827–847. doi:10.1177/1461444807081228

Dahlgren, P. (2006). Civic participation and practices: Beyond deliberative democracy. In Carpentier, N., Pruulmann-Wengerfeld, P., & Nordenstreng, K. (Eds.), *Researching media, democracy and participation* (pp. 23–35). Tartu, Estonia: Tartu University Press.

Davis, R. (1999). *The Web of politics: The Internet's impact on the American political system.* Oxford, UK: Oxford University Press.

de Certeau, M. (1984). *The practice of everyday life.* Berkeley, CA: University of California Press.

Deleuze, G. (1988). *Foucault.* Minneapolis, MN: University of Minnesota Press.

Deleuze, G. (1992). *The fold, Leibniz and the baroque.* Minneapolis, MN: University of Minnesota Press.

Deleuze, G. (1995). *Negotiations.* New York, NY: University Press.

Deleuze, G., & Guattari, F. (1988). A thousand plateaus: Capitalism and schizophrenia: *Vol. 2. (trans. Brian Massumi).* London, UK: Athlone.

Deleuze, G., & Parnet, C. (2002). *Dialogues.* New York, NY: Columbia University Press.

Dunne, K. (2007). *The possible use of political online forums to engage young people in local politics.* Paper presented at the Institute of Communication Studies (ICS) Postgraduate Conference, Leeds, United Kingdom.

Farrell, T. J. (1979). The female and male modes of rhetoric. *College English, 40*(8), 909–921. doi:10.2307/376528

Foucault, M. (1977). *Discipline and punish: The birth of the prison.* New York, NY: Random House.

Foucault, M. (2008). *The birth of biopolitics: Lectures at the College de France, 1978-1979.* New York, NY: Palgrave MacMillan.

Fraser, N. (1992). Rethinking the public sphere: A contribution to the critique of actually existing democracy. In Calhoun, C. (Ed.), *Habermas and the public sphere* (pp. 109–142). Cambridge, MA: MIT Press.

Gastil, J., & William, K. M. (2005). A nation that (sometimes) likes to talk. In Gastil, J., & Levine, P. (Eds.), *The deliberative democracy handbook* (pp. 3–19). San Franciso, CA: Wiley & Sons/Jossey-Bass.

Greffet, F., & Wojcik, S. (2008). Parler politique en ligne. Une revue des travaux français et anglo-saxons. *Reseaux, 150,* 19–50.

Hargittai, E., & Walejko, G. (2008). The participation divide: Content creation and sharing in the digital age. *Information Communication and Society, 11*(2), 239–256. doi:10.1080/13691180801946150

Hibbing, J. R., & Theiss-Morse, E. (2002). *Stealth democracy: Americans' beliefs about how government should work.* Cambridge, UK: Cambridge University Press. doi:10.1017/CBO9780511613722

Hill, K. A., & Hughes, J. E. (1998). *Cyberpolitics: Citizen activism in the age of the Internet.* Lanham: Rowman & Little.eld.

Iyengar, S., & Jackman, S. (2003). *Technology and politics: Incentives for youth participation.* Paper presented for the presentation at the International Conference on Civic Education Research, New Orleans, USA.

Jankowski, N., & Van Os, R. (1998). Internet based political discourse: A case study of electronic democracy in Hoogveen. In Shane, P. M. (Ed.), *Democracy online. The prospects for political renewal through the Internet* (pp. 181–195). London, UK: Routledge.

Janoski, T. (1998). *Citizenship and civil society. A framework of rights & obligations in liberal, traditional and social democratic regime.* Cambridge, UK: Cambridge University Press.

Latour, B. (1987). *Science in action: How to follow scientists and engineers through society.* Milton Keynes, UK: Open University Press.

Latour, B. (1993). *We have never been modern.* New York, London: Harvester Wheatsheaf.

Latour, B. (1999). *Pandora's hope. Essays on the reality of science studies.* Cambridge, MA; London, UK: Harvard University Press.

Latour, B. (2005). *Reassembling the social: An introduction to actor-network theory.* Oxford, UK: Oxford University Press.

Latour, B. (2008). Pour un dialogue entre science politique et sciences studies. *Revue Francaise de Science Politique, 58*(4), 657–678. doi:10.3917/rfsp.584.0657

Latour, B. (2010). *Making law. An ethnography of the Conseil d'Etat.* Cambridge, UK: Polity Press.

Manin, B. (1987). On legitimacy and political deliberation. *Political Theory, 15*(3), 338–368. doi:10.1177/0090591787015003005

Manin, B. (2002). L'idée de démocratie délibérative dans la science politique contemporaine. Introduction, généalogie et éléments critiques. *Politix, 15*(57), 37–55.

Manin, B. (2005). Délibération et discussion. *Swiss Political Science Review, 10*(4), 34–46.

Mansbridge, J. (1983). *Beyond adversary democracy.* Chicago, IL: University of Chicago Press.

Mansbridge, J. (1999). Everyday talk in the deliberative system. In Macedo, S. (Ed.), *Deliberative politics* (pp. 211–242). Oxford, UK: Oxford University Press.

Monnoyer-Smith, L. (2006a). Citizen's deliberation on the Internet: An exploratory study. *International Journal of Electronic Government Research, 2*(3), 58–74. doi:10.4018/jegr.2006070103

Monnoyer-Smith, L. (2006b). How e-voting technology challenges traditional concepts of citizenship: An analysis of French voting rituals. In Krimmer, R. (Ed.), *Electronic voting 2006* (pp. 61–68). Bonn, Germany: GI Lecture Notes in Informatics.

Monnoyer-Smith, L. (2007). Citizen's deliberation on the Internet: A French case. In Norris, D. (Ed.), *E-government research: Policy and management* (pp. 230–253). Hershey, PA: IGI Publishing.

Monnoyer-Smith, L. (in press). The technological dimension of participation. A comparison between on and off-line participation. In Shane, P. M., & Coleman, S. (Eds.), *Connecting democracy: Online consultation and the future of democratic discourse.* Cambridge, MA: MIT Press.

Monnoyer-Smith, L. (2009). Deliberation and inclusion: Framing online public debate to enlarge participation. A theoretical proposal. *I/S: A Journal of Law and Policy for the Information Society, 5*(1), 87-116.

Muhlberger, P. (2004). Access, skill, and motivation in online political discussion: Testing cyber-realism. In Shane, P. M. (Ed.), *Democracy online* (pp. 225–238). London, UK: Routledge.

Muhlberger, P. (2005). *Attitude change in face-to-face and online political deliberation: Conformity, information, or perspective taking?* Paper presented at the American Political Science Association, 2005 Annual Meeting. Retrieved April 24, 2010, from http://www.geocities.com/pmuhl78/AttitudeDelib.pdf

Noveck, B. S. (2008). Wiki government. *Democracy Journal, 7.* Retrieved April 24, 2010, from http://www.democracyjournal.org/pdf/7/031-043.noveck.final.pdf

Peixoto, T. (2008). *E-participatory budgeting: e-democracy from theory to success?* Working paper. Retrieved April 24, 2010, from http://edc.unige.ch/edcadmin/images/Tiago.pdf

Price, V. (2006). Citizens deliberating online: Theory and some evidence. In Davies, T., & Noveck, B. S. (Eds.), *Online deliberation: Design, research, and practice* (pp. 37–58). Chicago, IL: University of Chicago Press.

Rajchman, J. (2000). *The Deleuze connections.* Cambridge, MA: MIT Press.

Ranerup, A. (2000). Online forums as an arena for political discussions. In Ishida, T., & Isbister, K. (Eds.), *Digital cities. Technologies, experiences, and future perspectives* (pp. 209–223). Berlin, Germany: Springer.

Raynes-Goldie, K., & Walker, L. (2008). Our space: Online civic engagement tools for youth. In L. Bennett (Ed.), *Civic life online: Learning how digital media can engage youth.* (pp. 161-188). The John D. and Catherine T. MacArthur Foundation Series on Digital Media and Learning. Cambridge, MA: MIT Press.

Sanders, L. (1997). Against deliberation. *Political Theory, 25,* 347–375. doi:10.1177/0090591797025003002

Schudson, M. (1997). Why conversation is not the soul of democracy. *Critical Studies in Mass Communication, 14*(4), 297–309. doi:10.1080/15295039709367020

Seyle, D. C., McGlohen, M., Ryan, P., Durham-Fowler, J., & Skiadas, T. (2008). *Deliberative quality across time and gender: An introduction to the effectiveness of deliberation scale.* Poster presented at the annual meeting of the ISPP 31st Annual Scientific Meeting, Paris, France. Retrieved April 24, 2010, from http://www.allacademic.com/meta/p245886_index.html

Shappin, S., & Shaeffer, S. (1985). *Leviathan and the air pump.* Princeton University Press.

Sintomer, Y., Herzberg, C., & Röcke, A. (2008). Participatory budgeting in Europe: Potentials and challenges. *International Journal of Urban and Regional Research, 32*(1), 164–178. doi:10.1111/j.1468-2427.2008.00777.x

Steiner, J., Bächtiger, A., Spörndli, M., & Steenberge, M. (2004). *Deliberative politics in action. Analysing parliamentary discourse.* Cambridge, UK: Cambridge University Press.

Talpin, J. (2007). Who governs in participatory governance institutions? The impact of citizen participation in municipal decision-making processes in a comparative perspective. In Dewitt, P., Pilet, J.-B., Reynaert, H., & Steyvers, K. (Eds.), *Towards DIY-politics. Participatory and direct democracy at the local level in Europe* (pp. 103–125). Bruges, Belgium: Vanden Broele.

Talpin, J., & Monnoyer-Smith, L. (2010). *Talking with the wind? Discussion on the quality of deliberation in the Ideal-EU project.* Paper presented at the International Political Science Association International Conference, Luxemburg. Retrieved April 24, 2010, from http://www.luxembourg2010.org/sites/default/files/Lux%20paper%20Talpin.pdf

Talpin, J., & Wojcik, S. (In press). When the youth talk about climate change. A comparison of the learning potential of online and face-to-face deliberation. *Policy and the Internet, 1*(2).

Tedesco, J. C. (2007). Examing Internet interactivity effects on young adult political information efficacy. *The American Behavioral Scientist, 50*(7), 1183–1194. doi:10.1177/0002764207300041

Toomey, B. (2008). Can the use of technology encourage young people to take an active part in urban regeneration consultations? A case study from East London. *Local Economy, 23*(3), 247–251. doi:10.1080/02690940802197473

Wilhelm, A. G. (2000). *Democracy in the digital age: Challenges to political life in cyberspace.* London, UK: Routledge.

Wilhelm, A. G. (2000). Virtual sounding boards: How deliberative is online political discussion? In Hague, B. N., & Loader, B. (Eds.), *Digital democracy: Discourse and decision making in the information age* (pp. 154–178). London, UK: Routledge.

Witschge, T. (2002). *Online deliberation: Possibilities of the Internet for deliberative democracy.* Paper presented at the INSITES conference: Prospects for Electronic Democracy. Pittsburgh, Carnegie Mellon University. Retrieved April 24, 2010, from http://java.cs.vt.edu/public/projects/digitalgov/papers/onlinedeliberation_Nl.pdf

Witschge, T. (2004). Online deliberation: Possibilities of the Internet for deliberative democracy. In Shane, P. M. (Ed.), *Democracy online. The prospects for political renewal through the Internet* (pp. 109–122). London, UK: Routledge.

Witschge, T. (2008). Examining online public discourse in context: A mixed method approach. *Javnost - The Public, 15*(2), 75-92.

Wojcik, S. (2008). Les forums électroniques municipaux: Un espace délibératif inédit. *Hermes, 45*, 177–182.

Woolgar, S. (2001). Configuring the user: The case of usability trials. *Sociological Review. Mongraph, 38*, 57–102.

Wright, S. (2005). Design matters: The political efficacy of government-run discussion forums. In Gibson, R., Oates, S., & Owen, D. (Eds.), *Civil society, democracy and the Internet: A comparative perspective* (pp. 80–99). London, UK: Routledge.

Wright, S., & Street, J. (2007). Democracy, deliberation and design: The case of online discussion forum. *New Media & Society, 9*(5), 849–869. doi:10.1177/1461444807081230

Young, I. M. (1990). *Justice and the politics of difference.* Princeton, NJ: Princeton University Press.

Young, I. M. (1996). Communication and the other: Beyond deliberative democracy. In Benhabib, S. (Ed.), *Democracy and difference: Contesting the boundaries of the political* (pp. 120–135). Princetown University Press.

Young, I. M. (1999). Difference as a resource for democratic communication. In Bohman, J., & Rehg, W. (Eds.), *Deliberative democracy* (pp. 387–398). Cambridge, MA: MIT Press.

Young, I. M. (2002). *Inclusion and democracy.* Oxford, UK: Oxford University Press. doi:10.1093/0198297556.001.0001

ENDNOTES

[1] I refer here to Andrew Barry's *Political Machines* which also refers to Deleuze in its analysis of *Diagram of Interactivity*, see below.

[2] One problematic issue, for example, from T. Wischge's article "Online Deliberation: Possibilities of the Internet for Deliberative Democracy" where she states: "The aim of this chapter is to examine whether or not the Internet holds possibilities for deliberative democracy in terms of meeting the criteria of difference and disagreement." (2004, 110).

[3] See however the experiments of P. Muhlberger op.cit. and V. Price. In France however most experiments have been virtual and face-to-face since mass market access to the Internet. It would thus be odd for a local authority to have only a virtual presence: public meetings and various neighbourhood associations are a long established political tradition in France (Monnoyer-Smith, 2006, 2007). We therefore can explain the lack of comparison by a disciplinary segmentation which has led political sciences towards F2F and communication studies towards online consultations. It is only very recent

that national calls for projects have brought together those two disciplines.

4   For evidence, see the following from the lead article in the French political science review Politix: "this issue understandably takes issue with that dualistic idealist or cynical attitude and aims to contribute towards changing these emerging forms of democracy into full sociological objects." This issue marks a turning point in French research by aiming to "shift focus and questions usually directed at this type of object by recourse to a resolutely 'internalist' approach to participative procedures. Blondiaux, Cardon, 2006, p.4.

5   My translation from the French version, *Ce que Parler veut dire*, Paris, Fayard,1982, pp 104, 107;

6   This holds at least in modern democracies where legitimacy is now procedural, not Rousseauist: its source is in the opinion building process, not public opinion itself, i.e. "law is a product of general deliberation, not…public opinion (Manin, 1987). Sixteen years later, Manin (2002, 38) added: I was arguing that the value of a collective decision and its authority over all citizens, minorities included, results from the fact that the decision was made after discussion open to all but not that it should, or could, have secured unanimous consent." (Manin, 2002, 38).

7   Deleuze uses the French term "agencement".

8   Deleuze (1992 [1988]) expands on the notion of the *Pli*, or "pleat" derived by Gottfried Liebniz from the curvature of the planet. The pleat is therefore the product of the subject's (or monad's) view of the world. In a curved world, any perspective involves a series of points of inflexion that mask pleats which encapsulate some part of reality invisible to the human eye. Thus, each perspective offers

a specific mix of pleats and observables that only abstraction can unpleat and explicit.

9   Latour borrows Deleuze's notion of setups (*agencements*) as a heterogeneous set of groupings and artifacts in a state of change.

10 "A technological society is one which takes technical change to be the model for political invention. The concept of a technological society does not refer to a stage I history, but rather to a specific set of attitudes towards the political present which have acquired a particular contemporary intensity, salience and form." (Barry, 2002, 2)

11 For details, see T. Janoski, 1998, pp 28+ *et seq.* The active dimension of citizenship covers two types of rights depending on the spheres they are exercised on. Political rights correspond to personal organizational, oppositional, etc. rights, as participation rights correspond to wider control rights over public or private bodies.

12 "Panoptism is a general function of seeing while remaining unseen (that) applies to any multiplicity." (Deleuze, 2002, 2)

13 Feudalism is one example of a setup that establishes new relationships between man, horse, soil, dislocations (Crusades or knightly jousts) and women (chivalry). The arrays may be totally insane but remain historically attributable nonetheless. (Deleuze, 2002 [1977, 4])

14 Translation from the French version, *Qu'est-ce qu'un dispositif ?*, Paris:Payot, 2007.

15 Deleuze and Guattari use the term *lignes de fuite* which could be understood both as lines of escape for individuals and leaks within a setup or a diagram. For clarification on Deleuze's work, see Rajchman, 2000.

16 This is especially true in European contexts in which national of regional debates take place.

Chapter 3
Communicative Mechanisms of Governance:
E–Democracy and the Architecture of the Public Sphere

Lori Anderson
Radford University, USA

Patrick Bishop
Lancaster University, UK

ABSTRACT

Significant claims have been made that developments in Information Communication Technology (ICT) can lead to e-democracy. The league tables that are regularly published rating different governments' performance and the laudatory tones in which governments identify their own actions as more democratic in the field of e-government need to be treated with some caution. This chapter starts with a review of some of these studies of e-government and e-democracy trials. Finding these studies largely unsatisfactory for determining advances in democracy, the chapter then looks at the kinds of communication that are needed to facilitate the political conversation of deliberative democracy. In particular, the chapter introduces a communication typology, based on the work of David Bohm, to see how the new technology might be used to shape the architecture of the public sphere to create political conversation.

INTRODUCTION

In this chapter we look first at one way in which E-democracy has been evaluated in a global

context through the series of studies undertaken by Darrell West of Brown University. The results of this series of surveys are then compared to the Freedom House International ranking of important democratic indicators such as human rights and press freedom to show that apparent

DOI: 10.4018/978-1-60960-159-1.ch003

success in technological functionality is not correlated to improvements in democracy. We then look at a particular site in a mature western liberal democracy that has been claimed to "world leading" to see if its presence has had any impact on the practice of democracy in such a regime. Evidence is retrieved from the commencement of that site in 2000 to more recent times in order to evaluate its impact on the practice of state government politics. What we are evaluating is if the E democracy site is meeting any of the criticism that have been directed at the practice of liberal democratic regimes, what Robert Dahl calls "polyarchy,"(1971) by authors such as Carole Pateman (1970) and Benjamin Barber (1984) and, more recently by the deliberative democrats discussed below, that such forms of democracy have little claim to being true democracy. By investigating experiments in e-democracy and e-government practices we consider how the public sphere might be shaped to improve democracy through the use of Information Communication Technology (ICTs). While e-democracy is a fluid and imprecise term, it has been applied to trials and as an evaluative term. Many evaluations of ICTs and its democratic credentials merely catalogue the reach of the new technology or act as a form of 'boosterism' for the new technology. The aim of this chapter is first to look at the way in which some studies have failed to adequately asses the new phenomenon and then to evaluate the different kinds of communication that operate in politics and how these might be utilized to facilitate genuine political conversations in e-democracy. In doing so we consider how ICTs have, to date, been restrictive in their use of communicative mechanisms of governance and how they can be utilized to improve political communication. To do this we develop an account of how innovations can be directed towards creating the architecture of a more democratic public sphere.

EVALUATING THE NEW TECHNOLOGY

Initial predictions of the reach of the new technology were overly optimistic, especially in regards to how it might impact on the practice of democratic politics. Early enthusiasts such as Dick Morris saw the new technology as dispensing with the need for parliaments or the US Congress. (Morris 1999) These 'New Athenians' saw in the possibilities of the new communication technology an answer to representative democracy's status as, at best, a compromised ideal. While this early enthusiasm has died down, or at least the claims are becoming less dramatic, there is an eagerness to make progress that pervades discussions around e-government, leading to an apparent tech race between national administrations. This is captured in the series of Brown University studies that has now had seven iterations. The methodology from the initial survey in 2002 onwards focuses on website functionality. In the first year 1,197 websites from 198 countries were tested and evaluated in terms of citizen accessibility. By the most recent survey the figure has risen to 1,667 from the same 198 countries (West 2008) The data collected covers an extensive list of features including reference to physical addresses and phone numbers as well as facilities to pay online, online databases, online publications, video and audio clips, foreign and non native language translations, commercial advertising, links to non-government sites etc. The system was also tested for functionality by utilizing any email request systems with a test email.

The flavour of the way in which this study has been promoted emerges in a press release to announce the second report in 2002.

Last year's global leader in digital government, the United States, dropped to fourth place (60.1), behind Taiwan (72.5), South Korea (64) and Canada (61.1). Chile moved up to fifth place with 60 points, followed by Australia with 58.3 points. (Brown University 2002)

Table 1. E-government rank (2002) compared to Freedom House rank of political rights, civil liberties and press freedom[5]

West Rank (2002)	Country	Political system	Freedom House Rank 2009	
			Press Freedom Range /100	Combined Freedom Index Range 1-7
1	Taiwan	Democracy	Free 23	1.5
2	South Korea	Democracy	Free 30	1.5
3	United States	Democracy	Free 18	1
4	Canada	Democracy	Free 19	1
5	Chile	Democracy	Free	2
6	Australia	Democracy	Free 22	1
7	China	Non democracy	Not Free 85	6.5
42	Austria	Democracy	Free 21	1

A comparison with the third iteration in 2003 shows dramatic advances and reversals in rankings. For example, in the 2002 survey, Austria ranked forty-second. This was a surprising result following our own examination in 2001 and through interviews with the architects of the extensive *Help.gv* site of the Austrian Government. Their self-perception was that they were close to 'European Best Practice'[1]. By the 2003 survey they ranked at number ten. The most surprising slide from 2002 to 2003 was South Korea. At a government-sponsored conference in South Korea in November 2002[2] their ranking of number two was mentioned regularly amid considerable self-congratulation. Their ranking at thirty in the 2003 survey must have led to considerable consternation in the same South Korean agencies that had been so pleased at the 2002 result. While any measurement of the impact of new technologies on a diverse social and political landscape in not easy, the report does not go into details as to how or why this dramatic slide occurred.[3] Publishing and publicizing results as a league table implies that there are winners and losers in e-government performance and that better performance in this area is desirable. What is being evaluated, if not celebrated, by this survey?

In some cases what the survey reports as successful e-government is occurring in countries that do not have good track records in democracy. Some of the most successful countries are not even democratic states. In 2003 the number one country, Singapore, is an authoritarian regime. Taiwan and South Korea rank second in terms of political rights and civil liberties according to the rights watch organisation Freedom House.[4] (See Table 1 and Table 2) China, ranked seven in 2002 and eleven in 2003, has the lowest ranking for political rights, and is not alone amongst high-ranking e-government performers in lacking a free press. Malaysia, Singapore and Turkey (ranked 'partly free') also miss out in this crucial indicator. In fact, no country in the top ten for e-government performance features in the top rank for press freedom in the Freedom House survey.

Subsequent versions of this particular study have also delivered widely ranging results. Malaysia for example fluctuated from being as high as eight in 2003 to being 157 in 2005 and back to twenty five in 2007. South Korea returned to the number one position in 2006 and 2007, but not before plunging to 86 in 2005. These fluctuations point to possible methodological weaknesses that we are not investigating here but as

Table 2. E-government rank 2003 compared to Freedom House rank of political rights, civil liberties and press freedom[6]

West Rank (2003)	Country	Political system	Freedom House Rank 2009	
			Press Freedom Range /100	Combined Freedom Index Range 1-7
1	Singapore	Non democracy	Not Free 68	4.5
2	United States	Democracy	Free 18	1
3	Canada	Democracy	Free 19	1
4	Australia	Democracy	Free 22	1
5	Taiwan	Democracy	Free 23	1.5
6	Turkey	Democracy	Partly Free 50	3
7	Great Britain	Democracy	Free 19	1
8	Malaysia	Non democracy	Not Free 71-80	5
9	Vatican	Non democracy	No data	-
10	Austria	Democracy	Free 21	1
11	China	Non democracy	Not Free 85	6.5
30	South Korea	Democracy	Free 30	1.5

our comparison with the Freedom House ranking shows the survey covers a variety of qualitatively different political regimes. To account for this Darrell West (2003) simply rules regime type out as a variable. "In each system analysed, we employ the same type of criteria in order to be able to compare the results across countries." (West 2003, 3) It is perhaps unfair to expect such a data gathering exercise to deliver results relating to democracy when it is specifically devised to measure only technical performance. However, in presenting or promoting the reports, press releases make much more qualitative claims; that better e-government is in some way benefits the citizen/customer.

Governments should promote features that allow citizens to post comments or otherwise provide feedback about a government agency. They also should consider market research, public opinion surveys, or focus groups that would provide them with information on how citizens feel about e-

government websites and what features would attract them to use these sites. (West 2002)

In the 2003 study West is even clearer as to the benefits of e-government.

E-government offers the potential to bring citizens closer to their government. Regardless of the type of political system that a country has, the public benefits from interactive features that facilitate communication between citizens and government. (West 2003 p.7 emphasis added)

The democratic promise is still there in the executive summary of the 2008 survey.

Electronic government offers the promise of utilizing technology to improve public sector performance as well as employing new advances for democracy itself. In its boldest formulation, technology is seen as a tool for long-term system transformation. (West 2008)

Table 3. E-government rank 2007 compared to Freedom House rank of political rights, civil liberties and press freedom[7]

West Rank (2007)	Country	Political system	Freedom House Rank 2009	
			Press Freedom Range /100	Combined Freedom Index Range 1-7
1	South Korea	Democracy	Free 30	1.5
2	Singapore	Non - Democracy	Not Free 68	1.5
3	Taiwan	Democracy	Free 23	1.5
4	United States	Democracy	Free 18	1
5	Great Britain	Democracy	Free 19	1
6	Canada	Democracy	Free 19	1
7	Portugal	Democracy	Free 16	1
8	Australia	Democracy	Free 22	1
9	Turkey	Democracy	Not free 50	3.0
10	Germany	Democracy	Free 16	1
51	China	Non democracy	Not Free 85	6.5
31	Austria	Democracy	Free 21	1

In this executive summary of the most recent survey conducted by the West team there is also the qualified finding that:

In general, e-government is not radically transforming the public sector. While some countries have embraced digital government broadly defined, the United States is falling behind in broadband access, public sector innovation and in implementing the latest interactive tools to government websites. This limits the transformational potential of the Internet and weakens the ability of technology to empower citizens and businesses. Government websites must make better use of available technology, and address problems of access and democratic outreach. (West 2008)

In a survey that only evaluates sites analysing at best a cyber reality and where the type and qualities of the broader political regime are purposefully excluded, normative assertions of desirable systems of government cannot be supported by the data. For example, whether it is prudent for

citizens to respond to a government request to post comments surely depends on whether the regime is democratic or authoritarian.

Therefore, it seems possible to have extensive e-government without democracy, even in its most minimal form. Throughout these surveys a government can be placed highly on the e-government scale and still remain at, or near, the bottom when it comes to measures of political rights, civil liberties and press freedom. By the 2007 interation there is only one non-democracy in the top ten (See Table 3).

The United Nations has also offered an annual survey of e-government through its E-Government Readiness Index. (See Table 4) This index is not given to such wide fluctuations and also has consistently high scoring countries on the Freedom House rankings in the top ten. Interestingly the three top performers are countries that do not feature at all in the top rank of the West studies.

In both these studies, however, what is being measured implies that the impact of the new

Table 4. 2008 UN E government Readiness Index (United Nations 2008)

Rank	Country	Index
1	Sweden	.9157
2	Denmark	.9134
3	Norway	.8921
4	United States	.8644
5	Netherlands	.8631
6	South Korea	.8317
7	Canada	.8172
8	Australia	.8108
9	France	.8038
10	United Kingdom	.7872
23	Singapore	.7009

technology is politically neutral, certainly if the benefits are as evident in authoritarian regimes as in democracies. Good performance in E-government cannot stand alone as an indicator of successful democratic benefits. In fact, in a regional statistical survey of e-government in South America, David Altman suggests that countries with "high levels of satisfaction with democracy are where e-government is less likely to develop" (Altman 2002, p.16) and raises the question whether e-government actually has positive effects on satisfaction with democracy and democratic accountability. (Altman 2002) The very high ranking of Singapore throughout the surveys and the high scores of China, and Malaysia, in the *absence* of democratic government, may show that the new technology is one way for regimes to build trust using the new the technology while bypassing democratisation.

West (2004 p.25; 2008) still sees the cost of specific e-government infrastructure as a "pressing challenge" to further adopt new technology but even if an efficiency dividend could be established it is not, of itself, a democratic value. The most dramatic way we can see the delivery of government services via electronic technology assisting in building trust in government, that deliver a democratic dividend, is through its potential to remove petty corruption at the local level, the 'kickback' or bribe. That is, the transaction is rendered consistently transparent be removing the role of the potentially corrupt actor. This procedural fairness argument is a strong one. A commitment to equal treatment, however, might deny one of the most effective commercial mechanisms for building Internet usage of service delivery, the online discount. Airlines, hotel chains, car rental firms have all built Internet usage of their services through providing their best rates on the Internet. When adopted by government, these commercial incentives cut across government commitments to provide the same level of service and the same fee to all citizens, a sense of equality we argue is characteristic of democracy.

AUSTRALIAN EXPERIENCE

We now consider an experiment conducted to specifically advance the concept of e-democracy in the context of representative government. The case study comes from the Australian state of Queensland and was evaluated by Stephen Clift[8], in a report commissioned by the Commonwealth Centre for Electronic Governance. Generally laudatory, Clift concluded that he was "extremely bullish on the future of e-democracy in government in Australia and New Zealand." (Clift 2002) Initiatives he endorsed as "important and exciting", however, need more critical investigation, beyond these adjectives, to assess their impacts on existing institutions of representative democracy and if they offer any advance in democracy itself.

Of the Queensland e-democracy initiative Clift also says it "is the clearest sign of political support for e-democracy issued by a government in the region, perhaps anywhere in the world to date." (Clift 2002) The Queensland government has certainly been active in promoting its e-democracy profile. In November 2001 it restructured the Department of the Premier and Cabinet to include the

Community Engagement Division. In announcing the initiative, Premier Peter Beattie asserted, "the role of Government is changing. The community is seeking better Government leadership through increased public participation in decision-making. I am willing to accept this challenge." (Premier Beattie cited in Clift 2002) The reform was aimed at "strengthening relations with citizens", which the Premier saw as "a sound investment in better policy-making by allowing government to tap new sources of relevant ideas, information and resources when making decisions." (Premier Beattie cited in Clift 2002)

In a move that Clift identified as "the highest level of formal e-democracy policy interest that I have seen in any government" the Community Engagement Division's 'Direction Statement', contained a commitment by the Premier to a Queensland E-Democracy Three Year Trial, approved by Cabinet and assigned to the Community Engagement Division to develop. While he also notes, "current developments in the UK will certainly place it in the lead on a national scale", he sees Queensland as "the place to watch in terms of measurable and identifiable outcomes due to its relatively modest population of around 3 million people." (Clift 2002)

As proclaimed on the government's own website, the commitment included "exploring the many new opportunities the Internet brings and to discovering ways in which this medium can strengthen participative democracy within Queensland – *The Smart State*[9]."(Queensland Government 2003) Despite mention of 'participative democracy' the definition places the trial squarely in the bounds of existing representative political structures. E-democracy here is seen as being "at the convergence of traditional democratic processes and Internet technology." (Queensland Government 2003) From the government's perspective, "it refers to how the Internet can be used to enhance our democratic processes and provide increased opportunities for individuals

and communities to interact with government." (Queensland Government 2003)

The institutional placement of the e-democracy experiment is significant and is reiterated when the definition is expanded to comprise "a range of Internet based activities that aim to strengthen democratic processes and institutions, including government agencies." (Queensland Government 2003) Specifically this amounts to "providing accessible information resources online; conducting policy consultation online; and facilitating electronic input to policy development." (Queensland Government 2003) Further, the initiative is government led, where it retains the responsibility "to expand the channels of communication to reach as many citizens as possible." (Queensland Government 2003) The preamble concludes, "the Internet is not inherently democratic, but it can be used for democratic purposes. The full implications of how the Internet will enhance this interaction are yet to be explored." (Queensland Government 2003)

The trial included a commitment over three years to, "post a number of issues on the website on which the Government desires wide consultation and feedback; provide online access to Government consultation documents relevant to those issues, such as discussion and policy papers and draft bills; broadcast Parliamentary debates over the Internet; and develop a system to accept petitions to the Queensland Parliament online." (Queensland Government 2003)

The trial was completed and each of the initiatives continue to the present day. E-petitions are regularly submitted and parliamentary debates are now available by audio streaming. The first practice, while utilizing the new technology, directly mirrors the analogue environment. That is, it has only generated a new method for *submitting* petitions, it has not altered their status; they still only have the capacity to influence decision-makers if they choose to take notice. They do not, as is the case in California, have any direct constitutional power to become ballot propositions, or to recall elected officials. While Queensland State parliament debates are, for the first time, available to a wider audience than those who actually attend, the technology is only being used as a narrowcast system. The technically possible opportunity to send in comments directly to parliamentarians via the Internet, in real time, for example, has not been adopted.

The posting of e-democracy initiatives for comment presents the most problems for administrators given the avowed place of these initiatives within representative democratic decision-making structures. The questions posted are relatively uncontroversial and response rates are quite low. The problems occur in the amount of management that a government-operated site requires. To make sure there wasn't a clash between the governmental and private spheres or that possible damage from harsh comments were limited, a system of double-posting was adopted. Items would only get on the public website once they were subject to approval by public servants. While this is prudent for a government-sponsored site, it also generates problems. Groups in the community who are suspicious of any involvement with government simply won't participate if they know they will be subject to censorship. On the other hand, racist comments or views can be posted in subtle ways that are not always detected. In a similar process with Regional Community Forums, for example, submissions apparently from advocates of Esperanto, a universal language, (itself not racist) were accepted without realising that their rationale was to deny the teaching of any other languages apart from English or Esperanto, a xenophobic, if not an outright racist proposal, in a multicultural society. (Queensland Government 2000)

From these examples it is clear that many of the more deliberative possibilities of the Internet are not being used in Queensland. The potential for expanding democracy is not fully explored. In fact, its whole existence is dependant on the whim of the leader. The unit that was formed to set up the trial has since been disbanded, meaning that there is no ongoing commitment to further

innovations. As the following example shows, it has failed to reshape governance in that state and remains largely window dressing.

By far the most successful of the e-petitions, in terms of recruiting numbers, has been for a trial of daylight savings time for the summer. This move would bring Queensland into line with the other Eastern states. The first petition was submitted in 2006 with some 62000 signatories and a second in 2007 with 77000 signatories. (Few e-petitions get more than 1000 responses) The then acting Premier's first response, dated 20 May 2006, refers to a previous referendum on the matter:

A majority of Queenslanders rejected the intro-duction of daylight saving in a 1992 referendum. The State Government has no intention currently to hold another referendum or introduce any of-ficial changes related to daylight saving. ...I am unaware of any current workable model for state-wide daylight saving that would be supported by the majority of Queenslanders. (Bligh 2006 p.1)

The second reply, on 21 December 2007, is more detailed citing research by AC Nielsen in April of that year that 59% of all those surveyed supported the introduction of daylight savings time across Queensland. It also showed strong opposition to daylight savings time in regional Queensland, with 52% of residents opposed to its introduction across the state. The research also found that the compromise of a split time zone was opposed by 63% in rural and regional areas and 45% in the urban south east.

Premier Bligh continues:

To hold a referendum on this issue would cost approximately $12m to $13m. This cost would be equivalent to the employment of approximately 86 additional police officers, 118 additional nurses, 121 additional ambulance officers or 155 additional teachers in one calendar year. (Bligh 2007 p.2)

The emphasis on cost and subsequent statistics relating to the delivery of government services draws the reader away from what her reply doesn't emphasise: that, according to the research, community attitudes have altered since the 1992 referendum to the extent that a referendum would *now pass*. As the research also shows, this would be a divisive outcome for the state. This is representative democracy as usual, not electronically-transformed direct democracy.

Stephen Clift, while still promoting the Queensland government's unique commitment, is less ebullient about the process of e democracy itself.

After speaking hundreds of times across 24 countries, mostly to e-democracy interested governments, it is clear to me that what is possible is not probable. The best practices and e-democracy technologies are not being effectively shared. If we want the demonstrated potential of the new medium to spread, democratic intent will be required. The default path I see, without a political and resource commitment, is democratic decline. (Clift 2004)

This governmental activity takes place in an increasingly crowded cyber space. While such government postings are still relatively rare and carefully managed, there are many existing media sites, where 'votes' are sought in a sensationalist manner that aims for, rather than avoids controversy. "Have your say!" the sites encourage about the latest controversy. Here, questions are posed to be controversial and only yes/no answers are possible. Such sites, now part of mainstream media, may have already generated expectations that compete with any new government initiatives. If government postings are benign, bland or feel good, it may well add to, rather than address, community cynicism.

As yet, the primary concern of public sector mangers designing and maintaining these sites has been to meet the political objective of having an e-democracy presence.[10] They have done this without giving due consideration to the possibility that some forms of consultative practice may actually be harmful to governments and the policy process (See Irvin and Stansbury 2004; Kane and Bishop 2002). Despite the somewhat patronising tone of Clift's conclusion,[11] our interviewees in Queensland have invariably drawn attention to their respective endorsements from Steven Clift. This endorsement has also led to complacency when it comes to exploring the possible ways in which these initiatives may either fail to deliver on raised expectations of more participatory democracy or, a more pressing concern, the potential for this failure to embarrass governments rather than meet their objective, to improve their standing in the eyes of the public.

E-GOVERNMENT AND E-DEMOCRACY

The studies discussed above blur the distinction between e-democracy and e-government. E-government is about the electronic delivery of government services, and as our earlier comparisons showed, is neutral as to what type of government regime. We believe that e-democracy involves more qualitative assessments and is usually identified as some level of engagement, via the web or the Internet, with citizens' views about what should and shouldn't be government policy. This distinction has been blurred, for example, by the exhortation from West that a push for more citizen feedback somehow improves e-government performance or by the ringing endorsements and the title of Stephen Clift's report on Australia, *from e-governance to e-democracy*, (Clift 2002) that imply a normative argument without making clear how these new initiatives improve representative democracy. A policy brief from the OECD makes a more sober point. "E-government is more about government than about 'e'." (OECD 2003, p.1) It is even more the case that 'e-democracy' is about 'democracy'. The challenge presented by the new technology is not merely about what is now possible but what in fact is desirable. It is, in other words, fundamentally a theoretical problem regarding the ideals of democracy itself. (See Bishop *et al.* 2002) If it is to make projections about the development of e-democracy, any study of e-government must assess the *qualities* of government that new techniques and technologies engender.

EVALUATING E-GOVERNMENT INITIATIVES AS AN ADVANCE OF DEMOCRACY

The series of *Global E-government* surveys evaluate the relative success or failure of the application of new technology to the practice of government. The government-promoted e-democracy trial discussed above has also been evaluated primarily in terms of its application of technology. As a management technique adopted by governments and administrators, the new technology can produce benefits that are internal to government such as increased managerial efficiency and effectiveness, and also deliver benefits external to government, by improving information flows and providing services to citizens and businesses. While the examples above emphasise and celebrate the external citizen relationship, they also propose internal benefits. West, for example, suggests that benefits accrue to government in gaining diverse perspectives from citizens and also recommends regional alliances so that site development costs can be shared. (West 2002, p.14) The Premier in the Australian case acknowledges that e-government trials enhance and exemplify his broader political agenda.

The technological focus of much e-government evaluation means that actual, or potential, democratic impacts are not measured; in fact, they are overlooked. Benefits are touted and celebrated but not defined. The Clift review, the West surveys and the UN Index present or imply a staged model

of the development of e-government. Benefits flow through a progression from less to more technological sophistication. As with other models of consultative practice (See Bishop and Davis 2002) stages flow from information dissemination, to two-way communication, to service and financial transaction, to vertical and horizontal integration and finally to political participation. (Moon 2002, p.426) While this is a logical and useful framework from a governmental perspective focusing on what is and can be available through technology, it implies rather than specifies any particular democratic components of the practice.

What we address here is the relationship between e-government and e-democracy. Primarily we are arguing that technology needs to be seen as an aid to communication rather than the determining factor in exploring the democratic potential in the use of ICT in government and governance.

TECHNOLOGY AS A COMMUNICATION TOOL

While many discussions of ideal communication take as their starting point Jürgen Habermas's *Theory of Communicative Action,* (Habermas 1981) for this analysis we chose the work of David Bohm to provide our communication matrix, in particular for the distinction he develops between discussion and dialogue. David Joseph Bohm (1917 – 1992), a U.S. born, British physicist, collaborated with Basil J. Hiley to develop the ontological interpretation of quantum physics, a critique of the Copenhagen interpretation. Concurrent and integral with this theory, Bohm developed a philosophy of consciousness. Both are based on an *implicate order*, a theoretical construct for explaining the manifestation and relationship of matter and consciousness. For Bohm, matter and consciousness are not separate entities. (Bohm 1993; Nichol 2003) Bohm identifies the current *inherited order*, or generalized, societal paradigm as *mechanism*, a view that natural phenomenon exist in an external relationship with one another that displays discrete and observable cause and effect. A century of quantum physics suggests otherwise. Therefore the mechanistic paradigm that informs modern metaphysics is incongruent with scientific research. (Nichol 2003) More congruent with this century long tradition of research in quantum physics, Bohm proposes a *philosophy of the implicate order* that views the natural world as a whole and human existence as embedded within it. It is within this philosophy that he introduces the concept of dialogue. (Bohm 1993, 1991; Bohm and Peat 2000; Nichol 2003)

Our claim here is not that one form of communication is more valid than another, however, when it comes to resolving political matters, deliberation will tend to produce a more considered, nuanced and finessed public policy and legislation. In a democracy this will always be done through a combination of inputs, both directly from citizens and via representatives, as well as policy expertise from public servants, academics, policy experts and lobbyists. The immediate thrust of ICTs, however, has tended to emphasise one-way communication. It has been much easier to create the electronic referendum in the form of the e-petition or the unmediated space of the 'blogosphere' than it has been to create the kinds of political circumstances that shape deliberative forums.

As we have argued above, evaluation of the new phenomenon via the technology obscures the public communicative character necessary for democracy. If we are to explore the democratic governance potential of technology, not as an end itself, but as a communicative tool, we need to disentangle the technological innovation from democracy so we can see in what way the new technology might be used to form better democracy. As a democratic tool, technology's role needs to be expanded to facilitate public discourse and create a communicative mechanism of governance, serving rather than shaping governance goals.

This lens shifts the focus from the technological to the democratic.

Technology has the potential to facilitate a series of communication tools, ranging from the simplest to the most sophisticated. The simplest form of political communication is information dissemination or one-way communication. In this form of communication one party provides information to another party without feedback or response. For example, information posted on a government website where there is no opportunity for the viewer to respond to the posted information is an example of information dissemination.

Another form of political communication is information exchange or two-way communication in which both parties exchange information without confirming that the communication has been understood. A web-based survey posted on a government website is and example of information exchange. Information has been exchanged between the government and the viewer, yet neither has confirmed their communication has been understood. In this schema of communication tools, ICTs provide information dissemination and information exchange but do not offer any qualitative advances over older technologies, such as letter writing, petitions and media broadcasts. These modes of communication are also the most common to be adapted to the new ICT. While necessary for democratic governance they are forms of communication that offer the least potential to reshape the public sphere toward more deliberative and dialogic mechanisms of communication.

A third form of political communication is political contest, which utilizes discussion. As defined by Bohm and Peat, there is a distinction between discussion and dialogue that assists our exploration of the different communicative qualities implied by e-democracy (as distinct from e-government). In discussion, participants present and defend their fixed views. Individuals talk to persuade others; their goal is to convince other participants of their view. Agreement may be reached and compromise is likely, where the

Table 5. Discussion and Dialogue Contrasted (Bohm 2002)

	Method	Goal	Outcome	Generates
Discussion	Talk to Persuade	Convince Other Participants	Decision & Action	Competition
Dialogue	Listen to Understand	Identify Values	Understanding & Creativity	Meaning & Learning

two parties gain and concede something of minor significance. When issues are of high significance, parties rigidly hold to their positions and negotiations cease as communication deteriorates into either destructive confrontation or avoidance. Creative solutions are not likely from this viewpoint. (Bohm and Peat 2000; Nichol 2003) The more positive political effects of discussion are decision making and subsequent action. In Western societies discussion is the most frequent, familiar and primary mode of verbal communication. It is the communication mode in which most individuals are comfortable, practiced and skilled. Even when the tone is congenial or friendly, discussion generates competition. Most political discourse is based on discussion and is congruent with the adversarial political party exchanges familiar to observers of key institutions of representative democracy such as the US Congress or parliaments. It is also often the communicative mode of political interest groups and lobbyists and the form of communicative interaction most consistent with many practices of pluralist, representative democracy.

Finally, political conversation is based on dialogue. Relying on the work of psychiatrist Patrick de Mare', Bohm and Peat discuss dialogue as a free flow of meaning between people. (Bohm and Peat 2000) In contrast to discussion, participants in dialogue listen to understand. Each participant watches for and exposes his or her own assumptions, as well as the assumptions and biases of the other participants. The goal of dialogue is to identify values and examine them. Participants expose and suspend their own and others' positions so that all points of view and their underlying assumptions and values may be

explored for their meaning. By engaging in this suspension, exposition, and examination of varying points of view, dialogue creates the cognitive space where creative and innovative solutions can arise. Therefore, dialogue is about more than an examination of the various positions present at the start of the process, it's great value is the creation of new possibilities, not originally present at the start of the communication. The spirit of dialogue, then, is to hold multiple views in suspension, while also seeking to create a common meaning. The dialogue itself is more important that the outcome of the dialogue. In other words no point of view is worth holding at the cost of ending the dialogue. Bohm and Peat refer to this as *unity in plurality*. Understanding and creativity are the outcomes of dialogue and dialogue generates meaning and learning. (Bohm and Peat 2000; Nichol 2003) An example of this political conversation occurs in focus groups and deliberative forums where government representatives non-defensively listen to understand the views of the consumers of governmental services.

Both discussion and dialogue are appropriate modes of political communication for most interactive contexts. (See Table 5) In the public arena, dialogue and discussion are potentially complimentary. Dialogue explores complex and subtle issues not evident in most discussions and offers an opportunity for shared meaning, creativity and learning. Discussion allows positions to be articulated, decisions made and actions to be taken.

Surprisingly, a number of practices that might be seen as direct democracy employ only information dissemination. In a referendum, it is the citizen who informs the government of his or her opinion. While direct democracy is often presented as the most desirable form of democracy, it utilizes the least sophisticated form of communication, information dissemination or one-way communication. There is no information exchange, contest or conversation in this kind of direct democracy. This simplest form of communication is also the mode found on media websites offering yes/no voting on sensationalist propositions or via phone responses at the end of public affairs television programs.

Australia, where the referendum is the mechanism to alter the national constitution, provides a good example of how this form of direct democracy where decision-making authority resides with the citizens, is not conducted as a dialogue but as simple information dissemination, with very clear political consequences. While opinion polls showed some 80% of Australians wanted to become a republic, the referendum format with the presentation of a 'Yes' and 'No' case, and the way in which the political campaign was subsequently waged, meant that the desired option was not achieved because the method of communication was at the level of information dissemination. (McAllister, 2001; See also Uhr 2000 for a discussion of the use of deliberative polling in the same election) Rather than generating dialogue, or even discussion, the move to the referendum simply reverses the role of decision maker from representative to citizen.

Most e-government practices, where they are undertaken in democracies, occur in the context of representative democracy. All technological innovations do not necessarily enhance democratic character. The 2004 nomination race for the US Democrat Presidential candidate saw the emergence of new technology in the quest for campaign funding when candidate former Vermont Governor Howard Dean sought to raise a considerable amount of money via the Internet[12] but this in itself wasn't e-democracy. While lists of contributors form a campaign database, it does not give them any input into subsequent policy development if he were to be elected. In a repre-

sentative democracy, whoever is elected works in the interests of the public – all the public – not just those who supported the candidate. Even if purchased at a lower cost by more people, preferential treatment for campaign contributors is still undue influence. In his survey of 2000 American political campaign Internet and web usage, David C. King concludes that, despite growing innovation in its use, the web is unlikely to change the way members of the US Congress deliberate. (King 2002, p.115)

In the most recent US Presidential campaign Senator Barack Obama utilized the Internet as part of a fundraising strategy to raise vast sums. However, his campaign also showed a different and more discursive use of the Internet. While the use of viral email campaigns emerged during the President George W. Bush / Senator John Kerry presidential race, it reached a crescendo in the Obama campaign. The campaign's response was to fight the misinformation that was circulating about the candidate's birth; about his religion and about his relationship with people identified as terrorists with a website dedicated to exposing the myths. (Denton 2009; Talbot 2008) Despite these innovations in campaign technique we believe King's point that the Internet is not having an impact on US Congressional deliberation still holds true. That is, email campaigns lack impact on deliberations and the potential for ICTs to be utilized to facilitate meaningful dialogue between constituents and representative has not been developed.

For e-democracy to be an advance on current forms of representative democracy, it needs to incorporate dialogue between representatives and citizens and amongst citizens and interest groups. Clearly in some cases the representative would rather rely on contest than conversation but there may be some instances where there is a need to work through difficult or intractable problems in which an Internet based forum could be used to include citizen dialogue to reach the kind of considered outcome that Bohm outlines.

Representative democracy currently utilizes information dissemination, information exchange, and political contest. The trustee and agent models of representative democracy (Mansbridge 1998, Bishop *et al* 2002) primarily employ information dissemination. In the trustee model, a citizen communicates with his or her representative primarily through voting. The citizen entrusts daily governmental decisions to the representative. Although it is under-utilized, the representative has an opportunity to communicate decisions and decision rationale to the constituency, making greater use of information exchange. In the agent model as proposed by some e-democracy advocates (Latham 2001; See also Bishop *et al,* 2002) the citizen informs his or her representative about preferences regarding specific governmental actions and the representative undertakes to act on it. Political contest remains the cornerstone of current representative democratic practice as interest groups and representatives negotiate and compromise toward political decisions. Despite claims of more consultative government, most interactive governmental forums such as town meetings and public hearings exemplify political contest, employing discussion as their primary communication mode. Relying on dialogue, political conversation is currently rare. The discerning factor between political contest and political conversation is that political conversation is characterized by a commitment by both the government and citizens to listen to understand with a willingness to change their original position.

To map these distinctions across current practice, e-government and e-democracy, we have developed a framework of communicative mechanisms of governance, a democracy centered and communication driven model that does not shift ultimate decision-making authority. To reflect current practice and the apparent aims of current government e-democracy trials, decision-making authority under this framework remains with the representative. Government representatives would be prudent to explicitly define their decision-making responsibility and authority when utilizing political conversation because as interaction increases, so will expectations for influence and control. However, because of the retention of legitimate decision-making authority in the representative body, increased equality of communication does not necessarily correspond to increased equality in decision-making authority.

THE DELIBERATIVE TURN

A number of theorists have focussed on deliberative democracy as a way of overcoming a perceived deficit in representative democratic practice. Seeking to overturn the aggregation of voting choice that is at the heart of the institution of representative democracy, they argue for more sites for citizen deliberation in determining policy and legislation. (Cohen 1989, Benhabib 1996, Dryzek, 2000) John Dryzek identifies a constitutional strand of deliberative theory, associated with the work of James Fishkin (1993) and his own more discursive and radically critical version of deliberation. Dryzek and Simon Niemeyer bring back the notion of representation but in a discursive form which, he argues, will help "render policy making more rational, respect individual autonomy by more fully representing diverse aspects of the self, assist in realizing the promise of deliberative democracy and make democratic theory more applicable to a world where the consequences of decisions are felt across national boundaries." (Dryzek and Niemeyer 2008, p.492) Some proponents of deliberative democracy have directly related it to the use of the new technology (Leib 2004). In all cases deliberative theory is looking for deliberation to be a method whereby multiple views are brought into dialogue and where dialogue can lead to a transformation of views to a more genuinely democratic outcome. In these final sections we consider how ICTs might be applied to more deliberative practices in a reshaped public sphere.

THE ARCHITECTURE OF THE PUBLIC SPHERE

The complete liberty of the Internet and the 'blogosphere' (Barlow 2007) means that, while some sites offer dialogic possibilities, there is little to constrain other modes of communication, one-way shouting, prejudiced ranting or two-way competitive discussion. From our observation of developments thus far, little use has been made of the technology to foster political conversation. For democracy in its historic, representative guise liberty is always constrained either by constitutions or conventions that create not only the realm of government but also provide a demarcation between the public and private spheres. In regimes that have strong party systems such as the United Kingdom and Australia, parliament offers the spectacle of lively debate, but it is more often than not the arena for grandstanding and political point scoring. The aim in such bear pits is competition; to show the government in a poor light rather than to foster debate directed toward the best policy solution. However, other forums within government do create a more dialogic and deliberative space. In Australia, for example, the work of standing or *ad hoc* legislative committees with membership from all parties, have become opportunities for less conflict and more deliberative dialogue. (Uhr 1998) Other deliberative forums have been set up in Britain, Denmark, Australia, and in the US states of Oregon, Texas and Connecticut to address a range of issues including health policy, national reconciliation with indigenous citizens and resource planning of electric utilities. (Fishkin 2004) Techniques such as citizens' juries have also been adopted to respond to environmental issues. (Hendriks 2002) All of these forums require rules or practices for those who participate to know that their efforts will be considered. These are also necessary to ensure that all share responsibility for the outcome. In representative democracies elected officials are charged by their constituencies with the responsibility to govern, but also have

the more practical concern of the certainty of the next election to keep them accountable for their actions. What the public sphere as created by ICTs requires for serious deliberation to take place is a new *architecture* to create a public space that encourages and constrains actors to ensure that what occurs is genuinely deliberative. There is, we believe, a need to design spaces with rules, constitutions or conventions that apply in the online environment to ensure that engagements are productive.

COMMUNICATIVE MECHANISMS OF GOVERNANCE

Anchored in democracy, our communicative mechanism framework (See Table 6) redefines technology as a communication tool subservient to democracy.

This framework is devised on the quadrant to remove any implied scale from less to more democracy. The shaded three quadrants show the

Table 6. Communicative Mechanisms of Governance

Political Conversation Dialogue - Desire to get the best outcome - Accumulation of knowledge - Diffusion - Partnerships - Deliberation **E-technologies** - new technology creates dialogic space.	Information Dissemination One-way communication - Transparency - Informing **E-technologies** - Petitions - Audio streaming of Parliament
Political Contest Discussion - Polarizing debate - Interest group negotiation - Pluralism - Escalation - Participation **E-technologies** - Political activists web sites - Media websites - Seeks controversial	Information Exchange Two-way communication - Accountability - Public justification - Trust **E-technologies** - Surveys - Online consultation

modes of political communication that currently dominate in representative democracies; that are carried out without the aid of new technology but that new technology has been applied without challenging the existing practice. The quadrant also does not imply that governance communication can only operate in one quadrant. For example, information dissemination and exchange can be a significant preliminary to political contest and political conversation. The use of ICTs may increase availability and add new opportunities for communication but they do not provide a qualitative advance representative democracy.

CONCLUSION

Democratisation is usually a term applied to developing countries or to former dictatorships or totalitarian regimes. (Grugel 2002) The term can also be usefully applied to existing western liberal democracies to look at the phenomenon, of which there are a number of examples in this chapter, of governments attempting to make existing representative democracy *more* democratic.

We need to understand the phenomenon of government initiated e-government and e-democracy. We have looked at this here and elsewhere (Anderson and Bishop 2005) first as a transformation from e-government to e-democracy. This trend does not, however, take sufficient account of the institutional structures of representative democracy and the differing modes of communication required. If we look, for example, at the Queensland initiatives, they are placed firmly within government control and designed primarily to reflect well on the activities of the current Labor administration. This is not a criticism. It only reaffirms the initiative as part of 'business as usual' in terms of party government in a representative democracy. The initiatives reinforce the existing structure by showing that the representatives are listening to the public. Like other initiatives of the government, it is designed to restore faith in existing institutions, albeit by novel means. As we can see these initiatives may provide an impetus that can meet the aim of building trust in government. They do not, as yet, offer an advance in democracy to the point where the label e-democracy connotes a qualitative advance on the traditional representative democratic compromise.

When looking at the turn towards more deliberative forms of democracy we see that different forms of communication are needed. Protagonists for deliberative democracy see it as a means whereby complex cross-national issues can be considered in a manner that produces rational solutions that are respectful of individual autonomy. (Dryzek and Niemeyer 2008) Here we have argued that to achieve this level of deliberation via the new ICTs requires considerable effort in the design of the architecture of the public sphere to encourage Bohmian dialogue that has as its focus the development of shared meanings to provide creative solutions to complex policy problems. The challenge that remains for the technology lies in the unshaded fourth quadrant of our framework: to devise a system that seeks and promotes dialogue within a representative institutional context that still leaves ultimate decision-making to the elected representatives. This would certainly be a qualitative advance in representative democratic practice, incorporating aspects of the agent model with the representative's current trustee status in response to the criticism that the current political discourse is somehow 'broken'. (Kane and Patapan 2004; Latham 2001) It could also facilitate democracy through a dialogic e-democracy that is not merely new technology applied to old techniques but could fulfil the promise of a truly deliberative democracy.

REFERENCES

Altman, D. (2002). Prospects for e-government in Latin America. *International Review of Public Administration, 7*(2), 5–20.

Anderson, L., & Bishop, P. (2005). E-government to e-democracy: Communicative mechanisms of governance. *Journal of E-Government, 2*(1), 5–26. doi:10.1300/J399v02n01_02

Barber, B. (1984). *Strong democracy*. Berkeley, CA: University of California Press.

Barlow, A. (2007). *The rise of the blogosphere*. Westport, CT: Praeger.

Benhabib, S. (1996). Toward a deliberative model of democratic legitimacy. In Benhabib, S. (Ed.), *Democracy and difference: Contesting the boundaries of the political* (pp. 67–94). Princeton, NJ: Princeton University Press.

Bishop, P., & Davis, G. (2002). Mapping public participation in policy choices. *Australian Journal of Public Administration, 61*(1), 14–29. doi:10.1111/1467-8500.00255

Bishop, P., Kane, J., & Patapan, H. (2002). The theory and practice of e–democracy: Agency, trusteeship and participation on the Web. *International Review of Public Administration, 7*(2), 21–31.

Bligh, A. The Hon, Premier of Queensland. (2006). *Response to petition 553-05*. Retrieved from http://www.parliament.qld.gov.au/view/EPetitions_QLD/responses/553-05.pdf

Bligh, A. The Hon, Premier of Queensland. (2007). *Response to petition 931-07*. Retrieved from http://www.parliament.qld.gov.au/view/EPetitions_QLD/responses/TP2778-2007.pdf

Bohm, D. (2003). *The essential David Bohm*. New York, NY: Routledge.

Bohm, D., & Edwards, M. (1991). *Changing consciousness: Exploring the hidden source of the social, political, and environmental crises facing our world*. San Francisco, CA: Harper.

Bohm, D., & Hiley, B. (1993). *The undivided universe: An ontological interpretation of quantum mechanics*. London, UK: Routledge.

Bohm, D., & Peat, D. (2000). *Science, order, and creativity*. London, UK: Routledge.

Brown University. (2002). *Second annual global e-government study shows Taiwan, South Korea, and Canada overtaking United States*. Press release. Retrieved from http://www.insidepolitics.org/PressRelease02int.html

CBS News. *(2003, June 4)*. Howard Dean's Internet love-in. *Retrieved from* http://www.cbsnews.com/stories/2003/06/04/politics/main557004.shtml

Clift, S. *(2002)*. E-governance to e-democracy: Progress in Australia and New Zealand toward Information-Age democracy. *Retrieved from* http://www.publicus.net/articles/aunzedem.html

Clift, S. (2004). Saving democracy from the Information Age. *CIO Government Magazine, Australia*. Retrieved from http://stevenclift.com/?p=114

Cohen, J. (1989). Deliberation and democratic legitimacy. In Hamlin, A., & Pettit, P. (Eds.), *The good polity* (pp. 17–34). Oxford, UK: Basil Blackwell.

Dahl, R. A. (1971). *Polyarchy: Participation and opposition*. New Haven, CT: Yale University Press.

Denton, R. (2009). *The 2008 presidential campaign: A communication perspective*. Lanham, MD: Rownam & Littlefield.

Dryzek, J. S. (2000). *Deliberative democracy and beyond: Liberals critics, contestations*. Oxford, UK: Oxford University Press.

Dryzek, J. S., & Niemeyer, S. (2008). Discursive representation. *The American Political Science Review, 102*(4), 481–493. doi:10.1017/S0003055408080325

Fishkin, J. S. (1993). *Democracy and deliberation: New directions in democratic reform*. New Haven, CT: Yale University Press.

Fishkin, J. S. (2004). Consulting the public through deliberative polling. *Journal of Policy Analysis and Management, 22*(1), 128–133. doi:10.1002/pam.10101

Grugel, J. (2002). *Democratization: A critical introduction*. Houndmills, UK: Palgrave.

Habermas, J. (1981). Theory of communicative action: *Vol. 1*. (*trans. Thomas McCarthy*). Boston, MA: Beacon Press.

Hendriks, C. (2002). Institutions of deliberative democratic processes and interest groups: Roles, tensions and incentives. *Australian Journal of Public Administration, 61*(1), 64–75. doi:10.1111/1467-8500.00259

Irvin, R., & Stansbury, J. (2004). Citizen participation in decision making: Is it worth the effort? *Public Administration Review, 64*(1), 55–65. doi:10.1111/j.1540-6210.2004.00346.x

Kamarck, E. C., & Nye, J. S. Jr., (Eds.). (2002). *Governance.com: Democracy in an Information Age*. Washington, DC: Brookings Institution Press.

Kane, J., & Bishop, P. (2002). Consultation or contest: The danger of mixing modes. *Australian Journal of Public Administration, 61*(1), 87–94. doi:10.1111/1467-8500.00261

Kane, J., & Patapan, H. (2010). The promise of e-democracy. *Griffith Review, 1*(3).

King, D. C. (2002). Catching voters on the Web. In Kamarck, E. C., & Nye, J. S. Jr., (Eds.), *Governance.com: Democracy in an Information Age* (pp. 104–115). Washington, DC: Brookings Institution Press.

Latham, M. (2001). Direct democracy in Werriwa. In Bishop, P., Kane, J. & Patapan, H. (2002) The theory and practice of e–democracy: Agency, trusteeship and participation on the Web. *International Review of Public Administration, 7*(2), 21–31.

LeDuc, L., Niemi, R., & Norris, P. (Eds.). (2002). *Comparing democracies* (*Vol. 2*). London, UK: Sage.

Leib, E. J. (2004). *Deliberative democracy in America: A proposal for a popular branch of government*. University Park, PA: Pennsylvania State University Press.

Mansbridge, J. (1998). The many faces of representation. Retrieved from http://www.ksg.harvard.edu/prg/mansb/faces.htm

McAllister, I. (2001). Elections without cues: The 1999 Australian republic referendum. *Australian Journal of Political Science, 36*(2), 247–269. doi:10.1080/10361140120078817

Moon, M. J. (2002). The evolution of e-government among municipalities: Rhetoric or reality. *Public Administration Review, 62*(4), 424–435. doi:10.1111/0033-3352.00196

Morris, D. (1999). *Vote.com: How big money lobbyists and the media are losing their influence and the Internet is giving power back to the people*. New York, NY: Renaissance Books.

Nichol, L. (Ed.). (1996). *On dialogue*. London, UK: Routledge.

Nichol, L. (Ed.). (2003). *The essential David Bohm*. London, UK: Routledge.

OECD. (2003). *The e-government imperative: Main findings*. March policy brief.

Pateman, C. (1970). *Participation and democratic theory*. Cambridge, UK: Cambridge University Press.

Queensland Government (2000). *Regional communities 2000 report*.

Queensland Government. (2003). *About us*. Retrieved from http://www.premiers.qld.gov.au/about/community/pdf/edemocracy.pdf

Talbot, D. (2008). How Obama really did it: The social networking strategy that took an obscure Senator to the doors of the White House. *Technology Review*.

Uhr, J. (1998). *Deliberative democracy in Australia: The changing place of Parliament*. Melbourne, Australia: Cambridge University Press.

Uhr, J. (2000). Testing deliberative democracy: The 1999 Australian republic referendum. *Government and Opposition*, *35*(2), 189–210. doi:10.1111/1477-7053.00023

United Nations. (2003). *UN global e-government survey 2003*. New York: Department of Economic and Social Affairs, Division for Public Administration and Development Management.

United Nations. (2004). *UN global e-government readiness report 2004: Towards access for opportunity*. New York: Department of Economic and Social Affairs, Division for Public Administration and Development Management.

United Nations. (2005). *UN global e-government readiness report 2005: From e-government to e-inclusion*. New York: Department of Economic and Social Affairs, Division for Public Administration and Development Management.

United Nations. (2008). *UN e-government survey 2008: From e-government to connected governance*. New York: Department of Economic and Social Affairs, Division for Public Administration and Development Management.

West, D. M. (2002). *Global e government 2002*. Retrieved from http://www.insidepolitics.org/egovt02int.PDF

West, D. M. (2003). *Global e government 2003*. Retrieved from http://www.insidepolitics.org/egovt03int.pdf

West, D. M. (2004). E-government and the transformation of service delivery and citizen attitudes. *Public Administration Review*, *64*(1), 15–27. doi:10.1111/j.1540-6210.2004.00343.x

West, D. M. (2007). *Global e-government 2007*. Brown University, United States. Retrieved from www.InsidePolitics.org

West, D. M. (2008). *Global e-government 2008*. Retrieved from http://www.brookings.edu/reports/2008/0817_egovernment_west.aspx

ENDNOTES

[1] Interview with Dr Ernst Kouba of *Help.gv* project of the Austrian Government, Vienna, 16 February 2001

[2] Global e- Policy e- Government Forum, SungKyunKwan University Seoul South Korea 6-7 November 2002

[3] There has been no change in regime or to the bureaucracy's high level of commitment to the new technology between 2002 and 2003. This dramatic slip may point to a methodological problem with the 'snapshot' technique West had to adopt to cover so many sites. A temporary problem with the technology could mean, for example, that 'accessibility' is recorded lower than the optimal design standard, skewing the overall rank.

[4] While there is no absolute standard by which to measure democracy the The Freedom House indicators are used here as comparative democratic indicators on the basis that they have also been used in other well known studies. See for example Lawrence LeDuc, Richard Niemi and Pippa Norris eds. Comparing Democracies 2, Sage London 2002

[5] Derived from: Darrell M, West (2002)*Global e government 2002*http://www.inside-

[6] politics.org/egovt02int.PDF ; and Freedom House website: http://www.freedomhouse.org

[6] Derived from Darrell M West 2003*Global e government 2003*http://www.insidepolitics.org/egovt03int.pdf and Freedom House website http://www.freedomhouse.org

[7] Derived from Darrell M West 2007, *Global e-Government 2007*, www.InsidePolitics.org and Freedom House website http://www.freedomhouse.org

[8] Stephen Clift was the originator of the ground-breaking Minnesota e-democracy site and has been a frequent speaker at conferences and consultant to governments on the application of new technology.

[9] 'The Smart State' is the current government's strategic slogan to attract high tech businesses to the region

[10] This is often no easy task. The Queensland initiative, for example, was the result of a campaign promise by the Premier that, as *The Smart State*, Queensland would have an e-democracy trial. What it might entail, how it was to be developed, what the potential pitfalls were, was left to government officers to sort out.

[11] "They have a unique perspective on the world that encourages them to gather innovative ideas and applications from far away places and adapt them to their very practical cultures. In North America and Europe, sometimes you are too close to the action to see what is really important or gain the perspective required to fully appreciate what really works."(Clift 2002)

[12] CBS new reported in June 4 2003: "The Dean Meetup group is already having an impact where it really matters – fund-raising. So far, the Meetuppies have contributed almost $400,000 to the campaign. Over $1.25 million has been raised online, says [Campaign Manager Joe] Trippi. The "Meetup Challenge" was started in March by a New York member who asked others to send in checks for $10.01. (The extra penny made it easy for the donations from Meetuppies to be tracked.) Trippi says they've received thousands of contributions as a result." (CBS 2003)

Chapter 4

Habermas, Networks and Virtual Public Spheres:
A Blended Deliberative Model from Developing Countries

Veena V. Raman
Pennsylvania State University, USA

ABSTRACT

This chapter examines Habermas' conceptualization of the public sphere as it applies to a non-Western context, in Bangalore City, India. It provides examples of how Information and Communication Technologies are being used to empower ordinary citizens to participate in local governance, though deep digital divides persist. The chapter highlights problematic aspects of using technologies to promote better governance in the face of pervasive asymmetries in access to resources, power to leverage networks, and in levels of civic competencies. Drawing on the capabilities approach, it argues that there is need for a blended model of deliberative 'e-democracy' that does not privilege online venues and interactions, but employs technologies in strategic combinations with existing civic networks to improve governance in developing countries.

INTRODUCTION

This chapter examines Habermas' conceptualization of the public sphere as it applies to a non-Western context, in Bangalore City, India, to understand how information and communication technologies are used to help ordinary citizens participate in local governance, though deep digital divides persist.

DOI: 10.4018/978-1-60960-159-1.ch004

In Habermasian terms, the public sphere is seen as comprised of institutional communicative spaces that facilitate the formation of public opinion and political will, a sphere that mediates between the private domain and the realm of public authority by allowing free access and free flow of information and ideas (Habermas, 1991). With the proliferation of new media technologies, it is expected that the virtual public sphere will empower citizens to engage in effective public discourse and effect political change. The concept of deliberative democracy follows the notion of the public sphere and is rooted in Habermas' idea of communicative rationality. Deliberative democracy underscores the notion of providing reasons for decisions taken and the concept of reciprocity where decision makers owe it to the people to justify their decisions. These ideas are foundational to governance, if we define governance as inclusive of the role of citizens in the policy process and how groups within a society organize to make and implement decisions through the processes of differentiation, networks, trust, diplomacy and coalition building (Rhodes, 1997). Deliberation, reciprocity, and mutual respect are critical to civic interactions that occur within governance, particularly in situations where deep differences exist, where consensus is not likely, and people have to arrive at acceptable solutions via dialogue.

There have been many critiques of the Habermasian model of the public sphere as a civic arena of deliberation and opinion-formation (Fenton & Downing, 2003) and of deliberative democracy (Besson & Marti, 2006). The role of information and communication technologies in facilitating an online public sphere is also vigorously debated (Papacharissi, 2009). Ultimately, if we define publics as groups of people engaging with issues through discursive interactions, they can be constituted either through face-to-face interactions or through various mediated forms and in online venues. An interactional public sphere emerges when political issues become actualized through talk and other forms of civic action.

The level of complexity in examining the role of the virtual public sphere in empowering ordinary citizens increases in the context of developing countries where people are engaged in conflict and political struggle to gain access to basic resources such as clean drinking water and infrastructure such as paved streets. In addition, in most developing countries, there are many digital divides (Keniston, 2004) that limit the role of information and communication technologies (ICTs) in governance. Thus, the use of online networks as a basis for a new politics of alliance and governance, to contest the mainstream and offer alternative views and politics, becomes subject to bridging the many digital divides that currently exist.

This chapter examines these issues using ethnographic and participant observation data from two citizen initiatives in Bangalore City, India and a case study of a partnership between a not-for-profit eGovernments Foundation with city governments to provide free e-governance software, with built in information transparency requirements. It highlights the issues that are not addressed within the virtual public sphere and online deliberative democracy theories such as the normalizing and exclusion that come with designating a specific form of communication as the rational and legitimate norm, and not recognizing these spheres as venues for cultural power struggles. It examines the problematic ethical aspects of using information technologies to promote better governance in the face of pervasive asymmetries in access to resources, power to leverage networks, and in levels of civic competencies. Drawing on Sen's (1987) capabilities approach, it argues that there is need for a blended model of deliberative 'e-democracy' that does not privilege online venues and interactions, but employs technologies in strategic combinations with existing civic networks to improve governance in developing countries.

BACKGROUND

ICTs, Public Sphere, Democracy and Deliberation

Proliferation of information and communication technologies, internet-enabled devices and mobile media has led to many expectations about their potential to reshape democratic life. Scholars have been animated about transformations in politics (Morris, 1999; Dahlberg, 2001; Shane, 2004) or very skeptical about changes (Margolis & Resnick, 2000; Wilhelm, 2000). Internet enthusiasts have suggested that it could lead to increased political engagement, provide direct links to policymakers; and expand opportunities for political deliberation (Norris 2001). A few empirical studies provide evidence for this claim (Wilkund, 2005). Other research suggests that there is a negative correlation between ICTs and civic engagement (Bimber, 2003), with ICTs perpetuating established patterns of political communication, widening gaps between elites and non-elites (Norris, 2001; Bimber, 2003). Thus, the Internet may be used to establish privileged networks that leave out many and create social exclusion. It can also be considered a new form of public space since its decentralized nature allows many voices to be heard. If the public sphere is "a network for communicating information and points of view" (Habermas, 1996, pp. 360), it is not surprising that digital networks have been considered critical to the viability of the public sphere (Castells, 2008), and there is discussion of a global public sphere (Volkmer, 2003).

However, these conceptualizations have been controversial (Fraser, 2007), since the Habermasian model of the public sphere as a civic arena for deliberation and opinion-formation has been problematic. It has been critiqued by scholars such as Fraser (1992), Eley (1992) and others on the basis that it is not gendered; does not take into account power differentials; over emphasizes use of reason and persuasion; fails to consider social identities as part of public attitudes of individuals; is rigid in separating the public from the private and everyday life; and glosses over the role that political conflict or struggle plays. A direct application of Habermasian public sphere theory to the internet is open to the same critique. Kahn & Kellner (2005) and Kellner (1999) have argued that the Internet should be seen as a site of struggle, as contested terrain where exclusion, domination as well as solidarity and resistance are reproduced. Chadwick (2009) suggests that though interactive web 2.0 technologies can promote citizen engagement, they require a plurality of different sociotechnical values and mechanisms to be of real value in online consulting and public policy making. Thus, the role of the internet in the public sphere literature has been controversial and Papacharissi (2002, 2009) has argued that while the Internet may create a public space for people to engage in self-serving expression and conversations; the technology itself does not decide whether a public space can transcend to a public sphere.

Analogous to the discussion above, there is great diversity of opinion and evidence about the relationship between the internet and democratic practice. Morrisett (2003) identified six ways ICT use could enhance the democratic process: providing widespread and effective access to decision-makers; provision of relevant and timely information; interaction within and between institutionally, politically or geographically distinct networked communities; access to various positions in relation to policy issues; the capacity to register choices, and awareness of the implications of different choices; and evidence that such deliberations have informed actions by governing institutions or elected representatives in relation to those issues. While researchers such as Jenkins & Thorburn (2004) and (Mossberger, Tolbert, & McNeal, 2007) provide hopeful assessments about the impact of the internet and ICTs, Hindman (2008) challenges claims that the internet has led to expansion of public voices, weakened gate keeping powers and engaged citizens in politics. Hindman presents strong evidence to argue that politics is a very small part of what internet users actually do, and while blogs, chat rooms and other venues enable individuals to speak, they are rarely heard and have relatively little impact, and that the most powerful political voices online are socially elite.

Within the internet democracy scholarship, there are three distinct variations on how the internet could change the status quo. Liberal individualist democracy researchers see the internet as the means of providing citizens with political information, to express opinions, and directly contacting elected representatives (Mossberger, Tolbert, & McNeal, 2007). The second model emphasizes the possibility of internet-based groups and networks working as collectives to work on specific agendas (Dahlberg, 2001a). Lim & Kann (2008) provide a concise summary of evidence for this model. The third model incorporates deliberative democracy and public sphere theory into the discussion of internet democracy. This is consistent with Barber's (2000) call for e-democracy to focus on participation of citizens in discussion and deliberation of public matters. Defining deliberative democracy as a form of government in which free and equal citizens … justify decisions in a process in which they give one another reasons that are mutually acceptable and generally accessible (Gutmann and Thompson, 2004), scholars in this area see the internet as a means to expand citizen deliberation and formation of rational public opinion to hold official decision makers accountable (Thompson, 2008; Janssen & Kies, 2005; Gimmler, 2001). Recently, researchers (Chadwick, 2009; Thompson, 2008; Price, 2006) have provided guarded assessments about the role of online deliberations in civic action.

The arguments and claims of this model are examined in greater detail here since the chapter focuses on a blended deliberative model based on the public sphere theory. Deliberative public sphere researchers are interested in the extent and quantity of argumentation online. Many publications in this area focus on developing technologies and moderation systems for online deliberations, and case studies examine the degree to which these communicative spaces facilitate argumentation (Carpini, Cook, & Jacobs, 2004; Wright, 2005; Stromer-Galley, 2007; Wright & Street, 2007; Thompson, 2008).

While there is disagreement about the definition of rational deliberation, usually deliberations have to meet the following criteria: inclusive, free, equal, sincere, respectful, reasoned and reflexive (Dahlberg, 2007). These criteria constitute the ideal. However, most empirical research demonstrates that arguments and the deliberative processes as a whole are affected by the social, cultural and political positions of participants, the form of mediation employed, the distribution of social, cultural and economic capital, and the degree to which citizen interactions are free from state mechanisms and economic systems (Thompson, 2008).

'Mini publics' have been proposed as an option to remedy some of these issues (Fung, 2003). Mini publics are groups that are small enough so they can genuinely deliberate and be representative enough to be genuinely democratic, though they are not representative electorally or in a statistical sense. Such groups include deliberative polls, consensus conferences, citizens' juries, and planning cells among others. Goodin and Dryzek (2006) catalogue the various ways minipublics can affect the macro-political system, though they argue that more actual mini publics are required before the explanations for conditions that lead to successful deliberation can be tested.

These issues have led to a need for research about the impact of digital divides, communicative competencies, how people use the internet and navigate online, and the impact of interest groups and corporate ownership practices on online deliberation. The importance of these questions is magnified in the case of a developing country like India.

HABERMAS AND THE INDIAN PUBLIC SPHERE

India, with a population of more than 1.2 billion people, speaking eighteen major languages and sixteen hundred minor languages and dialects, with more than six major religions, from six main ethnic groups, divided into 6400 castes and sub castes and fifty-two major tribes presents a varied, complex, and interesting political space (Behar & Prakash, 2004). The country's plurality and diversity and status as the most populous democracy present multiplicity of experiences. By the traditional measures of freedom of speech (Schwartzberg, 2008), and availability of numerous media channels (Thomas, 2006), India can be seen as possessing a vibrant public sphere, albeit a skewed one since citizens have to navigate gender, religion, caste, and class issues as they try to access resources and demand recognition of their claims. Various social and institutional arrangements that create exclusion from participation (Manor, 1993) continue to exist. Rajagopal (2009) provides a good overview of the Indian public sphere; the discussion here will focus mainly on the differences between the Habermasian conceptualization and the Indian context.

There are studies that indicate the Indian public sphere is not entirely secular, rational-deliberative or equitable (Reifeld & Bhargava, 2005). In this context, it becomes necessary to go beyond the public use of reason and expand our analysis to understanding how publics are formed, and broaden the spaces in and through which publicness operates. In addition, rather than just focusing on the macro level public sphere, there is a need to focus on sites integrated into everyday practices of social actors and situated in horizontal forms of sociability, such as the family, the house and the neighborhood.

While thinking about the public sphere and its relation to conflict and political struggle in the Indian context, it is useful to employ Turner's (1974) concept of liminality, a threshold on the periphery of everyday life – those spaces where structural and norm-bound constraints are lifted, opening up venues for collective agency. Traditional Western models of public spheres such as stratified (characterized by the counter discourses of subordinated groups) and egalitarian (where members of more limited publics talk across lines of cultural diversity) cannot adequately account for the creative tension which emerges when multiple public spheres exist simultaneously, some are mutually constitutive and people move in and out of these spheres, others are based on mutually exclusive social groups such as the untouchables and Dalits who were historically marginalized by dominant groups (Guru, 2005).

Between kinship ties on one end of the spectrum and the state on the other, human beings experience a diversity of social relationships and groupings which in modern western thought has been labeled civil society. Though Habermas's public sphere may seem remote from a large swath of social reality, it is still closely linked to the liberal conception of civil society. Habermas explicates not just the difference between a public and a private realm; he discusses those two realms in the context of juxtaposition: the state versus civil society.

While India has a robust civil society, this version of civil society does not neatly fit into Habermas' juxtaposition. Though a large section of Indian civil society, working at the micro level, has argued for development embedded in the discourse of empowerment, and rights, there have been state interventions, and instances of cooption of civil society by state authority (Behar & Prakash, 2004). The connection between the public sphere and civil society in India becomes stronger if we understand civil society in a broad sense, as involving the investigation of everyday social practices, and the elusive power relations and shared moralities that hold communities together.

India's history includes striking achievements in some sectors and considerable failures in dimensions of human development such as illiteracy, and malnutrition (World Bank, 2009), since economic benefits have not reached the poor and the marginalized. In this context, the contributions of civil society have been contingent on political opportunity, and constraints, the strength and role of the state and political party. Indian civil society has been the site to contest the state and its institutions with its discourse of rights in a democracy for the marginalized groups. These groups have played a critical role in bridging the gap between institutional democracy and the substantive aspects of democracy. It has been the realm of non state organizations, the site of discourse and power struggle, and a realm to negotiate the meaning of governance.

Recently, religious and caste identity movements have significantly altered the contours of civic space[1]. There has also been greater communalization and blending of religion in the Indian sphere since the 1990s. Most of the thinking about the public sphere has been secular; following Rawls' formulation that public reason requires arguments conducted entirely in secular terms. However, our concept of the public sphere is challenged by the visible influence of religion in public life since it is inherent in how people organize and vote. In India, the contradictions abound. Nigam (2005) demonstrates the incongruity in a liberal and bourgeois civil society trained in Nehruvian secular and rational discourse diverging from an Indian population that operates within the framework of Hindu and Muslim orthodoxy and communalism. Civil society groups have been instrumental in offering communication spaces to groups associated with marginalized discourses to develop counter-publics and alternative arenas to challenge dominant narratives.

INDIA: DIGITAL DIVIDES AND GOVERNANCE

India is a relatively large country with tremendous diversity in technological development and politi-

cal culture across its states. While it has recently been prominent for the growth of its information services sector, it contains characteristics both of an agricultural society transitioning to an industrial one and an industrial society evolving into an information society. Internet adoption has continued to grow, though at a slow pace. Of the total population of 1.2 billion, there were about 81 million internet users and 3.1 million internet hosts in 2009 (CIA, 2009). Statistics indicate that there are an estimated 126.9 million wireless internet subscribers (TRAI, 2009). Though there were 427.3 million mobile telephone users, internet access through mobile phones is expensive and has not become very popular in rural India, where 71% of the population lives. India has experienced economic growth in recent decades and has had some success in reducing poverty, though 42% of India's population falls below the international poverty line of $1.25 a day (Ravallion, 2009). An IT & Telecom Ministry initiative makes computers available for purchase below 10,000 rupees (US $226). However this has to be viewed in the context of the poverty rate discussed above.

Digital divide remains a major issue. The most affluent groups, concentrated in major cities, with good knowledge of English, education and cutting edge IT knowledge constitute the vast majority of users (TRAI, 2009). Keniston (2004) identifies four areas which manifest the digital divide: Disparities in access to ICTs between rich and poor nations, a linguistic-cultural gap online between the dominant Anglo-Saxon culture and other cultures, the gap within a country between the digitally empowered rich and the poor; and the emerging gap between an affluent elite digerati from the rest of the people since they live in special enclaves and disregards local conventions, authority and traditional hierarchies. A majority of India's population lives in rural areas, is poor, and has limited access to ICTs. India's adult literacy rate is 66% (males 73%, females 47%; CIA, 2009) and this poses challenges to internet use since a majority of the content continues to be text based. Initiatives such as the experimental Computer-based functional literacy (CBFL) program of the Tata Group, illustrates that ICTs can play a role in addressing illiteracy. In addition, there is also a great need for development of Indian language fonts to remove language barriers and facilitate localization of content.

To address the issue of multiple languages, initiatives such as the Simputer or Simple Computer that costs about US $ 200, that can read a smart card, and has advanced audio and text processing capabilities in several Indian languages, have been created as pilot projects. The lack of standardization of code for major Indian languages creates inter-operability problems between programs involving distinct codes. The Centre for the Development of Advanced Computing, has been working on Indian language fonts and software for over a decade. Many rural ICTs projects use its fontographic standards or text-processing software. A pilot project in machine language translation called Anusaraka promises to allow Indian language users translation between various Indian languages (CDAC, 2010). These are all pilot projects and their success cannot be evaluated at this time. In this context, the use of online networks as a basis for a new politics of alliance and governance to contest the mainstream, and offer alternative views and politics is challenging.

Keniston and Kumar (2004) argue that there is a need to reframe the question of ICT implementation by asking, how, if at all, ICTs can be used to ensure the fulfillment of basic human needs and to further basic human rights. This reframing highlights the need for community participation in dialogue so that ICTs, if relevant, are woven into the contextual and situated solutions generated by each community. This is particularly true because ICT use is not just a question of investing in computers but also has ongoing implications for communities in terms of the investments in expertise, content generation, time, and resources required for administration and maintenance of ICT systems (Dederich, Hausman, & Maxwell, 2006). Kanungo (2004) has argued that there are

no established patterns of research about how to build effective, emergent and emancipatory information systems that explicitly address the larger development issues of poverty, health, education and employment in poor, rural regions. Taking advantage of ICTs requires social, cultural and political environments that themselves are historically situated and influenced by a range of human and social factors (Ganesh & Barber, 2009).

In India, the great diversity of local environments demands fabrication of hardware such as Intel-powered Community PC platforms to be deployed in rural kiosks and software devices such as making available local language software tools and fonts in the public domain through the Centre for Development of Advanced Computing, in Tamil, Hindi and Telugu languages under Language Technology Mission, for citizens with different levels of educational attainment, informational capacity, initiation, age groups, gender, etc. While telecenters and rural kiosks have been promoted as important ways to address the digital divide in India, both those options have had mixed success. Rao (2008) provides a critical review of the role of telecenters in addressing the digital divide by reviewing the experiences of a few Indian telecenter initiatives such as Gyandoot, Drishtee and e-Choupal. Best & Kumar (2008) review the Sustainable Access in Rural India (SARI) project and assess variation in a kiosk lifespan and Mukerji (2008) provides a typology of telecenters in rural India. These studies illustrate the challenges in providing sustainable ICT solutions in a country like India.

A second area that needs consideration in the Indian context is governance. The term is defined in various ways by organizations such as the World Bank (Kaufmann, Kraay & Mastruzzi, 2008) and the United Nations (2008). Most of the work by these international institutions has centered on administrative reforms, structured around the 73rd and 74th amendments to the Indian Constitution that gave greater powers to local governments, including increased financial and administrative autonomy (World Bank, 2009a). Their basic argument for this focus was that reform in government would lead to greater accountability to the people and good governance would lead to growth (Kaufmann and Kraay, 2002). In contrast, academic researchers see governance as a broader and more inclusive term than government in that it encompasses the activities of a range of groups – political, social and governmental – as well as their interrelationships (Stren & Polese, 2000). The term governance includes the relationship between government and state agencies on the one hand and communities and social groups on the other and is not tied specifically to a place. It refers to the role of citizens in the policy process and how groups within a society organize to make and implement decisions. Governance stresses the role of citizens in the policy process- from issue identification, to implementation, feedback and evaluation of results. Citizens maximize their chances of representation for their interests by playing out strategies in the networks of relationships between various institutions. Thus, technologies such as the internet that operate on network logic are seen as playing an important role in governance. While these two conceptualizations of governance are obviously linked, the broader more inclusive definition is used in this chapter.

In India, governance as administrative reform has been examined for more than a decade (Court, 2003). A common theme among the reports has been that policy-making is detached from the people, particularly the poorest members of society, and that corruption and inefficiency pose important challenges. ICTs have been promoted as tools to address these challenges. For example, the United Nations Development Program has funded projects in India to foster governance reform and accountability while providing work opportunities to people in rural areas. It has supported citizens' monitoring capacities, through the use of public disclosure tools such as social audit, governance 'report cards', the Right to Information Act, and ICT-based systems (UNDP, 2009). However,

the results of these programs have been uneven; success has been dependent on local political, economic and social contexts.

To summarize, ICTs can be used in democracies in many ways: for increasing transparency in government, improving citizen satisfaction by delivering efficient services, providing opportunities for electronic ballot casting, stimulating citizen involvement through civic consultation and creating a virtual sphere to facilitate citizen deliberation. However research suggests that in most countries, and particularly so in developing countries, ICTs have largely been employed in streamlining labor-intensive bureaucratic transactions rather than in participatory or consultative efforts to promote democratic practices (Bekkers & Homburg, 2007; Norris, 2003; Chadwick & May, 2003).

Citizen participation and engagement is not deterministically driven by adoption of information technology. It is contingent upon individual resources, capacities, and predispositions and on how collective action organizations and other groups use the greater access to information now available to them to influence and mobilize people. Though ICTs allow connections to be made, they are tools; they do not facilitate deliberative engagement on their own. Facilitation of such engagement is a cultural-democratic function. ICTs offer another communication channel, but they cannot address factors such as availability and utilization of resources, ability, and inclination for political action.

ISSUES NOT ADDRESSED WITHIN THE INTERNET DELIBERATIVE DEMOCRACY LITERATURE

Deliberative democracy theories discuss power as operating in positive and negative ways. In the positive sense, good arguments transform individuals into critical-reflexive citizens and lead to rational resolution for disputes. They try to minimize the use of power in a negative sense, by guarding against coercion and constraints placed on participants. However, these theories do not address the normalizing and exclusion that come with designating a specific form of communication as the rational and legitimate norm (Dahlberg, 2007). The norming process is exclusionary since it fixes the boundaries of legitimate public sphere deliberation. In addition, some participants are advantaged over others since some participants' naturalized mode of communication are closer to the legitimate normative mode than others. Thus, the whole process involves cultural power struggles. This is true even of the radical public sphere as conceptualized by Dahlberg (2007). When social crises occur, opportunities to interrupt dominant discursive structures emerge, and those at the margins can participate.

Secondly, online discourses can be constrained just as those in the offline world. A lot of discussions about ICT and democracy focus on the availability, accessibility and affordability of technologies. Recent literature has examined the role of skill levels (Hargittai, 2006). However, in the context of using ICTs for deliberation, there is a need to recognize other barriers such as low literacy, language barriers, low self-efficacy about IT use, and social and cultural barriers. It is assumed within literature that all the information that people need to make informed decisions and participate in civic discussions is available; this is not true particularly in developing countries. Though entertainment content abounds, the information needed to participate in local governance is often not easily accessible. Besides, there is the issue of what motivate people to participate and how they use ICTs when they are not a part of experiments or special civic initiatives is not well researched within the deliberative context.

Finally, one problematic issue that is not widely discussed is what Dean (2005) calls the technological fetish that allows communicative citizens to feel that they are engaged, while relieving them of the guilt of not being active, thus foreclosing political participation that actually effects change.

How Can ICTs Be Used in Developing Countries to Foster Citizen Deliberation and Participation in Governance?

In the context of the challenges discussed above, it is fair to ask; can people in developing countries participate in local governance and use ICTs? What role can technology play? This chapter tries to answer this question through a case study from Bangalore City, India.

Bangalore City, the capital of Karnataka State, is the fifth most populous city in India with 6.52 million residents. It is known as the information capital and Silicon Valley of India. Bangalore is the source of 45 % of India's software exports and has been the favored destination for information technology (IT) companies, since it is home to one third of all IT professionals in India (Department of IT,BT and S&T, 2009). It is one of the 'technopoles' (Castells, 2008), a hub integrating the region to the global information economy. It has been ranked in a UNDP survey (UNDP, 2009) as the world's fifth largest technology hub.

Yet, sizable portions of the city's 6.52 million people remain beyond this information economy. There is tension between participation in global operations and the local socioeconomic context. Bangalore exhibits pervasive forms of asymmetry between those who can participate in the global information economy and those who cannot (Madon, 1997). However, the state and the local government's use ICTs for e-government initiatives and have specific policy documents highlighting their goals. In its official policy, Mahiti – The Millennium IT Policy of 1997, the Karnataka State government declares that its goal is to use "e-Gov as a tool and deliver a government that is more proactive and responsive to its citizens(Department of IT,BT and S&T, 2009). In a policy document titled document 'e-Governance strategy for Karnataka', the government defines e-government as involving "the application of Information and Communication Technologies to bring about more speed, transparency and responsiveness to the various areas of governmental activities resulting in enhanced accountability and empowerment of people. The policy declaration states that the government is convinced that e-Governance can help bridge the gap between the rich and the poor, between the developed and the less developed, between the urban and the rural population by providing equality of opportunity and empowering the poor. (Department of IT,BT and S&T, 2009).

As the capital of Karnataka State, Bangalore was seen by the state government as critical to its projected image as the 'software destination of India' and the local city government (called Bangalore City Corporation) was among the pioneers of e-governance initiatives. Raman (2008) provides an overview of the online services available and their use by citizens in Bangalore City and argues that while the local government was publishing information and had established a presence online, there were few transactional features and the government's policy goal of facilitating democratic outreach did not materialize on the official websites or as part of formal e-governance initiatives.

This assessment holds true if we make technology use central to our conceptualization, and rely exclusively on citizens employing ICTs to interact with their government as constituting the definition of e-governance. However, such an analysis would be misleading. The next section examines two citizen initiatives that provide contrary evidence.

As Bangalore City became a major destination for software development in India in the early 1990s, many companies set up offices in the city, attracting job seekers from all over India. This resulted in increasing pressure on the city's infrastructure and greater service demands from the growing population. The city did not have the financial power to undertake infrastructure projects on its own and had to approach international capital markets for funding. To obtain such funding, the city government was required to move its accounting system from an analog mode to a digital system and a management information system was put in place. This change in system led to a complete overhaul of the public works management system. The City Corporation could provide specific details of finances, public works undertaken and status of infrastructure initiatives through the Internet, through email and through traditional means such as print outs. Thus the stage was set to enable the city government to respond to requests for information from members of the public. This provided an opportunity for citizen groups to request information from the city government about budgets (an initiative called Public Record Of Operations and Finance, PROOF) and public works undertaken within their neighborhoods (a program called WardWorks).

Historically, citizen participation in governance has not been encouraged. Traditionally, Karnataka State has retained a high level of concentration of power at the level of the state government. Some of this has been attributed to colonial legacy practices. Bangalore City figured prominently in colonial government as a cantonment for British troops and this affected how democratic traditions evolved in local government. The Nagarapalika Act of 1993 mandated major changes in urban government. All of the provisions were aimed at promoting local democratic participation in municipal government. Yet, decentralization and devolution of power was thwarted in Karnataka during the implementation of the Nagarapalika Act (Heitzman, 1999). Without transparency, financial reporting, and structured disclosure norms from government institutions, citizens cannot participate in governance. It is in this context that we have to view the PROOF and WardWorks.

While citizens and the Bangalore City Corporation have a common interest in the city's functioning, there was no formal mechanism for them to work together prior to PROOF. Citizens working through four civic groups, Janaagraha, VOICES, Public Affairs Center, and Center for Budget and Policy Studies mobilized the community groups to participate in PROOF meetings. Beginning in July 2002, the Bangalore City Corporation has made public its financial statements to provide full and accurate performance information to the city's various stakeholders.

Each quarter, a public meeting is held where city government officials meet citizens to discuss the city's standardized financial statements, a set of performance indicators, as well as a report that contains the city government's management discussion and explanatory statements. Citizens question specific expenditure items and request clarifications on decisions made. In the public meetings, citizens present their analysis of the budget. They point out discrepancies in the budget and the Additional Commissioner of Finance responds. This is followed by an open house where citizens question the corporation officials about specific expenses.

Citizens also participate in the formulation of the Corporation's budget. To facilitate this process, three retired officials from government finance departments lend their expertise to citizens' discussions and planning during weekly discussions. They prioritize public works from their local areas such as road repairs, footpaths, and drainage; examine ways to improve the budget, and enhance revenue collection. Citizens have been involved in proposing methods to double property tax receipts by researching various issues such as assessment of tax on government residential properties. They also examine whether all the obligatory functions of the Corporation are being carried out. This system operates on the rationale that disclosure of accurate and timely information is a necessary condition for good governance.

In addition to participating through PROOF, Bangaloreans also participate at the level of their local wards through an initiative called Ward-

Works. WardWorks is citizen follow up on public works going on in their wards, relying on the same accounting and information management system that made PROOF possible. Adoption of the new computerized accounting system helped the Corporation streamline application of resources, plan for the future, and facilitated prioritization of activities that needed funds. It also facilitated the generation of a monthly report called Arthika Darpana. This allowed for the generation of a ward-wise budgetary allocation index. The Corporation could also provide online access to ward level budgets. Citizens make use of this information to hold their elected representatives and service providers accountable and influence decisions about projects to be undertaken.

While ward level works constitutes a relatively small item in the city budget (6%), it allows citizens to participate in selection, prioritization and implementation of various local works. When field research was completed by the author for this project in 2006, Bangalore City had 100 administrative units called wards; of those citizens from 10 wards were active participants in WardWorks. The leadership of the City Corporation was persuaded by citizens working through the Janaagraha civic group to mandate attendance by their ward engineers, health officials and other employees to a monthly review meeting. It was established that points raised at the meetings would be part of the official record. The monthly review meetings involve accessing the ward works index for each ward for a given month and discussing the progress of works with the officials responsible for them.

This gave citizens an overview of how money had been spent and provided a critical formal space for citizens to hold the agencies responsible for ward-level issues and press forward with the agenda of their neighborhood vision documents they have generated. Communities in different wards held monthly review meetings each month, where they met with their corporators, engineers, police inspectors, and other officials dealing with electricity, water and sanitation to discuss ward works and work together in tackling civic problems. Some of the most successful wards have been those with serious infrastructure problems. Constructive engagement with government officials has occurred where residents selected specific issues and employed a focused approach to actively participate in meeting officials, pursuing them over time and kept following up on their issues until they were satisfied with the solutions. These initiatives have some similarities to citizen participation in Porto Alegre in Brazil (Baiocchi, 2005).

What Has Been Achieved By These Initiatives?

These two initiatives are unique in the extent to which citizens are able to require transparency and accountability from their local government in addition to participating in the budgeting process. The public meetings have provided a formal mechanism for citizens to question the local government officials on their priorities for the city and request clarifications. Through Ward Works, citizens engage in participatory budgeting for the first time in Bangalore. They identified Rs 100 million of ward works as priorities for the financial year 2002-03 of which Rs 50 million of works was included in the Program of Works. The process of prioritization led to citizens engaging in dialogue with other citizen groups/associations in their wards. Instead of collapsing into chaos, these meetings proved that with enough information and opportunities to participate in decision-making citizens could work effectively. They made compromises when they saw the process as fair and transparent. They also monitored implementation of works to improve the output for their tax rupees and make their neighborhoods more livable. This model of using data management systems to promote transparency and accountability and enable citizen participation in governance is now being employed by a non profit group, eGovernments Foundation in 75 different cities across India.

These initiatives to a degree relied on the opportunities provided by information technologies to gain access to information. However, the deliberation and participation took place in local neighborhoods away from the virtual sphere, in sites integrated into local everyday practices.

Citizens who participated in these meetings brought their religious, linguistic, gender, class and caste identities with them and had to negotiate deliberating in spaces that were not always equitable communicative spaces. For example, meetings between citizens groups in wards 90 and 94 and their construction of a local public sphere provide data we can use to rethink the public sphere in its event-character, and in its relation to conflict and political struggle. Ward 90 and 94 are adjacent areas and residents from the two wards share many amenities and organizations including a resident welfare association. Ward 94 is composed of community members from diverse religious (Hindu, Muslim, Christian) and linguistic (local languages: Kannada, Tamil, Urdu) backgrounds. Communalization of national politics in the 1990s led to the rise of religious clashes between majority Hindus and Muslim minorities in Bangalore. Thus, religious identity is a subtext to the public stance of individuals residing there. This tension led to the creation of a new residents' welfare association and the founding president provided a rationale that it was necessary to reach out to residents in a language (Urdu) that they could not only identify with, but also use to communicate their own ideas. This rationale underlines the divisions along linguistic and religious boundaries; though geographically these residents were neighbors, their identity politics place them in different public spheres. Their media consumption patterns and social activity groups were also distinct. However, lack of functioning sewer lines brought the various groups together. Crossing over identity boundaries, the various associations worked together to crowdsource information about which homes and streets lacked amenities, they petitioned local agencies by collecting hundreds of signatures from residents, and debated to prioritize works to be undertaken. Due to their collective efforts, sewer line construction was started.

While scholars may broadly classify these tensions as a problem of minority rights within a democracy, common problems of inadequate infrastructure created a liminal space of contact that blurred the otherwise rigidly drawn boundaries between the groups. They found themselves generating new practices and responding to new demands. Reasoned or otherwise, debate and negotiation then became inevitable between state and non-state actors in the Wards, though the same did not hold on the regional or national scale. They initiated and refined numerous local practices of democratic governance bringing different class constituencies, religious associations and local political party members together in a deliberative processes. An urban space that was polarized by ideological divisions was re-appropriated by locals and a public space of action and interaction was created among a plurality of actors.

Within the grand narrative of demanding resources from the state, a public sphere in which the dominant norms and structures of collective life were modified through actual practices in a time of crisis emerges. The Muslim women who signed these petitions engaged in crossover performances in spaces formerly forbidden to them both by secularists and by tradition, enacting a liminal way of being public. Most people engaged in these meetings were neither Hindu nor Muslim nor completely modern, neither private nor republican, but between established social identities and codes. The mode of publicness that ensued was negotiated in a series of micro-practices that modify the existing space of appearances. In this context, liminal publicness is a field of possibility.

A BLENDED DELIBERATIVE MODEL

If we apply the criteria found in past literature, the two initiatives discussed above do not qualify as virtual public spheres. In fact, the larger Indian public sphere would not qualify as one under the Habermasian model of the public sphere. However, the two initiatives discussed in this chapter are exercises in deliberative democracy if we apply the core principles of deliberative democracy: a focus upon tangible problems, involvement of both people and public officials who are close to the problem, and a collaborative approach to generating solutions (Fung and Wright 2001: 17-19). They are closer to Fung's (2003) conceptualization of mini publics.

If we use the internet democracy literature, these two examples are not cases of e-consultation or e-deliberation. Yet, as demonstrated in the previous section, there are cases where, without heavily relying on ICTs, people use them to engage in deliberation and participate in governance. Thus, it is necessary that we conceptualize a blended model of deliberation.

In this model, use of ICTs to achieve democratic ends is present but not privileged. In the blended model, empowering people is about improving the governance process through enabling use of information technologies within strategic areas. Thus, ICTs provide opportunities for generating and accessing information that can lead to participation and deliberation that occurs through talk, that is either face to face or through mobile phones. Civic agency here involves a variety of practices beyond talk to include collective bargaining and action.

The rationale for the blended model is derived from Amartya Sen's capability approach. In describing his capability approach to development, Sen (1999) makes a crucial distinction between 'functionings' and 'capabilities'. According to him, functioning is an achievement, whereas a capability is the ability to achieve.

Functionings are directly related to living conditions, they indicate the current status of being. Capabilities are one's freedom to achieve the well-being that he or she values, and the ability to utilize resources to achieve those desired goals. Thus positive developments include expansion of capabilities or introduction of new capabilities among those who are currently deprived from it. For Sen (1999), expansion of freedom is 'both as the primary end and as the principal means of development'.

Based on this approach, we can argue that Bangaloreans who were involved in PROOF and WardWorks were able to expand their capabilities to participate in deliberation by using ICTs to access information and share it among community members. In this context, the role of digital technologies was to expand the opportunities and choices for engaging in civic action.

Citizens were able to achieve their desired goals of improving their quality of life by using technological means of information gathering and harnessing the power of collective action to effect local political change.

This model is also consistent with Agre's theory of amplification that the Internet will serve to enlarge and accelerate processes already in place in societies and organizations, rather than create entirely new forces, since it is embedded in larger networks of societal processes and amplifies existing social forces when appropriated by participants for communication processes (Agre, 2002:315–6).

FUTURE RESEARCH DIRECTIONS

There are interesting questions to be examined within the area of virtual public spheres in non-Western contexts. Conceptualizing the public sphere in non-Western contexts requires us to revisit the relationship between the public and private spheres, while considering the specific history and culture that inform the formation of those spheres. In many non-Western contexts, the philosophical, ideological, and political foundations on which the public spheres are based are very different from the Habermasian model. They often have different rhetorical traditions and deliberation styles, and diverse opinion and consensus formation styles that shape their public spheres.

Another area that has to be reconsidered is the relationship between the State and the civic sphere. This can be a blend of various degrees of confrontation, co-option and collaboration as seen in India. A good example of public-private collaboration is the eGovernments Foundation in Bangalore City, a not-for-profit foundation started by a Silicon Valley IT entrepreneur who returned to India and has held various advisory positions within committees advising governments. It operates on moneys contributed by the Co-Chairman of Infosys, one of India's largest IT companies based in Bangalore. It draws on expertise from volunteers around the world and from local knowledge sources such as the Director of the Indian Institute of Information Technology, a strategy reminiscent of crowdsourcing. The Foundation has provided a whole suite of municipal e-governance products such as property tax collection, public grievance systems, interfaces to web and phone systems, geographical information systems, accounting systems and comprehensive city presence on the Internet in addition to local language support. The Foundation has been able to convince governments to make information available to citizens, though citizen participation in governance is not the goal of all politicians and bureaucrats. Strategies for managing the tensions of power sharing in a democracy differ based on the country and they have to be studied.

Habermas' idea of the rational-critical debate as central to the public sphere has to be reexamined in the non-Western context since many forms of talk such as personal emotive narratives and images are also part of the public sphere where people perform street plays and mime, burn effigies or garland images of politicians or party symbols with flowers or shoes in public spaces to indicate support or protest when they have no seat at the discussion table. This is also true in the digital context where public speech and social mobilization can occur through Twitters (140 character messages sent through online and cell phone venues) and political satire or a call to action is communicated through text messages. Further research has to be conducted on these questions to understand and expand the notion of the public sphere.

Finally, we have to revisit what constitutes a virtual sphere and what role ICTs can play in developing countries. If we focus on ICT use, achieving citizen participation through e-consulting or e-engagement seem impossible goals even in Bangalore City, the information capital of India. This is because a majority of the population has to deal with issues of physical access to technology, lack of infrastructure such as reliable electricity, lack of relevant content in local languages and disparate skill levels, besides issues related to low literacy rates, language barriers since local language fonts and content is relatively rare, and low self-efficacy about ICT use. If we assume that educated and skilled citizens, appropriate technical infrastructure, and online venues are preconditions for deliberative democracy using information technologies, most developing countries will have to wait a very long time before there is any evidence of citizen engagement and civic empowerment through ICT use. However, if our chief concern is to achieve genuine democratic dialogue, we have to start from the perspective of citizen participation, and our questions will be very different. If governance is the process where citizens mobilize, network and try to influence their governments, it is already happening in developing countries in different ways without extensive use of information technologies. Thus, ICT use in many instances is manifested as amplifying the power of existing social networks and providing them new opportunities to effect political change. In this context, the research questions are related to how citizens engage in effecting political change through institutional structures such as legislations or the budget and what role information technologies might play or how new technologies interact with and transform these processes. This would also avoid the technological fetish that Dean (2005) talks about.

CONCLUSION

This chapter considered Habermas' conceptualization of the public sphere in a non-Western context, in Bangalore City, India. Through two specific examples, it examined how information and communication technologies are being used to empower ordinary citizens to participate in local governance, though deep digital divides persist. The chapter highlighted the problematic aspects of using technologies to promote better governance in the face of pervasive asymmetries in access to resources, power to leverage networks, and in levels of civic competencies. Drawing on the capabilities approach, it argued that there is need for a blended model of deliberative 'e-democracy' that does not privilege online venues and interactions, but employ technologies in strategic combinations with existing civic networks to improve governance in developing countries. If our objective is to understand how deliberative democracy is occurring in non-Western contexts, we have to consider the current civic engagement practices of citizens and civic groups and how they use ICTs within this process.

REFERENCES

Agre, P. E. (2002). Real-time politics: The Internet and the political process. *The Information Society*, *18*, 311–331. doi:10.1080/01972240290075174

Baiocchi, G. (2005). *Militants and citizens: The politics of participatory democracy in Porto Alegre.* Palo Alto, CA: Stanford University Press.

Barber, B. (2000). Which technology for which democracy? Which democracy for which technology? *International Journal of Communications Law and Policy, 6.* Retrieved December 11, from http://www.ciaonet.org/olj/ ijclp/ijclp_6/ijclp_6e. pdf

Behar, A., & Prakash, A. (2004). India: Expanding and contracting democratic space . In Alagappa, M. (Ed.), *Civil society and political change in Asia* (pp. 192–222). Stanford, CA: Stanford University Press.

Bekkers, V., & Homburg, V. (2007). The myths of e-government: Looking beyond the assumptions of a new and better government. *The Information Society, 23,* 373–382. doi:10.1080/01972240701572913

Besson, S., & Marti, J. L. (Eds.). (2006). *Deliberative democracy and its discontents.* Hampshire, UK: Ashgate.

Best, M. L., & Kumar, R. (2008). Sustainability failures of rural telecenters: Challenges from the sustainable access in rural India (sari) project. *Information Technologies and International Development, 4*(4), 31–45. doi:10.1162/itid.2008.00025

Bimber, B. (2003). *Information and American democracy: Technology in the evolution of political power.* Cambridge, UK: Cambridge University Press. doi:10.1017/CBO9780511615573

C-DAC. (2010). Language technology initiatives at C-DAC Noida. Retrieved December 11, 2009, from http://tdil.mit.gov.in/ cdacnoidaapril03.pdf

Carpini, M. X. D., Cook, F. L., & Jacobs, L. R. (2004). Public deliberations, discursive participation and citizen engagement: A review of empirical literature. *Annual Review of Political Science, 7*(1), 325–344. doi:10.1146/annurev. polisci.7.121003.091630

Castells, M. (2008). The new public sphere: Global civil society, communication networks, and global governance. *The Annals of the American Academy of Political and Social Science, 616*(1), 78–93. doi:10.1177/0002716207311877

Chadwick, A. (2009). Web 2.0: New challenges for the study of e-democracy in an era of informational exuberance. *I/S: A Journal of Law and Policy for the Information Society, 5*(1), 9-41.

Chadwick, A., & May, C. (2003). Interactions between states and citizens in the age of the Internet. 'E-government' in the United States, Britain and the European Union. *Governance, 16*(2), 271–300. doi:10.1111/1468-0491.00216

CIA. (2009). *The world fact book–India.* Retrieved December 11, 2009, from https://www.cia.gov/ library/publications /the-world-factbook/geos/ in.html

Coleman, S. (2004). Connecting parliament to the public via the Internet: Two case studies of online consultations. *Information Communication and Society, 7*(1), 3–22.

Coleman, S., & Gøtze, J. (2001). *Bowling together: Online public engagement in policy deliberation.* London, UK: Hansard Society Publishing.

Court, J. (2003). Assessing and analyzing governance in India: Evidence from a new survey. World Governance Assessment, Overseas Development Institute, UK. Retrieved December 11, 2009, from http://www.odi.org.uk/ resources/ download/3145.pdf

Dahlberg, L. (2001a). The Internet and democratic discourse: Exploring the prospects of online deliberative forums extending the public sphere. *Information Communication and Society, 4*(4), 615–633. doi:10.1080/13691180110097030

Dahlberg, L. (2001b). Democracy via cyberspace: Examining the rhetorics and practices of three prominent camps. *New Media & Society, 3*(2), 187–207. doi:10.1177/14614440122226038

Dahlberg, L. (2007). The Internet, deliberative democracy, and power: Radicalizing the public sphere. *International Journal of Media and Cultural Politics*, *3*(1), 47–64. doi:10.1386/macp.3.1.47_1

Dean, J. (2005). Communicative capitalism: Circulation and the foreclosure of politics. *Cultural Politics*, *1*(1), 51–74. doi:10.2752/174321905778054845

Dederich, L., Hausman, T., & Maxwell, S. (2006). *Online technology for social change: From struggle to strategy.* New York, NY: dotOrganize

Department of IT. BT and S&T, Government of Karnataka. (2009). *Home page.* Retrieved November 23, 2009, from http://www.bangaloreitbt.in/

Eley, G. (1992). Nations, publics, and political cultures: Placing Habermas in the nineteenth century . In Calhoun, C. (Ed.), *Habermas and the public sphere* (pp. 318–331). Cambridge, MA: MIT Press.

Fenton, N., & Downing, J. (2003). Counter public spheres and global modernity. *Javnost/The Public*, *10*(1), 15–32.

Fraser, N. (1992). Rethinking the public sphere: A contribution to the critique of actually existing democracy . In Calhoun, C. (Ed.), *Habermas and the public sphere* (pp. 109–142). Cambridge, MA: MIT Press.

Fraser, N. (2007). Transnationalizing the public sphere: On the legitimacy and efficacy of public opinion in a post-Westphalian world. *Theory, Culture & Society*, *24*(4), 7–30. doi:10.1177/0263276407080090

Fung, A. (2003). Recipes for public spheres: Eight institutional choices and their consequences. *Journal of Political Philosophy*, *11*(3), 338–367. doi:10.1111/1467-9760.00181

Fung, A. (2006). Varieties of participation in complex governance. *Public Administration Review*, *66*, 66–76. doi:10.1111/j.1540-6210.2006.00667.x

Fung, A., & Wright, E. O. (2001). Deepening democracy: Innovations in empowered participatory governance. *Politics & Society*, *29*(1), 5–44. doi:10.1177/0032329201029001002

Ganesh, S., & Barber, K. F. (2009). The silent community: Organizing zones in the digital divide. *Human Relations*, *62*(6), 851–874. doi:10.1177/0018726709104545

Gimmler, A. (2001). Deliberative democracy, the public sphere and the Internet. *Philosophy and Social Criticism*, *27*(4), 21–39. doi:10.1177/019145370102700402

Goodin, R. E., & Dryzek, J. S. (2006). Deliberative impacts: The macro-political uptake of min-publics. *Politics & Society*, *34*(2), 219–244. doi:10.1177/0032329206288152

Government of Karnataka. (1997). Mahiti–the millennium IT policy. Retrieved November 23, 2009, from http://www.bangaloreitbt.in/word document/pdf/IT%20policy.pdf

Guru, G. (2005). Citizenship in exile: A Dalit case . In Reifeld, H., & Bhargava, R. (Eds.), *Civil society, public sphere and citizenship: Dialogues and perceptions* (pp. 260–276). Thousand Oaks, CA: Sage.

Gutmann, A., & Thompson, D. (2004). *Why deliberative democracy?* Princeton, NJ: Princeton University Press.

Habermas, J. (1991). *The structural transformation of the public sphere.* Cambridge, MA: MIT Press.

Habermas, J. (1996). *Between facts and norms: Contributions to a discourse theory of law and democracy.* Cambridge, MA: MIT Press.

Hargittai, E. (2006). Hurdles to information seeking: Spelling and typographical mistakes during users' online behavior. *Journal of the Association for Information Systems*, *7*(1), 52–67.

Heitzman, J. (1999). Democratic participation in Bangalore: Implementing the Indian 74th amendment. Cited in Madon, S., & Sahay, S. (2000). Democracy and information: A case study of new local governance structures in Bangalore. *Information Communication and Society*, *3*(2), 173–191.

Janssen, D., & Kies, R. (2005). Online forums and deliberative democracy. *Acta Politica*, *40*, 317–335. doi:10.1057/palgrave.ap.5500115

Jenkins, H., & Thorburn, D. (2004). *Democracy and new media*. Cambridge, MA: MIT Press.

Kahn, R., & Kellner, D. (2005). Oppositional politics and the Internet: A critical/reconstructive approach. *Cultural Politics: An International Journal*, *1*(1), 75–100. doi:10.2752/174321905778054926

Kanungo, S. (2004). On the emancipatory role of rural information systems. *Information Technology & People*, *17*, 407–422. doi:10.1108/09593840410570267

Kaufmann, D., & Kraay, A. (2002). *Growth without governance*. (World Bank Policy Research Working Paper No. 2928), Washington, D.C. Retrieved November 23, 2009, from http://www.worldbank.org/wbi/governance/pubs/growthgov.html.

Kaufmann, D., Kraay, A., & Mastruzzi, M. (2008). *Governance matters VII: Aggregate and individual governance indicators, 1996-2007*. (World Bank Policy Research Working Paper No. 4654), Washington, D.C. Retrieved November 23, 2009, from http://www.worldbank.org/wbi/ governance/pubs/aggindicators.html

Kellner, D. (1999). New technologies: Technocities and the prospects for democratization. In Downey, J., & McGuigan, J. (Eds.), *Technocities*. London: Sage.

Keniston, K., & Kumar, D. (Eds.). (2004). *IT experience in India: Bridging the digital divide*. New Delhi: Sage.

Lim, M., & Kann, M. E. (2008). Politics: Deliberation, mobilization, and networked practices of agitation. In Varnelis, K. (Ed.), *Networked publics* (pp. 77–108). Cambridge, MA: MIT Press.

Madon, S. (1997). The information-based global economy and socio-economic development: The case of Bangalore. *The Information Society*, *13*(3). doi:10.1080/019722497129115

Manor, J. (1993). *Power, poverty and poison: Disaster and response in an Indian city*. New Delhi: Sage.

Margolis, M., & Resnick, D. (2000). *Politics as usual: The cyberspace revolution*. London, UK: Sage.

Morris, D. (1999). *Vote.com: How big-money lobbyists and the media are losing their influence, and the Internet is giving power back to the people*. Los Angeles, CA: Renaissance Books.

Morrisett, L. (2003). Technologies of freedom? In Jenkins, H., & Thorburn, D. (Eds.), *Democracy and new media* (pp. 21–31). Cambridge, MA: MIT Press.

Mossberger, K., Tolbert, C. J., & McNeal, R. S. (2007). *Digital citizenship: The Internet, society, and participation*. Cambridge, MA: MIT Press.

Mukerji, M. (2008). Telecentres in rural India: Emergence and a typology. *The Electronic Journal on Information Systems in Developing Countries*, *35*(5), 1–13.

Nigam, A. (2005). Civil society and its underground: Explorations in the notion of political society . In Reifeld, H., & Bhargava, R. (Eds.), *Civil society, public sphere and citizenship: Dialogues and perceptions* (pp. 236–259). Thousand Oaks, CA: Sage.

Norris, P. (2001). *A digital divide: Civic engagement, information poverty, and the Internet in democratic societies*. New York, NY: Cambridge University Press.

Norris, P. (2003). *Deepening democracy via e-governance*. Report for the UN World Public Sector Report. Retrieved December 11, 2009, from http://ksghome.harvard.edu/~pnorris/ ACROBAT/e-governance.pdf

Papacharissi, Z. (2002). The virtual sphere: The net as a public sphere. *New Media & Society, 4*(1), 5–23. doi:10.1177/14614440222226244

Papacharissi, Z. (2009). The virtual sphere 2.0: The Internet, the public sphere, and beyond . In Chadwick, A., & Howard, P. (Eds.), *Routledge handbook of Internet politics* (pp. 230–245). New York, NY: Routledge.

Price, V. (2006). Citizen deliberating online: Theory and some evidence . In Davies, T., & Noveck, B. S. (Eds.), *Online deliberation: Research and practice*. Chicago, IL: Chicago University Press.

Rajagopal, A. (Ed.). (2009). *The Indian public sphere: Readings in media history*. New York, NY: Oxford University Press.

Raman, V. (2008). Examining the 'e' in government and governance: A case study in alternatives from Bangalore City, India. *Journal of Community Informatics, 4*(2), 405-437. Retrieved November 23, 2009, from http://ci-journal.net/index .php/ ciej/article/view/437/405

Rao, S. S. (2008). Social development in Indian rural communities: Adoption of telecentres. *International Journal of Information Management, 28*(6), 474–482. doi:10.1016/j.ijinfomgt.2008.01.001

Ravallion, M. (2009). *A comparative perspective on poverty reduction in Brazil, China and India*. (Policy Research Working Paper 5080). The World Bank Development Research Group. Retrieved December 11, 2009, from http://www. wds.worldbank.org/ external/default/WDSContentServer/ IW3P/IB/2009/11/30/000158349_ 20091130085835/Rendered/ PDF/WPS5080.pdf

Reifeld, H., & Bhargava, R. (Eds.). (2005). *Civil society, public sphere and citizenship: Dialogues and perceptions*. Thousand Oaks, CA: Sage.

Rhodes, R. A. W. (1997). *Understanding governance, policy networks governance reflexivity and accountability*. Buckingham, UK: Open University Press.

Schwartzberg, J. E. (2008). *India*. Encyclopedia Britannica.

Sen, A. (1999). *Development as freedom*. New York, NY: Knopf.

Shane, P. M. (Ed.). (2004). *Democracy online. The prospect for political renewal Through the Internet*. New York, NY: Routledge.

Stren, R., & Polese, M. (2000). *The social sustainability of cities: Diversity and the management of change*. Toronto, Canada: University of Toronto Press.

Stromer-Galley, J. (2007). Measuring deliberation's content: A coding scheme. *Journal of Public Deliberation, 3*(1), 1–37.

Thomas, R. G. C. (2006). Media . In Wolpert, S. (Ed.), *Encyclopedia of India* (*Vol. 3*, pp. 105–107). Farmington Hills, MI: Thomson Gale.

Thompson, D. F. (2008). Deliberative democratic theory and empirical political science. *Annual Review of Political Science, 11*, 497–520. doi:10.1146/annurev.polisci.11.081306.070555

TRAI. (2009). The Indian telecom services performance indicators, April-June 2009. Retrieved Dec 11, 2009, from http://www.trai.gov.in/WriteReadData/trai/upload/Reports/48/Indicator-Report1oct09.pdf

Turner, V. (1974). *Dramas, fields and metaphors: Symbolic action in human society*. Ithaca, NY: Cornell University Press.

UNDP. (2009). United Nations Development Programme, India: Democratic governance. Retrieved December 11, 2009, from http://www.undp.org.in/index.php?option=com_content&view=article&id=20&Itemid=255

United Nations. (2008). *UN e-government survey 2008: From e-government to connected governance*. United Nations e-Government Readiness Knowledge Base. Retrieved March 23, 2009, from http://www2.unpan.org/egovkb / global_reports/08report.htm

Volkmer, I. (2003). The global network society and the global public sphere. *Development, 46*(1), 9–16. doi:10.1177/1011637003046001566

Wilhelm, A. G. (2000). *Democracy in the digital age: Challenges to political life in cyberspace*. New York, NY: Routledge.

Wilkund, H. (2005). A Habermasian analysis of the deliberative democratic potential of ICT-enabled services in Swedish municipalities. *New Media & Society, 7*(5), 701–723. doi:10.1177/1461444805056013

World Bank. (2009). India country overview 2009. Retrieved Dec 11, 2009, from http://www.worldbank.org.in/WBSITE/ EXTERNAL/COUNTRIES/ SOUTHASIAEXT/INDIAEXTN/0, contentMDK:20195738~menuPK:295591 ~pagePK:141137~piPK:141127~theSitePK:295584,00.html

World Bank. (2009a). Governance in India, governance and public sector management in South Asia. Retrieved Dec 11, 2009, from http://go.worldbank.org/BNHP6XVL60

Wright, S. (2005). Design matters: The political efficacy of government-run discussion forums . In Gibson, R., Oates, S., & Owen, D. (Eds.), *Civil society, democracy and the Internet: A comparative perspective* (pp. 80–99). London, UK: Routledge.

Wright, S., & Street, J. (2007). Democracy, deliberation and design: The case of online discussion forum. *New Media and Society.*

ENDNOTE

[1]   According to the 2007 State of the Nation survey conducted by the Centre for the Study of Developing Societies among Indians, the level of religiosity has gone up considerably in the past five years. A mere five per cent of respondents said that their religious belief had declined, while 30 per cent said they had become more religious. The same poll found that education and exposure to modern urban life seem to make Indians more, not less, religious

Chapter 5
Issues of Digital Disempowerment and New Media Networking (NMN) in Relation to E-Government

Kenneth L. Hacker
New Mexico State University, USA

Eric L. Morgan
New Mexico State University, USA

ABSTRACT

Emerging media technologies are increasingly reconfiguring the public sphere by creating new spaces for political dialogue. E-democracy (digital democracy) and e-government can be usefully served by these emerging technologies; however, their existence does not automatically equate to increased political participation. There is still a need to develop specific and theoretically-oriented approaches to a newly reconfigured public sphere. Employing a structurational perspective, this essay addresses the relationship between political participation, emerging media, new media networking, and e-democracy. While new media networking increases the potential for political participation, depending on various factors such as access, usage and skills, the potential exists for increasing disempowerment as well. The chapter concludes with recommendations for the use of new media networking in ways that enhance e-democracy.

INTRODUCTION

Emerging media technologies are increasingly important for people as they connect with others

DOI: 10.4018/978-1-60960-159-1.ch005

in a variety of contexts including politics and government. As this occurs, the public sphere becomes reconfigured, opening up new spaces for discourse while possibly obscuring others. The concept of the public sphere has been subjected to many decades of debate. With new media and new media networks offering new potential for citizens to engage each other and various levels of government in political dialogue, the concept of public sphere is once again susceptible to new conceptualizations. This is particularly true in intellectual writings concerning e-democracy and e-government. While e-democracy (digital democracy) and e-government can be served well by the new media, there is no automatic improvement from previous means of political interaction. There is a need to develop specific and theoretically-oriented views of new public sphere potential. In this way, it will be possible to relate new forms of political participation to issues of how to use e-government to maximize participation for as many citizens as possible.

The purpose of this chapter is to address the concerns of e-government and disempowerment since new media networking (NMN) can both increase and decrease the abilities of citizens to substantially increase their voice and input into democratic politics. Of particular concern here is the persistent problem of the Digital Divide and its gaps which sometimes narrow and other times open depending on what aspect of digital access, usage, or skills is being examined. The most significant problem with the Digital Divide is the possible exclusion from valuable networks for many people who do not have the networking abilities to well position themselves in new media networks. A related problem concerns the various forms of political skills that are related to creating, expanding, and modifying networks of communication that generate political influence.

From its beginning, the Internet has been about interconnection. While it is common to hear how new media networks empower individuals by giving them access to information which they have previously had little access to, there are difficult realities about those who are not so empowered. When examining the potential of new media networking for digital democracy and electronic government (e-government), scholars and practitioners need to take stock of how the

new media and networking technologies are being used to create new personal and social networks. This focus forces a shift away from old ideas of computer-mediated communication (CMC) and toward newer concepts like emerging media, social media, social software, and social computing. It also encourages us to examine the irony that the same technologies which empower individuals to create more networking than at any time before, can function to minimize their role in significant and meaningful political communication.

A guiding assumption of this chapter is that NMN is replacing the one-dimensional concepts associated with computer-mediated communication. The latter refers to predominantly single channeled genres of communication such as email alone, cell phone alone or any other singularly purposed communication device. Email alone or Twitter alone are less important from a networking perspective than the use of email with Twitter and other channels of communication that form a technological network that facilitates a social network. NMN is based on converging communication technologies with shared electronic (Internet) networks. With NMN, we see that cell phones become smart phones, and smart phones become major hubs of personal communication technology intersections that are capable of affecting political communication.

The study of NMN is therefore the study of social behavior as opposed to individual behavior. Shirky (2008) argues that the study of human communication must focus more on networks because human behavior and communication involve linkages with other people. In his view, "Bees make hives, we make mobile phones." (Shirkey, 2008, p. 17). NMN allows us to expand cooperation and collective action and this increase can be done outside of traditional and institutional frameworks. Increasing amounts of former professional-only types of communication are moving into general public uses in what Tim O'Reilly calls an "architecture of participation[1]." Features of single communication technologies such as email become less important and less interesting than technologies used in networking. This is because communication technologies aid our social capabilities and are closely related to networking. Social behavior cannot be explained by only studying individuals (Shirky, 2008).

NMN is creating new forms of communication, and with those forms come a reconfiguring of communication research. Fading into the archives of communication research is the split between schools of thought that argue the dichotomous positions of the Internet either aiding or not aiding processes of participation within democratic political systems. Rather, research about how people organize, challenge, form, and change politics by how they work with the new media networks and how they form some of these networks themselves is gaining prominence (e.g., van Dijk, 2006). While extreme positions can be found about Digital Divide gaps for all forms of online communication, more realistic assessments note where gaps that are significant in terms of usage that might have actual political effects. Despite this fact, there is a profound optimism by many scholars for what online communication can contribute to government and democracy.

This optimism can lead to a bifurcation of understanding of NMN such that it is still possible to use the old dichotomous terms of "technologies of freedom" versus "technologies of control" to discuss NMN. Doing so, however, runs the risk of obscuring more complex effects. We believe it is more fruitful to look at new media and NMN as sites of competition and contestation by citizens, governments, consumers, corporations, and activist organizations. While NMN can be used for citizen empowerment, it can also be used for citizen disempowerment. There is no mystery to this claim because it is a general principle that has applied to the emergence and adoption of all communication technologies in human history and goes hand in hand with communication industry polemics of cultural revolution going back to the introduction of radio. The key issue for scholars

and policy makers is how to maximize the empowerment of citizens through e-government structures and processes.

To accomplish our analysis, we will first discuss the differences between e-government and e-democracy (digital democracy) as it is important to recognize that these are distinct phenomena that will engage NMN differently. We will then move into a discussion of the technological trends that have led to increased capabilities for e-government and e-democracy. While discussion of technological trends will allow for an understanding of these processes from a particular standpoint, we will focus the majority of our argument on the sociological and communicative dimensions of what is increasingly a networked society. The network society discussion will lead into a consideration of the key empowerment and disempowerment issues (i.e., Digital Divide issues) as well as an argument concerning the nontrivial nature of low participation in a networked society. The chapter concludes with a discussion of future directions for research.

DIGITAL DEMOCRACY AND E-GOVERNMENT

Digital democracy and e-government are both important concepts in political communication, but they are not the same. Additionally, they are not isolated but rather, related concepts. E-government in the service of e-democracy is qualitatively different than e-government in the service of nondemocratic governance. E-government is generally defined as the use of information and communication technologies for the purpose of improving public services as well as the internal communication of governments (van Dijk, forthcoming). E-government can serve e-democracy by offering citizens a more transparent and citizen-services oriented government. On the other hand, e-government can work against e-democracy by obscuring governance in ways that foster low political interactivity and high surveillance of citizens (van Dijk, forthcoming). We argue that the partnership of e-government with NMN can significantly increase the connections of e-government to e-democracy.

E-government includes basic services such as services directories and documents provision. Beyond such basic efficiency services, e-government can serve e-democracy by increasing interactivity between citizens and government sites in forms such as extended search features, input channels, and email contact channels. It can also increase interactivity between citizens and government officials by providing social media features such as blogs and short message service. In combining e-government with NMN, the former helps citizens and government officials to constitute a networked form of governance that is conducive to optimizing the use of new communication technologies for interactivity within internal government, between citizen and government, and among citizens. Digital communication technology clearly makes it possible to increase governmental efficiency; yet, efficiency, while supportive of democracy, is not enough to enhance or provide democracy. Democracy involves citizen input, deliberation, and involvement with public spheres. Networking efficiency can help responsiveness to citizen needs as in the case of inter-agency coordination during crises (van Dijk, forthcoming).

A constant limiting factor to the use of e-government in facilitating e-democracy is the limited number of citizens who are capable of and motivated to use online interaction with their government. Digital skills necessary for using the Internet in general, become more complicated as users move into NMN. While costs may be low after having computer and network connectivity, amount of effort increases when it comes to website design, blog updating, and social media interlinking. Studies show that there is an association between usage of e-government and digital skills (van Dijk, forthcoming). van Dijk (forthcoming) argues that simply digitizing

government services might do nothing for digital democracy. It is necessary to empower citizens to become more involved with government as they become more involved with the new media of government. With this approach, citizens can learn more about how their government works and possibly increase their trust in government as they do so.

Viewing e-government in light of the rapid acceleration of NMN allows us to think of e-democracy and e-government from a perspective that differs from the site-to-public models that have been commonly discussed. The government-public communication models of e-government admirably stress increasing the political interactivity between governments and citizens. A shifting focus on NMN allows citizens to create their own public spheres in communication with each other before or while they communicate with government. It even allows members of one network to become members of the other network. In other words, government representatives can deliberate in public spheres and members of the public can communicate within government spheres. These new possibilities are a direct result of increased technological capabilities of the new media.

THE TECHNOLOGICAL TRENDS

Perhaps the single most dominant trend among emerging media is the move toward social networking. Social networking refers to the capability of users to connect with other users for a variety of purposes. This networking is done through email, websites, gaming, texting, and cell/smart phones (Grant & Meadows, 2008). Social networking commonly occurs via particular platforms such as Facebook, Twitter, Meetup, and MySpace. These sites allow individuals to increase their social links across many interest groups. While connectivity among members of a social network is enhanced, communication scholars are more interested in how new forms of communication are organized than in simple increases of social linkages. In other words, these emergent new media allow, and often require, different structures underlying communication processes. Two fundamental characteristics of emergent media and NMN are self-organization and increases in collaborative relationships.

The technological attribute of self-organization refers to the ability of users to generate their own communication networks. Barry Wellman and other scholars refer to this as networked individualism (Castells, 2001; van Dijk, 2006). NMN makes possible new and creative forms of self-organization for groups of people. The self-organizing groups can operate without formal structures, institutional imperatives, or permission. They can be more widely distributed than at any time in the past (Shirky, 2008). Group self-organization involves processes of sharing, cooperating, coordinating, and collaborating, all of which are aided by NMN. Because the groups are self-organizing rather than driven by authorities, they may be conducive to digital democracy. This is especially true if what counts more in examining e-democracy is communication networking rather than personal identity. Collaborative production and community formation appear to work together and we know from history that democracy and community work together (Hacker & Todino, 1996).

New media networks are also characterized by mobile individuals that are no longer tethered to particular places as with telephones in the past (Grant & Meadows, 2008). This mobility undercuts a primary assumption of telecommunication of old in that no longer are communication partners reliant on schemata of places when interacting with others. Thus, a new self-organizing and (at times decreasingly) self-regulating system is created for communication, including political communication. This more clearly highlights the second characteristic of collaboration. New media users are able to engage in "integrative collaboration" through audio, text, video, and other forms of new media interaction (Ogden, 2008, p. 322).

The collaborative characteristic is particularly important in e-government and e-democracy. NMN provides a platform for users to perceive that they are engaged in political discourse in a collaborative sense, that is, by working with others.

The community aspect of some NMN is essential to newly forming power in certain groups. With community, there is higher density of interaction or what Shirky (2008) calls "social density." (p. 85). We have long known that interactivity is important to communication in general and to political communication in terms of citizen involvement with government (Hacker, 1996). NMN increases the potential for interactivity but interactivity can lessen as networks get larger and larger. As we will see later, this is why some scholars argue for the value of smaller online public spheres as opposed to larger mass media public spheres. Essentially, online spheres are restricted in interactivity due to the number of users involved.

Formerly singular media are increasingly integrated into multimedia technologies (Dallow, 2007). While communication research could once productively analyze the use of single media or channels of communication, convergence of communication modalities has made this less likely. As Grant & Meadows (2008) note, "No single technology can be understood without understanding the competing and complementary technoloogies and the larger social environment within which these technologies exist" (pg 3). Contrary to claims about new media replacing old media, empirical observations of the new technologies and their supporting industries instead show a marriage of the old and new media. Television, radio, music, and movie content are found in both old and new media and NMN involves a combination of personal media (e.g., tablet computers like iPad), smart phones, mass media, and various mutlimedia devices that facilitate the portability and easy transfer and storage of all forms of communication content (Brown, 2008). Ostensibly, there are increasing channels of interaction and content access that continue to create a complex NMN environment. The concept of "unified communication" extends the notion of convergence and implies that digital communication is not about single applications of communication technologies but about linked technologies like instant messaging (IM), email, cell phone, social networking, etc. (Ogden, 2008, p. 330).

Going beyond multimedia, there are new forms of communication resulting from emerging and extended media and what are referred to as extensible media (Dallow, 2007). These changes are related to Web 2.0 developments and include trends that are both summative (communication technology convergence) and exponential (emerging media). Interactivity, convergence, and connectivity are all increased in NMN and new forms of interrelationships are made possible (Dallow, 2007). Social networking sites have followed the dynamics of online communities as well as online collaboration by facilitating the sharing of information, ideas, and impressions (Dallow, 2007). Another form of collaboration involves open access to software code. This is done freely and the improvements made to the coding are openly shared with other users (Dallow, 2007).

Cell phones and smart phones provide devices that can act as hubs for emerging networks. Applications integrated into one small and portable device include photography, email, telephone, and Web access (Grant, 2008). Digitization, convergence, and tecnnical inter-operability have made digital communication capable of making any type of information a digital data stream. Thus, messages created in one form of communication can easily migrate to another. (Grant, 2008). Social institutions and ways of social organizing are susceptible to the changes made in extensible media and emerging media networking. Smart phones will increasingly bring together computer applications like word processing and global positioning systems (GPS), mass media such as television, and interpersonal interaction through email and telephone (Grant, 2008). Along with convergence and extensible networking, we also

see a ubiquity of communication access for those who can afford the networking access and smart phone interfaces. This ubiquity allows those who can learn the digital skills necessary an opportunity for creating personal networks of communication involving the new media.

Communication researchers have noted how easily NMN makes social organizing and political mobilization. Transaction costs and barriers can be dramatically lowered for those who have access and digital skills. In network societies found in the United States, many nations in Europe and cities in other parts of the world that have high percentages of their populations using new media, there is a shift in political communication from reliance on mass media to one that combines mass media with NMN. To appreciate the significance of this, it is necessary to see how different NMN is from using mass media alone for political information and communication.

Shirky (2008) notes that new media have a given us a condition where "never have so many people been so free to say and do so many things with so many other people." (p. 123). What is known in advertising as viral marketing (spreading messages quickly through interpersonal networks) is made faster and easier than ever before with NMN and not just for commercial persuasion. This can be positive when valid information is diffused and negative when rumors and urban legends are disseminated. Shirky (2008) notes that NMN is not creating collective action but is making it easier.

The technologies of NMN allow users to participate in communication that is high in interactivity and which is also multidirectional and iterative (Drapeau & Wells, 2009). NMN users are involved in the production of messages, content, and networking. Some users are more comfortable getting information from their personal online networks than from traditional news media (Drapeau & Wells, 2009). This is a critical point to realize for those working with e-government and seeking to influence message diffusion. Users of new media are not audience members only as they can alternate between the role of audience member (reading, viewing, listening) and author (writing, speaking, sharing content).

One interesting application for e-government involves taking advantage of the new networks that citizens now employ to seek and distribute information. For example, a government can post news on YouTube and then gain feedback both through YouTube and other new media channels such as blogging. As noted earlier, citizens in democracies appreciate interactivity with their governmental representatives. NMN channels such as Twitter and live Internet video channels like Qik can be used to increase representative-constituent interaction (Drapeau & Wells, 2009). Even the U.S. State Department, Air Force, and Coast Guard are taking advantage of the rapid message diffusion capabilities of Twitter and other social media (Drapeau & Wells, 2009).

Political participation is not simply about citizens interacting with government but also with each other. NMN can and should facilitate both. Technical barriers to political participation are dramatically lowered to those who can use new media. Yet, as we will address in more detail later, as total participation increases, inequalities in participation can persist.

NETWORK SOCIETY

van Dijk (2006) defines network society in terms of communication networks that shape the most important forms of organization in a society. In what we have known for decades as mass society, citizens have been informed and entertained by mass media while remaining somewhat disconnected from people outside of their primary (e.g. family, friends) and secondary social groups (e.g. workplace). Where network socities begin to emerge, increasing numbers of social structures involve interconnected individuals using computer networks to seek out information, relationships,

and networks of influence. In these structures, political power and politics are more about relationships among people than characteristics of individuals (van Dijk, 2006). Dimensions of geographical space are accompanied by a technological space. This space is sometimes referred to as social geography, wherein social networks rather than physical space become the basis for closeness or distance. Political systems, which traditionally have been modeled as top-down organizational charts, may be more accurately reflected as polycentric systems of power in which political power is based more on network position than on traditional roles (van Dijk, 2006).

The consequences of people being connected to the new communication networks of network society are becoming more significant as participation in these networks is increasingly linked to tangible benefits. Network society perspectives of social organization and communication technologies include economics as well as politics. Indeed, economic reorganization is seen historically as the main impetus for the emergence of network societies (Stalder, 2006). Globalizing trade and finance make up an informational economy with the center of the global economy as finance (Stalder, 2006). Organizations become more flexible to meet changing markets and governments where changes and discontinuities constitute a new focus.

Communication technologies have always been central to both the exercise of power by the state and to the formation of public spheres of deliberation made available to citizens (Barney, 2004). Power in network society social, economic, and political contexts can be viewed more as matters of position and network relations than of material or content advantages. Power in previous paradigms like Fordism or Weberian organizational assumptions was about getting others to do one's will. In contrast, power in networks is more about flows of influence, investment, and planning (Stalder, 2006). Barney (2004) argues that "access to networks and power to determine what flows over them is a significant marker of systemic advantage and disadvantage domestically and globally" (p. 178). While there is little evidence that NMN yet has strong empowerment effects for those without extant power, there is a sense of democratic potential that does have empirical support.

In July, 2009, 42% of American Internet users said they had visited government websites (Comscore, 2009). Some of the most visited sites were the Department of Commerce, the Department of Education, the National Institute of Health, the White House, and the Social Security Administration. Recent Pew research shows that 64% of adult Americans have home broadband access to the Internet (Horrigan, 2009). Sixty eight percent of these users say that the access is important for learning about events in their community, 65% for communicating with health care professionals, and 58% for sharing their views with others (Horrigan, 2009). Other Pew research indicates that during the 2008 U.S. presidential election, about 74% of Internet users were using online sources for information and news about the campaign (Smith, 2009). Thirty eight percent used the Internet for interactions with others about the campaign. Fifty nine percent used online campaign tools like email, instant messaging, texting, and Twitter (Smith, 2009). Annenberg School of Communication data indicate that 81% of online community members report that they participate in online communities related to social causes (Cole, 2009). However, only 25% of respondents said that the Internet can be used to encourage political leaders to care more about the concerns of citizens (Cole, 2009). While such reports are interesting and useful, we need data about networking positions and perceptions.

Such data is not as common as simple usage statistics, but we can see from recent reports that more people in the United States are using new media for political information and communication. Most Americans (92%) get their news from a variety of sources which mix old media with new media – radio, TV, Internet, newspapers, etc. (Purcell, Mitchell, Rosentiel, & Olstead, 2010).

Only 6% of Americans are getting their daily news from a single platform. The Internet is the third most popular platform (Purcell, Mitchell, Rosentiel, & Olstead, 2010). Thirty-three percent of American cell phone owners access news on those phones. A key finding for networking analysis is that 37% of American Internet users have contributed to the creation of news or the posting of news on social media sites like Facebook (Purcell, Mitchell, Rosentiel, & Olstead, 2010). Also important is the finding that 75% of American online news consumers report getting news forwared to them through email or postings on social networking sites (Purcell, Mitchell, Rosentiel, & Olstead, 2010).

Networks are comprised of nodes; these nodes are connected by communication and join together to become influence networks (Castells, 2000). When a node does not connect to other nodes, it may be dropped from the network. Such nodes are then excluded from exercising influence on social organization. Those who are part of the networks that exert influence on society can work to increase the impact of their influence by stimulating changes in, or reinforcing, existing patterns in the social structures that are beneficial to them. According to Castells (2009), the function and meaning of a node (person) in a network is dependent on the programs of the network and the node's interactions with other nodes. Members (nodes) of networks that are most valued and empowered are those that most help the network to achieve its goals. Conversely, members that do not help network goals can be dropped or replaced (Castells, 2009). Castells observes that valued members of networks have not only a skill set, but also a creativity in working with information and knowledge, and with making their contributions to the network necessary and valued. Networking power entails bringing more valued nodes into a network and keeping ones that will not be useful out of the network. Castells (2009) notes that the cost of being excluded from a network increases faster than the benefits of inclusion because of the fact that node values increase exponentially with network size increases.

As the Internet and NMN become embedded with economic, social, and political activities, citizens are likely to develop stronger needs to use the networks in order to maximize their abilities to participate in online opportunities, resources, or social formations. Those who become most skilled and active with NMN networking are more likely to gain power than those without these skills and activities. This means there may be accelerating gaps in network sophistication. As van Dijk (2002) notes, digital skills are cumulative. Accordingly, the inequalities resulting from their increasingly embedded nature are cumulative as well. Holderness (1998) argues that the Digital Divide gaps that we have been discussing may become self-reinforcing. Those individuals and nations who accelerate their use of NMN systems build their communication capital at rates that perpetuate how far they stay ahead of others in networking.

It is generally accepted that the increasing organization of societies with the use of NMN technologies facilitates the importance of information and knowledge for economic growth and a shift of importance from densely-knit bounded groups to computer-supported social networks (United Nations, 2004). The emergence of network societies entails social and organizational formations that are constructed in relation to flows of symbolic interaction more than in relation to traditional institutional, governmental, and organizational boundaries (Contractor & Monge, 2003).

Those with the most power and resources tend to be the early adopters of new technologies, and their influence shapes the evolution of technological changes in society (van Dijk, 2006). Thus, social inequalities may be perpetuated as those who use the technologies are increasingly organizing social networks around them. The inability to access or make effective use of the Internet and NMN becomes increasingly significant as those with power make their use increasingly prominent in all areas of society. Those who do not have ac-

cess to new forms of communication technology are increasingly excluded from the organization of society on many levels. This suggests that increasing networking that is accompanied by increasing gaps in usage for government and political communication may disempower many citizens in any nation moving toward network society structures.

Given the above discussion, we can conclude that new power in network societies is strongly linked to influence over system configurations, position within networks and control over information flows. It is no longer surprising that those with greater connectivity, centrality, and interactivity are those in a society that will benefit the most from network technologies of communication. Moreover, simply being connected to new communication networks does not assure any degree of influence or power. In fact, connection without power is likely to assure that the connected person is subjected to new forms of domination by those with more control over the information flows and configurations of the networks (Barney, 2004).

FROM MASS MEDIA PUBLIC SPHERE TO NETWORKED PUBLIC SPHERES

As John Keane (2000) has argued, there is no single Habermasian public sphere in digital communication, but rather muliple types of public spheres at many layers of society. Keane (2000) notes that much discourse about "the public" (public good, public opinion, public spheres) was used in history to resist the actions of political leaders who seemed to care more about themselves than their subjects. Discussions about a public sphere have been built on the hope that rational, informed, and democratic communication among citizens could challenge the control of communication by either market or governmental forces. Keane (2000) further argues that NMN involves three levels of public spheres today -- micro, meso, and macro. The micro-level involves the coffee house chats, town hall meetings, and other forms of social interaction in which citizens argue, complain, and challenge all sorts of political actions and policies. Keane (2000) argues that these forms of communication are important because they involve identity and meaning formation. He even calls them "the laboratories in which new experiences are invented and popularized" (p. 78). With NMN, micro-level political interaction can involve any channel or any combination of channels that helps citizens to "question and transform the dominant codes of everyday life (Keane, 2000, p. 78). This focus on the power of micro-level social interaction is consistent with structuration theory which explains how structures in society are (re)instantiated through interaction (Giddens, 1984). At the meso-level of public sphere, Keane (2000) argues that current affairs are debated in mass media venues. Global media constitute the macro-level of public spheres in Keane's argument. While global media corporations are propelled by profit seeking, they often are agents in stirring up public controversies and concerns when they cover dramatic political events such as the suppression of students in China at Tiananmen Square in 1989 (Keane, 2000).

The challenge to the traditional Habermas concept of public sphere as an alternative space of political communication freed from both commercial and governmental manipulation is the argument that multiple public spheres (rather than one free zone such as public broadcasting) are the zones where citizens can generate communication that challenges all forms of domination. Keane (2000) even goes so far as to argue that such communicative challenges can occur within civil society, markets, and even governments. Of course, he adds the caveat that not all political discussion has significant political effects. For our purposes, it is important to recognize the multiplicity of possible sites of political structuration, one of them being e-government.

With mass media dominating political news and discussion, public debate and the public sphere were largely the result of decisions made by those who control the media production companies, usually either governments or corporations (Benkler, 2006). The technical architecture of mass media is a hub-and-spoke structure with information generally transmitted linearly from one to many. Feedback from audiences to producers is possible, but not always significant and audience members receive messages in isolation from each other. News media have been seen as, and portray themselves as, monitors of politicians and governments for the people (Benkler, 2006). Cooperative relationships between governments and media corporations have been conducted with a discourse of protecting the "public good." (Benkler, 2006, p. 196). In all of this, the public sphere is limited to what mass media elites consider as necessary subjects for public deliberation and debate.

In the mass media public sphere communication moves from a small number of people to a much larger number of people, the latter having little say regarding the topics debated in the sphere. Filtering of issues is not done by the larger number as the smaller number sets the issue agenda. Feedback from receivers to senders is minimal (Benkler, 2006). Since the mid-19th century, the startup costs for a mass media business such as a newspaper, is well beyond the reach of most Americans (Benkler, 2006). In essence, the consumers of mass media political information are passive receivers of messages. The mass media public sphere involves scripted, filtered, and packaged deliberation about issues that are conceptualized and framed by media planners.

In contrast to mass media, new media and NMN offer the potential of what Benkler (2006) calls "the networked public sphere" (p. 177). He argues that this type of public sphere inverts the mass media public sphere, as public deliberation and debate are driven by clusters of individuals and the debating is freed from governmental and commercial control. In contrast to mass media public spheres, which offer citizens finished statements, the networked spheres offer citizens opportunities to engage in genuine debating practices. The hub-and-spokes architecture is challenged by a multidirectional architecture with nodes connected with others nodes with various many-to-many channels (Benkler, 2006).

A second key difference in the networked sphere is the dramatically lowered cost of becoming a message source. One can begin with a website, blog, Twitter account, SMS, etc. and expand into other channels of NMN. A third key characteristic of the networked sphere is that the agendas of debating are not set by single centers of power like media corporations but by coalitions or groups of citizens who do their own framing of political events. While the numbers of networked public spheres increase, it is possible that the number of speakers and participants in political debates will also increase.

A networked public sphere now has the possibility to intersect with e-government in novel ways. Usual concerns of e-government are efficiency and productivity in governments providing services to citizens through online access. Some scholars argue that e-government must move beyond this, however, and design NMN that facilitates and encourages more citizen political participation. As van Dijk (forthcoming) notes, the typical focus of e-government on improving the efficiency of government service delivery can serve either as a direction toward more citizen input into decision making or a direction toward increased government control and decreased citizen control of decisions. To increase citizen involvement in government, e-government design can be used to enhance how much input and interactivity is available for citizens, and also help citizens produce networked public spheres.

A study done in The Netherlands shows that there is a positive linear relationship between digital skills and the use of online government services (van Dijk, forthcoming). Despite this fact, however, digital skills are not enough. There

is also a need to encourage the motivation of citizens to use e-government and the creativity that is necessary to work with digital content and online social interaction (Castells, 2000). Citizens seek more than online service efficiency; they also seek more input into policies and decisions (van Dijk, forthcoming).

POWER AND NETWORKS

Arguments about NMN and politics that simply discuss political potential, a staple since the 1990s, do not use theories of communication or politics to explain the role of NMN in empowerment. Contemporary new media networking necessitates an explanation of power as related to networks since NMN is all about networks that employ new and emerging media. Structuration theory allows a theoretical view of networked power. The basic argument of structuration theory is that as actors act, they do so within a set of structures; however, in so acting, actors reinstantiate those structures. Citizens produce power in their lives partially by their station in society, but also by how they self-generate meaningful political actions (Castells, 2009). Structure, agency, and social dynamics are all interrelated in this view. Structuration occurs at various levels of social organization and communication ranging from micro to macro levels of communication.

Castells (2009) identifies four types of power in emerging communication networks. The first type of power is what he calls networking power. Such power refers to the ability to be included in networks as opposed to being excluded. He notes that the cost of exclusion from networks increases faster than the benefits of inclusion. He also argues that this is true because inclusion increases in value (as noted by Metcalfe's Law) at a slower pace than devaluation from exclusion increases. Another type of power is network power. This power involves influence over the rules of inclusion for networks. The third type of power observed by Castells is networked power. This refers to the ability to impose one's will over others because of structural domination in a network. Finally, there is networking-making power. This entails the ability to create networks and configure them in terms of goals (Castells, 2009).

Castells (2009) argues that political power today is also related to how power is related to meanings in the minds of citizens and how those meanings are influenced by networks of communication. By using his theory of communication power, it is possible to see how NMN depends upon and influences networks of cognition. It is also possible to recognize and study how cultural codes, cognition, and social networks are interrelated in systems of power. In his theory of communication power, Castells (2009) argues that there two other major forms of network power, that of programming and that of switching. Programming power involves agenda-setting and making decisions about operations. Switching power is the ability to manage the connections between two more networks (Castells, 2009). Challenges to network power, according to Castells (2009) come from "reprogramming networks around alternative interests and values." (p. 431). One aspect of NMN that increases democracy, according to Castells, is bringing new people into political activities, generating more "insurgent politics," and enabling new sources of political decision-making.

Governments have to respond to citizens who organize, mobilize, and participate in politics more with NMN. When citizens use networks to expose the lies of their leaders or to mobilize large-scale acts of resistance, government officials are forced to pay more attention to certain principles of democracy such as the people having rights of input into political decision-making (Castells, 2009). Unlike the conclusion reached by some scholars such as Hindman (2009), that the power of mass media is replicated in the power of new media corporations, Castells (2009) adopts a structurational view of new media and argues that

technologies alone cannot be expected to generate political change or to lower inequalities. NMN provides the opportunities for citizens to use the multi-modal and highly interactive networking potential to re-program various networks around values and concerns that simply do not cascade down from media corporations and governments. From a structuration theory perspective, this means that citizens can use the resources of new media, networks, and new forms of collaboration to generate new social structures that affect larger social systems. NMN provides more autonomy for citizens because they can generate and disseminate political content as well as perceive (mass media mode) it. Such increased agency is an important condition for being able and motivated to participate in democratic politics.

NEW MEDIA NETWORKS AND POLITICAL PARTICIPATION

The relationship between new media networks and political participation requires more examination because the networks are constantly changing as they allow novel forms of political participation. The 2008 U.S. presidential campaign provides a good example of the suspected links between NMN and political participation. Both major party candidates had websites devoted to allowing users to create profiles, connect supporters with like-minded others, and organize fundraising and "get out the vote" rallies (Krueger, 2008). These websites functioned much as the popular social networking sites Facebook and MySpace by encouraging users to feel more a part of the campaign through the personalization of profile sites. While the statistical effects of these websites remain to be seen in terms of voter participation, users did report that they felt more able to get involved (Krueger, 2008). Another more recent example is the European Parliament elections held in June, 2009. Prior to the election, the EP created profiles on both Facebook and MySpace in an effort to

Figure 1. The Power Law Curve

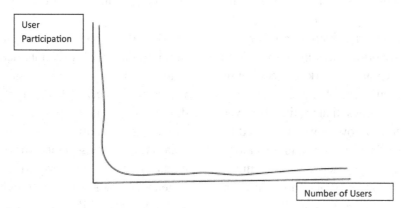

increase political participation (European Social Policy, 2009). One obvious question concerning these websites is whether they actually increased political participation or if those who are already politically involved found another mechanism to engage in political activity.

Indeed, while it is possible that some NMN users are increasing their political knowledge and participation; it is also possible that others are not. In other words, NMN can be empowering to some people while it is disempowering to others. This could particularly be the case for those individuals who have traditionally felt marginalized from changing technology, such as older voters. Internet-based communication appears to offer younger people new spaces for political dialogue and more private types of political communication (Vromen, 2007). As e-government becomes a part of a networked public sphere and as it is part and parcel of e-democracy, we can ask the question of who will have the networking power to engage these new forms.

There are many studies of Internet usage and political participation which attempt to answer the question of how much Internet usage contributes to significant increases in political participation. For example, Polat (2005) finds that the Internet enables expanded capabilities of political information seeking and dissemination. However, Polat (2005) also notes that studies indicate that people with higher levels of education are more likely to use the Internet in instrumental ways while people with lower levels of education are more likely to use the Internet for entertainment. Yet, consistent with Castells (2009), Polat (2005) sees the potential of new media and democracy lying more with deliberation potential than with information increases. In other words, there is potential for bottom-up effects stemming from deliberation in virtual public spheres. Because democracy depends upon a public sphere and public deliberation, NMN can be seen as increasing e-democracy by extending the public sphere (s).

THE NOTORIOUS POWER LAW

It is clear that increased networking has potential effects regarding political participation, but the question remains of how members of these networks may be impacted. While a Gaussian distribution or a bell curve may fit individual characteristics like height, weight, education, etc., it does not work well to summarize contributions of members in social networks. What describes the distribution of individual contributions in social networks more accurately is the Power Law curve where X equals number of users and Y equals user participation (see Figure 1).

Figure 2. Social Density and the Power Law

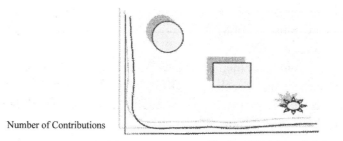

Number of Contributions

Number of Participants in Online Discussion

An article in a new media venue like Wikipedia might have 129 authors making 205 edits to the article. However, of the 129 authors, about 6 are likely to make 25% of the edits. On Flickr, the photo posting site, if 118 people upload photos about a particular subject, the top tenth of the submitters are likely to contribute over half of the photos (Shirky, 2008). Three-fourths of the contributors are below average in how many pictures they upload. Shirky (2008) observes that this pattern holds for new media in general. Hindman (2009) observes that power law distributions fit all kinds of new media political communication including websites and blogs. The distributions are like the economist Vilfredos Pareto's finding about wealth - 20% of the population controls 80% of the wealth (Hindman, 2009). In a power law distribution, the nth position has 1/nth of the rank of the first position (Shirky, 2008). The gap between the first and second position is larger than the gap between the second and third. In an online discussion group, the most talkative participant is far more active than the median participant so the concept of an average amount of participation is basically meaningless (Shirky, 2008).

Hindman's (2009) conclusion is that small numbers of sites on the Internet receive the most visitors, which indicates that new media, like old media, involve more political elitism than digital democracy. van Dijk and Hindman (forthcoming) conclude that the power law characteristic of NMN

requires increasing amounts of skill while there is no indication that increasing percentages of people are obtaining such skills in the subpopulations that are already behind in digital democracy such as those low in education. Shirky's (2008) conclusion is radically different. He argues that the 2% of Wikipedia contributors create amazing value for the 98% of readers who do not contribute (Shirky, 2008). In other words, the power law imbalance found in new media is not a problem, but rather something that drives large social systems and makes them work. This may seem like a strange argument to justify inequalities, but large social systems are not collections of alleged average users. The behaviors of people in a new media network are not independent so that the actions of everyone, whether high or low in frequency, affect the systems. Shirky even argues that there is power on the low end of the power law that we should not miss. In Figure 2, we can see a power law in terms of size of group and amount of social density. Social density is higher with the lower numbers of participants, not the higher ones.

In the curve above, for example, the highest amount of participants (upper left circle) results in a broadcasting form of new media. In this case, there is no significant difference between traditional forms of mass media and NMN. The middle figure (rectangle) shows loosely structured new media conversation, while the lower right figure indicates tight conversation and high *interactivity* (Shirky, 2008). In contrast to Hindman's argument that the rich and famous in the upper left broadcasting model of new media have a monopoly on digital democracy, Shirky (2008) argues that the power of the lower end does not come from numbers of participants but rather their community structure and commitment where each member can both send and receive (interactive) and the community can network with others. With an absence of network theory, structuration theory, diffusion theory, and communication theory, such power of small groups can be neglected. In other words, a clear understanding of NMN requires a theoretical approach to collective behavior because NMN is about social and collective behavior rather than individual actions alone.

Furthermore, NMN allows such collective action to occur more rapidly and easily. From the example of East Germany in 1989 to the protest in the Philippines against the Estrada government, history is replete with examples of communities organizing and creating social change. Because these examples of NMN helping large collective mobilizations, some observers assume that digital democracy is not being served all that well. However, the fact of the matter is that some of these cases indicate that democracy was helped along because people were able to participate in ways that were not available to them prior to new media.

As noted previously, Castells (2009) observes that NMN can create what he calls "insurgent politics." One example he cites is the Barack Obama presidential campaign in 2008. The Obama campaign used NMN fully as it used the Internet to disseminate messages, social networking sites to stimulate dialogue about the campaign, blogs for debating, and YouTube videos for advertising (Castells, 2009). The campaign hired Chris Hughes, a co-founder of Facebook to coordinate social networking efforts. Castells (2009) argues that the NMN efforts of the Obama campaign enabled the candidate to succeed at "mobilizing millions of citizens, including many who were withdrawn from the political system..." (p. 405). Voting turnout was the highest (percent of eligible

voters - 63%) since 1960 for participation of young voters (Castells, 2009).

EMPOWERMENT AND DISEMPOWERMENT ISSUES FOR ELECTRONIC GOVERNMENT

Discussions of increasing NMN within political discourse, networked public spheres, and e-democracy lead inexorably to a reconsideration of empowerment issues within political participation. There is little indication that NMN is drawing new people into democratic political processes, but there is substantial evidence that people who already participate are becoming more enabled in their participation (Bimber & Davis, 2005; van Dijk & Hacker, 2000). It is easier for NMN users to contact governmental officials, obtain government documents, and join political discussions with people they do not know (Pratchett, Wingfield, & Polat, 2006; van Dijk, 2004). Weerakkody & Dhillon (2008) note that in the U.K., electronic government now exists in a transformational phase that could allow for increased civic participation. On the other hand, Bimber & Davis (2005) argue that NMN is providing effective tools for political activities and mobilization, but that "the divide between those who are political activists interested in electoral campaigns and those who are not will expand" (p. 168).

Without the knowledge and ability to evaluate policies and potential leaders, citizens cannot engage in the democratic process in its true sense (Barber, 1984; Yankelovich, 1991). However, as Yankelovich (1991) maintains, information given to citizens in a downward flow means that they possess only that information passed onto them by elites. Receiving information in this type of downward flow pattern does not necessarily empower citizens; rather, it can serve to reinforce existing power structures as citizens maintain the passive role of consumers of information generated by the elite, who maintain control over all information

(Bordewijk & van Kaam, 1986; van Dijk, 1996). If high NMN users have more multilateral political communication than low NMN users, the latter are less likely to develop empowering roles for themselves in the polycentric power structures that appear to be part of network societies.

Political movements now employ the Internet to organize their struggles, and some of these users are developing a practice known as "self-directed networking" (Castells, 2000, p.55). Self-directed networking involves people inventing personal ways of organizing and disseminating information. As more formal political structures such as civic organizations have less public membership today, political movements can employ NMN to effectively mobilize political action (Castells, 2001). Those who are involved with online politics have an advantage over those with less involvement since online politics are becoming more common and influential as clearly demonstrated by the Obama campaign in 2008.

With the use of NMN, users need not only the digital skills of Internet, computer, website, new media, social media, and software usage, but also skills of building the networking power described by Castells. As noted earlier, dense small and interactive networks look weak in terms of the power law but have force in terms of their high levels of interactivity and possible linkages with other small dense networks. What makes the Small Worlds phenomenon work, for example, is that within one's small networks there is a high likelihood that one person knows someone more connected and important in society than the other members of the network (Shirky, 2008). The more one can be a connector or linking pin between networks, the more influence they can have in terms of who they know and how much networking power they have. However, discovering and expanding such influence may require education and social capital that many people do not possess.

E-government can be used in any type of political system. Issues of digital disempowerment may not be weighted highly in totalitarian societies that use e-government solely for efficient delivery of information and collection of information from citizens. In democratic systems, those who administer e-government must confront the expectations of citizens concerning active influence of the people on how their government reaches decisions, sets policies, and interacts with citizens. Structural inequalities work against democratic governance because structural inequality is related to positions in networks that privilege various groups of citizens over others (van Dijk, 2006).

One important area of digital empowerment concerns user-generated content (UGC) in NMN. With UGC, people can use social networking to create digital information and then to share it. UGC can challenge traditional forms of news, entertainment, education, and ways of gaining political information. YouTube videos are a classic example of UGC. One interesting form of UCG involves collaborative generation of content as in the case of Wikipedia (Meadows, 2008). Another example may be the increased usage of peer-to-peer (p2p) communication. This form involves file sharing and can also challenge reliance on more traditional or institutional forms of information distribution. UGC is easily available or distributed in blogs, websites, Twittering, file sharing, discussion lists, and chat rooms. While the audience size for personally produced content is most likely to be minuscule compared to mass media offline and online source content, there is still the opportunity to challenge traditional sources of political information and news. UGC can contribute to citizen expectations of empowerment. Still, development of good-quality UGC and gaining an audience for UGC is not as easy and affordable as often made to sound. As with the case of the Power Law phenomenon in online discussions, there is the same problem with UGC. There are new online elites that fulfill the role of their offline mass media counterparts (van Dijk & Hindman, forthcoming). Empirical research shows that online elites, such as the most popular bloggers, are not representative of the general population, but rather are more educated and affluent (Hindman, 2008).

The involvement of citizens in terms of access, skills, and creativity remains to be sufficiently addressed by both scholars and government officials. A fundamental characteristic of communication networks is that they can exclude people as much as include them (van Dijk & Hindman, forthcoming). Unlike some claims of this binary nature of networks, however, it should be noted that there are degrees of both inclusion and exclusion. In other words, one's position within a communication network determines one's level of influence potential in that network. Access to e-government is not the same thing as either connectivity or interactivity. Connectivity refers to the number of other people one is connected to in a network and interactivity refers to the back-and-forth message exchanges that occurs between nodes (individuals) in a network.

Other problems with online political communication concern the providers of Internet services. While we so often hear that NMN ends the old gatekeeping practices of the old media corporations, new media corporations are involved in newer forms of privileging some forms of content over others. An example of this is the way that search engines like Google list websites for searches. Google for example, uses software algorithms that places sites on top of search lists when those sites are linked to many other sites. When searching for political information, ten popular sites account for over one half of total links (Hindman, 2008). Two fallacies have emerged in existing claims about information and the Internet. One says that online searching would reveal a more expansive range of diversity in total information seeking. The second one says that because selective perception occurs in online searching as it does in mass communication, there would be fragmentation among citizens with everyone paying attention to their favorite sources. In fact, Hindman (2008) and others have found that Internet news and political information sources are more concentrated than news and information sources in the mass media.

Castells (2009) notes that political empowerment helps citizens to take actions that help with their interests and can challenge the interests of others. He argues that power is always relational. In this perspective, power is not an attribute but is rather a relationship. Influence, like communication, moves back and forth, but power involves asymmetrical relationships where one party has more influence than the other (Castells, 2009). Those in power who have the force of domination can use communication to create a rhetorical legitimation of their dominance. On the other hand, political resistance to domination can occur when compliance and acceptance are rejected by those who are dominated (Castells, 2009). The power of such resistance is found in the abilities of the dominated to challenge the values and interests of others. In terms of how empowered citizens actually are in relation to the digital age, then, involves interesting questions of just what political engagement, empowerment, and participation actually mean in relation to power and communication.

THE NONTRIVIAL NATURE OF LOW PARTICIPATION IN NETWORK SOCIETY

Recent Pew Research Center data indicate that traditional political activity, whether online or offline, is largely done by those with higher levels of education and income (Smith, 2009). This holds true for the online population as political engagement is more common for those higher in education and income (Smith, 2009). Use of new media is now part of the ways that many people communicate. In the United States, for example, half of those involved in civic or political groups use new media for communication with others in their groups (Smith, 2009).

The basic pattern of Internet use and political participation appears to be the same online as offline; those with power get more power. However, the usage of social networking may change this pattern over time. Pew Research Center data in 2008 indicated that 33% of Internet users in the United States had a social networking site profile (Smith, 2009). Of these, 31% reported either civic or political engagement. Some of the change reflects generational differences in technology usage. While 17% of Internet users aged 30-49, 12% of those 50-64, and 10% of those over 65 use blogs or social network sites for civic or political engagement, 37% of those aged 18-29 do so (Smith, 2009). The younger group is less educated and less affluent than the older groups, but it should be noted that income and education associations with political activity exist with all age groups.

The Pew data confirm Digital Divide observations from many years of observation in the United States. One continuous pattern since the 1990s is that the offline tendency of the higher educated and higher income citizens being most involved in politics continues online (Smith, Schlozman, Verba, & Brady, 2009). Despite this constant disappointment, however, there is the expansion of political activity enablement made possible by new media. So whether or not the Digital Divide gaps narrow or persist with new media, there are issues of gaps in networking that are even more important than the past issues of who has access to the Internet and who gains the most from new media activity. The stronger issues of empowerment and disempowerment now concern who is networking the most. One sign of hope for breaking the persistent Divide pattern concerns blogging and social networking. The Pew data indicate that the pattern noted above is weaker for those forms of political communication (Smith, et al., 2009).

A recent FCC report reveals that data indicate that there are problems with which segments of society are most likely to use NMN for communication that will consequently bring them into engagement with e-government and e-democracy. While about 65% of Americans have broadband access to the Internet in their homes, only 49% of Hispanic Americans (respondents in both English and Spanish), 59% of African Americans, 42% of people with disabilities, and 35% of those over the age 65 have such access (Horrigan, 2010). For those with a high-school education, 46% have home broadband access while 82% of those with a some or complete college education have such access. For those with lower incomes (<$50k/yr), 52% have home broadband, while 87% of those with higher incomes have such access (Horrigan, 2010). This would indicate a particular type of concentration of users that may coincide with traditional points of marginalization in the U.S. People with influential network positions and flows are more likely to be more interest-bound than place-bound in how they associate and work with others. Those who are left as more place-bound become less and less important to those who are sharing capital flows in cosmopolitan networks of association and influence. Barney (2004) argues that the less connected are likely to be passive consumers of communication content rather than active creators of messages and content.

E-governments can exacerbate the problems just described when they do not add political value to service provision. In other words, e-governments have opportunities to encourage more political participation in governance as well as more transparency in decision-making, but they rarely seize these opportunities. For example, Norris (2001) observes that government websites rarely publish information like citizens' reactions to policy proposals. E-government is more likely to be used to enhance the efficiency of information access than the democratization of governance (Barney, 2004).

The data regarding Digital Divide issues show three important generalizations which when added together indicate the likely digital disempowerment trend for many people in the world. First, NMN usage continues to accelerate the expansion of networks that link people to economic and political influence. Second, NMN usage is related to tangible benefits such as increasing one's social capital. Third, NMN usage gaps and poor positioning in network society networks are related to diminished opportunities in networked societies when compared to high usage and effective positioning.

When a new avenue of access becomes available that would facilitate citizens' ability to make informed decisions about policy, to communicate with representatives, and allow for more equal opportunities to influence decision-making, it would seem to follow that governments should take measures to enable access to this important platform of social and political communication, serving as a check to ensure equal access to the process. Muhlberger (2002) argues that if the Internet enables citizens to exert political influence and obtain political information, then its representativeness is at issue. "Those concerned with the development of a democratic public sphere need to be aware of the representativeness of Internet political activity," because "... an Internet that over-represents some political views advantages those views relative to others" (Muhlberger, 2002, p. 2). If we accept that the possibility of increased political influence exists via the Internet, then we must consider that the potential for power imbalances to be created (or exacerbated) also exists when some members of a society may exercise this influence, while others are excluded due to economic, educational, and other social factors. While Internet access costs go down as do transactions costs for new media, costs for networking power and skills can increase.

The research on the Digital Divide makes it clear that connectivity remains an unsolved problem for realizing digital democracy. Within the United States, there are pockets of Americans who are living more and more on the periphery of the network society. Hoping that digital democracy can repair the problems of offline democracy is a strong issue for intellectual debate. However, the

longer significant groups of people lack meaningful participation in their political system, the more likely that the system will not change for the better and that structural inequalities will stabilize. Hacker (2002a, 2002b, 2004) argues that the issues of Digital Divide gaps, whether national or global, will not be resolved without political will that is deliberately aimed at increasing citizen participation in digital democracy. Political will stems from political culture and the abilities and willingness of leaders and citizens to make practices match values.

A global economic infrastructure, as envisioned by Bill Gates and others, is not the same thing as the public spheres for democratic communication envisioned by scholars of political communication. Couldry (2003) argues that most developed national governments have focused more on global digital economies than on digital democracies. This focus holds more concern for expanding markets than concern for making sure that citizens are not socially excluded from important spaces of political deliberation. This focus also neglects the need for content that helps disadvantaged people find sources and spaces to improve their social and political positions by helping them with job training, job searches, and other information that is useful for them. As Menou (2002) maintains, the focus of many efforts by the private sector to close the Digital Divide is to make consumers out of the poor. "What should really be at stake is social change and not the marketing of ICT's" (Menou, 2002, para. 3).

Political interactivity can increase more with NMN than with mass media approaches to public spheres and political participation in government. As such, both e-government and e-democracy are better served. This is because NMN involves citizens as members of political communities rather than as isolated citizens and as active citizens who are capable of distributing their views easily and quickly. This is beneficial to e-government as officials and leaders can learn more about how citizens are reacting to policies and can also extend their transparency of policymaking and involvement with citizens in making decisions. (Drapeau & Wells, 2009).

DIRECTIONS AND CONCLUSION

Public spheres of deliberation are vital to democratic political systems. Electronic government technologies that add more citizen deliberation, political interactivity between leaders and citizens, and greater debate about various issues, are likely to help citizen motivation for getting involved with electronic government and digital democracy (Chen & Dimitrova, 2006). However, studies show that governments rarely use their network technologies to do these things (Barney, 2004). The combination of e-government and NMN allows citizens to self-organize themselves as political constituencies, drawing upon traditional mass media as needed, and interacting with government sites in order to move debate and decisions along in directions they feel are important.

High NMN exclusion does not mean that people have no voice in governance, but rather that they have less than they would if they were able to employ NMN as a key resource in creating or changing social structures related to political issues and causes. The provision of universal access, similarly, does not guarantee radical social restructuring. Menou (2002) argues that the focus of Digital Divide debate should not be how to bring the technology to the marginalized, but to discover the best ways for those who need the technology to put it to use and improve their network positions. It is important to keep in mind that online inequalities often mirror offline ones, and existing social problems will not be undone by technology. It is also necessary to understand the role of NMN in political structuration and how it may magnify or mitigate inequalities.

By employing communication theories such as structuration theory to e-government, it should

be possible to directly confront the factors of digital disempowerment that can be mitigated in order to build citizen empowerment through e-government. Some early factors that appear relevant to facilitating participation with NMN are a) greater interactivity between government workers and citizens on government websites, b) facilitation of citizen-citizen interaction about political policies in public spaces in (fora, etc.), c) encouragement of citizen motivation, skills, and creativity in using e-government, and d) developing policies that encourage access, training, and diversity in content. More theory and research are needed concerning all of these factors.

Policies vs. Promises

Communication policies generally attempt to balance interests of citizens with the freedom of the marketplace (Berquist, 2008). They are also aimed at encouraging industry competition to an extent, program diversity, and a general commitment to pubic goods and interests (Berquist, 2008). Advocates of what is known as network neutrality, such as Tim Berners-Lee who invented the World Wide Web, argue that Internet channels or "pipes" should be free from corporation discrimination of content or amount of content. In 2008, Comcast was accused of delaying Internet traffic on its channels for the file sharing service BitTorrent (Berquist, 2008). Comcast was said to be secretly blocking connections between file sharing computers (Wilkinson, 2008). After investigations, Comcast announced that it would respect network neutrality (Wilkinson, 2008).

To make government work for its citizens, it may be necessary to give local governments the ability to regulate and control online services for communities more than ever. While this may require turning a deaf ear to the communication industries that demand de-regulation, their track record of not caring enough for the public good belies their future intentions. This means that e-government should be treated as necessity and as both a means to automate government services and to involve citizens more in political deliberation and participation, thus increasing e-democracy. Public interests can be held up as the main concern for new media related to e-government so that more citizens can gain networking power. Not only can citizens learn how to use emerging media networking to build personal networks; they can also learn the vital skills of networking power.

The digital landscape is changing as fast as we can write about it. Governments might learn the lessons of new media that have been absorbed by some traditional journalism organizations such as newspapers. That lesson is that social media and new media networking should be integrated into what reporters use as sources and where they disseminate their reporting. By monitoring social media, for example, they can detect what concerns many people very quickly, what rumors are spreading, and what trends are emerging. A reporter for the *Austin American-Statesman* (Gleason, 2010) observes "During Hurricane Ike in the fall of 2008, we set up a special account just for the hurricane called @trackingike. That weekend we drove over 300,000 visitors to our site from Twitter alone" (pp.6-7).

There are specific necessary conditions for e-democracy that can be identified for e-government to facilitate political participation in democracy. For participation in networked public spheres, it is first necessary to be sure that access to the spheres is as open to as many people as possible, and that the people are taught how to use the access and input technologies of NMN that create the spheres. This means that public policies which bring in new system participants into the deliberation spaces is required (Polat, 2005). A second necessary condition is that the spheres are free from corporate and governmental dominance (Polat, 2005). Third, power law issues and inequality issues must be addressed to avoid structural inequalities from becoming embedded in newly forming networks and networked public spheres.

One way to do this is to recognize that the power law is a function of collective behavior in general and that fragmentation by selective exposure is common to both mass media and new media usage. At the same time, however, it can be recognized that even the small online communities can organize, mobilize and give citizens direct mechanisms for participating in political debate, deliberation, and collective action. Again, from a strucuturational view, there is the opportunity to expand lower-level interactions into higher-level interactions that result in new social structures while expanding political participation. Another necessary condition is giving people the ability to organize around the issues they themselves find most important. Information is not enough. As we knew in the 1900s with mass media, citizens want political efficacy, the knowledge that their communication produces meaningful effects.

REFERENCES

Barber, B. (1984). *Strong democracy: Participatory politics for a new age*. Berkely, CA: University of California Press.

Barney, D. (2004). *The network society*. Malden, MA: Polity Press.

Benkler, Y. (2006). *The wealth of networks: How social production transforms markets and freedom*. New Haven, CT: Yale University Press.

Berquist, L. (2008). Communication policy and technology. In Grant, A. E., & Meadows, J. H. (Eds.), *Communication technology update and fundamentals* (11th ed., pp. 66–76). Boston, MA: Focal Press, Elsevier.

Bimber, B., & Davis, R. (2005). *Campaigning online*. New York, NY: Oxford University Press.

Bordewijk, J. L., & van Kaam, B. (1986). Towards a new classification of teleinformation services. *Intermedia, 14*, 16–21.

Brown, D. (2008). Historical perspectives on communication technology. In Grant, A. E., & Meadows, J. H. (Eds.), *Communication technology update and fundamentals* (11th ed., pp. 10–40). Boston, MA: Focal Press, Elsevier.

Castells, M. (2000). Toward a sociology of the network society. *Contemporary Sociology, 29*, 693–699. doi:10.2307/2655234

Castells, M. (2001). *The Internet galaxy: Reflections on the Internet, business, and society.* New York, NY: Oxford University Press.

Castells, M. (2008). The new public sphere: Global civil society, communication networks, and global governance. *Annals of APSS, 616*, 93.

Castells, M. (2009). *Communication power.* New York, NY: Oxford University Press.

Chen, Y., & Dimitrova, D. (2006). Electronic government and online engagement: Citizen interaction with government via Web portals. *International Journal of Electronic Government Research, 2*(1), 54–76. doi:10.4018/jegr.2006010104

Comscore. (2009). *81 million Americans visited a government website in July.* Retrieved from http://comscore.com/Press_Events/Press_Releases/2009/9/81_Million_Americans_Visited_a_Government_Web_Site_in_July

Contractor, N., & Monge, P. (2003). *Theories of communication networks.* New York, NY: Oxford.

Couldry, N. (2003). Digital divide or discursive design: On the emerging ethics of information space. *Ethics and Information Technology, 5*, 89–97. doi:10.1023/A:1024916618904

Dallow, P. (2007). Mediatising the Web: The new modular extensible media. *Journal of Media Practice, 8*, 341–258. doi:10.1386/jmpr.8.3.341_1

Drapeau, M., & Wells, L. (2009). *Social software and national security: An initial net assessment.* Center for Technology and National Security Policy, National Defense University.

EP. (2009). *European social policy.* (pp. 249-336). Retrieved December 21, 2009, from http://find.galegroup.com/gtx/start.do?prodId=EAIM&userGroupName=nm_a_nmlascr

Fallows, D. (2007). *Chinese online population explosion: What it may mean for the Internet globally...and for US users.* Pew Internet & American Life Project. Retrieved November 11, 2007, from http://www.pewinternet.org/pdfs/China_Internet_July_2007.pdf

Giddens, A. (1984). *The constitution of society: Outline of the theory of structuration.* Los Angeles, CA: University of California Press.

Gleason, S. (2010). Harnessing social media. *American Journalism Review, 32*, 6–7.

Grant, A. (2008). The mobile revolution. In Grant, A. E., & Meadows, J. H. (Eds.), *Communication technology update and fundamentals* (11th ed., pp. 343–350). Boston, MA: Focal Press, Elsevier.

Grant, A., & Meadows, J. (2008). *Communication technology update and fundamentals* (11th ed.). Boston, MA: Focal Press, Elsevier.

Hacker, K. (2002a). Network democracy and the fourth world. *European Journal of Communication Research, 27*, 235–260.

Hacker, K. (2002b). *Network democracy, political will and the fourth world: Theoretical and empirical issues regarding computer-mediated communication (NMN) and democracy. Keynote address to EURICOM.* The Netherlands: Nigmegan.

Hacker, K. (2004). The potential of computer-mediated communication (NMN) for political structuration. *Javnost/The Public, 11*, 5-26.

Hacker, K., & Todino, M. (1996). Virtual democracy at the Clinton White House: An experiment in electronic democratization. *Javnost/The Public, 3,* 71-86.

Hindman, M. (2009). *The myth of digital democracy.* Princeton, NJ: Princeton University Press.

Holderness, M. (1998). Who are the world's information poor? In Loader, B. (Ed.), *Cyberspace divide* (pp. 35–56). London, UK: Routledge.

Horrigan, J. (2010). *Broadband adoption and use in America.* Washington, DC: Federal Communications Commission.

Keane, J. (2000). Structural transformations of the public sphere. In Hacker, K., & van Dijk, J. (Eds.), *Digital democracy: Issues of theory and practice* (pp. 70–89). London, UK: Sage.

Krueger, C. (2008, August). Campaigns connect on-line, in person. *St. Petersburg Times,* 3B.

Meadows, J. H. (2008). Conclusions. In Grant, A. E., & Meadows, J. H. (Eds.), *Communication technology update and fundamentals* (11th ed., pp. 351–354). Boston, MA: Focal Press, Elsevier.

Menou, M. J. (2002). *Digital and social equity? Opportunities and threats on the road to empowerment.* Paper prepared for The Digital Divide from an Ethical Viewpoint, International Center for Information Ethics Symposium, Ausberg, Germany.

Muhlberger, P. (2002). *Political values and attitudes in Internet political discussion: Political transformation or politics as usual?* Paper presented at the Euricom Colloquium: Electronic Networks & Democracy, Nijmegen, Netherlands.

Norris, P. (2001). *Digital divide: Civic engagement, information poverty, and the Internet worldwide.* Cambridge, UK; New York, NY: Cambridge University Press.

Ogden, M. R. (2008). Teleconferencing. In Grant, A. E., & Meadows, J. H. (Eds.), *Communication technology update and fundamentals* (11th ed., pp. 321–342). Boston, MA: Focal Press, Elsevier.

Pew Research Center. (2008). *The Internet's broader role in campaign 2008: Social networking and online videos take off.* Retrieved February 19, 2008, from http://people-press.org/report/384/internets-broader-role-in-campaign-2008

Polat, R. (2005). The Internet and political participation: Exploring the explanatory links. *European Journal of Communication, 20,* 435–459. doi:10.1177/0267323105058251

Pratchett, L., Wingfield, M., & Polat, R. K. (2006). Local democracy online: An analysis of local government websites in England and Wales. *International Journal of Electronic Government Research, 2*(3), 75–92. doi:10.4018/jegr.2006070104

Purcell, K., Mitchell, A., Rosentiel, T., & Olmstead, K. (2010). *Understanding the participatory news customer.* Pew Internet and American Life Project. Retrieved from http://pewinternet.org/Reports/2010/Online-News/Part-1.aspx?r=1

Shirky, C. (2008). *Here comes everybody: The power of organizing without organizations.* New York, NY: Penguin Books.

Smith, A. (2009). *Civic engagement online: Politics as usual.* Retrieved from http://pewresearch.org/pubs/1328/online-political-civic-engagement-activity

Smith, A., Schlozman, K., Verba, S., & Brady, H. (2009). *The internet and civic engagement.* Pew Internet and American Life Project.

Stalder, F. (2006). *Manuel Castells: The theory of the network society.* Malden, MA: Polity Press.

United Nations. (2004). *United Nations economic and social commission for Western Asia interim report. Foundations of ICT Indicators Database.* New York, NY: United Nations.

United Nations Development Programme. (2004). *Human development report 2004: Cultural liberty in today's diverse world*. New York, NY: United Nations Development Programme.

van Dijk, J. (1996). Models of democracy-behind the design and use of new media in politics. *Javnost/The Public, 3*, 43-56.

van Dijk, J. (2002). A framework for digital divide research. *The Electronic Journal of Communication, 12*(1-2). Retrieved July 31, 2005, from http://www.cios.org/getfile/vandijk_v12n102

van Dijk, J. (2004). *The deepening divide: Inequality in the information society*. London, UK: Sage.

van Dijk, J. (2006). *The network society* (2nd ed.). London, UK: Sage.

van Dijk, J. (In press). E-government and democracy. In van Dijk, J., & Hacker, K. (Eds.), *Digital democracy in a network society*. Hampton Press.

van Dijk, J., & Hacker, K. (2000). Summary. In Hacker, K., & van Dijk, J. (Eds.), *Digital democracy: Issues of theory and practice*. London, UK: Sage Publications.

Van Dijk, J., & Hindman, M. (In press). Network propeterties and demcoracy. In van Dijk, J., & Hacker, K. (Eds.), *Digital democracy in a network society*. Hampton Press.

van Duersen, A., & van Dijk, J. (2009). Using the Internet: Skill related problems in users' online behavior. *Interacting with Computers, 21*, 333–340.

Vromen, A. (2007). Australian young people's particpatory practices and Internet use. *Information Communication and Society, 10*, 48–68. doi:10.1080/13691180701193044

Weerakkody, V., & Dhillon, G. (2008). Moving from e-government to t-government: A study of process reengineering challenges in a U.K. local authority context. *International Journal of Electronic Government Research, 4*(4), 1–16. doi:10.4018/jegr.2008100101

Wellman, B., & Haythornwaite, C. (2002). The Internet in everyday life: An introduction. In Wellman, B., & Haythornwaite, C. (Eds.), *The Internet in everyday life* (pp. 3–41). Oxford, UK: Blackwell Publishing.

Wilkinson, J. S. (2008). IPTV: Streaming media. In Grant, A. E., & Meadows, J. H. (Eds.), *Communication technology update and fundamentals* (11th ed.). Boston, MA: Focal Press, Elsevier.

Yankelovich, D. (1991). *Coming to judgment: Making democracy work in a complex world*. Syracuse, NY: Syracuse University Press.

ENDNOTE

[1]   As cited in Shirkey (2008), p. 17.

Chapter 6
'Videoblogging' Human Rights on YouTube:
An Ethical Dilemma

Jacques DM Gimeno
Institute of Political Economy, University of Asia and the Pacific, Philippines

Bradley C. Freeman
Nanyang Technological University, Singapore

ABSTRACT

This chapter discusses what happens when, instead of co-existing, our online and offline worlds clash. In an age where the difference between virtual reality and real life becomes almost impossible to distinguish, a re-examination of core values and ethics becomes a necessity to ensure that human decency is not abandoned and that ethical standards become a core part of virtual public spheres. This chapter discusses a fundamental theme of modern human communication that involves a shift from traditional face-to-face interaction to one that is heavily mediated. Specifically, this chapter focuses on the role of different websites in providing a virtual public sphere, one exemplified by YouTube, where anonymity and immediacy greatly influence human communication in ways that may result in either fomenting greater divisions among societies and propagating a culture of carelessness and disregard for human rights, or one where human rights abuses are exposed, but victims' identities are concealed and carefully protected.

INTRODUCTION

An Internet journal (weblog) used to be limited to text and audio and mainly hosted for free on an individual webpage where the number of hits or visits from other users usually reflects its popularity. However when YouTube came into the picture, the world of blogging drastically changed. Before video streaming, a text-based blogger would have to write about controversial issues to merit regular following; but on YouTube, despite millions of videos being uploaded every day, many

DOI: 10.4018/978-1-60960-159-1.ch006

videobloggers can expect to get hundreds of hits in just a few minutes after posting.

One of the factors that has led to YouTube's popularity is its community-oriented format which allows users to videoblog on a single common platform accessible to everyone (individually-hosted blogs are viewed mostly by people within the blogger's circle). YouTube constitutes a virtual public sphere, one where the marketplace of ideas is so vast and disorderly that one can barely keep track of all the information being exchanged. Of the many concerns regarding online communication, this chapter will focus on ethics; specifically, the ethics of videoblogging involving human rights videos. For the purposes of this chapter, we define human rights videos as those that include actual footage of where a person or persons' human rights are seen or understood as being violated. In 2007, for example, an amateur video of a woman being stoned to death in Iraq was circulated on the Internet and posted on YouTube. As a consequence of the Internet's accessibility, speed, and immediacy, verification of information can be compromised when videobloggers compete for attention by posting these videos before they first verify their accuracy. Furthermore, videobloggers are posting without regard for the safety of the victims – as is evidently happening on YouTube in videos involving torture, mass killings, violations of children's rights, among others.

Since videoblogging is a form of online communication that facilitates active interaction among members, this chapter will discuss how such interaction on YouTube, in the context of human rights violations, becomes a threat when videobloggers fail to adhere to ethical guidelines protecting the victims from further harm. To support this thesis, this chapter will make a case of the downside of the use of the new medium with respect to human rights activism amid claims that the technology helps champion human rights around the world. This chapter will revolve around the ethics of videoblogging (this term will be used interchangeably with blogging in this chapter) by discussing issues pertinent to online communication namely freedom of expression, right to information, human rights victims' right to privacy and dignity, anonymity, and immediacy. In order to understand the movement behind activism on the Web, Habermas' concept of communicative action will be discussed as a starting point in this chapter. Moving forward from previous and current scholarship on media ethics, a case study comprised of an analysis of videos on YouTube and a worldwide survey of YouTube users conducted by the authors will likewise be presented. As a contribution to the ongoing debate on ethical blogging practices, the authors recommend a set of guidelines for proper blogging. The authors hope that this chapter will further the cause for scholars and media practitioners to seriously consider the establishment of a universal code of ethics for videoblogging in light of human rights as a universal concept.

BACKGROUND

The YouTube Phenomenon

Boasting more than one hundred million unique monthly visitors in the U.S. alone, YouTube is the fastest growing video website in terms of audience share (Nielsen Company, January 2011) and with more than 8 billion streams[1] in January 2011, it is at the top of the ten most successful online video websites in the U.S. (see Table 1).

Founded in 2005 by former Paypal employees, Chad Hurley, Steve Chen, and Jawed Karim, the website allows users to upload, view, and share videos of almost any sort – from simple everyday life such as one's pet performing tricks to complex political issues such as the conflict in Darfur and recent political uprisings in Arab countries.

Barely a year after it was launched, YouTube became the fastest growing website from January

Table 1. Top online video brands in the U.S. ranked according to streams and number of unique visitors for January 2011

Video Brand	Total Streams (000)	Unique Viewers (000)
YouTube	8,460,419	112,764
Hulu	813,169	11,924
VEVO	346,764	32,230
MSN/WindowsLive/Bing	246,675	17,285
Netflix	200,223	7,394
Yahoo!	186,606	25,511
Facebook	159,075	32,328
Nickelodeon Family & Parents	136,555	---
Megavideo	135,925	---
MTV Networks Music	135,535	---

Source: The Nielsen Company. Note: The last three brands did not make the Top 10 in terms of monthly unique visitors.

to June 2006, totaling 20 million unique visitors in the US alone a growth of 297% from roughly five million in January (Nielsen/Netratings, 2006). This growth did not go unnoticed when in October 2006, Google, Inc. announced that it would be purchasing YouTube for $1.65 billion in stock, making the video sharing site the second largest purchase by Google (Levy, 2008). YouTube's quick ascent to popularity can be attributed to several factors. Joining its community is relatively simple, even for novice computer users. People are free to watch the site's vast collection of videos in complete anonymity, but have to create an account to upload videos and join in the discussions. Creating an account, however, is free and does not require a person to give out too many personal details. Concerns about the privacy of identity are also addressed since YouTube does not require people to use their real names, which allows anyone to create multiple accounts, effectively maintaining almost total anonymity. Among the benefits of registering is the unlimited access to

features such as building playlists and "friends" lists, joining or starting discussions and groups, exchanging private messages, controlling privacy, and subscribing to other people's videoblogs.

As YouTube's popularity rose, so too did the number of videos posted, most of which it seems were not be subject to any "gatekeeping" functions such as are known in the traditional media. In November 2006, for example, the video of the brutal torture and rape of Egyptian Emad al-Kabir at the hands of two Egypt policemen was posted on the Internet around the same time as images of the abuse came out in a Cairo newspaper (Amnesty International, 2007). Since then it has been viewed more than 13,000 times on YouTube (before it was removed in 2007) and is still available on LiveLeak with over half a million views as of February 18, 2011. The incident caused widespread protests from human rights organizations and the subsequent interest from the mainstream media compelled the Egyptian government to investigate the alleged crime. Due perhaps to the popularity and reach of YouTube, what followed was a frenzy of uploading videos depicting violence towards victims of oppressive governments and groups such as the case of the beheading of Wall Street Journal's Daniel Pearl and the popular uprisings in Iran, Egypt, and Tunisia that lasted for many weeks.

A technological determinist would simply conclude that the video sharing application has actually helped in democratization by providing an avenue for exposing atrocities in their societies. However, previous scholarship on public discourse would point to the fact that dissatisfaction in the society motivates people to come together to fulfill a common need regardless of the presence or absence of a technology. In the next section, we present a theoretical underpinning for democratic public discourse in Habermas' communicative action.

Reaching Common Ground: Communicative Action

The apparent phenomenon of videoblogging on YouTube is not accidental because there could have been a communal void that needed to be filled. Jürgen Habermas's theory of communicative action can be used to explain the mobilization of activism on the Internet (Habermas, 1987). He explains that changing structures in the society, due to interactions between societal groups, make "value generalization" (p. 180) more complex. Value generalization is defined as the process in which societal norms undergo changes due to an ever-evolving society where similar beliefs come together to push for widespread reforms. New norms are formed when members and/or stakeholders come to an understanding that certain practices in the society no longer apply and therefore need modification. For instance, certain paternalistic cultures have made significant developments in promoting women's suffrage on the basis of, among other things, the realization of gender equality. However, since members in a society do not always have a fixed and shared understanding of things, staying within the bounds of certain norms differs from person to person due largely to individual motives, personal experiences, and personal agenda. Therefore, as individual motives are communicated to the rest of the society and find support among other members, established norms are challenged. This is what Habermas refers to as communicative action. When simply obeying laws or following social norms is no longer enough for individuals, they work towards being understood and accepted by the larger public. Furthermore, Bolton (2005) points out that communicative action is a process whereby social actors communicate to reach a common understanding of issues and "coordinate actions through reasoned argumentation, consensus, and cooperation rather than strategic action" (p. 1) to pursue individual goals. In order to understand how social actors operate, public discourse

theorists use a three-world concept that categorizes the means of the actions and what ends that they pursue. The three worlds are known as *objective, social,* and *subjective.* Cecez-Kekmanovic and Janson (1999) defined the objective world as being "the totality of what is the case" (p. 2) where true propositions are possible and people's opinions and beliefs are judged as either absolutely true or false according to what is really happening in the society. Habermas (1984) defines the social world as consisting of a "normative context that lays down which interactions belong to legitimate interpersonal relations" (p. 88). The social world operates according to "norms, rules, and values" (Cecez-Kekmanovic & Janson, 1999, p. 3) where actions are judged based on whether they conform to norms. Another aspect of the three-world concept accounts for a person's experiences which are seen as exclusive to him and are contained in the subjective world. Habermas (1984) believes that individual experiences differentiate people from each other, hence, they communicate with the aim of being understood. Moreover, communicative action seeks to establish a common ground among members of the society when certain perceptions fall outside the norms, keeping in mind that there are no definite parameters set. Moreover, Edgar (2006) differentiates communicative action from strategic action; the latter does not work towards establishing understanding but simply attempts to manipulate.

Communication, with specific attention to human rights activism (that is, actions whose aim is to expose abuses in the society), can therefore be understood in the context of communicative action. Also, it needs to be taken into account the different cultures that come into play since globalization and technology have made it easier for people around the world to participate in the discourse. Human rights activists attempt to direct their appeal to a wider audience so as to expose what they perceive as deviant practices and convince others in the community and outside that such practices ought to be strongly criticized, if not fully stopped. It is important to note here that for communicative action to realize its goals, political democracy has to be a major force in society; and the Internet, often hailed as a democratizing tool, has an important role as we examine online and offline settings wherein communication takes place. Schuldt (2004) explains that society is now characterized by online and offline aspects where activities that occur online are gradually crossing into the offline world. It is therefore equally important to discuss how freedom of expression and human rights activism are gradually moving from offline to online discourse.

THE ETHICS SIDE OF ICT

Freedom of Expression and Human Rights Activism on the Internet

From Socrates to the USA's PATRIOT Act, the history of freedom of expression can be seen as a history of contentious interpretations manifested in events that either advocated for (e.g., The Declaration of the Rights of Man of the French Revolution, the First Amendment of the US Bill of Rights, and the Universal Declaration of Human Rights, among others) or against (e.g., Galileo Galilei before the Inquisition, the banning of D.H. Lawrence's *Lady Chatterley's Lover*, and the slaying of Dutch filmmaker Theo van Gogh) this form of freedom (Smith & Torres, 2006). The debate about freedom of expression has taken on many different angles and aspects, among others: as a human right (Alexander, 2005); as a privilege (Meiklejohn, 1965, cited in Scanlon, 1972) and; as a culture (Prott, 1986). The Internet has added to this debate a new dimension; according to Balkin (2004), it is important that we make adjustments in our theories of freedom of expression to accommodate the new medium because it changes the way societies communicate.

A 1998 joint report, *Regardless of Frontiers*, by the Center for Democracy & Technology (CDT) and the Global Internet Liberty Campaign (GILC) highlighted Article 19 of the Universal Declaration of Human Rights and asserted that "…for the first time since the 1948 proclamation of the international human right to freedom of expression, the citizens of the world have the ability to exercise that right on a truly global basis 'regardless of frontiers'" (Dempsey & Weitzner, 1998, p. 1). The report's purpose was to establish the groundwork for Internet activists to demand that international protection for the freedom of expression be applied to the Internet because of its unique qualities. In 2001, The Freedom House came up with a survey it said was "the first assessment of the degree of freedom on the Internet" that involved 131 countries categorized under "most restrictive", "moderately restrictive", or "least restrictive" (Sussman, 2001). Only 10% of the countries were judged most restrictive compared to the 33% judged to be highly restrictive in a larger traditional survey for print and broadcast media involving 181 countries.

One activity on the Internet that is capitalizing on freedom of expression is *cyberactivism*. McCaughey and Ayers (2004) believe cyberactivism "crosses disciplines, mixes theories with practical activist strategies, from online awareness campaigns to Internet-transmitted laser-projected messaging" (p. 2). Similarly, Vegh (2003) highlighted online political activism in his examination of what he called "cyberprotests" against the World Bank following the 9/11 attacks. He presented a very simple scenario of online activism as traditional activists taking advantage of the new technology to reach traditional goals. An example of traditional human rights activists turning to the Internet, according to Caldwell (2006), is the international human rights organization Witness (www.witness.org), which uses "video advocacy" to take freedom of expression on a global stage. In their latest annual report (2005), the organization stressed that their videos and other initiatives reached millions of viewers worldwide with an audience of 21.3 million in Croatia, Germany, Sierra Leone, and the

US. Their website lists cases where their videos had been used, for instance, in the investigation of Slobodan Milosevic's crimes against humanity. Despite the Internet's vast potential there are also multiple causes for concern. An extensive study by Weimann, et al. (2006) identified terrorism as a form of freedom of expression that is a cause for worry. From 1998 to 2005, Weimann et al. studied 4,300 sites for terrorists and their supporters, which led him to conclude, "The great virtues of the Internet have been converted to the advantage of groups committed to terrorizing societies in order to achieve their goals" (p. 29).

Human Rights Victims' Right to Privacy and Dignity

Probably one of the most contentious issues surrounding the Internet is user privacy. If users invoke freedom of expression on almost every occasion, to what extent can they push this right and not intrude on others' right to privacy? In their book, *Media Ethics,* Christians et al. (1997) stated that although American laws protecting privacy depend on individual jurisdictions and states, the general idea is to protect "against deep intrusions on human dignity by those in possession of economic or governmental power" (p. 19). In the case of video sharing on the Internet, Marcus and Perez (2007) stressed that websites like YouTube make it possible for users to post videos expressing almost anything to their personal or professional networks; and according to Abril (2007), this is creating more serious concerns regarding personal privacy because of the digital nature of the new technology, which makes information permanent, searchable, replicable and transformable—hence making its effects even more damaging. The problem starts when the information has the potential to harm a person, for instance, images (moving and still) of human rights violations. Elliot (2004) stated when these are used unethically, they can harm someone directly or indirectly.

In the book *Video for Change: A Guide for Advocacy and Activism* produced by Witness, Cizek (2005) presented cases where victims were further harmed because the filmmakers failed to protect the former's identities. For example, Tibetans living under the Chinese government in the province have experienced extreme difficulties following irresponsible practices by many journalists covering the conflict during the 1980s and 1990s. Films documenting torture and abuses in the territory revealed enough identifiable features of those who were interviewed by the journalists or filmmakers, which made it easy for the Chinese government to identify Tibetans who were involved in the making of the films – either those who provided information or simply provided accommodations to the filmmakers. Reports on retribution from the Chinese government surfaced thereafter. The report of the International Commission of Jurists (ICJ) echoed the same concerns in its 2005 report, *Iraq: The Trial of Saddam Hussein and The Rights of the Victims*. One of the Commission's major concerns was the safety of the victims and their families especially when they were called to testify against Hussein and his cohorts. It alleged that, "International standards place a heavy responsibility on governments to ensure the effective safety of victims and witnesses *before*, *during*, and *after* the trial" (ICJ, 2005, p. 9). The report further emphasized that the Iraq government should take steps to make sure that victims and witnesses are protected against intimidation and retaliation.

Given the cases mentioned, more scholarly studies are needed to examine similar practices on the Internet involving video sharing platforms where problematic treatment of images occurs. To fully appreciate the urgency to address this problem, we refer below to how mainstream journalism deals with issues similar to one we have raised above.

Image Ethics in Mainstream Media

Arguably, the coverage of violence and tragedy by the mass media has taken on more prominence in recent years and it has been quite evident that the presentation of images illustrating these events has come under close scrutiny by the public and members of the media themselves (International Council on Human Rights Policy, 2002; Keith, Schwalbe, & Silcock, 2006; Simpson & Cotè, 2006). Concerns are mounting over the ethical or unethical treatment of persons in these images; concerns that pose a challenge to the mainstream journalist (Keith et al., 2006) whose intention and professional credibility are being questioned with regard to whether the practitioners simply exploit subjects of news stories to give a sense of "compelling edge" to their presentation (Simpson & Cotè, 2006, p. 2). Moreover, since most of the public harbors suspicions of the motives behind those publicizing victims' pain and the media's practices in framing such suffering (Seaton, 2005), and the notion that journalists substantiate their reports from what sources give them (Gans, 2004), journalists thus take the brunt of the public's disdain for the resulting discomfort from "exposure to tragedy" (Simpson & Cotè, 2006, p. 2). In other words, according to Lester (1995), journalists (more specifically, photojournalists) are severely criticized on their use of disturbing images. This is perhaps why, in Griffin's (1995) study of ethical considerations surrounding the use of news images in Australia, he found that most Australian press photographers go about leaving ethical decisions of publishing pictures to their editors; although he was quick to add that these photographers were prepared and interested in addressing ethical issues when challenged.

Such a challenge had been directed at journalists in several other high-profile cases involving contentious coverage by the mainstream media, most notably those involving the images from the US-led war against Iraq (Keith et al., 2006; Taylor, 2005) from the troubling image of the corpses of

Saddam Hussein's sons (Romano, 2003, cited in Keith et al., 2006) to the humiliation of the prisoners at the Abu Ghraib prison (Hersh, 2004, cited in Keith et al., 2006; Taylor, 2005). In the same light, the depiction of tragic images from September 11, 2001 testifies to the difficulty for journalists as they attempt to deal with the clash of national security and the people's right to know (Fahmy, 2005). Outside the US, the image of assassinated Dutch politician Pym Fortuyn caused a great stir among readers in Australia when a major newspaper, *The Australian,* ran the story with a full photograph of his dead body on the front page (Harrison, 2004). The backlash the paper got was strong enough for its editor to go public with an explanation and apology (ibid.). Similarly in 2004, images from the train bombing in Madrid and the massacre at a Beslan school in Russia proved to be tough editorial decisions for the media (Keith et al., 2006). The images of the London Underground bombings in 2005 were no different as questions on the ethics of publishing images of tragedy were again directed at the mass media (ibid.). The list of perceived questionable practices by the major news media with regard to violent news images goes on, and this raises the question of whether ethical guidelines are in place for professionals in this industry.

The Society of Professional Journalists (SPJ), an organization in the US that boasts of almost 10,000 members across the country, states on its website their core dedication of "stimulating high standards of ethical behavior." Furthermore, the SPJ specifies in their code of ethics the journalist's responsibility to minimize harm by being "sensitive when seeking or using interviews or photographs of those affected by tragedy or grief" (Society of Professional Journalists, www.spj.org/ethicscode.asp). This and other codes of ethics observed by professional journalists provide straightforward guidelines as to how journalists should conduct their business when it comes to covering violence and tragedy. However, Keith et al. (2006), in their analysis of 47 journalism codes of ethics, stated that although those who have provisions covering news of this nature largely agree on what constitutes a problematic image and are open to improving practices, only nine specifically address image ethics in reporting during wartime. Similarly, studies have examined the context of journalism codes of ethics from the history and theory of how good journalism is defined (Wilkins & Brennen, 2004), comparing codes of ethics across cultures (Hafez, 2002), determining how the public views ethical journalism (Lester, 2006; Ward, 2005), applying journalistic protocol in education (Roberts & Webber, 1999) and to studying the possibility of coming up with a standard and universal code of ethics (Herrscher, 2002; Perkins, 2002; Ward, 2005). Among the issues most tackled regarding image ethics in journalism are privacy and moral rights of subjects (Gross, Katz, & Ruby, 1988; Hodges, 2002; Lester, 1995; Tulloch, 2006), manipulating images (Gross, Katz, & Ruby, 2003; Lester, 1995; Pavlik, 2005; Roberts & Webber, 1999; Taylor, 2005), and the effects of graphic images on the audience (Fahmy & Wanta, 2007; Kitch, 2006; Ward, 2005).

Gross, et al. (1998) quoted in their book, *Image ethics: the moral rights of subjects in photographs, film, and television,* a statement made by the editorialist of *The Independent* one hundred years ago: "As regards photography in public it may be laid as a fundamental principle that one has a right to photograph anything that he has a right to look at (*The Independent*, 1907)" (p. v). According to Gross et al, the statement served little to address issues of ethics and morality with regard to how the camera is used. Ultimately, the question of privacy involves concepts of personal boundaries and which part of the self should be exposed and which should be kept private. In explaining how people set boundaries in their social lives, Henderson (1998) cited Goffman's (1971) "territories of the self" that include personal space, use space, turns, sheath of skin and clothing, possessional

territory, information preserve, and conversation preserve. Of these territories, Henderson's concern lies on the informative preserve – "the set of facts about himself to which an individual expects to control or access while in the presence of others" (p. 93), and this explains the awareness among photographers of the threat they pose to privacy when they are in public (ibid.). The effect of this threat is further explained by Viera (1988) in the context of the resulting social problems encountered by an individual in trying to safeguard their privacy. Sadly, in the case of graphic images in news, Lester (2006) conceded that violence and tragedy were "staples of American journalism" (p. 254). The threat further extends to the potential harm to the subjects of news as mentioned earlier regarding the cases cited by Cizek. More recently, Hodges (2002) presented the case of the publishing of the images of Daniel Pearl's beheading in Pakistan to several journalists and journalism scholars for commentary. The commentaries touched on the ethical aspects of producing such images that ranged from the presentation of the truth to the violation of moral sensitivities. Despite numerous scholarly inquiries into journalism ethics, Keith et al. (2006, p. 245) stressed that there have not been enough studies on existing codes of ethics and how they address what journalists should actually do in situations they call special issues – "truth telling in wartime" and presenting disturbing images. Another issue that should be considered when discussing the right to privacy is the right to information, which evokes equally strong sentiments. We discuss the tension between these two rights in the next section.

Right to Privacy vs. Right to Information

An individual's right to privacy remains a difficult concept to fully explicate. These rights exist on a wide continuum; different societies have different approaches when it comes to the notion of privacy rights, Whitman (2004) argued that questions on privacy cannot be addressed "by assuming that all human beings share the same raw intuitions about privacy (p. 1160)". An additional complication arises when these rights come into conflict with the oft-cited "public right to know" or "free flow of information" -- it is seldom possible to find a hard-and-fast rule that balances these competing rights in every circumstance across the globe. On this matter, Levinson (1990) wrote: "Almost every assertion of a privacy right to limit access to information can be met with a plausible "right to know" claim based on the public benefits attached to wide access to the information in question." To be sure there are many people in activist communities who would agree with this and would further argue that any available tool for use must be wielded to expose wrong-doing or corruption. As a result, in certain instances, these activists assert the ability to mobilize opinions and sway attitudes will be found to outweigh ethical considerations of a victim's rights regardless of any form of request for confidentiality from any source.

Any discussion of the right to privacy, when weighed against the right to know, would not be adequate without reference to the famous 1890 article by Samuel D. Warren and Louis D. Brandeis. More than a century later, their article remains one of the most cited works on the right to privacy (Whitman, 2004), and is considered to have reached "legendary status" (Bratman, 2002) in the debate concerning the aforementioned rights. Warren and Brandeis argued for privacy to be accepted in American jurisprudence as a right that evolved in common law (Gormley, 1992) and should therefore one to be afforded due protection because at the time as they lamented:

The intensity and complexity of life, attendant upon advancing civilization, have rendered necessary some retreat from the world, and man, under the refining influence of culture, has become more sensitive to publicity, so that solitude and privacy have become more essential to the individual; but modern enterprise and invention have, through invasions upon his privacy, subjected him to mental pain and distress, far greater than could be inflicted by mere bodily injury (Warren & Brandeis, 1890, pp. 2-3).

However, Warren and Brandeis' concept of the right to privacy received as much criticism as praise especially from American scholars who believe that the type of privacy they espoused was closer to the European model and would be unlikely to be transplanted intact into American society. Whitman (2004) argued that Warren and Brandeis had failed to sell their idea, on grounds that freedom of expression and freedom of the press have always been more important in American laws and are the biggest obstacles to European-style privacy. Elsewhere outside the US, the take on privacy has a somewhat more specific stance. In particular, privacy is seen as a fundamental right and promoted in the Charter of Fundamental Rights of the European Union and upheld by the highest court in Canada (Lasprogata, King, & Pillay, 2004), among others. Hence, it is often a very challenging balancing act between the right to information and the right to privacy, especially when examined in light of what is ethical and what is not.

Changing society, as stated by Warren and Brandeis, has an even greater impact in the information age where technological innovation occurs at an unprecedented speed. How has information dissemination evolved amid the changing roles of actors – where recipients of news compete with traditional providers – and a wider, more competitive space? In the next section, we discuss how the effects of immediacy and anonymity make things even more complicated in cyberspace.

THE DOWNSIDE OF A VIRTUAL PUBLIC SPHERE

Anonymity: Online vs. Offline Communication

The evolution of communication can be observed in light of the development of technology, which saw the changing dynamics of how people interacted with one another. Before the Internet, communication was a linear process of one person to another person with face-to-face as the "most familiar and obvious" mode (Adler & Rodman, 2006, p. 12). Electronic media changed not only our concept of space and time but also the social dynamics of our interpersonal communication. For instance, people feel less restrained communicating online because social inhibitions can be masked or completely abandoned through the luxury of an anonymous identity. Think of it this way: two complete strangers who strike up a conversation in Starbucks would more likely exchange names a few minutes into their conversation, but would be restrained in exchanging personal or intimate details about themselves. Compare this situation to one in which two strangers on Yahoo! Personals begin exchanging intimate details through e-mail messages or instant messages long before they make each other aware of their real life identities. The absence of inhibitions in the online setting is due largely to a person not being "physically there" with the person on the other end of the conversation. In other words, because physical attributes are not exposed to scrutiny, people become less self-aware and, therefore, less inclined to feel responsible to provide their real identity as compared to face-to-face conversation where people expect a name to go with a face. Simply put, people's online practices are often different from their offline behaviors.

Non-disclosure of identity online is very much valued by Internet users because this feature gives them a reassuring feeling that they are able to break from social constraints (Wood &

Smith, 2005), which consequently gives rise to instances where "identity verification becomes problematic" (Veraar, 2006, p. 54). This practice is more often observed in online communities such as social networking sites. It seems that participating anonymously in discussions within a large group of people makes non-disclosure of identity more prevalent especially when one is allowed to use multiple identities or usernames. For instance, a member can create several user accounts on YouTube so long as each account is registered with a valid e-mail address and, for most websites, e-mail account validation (though not identity validation) is done through e-mail. On the other hand, membership with a country club or a gym entails a more rigorous process of identity verification. Reiter and Rubin (1998) calls this mechanism or process *crowds* wherein anonymity becomes very well entrenched in a group of either random or select individuals who come together to build an online community and, in the process, remain anonymous: "hiding one's actions within the actions of many others" (p. 67). Social scientists call this *deindividuation,* which is not exclusive to online settings. In other words, instances wherein, acting within a group, individuals lost their self-identity and committed acts they wouldn't normally do when acting alone. According to Myers (1999), experiments conducted on *social facilitation*[2] and *social loafing*[3] show how groups mobilized individuals into behaving beyond what is deemed acceptable. This is not to say that social behaviors brought about by groups result only in destructive outcomes. History, for example, shows that popular movements around the world have toppled authoritarian regimes, pushed for policy changes, and successfully carried out a cause with little or no violence. Physical presence is an important factor for spontaneous activities in the offline setting while group behavior online is manifested differently. Thus, instead of deindividuation, online groups tend to *depersonalize* because of constructed social identity, which is more fluid online due to anonymity that tends to minimize personal accountability. This begs the question of whether online group communication can actually promote more aggressive participation amid the atmosphere of decreased responsibility. This is the premise of the 2008 movie thriller *Untraceable* about a serial killer who perpetrates murders on his untraceable website *killwithme. com*. The methods he employs are horrendous and the victims are killed via contraptions that are set off as more and more people log onto the website to watch the murders as they occur. The spectacle of seeing someone die right before their eyes was the leverage used by the killer, passing off some degree of responsibility to the audience who provided encouragement to the killer through their participation in his website. The movie asks: "can the online audience be held responsible for the deaths of others offline?"

For some human rights activists among a segment of the YouTube population, videos of rights abuses are posted to encourage people to help to campaign against similar abuses. Alterman (2006) explains that participation in social networking sites allows people to "touch and feel" (p. 39) a cause or issue. However, social psychologists contend that when operating under the veil of anonymity, people tend to be less helpful for the simple reason that they cannot be held accountable. Anonymity can also work against activists themselves because their credibility and the veracity of their claims are questioned when they do not properly identify themselves. But how rigorously do people actually question and verify claims made online? Given the Internet's capacity to store information and the speed with which news can be carried, verification requirements become cumbersome and may even lead to *desensitization*. Desensitization occurs when there is "repeated exposure to emotionally-arousing media" (Bushman & Wessman, 2006, p. 349), which may result in a passive response from the audience. Therefore, along with anonymity, desensitization may account for people's seemingly detached attitude towards violence. Consequently,

this detachment (or insensitivity) does not result in the expected response for the victims who are the subjects of human rights videos; for while activists recognize the medium's capability for immediacy, most are seemingly unaware of the possibility of desensitization that exists, not to mention the consequences to the victims of greater vulnerability and further harm as a result of their increased exposure.

When Immediacy Hurts

When we think of immediacy in the case of videos on YouTube and videobloggers functioning as information providers, we tend to think of the speed in the delivery of the information. Basically, immediacy in this context includes not just the notion of the speed of information being disseminated to the public but also the speed in searching information on the Internet. In a study by Omar (2007) on the perception of immediacy between online and print newspapers, they found that those who valued immediacy in online media scored higher in surveillance gratification seeking and current issues knowledge. With the notion of immediacy associated with the expeditious delivery and receipt of the news, traditional gatekeepers are left out of the process. This scenario, moreover, may very well be championed by those who advocate for freedom of expression and right to information; but we beg to differ, if only in the case of human rights videos on YouTube; and because, given the apparent speed that the new technology offers, immediacy can inadvertently contribute to harming the subject of the message.

Immediacy is the "right here, right now" attitude often seen among many journalists (Deuze, 2004, p. 283) in the age of 24-hour cable TV and online news. Since videobloggers increasingly take on the functions of journalists in an online community where news dominates the agenda, there is a tendency for these videobloggers to constantly share up-to-date information to sustain active discussions. However, since most videobloggers prefer to be anonymous, they cannot easily be held responsible for misinformation. Although members of some online communities take verification of information seriously and actually take time to gauge whether the presentation of news adheres to ethical journalism, these ideals can get lost in the deluge of information that can easily overwhelm the audience. Furthermore, because information technology has made it possible to provide people with "byte-size" news on-the-go and therefore less time is spent scrutinizing the veracity of information, news is often taken at face value as long as salient details are present. Deuze (2004), for example, explains that the newsroom culture is one of fast-paced operations and tight deadlines that does not give space for diversity; thus, preventing a holistic approach that should ideally include diverse opinions from different members of the society. Experts further emphasized that in the profession, journalists do not typically invest enough time getting deeply acquainted with a community and therefore miss out on the salient features of a culture (ibid.). Despite these and other shortcomings, professional journalists must still be held to the highest standards of credibility in news-gathering and that calls for an effective verification of facts. This is why many journalists reserve judgment regarding the Internet and are still resistant to the idea that bloggers ought to be placed with them in the same category. This is not to say that bloggers do not verify information they share; the issue is the lack of ethical standards they apply in the course of gathering, verifying, and presenting news. Moreover, the anonymity in which many of them operate casts doubt on their credibility because of the lack of accountability.

Nowhere is this lack of ethical standards more apparent than when videobloggers share human rights videos, which are clearly not lifted from mainstream media, jumpstarting a flurry of comments ranging from condemning the acts to questioning the authenticity of the material. Even more importantly, bloggers are not required to adhere to any code of ethics, specifically in the treatment of images of victims.

A UNIVERSAL CODE OF ETHICS FOR VIDEOBLOGGING

If we were to consider the previous scholarship presented above on media ethics and on the rights of expression, information, privacy, and dignity, the argument for establishing a universal code of ethics becomes more powerful. More importantly, since bloggers take upon themselves the task of journalists, that is, "the role of news source, analyst, and interpreter" and function as their own editors and commentators in reshaping news items from other sources (Beers, 2006, p. 118), it becomes reasonable that they should adhere to the same ethical guidelines set for professional journalists. Kuhn (2007) identified two important attempts at establishing a code of ethics for bloggers who function as journalists: one by Rebecca Blood, an author and a blogger, and another by Jonathan Dube, the founder of Cyberjournalist.net. According to Kuhn, both attempts effectively addressed how bloggers could increase their credibility by following certain codes of ethics similar to those followed by professional journalists. However, these same attempts limited the usefulness and relevance of ethics to only a group of bloggers who function as journalists and "overlooked the interactive and human aspects of the blogging form" (p. 20). Hence, Kuhn asserts that "a code of blogging ethics should be both normatively based; drawing upon the interactive nature of blogs, and dialogically derived" (p. 21). To this effect, Kuhn came up with his own blogging ethics scrutinized in a blogging conference organized by Harvard University but which remains in need of more debate and fine-tuning.

An analysis of the present situation of blogs in the legal realm was recently presented by Kulesza (2009) as a recap of current efforts to provide legal standards applicable to blogging in Europe.

Apparently, some measures have been taken to effectively define bloggers apart from the press, while some have also tried to treat bloggers as no different from the press. This article by Kulesza touched on an issue that remains at the heart of the debate: Which blogs should be treated legally as press (or which bloggers should be treated like mainstream journalists) and which should not? The author opined that because the definition of a weblog is so broad as to actually encompass all activities undertaken by bloggers, the task of coming up with similar all-encompassing rules would be so difficult as to seem almost impossible. The solution, therefore, is to clearly define blogs that compete with or function similarly to the mainstream press, which would make the determination of appropriate and applicable rules easier for a government to assign in cases when such bloggers violate terms of use. Furthermore, these bloggers would be required to disclose the nature of their blogs and register them for proper identification. To achieve this, Kulesza stated that the definition of press would have to be expanded to include blogging activities similar to the press that were not included in its current definition. Other blogs falling outside the new definition would be treated as personal whose primary function is social interaction. Although many more debates will come out of such a proposal, it is important to note that such efforts are directing attention to some serious problems in the blogosphere.

The discussion on blogging ethics would not be complete without also including input from the bloggers themselves. Like scholars and media experts, bloggers are divided in the issue of a code of ethics, especially when many are hailing blogs as the new providers of fast and in-depth information and when the mainstream media find it increasingly challenging to sustain loyal following and support from their audience. To contribute to the growing literature on and attention to ethical practices in the blogosphere, we conducted a survey of YouTube users (Gimeno & Freeman, 2009) to examine a fraction of the blogging community's side of the issue.

THE CASE OF HUMAN RIGHTS VIDEOS ON YOUTUBE

The exploratory case study was conducted, through a content analysis of videos on YouTube (Gimeno, 2008) and a worldwide survey of YouTube users. We looked into how the Internet is facilitating information exchange among videobloggers. More specifically, we focused on human rights videoblogging on YouTube that is a major part of community discussions on the Web site. YouTube is very effective and attractive both as a platform and a medium in the discussion of human rights issues primarily because it accommodates as much participation as possible from millions of users. Moreover, where early forms of blogging fail to generate as much interest, videoblogging on YouTube revolutionized communication by making discussions much more vibrant as it provides both visual and auditory content. Through videoblogging, YouTube members can discuss issues accompanied by both moving and still pictures. In some instances, members respond to each other through video clips thereby eliminating the language barrier, which results in increased participation that crosses cultures. In our study, we attempted to find out whether YouTube has adequate guidelines for proper video sharing through a content analysis of selected human rights videos. We conducted a survey of 379 YouTube users thereafter to solicit their opinions regarding unethical videblogging on YouTube.

Analysis of the Videos

At the time of the study from February 10 to October 14, 2007, there were 22,959 videos on YouTube that corresponded to a set of keywords: armed conflict, children's rights, child soldiers, execution, genocide, honor crimes/honor kill-

Table 2. Videos analyzed

Name & Length of Video	Description
Sodomy Video[†] 00:00:38	The torture and rape of Emad al-Kabir in Egypt in the hands of policemen.
Pakistan Torture 00:00:31	Police brutality in Pakistan.
Egypt Torture* 00:00:11	Policemen laugh and strike a man repeatedly.
Egypt Police* 00:00:52	A policeman lands a blow on a man's head.
Female Torture 00:00:32	This video of the torture of a suspected female murderer in Egypt shows the woman's ankles and wrists bound to chairs that keep her suspended in mid-air.
Child Soldier 00:01:24	The victim, a former child soldier who escaped from his captors, talks straight to the camera with his face at a very close range. The child talks about his experiences being captured by rebels in Sri Lanka and escaping from them.
War Child 00:03:44	From the description that came with the video, the child talks to an interviewer about his experience as a child soldier. The conversation is not in English and there are no subtitles; analysis of this clip was based on the short description on YouTube and the good quality of the video.
Saddam Hussein Execution 00:02:36	The video shows Hussein during his last moments leading up to his execution.
Juvenile Beatings 00:03:07	A policeman can be seen beating up a juvenile prisoner in Saudi.
Young Girl 00:00:42	Shows a 3-year-old girl in what looks like a public service announcement (PSA) against child abuse. There is neither a description nor an explanation of whether the child is just an actor or a real rape victim.
Mass Killings* 00:06:43	Several dead bodies can be seen in the video, including those of children who had been hacked to death by machetes; severed heads in about two scenes; and badly mutilated bodies.

[†]Sodomy Video had been taken out of the Web site but is still available on LiveLeak.com.

* Taken out of the Web site as of February 20, 2011.

ings, mass killings, police misconduct, prisons, rape and sexual abuse, slavery, and torture/ill-treatment. These keywords were adapted from a list of human rights categories from Witness.com, a YouTube-like Web site that caters specifically to online human rights activism. Since it would have been impossible to analyze almost 30,000 videos, we narrowed the number down to 11 videos (see Table 2) that met the following criteria: 1) the video must be raw footage (not production footage), 2) the video must not have been lifted from mainstream media, 3) the videos are not "just for fun videos" created by users (i.e. pretend torture, re-enactment, etc.), and 4) the video must have been viewed more than 1,000 times.

We employed qualitative content analysis on the selected videos. The coding was conducted by two independent coders who were graduate students at the time of this study (see Appendix A for the complete coding system) and were trained prior to coding. Inter-coder reliability was established through member-checking between the coders. The videos were analyzed using three factors: *appropriateness* (whether the video is appropriate or not for public viewing), *violence* (degree of violence shown in the video), and *identity* (how recognizable and clear were the victims' faces). These factors were adapted and modified from the rating guidelines of the Motion Pictures Association of America (MPAA), the guidelines from Witness' Human Rights Video Hub Pilot, and cases presented in the book *Video for Change: A Guide for Advocacy and Activism*.

We found that all the videos in question violated YouTube's user guidelines. Most of them, however, were not reported as inappropriate material and therefore remained available on the web site for several months, even years. Upon closer look, the web site's user guidelines clearly state that material containing pornography, sexually explicit acts, danger, and violence are strictly prohibited. Given that these guidelines are present, we find it very disturbing that videos with these descriptions are still proliferating. Despite the fact that YouTube has a tool called "flag" that enables users to report inappropriate videos, many of these videos still find their way onto the Web site where some are even re-posted several times by different users. For instance, there were almost 500 separate uploads of the video of Saddam Hussein's execution. YouTube thus leaves the policing of videos largely to the members of the community; the web site's management will only act upon receipt of reports chiefly because screening millions of videos is just not feasible. Therefore, despite the presence of guidelines, the lack of effective implementation and enforcement results in users violating them with seeming impunity.

Seven of the videos are still available on the Web site as of February 20, 2011; and from the discussions that typically follow a video on YouTube, we can observe how users capitalize on the anonymity afforded to them by the web site. Without the pressure of having to disclose their identity, members of the YouTube community can express their beliefs freely; whether the rest of the community agrees or not. Consider the following case involving activism in Egypt. Mainstream media reported that while the government blocked the Internet and arrested several pro-democracy demonstrators in February 2011, the anti-government opposition continues on YouTube, Facebook, and Twitter via a few bloggers who were able to go online documenting events as they happen. Thus online communication and offline communication differ when an event galvanizes people for a cause.

Since the offline setting provides greater physical proximity and transparency among members of the group, there is also greater immediacy in action. However, since we are living in the Information Age and technologically competent individuals are everywhere increasing in number, online presence therefore makes up for geographical boundaries and immediacy in information dissemination becomes an advantage over the offline setting.

YouTube Human Rights Activists Have Their Say

In addition to the content analysis of human rights videos, we conducted an online survey involving 379 YouTube videobloggers (since they use videos to blog) from March 19 to June 15, 2008 through a web-based survey company; prospective respondents were directed to a link for the survey. Out of the eleven videos we analyzed, three were presented to solicit reaction from the respondents of the survey. The videos were unedited versions of actual violations exposing the violent acts and the identity of the victims and including such violent acts as torture, rape, exposure of at-risk minors (child soldiers), execution, and police brutality.

The main points raised by the respondents in support of using human rights videos include the ability of blogs to provide information, promote awareness, and aid in bringing about justice to the victims. However, the same respondents also acknowledged that two of the videos were recklessly displayed without regard for the victims' safety and dignity. For instance, when the video of an escaped child soldier was presented, 70% the respondents stated that it could compromise the child's safety because it was possible that the child would be identified and harmed by his former captors; some of the respondents added that the blogger should have taken measures to protect the victim's identity by reducing the pixels in the boy's image until it was unrecognizable. This goes to show that some bloggers are themselves torn between the potential of videoblogs to raise awareness about atrocities in societies that might otherwise have gone unnoticed and the ethical use of images of victims. We argue that exposing the identity of a victim does not make the severity of a violation greater. Although some would counter that violent images make for more compelling storytelling; nevertheless, it does not take away the fact that the risk and danger for the victims remain real and that the victims would benefit more from the exposure of the violation along with the protection of their identities. Certainly professional journalists (albeit not all) often take extra precautions to protect victims from further harm without sacrificing accurate storytelling to tell a compelling news story.

On the issue of whether there should be a universal code of ethics for the blogosphere, 65% of the respondents support the idea but not without reservations. The major hindrance they see is the diversity of world cultures that would make a universal set of ethical guidelines difficult to come up with. Another is the question of whose responsibility it would be to implement and enforce such a code on the World Wide Web, which knows no borders and recognizes no national laws. We argue that, given the existence of the Universal Declaration of Human Rights (which posits that certain human rights cut across cultures), a code of ethics for blogging human rights violations could serve similarly as a model for more responsible treatment of sensitive materials. Furthermore, if such a code were formulated with the input of bloggers around the world, a sense of ethical responsibility would likely be felt in the blogging community, which could ultimately lead to a common ground of understanding among bloggers and their followers. Thus we propose a series of recommendations regarding a code of ethics for the blogosphere as the first step in establishing a truly global virtual public sphere.

Solutions and Recommendations

We acknowledge that current and past efforts to address unethical blogging practices have made significant contributions to attracting attention to a serious problem in online communication. Our objective is to contribute to the current endeavor by specifically providing some ethical considerations for human rights blogging:

Verify Source of Information

Given that the Internet contains a cornucopia of information and that erroneous ones infiltrate this vast space, efforts should be made to verify information.

- Cross-check with primary sources (if blogger is not primary source).
- Cross-check with other reliable sources that in turn exhaust other sources.
- Cite reliable sources either by linking to their websites or posting their write-ups.

If verification is not possible, do not blog about the information. Rather, write in broad terms without going into any specifics that would point directly to people or events involved. It is always better to err on the safe side.

Protect the Subject of the News or Information

Handle sensitive and/or incriminating materials (still or moving images).

- Obtain consent from people involved (if possible).
- Inform subject of the objective of the blog (if possible).
- Do not manipulate material to convey a different message.

- Do not allow others to manipulate material.

If obtaining an informed consent is not possible, conceal the identity of the subject.

If subject is in a delicate situation (i.e. minor, political dissident, ostracized, etc.), conceal identity even if consent is given.

Provide Readers with Updates

- Monitor and blog about developments and provide links to reliable sources following the case.

Promote Interactivity

- Allow readers to comment on or discuss the subject.
- Allow readers to link to the blog for effective information dissemination.

By consolidating our proposed ethical guidelines and others currently being considered in the field through extensive dialogs with bloggers, human rights specialists, professional media practitioners, and the victims themselves, we can move from simply debating the formulation of a universal code of ethics to actually establishing one and making it work.

FUTURE RESEARCH DIRECTIONS

The task of coming up with a code of ethics that would encompass most, if not all, blogging practices is a herculean task because considering the welfare of stakeholders, identifying strengths and weaknesses, and anticipating opportunities and threats require rigorous gathering of facts. In line with conducting a deeper exploration of ethics for blogging, we would need to involve journalists in a worldwide survey to gather insights on the issue from the point of view of professional media

practitioners. More significantly, scholars may also want to look into the experiences of victims from the exposure of human rights videos that rendered the subjects recognizable and identifiable to build a stronger argument on the need for a code of ethics.

CONCLUSION

After all is said and done, the fact remains that people will continue to fight for human rights and answering the question of which right should be placed above all others will never be successfully resolved. However, this is the essence of Habermas' theory of communicative action. Thus, while prevailing norms serve as the standards for human behavior, some will question the applicability of such practices amid social changes, ones that call for adjustments in the treatment of certain rights that become more apparent as human interaction experiences a shift in form and matter. To be certain, a unanimous view on privacy as a fundamental right can never be reached since— to refer to Habermas once again—no society is characterized by a completely uniform way of thinking about rights and personal motives are always a factor in these diverse opinions regarding rights; thus, the importance of a virtual public sphere that includes an ethical approach to human rights videoblogging. However, in our study of YouTube videobloggers, we were able to establish that following a set of guidelines is not enough to ensure proper behavior. Proper behavior is of course yet another point for debate especially in the context of an Internet that is nortoriously a breeding ground for many forms of freedom still suppressed in some societies, e.g., China. We have observed and noted changes in human communication and interaction, more specifically the treatment of anonymity and immediacy, and we have reached the conclusion that these behaviors simply do not apply for all the one-billion plus

Internet users around the world. It is that same diversity that inspired the authors of this chapter to propose a universal code of ethics much in the same vein as how privacy is universally considered a right of citizens around the world albeit amid different conceptualizations and treatments under each country's laws. The presence of a universal code of ethics for videoblogging, we believe, would not undermine other forms of freedoms or respective laws but its presence could serve as a model, which we hope would cut across cultures just like its platform, the Web, can. We acknowledge that the adaptation of such code has a long way to go. But if we take the inspiration from the work of Warren and Brandeis along with the Universal Declaration of Human Rights and the Charter of Fundamental Rights of the European Union, then finding a common ground for ethical videoblogging is not a pipe dream.

The Universal Declaration of Human Rights includes both the right of a person to protect his honor and reputation (Article 12) and the right to freedom of opinion and expression (Article 19). The age-old debate about the conflicting fundamental principles embodies in these inherent human rights will never be resolved; add to this the heavily contentious freedom of the press and the public's "right to know" and you have a series of irreconcilable opinions where a clear-cut consensus is very difficult, although still possible, to attain. This is the beauty of communication; as the advancement of technology continues, changes in society that can lead to both improvements and to conflicts are part and parcel of the grand scheme of things. However, in the subject of human rights videos proliferating on the Web, we maintain that the right of the victims to be protected against further suffering must be given more importance than freedom of expression and the right to know regardless of the potential liberating effect that technology brings.

REFERENCES

Abril, P. S. (2007). A (My)Space of one's own: On privacy and online social networks. *Northwestern Journal of Technology and Intelelctual Property, 6*(1). Retrieved June 16, 2009, from http://www.law.northwestern.edu/journals/njtip/v6/n1/4/?title=A+(My)Space+of+One's+Own:+On+Privacy+and+Online%0D%0ASocial+Networks&author=Patricia+ Sanchez+Abril&pagination=&startpage=& endpage=&issueTitle=&issueDate=Fall+ 2007&vol=6&n=1&jTitle=Northwestern+ Journal+of+Technology+and+Intellectual +Property&cite=

Adler, R. B., & Rodman, G. (2005). *Understanding human communication* (9th ed.). New York, NY: Oxford University Press, Inc.

Alexander, L. (2005). *Is there a right of freedom of expression?* New York, NY: Cambridge University Press. doi:10.1017/CBO9780511614668

Alterman, E. D. (2006). The social context. In Germany, J. B. (Ed.), *Person-to-person-to-person: Harnessing the political power of online social networks and user-generated content* (pp. 37–40). Washington, DC: Institute for Politics, Democracy & the Internet.

Amnesty International. (2007). Egypt–systematic abuses in the name of security. Retrieved October 31, 2007, from http://www.amnesty.org/en/library/asset/ MDE12/001/2007/en/ dom-MDE120012007en.pdf

Balkin, J. M. (2004). Digital speech and democratic culture: A theory of freedom of expression for the information society. *New York University Law Review, 79*(1), 1–55.

Beers, D. (2006). The public sphere and online, independent journalism. *Canadian Journal of Education, 29*(1), 109–130. doi:10.2307/20054149

Bolton, R. (2005). *Habermas's theory of communicative action and the theory of social capital.* Paper presented at the Association of American Geographers meeting. Denver, Colorado. Retrieved March 31, 2007, from http://www.williams.edu/ Economics/ papers/Habermas.pdf

Bratman, B. E. (2002). Brandeis and Warren's *The Right to Privacy* and the birth of the right to privacy. *Tennessee Law Review, 69*(623), 623–651.

Bushman, B. J., & Wessman, L. R. (2006). Short-term and long-term effects of violent media on aggression in children and adults. *Archives of Pediatrics & Adolescent Medicine, 160,* 348–352. doi:10.1001/archpedi.160.4.348

Caldwell, G. (2005). *Witness 2005 annual report.* Retrieved April 6, 2007, from http://www.witness. org/images/stories/ pdf/Annual_Report_2006h. pdf

Cecez-Kemanovic, V., & Janson, M. (1999). *Rethinking Habermas's theory of communicative action in Information Systems.* Paper posted to University of Missouri-St. Louis. Retrieved March 30, 2007, from www.umsl.edu/~mjanson/ myarticles/habermas.pdf

Christians, C. G., Fackler, M., Rotzoll, K. B., & McKee, K. B. (1997). Invasion of privacy. In *Media ethics: Cases and moral reasoning* (5th ed., pp. 109–124). USA: Longman.

Cizek, K. (2005). Safety and security. In S. Gregory, G. Caldwell, R. Avni, & T. Harding (Eds.), *Video for change: A guide for advocacy and activism* (pp. 20-73). Retrieved April 9, 2007, from http://www.witness.org/images/stories/pdf/ VideoforChange_Safetyand Security_Titled.pdf

Dempsey, J., & Weitzner, D. (1998). *Regardless of frontiers: Protecting the human right to freedom of expression on the global Internet* (introduction & overview). Center for Democracy & Technology and the Global Liberty Internet Campaign. Retrieved April 5, 2007, from http://gilc.org/ speech/report/

Deuze, M. (2004). What is journalism? *Journalism, 6*(4), 442–464. doi:10.1177/1464884905056815

Edgar, A. (2006). *Habermas: The key concepts.* New York, NY: Routledge.

Elliot, D. (2003). Moral responsibilities and the power of pictures. In Lester, P. M., & Ross, S. D. (Eds.), *Images that injure: Pictorial stereotypes in the media* (2nd ed., p. 7). Westport, CT: Praeger.

Fahmy, S. (2005). U.S. photojournalists' & photo editors' attitudes & perceptions: Visual coverage of 9/11 & the Afghan War. *Visual Communication Quarterly, 12,* 146–163. doi:10.1207/ s15551407vcq1203&4_4

Fahmy, S., & Wanta, W. (2007). What visual journalists think others think. *Visual Communication Quarterly, 14,* 16–31.

Gans, H. J. (2004). Sources and journalists. In *Deciding What's News: A study of CBS Evening News, NBC Nightly News, Newsweek, and Time* (25th ed.) (pp. 117-118). Illinois: Northwestern University Press.

Gimeno, J. D. M. (2008). *YouTube and mainstream journalism: Strange bedfellows?* Paper presented at the 2008 International Communication Association (ICA) conference, Journalism Ethics Division, May 22-26, 2008, Montreal, Quebec, Canada.

Gimeno, J. D. M., & Freeman, B. C. (2009). *The ethics of videoblogging: Public journalists have their say on YouTube.* Paper presented at the University of Melbourne and the International Communication Association (ICA)'s Journalism in the 21st Century: Between Globalization and National Identity, July 16-17, 2009, University of Melbourne, Australia.

Gormley, K. (1992). One hundred years of privacy. *Wisconsin Law Review,* 1335.

Griffin, G. (1995). Shoot first: The ethics of Australian press photographers. *Australian Studies in Journalism, 4,* 3–29.

Gross, L., Katz, J. S., & Ruby, J. (Eds.). (1988). *Image ethics: The moral rights of subjects in photographs, film, and television.* New York, NY: Oxford University Press.

Gross, L., Katz, J. S., & Ruby, J. (Eds.). (2003). *Image ethics in the digital age.* Minnesota: University of Minnesota Press.

Habermas, J. (1984). *The theory of communicative action: Reason and the rationalisation of society (Vol. 1).* (McCarthy, T., Trans.). Boston, MA: Beacon Press.

Habermas, J. (1987). The uncoupling of system and lifeworld. In *The theory of communicative action: Lifeworld and system: A critique of functionalist reason (Vol. 2,* pp. 153–198). (McCarthy, T., Trans.). Boston, MA: Beacon Press.

Hafez, K. (2002). Journalism ethics revisited: A comparison of ethics codes in Europe, North Africa, the Middle East, and Muslim Asia. *Political Communication, 19,* 225–250. doi:10.1080/10584600252907461

Harrison, J. (2004). *From image to icon? Ethics and taste in photographic portrayals of the death of Pym Fortuyn.* The University of Queensland Web. Retrieved March 15, 2008, from http://espace.library.uq.edu.au/view.php?pid=UQ:10515

Henderson, L. (1998). Access and consent in public photography. In Gross, L., Katz, J. S., & Ruby, J. (Eds.), *Image ethics: The moral rights of subjects in photographs, film, and television* (pp. 91–107). New York, NY: Oxford University Press.

Herrscher, R. (2002). A universal code of journalism ethics: Problems, limitations, and proposals. *Journal of Mass Media Ethics, 17*(4), 277–289. doi:10.1207/S15327728JMME1704_03

Hodges, L. W. (Ed.). (2002). Cases and commentaries. *Journal of Mass Media Ethics, 17*(4), 318–327. doi:10.1207/S15327728JMME1704_07

International Commission of Jurists. (2005). *Iraq: The trial of Saddam Hussein and the rights of the victims.* Retrieved April 9, 2007, from www.icj.org/IMG/pdf/IQTrial_Saddam_R.victims_.pdf

International Council on Human Rights Policy. (2002). Human rights as a news topic. In *Journalism, media and the challenges of human rights reporting* (pp. 2–3). Vernier, Switzerland: ATAR Roto Press.

Keith, S., Schwalbe, C. B., & Silcock, B. W. (2006). Images in ethics codes in an era of violence and tragedy. *Journal of Mass Media Ethics, 21*(4), 245–264. doi:10.1207/s15327728jmme2104_3

Kitch, C. (2006). Useful memory in Time Inc. Magazines. *Journalism Studies, 7*(1), 94–110. doi:10.1080/14616700500450384

Kuhn, M. (2007). Interactivity and prioritizing the human: A code of blogging ethics. *Journal of Mass Media Ethics, 22*(1), 18–36.

Kulezsa, J. (2009). Which legal standards should apply To Web-logs? The present legal position of Internet journals in the European *iuris prudence* in the light of the European Parliament Committee's on Culture and Education report and Polish Supreme Court decision. *Lex Electronics, 13*(3), 1–22.

Lasprogata, G., King, N. J., & Pillay, S. (2004). Regulation of electronic employee monitoring: Identifying fundamental principles of employee privacy through a comparative study of data privacy legislation in the European Union, United States and Canada. *Stanford Technology Law Review, 4.*

Latane, B., Williams, K. D., & Harkins, S. (1979). Many hands make light the work: The causes and consequences of social loafing. *Journal of Personality and Social Psychology, 37,* 822–832. doi:10.1037/0022-3514.37.6.822

Lester, P. M. (1995). Photojournalism ethics timeless issues. In Emery, M., & Smythe, T. C. (Eds.), *Readings in mass communication*. Brown & Benchmark Publishers.

Lester, P. M. (2006). *Visual communication: Images with messages* (4th ed.). Belmont, CA: Wadsworth.

Levinson, S. (1990). Privacy vs. the public's right to know. *The World and I, 1990*(9).

Levy, F. (2008). *Becoming a star in the YouTube revolution*. New York, NY: Alpha.

Marcus, A., & Perez, A. (2007). m-YouTube mobile UI: Video selection based on social influence. In J. Jacko (Ed.), *Proceedings from the Human-Computer Interaction, Part III*. Heidelberg/Berlin, Germany: Springer-Verlag.

McCaughey, M., & Ayers, M. (Eds.). (2003). *Cyberactivism: Online activism in theory and practice* (pp. 1–21). New York, NY: Routledge.

Myers, D. G. (1999). *Social psychology* (6th ed.). USA: The McGraw-Hill Companies, Inc.

Nielsen Company. (2009). *Nielsen announces September U.S. online video usage data*. Retrieved December 13, 2009, from http://en-us.nielsen. com/main/news /news_releases/2009/october/ nielsen_announces Nielsen/Netratings. (2006). *YouTube U.S. Web traffic grows 75 percent week over week, according to Nielsen/Netratings*. Retrieved February 17, 2007, from http://www. nielsen-netratings.com /pr/pr_060721_2.pdf

Omar, B. (2007). The switch to online newspapers: Could immediacy be a factor? In *Proceedings from the Australian New Zealand Communication Association 2007 Conference*. Melbourne, Australia.

Pavlik, J. V. (2005). *Journalism competencies in the digital age: Twelve core principles*. Paper presented at the III Congrès Internacional Comunicació I Realitat, Barcelona, Spain. Retrieved March 15, 2008 from http://cicr.blanquerna.url.edu /2005/Abstracts/PDFsComunicacions /vol1/01/PAVLIK_John.pdf

Perkins, M. (2002). International law and the search for universal principles in journalism ethics. *Journal of Mass Media Ethics, 17*(3), 193–208. doi:10.1207/S15327728JMME1703_02

Prott, L. V. (1986). Cultural rights as people's rights in international law. *Bulletin of the Australian Society of Legal Philosophy, 10*(4), 4–19.

Reiter, M. K., & Rubin, A. D. (1998). Crowds: Anonymity for Web transactions. *ACM Transactions on Information and System Security, 1*(1), 66–92. doi:10.1145/290163.290168

Roberts, P., & Webber, J. (1999). Visual truth in the Digital Age: Towards a protocol for image ethics. *Australian Computer Journal, 31*(3), 78–82.

Scanlon, T. (1972). A theory of freedom of expression. *Philosophy & Public Affairs, 1*(2), 204–226.

Schuldt, B. A. (2004). MAMA on the Web: Ethical considerations for our networked world. In Quigley, M. (Ed.), *Information society and ethics: Social and organizational issues*. Hershey, PA: IRM Press.

Seaton, J. (2005). Painful news. In *Carnage and the Media: The making and breaking of news about violence* (p. 5). London, UK: Penguin Books, Ltd.

Simpson, R., & Cotè, W. (2006). Journalists and violence. In *Covering violence: A guide to ethical reporting about victims and trauma* (2nd ed., pp. 1–12). USA: Columbia University Press.

Smith, D., & Torres, C. (2006, February 5). Timeline: A history of free speech. *The Observer.* Retrieved April 21, 2007, from http://www.guardian.co.uk/ media/2006/feb/05/religion.news

Sussman, L. R. (2001). *The Internet in flux*. Press Freedom Survey 2001, Freedom House. Retrieved August 3, 2007, from http://epic.org/free_speech/pfs2001.pdf

Taylor, J. (2005). Iraqi torture photographs and documentary realism in the press. *Journalism Studies*, *6*(1), 39–49. doi:10.1080/1461670052000328195

Tulloch, J. (2006). The privatising of pain: Lincoln newspapers, mediated publicness and the end of public execution. *Journalism Studies*, *7*(3), 437–451. doi:10.1080/14616700600680922

Vegh, S. (2003). Classfying form of online activism: The case of the cyberprotests against the World Bank. In McCaughey, M., & Ayers, M. (Eds.), *Cyberactivism: Online activism in theory and practice* (pp. 71–93). New York, NY: Routledge.

Veraar, M. J. (2006). Identity formation in online social networking websites. In J. B. Germany (Ed.), *Person-to-person-to-person: Harnessing the political power of online social networks and user-generated content* (pp. 53-58). GW's Institute for Politics, Democracy & the Internet.

Viera, J. D. (1988). Images as property. In Gross, L., Katz, J. S., & Ruby, J. (Eds.), *Image ethics: The moral rights of subjects in photographs, film, and television*. New York, NY: Oxford University Press.

Ward, S. J. A. (2005). Journalism ethics from the public's point of view. *Journalism Studies*, *6*(3), 315–330. doi:10.1080/14616700500131901

Warren, S. D., & Brandeis, L. D. (1890). The right to privacy. *Harvard Law Review*, *6*(5), 1–23.

Weimann, G. (2006). New terrorism, new media. In *Terror on the Internet: The new arena, the new challenges* (pp. 15–32). Washington, DC: United States Institute of Peace Press.

Whitman, J. Q. (2004). The two western cultures of privacy: Dignity versus liberty. *The Yale Law Journal*, *113*(1153), 1151–1221. doi:10.2307/4135723

Wilkins, L., & Brennen, B. (2004). Conflicted interests, contested terrain: Journalism ethics codes then and now. *Journalism Studies*, *5*(3), 297–309. doi:10.1080/1461670042000246061

Wood, A. F., & Smith, M. J. (2005). *Online communication: Linking technology, identity, and culture* (2nd ed.). Mahwah, NJ: Lawrence Erlbaum Associates, Publishers.

ADDITIONAL READING

Alia, V. (2004). *Media ethics and social change*. London: Routledge.

Beyrer, C., & Kass, N. E. (2002). Human rights, politics, and reviews of research ethics. *Lancet*, *360*(9328), 246–251. doi:10.1016/S0140-6736(02)09465-5

Colarik, A. M. (2006). *Cyber Terrorism: Political and Economic Implications*. Hershey, PA and London, UK: Idea Group Inc.

Doostdar, A. (2004). "The Vulgar Spirit of Blogging": On Language, Culture, and Power in Persian Weblogestan. *American Anthropologist*, *106*(4), 651–662. doi:10.1525/aa.2004.106.4.651

Drezner, D. W., & Farrell, H. (2004). Web of Influence. *Foreign Policy*, *145*, 32–40. doi:10.2307/4152942

Godwin, M. (2003). *Cyber rights: defending free speech in the digital age*. Massachusetts: The MIT Press.

Griffin, J. (2008). *On Human Rights*. New York: Oxford University Press. doi:10.1093/acprof:oso/9780199238781.001.0001

Haas, T. (2005). From "Public Journalism" to the "Public's Journalism"? Rhetoric and reality in the discourse on weblogs. *Journalism Studies, 6*(3), 387–396. doi:10.1080/14616700500132073

Hauster, M. D. (2008). *Moral Minds: How Nature Designed Our Universal Sense of Right and Wrong*. London: Abacus.

Herring, S. C., Kouper, I., Paolillo, J. C., Scheidt, L. A., Tyworth, M., Welsch, P., et al. (2005). Conversations in the blogosphere: An analysis 'from the bottom up'. *Proceedings of the Thirty-Eighth Hawaii International Conference on System Sciences*. Los Alamitos, CA: IEEE Press.

Kahn, R., & Kellner, D. (2004). New media and internet activism: from the 'Battle of Seattle' to blogging. *New Media & Society, 6*(1), 87–95. doi:10.1177/1461444804039908

Keeble, R. (2009). *Ethics for Journalists* (2nd ed.). New York: Routledge.

Lasica, J. D. (2002). Blogging as a form of journalism. In Blood, R. (Ed.), *We've Got Blog. How Weblogs are Changing Our Culture* (pp. 163–170). Cambridge: Perseus.

Lenhart, A., & Fox, S. (2006). *Bloggers. A portrait of the internet's new storytellers*. Washington: Pew Internet & American Life Project. Available at http://www.pewinternet.org/pdfs /PIP%20Bloggers%20Report% 20July%2019%202006.pdf

Lievrouw, L. A., & Livingstone, S. (2002). The social shaping and consequences of ICTs. In Lievrouw, L. A., & Livingstone, S. (Eds.), *Handbook of New Media: Social Shaping and Consequences of ICTs* (pp. 1–15). London: Sage.

Matheson, D. (2004). Weblogs and the epistemology of the news: Some trends in online journalism. *New Media & Society, 6*, 443–468. doi:10.1177/146144804044329

Nardi, B. A., Schiano, D. J., Gumbrecht, M., & Swartz, L. (2004). Why we blog. *Communications of the ACM, 47*(12), 41–46. doi:10.1145/1035134.1035163

Perlmutter, D. D., & Schoen, M. (2007). "If I Break a Rule, What Do I Do, Fire Myself?" Ethics Codes of Independent Blogs. *Journal of Mass Media Ethics, 22*(1), 37–48.

Plaisance, P. L. (2007). Transparency: An Assessment of the Kantian Roots of a Key Element in Media Ethics Practice. *Journal of Mass Media Ethics, 22*(2&3), 187–207.

Schmidt, J. (2007). Blogging practices: An analytical framework [Electronic version]. *Journal of Computer-Mediated Communication, 12*(4), 13. Available at http://jcmc.indiana.edu/ vol12/issue4/schmidt.html. doi:10.1111/j.1083-6101.2007.00379.x

Singer, J. (2005). The political j-blogger. 'Normalizing' a new media form to fit old norms and practices. *Journalism, 6*, 173–198. doi:10.1177/1464884905051009

Subramanian, R. (2008). *Computer Security, Privacy, and Politics: Current Issues, Challenges, and Solutions*. London, Pennsylvania: IRM Press (an imprint of IGI Global).

Talbott, W. J. (2005). *Which rights should be universal?* New York: Oxford University Press. doi:10.1093/0195173473.001.0001

Tehranian, M. (2002). Peace Journalism: Negotiating Global Media Ethics. *The Harvard International Journal of Press/Politics, 7*(2), 58–83.

Trammell, K. D., Tarkowski, A., Hofmokl, J., & Sapp, A. M. (2006). Rzeczpospolita blogów [Republic of blog]: Examining Polish bloggers through content analysis [Electronic version]. *Journal of Computer-Mediated Communication, 11*(3), article 2. Available at http://jcmc.indiana.edu/ vol11/issue3/trammell.html

Tremayne, M. (Ed.). (2006). *Blogging, Citizenship, and the Future of Media*. New York: Routledge.

Viégas, F. B. (2005). Bloggers' expectations of privacy and accountability: An initial survey [Electronic version]. *Journal of Computer-Mediated Communication, 10*(3), 12. Available at http://jcmc.indiana.edu /vol10/issue3/viegas.html.

Vitaliev, D. (2007). *Digital Security and Privacy for Human Rights Defenders*. Dublin: Frontline: International Foundation for the Protection of Human Rights Defenders.

Walker, J. (2006). Blogging from inside the ivory tower. In Bruns, A., & Jacobs, J. (Eds.), *Uses of Blogs* (pp. 127–138). New York: Peter Lang.

Wilkins, L., & Coleman, R. (2005). *The Moral Media: How Journalists Reason About Ethics*. Mahwah, NJ and London: Lawrence Erlbaum Associates, Publishers.

ENDNOTES

[1] Webopedia defines streaming as "a technique for transferring data such that it can be processed as a steady and continuous stream" (http://www.webopedia.com/TERM/s/streaming.html). For instance, a video clip can be viewed on-site without the need to download (progressive download).

[2] According to Mullen and others (1997 cited in Myers, 1999, p. 294), significant evidence points to people feeling energized or aroused in the presence of others. This can be observed in riots among fans in a sporting event or between demonstrators and the police.

[3] Social loafing (Latané, Williams, & Harkins, 1979) is described as a situation in which people tend to put in less effort as they normally would when they act as part of a group, thus, diffusing responsibility.

APPENDIX A

Coding System for Qualitative Content Analysis

- **Category of Human Rights Violation:** the following categories are based on the list of human rights violations available on the website of Witness's Human Rights Video Hub Pilot Project.
  1) Armed conflict
  2) Children's rights
  3) Child soldiers
  4) Execution
  5) Genocide
  6) Honor crimes/ honor killings
  7) Mass killings
  8) Police misconduct
  9) Prisons
  10) Rape and sexual abuse
  11) Slavery
  12) Torture/ill-treatment
- **Identity Factor:**
  1) Very clear - victim's face is recognizable.
  2) Moderately blurred – not very clear, but victim's face is still recognizable.
  3) Blurred - victim's face will be recognized through facial and body features.
  4) Zero Visibility – victim's face is not recognizable at all.
- **Appropriateness Factor:** the following items are based on the principles followed by Witness's Human Rights Video Hub Pilot Project in determining which videos are not suitable for the project's website.
  1) Video carries a significant risk to someone's life or personal safety.
  2) Video contains a direct written or verbal incitement to violence or hate.
  3) Video contains nudity or sexual imagery.
  4) Video contains material that may compromise the capacity for decision making or ability to give consent – children (under 18), detainees/prisoners, and people with mental disability.
  5) Video features graphic violent imagery.
  6) Video contains material that is discriminatory and advocates intolerance on the grounds of ethnicity, race, gender, disability, national origin, sexual orientation or religion or is otherwise appropriate.
- **Violence Factor:** the following are based on the film rating system of the Motion Picture Association of America (MPAA).
  1) Violence is minimal to non-existent.
  2) There is some violence.
  3) There is violence, but is not extreme or persistent.
  4) There is intense and persistent violence.
  5) Violence is extreme; children 17 and under should not see it.

Chapter 7
Conceptualizing E-Participation in the Public Sphere

Jenny Backhouse
University of New South Wales, Australia

ABSTRACT

This chapter reviews the current understanding of the role of e-participation in democratic processes, in particular emphasizing the deliberative aspects of participatory democracy and the factors that impinge on successful participation initiatives. It considers what lessons can be learnt, if any, from related aspects of e-government and from e-business, in order to refine the concept of e-participation. The chapter concludes that e-participation has a role to play in a modern society where the Internet is increasingly the medium of choice for social communications. However, e-participation projects need to be appropriately developed so that they truly engage the citizenry and encourage meaningful participation in deliberative facets of democracy.

INTRODUCTION

The presidential campaign of Barack Obama in the United States in 2008 successfully integrated the use of Information and Communication Technologies (ICTs) into the campaign strategy, serving to involve and engage citizens in the campaign on a scale not seen before in electronic media election campaigning (2009, p. 12). This success has re-

newed hopes for a broader rejuvenation of citizen interest in political interaction and deliberation in the public sphere, supported by the use of ICTs (Garrett & Jensen, 2009).

However, election campaigning is only one aspect of democratic participation. To date, the mass appeal generated by the Obama campaign has been a high profile exception among the many well-intentioned initiatives developed using ICTs to support citizens' electronic participation (e-participation) and engagement in various facets

DOI: 10.4018/978-1-60960-159-1.ch007

of democracy and democratic processes (Garrett & Jensen, 2009; Gronlund & Astrom, 2009). It is clear that, if we consider that a vibrant democracy needs to engage its citizenry and that freedom and participation are key features of democracy, we need a better understanding of what role, if any, e-participation might play in encouraging this engagement.

The modern proliferation of ICT tools and technologies such as social networking has opened the possibility of a new virtual 'public sphere'. Habermas, who popularized the term 'the public sphere', explained the concept as private individuals freely assembling to "express and publish their opinions – about matters of general interest" (Habermas, 2001, p. 102). In sophisticated societies, this public sphere requires media, such as newspapers and television, to communicate these deliberations. The Internet, along with its associated 'e' technologies, provides an additional medium for "transmitting information and influencing those who receive it" (Habermas, 1991, p. 102). It also means that such assemblies of private citizens can now be virtual as well as physical.

THE NATURE OF DEMOCRACY

Democracy Models and the Citizen's Role

In considering e-participation, we need firstly to consider the nature of democracy itself since this impacts on the character of the citizen's deliberative or participatory role. The concept of democracy is not easily formally defined with many flavors of democracy extant in the modern world. One definition identifies the key features of democracy as the "basic principles of freedom and direct involvement in one's own self government " (King, 2006, p. 16). In current democratic practice, this involvement is generally indirect with citizens electing representatives who then make decisions on their behalf. Systems that use

referenda on a regular basis partially exercise direct democracy (Kersten, 2003).

The implementation of democracy and the resulting political structures vary from one democratic country to another and are set in different cultural contexts. "No two countries are alike and...national trajectories will be shaped by variables both within the public sector (including multiple levels of government) and across society at large." (UNPAN, 2008, p. xvi). Researchers generally distinguish between broad categories of democratic implementations. Gronlund (2009) discusses three categories of democracy models: 'quick', 'strong' and 'thin' democracy and the features which classify them.

In models implementing 'quick' democracy, the key role of citizens is as a decision maker. Citizens act directly as decision makers by voting on specific issues. The majority decision then forms the basis for the legitimacy of the resulting outcome and political representatives are bound by those decisions. Models implementing 'strong' democracy require public debate and deliberation as the basis for the legitimacy of decisions. The citizen therefore has a role in the formation of opinion and their representatives, after being elected, continue to interact and consult with citizens about decisions. In this type of model the "direct citizen involvement... is based on deliberation rather than voting" (Gronlund, 2009, p. 19). In models implementing 'thin' democracy, the key role of citizens is as a voter. The involvement of citizens is indirect in that once the representative is elected, he/she has an open mandate for decision-making. The basis for legitimacy is the representative's accountability at the next election.

In practice, in all three democracy models, citizens might be involved in a mix of participatory activities. However, the nature of the democratic model would influence the type of e-participation, if any, which would be most appropriate. In the case of 'quick' democracy, the focus of any ICT support would be mainly on the decision-making itself. For 'strong' democracy, ICT support would be focused on supporting discussion and debate. For 'thin' democracy, ICT would be mainly focused on the provision of information (Gronlund, 2009).

Direct democracy, having citizens participate directly as decision makers, is often presented as the ideal democracy model (LeDuc, 2003). However, most modern democracies are representative democracies, that is, they mainly exhibit the features of the 'thin' model of democracy. This model is often disparaged as not 'true' democracy (Behrouzi, 2008). It is criticized as distancing citizens both from the decision-making process and from their political representatives. A similar view is evidenced in research involving e-participation. Gronlund (2009) reviewed models which described the 'progress' towards e-participation. He critiqued the implicit assumptions, typical in these models, that "progress is equalled with more sophisticated use of technology, and direct democracy is seen as the most advanced democracy model" (Gronlund, 2009, p. 12). In practice, direct democracy as implemented in referenda or other initiatives, has limitations. As Le Duc discusses (LeDuc, 2003), referenda can be unduly influenced by elites or other special interest groups, voter turnout is often low and citizens may not have sufficient information to properly evaluate the issues. In California, voters have been presented with referenda on issues which are relatively trivial or contradictory and some referenda outcomes have caused the state to come close to bankruptcy (Kersten, 2003).

The Decision-Making Cycle

Democracy is not just about elections. Democratic governments typically follow a decision-making cycle consisting of agenda setting and analysis followed by creating, implementing and monitoring the policy (Gronlund, 2003; Macintosh, 2004). These stages are relevant for participatory democracy since, as Gronlund discusses (2003), the extent of the role for public participation depends on both the broad category of democracy

as mentioned earlier (quick, thin, strong) and the stage of the decision-making process. In the case of strong democracy, citizens could be involved in all stages of the policy cycle whereas, in thin democracy, their involvement is likely to be confined to the policy creation stage and possibly, the policy monitoring stage.

The inclusion of citizens in policy debate raises questions about how this might take place and what might be the features of such participation. The characteristics of political participation in a generic sense are relevant in conceptualising e-participation and the role that ICTs might play in supporting this participation. Pratchett (1999) highlights some salient dimensions of participation, which are relevant to both traditional and electronic forms.

- Whether the participatory opportunity is passively provided or actively encouraged.
- Whether the focus of participation is individual or group.
- Whether the participation supports a specific decision or a broader issue.
- Whether participants have an advisory role or real decision-making power.
- Whether the participation is designed to provide a representative sample of views or build capacity in marginalised groups.
- Whether the participation requires simple answers or more prolonged debate over time.

These sort of determinations need to be considered in the design of projects aiming to improve democratic deliberation and participation. The features need to suit the nature of the political system concerned, unless, of course, the aim is to spur fundamental change in that system. For a representative democracy, citizen participation in decision–making forums would typically play an indirect role in influencing the decisions made by their elected representative (Gronlund, 2003).

RELATED CONCEPTS

E-Government and E-Democracy

In conceptualizing e-participation, we need to set it in the context of the related concepts currently in use. Following Grant & Chau (2005 as cited in Beynon-Davies, 2007) in relation to e-government, it is enlightening to tease out the significant features of the concepts associated with e-participation.

The concept of 'e-government' came into being around the late 1990's following the growth of online technologies and the resulting realisation of opportunities, labelled e-business or e-commerce, for new approaches in the business world (Gualtieri in Bishop & Anderson, 2004). Researchers and practitioners saw a corresponding prospect for e-government: an opportunity to apply the demonstrated transactional capabilities and the streamlining of processes in the private sphere to the business processes and service delivery undertaken by government in the public sphere (Metaxiotis & Psarras, 2004). The term 'e-government', in turn, spun off a myriad of related, and potentially overlapping, terms including e-democracy, e-participation, e-voting, e-consultation, e-engagement and e-activism. As might be expected in the relatively new fields of research and endeavour these terms suggest, the boundaries have not yet been clearly and distinctly defined.

Researchers and practitioners in the e-government arena initially concentrated on the business-related aspects of efficiency, cost-reduction and service delivery (As-Saber, Hossain, & Srivastava, 2007; Beynon-Davies, 2007). It was quickly realized however that, for a democratic government, service delivery and business efficiency were not the only goals and the concept of e-government was used more broadly to acknowledge the goal of promoting greater interaction and involvement between citizens and government. For example, the Center for Democracy and Technology's e-

government handbook defines e-government as including "the promotion of civic engagement by enabling the public to interact with government officials" (as cited in Metaxiotis & Psarras, 2004, p. 142). Metaxiotis & Psarras themselves reinforce this definition by listing "new ways of debating and deciding strategies" and "new ways of listening to citizens and communities" amongst the concerns of e-government (2004, p. 149).

However, in modern democracies, there is a complex of social and technological interaction in the public sphere, not necessarily directly involving government or government officials. "Governance is now undertaken by a network of stakeholders not all of which are traditional political organisations or even public sector organisations" (Beynon-Davies, 2007, p. 11). Fang's explanation of e-government includes the goal "to provide greater opportunities to participate in democratic institutions and processes" (as cited in As-Saber et al., 2007, p. 157) thus acknowledging potential democratic interaction amongst a diversity of non-state actors as well as with government and traditional political institutions.

Accordingly the term 'e-government' broadened to encompass the public participative and democratic aspects of government along with the process and service-delivery aspects. At the same time, the term 'e-democracy' came to be used by researchers who referred more specifically to the participatory aspects of democratic government or to political participation outside of the government realm (Gronlund & Astrom, 2009). Nevertheless, much e-government research concentrated on the transactional and service delivery aspects of government. Correspondingly, systems which emerged to rank countries based on their e-government maturity tended to concentrate on these technical aspects of e-government as well. In fact, by some ranking systems, as Bishop and Anderson (2004) point out, a number of the countries ranking as top level e-governments have not been notably democratic. "It is possible to have extensive e-government without democracy, even in its most minimal form" (Bishop & Anderson, 2004, p. 6). Similarly, and more recently, the 5th Waseda University International Ranking on e-Government 2009 ranked Singapore, a country not known for the depth of its democracy, in first place (Obi, 2009). At the same time, the Waseda report does acknowledge the significant citizen-centric change in the global approach to e-government in the last few years and the corresponding moves for governments to meet the demands of citizens including establishing "virtual-spaces for citizens to have their voice" (Obi, 2009, p. 3).

E-Democracy and E-Participation

While e-government refers to "the electronic delivery of government services...e-democracy involves more qualitative assessments and is usually identified as some level of engagement, via the web or the Internet, with citizens views about what should and shouldn't be government policy" (Bishop & Anderson, 2004, p. 12). More recently the term 'e-democracy' has been constrained for some, particularly European, researchers by becoming associated specifically with 'e-voting' (Gronlund & Astrom, 2009). As Solvang points out "the term e-democracy... interprets democracy narrowly as voting procedures with statutory structural arrangements" (Solvang, 2009, p. 48). In consequence, the term 'e-participation' is being used as an alternative to highlight specifically the aspects of e-democracy that refer to citizen engagement and deliberation. One extant definition of e-participation is "the use of information and communication technologies to broaden and deepen political participation by enabling citizens to connect with one another and with their elected representatives" (Macintosh, 2006, as cited in Freschi, Medaglia, & Norbjerg, 2009, p. 36). This is the sense in which e-participation is used in this chapter.

The United Nations, in its E-government Survey (UNPAN, 2008), ranks countries on an E-participation Index. This ranking considers three categories:

- **E-information:** the information offered by the government website.
- **E-consultation:** the availability of e-consultation tools on the government website and the opportunity for citizens to use e-petitions to influence the debate.
- **E-decision-making:** the extent to which e-input received from citizens is actually considered in the decision-making process.

However, the UN's E-participation Index is specifically focused on formal governmental action since it is assessed based on " ... the extent to which governments proactively solicit citizen input" (UNPAN, 2008, p. 58). It does not therefore consider e-participation and interaction between third parties outside of the governmental realm. Additionally, the survey is restricted to websites or portals administered at the national level; regional and local sites are not taken into account. Such a comprehensive worldwide survey obviously has to work within the constraints of different governmental systems, differing levels of government and the practicalities of what is possible. Nonetheless, these limitations meant that, after the United Kingdom undertook the process of migrating its e-participatory initiatives from the portals at the national level to portals at the local government level, it dropped from 1st position in the E-participation Index rankings in 2005 to 24th position in 2008 (UNPAN, 2008). Many researchers and practitioners would consider local government the natural home for most e-participation initiatives (Coleman & Norris, 2005; Gronlund & Astrom, 2009) and thus find this result somewhat contrary.

CONSIDERING ANALOGIES FROM E-BUSINESS

Background

E-government has in some senses a close association with e-business since it came into being from corresponding developments in the private sphere. Researchers have examined the features of e-business and e-government to see whether such comparisons can better inform our understanding of these concepts (Scholl, Barzilai-Nahon, Ahn, Popova, & Re, 2009; Stahl, 2005). A comparison between e-business and the participatory role of e-democracy is also informative even given the fact that "the role of citizens in state and government is fundamentally different from the role of customers in a company" (Stahl, 2005, p. 12).

After some early failures, such as those experienced during the dot-com crash of 2001, the world of e-business has largely transitioned to mature technologies supporting a range of viable businesses (OECD, 2009). Sites such as Google, Amazon, iTunes and EBay have established a global presence. Where e-government involves Business–to–Government (B2G), it has also had considerable success in terms of the take-up trend by businesses (OECD, 2009). In contrast, e-government and participative e-democracy initiatives in many liberal democracies have struggled to provide successful engaging implementations (Coleman & Norris, 2005; Flew & Young, 2005; Stahl, 2005). On the e-government side, there has been a "dilemma between the promises of e-government, lagging user take-up and lack of satisfaction with e-government services" (OECD, 2009, p. 3). Disappointingly also for e-democracy enthusiasts, most applications have generally failed to fulfil the hopes that the applications would enhance democratic participation and decision making and "transform political cultures... and institutions" (Robbin, Courtright, & Davis, 2005, p. 417). In fact, many contemporary perceptions of e-democracy are "almost entirely conventional,

as they aim at facilitating, rather than transforming political action" (Insua, 2008, p. 175) It is instructive to consider why e-participation has not captured the public imagination on a wider scale.

Admittedly, it is probably unrealistic to expect e-democracy projects to achieve quite the same sort of profile as websites in the global e-business arena. Democratic processes and democratic deliberation are primarily local and national rather than global in nature. Additionally they typically do not involve motivators such as entertainment, financial gain or satisfaction of consumerist needs. Nevertheless, participative e-democracy in most countries has failed to live up to the expectations of many dedicated proponents. There is a "paucity of convincing empirical evidence that ICTs have altered political life" (Robbin et al., 2005, p. 417).

The conceptualization of e-participation may be informed by considering what factors, if any, affecting the success or otherwise of e-business may be pertinent to the development and implementation of e-participation projects. Over the last decade or more, researchers in the world of e-business have identified some of the necessary pre-conditions and drivers that contribute to success in e-business (Chaffey, 2006). These include appropriate communications infrastructure, relevant government regulatory frameworks, the nature of the business model, readiness of the population to engage in the process (motivation, trust, ease of use, availability of tools, appropriate skills).

Crucially, these factors hint at the wider socio-technical environment in which e-participation projects also sit. As Scholl et al observe in relation to e-commerce and e-government, such projects "are engrained in institutional and social settings leading to a mesh of socio, technical, and organizational complexities" (Scholl et al., 2009, p. 2). Ryder (2009) gives an example of the social issues in his discussion of a small group of wealthy retirees, not otherwise disadvantaged, who simply are not motivated to access the Internet despite numerous government efforts and money spent on pilot programs and encouragement (Ryder, 2009).

Access Channels

One component of managing a successful e-business is being aware of the "channels" via which customers access your business. Businesses that kept both a store front and an online presence had to consider whether this would increase sales or whether one business outlet would cannibalize the other. The rising popularity of mobile communications adds to the potential variety of access channels available to the consumer. An organisation's website now needs to be mobile friendly. If an organisation's strategy is to move customers online, they can give pricing signals, for example, a bank that charges a small fee for over the counter transactions that are free if completed online (Bishop & Anderson, 2004). For e-government transaction applications, this type of efficiency is not really an option. To ensure optimal access for all citizens, the public sector may need to maintain traditional access points (e.g. shop fronts) for many years.

Considering participation in a democratic sense, more points of access to government and policy decision makers means greater flexibility for the citizen to choose their preferred method. From a political activist point of view, it may make sense to provide citizens with a variety of access channels. As noted in the 2008 United Nations E-government Survey (UNPAN, 2008, p. 7), multichannel service delivery by government means that the delivery channels need to interoperate seamlessly. The multichannel approach could apply equally to deliberative and participatory democracy (Sabo, Rose, & Flak, 2008). An effective activist campaign, along the lines of those conducted by organisations such as MoveOn.org, GetUp.org.au and MeetUp.com often involves a blend of different strategies possibly including traditional tactics (e.g. street marches, advertise-ments in broadcast media), petition signing and online facilitation (Rodan & Balnaves, 2009).

Whilst an access channel is a facility for increasing citizen engagement, its effects can be perverse. Several researchers have noted that providing participatory and consultative facilities on government web sites means relying on politicians and administrators to approve and administer these initiatives. In some cases, as Dowe notes "Government administrators and politicians are not interested in using the new ideas put forth as it supposedly means more work and less power" (Dowe as cited in Coleman & Norris, 2005, p. 15). There are obviously exceptions to this view (e.g. some high-profile politicians who are regular bloggers) but they are just that: exceptions.

Citizen Engagement

In the e-business arena, customers generally have a clear motivation to participate in commercial transactions electronically. Successful business organisations and personnel work hard to engage customers by being responsive to their wants and needs. The profit motive serves as a key driver for business to cater to existing customers and recruit new customers. In some cases, businesses might choose to concentrate on particular customer segments such as their high value customers. Public service bureaucrats have an ethical, rather than a financial, motivation to treat citizens well and to ensure that opportunities are made available to all. Regarding e-participation, citizens generally have a less compelling motivation to participate in political deliberation. Some citizens obviously are keen to have their views heard but "citizens are not necessarily more willing to participate simply because net-services are provided for them" (Sabo, Rose, & Nyvang, 2009, p. 46).

Several surveys of bureaucrats confirm that many public administrators have negative attitudes to citizen engagement in the policy making process (As-Saber et al., 2007; Coleman & Norris, 2005; Kim & Holzer, 2006). Issues of concern included perceived increase in workload, loss of control over outcomes and doubts about the capacity of citizens to make such decisions. Initiatives may be established as tokenistic gestures designed to elicit government kudos but with no real intention to provide genuine deliberation. In reality, some members of the public may have particular expertise in certain areas and be better informed than bureaucrats and politicians who necessarily have to cover a wide area of expertise (Kim & Holzer, 2006). Members of the public need not formally be professionals in order to have informed opinions. They may have a particular motivation that drives their knowledge acquisition, for example, health policy initiatives informed by knowledge of a particular disease; planning policies related to their local area.

A legitimate criticism expressed by some bureaucrats is that forums may be un-democratic being dominated by narrow interests or be reduced to abuse and haranguing of other forum members. Similar reluctance and doubt has been noted by other researchers (Gualtieri as cited in Geiselhart, Griffiths, & Fitzgerald, 2003). The availability of ICT tools will not automatically engender in the citizenry the motivation and ability to process potentially complex information with an open mind. If the aim of e-participation is to widen the range of democratic engagement, then projects need to be designed carefully to encourage the desired result.

The enablement of citizen to citizen (C2C) interaction is a key component of e-business by virtue of auction sites and various other online forums. It is not normally seen as a channel relevant in the area of e-government but it is a crucial aspect of e-participation. As Beynon-Davies (2007) argues, it links the key functions of democratic accountability and policy-making. However, where citizen deliberation facilities are provided via consultative assemblies or in independent forums, elected officials could interpret these as removing significant powers from them and potentially acting as "substitutes for representative democracy" (Snider, 2008, p. 3).

Disruptive Technology

While the Internet has spurred the creation of new online businesses, it has also undermined the viability of some traditional businesses. Amazon was probably the first high profile online business that literally threatened even well established bookstore chains. Currently newspapers are experiencing an eroding of their revenue base, especially those that rely on classified advertising, a field which is inexorably moving online.

However the Internet may be similarly disruptive for democracy (King, 2006). It allows citizens to be removed from their geographical ties; to easily filter views so that they only interact with like-minded people, possibly reinforcing extremist views; to have undue clout via small interest groups perhaps lacking a coherent agenda; to expect direct links to political power and correspondingly quick replies and results. "The stable basis of participatory democracy, the need for something in common to help overcome the things on which we disagree, could be gradually eroded. Politics, the process of getting over these disagreements, could be undermined" (Crabtree, 2002, para 13).

Resources

In the early days of online business, a business could be sustained with a fairly simple website. For serious online businesses these days, maintaining a sophisticated website and the associated applications and infrastructure, is a significant cost. Customer expectations for functionality, appealing presentation, ease of use and the assurance of privacy have risen. Citizen expectations for e-democracy participatory services are probably similar. While many government sectors might be considered to have deep pockets and the appropriate technical expertise, the question arises of justifying the expenditure of public monies on e-democracy projects. This is particularly so if there are low levels of citizen involvement and the government needs to maintain the traditional resources as well. Moreover, the returns from projects designed to enhance citizen engagement in the public sphere are typically largely qualitative in nature. Conversely, where e-democracy sites are setup and maintained by community interest groups or other non-government organisations, they are likely to be subject to pressures such as financial stress and maintaining the enthusiasm of volunteer staff. "E-democracy projects involve more than set-up costs; it has often proved difficult to maintain them as permanent democratic features" (Coleman & Norris, 2005, p. 18)

The rise of e-business saw new players flood into the online market. Despite some spectacular successes, many online businesses were not sustainable. Over time, the well-established and well-resourced traditional companies have been able to re-establish their position in many market segments. Some e-democracy pessimists suggest that a similar situation may result from e-democracy initiatives. Rather than bring new players into the game, it may serve to entrench the access of the traditional political players, the so-called elites, lobby groups and major political parties (Norris & Curtice, 2006). Disintermediation Early e-business analysts emphasized the likely role of the Internet in disintermediation, cutting out the middleman or agent thus allowing customers to trade directly with product producers (Chaffey, 2006). This certainly eventuated in some areas. For example, many low-cost airlines have succeeded in moving most of their customers to direct online bookings, negating the need for travel agents to be involved in this process. Traditional airlines have followed suit by setting up their own online booking systems and eventually removing special pricing deals for the traditional middle man, the travel agents. While disintermediation has occurred in some instances, it has coincided with reintermediation in others. A whole new group of e-business intermediaries has arisen and proved effective in assisting online consumers to more efficiently perform desired functions, for example sites which aggregate available accommodation

or find the best deal on a particular product, online stock trading sites, sites for accessing music, search engines, etc. The search engine Google is currently in a powerful position because its search site is the first point of call for many Internet users. This new type of intermediary has given rise to a whole new industry, that of search engine optimisation, since many e-businesses want to ensure that their website is prominent and ranks highly in search results.

In the area of e-democracy participation, forums which are run independently of government perform a similar intermediary role replacing, to some extent, the traditional town meeting. As Gronlund notes, "intermediaries of different kinds have begun to interfere in those relations. This includes both service intermediaries... and 'democracy consultants'" (Gronlund, 2002, p. 1). Correspondingly, Caddy sees an enhanced role for intermediaries, such as the British Broadcasting Commission (BBC), who are trusted, branded and separate from government. "Citizens will look to them for packaging and facilitating the access to information" (Caddy in Coleman & Norris, 2005, p. 30). Intermediaries are also prominent in the participative area of political activism. Organisations such as moveon.org use ICTs to support activities such as rousing citizens, developing electronic petitions and helping to elect candidates who support their ideals.

Table 1 summarizes some of the key factors of commonality and difference between e-business and democratic e-participation.

DELIBERATIVE DEMOCRACY AND THE POLITICAL ENVIRONMENT

The Public Sphere

Over the past couple of decades, many liberal democracies have noted a decline in the participation of citizens in the public sphere, particularly as indicated by falling voter turnout at elections,

Table 1. Factors comparing e-business and e-participation

Factors	E-business	E-participation
Socio-technical Environment	• Need for appropriate infrastructure • Supporting regulatory framework	• Need for appropriate infrastructure
Access channels	• Careful management needed	• Variety of access channels is a plus
Citizen engagement	• Clear motivation – satisfying desires (social, financial: often a discount for online purchase, etc) • May target particular customer segments	• Motivation less compelling – citizen reluctance • Opportunities must be available to all • Prospect of domination by narrow interest groups
Disruptive technology	• New businesses created • Some existing businesses undermined	• Could undermine existing political power structures • May lead to expectations that can't be met (e.g. ongoing direct access to politicians)
Resources	• Need for appropriate infrastructure • Sophisticated sites require significant resources • Well-resourced companies re-establishing their position	• Need for appropriate infrastructure • Resources needed but return largely qualitative • Need to maintain enthusiasm of volunteer community groups • Reinforce position of elites?
Dis-intermediation	• Occurred in some areas (e.g. airlines) but new middlemen have arisen (e.g. sites for aggregating available accommodation)	• Independent forums; sites to co-ordinate and motivate political activism • Democracy consultants; trusted brands

reluctance to join political parties and voluntary associations or to attend public meetings (Russell, 2005; Scheuerman, 2005; Solvang, 2009). Other characteristics evidenced include citizen apathy, cynicism and a distrust of politicians and the political process. Scheuerman posits one factor as being "the growing misfit between the increasingly high-speed structural dynamics of modern society and the slow-going pace of traditional forms of liberal democratic citizenship" (Scheuerman, 2005, p. 457). In a similar vein, the OECD E-government Study partly blames the failure to deliver services specifically tailored to individual citizens on the "historically bound administrative cultures in a public sector" (OECD, 2009, p. 22) and Garrett notes the "individual and systemic resistances to change" (Garrett & Jensen, 2009, p. 29) in the political system.

While ICTs are seen as a potential tool to help redress this problem, designing engaging e-participation strategies is not a straightforward task. As Snider (2008, p. 2) notes, "The democratic ideal is a constantly moving target that must be regularly recalibrated to a higher standard as society becomes more complex". While town meetings, a traditional form of democratic deliberation, might be quite suitable for a village with a few thousand people, they are not practical for a country with a population in the hundreds of millions (Snider, 2008).

The Obama presidential campaign in the United States during 2007/2008 has highlighted the manner in which an innovative online strategy can contribute to citizen engagement in the public sphere and to effective campaigning. As Millard observes Obama's "… intelligent use of ICT in political fundraising and campaigning has opened a new chapter in eParticipation" (Millard, 2009, para 1). Key features of the campaign were the success of online fund-raising, recruiting volunteers, providing campaign news and connecting via social networks and other online forums. Obama supporters were particularly active online. "Obama voters took a leading role engaging in online political activism" (Smith, 2009, p. 10). For both sides of American politics, the 2008 presidential campaign was a watershed. A Pew Internet survey found that, for the first time "more than half the voting-age population used the Internet to connect to the political process during an election cycle" (Smith, 2009, p. 3).

Politicians in other countries took notice of the Obama style but success was not a forgone conclusion. The nature of political deliberation is closely tied to the political environment and the culture in which that deliberation is exercised. For the German elections of 2009, the politicians' website presences from the 2005 election were now augmented by a raft of social media. "These days every politician has a YouTube channel, Facebook page, Twitter feed and blog" (World e-Democracy forum, 2009, para. 4). It seems the strategy was not particularly effective the view being that these efforts were just for show, merely to indicate that those politicians were modern and up-to-date. "But their web strategies were just that: talk" (World e-Democracy forum, 2009, para. 4).

Social Media

The subtleties of designing citizen participation forums engagingly is dramatically illustrated by the rise of social media, technologies which allow general Internet users to easily contribute content and connect to other users. This popularity of social media, even in the political arena, provides a counterpoint to the numerous well-intentioned efforts over several years to encourage citizen participation in the public sphere, projects which generally had limited results. "Against the slow growth of e-government usage... it is somewhat ironic that … a new wave of applications, which now go under the name of Web 2.0, were launched with very little investment and encountered dramatic success in terms of take-up" (Osimo, 2008, p. 12). Systems to specifically support collaboration have been designed by universities and others at considerable expense and yet, frustratingly, the organically grown applications such as "YouTube, Facebook and other social networking sites readily available over the Internet offer tools for collaboration that are arguably more powerful" (Dutton, 2007, p. 19).

As Osimo notes, these interactive and social media technologies are affecting a variety of e-government domains, however "The most visible impact is certainly in the field of political participation" (Osimo, 2008, p. 7). Social networking sites can be particularly attractive to political actors (not to mention marketers), assisting them to hone their message for specific groups. Within these sites, user profiles and interactions inevitably reveal a lot of detail about the people themselves, along with their interests and preferences. "In the realm of political campaigns...social networking sites thus offer many advantages to political actors" (Chadwick, 2009, p. 14). Social media allows a two-way communication thereby adding a dimension of personalization, and potential engagement, to political interaction.

Deliberative Focus

Voting in elections is a crude instrument to convey citizens' views on issues of interest or concern on an ongoing basis (Pratchett, 1999). In recent times, the idea of greater citizen opportunity for deliberation and involvement in decision-making is achieving wider acceptance (Bayley & French, 2008). The involvement may take a variety of forms such as focus groups, online forums, stakeholder workshops or web polling. "Politicians are drawn to such instruments because greater public involvement seems to achieve greater acceptance of the ultimate decision and, arguable in more objective terms, a better decision" (Bayley & French, 2008, p. 195).

Democratic deliberation can take place at many levels. Different tiers of government obviously have different responsibilities and consequently different relationships with citizens. "National governments, responsible for the welfare of a whole country, are unlikely to understand the needs of communities in the same way as local government" (Shackleton, Fisher, & Dawson, 2004, p. 9). The type of decisions to be made also varies with the governmental level: local, regional, national. Decisions at the local level tend to be more immediate and clear cut, typically involving fewer people. It is not surprising therefore that the key focus of participatory technologies to date has been at the level of local government (Freschi et al., 2009).

At higher levels of government, decisions are often more complex and are likely to require a more sustained involvement and skill level for citizens to learn about the problem and understand the implications, constraints and alternatives (Kersten, 2003). Citizens need to be motivated to commit to participating in deliberation at this level and we should not underestimate the demands such projects may place on citizens. Additionally, "Systems capable of supporting participatory e-democracy need to provide tools for the generation of alternatives, simulation and analysis of the alternatives' environmental, economic and social impacts and their visualization and comparisons" (Kersten, 2003, p. 141). Social media and the current tools used to support political participation, typically online forums and groupware applications, may be useful for engendering citizen engagement. However they do not provide the more sophisticated level of argumentation support required for more complex deliberative decision-making (Macintosh, Gordon, & Renton, 2009).

Another dimension of the deliberative focus is the stage of the policy cycle at which citizen participation occurs: agenda setting, analysis, policy creation, implementation and monitoring (Macintosh, 2004). Different skills may be needed in particular stages and different people may be more appropriate participants. Gronlund, for example, found that "to achieve high participation consultations should be applied at the analysis or decision making stage in the policy process, that is the later stages in the process" (Gronlund & Astrom, 2009, p. 97).

CONCLUSION

Modern ICTs provide a viable base for facilitating elements of deliberative democracy and thus reinvigorating the citizen's relationship with government and encouraging the citizen's wider participation in the public sphere. Since the Internet is increasingly dominant in the lives of many people in liberal democracies, the concept of e-participation is relevant although traditional methods may also be part of the mix. Participation initiatives need to be appropriately tailored to the needs and skills of the stakeholders and the nature of the decisions to be made. Participatory projects also need to be well designed to ensure real engagement, equity of opportunity and validity of outcomes. More sophisticated applications are required to adequately support more complex decision making scenarios.

Dutton observes that "the Internet is becoming not only a new source of information, but also a platform for networking individuals in new Internet-enabled groups that can challenge the influence of other, more established, bases of institutional authority" (Dutton, 2007, p. 19). This networking effect is already evident in many areas of the private sector. To ensure the viability and legitimacy of modern democracies, it should also be evident in the public sphere by providing a means by which civil society renews its engagement with governmental and political institutions.

REFERENCES

As-Saber, S., Hossain, K., & Srivastava, A. (2007). Technology, society and e-government: In search of an eclectic framework. *Electronic Government: An International Journal, 4*(2), 156–178. doi:10.1504/EG.2007.013981

Bayley, C., & French, S. (2008). Designing a participatory process for stakeholder involvement in a societal decision. *Group Decision and Negotiation, 17*(3), 195–210. doi:10.1007/s10726-007-9076-8

Behrouzi, M. (2008). The idea of democracy and its distortions: From Socrates to Cornel West. *Journal of Public Deliberation, 4*(1), 13. Retrieved from http://services.bepress.com/jpd/vol4/iss1/art13.

Beynon-Davies, P. (2007). Models for e-government. *Transforming Government, People. Process and Policy, 1*(1), 7–28.

Bishop, P., & Anderson, L. (2004). *E-government to e-democracy: High tech solutions to no tech problems.* Paper presented at the Australian Electronic Governance Conference, Melbourne, Australia. Retrieved from http://www.public-policy.unimelb.edu.au/egovernance/papers/05_Bishop.pdf

Chadwick, A. (2009). Web 2.0: New challenges for the study of e-democracy in an era of international exuberance. *I/S: A Journal of Law and Policy for the Information Society, 5*(1), 1-32.

Chaffey, D. (2006). *E-business and e-commerce management* (3rd ed.). London, UK: FT Prentice Hall.

Coleman, S., & Norris, D. F. (2005). *A new agenda for e-democracy.* (Forum Discussion Paper No. 4). Retrieved Nov 2009, from http://www.oii.ox.ac.uk/resources/publications/FD4.pdf

Crabtree, J. (2002). *Is the Internet bad for democracy?* openDemocracy. Retrieved December 2009, from http://www.opendemocracy.org/media-edemocracy/article_822.jsp

Dutton, W. H. (2007). *Through the network (of networks)-the fifth estate.* Oxford Internet Institute. Retrieved November 2009, from http://people.oii.ox.ac.uk/dutton/wp-content/uploads/2007/10/5th-estate-lecture-text.pdf

Flew, T., & Young, G. (2005). *From e-government to online deliberative democracy.* Paper presented at the International Conference on Engaging Communities, Brisbane, Australia. Retrieved from http://www.engagingcommunities2005.org/abstracts/Flew-Terry-final.pdf

Freschi, A. C., Medaglia, R., & Norbjerg, J. (2009). A tale of six countries: e-participation research from an administration and political perspective. In Macintosh, A., & Tambouris, E. (Eds.), *Electronic participation* (pp. 36–45). Springer. doi:10.1007/978-3-642-03781-8_4

Garrett, R. K., & Jensen, M. J. (2009). *E-democracy writ small: The impact of the Internet on citizen access to local elected officials.* Paper presented at the Annual Meeting of the International Communication Association, Chicago. Retrieved from http://www.allacademic.com/

Geiselhart, G., Griffiths, M., & Fitzgerald, B. (2003). What lies beyond service delivery-an Australian perspective. *Journal of Political Marketing, 2*(3-4), 213–233. doi:10.1300/J199v02n03_12

Gronlund, A. (2002). Emerging infrastructures for e-democracy: In search of strong inscriptions. *e-Service Journal, 2*(1), 62-89.

Gronlund, A. (2003). e-democracy: In search of tools and methods for effective participation. *Journal of Multi-Criteria Decision Analysis, 12*(2-3), 93–100. doi:10.1002/mcda.349

Gronlund, A. (2009). ICT is not participation, is not democracy – eParticipation development models. In Macintosh, A., & Tambouris, E. (Eds.), *Electronic participation* (pp. 12–23). Springer. doi:10.1007/978-3-642-03781-8_2

Gronlund, A., & Astrom, J. (2009). Do IT right: Measuring effectiveness of different e-consultation designs. In Macintosh, A., & Tambouris, E. (Eds.), *Electronic participation* (pp. 90–100). Springer. doi:10.1007/978-3-642-03781-8_9

Habermas, J. (1991). *The structural transformation of the public sphere: An inquiry into a category of bourgeois society.* Cambridge, MA: MIT Press.

Habermas, J. (2001). The public sphere: An encyclopedia article. In Durham, M. G., & Kellner, D. M. (Eds.), *Media and cultural studies: Keyworks* (pp. 102–107). Oxford, UK: Blackwell Publishers.

Insua, D. R. (2008). Introduction to the special issue on e-democracy. *Group Decision and Negotiation, 17*(3), 175–177. doi:10.1007/s10726-007-9077-7

Kersten, G. E. (2003). e-democracy and participatory decision processes: Lessons from e-negotiation experiments. *Journal of Multi-Criteria Decision Analysis, 12*(2-3), 127–143. doi:10.1002/mcda.352

Kim, C.-G., & Holzer, M. (2006). Public administrators' acceptance of the practice of digital democracy: A model explaining the utilization of online forums in South Korea. *International Journal of Electronic Government Research, 2*(2), 22–48. doi:10.4018/jegr.2006040102

King, J. (2006). Democracy in the information age. *Australian Journal of Public Administration, 65*(2), 16–32. doi:10.1111/j.1467-8500.2006.00479.x

LeDuc, L. (2003). *The politics of direct democracy: Referendums in global perspective.* Ontario, Canada: Broadview Press.

Macintosh, A. (2004). *Characterizing e-participation in policy-making.* Paper presented at the 37th Annual Hawaii International Conference on System Sciences. Retrieved from http://ieeexplore.ieee.org/xpls/abs_all.jsp?arnumber=1265300

Macintosh, A., Gordon, T., & Renton, A. (2009). Providing argument support for e-participation. *Journal of Information Technology & Politics, 6*(1), 43–59. doi:10.1080/19331680802662113

Metaxiotis, K., & Psarras, J. (2004). e-government: New concept, big challenge, success stories. *Electronic Government: An International Journal, 1*(2), 141–178. doi:10.1504/EG.2004.005174

Millard, J. (2009). e-participation. *European Journal of e-Practice, 7.*

Norris, P., & Curtice, J. (2006). If you build a political website, will they come? *International Journal of Electronic Government Research, 2*(2), 1–21. doi:10.4018/jegr.2006040101

Obi, T. (2009). The 2009 Waseda University international e-government ranking. Retrieved from http://www.giti.waseda.ac.jp/GITS/news/download/e-Government_Ranking2009_en.pdf

OECD. (2009). *Rethinking e-government services: User-centred approaches.* OECD e-government studies.

Osimo, D. (2008). *Web 2.0 in government: Why and how?* European Commission, Joint Research Centre, Institute for Prospective Technological Studies Report.

Pratchett, L. (1999). New fashions in public participation: Towards greater democracy? *Parliamentary Affairs, 52*(4), 617–633. doi:10.1093/pa/52.4.616

Robbin, A., Courtright, C., & Davis, L. (2005). Policy: ICTs and political life. *Annual Review of Information Science & Technology, 38*(1), 410–482. doi:10.1002/aris.1440380110

Rodan, D., & Balnaves, M. (2009). Democracy to come: Active forums as indicator suites for e-participation and e-governance. In Macintosh, A., & Tambouris, E. (Eds.), *Electronic participation* (pp. 175–185). Springer. doi:10.1007/978-3-642-03781-8_16

Russell, A. (2005). Political parties as vehicles of political engagement. *Parliamentary Affairs, 58*(3), 555–569. doi:10.1093/pa/gsi051

Ryder, G. (2009). The digital divide: Investigating the Isle of Man's dilemma using exploratory research to resolve the problem. In Z. Irani, A. Ghoneim, M. Ali, S. Alshawi, O. Y. Saatcioglu, & A. G. Cerit (Eds.), *European and Mediterranean Conference on Information Systems*. Izmir, Turkey. Retrieved from http://www.iseing.org/emcis/EMCIS2009/_private/Accepted%20Refereed%20papers.htm

Sabo, O., Rose, J., & Flak, L. S. (2008). The shape of e-participation: Characterizing an emerging research area. *Government Information Quarterly*, *25*(3), 400–428. doi:10.1016/j.giq.2007.04.007

Sabo, O., Rose, J., & Nyvang, T. (2009). The role of social networking services in e-participation. In Macintosh, A., & Tambouris, E. (Eds.), *Electronic participation* (pp. 46–55). Berlin/Heidelberg, Germany: Springer. doi:10.1007/978-3-642-03781-8_5

Scheuerman, W. E. (2005). Busyness and citizenship. *Social Research, 72*(2), 447–471.

Scholl, H. J., Barzilai-Nahon, K., Ahn, J.-H., Popova, O. H., & Re, B. (2009). *E-commerce and e-government: How do they compare? What can they learn from each other?* Paper presented at the 42nd Hawaii International Conference on System Sciences.

Shackleton, P., Fisher, J., & Dawson, L. (2004). *Evolution of local government e-services: The applicability of e-business maturity models.* Paper presented at the 37th Annual Hawaii International Conference on System Sciences. Retrieved from http://ieeexplore.ieee.org/iel5/8934/28293/01265308.pdf?isnumber=&arnumber=1265308

Smith, A. (2009). *The Internet's role in campaign 2008*. Pew Internet & American Life Project. Retrieved from http://www.pewinternet.org/Reports/2009/6--The-Internets-Role-in-Campaign-2008.aspx

Snider, J. H. (2008). Crackpot or genius? Canada steps onto the world stage as a democratic innovator. *Journal of Public Deliberation, 4*(1), 12. Retrieved from http://services.bepress.com/jpd/vol4/iss1/art12.

Solvang, B. K. (2009). Political participation and democracy in the digital age: Effects of ICT-based communication forms between the authorities and the citizens on traditional channels of participation and democracy In *Proceedings of the Third International Conference on Digital Society,* (pp. 46-51). Cancun: Mexico: IEEE Computer.

Stahl, B. C. (2005). The paradigm of e-commerce in e-government and e-democracy. In Huang, W., Siau, K., & Wei, K. K. (Eds.), *Electronic government strategies and implementation* (pp. 1–19). Hershey, PA: Idea Group.

UNPAN. (2008). United Nations e-government survey: From e-government to connected governance. Retrieved November 2009, from http://unpan1.un.org/intradoc/groups/public/documents/UN/UNPAN028607.pdf

World e-democracy forum. (2009). Germany: Political parties test unsuccessfully Obama method. Retrieved December 2009, from http://www.edemocracy-forum.com/2009/09/germany-election.html

Chapter 8

An Investigation of the Use of Computer Supported Arguments Visualization for Improving Public Participation in Legislation Formation

Euripidis Loukis
University of the Aegean, Greece

Alexander Xenakis
Panteion University, Greece

Nektaria Tserpeli
Kapodistrian University of Athens, Greece

ABSTRACT

It has been argued that representative democracy, in order to be effective and address the problems and needs of different groups, and also at the same time legitimate and acceptable, should be combined with public participation (both off-line and on-line) of individual citizens and the civil society. However, the participation of citizens (either as individuals or as representatives of groups or any type of collective entities) in political debates in order to be meaningful and effective needs to be informed, which necessitates extensive study of large amounts of relevant material, such as reports, laws, committees' minutes, opinions expressed by experts, stakeholders, political parties, et cetera. Most of this material is in a legalistic or in other specialist languages, or in a political rhetoric style that hides their substance, making it less discernible. The above problems are putting barriers to a meaningful and effective participation. This chapter presents research on the use of 'Computer Supported Argument Visualization' (CSAV) methods for addressing these problems and supporting and enhancing public participation in the legislation formation process. Based on an analysis of this process and its main documents, a comprehensive approach to the use of CSAV in the legislation formation process is designed, which covers

DOI: 10.4018/978-1-60960-159-1.ch008

all its fundamental stages and documents, and assists citizens and civil society groups to participate in it in a meaningful and effective manner with a reasonable amount of effort. It is based on the issue-based information systems (IBIS) framework. This approach has been implemented in a pilot e-participation project in the Greek Parliament, which was then evaluated based on the 'Technology Acceptance Model' (TAM) with positive results. Based on the conclusions of this evaluation an enrichment of the IBIS framework has been developed for improving the visualization of the main content (articles) of bills and laws.

INTRODUCTION

It has been argued that representative democracy, in order to be effective and address the problems and needs of different groups, and also at the same time legitimate and acceptable by the society, should be combined with public participation of individual citizens and the civil society. This line of thought, in combination with the declining trust of citizens in government and lower interest in politics, gave rise to new model of democracy, termed as "participatory democracy" (Pateman, 1970; Macpherson, 1977; Barber, 1984; Held, 1987; Fishkin, 1991). A key principle of this model is that "the equal right to self-development can only be achieved in a participatory society, a society which fosters a sense of political efficacy, nurtures a concern for collective problems and contributes to the formation of a knowledgeable citizenry capable of taking a sustained interest in the governing process" (Held, 1987, p. 262). A major value of this model of democracy is public participation, defined by Row & Frewer (2004) as 'the practice of consulting and involving members of the public in the agenda-setting, decision-making and policy forming activities of organizations or institutions responsible for policy development'; they view it as a move away from an 'elitist model', in which managers and experts are the basic source of regulations and public policies, to a new model, in which citizens have a more active role and voice. However, the objective of participatory democracy is not the overthrow of the establishment and the implementation of a new

order; it aims mainly to function as a remedial and not as a revolutionary measure. It does not foster conflicts among social groups of each society, but tries to feature a practical way of coexistence; the basic idea of this model is the exchange of views among citizens, in order to form a core, a synthesis of their opinions. In this direction Barber (1984, p. 174) argues that discussion among opposing views 'entails listening no less than speaking, it is affective as well as cognitive...'.

Governments of many countries all over the world have attempted to put in practice the above ideas, promote public participation and strengthen their relations with the citizens, regarding them as sound investments in better policy-making and as a core element of good governance (Organisation for Economic Cooperation and Development, 2003a, 2003b and 2004a). The explosive increase of the penetration and use by more and more citizens of Information and Communication Technologies (ICT), and especially the Internet, gave rise to the development of e-participation. Governments of many countries attempt to extend citizens' participation in public policies formulation and politics in general through the use of ICT for supporting i) the provision of relevant information to the citizens, ii) the consultation with them and also iii) their active participation (Macintosh, 2004; Organisation for Economic Cooperation and Development, 2004b; Timmers, 2007).

It is widely recognized that the above two higher levels of e-participation, aiming at the consultation with the citizens and their active participation, have as basic precondition the first one, aiming at the provision sufficient relevant information to them. The quality of both the 'traditional' off-line participation and the more recent e-participation, and in general of any type of political debate, relies critically on how informed the participating citizens are on the problem under discussion, its multiple dimensions and the opinions that have been previously expressed on it. Elliman, Macintosh & Irani (2007, p. 33) state that 'Democratic political participation must involve both the means to be informed and deliberative mechanisms to take part in the decision-making'. However, most public policy design problems (e.g. development of plans, programs, regulations, legislation) are 'wicked' (Rittel & Weber, 1973), being characterised by high complexity, many different perspectives and dimensions, and multiple and usually conflicting stakeholders' groups with heterogeneous views, values and concerns. Therefore citizens interested to participate in such debates, in order to be sufficiently informed and make a meaningful contribution, should study large amounts of relevant material, such as reports, plans, laws, committees' minutes, opinions expressed by experts, stakeholders, political parties, etc. Most of this material is in a legalistic or in other specialist languages, or in a political rhetoric style that hides their substance making it less discernible. At the same time many citizens today do not have enough time for such extensive study, and some of them lack the required education and analysis skills. The above problems are putting barriers to a meaningful and effective public participation (both 'on-line' and 'off-line'). Furthermore, the increasing complexity of social problems and needs recently (e.g. due to the internationalization of the economy, the new technologies, the environmental threats) make more citizens think that it is not possible to understand them and form meaningful opinions and positions; this drives a gradual move back towards an 'elitist model', in which managers and experts have the main role in addressing the complex social problems and needs and public participation is limited.

In this chapter we present our research on the use of 'Computer Supported Argument Visualization' (CSAV) methods for addressing these problems, and supporting and enhancing public participation in one of the most important activities of democracy, the formation of legislation. Based on an analysis of the legislation formation process and its main documents in the Greek Parliament initially we designed a comprehensive approach to the use of CSAV in this critical process, which covers all its fundamental stages and documents, and assists citizens and civil society groups to participate in it in a meaningful and effective manner with a reasonable amount of effort. This approach has been implemented in a pilot e-participation project in the Greek Parliament, which was evaluated based on the 'Technology Acceptance Model' (TAM) with positive results. Based on the conclusions of this evaluation an enrichment of the IBIS framework has been developed for improving the visualization of laws. The research presented in this chapter has been part of the LEX-IS project ('Enabling Participation of the Youth in the Public Debate of Legislation among Parliaments, Citizens and Businesses in the European Union') (www.lex-is.eu) co-funded by the 'eParticipation' Preparatory Action of the European Commission (Loukis et al., 2007).

In next section the background of our research is outlined, while in the following section is described the development of a comprehensive approach to the use of CSAV in the legislation formation process. Next is presented the above-mentioned pilot application of this approach, and then its evaluation. They are followed by a section describing an enrichment of the IBIS framework we propose for improving the visualization of the main points of laws' content based on the results of the evaluation, while in the final section our conclusions are outlined.

BACKGROUND

Computer Supported Argument Visualization (CSAV) is the compact representation in a diagrammatic form of a set of arguments, usually contained in textual documents or expressed in debates, using a set of interconnected nodes of various types. It has been used successfully mainly in the domains of law and education, in order to teach critical thinking, presentation and defence of a point of view with arguments and provision of complex information in an organized manner, while their use in the political domain has only recently started (Macintosh, Gordon, & Renton, 2009). Arguments visualization was introduced by Wingmore (1913), who proposed a 'chart method' for representing in a simplified diagrammatic form the extensive material of legal cases, which assists in gaining a better understanding of the substantial elements and reaching conclusions; his charts show how different kinds of evidence (such as 'Testimonial Assertions' or 'Circumstances') are assembled in order to support or challenge various 'Propositions'. Toulmin (1958), building on Wingmore's work, developed a model (language) for formulation and analysis of arguments, which is based on a notation consisting of five components: facts or observations ('Datum'), which through logical steps ('Warrant' which can be supported by a 'Backing') lead to consequent assertions ('Claim'), though exceptions ('Rebuttal') can be also be added to them. This model, and in general Toulmin's analysis of the logical structure of arguments, was a sound foundation for many subsequent developments and applications.

The introduction and wide penetration of computers gave a boost to argument visualization, leading to the development of the CSAV domain, and also to the expansion of its practical application in various domains, such as education, products design, analysis of environmental impacts, commerce, research, etc. (Kirschner, Buckingham Shum & Carr, 2003). CSAV can be very useful

for solving a class of complex problems termed by Rittel & Weber (1973) as 'wicked', in contrast to the simpler 'tame' problems. Wicked problems lack mathematically 'optimal' solutions and pre-defined algorithms for calculating them, and have only 'better' and 'worse' solutions, with the former having more positive arguments in favour them than the latter. Kunz and Rittel (1979) suggest that wicked problems are most effectively countered by argumentation among stakeholders, in which each stakeholder group can express the particular issues and perspectives of the problem they regard as significant, possible actions for addressing them and also their advantages and disadvantages; CSAV can be very useful in supporting such an argumentation. Also, in the same paper is proposed the use for this purpose of 'Issue Based Information Systems' (IBIS), which aim to '*stimulate a more scrutinized style of reasoning which more explicitly reveals the arguments. It should help identify the proper questions, to develop the scope of positions in response to them, and assist in generating dispute*'. They are based on a simple but powerful framework for the representation of such problems, whose main elements are 'questions' (issues-problems to be addressed), 'ideas' (possible answers-solutions to questions-problems) and 'arguments' (evidence or viewpoints that support or object to ideas) (Kunz & Rittel, 1979; Conklin & Begeman, 1989; Conclin, 2003).

Most public policy design problems (e.g. development of plans, programs, regulations, legislation) belong to this class of wicked problems, since they are characterised by high complexity, many different perspectives and dimensions, and have multiple stakeholders with heterogeneous views and concerns. These characteristics have a negative impact on the quantity and quality of the political debates on most public policies, putting barriers to both 'on-line' and 'off-line' public participation. However, limited research has been conducted on how we can use methods of CSAV for conveying compact political information to the citizens on the substantial points and arguments of important political debates and documents in an easily and quickly understandable form, and how useful such an approach can be for the citizens. Renton & Macintosh (2007) identify this research gap stating that 'The use of argument visualization in a political context is still in its infancy', while more recently Macintosh, Gordon and Renton (2009) confirm this and argue that the use of these methods in the political domain 'is only just emerging'.

In the following we briefly review this limited previous research concerning the use of CSAV in the political domain. Renton (2006) investigates the use of CSAV in order to present in a compact and clear manner to the public complex political issues and arguments raised in Parliamentary debates. For this purpose he took the minutes of two debates from the Scottish Parliament concerning the introduction of the 'Terrestrial Trunk Radio Masts' (TETRA) and the 'Antisocial Behaviour', converted them into argument maps based on the IBIS framework using the 'Compendium' tool (Selvin, Shum, & Sierhuis, 2001) and then had them evaluated through qualitative interviews with members of the Scottish Civic Forum with positive results. He represented both these debates through argument maps showing the main questions raised by the Members of Scottish Parliament, ideas for addressing them, and also positive and negative statements on them; also, he connected some of these elements with relevant full text from the minutes of these debates. Renton & Macintosh (2005 and 2007) propose a systematic approach of using a set of maps for representing political debates concerning public policies and bills using icons and arrows, aiming to form in this way an electronic 'policy memory' for supporting policy development and citizens' engagement and deliberation. This approach includes the development of three kinds of maps: overview maps (providing a visualization of the main stages in the development of a bill), dialogue maps (showing the sequence of contributions of representatives of parties and stakeholders in a chronological order) and argument maps (showing in the form of decision trees the opinions expressed in this debate for various topics and questions). Also, they present an application of this approach for constructing a set of maps representing the discussion that took place in the Scottish Parliament concerning the 'Smoking in Public Spaces' policy. Ohl (2008) describes the application of CSAV for the diagrammatic representation of citizens' submissions in a public discourse on a draft South East Queensland Regional Plan, which aims to promote government transparency and accountability. For this purpose he uses an initial 'index map' visualizing the basic issues and questions posed by Queensland State Government, each of them being linked to a particular map visualizing citizens' opinions on it (for open questions), or showing relative frequencies of citizens' responses (for closed questions). All these maps are based on the IBIS framework and have been constructed using the abovementioned 'Compendium' tool.

Further research is required in order to formulate appropriate approaches and practices for using CSAV in the area of politics, in different stages of public policies, programs and legislation lifecycle, for different purposes and audiences, and also in order to evaluate in 'real-life' such approaches, practices and tools, and identify advantages, disadvantages and possible improvements. Our research is contributing in this direction by developing and evaluating a comprehensive approach to the use of CSAV in one of most important activities of democracy, the legislation formation process, which covers all the fundamental stages and documents this process includes. It aims to assist citizens and civil society groups to participate in the legislation formation process in a meaningful and effective manner with a reasonable amount of effort, and therefore to improve the quantity and quality of the relevant political debate.

A COMPREHENSIVE APPROACH TO THE USE OF CSAV IN THE LEGISLATION FORMATION PROCESS

In order to develop such a comprehensive approach to the use of CSAV in the legislation formation process, we adopted the following methodology:

i) initially we analyzed the process of legislation formation in the Greek Parliament, the stages it includes and its main documents,

ii) based on this analysis, we designed our approach with respect to the visualizations that should be constructed,

iii) then we designed our approach with respect to the most appropriate framework and tool to be used for these visualizations,

iv) as a next step we proceeded to a pilot 'real-life' application of the above approach for a bill under discussion in the Greek Parliament,

v) then we evaluated this pilot application,

vi) and finally, based on the conclusions of the evaluation, we made some improvements in our approach.

In particular, in order to understand and analyze the process, stages and documents of legislation formation we conducted interviews with three experienced officials of the Greek Parliament. Additionally we studied carefully and analyzed the justification reports and the main content (articles) of five laws from five different Ministries, which have been proposed to us by the above three officials of the Greek Parliament as being representative. Additionally, we studied carefully and analyzed the minutes of the sessions of the competent Parliamentary committees in which these laws were discussed, and also of the corresponding plenary sessions.

From this analysis it was concluded that the legislation formation process includes some fundamental stages, which are strictly defined by law, each of them adding some 'value' to the bill (sug-

gestions for modifications, improvements, etc.) and producing some fundamental documents in which this value added is documented. These fundamental documents are the justification report of the bill, its main content (articles) and the minutes of its discussion in the competent Parliamentary committee and also in the corresponding plenary sessions of the Parliament. Therefore in order to give to the interested citizens and civil society groups a full picture of a bill under formation in order to participate effectively in the formation process, it is necessary to provide them one hand 'individual' visualizations of these fundamental documents:

a) the justification report of the bill, representing clearly the main reasons that necessitate it (e.g. some social problems or needs) and the basic directions and solutions it provides,

b) the main content of the bill, representing clearly the issues settled by each article, and the particular settlements provided for them,

c) the opinions and positions on the bill of each of the stakeholders' representatives and experts invited in the competent Parliamentary committee (as recorded in its minutes), representing clearly the main strengths, weaknesses and suggestions he/she mentions,

d) the positions on the bill of each of the political parties' main speakers in the competent Parliamentary committee (as recorded in its minutes), representing clearly the main strengths, weaknesses and suggestions he/she mentions,

and on the other hand some 'synthetic' visualizations, such as:

e) a synthetic visualization of all strengths, weaknesses and suggestions mentioned by the stakeholders' representatives and experts invited in the competent Parliamentary committee for this bill,

f) a synthetic visualization of all strengths, weaknesses and suggestions mentioned by the main speakers of the political parties for this bill,

or even a combination of e and f (if it not too complex). Additionally, it is useful to construct an 'overview map' as well, as a starting point for the user, which includes nodes representing all the above visualizations, and also the corresponding textual documents, providing hyperlinks to them.

For these visualizations we decided to use initially the IBIS framework (Conklin & Begeman, 1989; Conclin, 2003), as implemented by the 'Compendium' tool (http://compendium.open. ac.uk/institute/) (Selvin, Shum, & Sierhuis, 2001), because they are mature, and have been used extensively in the past for arguments visualization in several domains, including the domain of politics, as mentioned in the previous section. They provide a simple, understandable and at the same time powerful typology of nodes, which have been proved to be sufficient for the representation of wicked problems in various domains, including politics. However, in the evaluation of the pilot application it will be assessed to what extent the nodes typology provided by the IBIS framework is sufficient for the above visualizations, and if not the required enrichments will be made.

A PILOT APPLICATION

A pilot application of the above approach to the use of CSAV in the legislation formation process was made, in an e-consultation conducted in the Greek Parliament as part of the LEX-IS project (www.lex-is.eu) (Loukis et al., 2007), on a bill concerning the 'Contracts of Voluntary Cohabitation'. This controversial bill regulated the matter of the formal voluntary co-habitation of two persons. It formalized an social situation existing for long time in Greece: many couples, especially among the younger age groups, are reluctant to proceed directly to marriage, and choose to live together for long periods of time; during that time many of them have children, share living expenses and buy property, just to mention some of their most important common actions, and these needed to be regulated.

Before the beginning of this e-consultation we constructed the visualizations mentioned in the previous section for this bill, which were provided to the participants, together with the corresponding textual documents, as basic reference material. From these visualizations some representative ones are shown below.

The initial overview map is shown in Figure 1. It includes four map nodes, representing the visualizations of the bill justification report, the bill content, the invited experts' opinions and the

Figure 1. Overview map

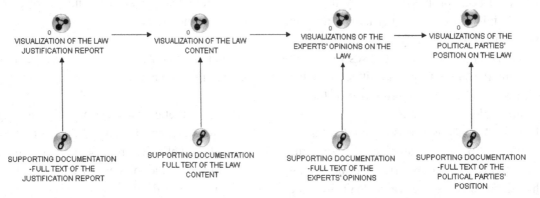

parties' positions on it, arranged horizontally in chronological order, which are hyperlinked to the corresponding visualizations; also, it includes four reference nodes hyperlinked to the corresponding textual documents.

The visualization of the justification report is shown in Figure 2. It includes three of the types of nodes supported by the tool, with an adaptation of their meaning: note/information nodes (adapted as 'clarification' nodes), question nodes (adapted as 'problem-need' nodes) and idea nodes (adapted as 'solution' nodes). It is structured in four layers. The first layer includes (modelled as clarification nodes) the reasons that create the need to legally regulate the voluntary cohabitation, which is modelled through a problem-need node in the second layer. The third layer represents this bill concerning the 'Contracts of Voluntary Cohabitation' as the basic solution for addressing this need, while the fourth layer includes the general directions of the law and the particular

solutions it provides (modelled through solution nodes), and also a clarification on it, further elaborated by two more clarifications (all modelled as clarification nodes).

The visualization of the main content of the bill that we constructed was quite lengthy, so we decided to break it into: i) one 'high level visualization', which shows the main issues regulated by the articles of the bill (as issue nodes) (Figure 3), and also ii) one 'lower level visualization' for the content of each article; since the bill includes 13 articles, we constructed 13 corresponding visualizations of them (in Figure 4 we can see the visualization of the content of the 7th article). For the visualization of the content of the bill we used four of the types of nodes supported by the tool with an adaptation of their meaning: question nodes (adapted as 'issue' nodes), idea nodes (adapted as 'settlement' nodes), note/information nodes (adapted as 'clarification' nodes) and map nodes (in the high level visualization, for provid-

Figure 2. Visualization of the justification report of the Bill

Figure 3. High level visualization of the content of the Bill

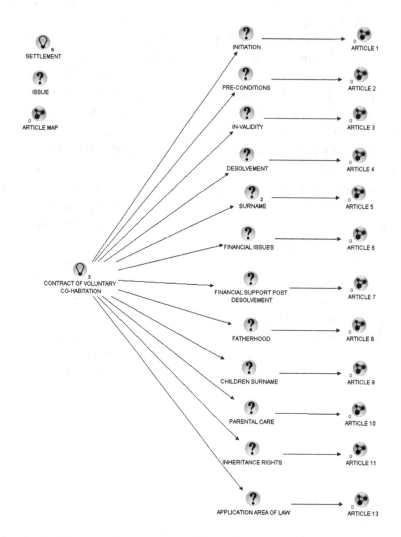

Figure 4. Lower level visualization of the content of the 7th article of the Bill

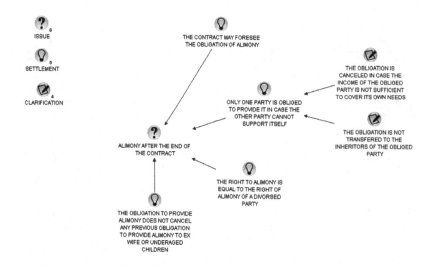

Figure 5. Visualization of the opinion of an expert

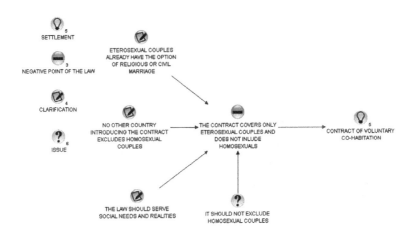

ing hyperlinks to the lower level visualizations of the articles).

The visualization of the opinion on the bill of one of the experts invited by the competent Parliamentary committee is shown in Figure 5. It includes four of the types of nodes supported by the tool, again with an adaptation of their meaning: one idea node (adapted as 'settlement' node) representing the whole bill, one contra-argument node (adapted as 'negative point' node), note/information nodes (adapted as 'clarification'

nodes), and one question node (adapted as 'issue' node). We can see that this expert mentioned one main weakness of this bill, which poses one basic issue, and also added three clarifications on this weakness.

In Figure 6 we can see the visualization of the position of one political party on this bill. It includes four of the types of nodes supported by the tool, with similar adaptations of their meaning: one idea node (adapted as 'settlement' node) representing the whole bill, contra-argument nodes

Figure 6. Visualization of the position of one political party

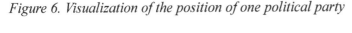

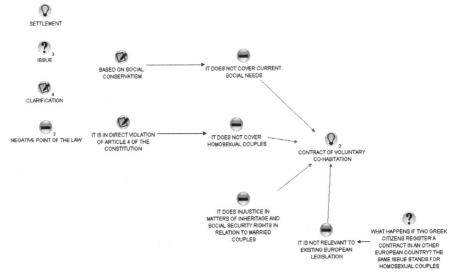

Figure 7. Visualization of the position of another political party

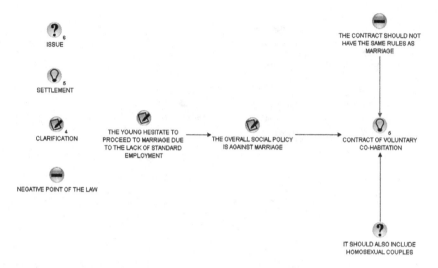

(adapted as 'negative point' nodes), note/information nodes (adapted as 'clarification' nodes), and one question node (adapted as 'issue' node). We can see that this political party mentioned four main weaknesses of this bill, and for two of them

added further clarifications; also they raised one issue associated with one of these weaknesses.

In Figure 7 we can see the visualization of the position of another political party on this bill. From a quick comparative look at the visualiza-

Figure 8. Synthetic visualization of the strengths, weaknesses and suggestions mentioned for this bill by parties, experts and stakeholders' representatives

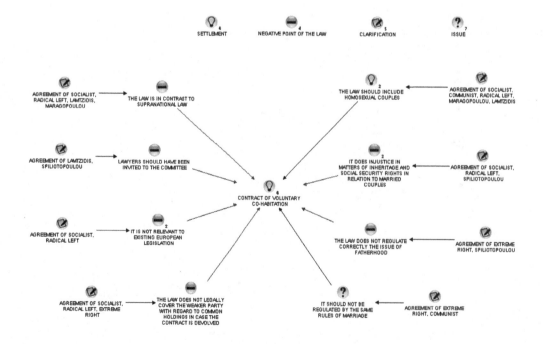

tions of Figures 6 and 7 we can immediately understand that the first party finds more weaknesses in this bill than the second, and that they have different focuses (e.g. the first party focuses on the lack compatibility of this bill with corresponding laws of other European countries and its practical implications, while the second focuses on the need in the co-habitation contracts to have different rules than in the traditional marriage); however, we can see that they agree on the necessity to cover in this bill the co-habitation of homosexual couples as well.

Finally, in Figure 8 we can see a synthetic visualization of all strengths, weaknesses and suggestions mentioned by the main speakers of political parties, the experts and the representatives of stakeholders for this bill. Its nodes have been arranged in 'co-centric circles'. In the middle of the map the bill has been modelled as a basic settlement node, and around it in the first inner circle have been placed six negative point nodes representing the main weaknesses mentioned; also, has been placed one settlement node representing the suggestion of some the parties, experts and stakeholder representatives to include homosexual couples as well, and an issue mode. In the second outer circle we have added for each of the inner circle nodes a clarification node showing who agrees on this particular point.

EVALUATION

The above pilot application of the proposed approach to the use of CSAV in the legislative process has been evaluated through a qualitative in-depth discussion of about four hours duration, held in a focus-group, consisting of four participants in this pilot e-consultation, a legal expert, a lawyer assistant to the member of the Parliament who was the main speaker of the governing party for the bill, and one official of the parliament. The evaluation was based on an established and mature foundation, the Technology Acceptance Model (TAM) (Davis, Bagozzi, & Warshaw, 1989; Davis, 1989), which has been widely used as a basis for the evaluation of various types of information systems. According to the TAM, the main determinants of the attitude towards using an information system of its potential or real users are:

- its perceived ease of use (PEU), defined as the extent to which users believe that using the system will be free of effort,
- its perceived usefulness (PU), defined as the extent to which users believe that using this IS will enhance their performance in a particular task.

Therefore in this in-depth discussion the main topics were the ease of use and the usefulness of the visualizations, and also possible improvements. With respect to the former, all the persons who participated in this discussion accepted that the visualizations were understandable to a rather good extent, after some initial time period required for getting familiar with the symbols of the nodes. However, it was mentioned that they would be easier to understand if all of them were read in the same direction (e.g. from left to right, harmonized with the direction of reading books), which should be clearly indicated. With respect to the usefulness, it was mentioned that the main advantages of visualizations are the time efficiencies created for the participants in such e-consultations, who usually do not have the time to go through all the lengthy relevant textual documents. It was also mentioned that the visualizations of the positions of the parties helped them to 'filter-out' the excessive rhetoric and the irrelevant or generic comments (not directly related to the bill under discussion), which are quite usual in such political speeches, and focus on the main points raised by them and also understand better their stance in the final balloting on the bill. The visualizations of the opinions of the experts and the positions of the parties were more understandable and useful (since the corresponding textual documents were quite lengthy), than the visualisations of the content (articles) of the bill and its justification report.

A major weakness of the visualizations of the articles of the bill was mentioned by the legal expert involved in this focus-group discussion. In particular, she argued that in the visualizations of the articles all the different types of settlements included were represented by a single type of node ('settlement node'); she added that this is not acceptable, since there are quite different kinds of legal rules, such as prohibitive, imperative, permitting and presumptions (Georgiadis, 1997; Lingeropoulos, 2002), which should be represented by different types of nodes. Also, in these visualizations of the articles the sequence of reading these 'settlement' nodes should be indicated, and follow their sequence of the corresponding settlements in the text of the bill, since some of them were associated with previous ones.

AN EXTENSION OF IBIS FRAMEWORK

Based on the conclusions of the evaluation we proceeded to an improvement of our approach to the visualization of the bills' articles. In particular, we enriched the typology of nodes provided by the IBIS framework and the Compendium tool, by refining the 'settlement' type, taking into account the classification of rules proposed by jurisprudence (Georgiadis, 1997; Lingeropoulos, 2002), into the following five types:

a) **Prohibitive Rule**: They are rules imposing to abstain from a particular behavior or excluding a particular outcome. Such prohibitions are often accompanied with sanctions in the case of violation (e.g. invalidity, forfeiture of a right, obligation of reimbursement). These rules are usually expressed using the verb "prohibit". For instance, a minor is prohibited, without the consent of his/her guardian, to acknowledge the obligation or expropriation of his/her property.

b) **Imperative Rule:** They are rules which impose a positive behaviour. These rules are usually expressed using the verbs "owes to", or "has to", or "must", etc. For instance, the banks have to report some types of transactions (e.g. ones for which there is a suspicion of association with fraudulent activities) to the Ministry of Finance.

c) **Permitting Rule:** They are rules which recognize to a person a certain authority or permit to it a certain action. These rules are usually expressed using the verbs "can", or "has a right to", etc. For instance, a minor who has completed his 14th year of age can dispose, without the consent of his/her guardian, everything that he/she gains from his/her work.

d) **Legal Presumption:** These are the outcomes which the law defines that should be initially deduced as far as unknown incidents are concerned, from other known ones, in order to facilitate the judge to find out the truth or the untruth of litigants' pleas, for which finding evidence is impossible or very difficult. For instance, a child who took birth during the marriage of his parents is initially presumed that has got for father the man to whom his mother is married to (except evidence for the opposite is presented).

e) **Settlement:** With this type will be modeled rules defined in bills' articles, which do not belong to any of the above four types

In Figure 9 we can see the new visualization of the content of the seventh article of this bill using the above enriched typology of nodes (its initial visualization appears in Figure 4).

CONCLUSION

In the previous sections has been described a comprehensive approach to the use of CSAV in the legislation formation process, aiming to support and enhance e-participation in it. This approach

Figure 9. New visualization of the content of the 7th article of the bill

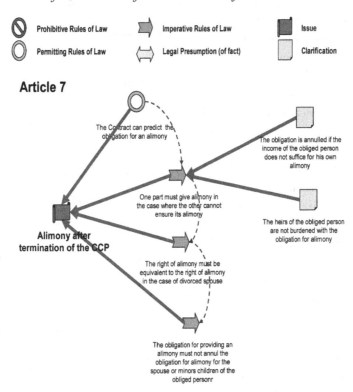

has been designed based on a careful and detailed analysis of this process, its stages and documents. This analysis revealed that the legislation formation process includes some fundamental stages, which are strictly defined by law, producing some fundamental documents. Therefore in order to give to the citizens and civil society groups interested to participate in the formation of a bill a complete picture of it, it is necessary to provide them a set of visualizations, including both i) 'individual' visualizations of these fundamental documents (justification report, main content of the bill (articles), position of each of the experts and stakeholders' representatives invited in the competent Parliamentary committee, position of each political party), and also ii) synthetic visualizations, combining information from several fundamental documents of parts of them (e.g. showing all strengths, weaknesses and suggestions mentioned by the stakeholders' representatives and experts invited in the competent Parliamentary

committee, or by the main speakers of the political parties). This was the base of our approach. Also, for these visualizations we decided to use initially the IBIS framework for representing wicked problems, as it is well established and mature, and at the same time provides a simple, understandable and powerful typology of nodes, which have been proved to be sufficient for the representation of wicked problems in various domains, including politics.

A pilot application of this approach has been conducted, as part of a pilot e-participation project in the Greek Parliament, concerning the bill on the 'Contract of Voluntary Cohabitation. This application has been evaluated through a qualitative in-depth discussion in focus-group based on the 'Technology Acceptance Model' (TAM). From this evaluation it has been concluded that these visualizations are understandable to a rather good extent, after some initial time period required for familiarization. Also, it has been concluded that they are useful, as they can significantly help citizens to understand more easily and quickly the content of the fundamental documents of the legislation formation process, enabling a more meaningful and effective participation in it. However, the IBIS framework was found to be insufficient for the representation of the different types of settlements that the articles of a bill include; for this reason an enrichment of this framework was developed, based on the classification of rules according to the jurisprudence, which improves the visualization of the main content of bills and laws.

Our findings provide a first evidence of a good potential of using CSAV in the legislation formation process for supporting and enhancing public participation in it (both off-line and on-line). Appropriate use of CSAV can make the complex political debate on new legislation more understandable by the citizens and the civil society, and therefore increase the quantity and quality of their participation; it can contribute to countering the observed trend towards an 'elitist model' of democracy, in which managers and experts have the main role in addressing the complex social problems and needs and public participation is limited. Therefore CSAV can have a positive impact on the 'public sphere', both in the traditional and 'virtual' sense (i.e. based on ICT and Internet), in all the three 'institutional criteria' suggested in the relevant analysis of Habermas (1962): inclusivity, disregard of status and common concern. The use of such technological tools can make the political debate more inclusive, so that more citizens (of various educational or knowledge levels and statuses) can express their opinions and concerns. Further research is required towards exploring and exploiting this potential of CSAV, in different stages of the lifecycle of public policies, programs and legislation, for different purposes, audiences and cultures.

REFERENCES

Barber, B. (1984). *Strong democracy*. Berkeley, CA: University of California Press.

Conklin, J. (2003). Dialog mapping: Reflections on an industrial strength case study. In Kirschner, P., Buckingham Shum, S., & Carr, C. (Eds.), *Visualizing argumentation: Software tools for collaborative and educational sense-making*. London, UK: Springer Verlag.

Conklin, J., & Begeman, M. (1989). gIBIS: A tool for all reasons. *Journal of the American Society for Information Science American Society for Information Science, 40*(3), 200–213. doi:10.1002/(SICI)1097-4571(198905)40:3<200::AID-ASI11>3.0.CO;2-U

Davis, F. D. (1989). Perceived usefulness, perceived ease of use and user acceptance of Information Technology. *Management Information Systems Quarterly, 13*(3), 319–340. doi:10.2307/249008

Davis, F. D., Bagozzi, R. P., & Warshaw, P. R. (1989). User acceptance of computer technology: A comparison of two theoretical models. *Management Science, 35*(8), 982–1003. doi:10.1287/mnsc.35.8.982

Elliman, T., Macintosh, A., & Irani, Z. (2007). A model building tool to support group deliberation. *International Journal of Cases on Electronic Commerce, 3*(3), 33–44.

Fishkin, J. S. (1991). *Democracy and deliberation*. New Haven, CT: Yale University Press.

Habermas, J. (in German 1962, English Translation 1989). *The structural transformation of the public sphere: An inquiry into a category of bourgeois society*. Cambridge MA: The MIT Press.

Held, D. (1987). *Models of participation. Cambridge, UK: Polity Press. Georgiadis, A. (1997). General principles of civil law*. Athens, Greece: Sakkoulas Publications.

Kirschner, P., Buckingham Shum, S., & Carr, C. (2003). *Visualizing argumentation: Software tools for collaborative and educational sense-making*. London, UK: Springer Verlag.

Kunz, W., & Rittel, H. (1979). *Issues as elements of Information Systems*. (Working Paper No. 131). Berkley, CA: University of California Press. Retrieved from http://www-iurd.ced.berkeley.edu/pub/WP-131.pdf

Lingeropoulos, A. (2002). *Lectures of Roman law. Classical legal library* (*Vol. 32*). Athens, Greece: Sakkoulas Publications.

Loukis, E., Wimmer, M., Charalabidis, Y., Triantafillou, A., & Gatautis, R. (2007). Argumentation systems and ontologies for enhancing public participation in the legislation process. In M. Wimmer, H. Scholl, & A. Grönlund (Eds.), *Proceedings of EGOV 2007 International Conference*, (LNCS 4656). Regensburg, Germany: Springer Verlag.

Macintosh, A. (2004). *Characterizing e-participation in policy making*. Paper presented at the 37th Hawaii International Conference on System Sciences.

Macintosh, A., Gordon, T. F., & Renton, A. (2009). Providing argument support for e-participation. *Journal of Information Technology & Politics, 6*, 43–59. doi:10.1080/19331680802662113

Macpherson, C. B. (1977). *The life and times of liberal democracy*. London, UK; New York, NY: Oxford University Press.

Ohl, R. (2008). Computer supported argument visualisation: Modelling in consultative democracy around wicked problems. In Okada, A., Buckingham Shum, S., & Sherborne, T. (Eds.), *Knowledge cartography: Software tools and mapping techniques*. London, UK: Springer.

Organisation for Economic Cooperation and Development. (2003a). *Citizens as partners–information, consultation and public participation in policy-making*. Paris, France: OECD.

Organisation for Economic Cooperation and Development. (2004b). *Promise and problems of e-democracy: Challenges of online citizen engagement*. Paris, France: OECD.

Organization for Economic Co-operation and Development. (2003b). *Engaging citizens online for better policy-making: Policy brief*. Paris, France: OECD.

Organization for Economic Co-operation and Development. (2004a). *Evaluating public participation in policy making*. Paris, France: OECD.

Pateman, C. (1970). *Participation and democratic theory*. Cambridge, UK: University Press.

Renton, A. (2006). Seeing the point of politics: Exploring the use of CSAV techniques as aids to understanding the content of political debates in the Scottish Parliament. *Artificial Intelligence and Law, 14*, 277–304. doi:10.1007/s10506-007-9040-6

Renton, A., & Macintosh, A. (2005). Exploiting argument mapping techniques to support policy making. In K. V. Andersen, A. Gronlund, R. Traunmueller, & M. Wimmer (Eds.), *Electronic government: Workshop and poster proceedings of the Fourth International Conference – EGOV*. Linz, Germany: Trauner Verlag.

Renton, A., & Macintosh, A. (2007). Computer supported argument maps as a policy memory. *Information Society Journal, 23*(2), 125–133. doi:10.1080/01972240701209300

Rittel, H. W. J., & Weber, M. M. (1973). Dilemmas in a general theory of planning. *Policy Sciences, 4*, 155–169. doi:10.1007/BF01405730

Rowe, G., & Frewer, L. J. (2004). Evaluating public-participation exercises: A research agenda. *Science, Technology & Human Values, 29*(4), 512–557. doi:10.1177/0162243903259197

Selvin, A., Shum, S. B., & Sierhuis, M. (2001). *Compendium: Making meetings into knowledge event*. Paper presented at Knowledge Technologies, Austin, Texas.

Timmers, P. (2007). *Agenda for e-democracy–an EU perspective*. European Commission.

Toulmin, S. (1958). *The uses of argument*. Cambridge, UK: University Press.

Venkatesh, V., Morris, M. G., Davis, G. B., & Davis, F. D. (2003). User acceptance of Information Technology: Toward a unified view. *Management Information Systems Quarterly*, 27(3), 425–478.

Wingmore, H. J. A. (1913). *The principles of judicial proof as given by logic, psychology, and general experience and illustrated in judicial trials*. Boston, MA: Little Brown.

Chapter 9
The Role of Trust in the Global Acceptance of E–Government

John J. Burbridge Jr.
Elon University, USA

Jayoti Das
Elon University, USA

Cassandra E. DiRienzo
Elon University, USA

ABSTRACT

Throughout the world, the number of e-government applications enabled by information and communication technologies (ICT) is proliferating. Some of the newer applications allow for interaction between government officials and its citizenry. As a result, the concept of a public sphere and e-democracy is becoming more of a reality. In all of these applications, one would expect that the level of trust within the society would be an important factor in determining the level of adoption. Using cross-country data from 140 countries, this empirical study extends past research by examining the impact of trust on the level of e-government where national diversity is used as a proxy of trust within a nation. The major empirical finding of this research shows that, even after controlling for the level of economic development and other socio-economic factors, trust as measured by ethnic and religious diversity, was a significant factor affecting e-government usage.

INTRODUCTION

In today's global economy, a country's level of e-government, or the use of information and communication technology (ICT) to provide government services, has emerged as an important policy tool for government. Recent studies indicate that

the use of e-government is growing throughout the world (Mossberger, Tolbert, and Stansbury, 2003 and Larsen & Rainie, 2002). Formally defined as "the delivery of government information and services online via the Internet or other digital means" (West 2000, page 1), e-government offers many benefits to its major stakeholders.

Implemented properly, it can be a cost effective method to deliver public services which can result

DOI: 10.4018/978-1-60960-159-1.ch009

in significant gains for the national economy. E-government initiatives also foster competitiveness by further enabling the integration of a country into the global community. A country that engages in e-government signals to the international community that it is open, transparent, and efficient, and creates an environment conducive to its users by streamlining procedures and providing easy access to a variety of public services (Thomas & Streib, 2003 and Peterson & Seifert, 2002). While the emphasis in e-government applications has been on providing information and services, a subtle shift has been occurring with ICT becoming the means to involve citizens in the democratic process. The recent election of President Barack Obama in the United States (U.S.) and some of the initiatives his administration is encouraging can best be described as open systems allowing the citizenry to have a stronger voice in arriving at national decisions or policy (Lyons and Stone, 2008).

As a result of such efforts and other worldwide initiatives, ICT is now enabling the concept of a public sphere, first proposed by Habermas (1962). The public sphere is a societal entity where people and groups can join together to freely identify and discuss issues, and possibly through such discussion influence political action. It's "a discursive space in which individuals and groups congregate to discuss matters of mutual interest and, where possible, to reach a common judgment" (Hauser 1998, pg. 86). Given its value to a country both in regard to domestic and international relations, it is important to understand the factors that encourage the use of e-government.

To date, the majority of e-government research studies are narrowly defined case studies which are qualitative in nature (Devadoss et al., 2002 and Ke & Wei, 2004). In regard to quantitative research, the primary focus has been on the availability of technical infrastructure and its usage at a country-level, while others have considered how digital technology and online services allow citizens to accomplish tasks easily (West, 2000 and

Steyaert, 2004). Broader studies by West (2003) and United Nations Department of Economic and Social Affairs (UNDESA) (2003) have explored how the use of ICT transforms the role of the government in regard to the level of economic and human development. However, only a few recent studies such as Kovačić (2005), Rose (2005), and Srivastava and Teo (2007) have explored which factors drive the level of e-government within a country. These studies have found that several "hard", socio-economic and institutional factors such as freedom of expression, civil rights, level of development, and infrastructure significantly affect a country's e-government usage. However, little to no research has considered "soft" factors such as trust that can also impact the successful implementation and adoption of e-government. These "soft" factors will become more critical as countries in their e-government pursues the concept of the public sphere and encourage greater participation of citizens in decision-making processes.

This study contributes to the advancements of e-government research by empirically exploring the relationship between trust and e-government globally. Using cross-country data from 140 countries, the relationship between trust and e-government is examined using regression analysis. In addition, cluster analysis is used to explore emerging global patterns in the use of e-government. If trust does indeed emerge as a significant factor as to why countries differ in the level of e-government, policy makers working to enhance e-government usage will also need to consider policies and methods to promote trust. Further, if trust is found to be an important precursor to successful e-government adoption, implementation, and promotion, this study will help lay the foundations for future analyses and provide the first roadmap for such policies and recommendations.

ROLE OF E-GOVERNMENT

At the national or local level, a major role of government is to provide services for its citizens. Major policy initiatives involving taxation and benefit programs such as Social Security could be delivered more effectively and efficiently using such technology. These applications involved massive databases and computation and required supercomputers and/or mainframes. However, the use of technology to deliver such services was not understood by citizens since it was somewhat invisible to them.

The Internet and World Wide Web (WWW) changed this. Using ICT, a transformation in the delivery of services and information has occurred with citizens becoming active participants. Web based interfaces can now be developed to facilitate the inputting of data or receiving information. For example, it is now possible for individuals to input all the relevant information associated with income and deductions and make payment for taxes. In addition, it is also possible for property owners to go online and see all the desired information associated with their properties including satellite pictures. Retirement and social security systems are also in the process of being developed to allow the citizen to access information concerning status. These are just a few of the wide array of applications available through e-government.

Moon (2002) developed a theoretical framework that breaks down the evolution of e-government into five stages – (1) information dissemination/catalog, (2) two way communication, (3) service and financial transactions, (4) vertical and horizontal integration and finally (5) political participation. Ho (2002) further points out that such a transformation is a shift from the standard bureaucratic model where government simply disseminates information to its citizens to a more participative style enabled by ICT. This newer model allows for more direct, transparent, and open communication between all parties.

Such a model is very similar to social networks. In social networks, individuals and/or organizations who share some relationship whether it be a friendship, a cause, or belief become interdependent and can easily interact using ICT. Increasingly, political parties, political platforms and causes, grass root organizations and even some government bodies such as the State of Virginia and Bahrain are using social networks such as Facebook as a means to enhance and encourage participation. Further, as discussed by Erman and Todorovski (2009), social network theory is an area that can be used to enhance e-government research. With social networking, the concept of a virtual public sphere is becoming a reality.

Thus, ICT allows governments today to become social networks with the possibility of engaging in high levels of interaction between the different stakeholders. Nevertheless, for such networks to promote and proliferate while engaging the stakeholders, certain attributes are crucial for members within the network to exist and maintain high levels of participation and continued interest. One fundamental characteristic is the degree of trust that exists between the members. For example, individuals and/or organizations would not participate in social networks if there was not some degree of trust between the members of the network. The "bridging or bonding" type of social capital (Putnam, 1995) that is often exploited by social networks depends crucially on the level of trust that exists between the members and, often this initial trust is the result of the relationship bringing the members together. As discussed in more detail below, groups that are more homogeneous in terms of their ethnicity, language, and religion tend to have similar value systems and greater social cohesion, and thus tend to have greater social capital. These more homogeneous groups tend to communicate more readily and exhibit higher levels of trust. Considering that trust is a factor in social networks, and ICT has allowed governments to function similarly, it can be theorized that trust plays a role in the success and growth of e-government.

ROLE OF TRUST

While the concept of 'social capital' has been contested in the social science literature, many researchers have considered trust as a dimension of 'social capital' or 'civil society'. In particular, Putnam (1995, pg. 67) defines social capital as the "...features of social organization such as networks, norms, and social trust that facilitate coordination and cooperation for mutual benefit". In reference to civil society, Gellner (1994) broadly defines the term as one form of social order, while Persell et al. (2001) describe civil society as consisting of two dimensions; institutional and qualitative. Persell et al. (2001, pg. 206) describe the institutional dimension of civil society as all of the organizations and associations to which people belong and the qualitative dimension of civil society as the "...social attitudes such as loyalty and trust, social practices such as civility and cooperation, and the health and safety of its members." Further, Leana and van Buren III (1999, pg. 538) define the term 'organizational social capital' as "...a resource reflecting the character of social relations within the organization, realized through members' levels of collective goal orientation and shared trust."

Regardless of how this social dimension is defined, a substantial number of studies have found evidence that higher levels social capital, which includes trust, is a catalyst for greater economic growth, development, and prosperity at the institutional, firm, and country-level. Specifically, at the country level, Knack and Keefer (1997) find that higher levels of social capital, as defined by trust and civic norms, lead to greater economic performance. Further, Putnam (1993) and Fukuyama (1995) theorize that social capital, largely defined as trust between social groups, can significantly affect growth and economic

success at the institutional level and Tsai and Ghoshal (1998) find that higher levels of social capital and trust significantly and positively affect product innovation at the firm level. Alesina and La Ferrara (2002, pg. 212) state "...a small but growing literature stresses that measures of 'trust' strictly defined or broader measures of 'social capital' are associated with effective public policies and more successful economic outcomes." In general, this literature finds that greater social capital and civil society, in which there are high levels of trust, leads to enhanced economic growth, development, and innovation. The underlying theory is that societies that enjoy higher levels of trust, or more broadly, societies with greater social capital, tend to have common value systems and communicate and collaborate more effectively. This enhanced communication and collaboration aids government officials and leaders in the implementation of large-scale initiatives such as e-government services. In order for e-government to be successful, it must be readily adopted and widely used. Thus, successful e-government implementation is more likely to occur in societies that exhibit higher levels of trust and are able to communicate and collaborate effectively. In other words, it is theorized that trust plays a critical role in a society's willingness to adopt new government initiatives such as e-government services.

Further, in regard to trust and communication, Granovetter (1973) states that based on social network theory, trust can be transferred to channels of communication which now include e-government. Trust can play an important role in facilitating the development of e-government within a country as any digital medium is a social platform through which individuals interact or transact with other citizens, businesses, or governments. Moore (1999) and Maskell (2000) have cited trust as an important factor in the development of new ideas and a prerequisite for any successful technological change as trust ultimately influences whether innovative ideas and new forms of communication are able to flourish. Further, Volken (2002) states that trust can be viewed as a cultural resource that facilitates innovative actions. Since e-government is considered an innovative technology, its success should be dependent in part on the level of trust between parties. Society must believe in the integrity of the applications and the controlling governmental entities. As discussed in Bélanger et al. (2002) and Lee and Turban (2001), there are privacy and security issues as well as reliability and integrity issues related to electronic commerce which also apply to e-government (Warkentin et al. 2002, and Carter & Bélanger, 2003; 2005).

As noted in the e-government Handbook (2007), the success of e-government projects and ultimately faith in e-governance depends on building trust between agencies, governments, businesses, and citizens. In this light, the success of e-government is dependent on the perceptions of trustworthiness among the stakeholders, as users need to have confidence both in the government and the technology in order to successfully engage in e-government.

With regard to trust itself, the literature provides definitions which generally differ based on the academic discipline (Bhattacharya et al., 1998). Personality psychologists define trust as an individual characteristic while social psychologists view trust from the perspective of behavioral expectations of others (Kim and Prabhakar, 2000). From an organizational behavior perspective, Currall and Judge (1995) define trust as an individual's reliance on another party under conditions of dependence and risk. Further, marketing research has defined trust as the willingness of one party to rely upon and have confidence in an exchange partner (Morgan and Hunt, 1994 and Mooreman et al., 1993). In regard to ethics, Baier (1986) defines trust as the reliance on others ability to properly care for things that have been assigned to their custody or supervision, which can include such tangible things such as money or children or intangible things such as democracy and societal norms (Tschannen-Moran and Hoy, 2000). In rela-

tion to information technology (IT), Gefen et al. (2005, pg. 54) states that to trust means to have expectations about others' behavior and that "One of the central effects of this trust in the context of IT adoption is to increase the perceived usefulness (PU) of Information Technology (IT) associated with the trustee's agency." It can be inferred from the above literature that trust is an important piece in the adoption and acceptance of e-government activities and services.

Measuring Trust

Given its intangible nature, trust is challenging to quantify and measure. In regard to social trust, Fukuyama (2001) discusses the difficulty of measuring it and Collier (2002) stated that trust is essentially impossible to measure directly and that for empirical evaluations, proxy indicators are necessary. Researchers have generally created measures of trust derived from surveys that were developed for specific studies or have used responses from the World Values Survey (WVS) (Knack and Keefer, 1997, La Porta et al., 1997, Glaeser et al., 2000, Collier (2002), and Johansson-Stenman et al., 2005). The studies which have developed their own surveys have generally focused on particular regions and are limited in scope and, as pointed out by Collier (2002), the data are only available for 45 countries and, of the country data available, the majority of the countries are industrialized and the transitioning countries are under-represented.

Alternatively, there is a growing literature which suggests that diversity, as measured by ethnic, linguistic, and / or religious heterogeneity, can be an appropriate proxy for the level of trust within a society. Other studies that use diversity as a proxy for trust, such as Putnam (1995), find that the greater the diversity within a community, the less likely neighbors will trust each other and, in general, greater diversity yields lower levels of trust. Similarly, Fukuyama (1995) argues that within a society there is a boundary of trust such that people in relationships within that boundary are trusted more than people outside that boundary and Glaeser et al. (2000) find that trust is easier to facilitate among people that are homogeneous ethnically, linguistically or religiously. Warkentin et al. (2002) establishes the connection between group diversity and the level of trust by stating that differences among groups will increase the likelihood of distrust between the groups. Newton and Delhey (2005) and Anderson and Paskeviciute (2006) find that greater levels of ethnic diversity are associated with lower levels of trust at the country level and Van Parijs (2004) suggests that the welfare of a nation or government is negatively affected by diversity. Further, in an Australian study, Leigh (2006) finds that trust is lower in ethnically and linguistically diverse communities and Johansson-Stenman et al. (2005) find that different religious affiliations significantly affect trust.

In summary, this research suggests that the greater the diversity, the lower the level of trust. The underlying theory in this literature is that diverse groups tend to have different value systems and different agendas, both socially and politically. Given these varied agendas and values, the implication is that there is less of the 'bridging and bonding' type of social capital and generally less social cohesion, communication, and collaboration. Thus, this increased fragmentation leads to lower levels of trust between groups. As stated above, it is challenging to quantify and measure trust, however, an appropriate proxy for trust is the degree of diversity within the society. While arguably not a perfect measure, diversity can capture the degree of fractionalization within the society and approximate the level of trust. Therefore, measures of diversity are used in this study to proxy trust.

Specifically, the Fractionalization Index created by Alesina et al. (2003), which separately measures ethnic (*E*), linguistic (*L*), and religious (*R*) diversity for 190 countries, is used in this study. Alesina et al. (2003) employs the Herfin-

dahl methodology and the index represents the probability that two randomly selected individuals from a population belong to different groups. The Fractionalization Index is computed in the following manner:

$$FRACT_j = 1 - \sum_{i=1}^{N} s_{ij}^{2},$$

where s_{ij} is the share of the group i ($i = 1,.....N$) in country j. A measure close to 0 would imply a less diverse or more homogenized society, while a measure closer to 1 suggests the opposite. Thus, the larger the fractionalization index the more diverse the society.

Using this measure, countries in Sub-Saharan Africa show the highest degree of fractionalization for all measures; ethnicity 0.66, linguistic 0.63, and religious diversity 0.50. The least ethnically fractionalized countries are South Korea and Japan. Countries in western and southern Europe reflects low levels of ethnic diversity (0.18), linguistic diversity (0.20), and religious diversity (0.31) on average, while the U.S. was found to be more ethnically, linguistically, and religiously diverse compared to most of Europe. Furthermore, South Africa, the U.S., and Australia were found to be the most religiously diverse countries. Low levels of religious diversity were predominantly Catholic (Italy and Ireland), Protestant (Scandinavia), and of course, Muslim countries.

Measuring E-Government

Several measures of e-government focus on either a country's potential to engage in e-government (Economist Intelligence Units, 2004), or a country's actual level of e-government related activities (World Economic Forum, 2007). The measure of e-government used in this analysis, the E-government Index 2005 (*EGOV*) developed by the United Nations (U.N.), incorporates both the potential for and the implementation of e-government and is

Figure 1. Composite Model Illustration

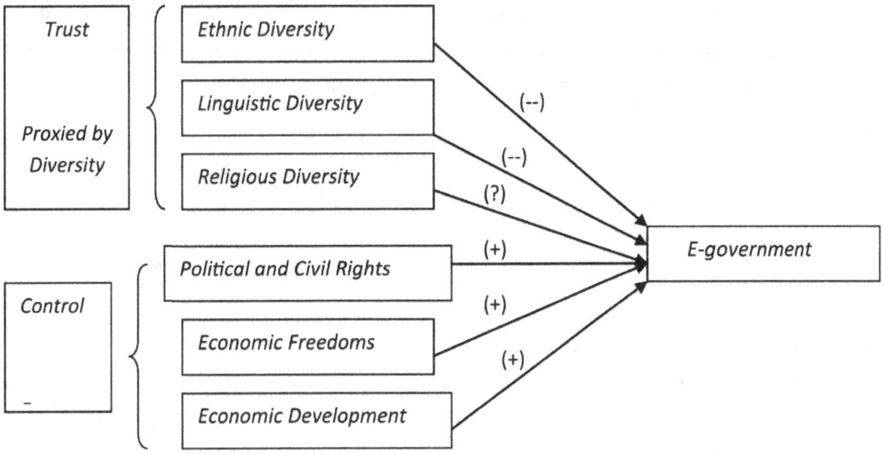

the most complete assessment of e-government across countries (Singh, et al. 2004).

The *EGOV* or e-government readiness index is an average of the (1) telecommunication infrastructure index, (2) the human capital index and (3) the web measure index as created and defined by the U.N. This composite index captures the overall ability of a country to engage and implement e-government. It is important to note that this index includes the two major factors important for presence and diffusion of e-government, infrastructure and education, while the web measure is intended to capture the attitude of governments to inform, transact, and network. The index ranges from zero (low levels of e-government) to one (high levels of e-government).

For example, the U.S. has the highest value of *EGOV* (0.9062) and is followed by northern European countries such as Denmark (0.9058) and Sweden (0.8983). Among the developing countries, the Republic of Korea (0.8727) and Singapore (0.8503) lead with Estonia (0.7347), Malta (0.7012), and Chile (0.6963) following. Regionally, Europe and North America generally have greater values of *EGOV* while South-Central Asia and Africa lag behind.

EMPIRICAL METHODOLOGY

This section describes the general model used to test the relationship between trust, as proxied by diversity, and e-government. A discussion of the regression model and the hypothesized relationships between the three different measures of diversity and e-government, in addition to the control variables and their data measures follows. In an effort to provide a visual synopsis of the discussion, Figure 1 provides a graphical representation of the research model.

Ethnic Diversity

Much research (Alesina & La Ferrara 2002; Delhey & Newton, 2004; Leigh, 2006; and Zak & Knack, 2001) has found that ethnic homogeneity raises social capital, which includes trust. Such research has found that social capital makes it easier to develop social networks that disseminate information and knowledge. In contrast, Collier (1998) finds that cultural and ethnic heterogeneity tend to hamper nation-building as such societies are more prone to polarization and social conflict. Further, Mauro (1995) finds a negative correlation between ethno-linguistic fractionalization and political stability, bureaucratic efficiency, and institutional efficiency, while Shleifer and Vishny (1993) find that ethnically diverse societies are likely to have higher rates of corruption and less trust. Annett (2001) and Ritzen et al. (2001) also find that ethnic diversity results in poor quality of government services and institutions. Several others such as Rodrick (1999) and Svensson (1998) note that ethnically polarized societies cause governments to marginalize investment in legal infrastructure. This research has also found that ethnically diverse countries tend to experience more bureaucratic, institutional, and political inefficiency as well as inferior government services and infrastructure. The underlying theory in this literature is that ethnic diversity creates barriers to communication between groups and weakens collaboration, which generally hinders country development and innovation, such as e-government implementation. Thus, it can be hypothesized that:

H1: *Countries that are more ethnically fractionalized than others experience lower levels of e-government.*

Linguistic Diversity

Linguistic heterogeneity reduces trust both at the native and immigrant level, as it often fails to promote equal treatment of the diverse languages and reduces the quality of information transmitted across different groups (Cook & Cooper, 2003). Leigh (2006) finds that trust is lower in linguistically heterogeneous communities; however, Delhey and Newton (2004) find no relation between linguistic heterogeneity and trust. Empirical studies by Mauro (1995), Annett (2001), and Barro (1999) find that linguistic diversity causes greater political instability and inefficient public policies due to increased transaction costs. However linguistically homogenous societies have historically been more effective in communicating new ideas among themselves making the adoption of a *lingua franca* important. Since e-government represents a platform for communication and networking

across agencies, and linguistic heterogeneity decreases the quality of information and, often, trust amongst its citizens and agencies, it can be hypothesized that:

H2: *Countries that are more linguistically fractionalized experience lower levels of e-government.*

Religious Diversity

Alesina and Ferrara (2002) state that trust is influenced by individual's religious beliefs as different religions have different attitudes toward social interactions. Some believe that religious fundamentalists are less trusting of diverse religious groups (Uslaner, 2002), while others contend that certain religious beliefs like protestant ethics promote higher levels of trust (Inglehart & Baker, 2000). Since most religious doctrines contain some elements that promote trust and some elements that set boundaries or limitations on trust, classifying some religious beliefs as promoting trust and not others is speculative. Further, while a religiously homogenous society may be more trusting of each other, intolerance towards a minority religion can develop and a more religiously diverse society can be more accepting of other religious affiliations and beliefs.

Studies examining religious allegiance and trust have not found a significant relationship between the two (Johansson-Stenman et al., 2006; Alesina & Ferrara, 2002; and Delhey & Newton, 2004). Although religious diversity has been linked with inefficiencies in the distribution of public goods and government, drawing any clear conclusion regarding the presence of different religions within a country and its effect on civic engagement and e-government is not readily apparent (Banerjee et al., 2005). Therefore, the hypothesis regarding religious diversity and e-government is stated:

H3: *A country's degree of religious fractionalization will have no impact on e-government.*

Control Factors

Before a statistical analysis examining the relationship between trust, as proxied by diversity, and e-government can be performed, the other socioeconomic and institutional factors that are known to affect e-government need to be controlled in order to prevent model misspecification. As noted by Easterly and Levine (2001) and Alesina et. al (1999) institutional factors such as education, role of governance, and political systems often mitigate the effect of diversity. For example, ethnic and linguistic diversity can have a greater adverse effect on a country's level of trust and e-government if there is a lack of institutional stability and democratic processes are hampered.

Political Rights and Civil Liberties

A democratic society usually reflects greater openness, freedom of expression, civil rights, and political stability and are generally more successful in regard to the development of e-government. Moon et al. (2005) state that countries with less democratic governments tend to marginally employ e-government as such governments generally do not want to engage in transparent and interactive relations with citizens or other agencies. Further, West (2003) suggests that a country's level of political development is critical in determining its level of commitment to e-government. Advocates of democracy and freedom of communication consider political and civil liberties as a necessity for greater access to government and public services (Zinnbauer, 2001). As stated by Rose (2005), the greater the acceptance of civil liberties and freedom of expression the greater the provision of any digital e-facility. Therefore, it can be hypothesized that:

H4: *Countries with higher levels of democratic and political freedom experience higher levels of e-government.*

The 2004 Political Rights (*PR*) and Civil Liberties (*CL*) indices by Freedom House are used to proxy the democracy afforded to the citizens. Freedom House conducts an annual survey concerning civil liberties and political rights in nations, emphasizing the importance of democracy and freedom. The indices are created using a survey method to judge all countries by a single standard which emphasizes the importance of democracy and freedom. In a free society, political rights allow people to participate freely in the political process, including the right to vote, compete for public office, and to elect representatives. Civil liberties include the freedom of expression and media independence, the right to associate and organize the rule of law, and personal autonomy without interference from the state. Rates are assigned separately to political rights and civil liberties on a scale of one to seven, with one representing the most free and seven the least. Following Klitgaard et al. (2005), the average of a country's *PR* and *CL* rates (noted *PCR*) is used in this analysis to represent a country's level of democratic freedom.

Economic Freedom

According to Ciborra and Navarra (2003), the pre-conditions for e-government are stability and an open economy and Watson and Mundy (2001) suggest that institutions favoring poor governance practices might actually resist the growth of e-government. Singh et al. (2004) state that an economically free nation with a stable legal and monetary system, efficient labor and product markets, and open trade and investment opportunities, provides a more competitive and dynamic environment in which e-government could flourish. Further, Rose (2005) states that if governments are more open with higher levels of institutional freedom, they are more receptive to e-government compared to countries with higher levels of economic and social instability and inefficient bureaucracies. Therefore, it can be hypothesized that:

H5: *Countries with higher levels of economic and institutional freedom experience higher levels of e-government.*

The 2004 Index of Economic Freedom (*EFI*) by the Heritage Foundation is used to capture distortions across institutional factors such as economic restrictions and barriers within a country. The EFI index considers 50 economic freedom variables which are divided into ten broad categories; trade policy, fiscal burden of government, government intervention in the economy, monetary policy, capital flows and foreign investment, banking and finance, wages and prices, property rights, regulation, and informal market activity. Each of these categories is assigned a score and then these 10 categories are averaged and an overall economic freedom score between one (most economically free) and five (least economically free) is assigned to each country. The Heritage Foundation classifies the economic freedoms afforded to a country in four broad categories: "Free", countries with an average overall score of 1.99 or less; "Mostly Free", countries with an average overall score of 2.00 to 2.99; "Mostly Un-free", countries with an average overall score of 3.00 to 3.99; and "Repressed", countries with an average overall score of 4.00 or higher.

Economic Development

Finally, it is necessary to control for the existing level of economic development within a country. Norris (2001) finds that more affluent industrialized economies are more conducive to online access to governments and the digital divide often creates a poor-information society. Hargittai (1999) finds economic wealth as measured by Gross Domestic Product (GDP) per capita to be an essential ingredient in promoting digital platforms. Further, Kaufmann (2004) states that countries

with higher per capita GDP are better able to afford and support e-government and Rose (2005) cites GDP per capita, urbanization, personal computers, and telephone lines per thousand people as being important in the development of e-government. Finally, Singh et al. (2004) emphasize the role of human capital and existing Information and Communication Technology (ICT) infrastructure in the growth and development of e-government. Therefore, it can be hypothesized that:

H6: Countries that enjoy higher levels of economic development will have higher levels of e-government.

GDP per capita (measured in constant 2000 U.S. dollars) is used to represent a country's level of economic development and was collected from the World Bank (2004). GDP per capita is selected to proxy economic development as other measures of economic development, such as the Human Development Index, include sub-indices that incorporate human capital measures. As discussed in the following section, e-government is proxied by an index that includes human capital. Thus, GDP per capita is employed in this study to proxy economic development in order to prevent model misspecification.

Descriptive Statistics

A sample of 140 countries is used to test the previously stated hypotheses. *EGOV* represents 2005 data, while the data for the control variables represents 2004 data, with the exception the *E*, *L*, and *R* which are only available for 2003. The control variables are appropriately lagged as their affect on *EGOV* cannot be expected to occur immediately. Table 1 provides a summary and descriptive statistics of the variables used in the analysis.

Table 2 provides the correlation matrix for all of the variables. Each of the variables was tested for normality using the Jacque-Bera test for nor-

Table 1. Variable Summary and Descriptive Statistics

Variable	Proxy	Mean*	St. Deviation*
E-government	E-government Index (*EGOV*)	0.465	0.204
Ethnic Diversity	Ethnic Fractionalization Index (*E*)	0.452	0.254
Linguistic Diversity	Linguistic Fractionalization Index (*L*)	0.397	0.284
Religious Diversity	Religious Fractionalization Index (*R*)	0.440	0.238
Political Rights / Civil Liberties	Freedom House (*PCR*)	3.275	1.858
Economic Freedom**	Economic Freedom Index (*EFI*)	1.076	0.235
Economic Development**	GDP per capita (*GDPPC*)	7.742	1.602

*n = 140

** A series of scatter plots and tests indicated that the relationships between *EFI* and *EGOV* and *GDPPC* and *EGOV* are log-linear and that the relationship between natural logarithm of each of these controls with *EGOV* was linear. Therefore, the natural log of both *EFI* and *GDPPC* were taken before the regression analysis was performed and the statistics above are based on the natural log of each of these variables.

mality. At 95% confidence, each of the variables, with the exception of *EGOV* was found to be non-normal. Given that one of the assumptions for the Pearson measure of correlation is normality, the Spearman rank correlation was used to measure the correlation between all of the variables and these results are presented in Table 2.

As seen in Table 2, *E* is positively and significantly correlated with *PCR* and *LnEFI* and negatively and significantly correlated with *LnGDPPC*. These correlation measures suggest that countries with greater ethnic diversity tend to have lower levels of political rights and civil liberties (higher values of the *PCR* index indicate less freedoms), economic freedoms (higher values of the *EFI* index indicate less freedom) and economic development. Similar to ethnic diversity,

L is positively and significantly correlated with *PCR* and *LnEFI* and negatively and significantly correlated with *LnGDPPC* which suggest that countries with greater linguistic diversity tend to have lower levels of political rights and civil liberties, economic freedoms, and economic development. Finally, there are no significant correlation measures between religious diversity and the control variables.

In regard to e-government, *EGOV* is significantly and negatively correlated with *E*, *L*, *PCR*, and *LnEFI*. These relationships suggest that countries with higher *EGOV* values tend to have less ethnic and linguistic diversity and more political rights, civil liberties, and economic freedom. *EGOV* is significantly and positively correlated with *LnGDPPC* which suggests that countries

Table 2. Spearman Correlation Matrix

	EGOV	E	L	R	PCR	LnEFI	LnGDPPC
EGOV	1						
E	-0.595**	1					
L	-0.494**	0.686**	1				
R	-0.023	0.267**	0.315**	1			
PCR	-0.679**	0.363**	0.280**	-0.014	1		
LnEFI	-0.708**	0.405**	0.326**	0.015	0.703**	1	
LnGDPPC	0.869**	-0.555**	-0.525**	-0.098	-0.597**	-0.724**	1

*p< 0.05 **p< 0.01

that are more economically developed tend to have higher levels of e-government. Finally, the correlation between religious diversity, *R* and *EGOV* is not significant. These correlations suggest existing interrelationships amongst the variables, without establishing any definite causal relationship. In order to explore the directional role of trust and e-government across countries, a regression analysis is performed.

FINDINGS

To test the previously stated hypotheses, an ordinary least squares regression analysis was performed. The regression equation is defined as:

$$EGOV = \beta_o + \beta_1 E_1 + \beta_2 L_2 + \beta_3 R_3 \\ + \beta_4 PCR + \beta_5 LnEFI + \beta_6 LnGDPPC$$

The Ordinary Least Squares (OLS) regression results are presented in Table 3. The significance levels of the coefficient estimates, the Adjusted R^2 value, and the *F* statistic indicate that the regression model provides a good fit to the data.

Tests for multicollinearity and heteroscedasticity validate the results shown in Table 3. The test of multicollinearity for each of the independent variables using the variance-inflation factor (VIF) shows that the VIF values range from 1.139 to 2.90. Given that VIF values greater than 5.3 have

been suggested as cutoffs (Hair et al., 1992), multicollinearity does not appear to be a problem in this analysis. Furthermore, White's (1980) general test for heteroscedasticity indicates that the residuals are homoscedastic suggesting that the regression results were not influenced by heteroscedasticity.

The regression allows the coefficients associated with *E, L*, and *R*, to be interpreted as the marginal effect of an increase in each of the factors on *EGOV*, holding all other independent variables constant. The results show that the coefficient on ethnic fractionalization is significant and negative suggesting that the marginal impact of becoming heterogeneous with regard to ethnic diversity (going from zero to one) results in an average decline of approximately 0.14 of a country's level of *EGOV*. This suggests that, while controlling for other factors known to affect e-government, countries with greater levels of ethnic diversity have lower levels of e-government on average, which supports H1.

The coefficient on linguistic fractionalization is negative, but not significant. The negative sign supports H2; however, the coefficient is insignificant which suggests that linguistic diversity does not significantly affect e-government which is contrary to H2. This result is not surprising as Alesina et al. (2003) state that there is a high correlation between ethnic and linguistic fractionalization measures and in regression analyses

Table 3. Regression Results

	Coefficient Estimates	Std Err	t Stat	VIF
Intercept	0.07507	0.10703	0.70	0
E	-0.13975**	0.04199	-3.33	2.204
L	-0.00351	0.03771	-0.09	2.218
R	0.08976**	0.03224	2.78	1.139
PCR	-0.01832**	0.00519	-3.53	1.806
LnEFI	-0.11249*	0.05224	-2.15	2.900
LnGDPPC	0.07692**	0.00761	10.10	2.880

Adj. R^2 = 0.8282 *F* stat = 112.68** *p <0.05; **p<0.01

often, linguistic diversity is insignificant when ethic diversity is included in the analysis. The implication is that when variables such as political and economic freedom and level of development are accounted for, linguistic diversity does not significantly affect e-government.

Finally, the coefficient on religious fractionalization was found to be positive and significant which does not support H3. As previously discussed, religious diversity can potentially have positive and negative effects on e-government and making general statements or hypotheses regarding the impact of religious diversity on e-government would be speculative. However, in this analysis, the positive effects, such as the possibility of religiously diverse societies to be more tolerant and trusting, outweighed the possible negative effects of religious diversity and countries with more religious diversity or religious freedom engage in higher levels of e-government on average. The marginal impact of becoming heterogeneous with regard to religion (going from zero to one) results in an average increase of approximately 0.09 of a country's level of *EGOV*.

All three of the control variables in this study prove to be relevant. The coefficient on *PCR* is statistically significant and negatively related to *EGOV* which confirms H4. Thus, countries with higher levels of democratic and political freedom experience higher levels of e-government on average. The coefficient on *LnEFI* was found to be negative and significant suggesting that countries with higher levels of economic and institutional freedom experience higher levels of e-government on average, thus supporting H5. Finally, the coefficient on *LnGDPPC* is positive and significant, supporting H6 that an economically prosperous country is more likely to advance e-government efforts.

In summary, the results of the cross country regression analysis suggest that both ethnic and religious diversity significantly affect a country's level of e-government even after controlling for such factors as democratic and economic free-

dom and economic development. The findings indicate that, on average, countries that are less diversified with respect to ethnicity, more diversified in terms of religion, have greater levels of political, civil, and economic freedoms, and higher levels of economic development enjoy greater levels of e-government. In other words, a developed country with higher levels of social ethnic cohesion and more freedoms accorded to them in terms of religion, politics and economics, are the ones likely to engage in higher levels of e-government indicating broader access to political thoughts and ideas based on a certain level of trust. Thus, trust does play a significant role especially among groups from similar ethinicity that bond across social platforms and dynamically engage in e-government.

The cross country regression results are general and show the broad relationships between the variables across all countries. In an effort to identify possible emerging global trends in e-government, a country-based cluster analysis is performed in the following section. The cluster analysis is designed to divide the countries into groups based on their similarity in regard to all significant variables from the regression analysis.

Cluster Analysis

A cluster analysis is used to group the 140 countries into distinct clusters using trust, socio-economic, and institutional variables as the criteria. The independent variables, with the exception of linguistic diversity (as it is not significant at 5% level), are used as the country characteristics upon which the clusters are formed. A cluster analysis groups objects, in this case countries, into groups such that the objects within a group are most similar to each other with respect to specified characteristics and least similar to objects in the other groups. In other words, the cluster analysis groups the individual countries based on how similar or "close" they are in regard to their ethnic and religious diversity, economic freedom, political and civil liberties and level of development.

A non-hierarchical cluster analysis is performed using the squared Euclidean distance as the measure of how close two countries are in regard to the five variables; *E, R, PCR, LnEFI,* and *LnGDPPC*. This particular type of cluster analysis requires that the number of clusters to be created in the analysis be set prior to performing the analysis. This is an exploratory process, and no hard guidelines have been suggested for determining the number of clusters to be created in a non-hierarchical analysis.

After considering different cluster analysis results, a grouping of two countries clusters was chosen and is presented in Tables 4 and 5. The results can be interpreted as follows. Country Cluster 1 represents the group of countries that are most homogenous in regard to their ethnic and religious fractionalization, political, civil, and economic freedoms, and economic development

Table 4. Country Cluster 1

Albania	Ghana	Nicaragua
Algeria	Guatemala	Niger
Armenia	Guinea	Nigeria
Azerbaijan	Guinea Bissau	Oman
Bahrain	Honduras	Pakistan
Bangladesh	India	Paraguay
Belarus	Indonesia	Philippines
Benin	Iran	Russia
Bolivia	Jordan	Saudi Arabia
Bosnia and Herzegovina	Kazakhstan	Senegal
Burkina Faso	Kenya	Sierra Leone
Cambodia	Kuwait	Sri Lanka
Cameroon	Kyrgyzstan	Swaziland
Central African Republic	Laos	Syria
Chad	Lebanon	Tajikistan
China	Lesotho	Tanzania
Colombia	Libya	Togo
Congo, Republic	Macedonia	Tunisia
Cote d´Ivoire	Madagascar	Turkey
Ecuador	Malawi	Uganda
Egypt	Malaysia	Ukraine
Equatorial Guinea	Mali	United Arab Emirates
Ethiopia	Mauritania	Uzbekistan
Fiji	Moldova	Venezuela
Gabon	Mongolia	Vietnam
Gambia	Morocco	Zambia
Georgia	Mozambique	Zimbabwe
	Nepal	

Table 5. Country Cluster 2

Argentina	Greece	Peru
Australia	Guyana	Poland
Austria	Hungary	Portugal
Belgium	Iceland	Romania
Belize	Ireland	Singapore
Botswana	Israel	Slovakia
Brazil	Italy	Slovenia
Bulgaria	Jamaica	South Africa
Canada	Japan	South Korea
Chile	Latvia	Spain
Costa Rica	Lithuania	Suriname
Croatia	Luxembourg	Sweden
Cyprus	Malta	Switzerland
Czech Republic	Mauritius	Thailand
Denmark	Mexico	Trinidad and Tobago
Dominican Republic	Namibia	United Kingdom
Estonia	Netherlands	Uruguay
Finland	New Zealand	USA
France	Norway	
Germany	Panama	

and most heterogeneous to the Country Cluster 2 with respect to these variables.

Given these country groupings, the differences in the level of e-government across the clusters should be detectable. To explore this theory further, Table 6 provides the mean *EGOV* value for each of the clusters. Cluster 1 has a lower level of *EGOV* compared to Cluster 2. Further, at 99% confidence, a *t*-test indicated that Cluster 1 has a significantly lower mean *EGOV*

Table 6. EGOV Means by Cluster

Clusters	Mean (*EGOV*)	Sample Size
Cluster 1 *Low E-government*	0.336	82
Cluster 2 *High E-government*	0.646	58

level than Cluster 2. Therefore, the cluster analysis demonstrates that if countries are grouped by their similarities in regard to their ethnic and religious fractionalization, political, civil, economic freedoms, and level of economic development, significant differences in their level of e-government can be detected.

Cluster 1 generally includes countries that are less developed and are in the process of enhancing their infrastructure, which will hopefully lead to increased e-government usage. Interestingly, Cluster 1 includes countries like China, India, and Russia that are clearly developing nations with a significant internet infrastructure in place, but perhaps are not as actively engaged in e-government. The urban centers of such countries may be heavy users of commercial internets, but it appears that they do not use the Internet for public service which would reach the greater majority of the population, especially across the rural parts of these countries. Alternatively, Cluster 2 represents countries with high e-government usage and includes developed countries such as the U.S., Sweden, and the United Kingdom as well as emerging nations such as Chile, Slovenia, and Romania that are actively engaged in e-government and represent countries with higher levels of social cohesion and religious as well as economic freedoms rendering higher levels of trust.

In other words, clusters of emerging as well as developed nations may provide a fertile ground for e-government while countries that have restrictive economic, political and civil freedoms with lower levels of development and appear to be more fractionalized do not experience the same level of e-government engagement. One of the crucial ways of disseminating and using public information to bring groups of people together in a civil society and have them actively engage in the democratic process is through e government. In this light, the cluster analysis helps us understand the global patterns in regard to country usage of e-government given the diversity and control variables previously discussed. The policy implications that seem apparent from the cluster analysis is that if nations are to forge ahead and engage in high levels of e-government, they need to first enhance their social and economic prosperity and establish trust among the diverse groups. In order for countries in cluster 2 to experience the same positive impact as countries in cluster 1, they must overcome the challenges faced by the inherent structural issues of ethnic diversity, and low levels of democratic and economic openness as shown by this study. Thus, successfully implementing e-government is not just enhancing ICT and technology across nations, but actually focusing on the social political and development aspects of the entire country in order to provide a successful social e-government networking platform.

DISCUSSION AND POLICY ANALYSIS

It has been argued that e-government promotes overall governance and enhances a country's competitiveness in the global community (Chevallereau, 2005). Countries with high levels of e-government are more open and transparent in their policies and practices. Such countries often engage in higher levels of corporate governance, are better connected with the regional and global community, and can be good investment opportunities as they generally experience lower financial risk. Thus, it is important to recognize the factors that lead to successful e-government adoption and widespread use.

E-government applications have also been linked to country competitiveness. As an example, Singapore has developed sophisticated systems for the assessment, collection, and enforcement of taxes (Kien and Siong, 2000) and facilitating trade with countries throughout the world (Applegate, Neo, and King, 1995). While Singapore's efforts were directed towards infrastructure applications, new applications throughout the world focus more directly on involving the public and, as shown in this study, the public and social capital element, especially in regard to trust, plays an important role in the successful adoption and implementation of e-government.

Overall, the empirical analysis finds that countries that are more ethnically homogeneous and religiously diverse, which may be an indication of religious freedom, and have higher levels of economic development, economic freedom, political and civil rights, also tend to engage in greater levels of e-government. These findings have relevant policy implications. Specifically, according to the cluster analysis, countries in cluster 1 that experience lower levels of e-government need to consider public and social issues influencing trust among groups while developing e-government applications. One way to address this issue is to pursue the perspectives associated with different minority groups in the design phase. Encouraging the involvement and participation of different groups can enhance communication and collaboration and, in turn, bolster trust and social capital and increase the likelihood that e-government services will be more widely accepted and adopted. Further, this study has found that more economically developed countries with higher levels of economic, political, and civil freedoms and rights also tend to be more successful adopting e-government services. These results suggest that policies aimed to enhance these freedoms should also serve in e-government implementation efforts.

While the above discussion clearly points to the importance of e-government and its relationship to trust, further research is still needed in this area. For example, as better measures of trust become available, future research can test the robustness of these results with larger cross-sectional data sets. Further, as more data is collected over time, especially measures of e-government usage and adoption, analyses can be conducted to explore how countries can transform through time and reap the benefits of policies aimed to enhance e-government usage and adoption.

In conclusion, though this study has established the importance of trust and the other factors such as level of development and freedom, this study has identified other factors that need to be considered in order to comprehensively analyze the differences across countries with regard to e-government. For example, some societies put a premium on interpersonal contact between governmental representatives and the citizenry and in such societies, a wider acceptance of governmental transactions via the Internet may be necessary. Thus, one can infer that a more holistic approach to the acceptance of e-government across countries should be adopted by policy makers.

REFERENCES

Alesina, A., Baqir, W., & Easerly, W. (1999). Public goods and ethnic divisions. *The Quarterly Journal of Economics*, *114*(4), 1243–1284. doi:10.1162/003355399556269

Alesina, A., Devleeschauwer, A., Easterly, W., Kurlat, S., & Wacziarg, R. (2003). Fractionalization. *Journal of Economic Growth*, *8*, 155–194. doi:10.1023/A:1024471506938

Alesina, A., & La Ferrara, E. (2002). Who trusts others? *Journal of Public Economics*, *85*, 207–234. doi:10.1016/S0047-2727(01)00084-6

Anderson, C., & Paskeviciute, A. (2006). How ethnic and linguistic heterogeneity influence the prospects for civil society: A comparative study of citizenship behavior. *The Journal of Politics*, *68*(4), 783–802. doi:10.1111/j.1468-2508.2006.00470.x

Annett, A. (2001). Social fractionalization, political instability, and the size of the government. *IMF Staff Papers*, *48*(3), 561–592.

Applegate, L., Neo, B.-S., & King, J. (1995). *Singapore tradeNet: Beyond tradeNet to the intelligent island*. Harvard Business School, case study.

Baier, A. C. (1986). Trust and antitrust. *Ethics*, *96*, 231–260. doi:10.1086/292745

Banerjee, A., Iyer, L., & Somanathan, R. (2005). History, social divisions, and public goods in rural India. *Journal of the European Economic Association*, *3*, 639–647.

Barro, R. J. (1999). Determinants of democracy. *The Journal of Political Economy*, *107*(2), 158–183. doi:10.1086/250107

Bélanger, F., Hiller, J., & Smith, W. (2002). Trustworthiness in electronic commerce: The role of privacy, security, and site attributes. *The Journal of Strategic Information Systems*, *11*, 245–270. doi:10.1016/S0963-8687(02)00018-5

Carter, L., & Bélanger, F. (2003). Diffusion of innovation and citizen adoption of e-government services. *The Proceedings of the 1st International E-Services Workshop*, (pp. 57–63).

Carter, L., & Bélanger, F. (2005). The utilization of e-government services: Citizen trust, innovation and acceptance factors. *Information Systems Journal, 15*(1), 5–25. doi:10.1111/j.1365-2575.2005.00183.x

Chevallereau, F. X. (2005). *The impact of e-government on competitiveness, growth and jobs*. IDABC eGovernment Erman Observatory Background Paper.

Ciborra, C., & Navarra, D. D. (2003). *Good governance and development aid: Risks and challenges of e-government in Jordan*. Paper presented at the IFIP WG 8.2 - WG 9.4, Athens, Greece.

Collier, P. (1998). *The political economy of ethnicity*. Washington, DC: World Bank.

Collier, P. (2002). Social capital and poverty: A microeconomic perspective. In Van Bastelaer, T. (Ed.), *The role of social capital in development* (pp. 19–41). Melbourne, Australia: Cambridge University Press. doi:10.1017/CBO9780511492600.003

Cook, K., & Cooper, R. (2003). Experimental studies of cooperation, trust, and social exchange. In Ostrom, E., & Walker, J. (Eds.), *Trust and reciprocity, interdisciplinary lessons from experimental research* (pp. 209–244). New York, NY: Russell Sage Foundation.

Currall, S., & Judge, T. (1995). Measuring trust between organizational boundary role persons. *Organizational Behavior and Human Decision Processes, 64*, 151–170. doi:10.1006/obhd.1995.1097

Delhey, J., & Newton, K. (2004). *Social trust: Global pattern or Nordic exceptionalism?* (Wissenschauftszentrum Berlin für Sozialforschung (WZB) Discussion Paper SP I 2004-202).

Devadoss, P. R., Pan, S. L., & Huang, J. C. (2002). Structurational analysis of e-government initiatives: A case study of SCO. *Decision Support Systems, 34*(3), 253–269. doi:10.1016/S0167-9236(02)00120-3

E-government handbook. (2007). *Handbook*. Retrieved March 15, 2007, from http://www.cdt.org/egov/handbook/trust.shtml

Easterly, W., & Levine, R. (2001). What have we learned from a decade of empirical research on growth? It's not factor accumulation: Stylized facts and growth models. *The World Bank Economic Review, 15*(2), 177–219. doi:10.1093/wber/15.2.177

Economist Intelligence Unit. (2007). *e-readiness rankings*. Retrieved January 10, 2007, from http://globaltechforum.eiu.com/index.asp?layout=rich_story&doc_id=6427

Erman, N., & Todorovski, L. (2009). Mapping the e-government research with social network analysis. *EGOV,* 13-25.

Freedom House. (2006). *Freedom of the world*. Retrieved January 10, 2007, from http://www.freedomhouse.org/

Fukuyama, F. (1995). *Trust: The social virtues and the creation of prosperity*. New York, NY: Free Press.

Fukuyama, F. (2001). Social capital, civil society and development. *Third World Quarterly, 22*(1), 7–20. doi:10.1080/713701144

Gefen, D., Rose, G., Warkentin, M., & Pavlou, P. A. (2005). Cultural diversity and trust in IT adoption: A comparison of potential e-voters in the USA and South Africa. *Journal of Global Information Management, 13*(1), 54–78. doi:10.4018/jgim.2005010103

Gellner, E. (1994). *Conditions of liberty: Civil society and its rivals*. New York, NY: Penguin Press.

Glaeser, E., Laibson, D., Scheinkman, J., & Soutter, C. (2000). Measuring trust. *The Quarterly Journal of Economics, 115*(3), 811–846. doi:10.1162/003355300554926

Granovetter, M. (1973). The strength of weak ties. *American Journal of Sociology, 78*(6), 1360–1380. doi:10.1086/225469

Habermas, J. (1962). *The structural transformation of the public sphere: An inquiry into a category of bourgeois society.* Cambridge, MA: The MIT Press.

Hair, J. F. Jr, Anderson, R. E., Tatham, R. L., & Black, W. C. (1992). *Multivariate data analysis.* New York, NY: Macmillian.

Hargittai, E. (1999). Weaving the Western Web: Explaining differences in Internet connectivity among OECD countries. *Telecommunications Policy, 23*(10/11).

Hauser, G. (1998). Vernacular dialogue and the rhetoricality of public opinion. *Communication Monographs, 65*(2), 83–107. doi:10.1080/03637759809376439

Ho, A. (2002). Reinventing local governments and the e-government initiative. *Public Administration Review, 62*(4), 434–444. doi:10.1111/0033-3352.00197

Inglehart, R., & Baker, W. (2000). Modernization, cultural change, and the persistence of traditional values. *American Sociological Review, 65*(1), 19–51. doi:10.2307/2657288

Johansson-Stenman, O., Mahmud, M., & Martinsson, P. (2006). *Trust and religion: Experimental evidence from Bangladesh.* Department of Economics, Göteborg University, Mimeo.

Kaufmann, D. (2004). *Corruption, government and security: Challenges for the rich country and the world.* Global Competitiveness Report 2004/2005. Retrieved January 11, 2007, from http://siteresources.worldbank.org/INTWBIGOVANTCOR/Resources/ETHICS.xls

Ke, W., & Wei, K. K. (2004). Successful e-government in Singapore. *Communications of the ACM, 47*(6), 95–99. doi:10.1145/990680.990687

Kien, S. S., & Siong, N. B. (2000). Reengineering effectiveness and the redesign of organizational control: A case study of the inland revenue authority of Singapore. In *Process think: Winning perspectives for business change in the Information Age.* Hershey, PA: Idea Group Publishing.

Kim, K., & Prabhakar, B. (2000). Initial trust, perceived risk, and the adoption of internet banking. *Proceedings of ICIS 2000,* Brisbane, Australia, Dec. 10-13, 2000.

Klitgaard, R., Justesen, M.K., & Klemmensen R. (2005). The political economy of freedom, democracy and terrorism. Dept. of Political Science and Public Management University of Southern Denmark, mimeo.

Kovačić, Z. J. (2005). The impact of national cultures on worldwide e-government readiness. *Informing Science Journal, 8,* 143–159.

La Porta, R., Lopez-de-Silanes, F., Shleifer, A., & Vishny, R. (1997). Trust in large Organizations. *American Economic Review Papers and Proceedings, 87,* 333–338.

Larsen, E., & Rainie, L. (2002). *The rise of the e-citizen: How people use government agencies' websites.* Pew Internet and American Life Project. Retrieved January 13, 2007, from http://www.pewinternet.org/reports/toc.asp?Report=57

Lee, M., & Turban, E. (2001). A trust model for internet shopping. *International Journal of Electronic Commerce, 6,* 75–79.

Leigh, A. (2006). Trust inequality and ethnic heterogeneity. *The Economic Record, 82*(258), 268–280. doi:10.1111/j.1475-4932.2006.00339.x

Lyons, D., & Stone, D. (2008, December 1). President 2.0. *Newsweek.*

Maskell, P. (2000). Social capital, innovation, and competitiveness. In Baron, S., Field, J., & Schuller, T. (Eds.), *Critical perspectives.* New York, NY: Oxford University Press.

Mauro, P. (1995). Corruption and growth. *The Quarterly Journal of Economics, 110*(2), 681–712. doi:10.2307/2946696

Moon, J. M., Welch, W. E., & Wong, W. (2005). What drives global e-governance? An exploratory study at a macro level. *Proceedings of the 38th Hawaii International Conference on System Sciences,* (pp 1-10).

Moon, M. J. (2002). The evolution of e-government among municipalities: Rhetoric or reality? *Public Administration Review, 62*(4), 424–433. doi:10.1111/0033-3352.00196

Moore, M. (1999). Truth, trust and market transactions: What do we know? *The Journal of Development Studies, 36*(1), 74–88. doi:10.1080/00220389908422612

Moorman, C., Deshpand, R., & Zaltman, G. (1993). Factors affecting trust in market research relationships. *Journal of Marketing, 57,* 81–101. doi:10.2307/1252059

Morgan, R. M., & Hunt, S. (1994). The commitment-trust theory of relationship marketing. *Journal of Marketing, 58*(3), 20–38. doi:10.2307/1252308

Mossberger, K., Tolbert, C., & Stansbury, M. (2003). *Virtual inequality: Beyond the digital divide.* Washington, DC: Georgetown University Press.

Newton, K., & Delhey, J. (2005). Predicting cross-national levels of social trust: Global pattern or Nordic exceptionalism? *European Sociological Review, 21*(4), 311–327. doi:10.1093/esr/jci022

Norris, P. (2001). *Digital divide: Civic engagement, information poverty, and the Internet worldwide.* New York, NY: Cambridge University Press.

Persell, C., Green, A., & Gurevich, L. (2001). Civil society, economic distress, and social tolerance. *Sociological Forum, 16*(2), 203–230. doi:10.1023/A:1011048600902

Peterson, E., & Seifert, J. (2002). Expectation and challenges of emergent electronic government: The promise of all things E? *Perspectives on Global Development and Technology, 1*(2), 193–212. doi:10.1163/156915002100419808

Putnam, R. D. (1995). Bowling alone: America's declining social capital. *Journal of Democracy, 6*(1), 65–78. doi:10.1353/jod.1995.0002

Ritzen, J., Easterly, W., & Woolcock, M. (2001). *On good politicians and bad policies: Social cohesion, institutions and growth.* Working Paper, Washington DC. World Bank

Rodrick, D. (1999). Where did all the growth go? External shocks, social conflict, and growth collapses. *Journal of Economic Growth, 1,* 149–187.

Rose, R. (2005). A global diffusion model of e-governance. *Journal of Public Policy, 25*(1), 5–27. doi:10.1017/S0143814X05000279

Shleifer, A., & Vishny, R. (1993). Corruption. *The Quarterly Journal of Economics, 108*(3), 599–618. doi:10.2307/2118402

Singh, H., Das, A., & Joseph, D. (2004). *Country-level determinants of e-government maturity.* Nanyang Technological University, Working Paper.

Srivastava, S. C., & Teo, T. S. (2007). What facilitates e-government development? A cross-country analysis. *Electronic Government, an International Journal, 4*(4), 365–378.

Steyaert, J. C. (2004). Measuring the performance of electronic government services. *Information & Management, 41*, 369–375. doi:10.1016/S0378-7206(03)00025-9

Svensson, J. (1998). Investment, property rights and political instability: Theory and evidence. *European Economic Review, 42*(7), 1317–1342. doi:10.1016/S0014-2921(97)00081-0

The Heritage Foundation. (2005). *Index of economic freedom.* Retrieved Dec 20, 2006, from http://www.heritage.org/research/features/index/

The Heritage Foundation. (2005). *Index of economic freedom.* Retrieved January 15, 2007, from http://www.heritage.org/index/

The World Bank Group. (2004). *Data.* Retrieved January 15, 2007, from http://www.worldbank.org/data

Thomas, J. C., & Streib, G. (2003). The new face of government: Citizen-initiated contacts in the era of e-government. *Journal of Public Administration: Research and Theory, 13*(1), 83–102. doi:10.1093/jpart/mug010

Tschannen-Moran, M., & Hoy, W. K. (2000). A multidisciplinary analysis of the nature, meaning, and measurement of trust. *Review of Educational Research, 70*(4), 547–593.

United Nations Department of Economic and Social Affairs (UNDESA). (2003). *World public sector report 2003: e-government at the Crossroads.*

Uslaner, E. M. (2002). *The moral foundations of trust.* Cambridge, UK: Cambridge University Press.

Van Parijs, P. (2004). *Cultural diversity versus economic solidarity.* Brussels, Belgium: De Boeck Universite.

Volken, T. (2002). Elements of trust: The cultural dimensions of internet diffusion revisited. *Electronic Journal of Sociology,* Retrieved March 10, 2007, from http://epe.lac-bac.gc.ca/100/201/300/ejofsociology/2005/01/volken.html

Warkentin, M., Gefen, D., Pavlou, P., & Rose, G. (2002). Encouraging citizen adoption of e-government by building trust. *Electronic Markets, 12*, 157–162. doi:10.1080/101967802320245929

Watson, R. T., & Mundy, B. (2001). A strategic perspective of electronic democracy. *Communications of the ACM, 44*(1), 27–30. doi:10.1145/357489.357499

West, D. M. (2000). *Assessing e-government: The Internet, democracy, and service delivery by state and federal governments.* Retrieved March 2, 2007, from http://www.insidepolitics.org/egovtreport00.html

West, D. M. (2003). *Global e-government.* Retrieved March 3, 2007, from http://www.insidepolitics.org/egovt03int.pdf

White, H. (1980). A heteroskedasticity-consistent covariance matrix estimator and a direct test for heteroskedasticity. *Econometrica, 48*(4), 817–838. doi:10.2307/1912934

World Economic Forum. (WEF). (2007). *The networked readiness index.* Retrieved March 2, 2007, from http://www.weforum.org/pdf/gitr/rankings2007.pdf

World Values Study Group. (1994). *World values survey, 1984-93.* Ann Arbor, MI: Inter-university Consortium for Political and Social Research.

Zak, P. J., & Knack, S. (2001). Trust and growth. *The Economic Journal, 111*, 295–321. doi:10.1111/1468-0297.00609

Zetter, K. (2009). *Nation's first open source election software released*. Retrieved December 1, 2009, from http://www.wired.com/threat-level/2009/10/open-source/

Zinnbauer, D. (2001). Internet, civil society and global governance: The neglected political dimension of the digital divide. *Information & Security, 7*, 45–64.

Chapter 10
Perspectives on E-Government in Europe

Sylvia Archmann
EIPA – European Institute of Public Administration, The Netherlands

Just Castillo Iglesias
EIPA – European Institute of Public Administration, The Netherlands

ABSTRACT

The e-government scene in the EU is undergoing profound changes. The gradual increase in online availability of services has now reached a point where new challenges are appearing, such as trust-building, increasing citizens' confidence and the use of existing services, as well as the need for new more efficient e-inclusion policies. Citizens of today have new demands which require new responses, also in terms of enhancing the participatory process. ICT and e-government have an important role to play in this respect.

INTRODUCTION

Today, as the first decade of the 21st Century comes to an end, the European eGovernment scene is at a turning point. The developments witnessed since the beginning of the decade have been remarkable: eGovernment in Europe has developed from being merely an informative platform, into becoming a true channel for interaction between citizens and governments, as well as a true channel for the online provision of governmental services. At the same time, in this decade we have witnessed the increased importance of information and communication technologies (ICT) and the internet in everyone's everyday life. Our way of shopping, communicating, understanding the world, obtaining services, etc. has been changed due to the incorporation of ICT. This increased presence of ICT in our lives has raised numerous questions on the potential impact that the incorporation of these technologies in our democratic participatory processes could have in terms of quality and accountability of our democracies. Moreover, the 'boom' of the social internet that has taken place

DOI: 10.4018/978-1-60960-159-1.ch010

in recent years has set an important example on how these technologies can transform reality. In this context, one only has to think of the implications that applications such as Facebook.com or Twitter have had in understanding such events as, for instance, the post-electoral crisis in Iran, and how the access to these technologies has given voice to the citizens. Although this is only an example, it illustrates perfectly the existing trend that gives the internet and ICT a crucial place, not only in the provision of services, but also as powerful tools for communication, networking and social participation.

In the eGovernment scene of the European Union these profound changes have become a major challenge and have, at the same time, brought about myriad opportunities. The needs and wishes of our citizens and business have grown more complex, and governments have to respond to the challenges posed by adapting to the new needs by offering new services when needed, and keeping a strong commitment to delivering the best value to its citizens and businesses. The financial crisis has, moreover, accentuated the need for significant use of ICT in order to achieve greater productivity and efficiency, and as a flexible element to provide better services. Nevertheless, this is a situation that has not only affected private enterprise. Public administration is faced with the need – and the opportunity – to become a driver for innovation and an example of good practice in this context of stagnation. Therefore, with the incorporation of ICT in public administration aimed at reducing unnecessary administrative burden and thus eliminating the need for citizens and businesses to bear extra costs in terms of time and money, the public sector can become a trigger for efficiency gains and cost reduction in European societies.

Success in these ambitions, however, will not depend exclusively on the capacity of European governments and EU institutions to introduce ICT as a preferential and more efficient channel for communication with citizens and businesses. Issues such as trust and confidence building, as well as the development of secure and interoperable auxiliary services, are of major importance (European Commission, 2009c). Moreover, and perhaps most importantly, the current ratios of ICT penetration in European households and businesses show an important need for improvement (Eurostat, 2009). Extending ICT penetration ratios and actively promoting eInclusion policies are *sine qua non* critical success factors for the future of eGovernment in Europe.

Therefore, the main challenges that European governments and EU institutions face today consist of concealing the necessity to satisfy the new needs of citizens and businesses to receive their required governmental services in a faster, cheaper and more efficient manner; while at the same time promoting the use of the existing services and extending the percentage of population with qualitative access and sufficient skills to take active part in the information society.

CHALLENGES: THE CHANGING GOVERNMENT AND THE CHANGING CITIZENS

Citizen-Government Relations: New Needs and New Demands

Our societies – often described as the 'knowledge societies' – are extremely dependent on information. However, thanks to this fact they also have an unprecedented potential for distributing knowledge in a more equal way and of offering job opportunities that overcome the traditional barriers of distance or physical space.

However, the widely available access to ICT and its advantages has not only changed the way people interact with each other or with the private sector; governments and public administration are enormously affected by this. When citizens know and become accustomed to receiving increasingly faster and more efficient commercial services with a better value through the internet, they also demand to be able to do the same when accessing public services. From an economic point of view, the avoidable costs incurred by citizens and businesses in order to comply with unnecessary governmental regulations assume an enormous burden in terms of time and money not only for individual citizens, but on the overall economy. At the same time, citizens and civil society increasingly demand to be given the opportunity to express their views in a more flexible way vis-à-vis the public authorities. This call for a revision and an enhancement of the participatory processes to be more inclusive and democratic is nowadays an issue of increasing concern within the different European countries. Political disaffection has been steadily rising across Europe during the past few years in what seems to be a crisis of the current models of participative democracy.

Nevertheless, all these challenges coming from both economic and participatory points of view are faced with significant problems. First of all, ICT have not reached everyone in our societies, nor have governments fully incorporated the potentials stemming from these technologies into their service delivery or decision-making processes. The challenges have to be met with prompt action taken by the European institutions and the Member States, which has to be articulated along the following four lines:

- Favouring eInclusion policies that bring the benefits of the information society to as many people as possible;
- Promoting the necessary changes, either technological, organizational or institutional within governments and public administrations in order to incorporate ICT in all aspects of governmental work and transition towards an administrative culture of shared services;
- Promoting trust and confidence in the citizens and encouraging the use of the services already put in place, in order to con-

vince the citizens of the convenience of eGovernment solutions;
- Setting up possibilities of participation for citizens through ICT in order to encourage its use.

eINCLUSION

eInclusion, according to the definition by the European Commission, aims at ensuring that disadvantaged people are not excluded due to their lack of digital literacy or internet access (European Commission, 2009a). Taking the defining words of Commissioner Reding, "we cannot allow anyone in Europe to be excluded from the benefits of information society, simply because of their age, disability, gender, income, education, or because they live in remote areas" (European Commission, 2005). eInclusion also means involving people more actively, by taking advantage of new opportunities offered by digital and technical services for the inclusion of socially disadvantaged people and less-favoured areas.

In 2006, the Riga Ministerial Declaration on eInclusion highlighted the necessity to improve e-Accessibility for people with special needs and the elderly, as well as increasing their competences, skills and familiarity with ICT – both in education and training, but also as part of the Lisbon Strategy for more and better jobs – by promoting socio-cultural changes that go in the direction of embracing the benefits of the knowledge society. It also promoted eInclusion in relation with the EU Regional policies, and aimed to bring the benefits of ICT to all regions of the EU through actions undertaken thanks to the cohesion and structural funds (European Commission, 2006). The November 2009 Ministerial Conference on eGovernment that took place in Malmö, Sweden, continued to highlight the importance of eInclusion, and set the willingness to achieve substantial improvements by 2015. EU governments will seek "to empower businesses and citizens through eGovernment services designed around users' needs, better access to information and their active involvement in the policy making process" (European Commission, 2009b).

The current situation in Europe in terms of eInclusion shows that a considerable disparity still exists between the different Member States. Besides the traditionally considered eInclusion gaps, such as age and gender, an additional challenge to be considered is overcoming the significant difference between the northern and central Member States with the southern and newly accessed ones (see Figures 1 and 2) (Eurostat, 2009).

Although this situation has improved significantly in comparison with previous measurements, the disparities still allow extensive room for improvement. On average, the percentage of individuals that regularly use the internet for any purpose in the EU-27 is approximately 43%. In the best-case scenarios, namely the Netherlands, Denmark, Sweden and Finland, these figures are approaching 70%; however, in several Member States, such as Romania, Bulgaria or Greece, to name a few examples, these figures are below 30%.

In general terms, promoting eInclusion policies and aiming at achieving greater ICT penetration ratios are issues directly linked with empowering the citizens. This empowerment has been recog-

Figure 1. Percentage of individuals who use the internet regularly. Source: Eurostat

nized repeatedly by the European Commission and the Member States as one of the key priorities for Europe both in terms of enabling governments to achieve greater efficiency rates, as well as in terms of favouring the competitiveness of the European economy.

The empowerment of the citizens, as a possibility in the hands of governments and public administrations, thus consists of the combination

Figure 2. Percentage of individuals using the internet regularly in Europe

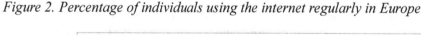

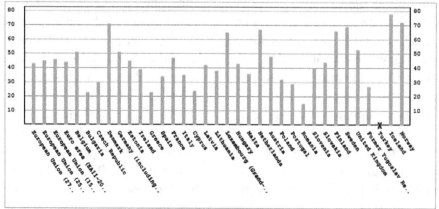

of offering the possibility to conduct transactions and obtain services fully online in the maximum number of occasions possible, while, at the same time, ensuring that segments of the population are not discriminated against by these benefits, simply because of their age, social position, their level of education or need for special attention; or simply because they live in remote areas. The periodical study on eGovernment availability in Europe conducted by Capgemini on behalf of the European Commission is an interesting source of information in this respect. The latest measurements, made available in November 2009 positively reveal that in a period of two years, from 2007 until 2009, a substantial improvement has been made in terms of full online availability of public services in the 27 Member States. While in 2007, 59% of the services were fully available online, this figure increased to 71% in 2009. In 2007, Austria was the only EU country with full online availability of its public services. While this continues to be true in 2009, the full online availability has now also been reached by Malta, Portugal and the UK, closely followed by Sweden and Slovenia (see Figure 3).

The European Commission-Capgemini study also offers figures on the evolution of online sophistication of its eGovernment services. In this case, a significant improvement has also been made, from 76% in 2007 to 83% in 2009. In 2007, Austria also had the most sophisticated online services available, while in 2009 this Member State has been slightly surpassed by Malta and Portugal; Sweden has also reached the same level of sophistication as Austria (see Figure 4).

Nevertheless, in both cases, the Capgemini study reveals the very significant differences between the Member States. Both measurements reveal the situation in several Member States ranking clearly below the EU average. These are figures that indeed have to be worked upon in order to reach better harmonization among the different Member States and to give the citizens of the Union the most similar possibilities to benefit from electronic public services as possible.

CHANGES IN GOVERNMENT

The incorporation of ICT in governmental and public administration work has increased the need for the latter to adjust their internal organization, systems and information management to enable interoperability, thus permitting administrations

Figure 3. Full online availability 2007-2009. (European Commission & Capgemini, 2009)

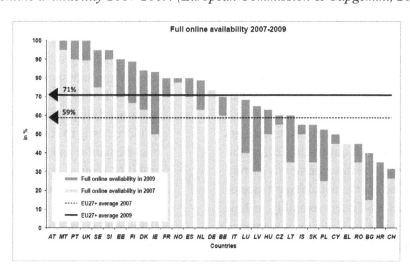

Figure 4. Online sophistication 2007-2009. (European Commission & Capgemini, 2009)

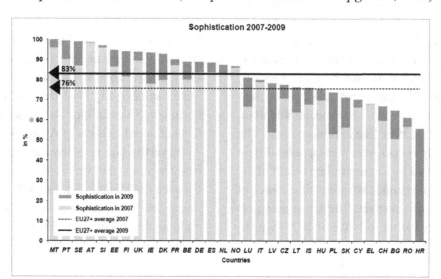

to interact, share information and set up common services. The importance of interoperability has increased substantially with the European integration process and the objectives to achieve a common market without electronic barriers to complement the existing common market for capital, goods and labour. By being an enabler for better eServices, and providing a better experience and fewer administrative burdens for citizens and businesses, the importance of interoperability in today's European eGovernment scene has been acknowledged by the European institutions, the Member States, the private sector and academia. Working on the interoperability of systems and governments does not only open up the possibility of developing services across different levels or instances of administration, but also between different Member States or even at a pan-European level.

Interoperability is not a uniquely technical matter, but a multidimensional one. In this regard, the 2007 MODINIS Study on Interoperability carried out by EIPA pointed out the equal importance of the four different layers of interoperability: technical, semantic, organizational and the governance layers (see Figure 5) (EIPA et al., 2007).

- The technical level refers to the ability of systems to communicate with one another and successfully process the exchanged information. This layer of interoperability thus aims at assuring the technical compatibility between different information systems; this being the easiest layer to achieve.

- Semantic interoperability aims at providing common interpretability of meanings, categories, etc. in order to achieve compatibility in interpreting the exchanged information and enable different administrations to operate with others' information systems.

- Organizational interoperability has to do with the ability of back-office systems to coordinate and share information and resources. Both semantic and organizational interoperability have been demonstrated to be more costly to achieve than the technical one. Semantic and organizational interoperability require engaging in re-organizational processes and intensive exchange of experiences within public administration: changes that are necessary due to the need for replacing old back-office – front-office

Figure 5. MODINIS II - The elements of Interoperability. Source: (EIPA et al., 2007)

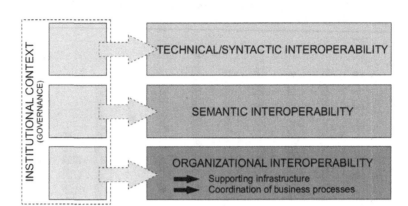

coordination by systems that are able to work within a culture of shared services and multilevel information exchange.

- Finally, the governance dimension of interoperability is concerned with the institutional context in which interoperability is to be achieved, including organization and management traditions, shaped by factors such as culture, language, history, geography, skills and competences, innovation and availability of economic resources.

Nevertheless, and despite the fact that interoperability has become one of the most crucial issues in the European eGovernment agenda of today, many of the changes needed in governments and public administrations in Europe related to the incorporation of ICT are of a non-technical nature. The need for changes in the working processes and customs that fully incorporate ICT as a natural element – and thereby acknowledging the need for a shared-services working culture, encouraging collaboration, networking and sharing of information of resources – is crucial if we are to achieve a truly European catalogue of eGovernment services which does not stop at the local, regional or national boundaries, but rather acquires a truly European dimension. Also in this case, although successful improvements have been made and several pan-

European pilot projects have been launched, the need for improvement and further work remains high (European Commission, 2004).

TRUST AND SECURITY

Trust, confidence building and the development of secure infrastructure and auxiliary services (e.g. eIDs) have become a major key issue today, particularly among the Member States that are at a more advanced stage in their online service provision and sophistication. For these more advanced countries, nevertheless, having comprehensive and fully available online services is not intrinsically linked to higher rates of actual use by the citizens and the businesses in comparison to countries which do not have such high availability or sophistication. Therefore, this issue becomes of utmost importance when one needs to evaluate the success of deploying certain services online or its return of investment.

Figure 6 illustrates the currently existing disparities between the actual use of the available online services in contrast to the ratios of provision. Unsurprisingly, in all analyzed cases, the supply side is ahead of the demand. Nevertheless, cases such as in Austria, where online availability reaches 100% but the actual use of these services

Figure 6. Figures showing the contrast between the availability of public services online and their respective demand by country. Source: (European Commission, 2009c, p. 121)

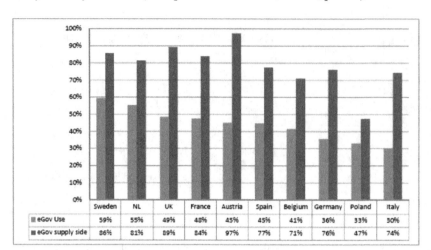

	Sweden	NL	UK	France	Austria	Spain	Belgium	Germany	Poland	Italy
■ eGov Use	59%	55%	49%	48%	45%	45%	41%	36%	33%	30%
■ eGov supply side	86%	81%	89%	84%	97%	77%	71%	76%	47%	74%

by the citizens remains slightly below at 50%, pose the question as to whether the investments and efforts should continue to be made towards steadily developing the supply side instead of promoting the use of these services, to ensure that citizens become familiar with their functioning and benefits (European Commission, 2009c).

Similarly, as it has been seen in terms of eInclusion, the percentage of citizens that use the internet to interact with public authorities in any way shows significant levels of disparity among the different Member States (see Figure 7). Although this number maintains a strong correlation with the number of citizens regularly using the internet in each country, the figures are in this case much lower. In the best-case scenarios – again the Nordic states and the Netherlands – the figures barely reach 55-60%. However, the average is situated between 20 and 30% for the whole of the EU-27 (see Figure 8).

Whilst this fact has very positive aspects, meaning that the use of eGovernment services still has good potential to increase, it remains that there are aspects to be worked upon, mainly related to trust and inclusion.

Besides encouraging use, security and trust are also key elements to be promoted here in this

context. As illustrated in Figure 9, those issues which have fewer implications in terms of privacy for citizens show higher rates of usage, and thus, a minor disparity between supply and use.

Moreover, the promotion of services already available as well as extending the feeling of security and trustworthiness among the citizens can have substantial payoffs in terms of better return

Figure 7. Individuals regularly using the internet for interacting with public authorities. Source: Eurostat

Legend (Data 2008)

6.4 - 14.0	14.0 - 18.2	18.2 - 29.2
29.2 - 41.6	41.6 - 57.7	N/A

Minimum value:6.4 Maximum value:57.7 eu25:26.8 eu15:29.5

Figure 8. Individuals regularly using the Internet in the last 3 months. (% of individuals ages 16 to 74). Individuals regularly using the Internet for interacting with public authorities. Source: Eurostat

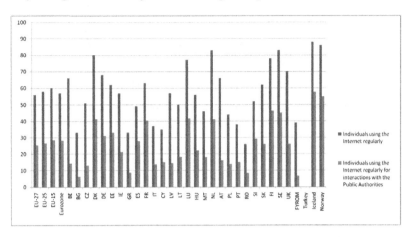

of investment for governments. In addition, the more citizens turning to the internet as a channel for interaction with public authorities and obtaining public services, the more resources – currently allocated to less preferable interaction channels – that can be employed in areas where such resources are more necessary. Interestingly, Figure 10 illustrates the likelihood of citizens and

businesses re-using electronic channels to interact with public authorities after the breakthrough first use has been successfully conducted. This is a crucial point also from the managerial point of view: when citizens try these channels and can successfully and efficiently conduct their transactions, the likelihood of a second use is very high. However, if insufficient efforts are dedicated to

Figure 9. Figures showing the contrast between the availability of the 12 basic public services online and their respective demand. Source: (European Commission, 2009c, p. 121)

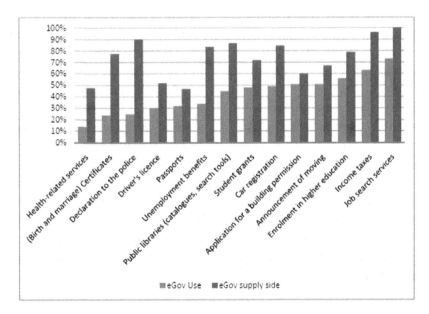

Figure 10. Likelihood of re-use of eGovernment services, per country. Source: (European Commission, 2009c)

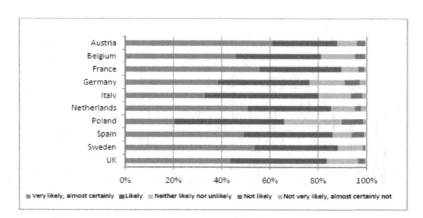

promoting this first use or if this is unsuccessful, the likelihood of this citizen not willing to try eGovernment services again is substantially high.

ePARTICIPATION

eParticipation is today, in many ways, the next great challenge in the European eGovernment scene. In the private sector and private lives of citizens, ICT and the internet have demonstrated enormous capability for facilitating communication, thus enabling people to share information, to network and work together in an easier, friendlier manner. The implications of this in the public sphere, if one thinks of the capacity of ICT for bringing people together in deliberative processes, are manifold.

eParticipation and eDemocracy, however, rely strongly on the points that have been treated earlier in this chapter. eGovernment, when seen as an alternative channel for public sector delivery that has increased efficiency and effectiveness, is indeed very positive; especially when those citizens that do not feel at ease using these services have other means of interacting with public authorities within their reach. However, when talking about eDemocracy and eParticipation, eInclusion becomes an even more important issue than in the

previous case (European Commission, 2009a; Macintosh, 2006; Millard). Enabling processes that rely on citizens to participate through the internet and ICT can have considerable negative effects if inclusion issues are not thoroughly considered and solved. The risk that a segment of the population can become excluded from the new ways of participating in public life because of age, skills or place of residence can be a shock to the core principles of our democracies.

Nevertheless, and despite these challenges that still remain to be solved in order to achieve a solid basis to enable eParticipation, several real cases have been deployed across Europe and have shown relatively successful results. Two of the most known cases are the city of Issy-les-Moulineaux in France, and the city of Trikala in Greece.

The first of these cases, in Issy-les-Moulineaux, has been considered one of the pioneers and still more advanced cases of eParticipation in Europe. Through the website of the city council, the residents of Issy can watch and actively participate in the City Council meeting live from their home or on the move. Active participation and citizen involvement in the process of the city's decision-making is encouraged and made possible through the internet and television. To take part in the City Council meeting, citizens only have to tune in, and ask questions or make suggestions through a toll-free telephone or by email[1]. The second case, the well-known "e-Dialogos" platform from the city of Trikala in Greece, is an innovative and fully fledged e-Democracy online platform for the citizens of Trikala to participate in the decision-making processes of the city[2]. The project aims at offering all citizens the opportunity to get involved directly with the process of development and implementation of city policies through an online platform of dialogue and participation, in an effort to reverse the disengagement of citizens with their elected representatives and the policy process. The e-Dialogos platform combines online deliberative and voting processes in a new way. The platform consists of five concrete steps embedded in each deliberative cycle: firstly, an e-Poll helps to set the agenda with the participation of citizens. This is followed by a moderated e-Forum with pre-determined discussion threads, e-Surveys to quantify opinions and, finally, interactive online real web-casting of the city council proceedings, where citizens can offer their feedback directly.

Many other similar projects have also been set up across Europe; although the most common cases are smaller-scale participatory processes with a very local dimension, e.g. enabling citizens to decide which is the best public work to be performed on a specific location. Nevertheless, the importance of these small-scale projects should not be underestimated. They can provide useful insights on how to rethink participatory processes in Europe through the active use of ICT at this point when political disaffection is on the rise and citizens demand their opinions and views to be better taken into account.

LESSONS LEARNT AND PROSPECTS FOR THE FUTURE: CONCLUDING REMARKS

Throughout this article, the different elements that have become a priority in the European eGovernment scene have been reviewed. eGovernment in Europe is at a crossroads, with different trends urging a profound transformation of public administration's working- and decision-making processes.

The article has reviewed how eGovernment has moved very rapidly over one decade, from becoming a merely informative platform into a true channel of service delivery. However, at the present moment, eGovernment in Europe is facing important challenges, namely: actively promoting eInclusion policies and skills in order to bring the maximum number of citizens possible to the information society; fostering the necessary innovations in governments and public administration so as to be able to fully work with ICT; and lastly, promoting trust and confidence in citizens to become active users of the services that are already put in place.

The financial crisis has exacerbated the need for active use of ICT in reducing administrative burden, which helps to reduce costs and time employed for conducting public transactions; however, the potential of ICT in improving our democracies and decision-making processes are considered to be the next challenge to meet, thus enabling us to have better and more representatives democracy.

A long journey has already been made in the European eGovernment scene, with significant improvements and challenges being met. The European integration process has indeed played a significant role in setting the agenda for advancing in the electronic provision of services in Europe and has triggered the existing efforts being carried out to achieve certain harmonization and similar levels of provision and use across the Member States. However, one cannot forget that Europe is a vast territory with an enormous diversity, both in terms of economic development, customs, education, etc.; thus, further common work at a European level is the real key success factor for more improvements to be made.

REFERENCES

EIPA. et al. (2007). *Study on interoperability at local and regional level, final version*. Retrieved from http://www.epractice.eu/en/node/281708

European Commission. (2004). *European interoperability framework for Pan-European e-government services IDABC*. Retrieved from http://ec.europa.eu/idabc/servlets/Doc?id=19529

European Commission. (2005). *Shaping Europe's digital revolution*.

European Commission. (2006). *Riga ministerial declaration on e-inclusion*. Retrieved from http://ec.europa.eu/information_society/events/ict_riga_2006/doc/declaration_riga.pdf

European Commission. (2009a). *e-inclusion*. Retrieved from http://ec.europa.eu/information_society/activities/einclusion/index_en.htm

European Commission. (2009b). *Malmö ministerial declaration*. Retrieved from http://epractice.eu/files/Malmo%20Ministerial%20Declaration%202009.pdf

European Commission. (2009c). *Study on user satisfaction and impact in the EU27*. Retrieved from http://ec.europa.eu/information_society/activities/egovernment/studies/index_en.htm

European Commission, & Capgemini. (2009). *E-government benchmarking survey. Smarter, faster, better e-government-8th benchmark measurement*. Retrieved from http://ec.europa.eu/information_society/eeurope/i2010/benchmarking/index_en.htm

Eurostat. (2009). *Statistics on information society*. Retrieved from http://epp.eurostat.ec.europa.eu/portal/page/portal/information_society/

Macintosh, A. (2006). *Challenges and barriers of e-participation in Europe?* Macintosh, A. (2006). E-participation in policy-making: The research and the challenges. In Cunningham, P., & Cunningham, M. (Eds.), *Exploiting the knowledge economy: Issues, applications and case studies*. Amsterdam, The Netherlands; Washington, DC: IOS Press.

Millard, J. (2006). *E-governance and e-participation: Lessons from Europe in promoting inclusion and empowerment*. Retrieved from http://citeseerx.ist.psu.edu/viewdoc/summary?doi=10.1.1.117.3155

ENDNOTES

[1]   http://www.epractice.eu/en/cases/issyicc

[2]   http://www.epractice.eu/cases/eDialogos

Chapter 11
Exploring the ICT Capabilities of Civil Society in Sub Saharan Africa:
The Zambian Case

Joshua C. Nyirenda
Saint Louis University, USA

ABSTRACT

Civil society is argued to have been the most significant force of many forces that eradicated entrenched authoritarianism in Africa, in the early 1990s, ushering most of these countries to multi-party democracies. And yet after such accomplishment, many of these new democracies have receded to undemocratic practices. With weak economies, civil society faces many challenges in resource mobilization and in mobilizing the masses for national causes. Information communication technologies, or ICTs, are increasingly being seen as an aid to the mobilization and organization challenges of civil society. However, advanced ICT capabilities are mostly in developed countries where civil society is already strong. Using e-governance as a proxy measure for ICT capabilities for civil society, this chapter conducts an exploratory study using secondary baseline data collected by international institutions on Sub Saharan Countries. The relationship between ICT capabilities and the several civil society development indicators (press freedom, civil liberties, and various other variables) is investigated. Later, the Nation of Zambia (a country with moderate ICT capabilities in the region) is used for a qualitative case study to explore how ICT capabilities and various contextual issues influence ICT applications by civil society organizations to enhance operational capabilities such as collaboration and mobilization efforts.

DOI: 10.4018/978-1-60960-159-1.ch011

INTRODUCTION

Civil society is argued to have been the most significant force of many forces that eradicated entrenched authoritarianism in Africa, in the early 1990s, ushering most of these countries to multi-party democracies. While other additional factors on the international scene, e.g. the demise of communism and pressure from foreign donors also deserve credit, the resourcefulness and tenacity of civil society is credited for beginning and carrying on the transition process (Gyimah-Boadi, 1996). Africa's civil society is a collage of several institutions and organizations, namely the church and ecumenical bodies, trade-unions, student union bodies, and non-governmental bodies among others. Gyima-Boyadi argues that having accomplished the pivotal role of democratization, civil society is facing the problem of consolidation, with its ability to strengthen democratic governance remarkably weak.

Some of the challenges that civil society faces are found in the governance practices of incumbent governments, where control over police forces for instance, enables them to crush dissenting views, while the control over the media and lack of press freedom controls the information that the masses get. Sub Saharan Africa is plagued by both the challenges of poor quality of political institutions and poorly performing economies. Most remarkable is that most of these nations are emerging democracies with immature institutions that are vulnerable to political manipulation and corruption. What is particularly intriguing is the re-emergence and persistence of undemocratic and authoritarian practices in some of Africa's nascent democracies, after the democratic wave of the 1990s, which have gradually weakened civil society's influence and autonomy as the fourth arm of government. This has often made civil society susceptible to cooptation traps by the state. Such susceptibility to corrupt government is more a reality given that most civil society organizations face contextual bottlenecks, such as lack of resources

due to poor economies. As a result civil society's ability to collaborate and mobilize support for social causes and action is seriously compromised under such circumstances. ICTs and internet based mobilization and social networking technology are increasingly being viewed as a potential shot in the arm of civil society, since challenges arising from authoritarian undemocratic tendencies (such as low democratic participation, a curtailing of the freedom of expression and the crushing political dissent), can be tackled by exploiting the benefits of ICTs in the public space. This is mainly because governments are generally perceived to have significantly limited control over ICTs. Hence civil society is able to circumvent reclusive regimes and their repressive information control, and is able to mobilize support for societal causes and sensitize the citizens on various issues and mobilize the masses for social action against undemocratic state practices. In this regard, ICTs present hope for these struggling democracies, which are characterized in part by low political participation and voter apathy, to increase participation and transparency by engaging citizens via cyber space and communication technology.

The objective of this chapter is to explore how ICT capabilities impact indicators of civil society development in Sub Saharan Africa. To measure ICT capabilities, the UN eGovernance readiness index is used because it captures both infrastructural and participation components, both of which are crucial elements for civil society development indicators. A statistical analysis of the relationship between measurement of eGovernance Readiness, press freedom, political freedom, good governance, and various other indicators for the development of civil society are conducted at the regional level. Using the case study of Zambia the study proceeds to investigate using a qualitative study how context and ICT capabilities lead civil society organizations in the region to apply ICTs to enhance inter-organizational collaboration, achieve intra organizational efficiency and achieve operational goals such as civic engagement (mobilization).

LITERATURE REVIEW

Civil Society

Foley & Edwards (1996) define civil society as "the realm of private voluntary association, from neighborhood committees to interest groups to philanthropic enterprises [which have] come to be seen as an essential ingredient in both democratization and the health of established democracies" (p.38). There is not an easy consensus on the meaning of this concept however. This is because the definition of civil society is a complex undertaking; several schools of thought on the characteristics and functions of civil society exist. Necessarily, these schools of thought yield different definitions.

There two major schools of thought from which stream several approaches. The first, the Lockean School of thought, views "civil society as a self-regulating realm, the ultimate repository of individual rights and liberties, and …[a] political culture of generalized trust, institutionalized into political structures underpinning rights" (Kunz, 1995, p.181). This is the basis for the orientation that emphasizes the independence of civil society from the state; a more polarized relationship between the two. The second school of thought, the Hegelian school, emphasizes a more complementary role between the state and civil society. This school distinguishes itself from the first by presenting "an integrationist or holistic picture of civil society and the state...perceiv[ing] the two rather in an organic or dialectical relationship, where they are overlapping, interdependent, or complementary"(Kunz, 1995, p.182). In this school civil society in seen, in the ideal situation, as a crucial input resource in policy formulation.

As a matter of course the roles that these contrasting schools espouse are different. The first school reflects civil society as a revolutionary force while the second one views it as an instrument of state consolidation. The former emphasizing autonomy, the latter -complementarity.

A definition that attempts to integrate both these schools of thought is that offered by Walzer (1992) defining civil society as "a dense network of civil associations…[that]…promote the stability and effectiveness of the democratic polity through both the effects of association on citizens' "habits of the heart" and the ability of associations to mobilize citizens on behalf of public causes" (89-107).

In line with the first school of thought, CIVICUS (2004) broadly defines civil society as "the arena, outside of the family, the state and the market, where people associate to advance common interests" (p. XVII). CIVICUS however qualifies this definition by stating that the boundaries between these sectors are fuzzy. Such a broad definition however, as correctly noted, raises concerns of definitional boundaries. Lack of constraints on the boundaries, can lead to problems of measurement of the concept or observation of the phenomenon. This also potentially raises focusing problems, which refer to the case where outputs are not defined ex facto, which leads to categorization and interpretation after the fact. Since types of associations that mobilize citizens for particular social causes can range from efforts by political actors to non political actors such as ecumenical bodies, or from private citizens to collective groups such as labor unions or student bodies.

Foley and Edwards (1996) extend this argument by advancing that while a civil society group may be non-political they may be involved in political affairs, such as an ecumenical body involved in poverty issues as a social justice issue. The definition of civil society by the London School of Economics Center for Civil Society captures this reality:

Civil society refers to the arena of uncoerced collective action around shared interests, purposes and values. In theory, its institutional forms are distinct from those of the state, family and market, though in practice, the boundaries between state, civil society, family and market are often complex, blurred and negotiated. Civil society commonly embraces a diversity of spaces, actors and institutional forms, varying in their degree of formality, autonomy and power. Civil societies are often populated by organizations such as registered charities, development non-governmental organizations, community groups, women's organizations, faith-based organizations, professional associations, trade unions, self-help groups, social movements, business associations, coalitions and advocacy group (Centre for Civil Society, 2004)

Implicit in this definition is the civil – political dichotomy where the former mobilizes support for action on broad common interest through voluntary participation and cooperation, whereas the latter mobilizes support for action on parts of a universe of conflicting interests and values, through competition. In the latter case, the losers are coerced by state authority to conform to the desires of the victors. Such political settlements can result in conflict which can essentially spill over to civil society.

Foley & Edwards (1996) argue that that it is important to evaluate the political settlement system since such systems have an influence on the character and nature of civil society. Indeed, being socialized into a system to some extent influences the perception of what civil society considers fair and unfair settlements. As Foley and Edwards posit, "political systems...are important determinants of both the character of civil society and of the uses to which whatever social capital exists might be put" (Foley & Edwards, 1997, p. 38).The corruption problems in SSA, hence, can have an influence on the quality of civil society.

Foley & Edwards (1996) identify two classes of the civil society debate; Civil Society I and Civil Society II. They argue that civil society I emphasizes "the ability of associational life in

general and the habits of association in particular to foster patterns of civility in the actions of citizens in a democratic polity" (p.39). This is congruent with Robert Putnam's idea of social Capital which he defines as the summation of the value derived from 'social networks' the associated sense of belonging that trigger reciprocity among members (Putnam, 1995). It is also defined as those stocks of social trust, norms and networks that people can draw upon to solve common problems. For Putnam, the chief virtue of civil associations lies in their capacity to socialize participants into the "norms of generalized reciprocity" and "trust" that are essential components of the "social capital" needed for effective cooperation.

A similar perspective is offered by Mahyar Arefi (2003) who argues that healthy social capital or civil society is denoted by its consensus building capabilities; that consensus building is a direct positive indicator of social capital. He argues that consensus is an indicator of "shared interest" among stakeholders that necessitates collective action.

Civil Society II on the other hand, emphasizes that civil society is "a sphere of action that is independent of the state and that is capable... of energizing resistance to a tyrannical regime" (Foley & Edwards, 1996, p.40). This is consistent with the Lockean school of thought.

The literature also discusses the importance of considering the context of a society and how such context shapes the nature and emphasis of its civil society. Context affects the emphasis by influencing what civil society considers as its priority mission. If faced with an autocratic regime, the emphasis or priority may be the establishment of democratic governance. If faced by a weak democratic system the emphasis may be consolidation of democratic governance while seeking to increase the accountability and responsiveness of governments may be the emphasis where government is generally perceived as unresponsive and unaccountable. These various scenarios affect the nature and behavior of civil society in as far as how it relates with government, in line with the various schools of thought; a confrontational relationship in the context of pre-democratic political systems and a complementary one where democratic consolidation is the emphasis. An extension of this argument, however is that even in cases of an unresponsive and undemocratic state where confrontation is the strategy for civil society, this strategy may be thwarted by the lack of democratic governance, suggesting that the impact of civil society is strongest in stronger democracies than in weaker ones where state policy may actively seek to repress or ignore citizens' efforts to mobilize and advocate for specific ends. The frustration that results leads to either militancy (the collapse of confidence in the political settlement systems e.g. war) or simply apathy. This, ironically, implies that civil society is expected to have more impact where it is 'less needed' and less impact where it is needed more, Foley and Edwards (1977), citing Walzer's concept of 'the civil society paradox' and Putnam, summarize this paradox well:

that a democratic civil society seems to require a democratic state, and a strong civil society seems to require a strong and responsive state. The strength and responsiveness of a democracy may depend upon the character of its civil society, as Putnam argues, reinforcing both the democratic functioning and the strength of the state. But such effects depend on the prior achievement of both democracy and a strong state. (Foley & Edwards, 1997, p.42).

ICTs AND DEMOCRACY / EGOVERNANCE-CIVIL SOCIETY LINK

It is these challenges to the functionality of civil society that have led some scholars to investigate the relationship between ICTs and democracy, in an effort to find systems of civil society organi-zation, such as the uses of the internet, that have the capacity to circumvent repressive regimes in mobilizing support from within borders and across borders for societal causes that may be at odds with the political establishment. In the literature, The ICT democracy relationship has two camps; optimists and pessimists.

Optimists contend that ICTs can be "the magic equalizer that allows hitherto marginalized segments of society to participate significantly in the political process" (Tettey, 2001, p. 135).

Cyber-libertarians, posit that technologies have certain intrinsic characteristics that en-hance the interaction between governments and citizens. They argue that ICTs provide unfettered "reciprocal interactivity among many people; a global network that is not constrained by territorial boundaries; uncensored speech; the ability to challenge and cross-check official views; and the development of transnational civil society" (Tettey, 2001, p. 135).

Hence optimists claim that ICTs are capable of changing the way citizens interact politically with each other and how, individually and collectively, they interact with their governments. This, they argue, empowers them and increases their influence over the government in its political decisions. As far as these technologies affect society's interaction with the state, this argument can be extended to include how such technology affects communication and mobilization efforts within civil society and its social capital.

Chatfield (1991) discusses the potential of ICTs to counteract governmental information control mechanisms through a centralized rather than hi-erarchically structured information dissemination process, which is also interactive. Optimists also, point to the possibility of penetrating reclusive societies in such a way that swift help from outside is obtained by victims of oppressive regimes after they call for help. They claim that this is made possible through reducing the reaction times from the international community and by-passing the 'under-surveillance' communication systems that insulate oppressive regimes from international scrutiny and intervention. This improved information flow also has a positive impact on civil society by strengthening social capital, its key component. Social Capital is a core characteristic of civil society which thrives where there is good communication. In as far as Social capital relies on communication, ICT is can be seen as contributors to the strengthening of social capital; by increasing the channels and means of communication, and more importantly, in their most critical role; their capability to increase political participation, and promote civic engagement levels.

Pessimists on the other hand "argue that ICTs … just produce a façade of democracy and popular participation because the elite manipulate information technologies to fit their institutional and personal agendas" (Tettey, 2001, p. 137). This criticism raises the legitimate argument concerning power relations in the use of technology in the democratic process.

Critics of the role of ICTs in democratization also point to power inequities in the structure of internet governance. For instance, they argue that there is a form of control in this domain that is characterized by a dominance of the world's communication system by a few businesses. Such internet governance, they contend, neither assures the participation of more people at the grassroots in the political process nor does it improve the democratic process. Another power related argument is that advanced by Clark and Themudo (2003) in which they claim that reliance on the internet may privilege certain groups, languages, or genders to the exclusion of others.

Pessimists are also concerned with increasing internet surveillance trends. In the name of national security many undemocratic governments thwart any efforts that threaten their hold on power, which can include social movements (Coombs, 1998; Kahn & Kellner, 2004).

Critics also raise the issue of context, arguing that various socio-economic and political context lead to different outcomes in the ICT-Democracy

relationship. Issues raised here include access to technology (both affordability and physical access) as well as political factors such as freedom of information. Others include education levels, gender, and geographical location.

Digital Divide

Considering the vital role that civil society plays in the democratic polity and the challenges that this institution faces in infant democracies, has led to the increased discussion in the literature regarding the role of ICT as a positive tool in mitigating these challenges. However, one major obstacle stands in the way of exploiting ICTs to this end: the digital divide. Numerous people in developing countries do not have access to ICT and there is a large gap between the elite, who can afford the technology, and the poor who cannot (Basu, 2004). Table 1 below illustrates the digital divide at the global level. The general public's access to ICT is critical to civil society's ability to engage them in social causes, as limited access cripples the extent that the reach of mobilization efforts by civil society can achieve.

Given the digital divide, and taking the ICT-democracy link as valid, an inference can be made that technologically disenfranchised people lack the ability to participate in governance issues or to circumvent repressive rule in expressing their interests and advocating responsiveness from government. The widely recognized capability of the internet in this regard is its ability to foster many-to-many communication, whereas previous technologies (such as the use of telephone, television and telefax), provide few- to–few and few-to-many communication at best. The internet however, provides a multi-way, even simultaneous many-to-many, live communication mode of communication. It also provides the convenience of allowing collaboration, participation and participant feedback without requiring physical convergence. It is these ICT capabilities that are absent where access to ICTs is limited, in which

Table 1. Internet usage by region of the world (Source: Argaez, E. D. (2009). The Internet Big Picture: World Internet Users and Population Stats)

World Regions	Population (2009 Est.)	Internet User 12/31/ 2000	Internet User Latest Data	Penetration (% pp'lation)	Growth 2000-09	Users % of Table
Africa	991,002,342	4,514,400	67,371,700	6.80%	1,392.4%	3.9%
Asia	3,808,070,503	114,304,000	738,257,230	19.40%	545.9%	42.6%
Europe	803,850,858	105,096,093	418,029,796	52.00%	297.9%	24.1%
Middle East	202,687,005	3,284,800	57,425,046	28.30%	1,648.20%	3.3%
North America	340,831,831	108,096,800	252,908,000	74.20%	134%	14.6%
Lt. Amer./ Carib.	586,662,468	18,068,919	179,031,479	30.50%	890.8%	10.3%
Oceania / Aust'lia	34,700,201	7,620,480	20,970,490	60.40%	175.2%	1.2%
WORLD TOTAL	6,767,805,208	360,985,492	1, 733,993,741	25.60%	380. 3%	100%

situations the ability of civil society to exploit them is limited.

Another issue that challenges the success of ICT utilization in less developed countries (LDCs) is the issue of technological capacity, which has two critical aspects for developing countries: technical capacity and infrastructural capacity. Tapscott (1996) discusses how developing countries' poor IT infrastructure constitutes a further obstacle for ICT use while low computer literacy rates further hinder the receptive base of people in those countries to participate in eGovernance.

SUB SAHARAN AFRICA

Sub-Saharan Africa (SSA) disproportionately has a majority of the Highly Indebted Poor Countries (HIPC) in the world (IDA, & IMF, 2007). Africa's population remains mostly rural with a majority subsisting on less than one dollar a day. Some development experts attribute Africa's economic woes to undemocratic rule and poor governance in general. Governments use undemocratic methods to repress opposition, while civic engagement levels are low and mechanisms to check government accountability are poor. Government control, among other factors, is argued to cause these

elements which essentially weaken the efficacy of the civil society.

As it stands, most African governments have been transitioning through two decades of political transformation. Tettey (2001) argues that this transition was possible due an interaction of internal and external factors, and that civil society played a role.

While this transition from authoritarian and single party systems to democratic and multi-party politics occurred during this period, the required subsequent consolidation of democratic governance eluded the continent in the following decade as corruption and poor governance indices still rocked the region. Civil society it is argued have been incapacitated by severe government control over their critical modes of operation and mobilization, consequently falling prey to governmental manipulation and cooptation due to lack of financial efficacy and civic values.

Tettey (2001) attempts to ascertain the validity of the causal linkage between ICTs and democracy in Africa, and argues that "while the technologies have expanded the amount and sources of information that are potentially available to citizens, they have not resulted in any significant transformations in the way government is run or how politics are conducted on the continent" (p.134-5) and that not as many people are engaged in or influence politics.

Many scholars emphasize the importance of viewing civil society not only as a network of social resources or as an infrastructure of organizations, (Helmut Anheier & Themudo, 2002) but also and more importantly, as a set of cosmopolitan values and identities (H. Anheier, Glasius, & Kaldor, 2001). This perspective can help explain the challenges faced by civil society in sub Saharan Africa, with the realization that in the same way that civil society helps shape the political culture, it is also affected by the same culture.

The colonial legacy still shapes government organization and political culture in Sub Saharan Africa, such that government officials and politicians keep most of the political power for themselves and citizens are perceived as 'subjects'. Such a culture breeds corruption and is venomous and if it is to a great degree a philosophical basis that civil society has been socialized into, as it will affect their interactions with the state their courage, authority and in general the lens through which they view all of such engagement. The African state itself is cited as being a major impediment to the success of civil society. "A formidable array of systemic and contextual factors are clearly responsible for slowing the development of civil society in Africa. Chief among them is the African state. Like its counterparts everywhere else in the world, the African state tends to seek hegemony" (Gyimah-Boadi, 1996, p. 125). Typically, the African state assumed a neopatrimonial form--in which the extremes of cooptation and repression were the main modes of state control over society.

The African context presents analytical challenges to civil society scholars given the foreign nature of the concept to the cultural context. Many scholars have argued about how democracy, being a foreign concept in most African societies, faces implementation challenges when it is at odds with local cultural practices and beliefs. I posit that such divergence between local cultural dispositions and the expectations of democratic

eGovernance can be a source of what I call 'negative social capital', at least from the western perspective. For instance, in traditional African society, paying tributes to traditional leaders was acceptable, which possibly solicited the favors from the leaders. In a similar way, 'helping each other' is part of communal society. Additionally, forms of reciprocity can include "scratch my back and I will scratch yours" and other anti-snitching mentalities. These attributes appear to be present in the African context and could present a challenge to the rule of law and good governance practices. While Africa's extended family system and strong associational and communal living can be observed at communal and family levels it is unclear whether this 'social capital' asset can be said of civil society organizations. This is because political organization based on ethnic and religious lines have been sources of conflict.

Associational life is dominated by traditional, ascriptive, and kin-based groups. These include clans, tribes, and ethnoregional formations; their neotraditional urban counterparts such as home-area improvement and cultural-preservation associations; and Islamic and Christian-millennialist religious groups. Yet these traditional and neotraditional groups tend to be preliberal or illiberal and to subscribe to gerontocratic, extremely hierarchical, patriarchal, and otherwise undemocratic values. Their leaders are socially and politically conservative and often view democratization with indifference (Gyimah-Boadi, 1996, p. 128-9).

As a result, civil society has fallen prey to the same problem: organizing itself or associating itself with ethno-regional, religious, and other identities in such as way that many progressive movements have disintegrated along such sectarian groupings. This sad reality is particularly a big challenge considering that African countries are characterized by multiethnic and multi-religious societies. The challenge is that it is often causes that are mobilized along these lines that have passionate and loyal supporters, a trap that civil society often falls prey to. On the other hand, seeking to remain in power, governments fuel such division in order to weaken the strength of anti-government sentiment, stressing the sectarian basis of any movement.

Coupled with the colonial legacy discussed earlier and high poverty levels, these contextual issues can be plausible causes of the culture of corruption. In as far as such tendencies are strengthened rather than undermined by social networks, such elements of the networks are negative social capital elements, which can undermine the strength of civil society. This can also explain why most civil society organizations are susceptible to cooptation by government and to corruption. While ICTs are critical for democratic progress, its adoption, is enhanced by good governance practice and conducive cultural practices-hence being bound in a circular cause and effect relationship.

A major source of weakness for civil society in Africa is its lack of fiscal independence. Most civil society organizations tend to depend (whether directly or indirectly) on government for financial resources. With the public sector constituting a large percentage of the economic sector and being the largest employer, most African trade unions have most of their members tied to governments. This has implications for the autonomy of trade unions given that prolonged labor standoffs with government jeopardize their own revenue interests, since their members' membership fees are dependent on their government salaries which decline during such labor disputes. A vibrant and large private sector is hence clearly crucial to the autonomy and success of civil society organizations. Those that are independent from the state and have international ties such as church organizations are better able to stand up to the government and not fear financial arm-twisting.

The dominance of the public sector, high unemployment rates, poor job security and lack of unemployment compensation compromise the integrity of many public officials including some civil society leaders, who are more concerned about their economic welfare and hence are more subservient than critical to political authority. This situation makes them susceptible to cooptation by neopatrimonial states.

It is these contextual issues that make the operationalization of ICT capabilities as merely infrastructural pre-requisites inadequate; necessitating the incorporation of contextual considerations. It is in this regard that the case study is incorporated.

METHODOLOGY OF THE STUDY

Measurement of Key Variables

The objective of this study is to explore the ICT capabilities of civil society in sub-Saharan countries and their capacity to use ICTs as tools for enhancing operational effectiveness. The operational definition for Civil Society's ICT capabilities includes not only equipment resources and infrastructure available to civil society organizations in particular and the wider society in general, but also the capabilities of the target audiences to acquire and use the technology. Additionally, it also includes the political environment and culture of participation and use of technology to partake in civic efforts. To assess the ICT capabilities, the UN eGovernance readiness index, which measures prerequisites for eGovernance, is selected. The index is selected in order to capture a wider set of predictors, focusing not only on the technical aspects but also the socioeconomic, cultural and political factors (Misuraca, 2006). This is because simply focusing on ICT infrastructure measurements and related technical requirements fails to capture political and socio-economic contexts which can influence utilization levels of ICT technology. For example, the mere count of computers and telephone subscriptions does not inform about people's ability to utilize them to specific goals. Using a wide range of predictors captures cultural and political aspects that can either help or hurt the ability of civil society organizations to actually embrace the use of technology (the culture). The political environment aspects that can impede or catalyze the general use of ICTs in countries and the socio-economic aspects such as the financial capabilities of nations to even invest in IT infrastructure in the first place are also encapsulated.

However, an ICT infrastructure does not consist simply of telecommunications and computer equipment. E-readiness and ICT literacy are also necessary in order for people to be able to use and benefit from [eGovernance] applications. Having the education, freedom and desire to access information is critical [and] ... Presumably, the higher the level of human development, the more likely citizens will be inclined to accept and use [the] services (Ndou, 2004, p.13).

In addition eGovernance is a good surrogate measure since it also provides the same platform (infrastructure and participation elements) which can be exploited by civil society for their organizational goals such as civic engagement. For instance, the telecommunication infrastructure used for eGovernance in a country is the same that civil society would use to strengthen their operational capabilities. Additionally, the state of eGovernance in a country is a reflection of how government and society at large interact in civic matters using technology with a key goal of increasing participation levels. As a result, eGovernance readiness, is composed of technical as well as political and cultural issues, making it a better reflection of ICT capabilities of civil society in SSA.

Civil society is measured by indicators that are resident in a democratic polity that portend to its success. As a concept civil society can be hard to measure (as discussed in the literature review). Instead of measuring civil society by counting the number of organizations that could qualify as civil society organizations (even if they do

not actually participate in civic issues or support social political causes) focus is on civil society development indicators that enhance its ability to influence the trajectory of politics and governance issues in a country.

Data Collection and Variable Selection

This study was conducted using relevant data gathered from several institutional datasets already collected for the Sub-Saharan region. In some cases the Sub-Saharan data had to be obtained from international datasets. These data sources were selected because data on SSA is rarely comprehensive. Data collected by international agencies or non-governmental organizations is more comprehensive and is more likely reliable than data self reported by individual governments. The data sources included Transparency International, the Ibrahim Governance Foundation, the World Bank, the International Telecommunication Union, and the Freedom House. Variables of interest that were compiled from these sources include the following:

- eGovernment Readiness index, (to measure ICT capacity)
- School life expectancy (prim- tertiary education) (to measure general literacy which affects computer literacy)
- Democracy 08 Rank (to measure the political environment)
- Political culture (pre-requisite for civil society)
- Civil liberties (pre-requisite for civil society)
- Internet Users per 100 inhabitants (to measure ICT capacity)
- Regional Corruption Rank (political environment)
- Press Freedom (political environment/ prerequisite for civil society)

- Participation and Human Rights (pre-requisite for civil society)
- Population below poverty line (to measure financial access to ICT services)

It was determined that these variables would provide a good perspective regarding the infrastructural capacity and other pre-requisite conditions of civil society and eGovernance. This approach would be a quasi political economy analysis providing the best insight into the political and, economic (Banaian, & Roberts, 2008), and infrastructural factors of the subject matter. Most ranking variables and index data were adapted and recoded in order to rank the countries within the region, and to also permit specific statistical analyses.

Since the collected data constitutes the entire 'population' or statistical universe (N), of the region under study, (i.e., all 48 countries in Sub-Saharan Africa), the main objective of the analysis was to investigate the existence of relationships and observe the nature of these relationships - not to seek inference to a broader population. One country however, Somalia, had data missing for most variables. This would have skewed analyses and so it was excluded from the study.

Scatter plot analysis was selected as the method of analysis in order to enable us to obtain a visual idea of the nature of the bi-variate relationship between the variables (Hair, et al., 2006). This method was selected because it provided a visual insight into the nature and direction of the various relationships and the plotting of ordered pairs also shows the correlation between the variables. As a result, a positive trend can be observed if, as one variable increased, the other variable plotted counter to it also increased; or a negative trend if, one variable decreased, the other variable also decreased. No trend exists if the ordered pairs show no correlation (Hair, et al., 2006). Additionally, some variables were selected for chi-square analysis in order to assess the degree of difference between various groups.

The second part of this study consists of the Zambia case study, which involves examination of the literature, research studies and policy documents of the Republic of Zambia, vis-à-vis policy and socio political environment affecting the vibrancy of civil society and determinants of ICT capabilities. This was undertaken to validate some of the observations made in the scatter plot analysis on Sub-Saharan region.

RESULTS

Scatter Plot Analysis

The number of telephone subscribers and internet users indicate the magnitude of the ICT-ready audience, in the event that civil society decides to use these as the tools for civic engagement. Figures 1 and 2 show that there is a positive relationship between internet users per 100 inhabitants and ICT capability; and between the number of telephone subscribers per 100 inhabitants and ICT capability respectively.

School life expectancy contributes to literacy levels, which can include computer literacy. Literacy can determine participation levels and the quality of participation which further affect the health of democracies. Similarly, it can determine the quality of social capital which is crucial for civil society. Computer literacy on the other hand helps to facilitate and enable the participation of the masses when civil society deploys ICTs for civic engagement in social causes.

Figure 3 shows that the lower the school life expectancy, the lower is a country's ICT capabilities (a positive relationship). Thus, Niger has the lowest ICT capability in Sub-Saharan Africa. The flip side are South Africa, Mauritius and Seychelles have the highest ICT capability and highest school life expectancy.

Freedom of the press is an indicator of the impact of civil society on the democratic polity. It can also be argued that this relationship is not

Figure 1. Scatter plot of internet users and ICT capabilities

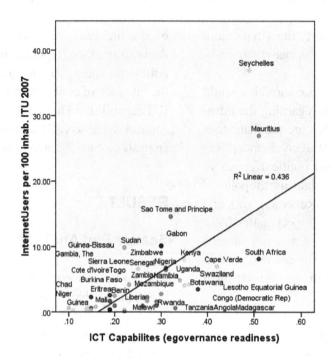

Figure 2. Scatter plot of "number of telephone subscribers" and ICT capabilities

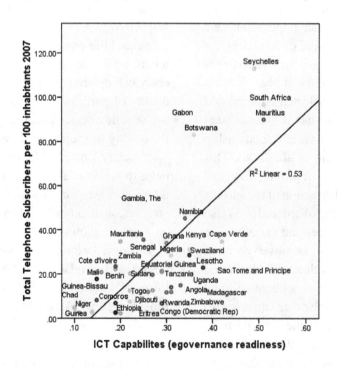

Figure 3. Scatter plot literacy levels (school life expectancy) and ICT capabilities

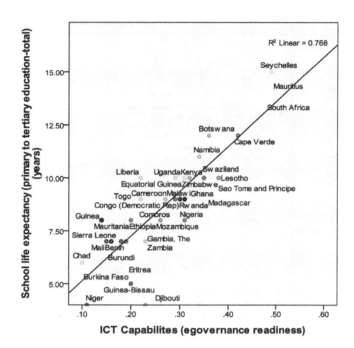

necessarily unidirectional, as a free press buttresses the efforts of civil society in the democratic process by providing vital information to stakeholders and citizens at large. Figure 4 shows that the better the freedom of the press ranking (1= best, 100= least), the better the ICT capabilities.

Civil and Political rights are another indicator of the vibrancy of civil society, and this plot shows that the higher the civil and political right, the better is the ICT capability environment.

Poverty affects earnings, which subsequently affect a population's ability to afford to purchase ICT equipment and/or services. Expectedly, the higher the unemployment rate the lower the ICT capabilities. Civil society organizations will have more challenges in utilizing ICTs under such circumstances (see Figure 5).

Discussion

The results indirectly confirm the discussion in the literature on the civil society paradox; that a minimum level of democracy is required for civil society to thrive. For instance, where civil liberties are limited, democracy is thwarted which limits the extent and quality of participation whether through conventional ways or through ICTs. Similarly, the results also show that a minimum level of development is required to achieve ICT capabilities. The development related outcomes shown in the results – school life expectancy, poverty levels, number telephone line subscribers and internet users, all have influence on ICT capabilities

ZAMBIA CASE-STUDY

Zambia ranks twenty seventh out of forty seven countries in the Sub-Saharan region in eGovernance readiness. It is nineteenth in the total number of internet subscribers within Sub-Saharan countries. The transition from one party rule to multiparty rule, through democratic elections after a campaign well coordinated by a civil society in

Figure 4. Scatter plot of "freedom of the press" and ICT capabilities

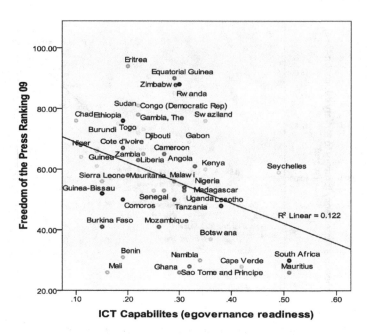

Figure 5. Scatter plot of "population below poverty line" and ICT capabilities

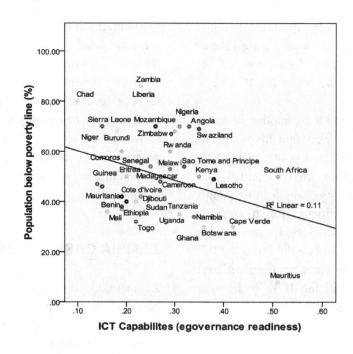

a brutally hostile political environment, elevated Zambia as a model of democracy in Sub-Saharan Africa. Events following this huge success have however been sobering and below expectations.

Civil Society in Zambia

In 1991, Zambia was the first country in post-independence Sub-Saharan Africa in which a change of government peacefully took place through the electoral process when power was transferred from President Kenneth Kaunda and the United National Independence Party (UNIP) to Frederick Chiluba and the Movement for Multi-Party Democracy (MMD) (Bartlett, 2000, p. 1). In line with Diamond's argument (1989) that civil society is more strongly precipitated by 'economic and social changes that give rise to new interests which demand voice and recognition' (p. 148-149) the 1991 'revolution' and the birth of Civil society in Zambia came from threatened business and economic interests when the Zambian government abandoned the New Economic Recovery Program (NERP) On 30 June 1989. With the economy already in dire straits, the manner in which the NERP was abandoned, with no public discussion, and the sudden renewal IMF- sponsored guided policies of structural adjustment programs brought a sense of disillusionment and despair. Leading the skeptics was the Economic Association of Zambia. It was widely acknowledged that the new economic policy trajectory required political reform such as the privatization of para-statal companies that had many ties to the one and only party in the country, UNIP, in order to set in place a free market economy (Bartlett, 2000). Echoing the ECZ on the need for political reform were trade union leaders through the umbrella body the Zambia Confederation of Trade Union (ZCTU) which made public its plans to campaign in favor of a referendum ballot measure in favor of the re-introduction of Multiparty Democracy (Bartlett, 2000).

The political atmosphere was characterized by increasing discontent with human rights abuses through a virtually permanent state of emergency, and a lack of true separation of powers, with the executive interfering in all branches of government. Adding their voice to calls for political reform the clergy expressed their support for political reform and in particular multi-party politics. Most notable was the pastoral letters to its members by the Catholic Church bishops, who have the largest following among Christian churches in the country.

Apart from established organizations voicing their discontent, the general populace joined in concert through mass demonstrations, the most remarkable of which was the food riots after a double price hike of maize meal. Student organizations were key in these protests as the immediate cause of the riots is argued to have been an attempt by police to thwart a peaceful student march by University of Zambia Students to the presidential residence to register displeasure against the price hikes and to voice support for multi-Party politics. The resultant riots and looting spread to several townships in the capital and later to other towns in the Copperbelt province. This mass combatant energy was later transformed into massive rally attendance for regime opponents.

In reaction to the pressure, the referendum plans were dropped and in December 1990 Kenneth Kaunda signed the Constitutional Amendment Act. The following day the NICMPD was reconstituted as a political party, the MMD. The MMD constituted individuals from some civil society organizations and professional associations that were critical of the political regime, its governance record and economic policies. Most notable among the constituent groups from which the party leadership was derived included: businessmen, trade unionists, churchmen, and academics and intellectuals (Bartlett, 2000). The most powerful of these groups were the trade unions and the church. The Church had great social influence, derived from what some observers described as a 'moral monopoly'. Strengthening its muscle was the fact that the church owned its own newspaper circulations, the *Mirror* and *Ichengelo,* which were uncensored by the state and offered an independent and critical view of the 'party and its government' in contrast to the state controlled and government owned daily newspapers.

Increasingly, progressives within the ranks of the founder organizations, particularly intellectuals, became disillusioned with the flooding of the movement with former UNIP leaders and new defectors from UNIP, whose leadership mentality and ethics had already been affected by the discredited regime (Bartlett, 2000).When the MMD took over government after a landslide victory in the 1991 elections, these concerns resurfaced as the government appointments were dominated by ex- UNIP members, and dominated by the Bemba ethnic group. This was followed by corruption scandals and allegations, and a number of government ministers announced resignations from government citing corruption and undemocratic governance. Progressives were increasingly sidelined and excluded and the eventual departure from the party of such progressives either in frustration by resignation or by expulsion after expressing dissenting opinion.. The re-declaration of the State of Emergency in March 1993, after which several opposition leaders were detained, was in the eyes of some observers, the beginning of the death of democratic aspirations as envisioned in the 1991 elections.

A new problem emerged: "While the one-party state had been abolished, multi-party elections were conducted and power was transferred under the Third Republic constitution: "older political logics" did not just disappear' (Bartlett, 2000, p. 88). What, transpired is that in effect the MMD institutionalized a de facto one-party state, the very thing they fought against. The emergence of the MMD created a façade of democratic governance and since it was established under the auspices of and in concert with other civil society organizations, such as the church, it took a while

for these organizations to start critically looking at the new regime, especially given that the new president had declared Zambia a Christian nation in a marked departure from the previous regime. The strength of civil society cannot solely be credited as the cause of the 1991 change of government in Zambia. In fact the change emerged more from the discontent of the masses, which was capitalized on by civil society to change the status quo. The governance record that ensued under the MMD government and the lackadaisical response of civil society, only served to expose the weakness of civil society. It can be argued that it was not until the birth of the Oasis forum that civil society in Zambia began to live to its true mission of being the fourth arm of government; keeping it accountable for its actions.

The Oasis Forum

The undemocratic practices of the MMD government continued as most of society watched helplessly in disbelief while the majority lost faith in politicians or simply became apathetic to politics. This trend went to a new low which gave birth to yet another civil society driven mobilization in opposition to abuse of office by the MMD. This was when Fredrick Chiluba was orchestrating party machinery to portray that the masses wanted him to run for a third term in office. This is was against the constitution, but the plot was to portray the public outcry as so strong that the constitution needed to be amended in order to enable him to re-contest. This gave rise to the Oasis Forum, formed in 2001.The Forum combined the efforts of the Law Association of Zambia (LAZ), the nation's three main Christian mother bodies (the Zambia Episcopal Conference, the Christian Council of Zambia, and the Evangelical Fellowship of Zambia), as well as the the NGO Coordinating Committee for the country's numerous women's organizations.

The forum presented a formidable union of "the legal authority of the lawyers, the moral authority of the Church, and the popular authority of the women's movement," (Gould, 2008, p. 282). This alliance was unprecedented. It broke the civil society fragmentation, overcome the characteristic power/resource struggles among civil society organizations. These struggles existed and still do exist in most part as a result of turf battles; with the aim of securing funding by drowning out competing organizations in order to emerge or to be regarded as the leading voice or institution for specific causes, and so secure government and donor funding. Thus, the union that the oasis forum presented became a success story in the midst of revenue challenges and the associated inter-organizational fiscal feuds.

During the conference the forum demanded President Chiluba to respect the constitution and abandon his third term bid. This was followed by a national campaign to mobilize support for their demands in what became known as the green ribbon and car honking campaigns. Essentially all who were against Chiluba's third term bid wore green ribbons everyday and honked their cars every Friday at 5:pm. The Forum managed to mobilize an energized non-violent civil protest around the country which eventually led to Chiluba's abandonment of the third term bid after succumbing to three months of constant pressure from the growing campaign. When their mission was accomplished, the forum resolved not to disband but rather maintain the alliance in order to advance the national interests such as promoting a culture of constitutionalism, the doctrine and practice of separation of powers, integrity and a culture and practice of accountability and transparency in governance.

IT Infrastructure and Access Challenges in Zambia

In order for civil society to use IT as a tool, the masses have to have access to the technology and that when they do have physical access that they can afford it. While Zambia has come a long way in infrastructural capabilities for telecommunication, the use of the internet to provide services remains limited. Structural rigidities in the IT sector, including the underdeveloped telecommunication infrastructure, as well as the over-centralized business and government institutions lead to inefficient bureaucracy.

IT Infrastructure

ZAMTEL, a wholly state-run entity, owns and operates the telecommunication infrastructure in the country. While the company is currently being considered for privatization, it has thus far had exclusive rights to the Mwembeshi Earth Station satellite and collects revenue from the private service providers using the satellite's facilities, including the international gateway. To date, the Zambian government has not deregulated the country's international communications gateway. The transmission network is predominantly analogue and is based mainly on microwave technology. Over time, this infrastructure has deteriorated, become outdated and its capacity has become outstripped. Additionally, Zambia lags behind its neighbors in telecommunications infrastructure investments. For instance, the country is behind in fiber optic backbone layout, which hampers its regional and national connectivity.

Given the high cost of deploying telecommunications infrastructure, such as fiber optic cable, there needs to be a holistic approach to social and economic infrastructure development strategy in the country. Zambia's Internet market is still in its infancy with approximately 12,000 internet subscribers and an additional 30,000 Internet users mainly patronizing Internet cafes. The infrastructural impediments in the technology sector are not restricted to the primary infrastructure as auxiliary infrastructure for ICT such as electricity of inadequate, which further stifles the demand of ICT services.

Zambia's policy document outlines a number of challenges for the ICT sector, such as low ICT literacy in the country, high cost of technology acquisition making it inaccessible to most Zambians, and the brain drain problem.

ICT Regulation and Market Structure/Conditions

The regulation of ICTs is in the hands of the Communications Authority which is under the jurisdiction of the Ministry of Transport and Communications. Until recently, ZAMTEL was the only licensed operator allowed to provide fixed telephone services to the public. Land phone lines are the predominant medium for internet connectivity. Cable and satellite alternatives still lag far behind. Protectionist regulation and heavy reliance on phone lines for both voice and data transmission create a monopoly for ZAMTEL, which results in uncompetitive prices and stifles innovation. Coupled with limited supply of telephone services, the billing system of phone services (mostly charged per minute) discourages prolonged usage of dial-up internet--the predominant mode of access in the country. ZAMTEL has failed to meet demand for land phone lines. Current World Bank data estimates Zambia's population at 11,669,534 million, with an installed capacity of 140,589

telephone lines on the Public Switched Telephone Network (with over 30,000 more applicants on the waitlist for phone lines), which roughly translates to a density of only 0.8. Additionally, Zambia has international Internet bandwidth of only 11 bites per person. Thus, Zambia has less than two phones available for every 100 people - one of the lowest telephone densities in Southern Africa.

Similarly, subscription for domestic and commercial internet services is low relative to the total population in Zambia. By mid 2002, estimates were that Zambia had about 7,500 paying customers spread across a total of five ISPs- Zamnet, Coppernet, ZAMTEL, Microlink and UUNet. Zamnet, Coppernet, and Zamnet received the lion share at 3,500, 1,800 and 1,500 respectively. Consequently, most individuals find it cheaper and more convenient to use Internet cafés for their Internet needs. Given Zambia's per capita income, however, the hourly and per minute charge rates of the Internet cafés are prohibitively expensive for prolonged use of internet services at these sites (see Table 2).

For the poor, especially in rural areas, a more significant factor is that, although the costs of telecommunication are generally high throughout the country, they are much higher in rural areas.

Table 2. Telephone Costs for Internet Access (The e-Brain Forum of Zambia, 2004)

Area (Province)	Cost Tel/ Hour To ISP*POP*	Aver Cost of 60 internet Hrs/month
Lusaka, Cop'belt, L'stone	Local Access $0.7 /hr	$21.00
Eastern – Chipata	$16.2	$486.00
Western – Mongu	$16.2	$486.00
North Western - Solwezi,	$12.15	$364.50
Kabompo, Zambezi	$16.20	$486.00
Luapula - Mansa,	$6.08	$182.40
Kawambwa	$12.15	$364.50
Northern - Kasama,	$12.15	$486.00
Mbala/Mpulungu	$16.20	$486.00
Southern – Choma	$6.08	$182.40

Note. This does not reflect current charges and is not intended to do so. It is rather intended to illustrate the geographical price discrepancies in IT's affordability. Factoring in inflation and the fact that the competition landscape remains virtually unchanged, the current prices may be actually higher.

This coupled with the per-unit rather than periodic billing marginalizes the rural poor, who mostly survive on less than a dollar a day. Given a centralized government and a concentration of businesses in the urban areas, the need for telecommunication is greater in rural areas, but that is also where the market works to make telecommunication more expensive. It could be argued that since most public outcries, riots and demonstrations in 1991 and 2001 took place in the urban areas, the efficiency of communication in those areas contributed to the public being well informed about planned demonstrations.

Case Discussion

The Civil society in Zambia offers considerable promise. Regarding the incorporation of ICTs to buttress it however, it can be argued to be still in its inception. Using eGovernance readiness as a proxy for the readiness or capacity of the society to use cyber social networking as a tool for civil society mobilization, the country ranks low. On a scale of a country's progress towards technology application, Zambia could be considered to be still at the first stage; it has not yet achieved the enhanced, interactive, and transactional forms of web presence. Thus the prospects of using ICT for civil society mobilization in the country are hampered by access and affordability issues, due to limited ICT infrastructure capacity, protectionist policies in telecommunication sector which impede competitive pricing, a market structure that is unfavorable for the rural poor and most importantly high unemployment, high poverty and low computer literacy levels. Given the economic situation, the limited communication capacity, the cost of technology and the political and organizational culture, the need for adopting affordable and appropriate technology is obvious.

Mobilization in the Zambian case in both the 1991 and the 2001 cases was through print media, radio and television while word of mouth was also key. While the 1991 multi-party campaign took

place in a more hostile environment, with tighter media control and restricted freedoms, the 2001 oasis led green ribbon and car honking campaigns took place in a much less hostile environment. While it could be argued that telephone and the internet communication were most likely used among the organizers, these modes of communication were clearly not employed in mobilizing the masses. Newspaper, radio and limited television adverts were used to mobilize support and attendance at rallies. The nature of the 'revolutions' in Zambia has been undergirded by mass public dissatisfaction which reached the critical mass and revolted against the political establishment. Since it has been mostly dependent on public outcry, the public whose issue attention cycle is constantly moving and shifts to other issues as soon as one is achieved, civil society causes have not been sustained. This reality is well encapsulated by Callaghy (1994) who argues that such mass movements are not necessarily a sign of the existence of civil society, but that rather viable economic bases are necessary for the autonomy of civil society organizations, because if a weak economic base precedes the change achieved such a situation will Persist and carry with it the associated culture of rent seeking and neopatrimonialism which threaten the viability and integrity of civil society. This culture persisted in the multiparty era and the Oasis forum alliance creates insulation from political manipulation that individual civil society groups can get from government and creates some stability and sustained agenda while increasing their bargaining power. With poor statistics for telephones/100, bandwidth per person, few internet subscribers and high poverty levels, the web presence has not matured enough to a stage where it can be meaningfully be used for mass mobilization or sensitization campaigns. They have to still rely on older forms of media which are more informatory than participatory like newspapers and the television and radio. With strict information controls and with the licensing authority for media organizations still heavily vested in government such modes receive challenges. With the majority of masses still not having access to phone lines, even this alternative is farfetched. This then validates Walzer's argument of the civil society paradox, which posits that for civil society to thrive, a certain level of good governance and the resultant economic development should be achieved first. This is true in the Zambian case and arguably to most other Sub-Saharan and developing countries in general.

CONCLUSION

The contextual imperatives of African civil society dictate that they focus on democratic consolidation, given that at least nominally, these countries have introduced competitive multi-party democracies. However, some undemocratic tendencies in these new democracies increase the chances of African civil society facing an identity crisis vis-à-vis their mission. This is because if the assumption of democratic establishment taking root is made then civil society's role and response would be expected to be that of democratic consolidation; collaboration with the state. On the other hand if emphasis is laid on the undemocratic tendencies then confrontation would be the expected response. The cultural impediments such as corruption, ethnic and religious factions, coupled with resource challenges also appear to pervade Africa's civil society and weaken its impact. These elements appear to undercut consensus building which according to (Arefi, 2003) is a key indicator of a vibrant civil society. The need for effective consensus building is demonstrated in the oasis forum case in Zambia.

While ICTs have the potential to overcome many of the logistical hurdles that nascent democracies in weak economies face, the discussion of ICTs capabilities of civil society and how civil society exploits these capabilities to achieve

organizational goals in these contexts cannot be of any import without the inclusion of the actual analysis of the contextual elements and the nature and strength of civil society itself. The results in this study corroborate the ICT paradox; that while ICTs can be a solution to aid civil society organizations overcome their contextual bottlenecks, it is in many cases these same contextual bottlenecks that limit civil society's ability to effectively apply technology to achieve their organizational challenges such as civic engagement or social mobilization. The study identified various hurdles that limit the ability of civil society to apply ICTs for civic engagement in any meaningful way. Policy instruments and political will, as the Zambian case shows, are key to making this a reality. ICT literacy levels are important and so are physical and financial access issues to ICT infrastructure, services and technology. The digital divide that exists even within regions of the SSA region is a cause of concern to the attainment of ICT capabilities in the region. What the Zambian case demonstrates also is that in order to access ICT capabilities not only the quantitative but the qualitative approaches should be undertaken. This is because, as Tettey (2001) would suggest, the contextual bottlenecks seem to be such that even the currently available capabilities and the associated potential for increased information sharing these opportunities present are not being used in ways that is transforming political discourse, or participation. Similarly, the extent of ICT driven civic engagement remains to be fully exploited.

REFERENCES

Anheier, H., Glasius, M., & Kaldor, M. (2001). Introducing global civil society. In Anheier, H., Glasius, M., & Kaldor, M. (Eds.), *Global civil society*. Oxford, UK: Oxford University Press.

Anheier, H., & Themudo, N. (2002). Organisational forms of global civil society: Implications of going public. In Glasius, M., Kaldor, M., & Anheier, H. (Eds.), *Global civil society*. New York, NY: Oxford University Press.

Arefi, M. (2003). Revisiting the Los Angeles Neighborhood Initiative (LANI): Lessons for planners. *Journal of Planning Education and Research*, *22*(4), 384. doi:10.1177/0739456X03022004005

Argaez, E. D. (2009). *The Internet big picture: World Internet users and population stats*. Retrieved February 12, 2010, from http://www.internetworldstats.com/stats.htm

Bartlett, D. M. C. (2000). Civil society and democracy: A Zambian case study. *Journal of Southern African Studies*, *26*(3), 429–446. doi:10.1080/030570700750019655

Basu, S. (2004). E-government and developing countries: An overview. *International Review of Law Computers & Technology*, *18*(1), 109–132. doi:10.1080/13600860410001674779

Callaghy, T. (1994). Civil society, democracy, and economic change in Africa: A dissenting opinion about resurgent societies. In Harbeson, J., Rothchild, D., & Chazan, N. (Eds.), *Civil society and the state in Africa*. Boulder, CO: Lynne Rienner.

Centre for Civil Society. (2004). *What is civil society?* Retrieved February, 13, 2010, from http://www.lse.ac.uk/collections/CCS/what_is_civil_society.htm

Chatfield, D. (1991). The information revolution and the shaping of a democratic global order. In Riemer, N. (Ed.), *New thinking and developments in international politics: Opportunities and dangers* (pp. 135–165). Lanham, MD: University Press of America.

CIVICUS: World Alliance for Citizen Participation. (2003/2004). *The CIVICUS civil society index toolkit*.

Clark, J., & Themudo, N. (2003). The age of protest: Internet-based dot causes and the anti-globalization movement. In Clark, J. (Ed.), *Globalizing civic engagement: Civil society and transnational action*. London, UK: Earthscan.

Coombs, W. T. (1998). The Internet as potential equalizer: New leverage for confronting social irresponsibility. *Public Relations Review*, *24*(3), 289–303. doi:10.1016/S0363-8111(99)80141-6

Diamond, L. (1989). Beyond authoritarianism and totalitarianism: Strategies for democratization. *The Washington Quarterly*, *12*, 141–142. doi:10.1080/01636608909443713

Diamond, L., Linz, J. J., & Lipset, S. M. (Eds.). (1988). *Democracy in developing countries: Africa (Vol. 2)*. Boulder, CO: Lynne Rienner.

Foley, M. W., & Edwards, B. (1996). The Paradox of Civil Society. *Journal of Democracy*, *7*(3), 38–52. doi:10.1353/jod.1996.0048

Foley, M. W., & Edwards, B. (1997). Escape from politics? Social theory and the social capital debate. *The American Behavioral Scientist*, *40*(5), 550–561. doi:10.1177/0002764297040005002

Gould, J. (2008). Subsidiary sovereignty and the constitution of political space in Zambia? In Gewald, J.-B., Hinfelaar, M., & Macola, G. (Eds.), *One Zambia, many histories: Towards a history of post-colonial Zambia*. Leiden, The Netherlands; Boston, MA: Brill Academic Publishers. doi:10.1163/ej.9789004165946.i-304.95

Gyimah-Boadi, E. (1996). Civil society In Africa. *Journal of Democracy*, *7*(2), 118–132. doi:10.1353/jod.1996.0025

Hair, J. F., Black, W. C., & Babin, B. J. Anderson, R. E. & Tatham R. L. (2006). *Multivariate data analysis*, 6th ed. Upper Saddle River, NJ: Prentice-Hall, Incorporated.

IDA, & IMF. (2007). *Heavily Indebted Poor Countries (HIPC) Initiative and Multilateral Debt Relief Initiative (MDRI) —status of implementation*. International Development Association (IDA) and International Monetary Fund (IMF).

International Telecommunication Union. (2007). *World telecommunication/ICT indicators*. Retrieved 12 September, 2008, from http://www.itu.int/ITU- D/icteye/Indicators/Indicators.aspx# K. Banaian & B. Roberts (Eds.). (2008). *The design and use of political economy indicators: Challenges of definition, aggregation and application*. New York, NY: Palgrave Macmillan.

Kahn, R., & Kellner, D. (2004). New media and Internet activism: From the battle of Seattle to blogging. *New Media & Society, 6*(1), 87–95. doi:10.1177/1461444804039908

Kunz, F. A. (1995). Review: Civil society in Africa. *The Journal of Modern African Studies, 33*(1), 181–187. doi:10.1017/S0022278X00020991

Ministry of Communication and Transport. (2006). *National information and technology policy*. Lusaka, Zambia: Government Republic of Zambia.

Misuraca, G. C. (2006). E-governance in Africa: From theory to action: A practical-oriented research and case studies on ICTs for local governance. *ACM International Conference Proceeding Series, 151*, 209-218.

Ndou, V. (2004). E-government for developing countries: Opportunities and challenges. *The Electronic Journal on Information Systems in Developing Countries EJISDC, 18*(1), 1–24.

Putnam, R. D. (1995). Bowling alone: America's decling social capital. *Journal of Democracy, 6*(6), 64–78.

Tapscott, D. (1996). *The digital economy*. New York, NY: McGraw Hill.

Tettey, W. J. (2001). Information Technology and democratic participation in Africa. *Journal of Asian and African Studies, 36*(1), 133–153. doi:10.1177/002190960103600107

The e-Brain Forum of Zambia. (2004). *Report of the Information and Communication Technology (ICT) in Local Government Workshop, ICTs for sustainability: Can local councils build capacity for change?* Lusaka, Zambia.

The Mo Ibrahim Foundation. (2008). *2007 Ibrahim index of African governance*. Retrieved.

Transparency International. (2007). *2007 Transparency International corruption perceptions index*. Retrieved September 12, 2008, from http://www.transparency.org/policy_research/surveys_indices/cpi/2007

UNDP. (2002). *E-governance an impetus for the private sector the Zambian case*. Paper presented at the Asia-Pacific Development Information Programme Workshop entitled "Promoting Cooperation in Information and Communication Technologies Development", Kuala Lumpur and Penang, Malaysia.

United Nations. (2008). *World urbanization prospects: The 2007 revision population database*. Retrieved September 12, 2008, from http://esa.un.org/unup

Walzer, M. (1992). The civil society argument. In Mouffe, C. (Ed.), *Dimensions of radical democracy: Pluralism, citizenship, community*. London, UK: Verso.

Chapter 12
Setting the Foundation for E-Democracy in Botswana:
An Exploratory Study of Interventions

Kelvin Joseph Bwalya
University of Johannesburg, South Africa

Tanya Du Plessis
University of Johannesburg, South Africa

Chris Rensleigh
University of Johannesburg, South Africa

ABSTRACT

The process of establishing appropriate institutional frameworks and information and communication technology (ICT) infrastructure backbones to support future development of e-democracy is not an easy task. Botswana has started building its e-democracy institutions as it accords citizens the opportunity to participate in the democratic process using appropriate ICT platforms out of the realization that participatory democracy is crucial in placing a country at a competitive edge in the contemporary global socio-economic value chains. Towards this goal, the first initiative has been the establishment of the e-government taskforce team, which has been mandated with the development of an e-government strategy commensurate with Botswana's local context. The establishment of the e-government taskforce team has been done in tandem with putting in place appropriate ICT infrastructures and legal, institutional, or regulatory frameworks. This chapter presents an exploratory study that aims to discuss the different interventions that are being put in place by the Botswana government and its co-operating partners as setting the foundation for implementing full-scale e-democracy applications such as e-forums and e-voting. The chapter also presents obstacles and challenges that have not been met, insofar as building virtual public spheres in the realm of participatory e-democracy in Botswana is concerned. Attention

DOI: 10.4018/978-1-60960-159-1.ch012

is given to how virtual public spheres should be used as collaboration and networking platforms both in the private and public sectors of Botswana. It is anticipated that the different approaches that have been employed by Botswana towards this course may prove useful to other emerging nations who may have intentions of implementing ICT infrastructure and encouraging virtual public spheres as a means to building viable e-democracy.

INTRODUCTION

Virtual public spheres (VPS) have made it possible for people of different socio-economic status to participate in decision-making of public matters. They have also enabled marginal individuals to participate in the various socio-economic activities; a phenomenon called social inclusion. VPS is one of the pre-requisites for effective e-democracy implementation. E-government is the use of ICTs in the interaction between the government and citizens or businesses for effective public service delivery. VPS allow both the public and private sector to interact effectively and exchange ideas for socio-economic development. This being the case, we may look at VPS along with e-government as being the two main pre-requisites for e-democracy.

This chapter defines a VPS as an open environment which allows interaction of different actors for the purpose of deliberation about the issues through ICT platforms. A platform of relevance to Africa's ICT users is that of mobile technologies. With the increase in the adoption and use of mobile technologies in Africa, it suffices to mention that more and more people will be able to take advantage and unleash the full potential of ICTs. Several African governments, with their goal to further promote decentralization to the household or individual level, have started implementing e-government, which, in turn, helps to promote the precursors to e-democracy. This public service delivery model of e-government has a huge promise for contributing to the socio-economic development agenda of Africa. In most parts of Africa, however, the potential of e-democracy is limited because of local culture's propensity to resist change.

We define e-democracy as the use of ICTs for ordinary individuals to participate in policy and decision-making, which will have an impact on their future and that of their children's. An example of e-democracy is e-Voting, which is defined as the use of ICTs in the voting process. E-democracy is an emerging phenomenon that makes it possible for ICT to be used in the formulation of policies and liberation of democracy (Stahl, 2005). E-democracy enables ordinary community members to determine their socio-economic course by enabling them to participate in decision and policy-making using ICTs at anytime and anywhere. It uses a bottom-up approach where participatory policy/decision making is the norm of the day and this ushers in a sense of ownership of the policies/decisions made. By allowing citizens to participate in the democratic processes using ICTs, citizens feel they own the policies that come out of government – citizen interaction and therefore buy-in to those policies.

The first step towards achieving e-democracy is successfully implementing e-government. Netchaeva (2002) argues that e-government ushers in a paradigm where transparency in public institutions is achieved; enables ordinary citizens to access public information freely and conveniently; and encourages wider participation of citizens in their democratic endeavors. ICT use in governance may intrinsically change relationships in society, help to achieve real democratic means and even transform people's social and political consciousness. Democracy is the ideal society where all citizens together decide how this society should be run and ruled. Stahl (2005, p.77) has identified the major constructs of e-government and e-democracy as follows: "e-government as the technological delivery of administrative services and e-democracy as the technological enhancement of primary democratic processes".

There are several conceptual distinctions between e-government and e-democracy. The former emphasizes the interaction between government and citizens or businesses, promotion of social inclusion, and seamless integration between the different departments of the government whereas the later emphasizes citizens' participation in the policy/decision-making processes. E-democracy makes it possible for the different members of the socio-economic structures such as civil society, all other private sector entities, and ordinary and marginal individuals to participate in the policy/decision-making processes. VPS, in this regard, acts as a collaborative or interactive platform, one that makes it possible for different socio-economic players to collaborate or participate in national policy development. VPS may contribute to ushering in the convergence and the socio-technical dynamism of e-democracy and e-government.

This chapter presents an exploratory study of the different interventions that are being pursued with the goal to eventually establish appropriate e-democracy institutions in Botswana. It discusses the role of civil society in utilizing the existing VPS for engagement with the government and other stakeholders for the sake of political and socio-economic development. The chapter also investigates the challenges faced by the Botswana government's efforts to promote its e-democracy agenda (it brings out the contextual issues in this regard) and investigates how ICT can be utilized as efficient tools in the e-democracy platform. It also questions whether Botswana has the basic ICT infrastructure to effectively promote e-democracy applications and how this must be adapted to the socio-economic hierarchies. The study is important in that it contributes to our understanding of

the development of e-democracy structures in developing societies and the recognition that the successful adoption of virtual public spheres in any environment depends on local factors such as culture, availability of appropriate ICT infrastructures, mindset of the people, and technical/usability aspects of the technological platform utilized. The discussions presented here draw from comprehensive literature and document reviews.

The chapter is organized as follows: in the next section, the background of this study is presented. In this section, the characteristics of the virtual public spheres and the status of VPS in developing countries are discussed. Then, a discussion on the current status of VPS's incorporation into the e-democracy framework and the different interventions being pursued in the realm of VPS in Botswana is presented. The analysis of the study is then discussed followed by a section on future work and recommendations. The chapter concludes by briefly summarizing this survey of interventions in setting the foundation for e-democracy in Botswana.

BACKGROUND

The Virtual Public Sphere and its Characteristics

Before we get into the discussion of VPS in Botswana, we must first look at some VPS prerequisites in general. For a VPS to be realized, the three major components required are the Internet, the connecting ICTs, and participants who access the VPS digital contents. Appropriate ICTs such as personal computers, personal digital assistants and mobile phones are the platforms through which the Internet is accessed. Providing ICT access in itself may not be adequate, VPS requires effective utilization of ICT that translates into e-Participation. The Internet provides a platform through which a VPS is realized and facilitates networking and interaction of different civil society organizations. Although this is the ideal, Aslama and Erikson (2009) wonder whether actual VPS facilitate participation and stimulate democratic debate characterized by networked information economy.

Effective e-democracy initiatives start from ensuring availability of effective ICT platforms to allow citizen and civil society engagement. ICT-readiness coupled with supportive political will, a developed civil society, appropriate institutional, legal and regulatory frameworks, and enthusiastic citizenry have a significant impact on the possibility of the ordinary citizens to participate in e-democracy. Tiamiyu and Aina (2008, p. 5) have broadly defined ICTs as "technologies that are used for capturing, creating, accessing, manipulating, presenting, communicating and transferring knowledge and information". ICTs include hardware, processes, and systems that are used for storing, managing, communicating and sharing information and these tools can be either analogue or digital (Duncombe and Heeks, 1999). ICTs can also be defined as technologies that allow users to participate in a rapidly changing world in which work and other activities are increasingly transformed by access to varied and developing technologies. For the purposes of this chapter, *ICT is defined as any technologies that are used in the context of information capturing, processing, storing and use and any gadgets or means through which information is exchanged between two or more entities.* In this context, notable examples of ICTs can be mobile phones, digital cameras, personal computers, telephone lines, radios, pagers, personal digital assistants (PDAs), and fax machines.

The importance of ICT cannot be overemphasized as it has been shown to positively influence production levels in industries and encourage higher efficiency levels (organizations, and even countries, can now efficiently manage information with more responsive and transparent resource management); promote faster and efficient information interchange and sharing;

and promote anywhere, anytime availability of information. Mutula and Van Brakel (2006) further point out that ICTs have improved service delivery and have been instrumental in opening up opportunities for socio-economic development and integration. This has further into the ushering in of an e-democracy paradigm which accords even marginal individuals to participate in the democratic process through VPSs. For the case of Botswana, emerging e-Democratic practices such as publishing of Botswana laws online (see http://www.laws.gov.bw) have raised the profile of the country by increasing transparency and foreign investor confidence. Further, ICTs have lead to the reduction of poverty from various levels of the socio-economic hierarchy, and in some circles, ICTs have led to massive employment creation. Having outlined all these benefits which only form a fraction of the gamut of spectrum of benefits of effective use of ICTs, it is important to look at the factors that may thwart the achievement of these worthwhile benefits.

E-democracy facilitates both bottom-up and top-down initiatives, helps empower civil society to have a voice in the democratic processes and encourage public private partnerships and engagements. Some of the common applications of e-democracy are e-Voting, e-Lobbying, e-Consultation and e-Participation in decision-making through participation in e-Forums concentrating on national issues so as to inform policy or decision-making.

Grönlund, Gross and Ives (2001) have outlined the major global challenges that affect e-democracy. Some of the profound issues are: 1) lack of a global or standardized definition of e-democracy. In this regard, different stakeholders define e-democracy according to different views and implementation strategies; 2) lack of appropriate institutional, regulatory and legal frameworks especially in less developed areas to inform e-democracy focus; 3) lack of general clear understanding of what e-democracy research should comprise. If this is the case, it means even coming up with an informed e-democracy implementation and adoption strategy is a far-fetched dream.

Rycroft (2007, p.2) posits that VPS builds "a new political culture that is more fluid, decentralized, diverse, and global than cultures of the past, which may move society beyond traditional political oligarchies towards greater participatory democracy, flexible coalitions and networks managing political affairs, and communication and information processes that are more influential than in previous generations". Thus VPS, coupled with e-democracy, will make it possible for marginalized voices to participate in the decision-making processes and to make sure their voices and concern on national matters are heard. VPS also allows sharing of information amongst the groups that compose civil society so that they can effectively participate in the democratic processes. VPS makes it possible to hold leaders accountable for the decisions they make and to ensure that national resources are managed with an acceptable level of precision and accountability by making transparent information from the government administrative processes. On the one hand, e-government makes it possible to streamline certain government processes; on the other, VPS contributes to e-democracy by encouraging effective and valued participation of the citizens in the democratic value chains. E-government and VPS also pressure the traditional media institutions to vigorously use the virtual architecture to disseminate information with a view towards challenging the hegemonic viewpoint of the state (Chan, 2005). All this contributes to the growth of e-democracy.

E-Democracy in Developing Countries

Most countries in the developing world have not done much at least in the way of establishing appropriate e-democracy institutions. As has been mentioned earlier, a prerequisite of implementing e-democracy is the establishment of e-government initiatives. Some of the developing countries that have made considerable strides on implementing e-government are India, Brazil, South Korea, Nepal, Singapore, Malaysia, South Africa, Ghana, Egypt and Mauritius. These countries have dedicated e-government strategies and adequately developed ICT infrastructure backbones. Some countries such as Tanzania, Botswana, Ghana and China have just started setting their e-government agendas and have started establishing the necessary institutional legal and regulatory frameworks towards the same. This indicates that e-democracy in developing countries is just emerging as most of the countries in the developing world are just now establishing e-government interventions. The reasoning behind this is that there can never be e-democracy without first being a significant degree of penetration and adoption of e-government by the ordinary citizens. This is because e-democracy represents a culmination and extension of the implementation of e-government in the political realm. As earlier stated, e-democracy emphasizes more citizen participation using ICTs in the political process (i.e., e-Participation). Most developing countries find themselves facing the opportunity cost of pursuing more citizen-centric, i.e., e-democracy, initiatives versus development endeavors such as creating roads. Suffice it to mention here that e-government strategizing and implementation often comes with huge socio-technical and economic costs that are beyond most of the developing countries' capabilities.

In a nutshell, one major challenge to nurturing the benefits of ICT usage in Africa has been its unreliable ICT infrastructures. As stated by Gerster Consulting (2008), unreliable infrastructures lead to high transaction costs, which make ICT use prohibitively expensive. This challenge has been compounded by negative cultural stances towards ICT in general on the part of the people. Generally, people do not feel secure in virtual public spheres and thus may not use them to interact with the government or fellow citizens effectively. This has had a direct negative impact on development of e-democracy and related institutions in Botswana. In the African context, generally, the factors that affect adoption of technologies, and by extension e-government and e-democracy, have much to do with lack of trust, low and unreliable ICT infrastructures, lack of adequate and appropriate ICT skills, and lack of dedicated legal, institutional and ICT regulatory frameworks. In the case of VPS, and correspondingly e-democracy, the issue of trust is amplified. However, this is not to state that the other issues are not of equally vital importance. Since e-democracy and virtual public spheres are multi-dimensional in nature, it is necessary to closely consider all the different factors that impact on them in the broadest possible context.

Botswana's E-Democracy Prospects

E-Government Adoption and Political Situation in Botswana

Botswana is located in the Southern African region and is a member of the vibrant socio-economic regional grouping known as the Southern Africa – the Southern African Development Community (SADC). In relation to its size of roughly 582,000 square kilometers, Botswana is sparsely populated with a population of just over 1.8 million people and with a growth rate of 2.5% per annum (Bedia, 2009). As of 2008, there have been 142,300 telephone main lines in use, 1.486 million mobile cellular telephone subscriptions, and mobile-cellular telephone density currently is about 80 per 100 persons (CIA, 2010).

Generally, Botswana has been frequently referred to as an "African miracle" because of its record of transparency in its government business processes and value chains. Soest (2009) performed an exploratory study on the current status of Botswana's government and ascertained that neopatrimonialism, which acts as a check on good and acceptable governance, seems to be very low in Botswana. Corruption levels in the major

sectors of its economy are also comparatively low as evidenced by the country's score on different corruption indices such as Corruption Perceptions Index (CPI) produced by the international NGO, Transparency International. Botswana maintains a multi-party political system and has a political environment where different stakeholders including civil society, church-based-organizations, diplomats, and individual citizens are given a platform to participate in the governance process. Most of the government line ministries and departments can be accessed online at the national e-government portal www.gov.bw. Botswana has an adequate presence on the Internet and has a dedicated e-government taskforce team, which has been mandated with developing a robust e-government implementation and adoption strategy. The political will is there to carry out government businesses online as is evidenced by the establishment of novel institutional and regulatory frameworks such as the Botswana Telecommunications Authority (BTA) and the Botswana Telecommunications Company (BTC), which regulate the ICT sector in Botswana and encourages its proliferation. Currently, there are attempts to make electronic signatures (e-Signatures) and documents (e-Documents) legally binding.

ICT Infrastructure Preparedness

In general, the majority of citizens in any society can access e-democracy applications only when appropriate ICT infrastructures have been put in place. Thus, it is important to ensure that the technological base of e-democracy, the infrastructure, allows easy and costless access, has proper usability qualities and is able to easily process information (King, 2006).

Given these criteria, the prospects for ICT infrastructure preparedness in Botswana is mixed when we recognize that the government and other co-operating partners have started implementing interventions that will revamp the ICT infrastructure and regulation landscape. To this end, appropriate legal, institutional and regulatory frameworks are currently being put in place to make sure that Botswana becomes an IT hub in Southern Africa. Botswana's government is dedicated to placing itself at the competitive edge of knowledge-based economies and in order to do this, it has realized that ICT infrastructure and the ICT sector in general should be developed to a significant degree. On the ICT regulatory, institutional and legal fronts, Botswana has established the BTA and BTC as ICT regulatory bodies and watchdogs, as noted above. Botswana has also put in place rigorous ICT policies (such as the Maitlamo ICT policy of 2006) in order to draw the ICT implementation roadmap for the country. On the infrastructure side, Botswana has just commissioned the Trans-Kgalagadi optical fibre network in 2008, and has also subscribed to the Eastern Africa Submarine Cable System (EASSy) considered the state-of-the-art ICT infrastructure initiative for African countries (Bwalya, 2009). Botswana also encourages universal service and access through the Universal Service and Access Policy of 2002. Another effort towards ICT adoption has been the country's participation in international forums such as the second conference of African Ministers in charge of Communication and Information Technologies, which adopted the reference framework for harmonization of telecommunication and ICT policies and regulation in Africa and Egypt (HIPSSA project, 2008).

Put succinctly, the cornerstones on which Botswana's ICT adoption framework is based are the following: well-informed public policy (e.g. Maitlamo ICT policy) including implementation follow-ups facilitated by alert ICT sector watchdogs; advocacy leadership (with leaders in the ICT sector and political leaders firmly dedicated and committed to the ICT growth agenda); transparency and accountability in ICT resource procurement and deployment; gender equity (where all citizens are empowered to take advantage of what ICT has to offer; and awareness campaign strategies on the benefits of ICTs, and infrastructure and easy accessibility.

Civil Society and Citizen Engagement

On a general level, civil society remains very weak in Botswana (Lekorwe, 1999). The Botswana Council of Non-Governmental Organizations, BOCONGO, has an online presence (www.bocongo.org.bw) and acts as coordinator of all NGOs in Botswana and as a networking platform. BOCONGO is an umbrella body that was formed to organize the basically weak civil society in Botswana. However, as a result of having a good record of governance and governmental transparency, civil society organizations continue to grow daily in Botswana. Civil society organizations supplement government's ongoing efforts at producing a corruption free society in Botswana and also keep check of government programming and service delivery models. Several of Botswana's civil society organizations have recently been using ICTs to promote collaboration, networking and engagement in various issues that affect humanity in general. Some of these issues include soliciting for funds from the donor community, fighting HIV/AIDS, fighting the plight of women in society (discouraging gender violence), employee protection, basic human rights, advice to government on different government issues and participation in the general democratic government processes.

Some civil society organizations in Botswana have been utilizing ICTs and other platforms to make sure that the marginalized individuals fully participate in socio-economic activities, including early efforts at e-democracy. An issue of high importance in Botswana in the recent past has been HIV/AIDS. To this end, a consortium of NGOs called Botswana Network on Ethics, Law and HIV/AIDS (BONELA) have created a VPS (www.bonela.org) as a means to collaborate with Botswana's citizens who are living with HIV/AIDS and with the appropriate organizations so that no one is discriminated against on the grounds of their HIV/AIDS status. Through this platform, HIV/AIDS positive people are also given a platform to participate in decision-making using ICTs such as the Internet, mobile phones and PDAs. Other civil society organizations which have formed VPS in Botswana include Women and Law in Southern Africa Trust (WLSA), Ditshwanelo (Botswana Human Rights Center), Emang basadi (Women's Association), and the Botswana National Youth Council (BNYC). The different civil society organizations which fight for the plight of the workers include the Botswana Federation of Trade Unions (BFTU), Botswana Teachers Union (BTU), Botswana Secondary Teachers Union (BOFETU) and the Botswana Primary Schools Association (BOPRITA). Despite these efforts, online participation is still in its infancy although it will be correct to state that a foundation is being laid for future potential massive online participation.

Barriers to Adopting E-Democracy in Botswana

At the current moment, Botswana is in the first stages of developing its e-democracy institutions and the different endeavors that are being put in place will serve, it is hoped, as the essential foundation for the full-scale implementation of e-democracy applications at a later stage. At the moment, however, no citizen input mechanisms can be established as this concept is only currently being introduced in Botswana. For example, the e-government portal found at www.gov.bw does not offer an interactive platform where citizens and businesses can connect with the government. This portal is mostly used by the citizens to obtain information on government departments, to find out what has been decided upon by the executive, and to read about the jobs advertised in different government departments. For businesses, this portal offers a platform for them to know what jobs or tenders have been awarded by the government, find information on specific taxes

that businesses are liable to pay and so forth. In short, the portal does not directly allow citizens and businesses to participate in decision-making nor does it have any forums where citizens can participate in decision-making. This means the input from these two important stakeholders in decision-making processes is not currently being considered when the government makes decisions. Thus, e-democracy cannot be said to be achieved to any appreciable extent as ordinary citizens are currently not given a chance to air their views on important national issues using the VPS or e-government.

Despite having accomplished some of the initial stages of the different interventions that, it is hoped, would later encourage the establishment of e-democracy in Botswana, there are still some challenges that remain. Blackhouse (2007) has argued that for e-democracy efforts to succeed, it is necessary to have more than information and service delivery, but there must also be the appropriate facilities which can facilitate the participation of the general citizenry into the actual decision-making processes. Since e-democracy is a multi-dimensional phenomenon, risks and barriers to e-democracy adoption may include social, political, technical, financial, legal, institutional or organizational, and cultural issues.

On the technological side, e-democracy remains very difficult to implement for several important reasons. First, due to a lack of stable power supply in many parts of Botswana (mainly rural zones), in many parts of the country, many people cannot even charge their mobile terminals or connect a computer to access the Internet. Second, there is also a lack of technological knowledge and a culture that is generally adverse to technology so that many people do not understand the possibilities that ICT has to offer, which is compounded by the lack of awareness campaigns from the government or other co-operating partners. Third, there are the difficulties to ensure an adequate return for technology investors due to the impoverishment of a large section of the population. Fourth, access points for ordinary individuals to computers or other ICTs such as mobile phones or PDAs to access the Internet are limited. Finally, is the limited ICT skills of the majority of the population, which serves to effectively curtail e-Participation. In order to overcome these barriers to e-democracy adoption in Botswana, there have been a number of major developments, which are discussed next.

Major Developments Towards the Future Adoption of E-Democracy

The Botswana government and other co-operating partners have pursued different types of interventions to increase the chances of realizing e-democracy in the future. What these different stakeholders acknowledge is that e-democracy is a multi-faceted phenomenon and realizing it involves consecutively tackling the different challenges that accompany e-democracy development and implementation. The first major step has been developing the ICT infrastructure backbone in major cities. The following are some of the different developments that have also been put in place:

- Promoting ICT skills literacy programmes at the community levels. This will, it is hoped, have a positive impact on building future e-democracy applications and increase e-Participation as most people will be able to access government information through ICTs.

- Encouraging ICT access through telecenters such as Community Access Centers (CAC) – Kitsong – which were initiated in 2006/07 to serve as gate-way to the Internet and access to other services in the rural areas. With this initiative, rural communities, which do not have access to the Internet and have no access to electricity such as Letlhakeng, Central Kgalagadi Game Reserve, Gumare and areas surrounding Okavango (Duncombe and Heeks, 1999)

will be empowered with Internet access. This should later help to encourage the building of e-democracy applications.

- Massive investments in setting up appropriate ICT infrastructures such as the funding of the trans-kgalagadi optical fibre network. This commitment can also be seen in the government's pledge of US $60 million to rehabilitate and fortify the national telecommunications network. The Kgalagadi (Trans-Kalahari) fibre optic project which runs approximately 2000 km is a multi-million Pula (Botswana currency) project funded by the government (Chengeta, 2003).

- With a goal to reduce the digital divide between the rural and urban dwellers ion Botswana, the Botswana Technology Center (BTC) is piloting a community user-information system. Rural communities are linked by means of an online computer to the capital city, Gaborone. These centers provide public access to Internet resources and provide them with a platform through which ordinary individuals can reach even the socially unreachable individuals. In the long run, it is anticipated that the centers will also provide small business services and offer basic computer literacy lessons.

- Botswana Telecommunications Corporation's launch of Very Small Aperture Terminals (VSAT) technology, which, it is hoped, will play a major role in bringing services to remote areas through the use of satellite and overcome limitations placed on traditional services by vast distances.

- The BTC is actively involved in connecting the metropolitan areas especially in Francistown and Gaborone. The Botswana government has established the government data network. This network makes it possible for information-sharing amongst different government departments and therefore enables streamlining of different government departments. This initiative is a necessary first-step towards what is hoped will be the eventual development of e-democracy.

- In the realm of creating appropriate ICT infrastructure, and towards Botswana's plans to place itself at the competitive edge of global socio-economic value chains, the government has identified three VSAT sites comprising a Tele-Education Centre (learning center) at the University of Botswana (UB), a Tele-medicine Centre (Patient-end-terminal) at Nyangabgwe Referral Hospital in Northern District and a very very important parts (VVIP) Location at the Office of the President (Bwalya, 2009).

- On the ICT infrastructure front, BTC has signatory status to three consortia that are intended to develop undersea optical fibre systems: the East Africa Submarine System EASSy, to run alongside the eastern coast of Africa from Port Sudan through East African seaports down to Mtunzini in South Africa; the West Africa Festoon System (WAFS), intended to run alongside the western coast of Africa from Nigeria through Gabon, DRC down to Angola, and possibly Namibia; and the Africa West Coast Cable (AWCC), proposed to run alongside the western coast of Africa from South Africa, Namibia through to the United Kingdom (Faye and Makane, 2000).

FUTURE WORK AND RECOMMENDATIONS

Whilst much has been done in promoting ICT infrastructure and regulatory frameworks in Botswana, it is evident that still a lot has to be done before e-democracy can be instituted. The planning and the implementation of institutional backbones for promoting ICT development are evident, as has been indicated above. The ICT infrastructure deployed so far is fairly adequate, and there appears to be the political will to complete an overhaul of parts of the socio-economic environment that influence ICT use. Despite this being the case, ordinary citizens in remote places may not even be aware of what the country is doing to facilitate VPS. With a population of just over 1.6 million people, it is evident that Botswana has not done enough with awareness campaigns of the ICT and e-democracy paradigm.

This raises the question of what should be done to increase the level of interaction in the virtual public domain. Specifically, this chapter recommends the following in order to advance the e-government and e-democracy agendas in Botswana:

- Encourage all sectors of the socio-economic hierarchies to participate in bringing about virtual public spheres.

- Regulation and management of the ICT sector is a mammoth task because of the issue of multi-dimensionality. There are many attributes attached to the sector. For this reason, it is important that the public sector should be part and parcel of developing basic IT infrastructure countrywide and therefore be responsible for provision of different ICT applications.

- There should be robust ICT policy implementation follow-ups in the form of monitoring and evaluation endeavors.

- The government and other co-operating partners should encourage the use of content in local languages so that the language barrier does not limit people participating fully in public virtual spheres.

- There is a need for combined public-private sector partnerships (PPPs). These concerted efforts should see continued commitment on the part of the government;

aggressive involvement by the private sector and other institutions.

The lessons learned may further shape the design of an e-government adoption model that may inform the implementation strategy of e-government in less developed countries that share the same socio-economic profile with Botswana. Future work includes the designing of a tailor-made e-democracy implementation strategy hinged on developing robust awareness and sensitization campaigns on the adoption and use of ICTs for participatory and inclusive governance.

CONCLUSION

This chapter has presented an exploratory study that discussed the different interventions being put in place to promote ICT usage in Botswana. Since e-democracy adoption requires a multi-stage process, the first step of which is to develop e-government, which is facilitated through ICT, an appropriate ICT infrastructure backbone is needed for e-democracy's adoption. ICT infrastructure, however, is not a comprehensive requirement of e-democracy as it has been shown that e-democracy is a multi-dimensional phenomenon and depends on various other factors including policy, culture, finance, as well as organizational and regulatory frameworks in order to occur. Botswana has come up with strategic efforts to make sure that the near future will see a Botswana that has adequate ICT infrastructure; one able to use the different ICT applications to the full. It is hoped that this will translate over time into the development of e-democracy.

The chapter has surveyed the impact of virtual public networks on the democratic landscape of Botswana and unearthed the challenges faced in the emergence of ICTs into socio-economical culture of Botswana. The culture and common attitudes of people in Botswana has an important impact on how e-democracy is perceived. Gener-

ally, people do not have adequate trust in the ICT medium, especially Internet-enabled platforms, because of privacy and security issues. Factors such as usability and language content utilized also have an impact on people's perception and adoption of ICT and by extension, e-democracy. Since this chapter has presented an exploratory study and although these issues have been identified, there is still need to carry out an empirical study to confirm these assertions.

Several recommendations have been offered especially on how to make sure there is an adequate ICT environment and infrastructure to support development of e-democracy in the future. Although the recommended interventions seem novel, it should be noted that a lot of future work needs to be done. One of the needs include coming up with implementation strategies on how to transform the already-existing policies into tangible results. With the different initiatives authored by the Botswana government and other co-operating partners, and the linking of these initiatives to the national developmental strategy (Vision 2016), there is considerable hope that e-democracy may be achieved by Botswana in the future.

REFERENCES

Ajzen, I. (1991). The theory of planned behavior. *Organizational Behavior and Human Decision Processes*, *50*, 179–211. doi:10.1016/0749-5978(91)90020-T

Al-Shafi, S., & Weerakkody, V. (2009). *Understanding citizen's behavioural intention in the adoption of e-government services in the state of Qatar*. Paper presented at 17th European Conference on Information Systems, ECIS 2009.

Aslama, M., & Erikson, I. (2009). *Public spheres, networked publics, networked public spheres? Tracking the Habermasian public sphere in recent discourse*. The Donald McGannon communication research center. Working paper.

Backhouse, J. (2007). E-democracy in Australia: The challenge of evolving a successful model. *The Electronic* [from www.ejeg.com]. *Journal of E-Government, 5*(2), 107–116. Retrieved March 16, 2010.

Bedia. (2009). *Botswana information and statistics*. Retrieved November 16, 2009, from http://www.bedia.co.bw/article.php?id_mnu=37

Bwalya, K. J. (2009). IT and role/analysis of information resource in decision making in Botswana. *Conference Proceedings, IST-Africa*, May 2009, Kampala, Uganda.

Carlsson, C., Carlsson, J., Puhakainen, J., & Walden, P. (2006). *Nice mobile services do not fly. Observations of mobile services and the Finnish consumers*. 19th Bled eConference eValues, Bled, Slovenia, June 5 - 7, 2006.

Chan, B. (2005). Imagining the homeland: The Internet and diasporic discourse of nationalism. *The Journal of Communication Inquiry, 29*(4), 336–368. doi:10.1177/0196859905278499

Chengeta, N. N. (2003). *The technology based incubation in Botswana*. Workshop Paper on Technology-based Business Incubators in SADC Countries; Mauritius: WAIT publication.

CIA. (2010). *The world factbook*. Retrieved November 8, 2009, from https://www.cia.gov/library/publications/the-world-factbook/geos/bc.html

Compeau, D. R., & Higgins, C. A. (1995). Application of social cognitive theory to training for computer skills. *Information Systems Research, 6*(2), 118–143. doi:10.1287/isre.6.2.118

Davis, F. D. (1989). Perceived usefulness, perceived ease of use, and user acceptance of Information Technology. *Management Information Systems Quarterly, 13*, 319–340. doi:10.2307/249008

Davis, F. D., Bagozzi, R. P., & Warshaw, P. R. (1992). Extrinsic and intrinsic motivation to use computers in the workplace. *Journal of Applied Social Psychology, 22*, 1111–1132. doi:10.1111/j.1559-1816.1992.tb00945.x

Dillon, A., & Morris, M. (1996). User acceptance of Information Technology: Theories and models. In Williams, M. (Ed.), *ARIST (Vol. 31)*. Medford, NJ: Information Today.

Duncombe, R., & Heeks, R. (1999). *Information, ICTs and small enterprise: Findings from Botswana*. (Development Informatics Working Paper Series, Working Paper 7), Institute for Development Policy and Management, Manchester, UK, 1999. Retrieved July 23, 2009, from http://www.man.ac.uk/idpm/idpm_dp.htm

Fishbein, M., & Ajzen, I. (1975). *Belief, attitude, intention and behaviour: An introduction to theory and research*. Reading, MA: Addison-Wesley.

Gerster Consulting. (2008). *ICT in Africa: Boosting economic growth and poverty reduction*. 10th meeting of the African Partnership Forum. Retrieved July 22, 2009, from http://www.gersterconsulting.ch/docs/ICT-Africa_Report_final_engl.pdf

Grönlund, Å., Gross, T., & Ives, B. (2001). *E-democracy: A panacea or Pandora's box? E-everything: E-commerce, e-government, e-household, e-democracy*. 14th Bled Electronic Commerce Conference, Bled, Slovenia, June 25 – 26.

HIPSSA Project. (2008). *Support for harmonization of ICT policies in sub-Sahara Africa*. Retrieved July 20, 2009, from http://ua-ue-frontend.irislink.com:8080/alfresco/d/d/workspace/SpacesStore/f32c4370-03e2-11de-a48b-3f161803b677/HIPSSA_Project.doc

King, J. (2006). Democracy in the information age. *Australian Journal of Public Administration*, *65*(2), 16–32. doi:10.1111/j.1467-8500.2006.00479.x

Lekorwe, M. (1999). Local government, interest groups and civil society. In *Public administration and policy in Botswana*. Kenwyn/ Cape Town, South Africa: Juta & Co. Ltd.

Mutula, S., & Van Brakel, P. (2006). An evaluation of e-readiness assessment tools with respect to information access: Towards an integrated information tools. *International Journal of Information Management*, *26*, 212–223. doi:10.1016/j.ijinfomgt.2006.02.004

Netchaeva, I. (2002). E-government and e-democracy. *The International Journal for Communication Studies*, *64*(5), 467–477.

Rycroft, A. (2007). *Young adults and virtual public spheres: Building a new political culture*. A long paper submitted as part of the requirements for Master of Arts in Professional Communication. Retrieved October 16, 2009, from http://SunshineCommunications.ca/articles/virtual_public_spheres.pdf. Victoria, Canada: Royal Roads University.

Soest, V. C. (2009). *Stagnation of a miracle Botswana's governance record revisited*. (Working Paper no.99, German Institute of Global and Area Studies). Retrieved September 23, 2009, from www.giga-hamburg.de/workingpapers.

Stahl, B. (2005). The ethical problem of framing e-government in terms of e-commerce. *The Electronic* [from www.ejeg.com]. *Journal of E-Government*, *3*(2), 77–86. Retrieved June 15, 2009.

Taylor, S., & Todd, P. (1995). Decomposition and crossover effects in the theory of planned behavior: A study of consumer adoption intentions. *International Journal of Research in Marketing*, *12*(2), 137–156. doi:10.1016/0167-8116(94)00019-K

Thompson, R. L., Higgins, C. A., & Howell, J. M. (1991). Personal computing: Toward a conceptual model of utilization. *Management Information Systems Quarterly*, *15*(1), 125–143. doi:10.2307/249443

Tiamiyu, M. A., & Aina, L. O. (2008). Information and knowledge management in the digital age: An African perspective. In Aina, L. O., Mutula, S. M., & Tiamiyu, M. A. (Eds.), *Information and knowledge management in the digital age: Concepts, technologies and African perspectives* (pp. 3–27). Ibadan, Nigeria: Third World Information Services Limited.

Tibenderana, P., & Ogao, P. J. (2008). Information Communication Technologies acceptance and use among university communities in Uganda: A model for hybrid library services end-users. *International Journal of Computing and ICT Research*, *1*(1).

Venkatesh, V., Morris, M. G., Davis, G. B., & Davis, F. D. (2003). User acceptance of Information Technology: Toward a unified view. *Management Information Systems Quarterly*, *27*(3), 425–478.

Chapter 13
Challenges of E–Disclosure in Romanian Local Public Authorities

Adriana Tiron Tudor
Babes-Bolyai University, Romania

Adina Simona Popa
University "Eftimie Murgu" of Reşiţa, Romania

Rodica Gabriela Blidişel
West University from Timisoara, Romania

ABSTRACT

There is a growing pressure on governments to broaden the scope of their financial responsibilities from accounting to accountability. Therefore, local public authorities (LPA) must provide clear, understandable and reliable information and should increase their transparency as part of their policy of good governance practice. Starting from the international context of good corporate governance characteristics, this chapter examines the implication level of the Internet in Romanian LPA as a tool of transparency improvement for the citizen's use. Due to the pivotal role played by citizens in participatory governance, the chapter analyzes the information disclosed by LPA websites focusing mainly on the financial information, as the financial resources have a special role in the local development and represent the base for a prompt reply to the citizen's needs. The final part proposes a Romanian LPA good e-governance model as well as e-disclosure improvements for citizen's trust in LPA information.

INTRODUCTION

In recent years, important changes have occurred in the way central and local governments act in relation with citizens. Governance has evolved in this time from hierarchical bureaucracy to participatory governance, where the role of citizens in public decision-making process is more direct. Romania, a young democracy reborn over the iron curtain of socialism, passed during the last decade

DOI: 10.4018/978-1-60960-159-1.ch013

through a reform of the public sector. Starting with the reform of the public management, both at central and at local level, the Romanian public sector has further passed through the public financial reform, especially through the law regarding the local public finances. Moreover, as regards the Romanian public accounting, accrual accounting (in accordance with International Public Sector Accounting Standards) was put into practice both at the local government and the central government levels starting in January 2006.

Starting from the recent reforms in Romanian public sector, our chapter focuses on the development of local government taking into account the relation with citizens, accountability for the management and control of public resources as well as the delivery of services and its transparency.

The chapter is organized in five sections. After this introduction, Section Two provides an overview of the evolution of governance models, public good governance concept and main characteristics and aspects related with good governance in the information age. Section Three begins with the introduction to the context of Romanian local public administration system, in particular the citizens' role, and the role of service users and Civil Society in Romanian LPA governance. Also, this section examines two of the characteristics of good governance: accountability and transparency as they are understood and implemented by Romanian LPA. The level of internet disclosure of Romanian LPA is measured and a regression model is built to determine if variables including city's revenues, citizen's participation and citizen's financial recommendation are influencing the level of e-disclosure of the LPA. Section Four proposes a model of good e-governance for Romanian LPA based on the results of the research performed in the previous section. Finally, the chapter concludes with a summary of the findings and recommendations.

BACKGROUND

Framework of the Public Governance Models Evolution

First, a distinction has to be made between government and governance. The government consists of the mechanisms of state vested with authority and legitimacy to act on citizens through the three main powers - legislative, executive and judicial – along with the institutions that concentrate power and implement decisions - in essence, referring to the official state institutions. In turn, *governance* refers to an alternative to official state action (United Nations Economic Commission for Europe, 2008), which aims at (re)distribution of power in public space by a (re)negotiation of authority and an incremental approach to partnership and network decisionmaking, one consisting of the social partners (government - employers - unions), public - private partnership (state structures - business) or civil partnership (public authorities - civil society).

The nature of governance consists of the way state-society relations are being structured and managed. Governance has evolved in time from hierarchical bureaucracy to participatory governance where the role of citizens is more direct in public decisionmaking process and the public authorities become organisations with multiple stakeholders characterized by strong democracy and transparency. Corresponding to this, the evolution stages of governance can be compared to those of public management: the classical model of public management, the new public management model and the public governance model (Bovaird, Bovaird &Loffler, 2003, p. 101) and refer to bureaucracy model, information management model, citizen participation model and public governance model.

As *the classical model of public management* defines the governmental entity as a hierarchical bureaucracy with separate powers; the *governance bureaucracy model* is characterized by top-down organization and is based on efficiency inside the government; on regulations and balanced budget laws, focused on bureaucratic compliance (conformity). The financial function is often described in terms of revenue collection and spending (cash base accounting and budget model), an invisible bureaucratic function that implements fiscal policies, and one that is uninvolved in policy decisionmaking.

Administrators are seen as technical professionals, they work without making use of their own judgment and strictly according to the desires of their political masters. Their purposes are budget maximization, legal compliance and financial control. In this model of governance, Civil Society is much undeveloped and stakeholders' participation is also very low.

In *the information management model* governments become aware of the role citizens' play in society and focus limited public services to their needs. Even though the citizens are informed by governments and the flow of services and other outputs between government and citizens is efficient, the reverse flow from citizen to government is not as efficient-citizens, do not participate in the decisionmaking process and the civil society is undeveloped.

One step toward a more evolved model of governance is linked to *the new public management* (NPM) model. The NPM postulates that the governmental entity is driven by a mission and operates strategically like a business unit, being conscious of cost efficiency. In this model, government bureaucracies turn into strategic business units, competing with each other, and citizens become customers. The focus shifts from laws and regulatory conformity to the "rules of the marketplace", that is, economy and efficiency; the accounting and the budget base are moved from cash to accrual basis. In this way, the financial function is reformed into one based on cost savings and incremental revenues. NPM also argues that privatization is the mechanism to establish efficiency, efficacy and quality in the delivery of public services, as Emanuel Savas asserts, "privatization is the New Public Management" (Savas, 2000, p 319). According to Cooper (2004) in NPM administrations are not ethically neutral from the electorate; they have ethical obligations to the citizens and citizens should participate in administrative decisions.

The citizen participation model theorizes that both sides, government and citizens, are interacting with each other; a complex area of services are open to public participation; and some of the features of good governance, including participation and transparency start to gather momentum while civil society is strong and active.

The Public Governance model (PGM) defines the governmental entity as an organization interacting with others in a network consisting of public, civic and business institutions. Governance is the process of decisionmaking and the process by which decisions are implemented. The organisation is in equilibrium when its managers succeed in balancing the contributions from, and the inducements given to, its stakeholders. In PGM governmental organizations work with their partners, stakeholders and networks to influence the outcomes of public policies; all stakeholders are actively and democratically involved participants in the act of governing. Civil Society is very mature, diverse and involved in governance process, therefore governmental transparency and democracy are very strong. In Kooiman's (1993, p.4) view, governance is the pattern or structure that emerges in a socio-political system as a "common" result or outcome of the interacting interventions efforts of all involved actors. This pattern cannot be reduced to the outcome produced by one actor or group of actors in particular. This definition of public governance, underlining the idea of a common decision – common result, is the one we use going forward.

Government and Governance in the Information Age

Internet impact in governance. Since the mid 1990s, when the Internet first gained the status of a public utility, the public sector, like its counterpart in the business sector, was concerned with how to use emerging technologies to build relationships with its stakeholders and to deliver services. Governments were more cautious, especially compared to businesses, in developing and providing online services for the purpose of improving and perfecting their governing process. But the Internet has since become a channel for public administration and politics and the number of government websites has grown rapidly.

Initially, governments throughout the developed world became seriously interested in the potential contribution of information and communication technologies (ICT) to transform public service and governance (Bellamy&Taylor, 1998). Since then, there have been huge changes in these technologies and in the ways they are used. At the United Nations World Summit on the Information Society in December 2003, governments from around the world adopted a plan of action to utilize ICT to achieve international development goals including: using the most innovative information and communication technologies, particularly web-based Internet applications, providing citizens and businesses with more convenient access to government information and services, improving the quality of the services and providing greater opportunities to participate in democratic institutions and processes.

In the context of ICT development, governance is now being approached from the electronic point of view. E-governance, for example, is the use of ICT with the aim of improving information and service delivery, encouraging citizen participation in the decision-making process and making government more accountable, transparent and effective in dealing with citizens.

E-governance refers to governance processes in which ICT plays an active and significant role. The role of ICT in the governance sphere could:

- Improve quality of governance products and services being currently provided;
- Provide new governance services and products;
- Enhance participation of people in choice & provision of governance products & services;
- Bring new sections of society into the governance sphere (including those who are most likely to remain excluded - namely the poor, the illiterate, the differently able, indigenous people, the migrants and displaced people) (Digital Governance.orgInitiative, 2010).

Meanwhile, ICT and especially the Internet have changed the way that government operates by facilitating information dissemination, communications and transactions. The main transformations that governments have to face on the impact of Internet includes: e-Government, e-Democracy, e-Disclosure, e-Services, e-Procurement, e-Health, e-Justice, e-Taxes, and e-Customs, among others. In other words, the exiting government functions are moved to an electronic base platform by the new ICT. Due to this transferral, some of the processes had to be improved and others will have to be replaced by new ones. The main transformations that governments have to face on the impact of the Internet applied to the full range of government functions consists of the following: information sharing (e-Disclosure); providing services (e-Services); facilitating online transactions (e-Transactions); developing online democracy (e-Democracy).

ICT can serve a variety of different ends for citizens, business and governments including: improve access to information and public services; eliminate bureaucracy and simplify the administrative process; improve information exchange between public administration and services; improve the quality of public services and better delivery of government services to citizens; improve interactions with business and industry; empower citizens through access to information, or more efficient government management. The new ICT like local area networks, new media networking and mobile computing have the ability to transform relations with citizens, businesses, and other government bodies, moving it closer to the users. The traditional interaction between citizens or businesses with a government agency is now moved from the government office to user's home or office. The resulting benefits can be less corruption, increased transparency, greater convenience, revenue growth, and/or cost reductions (World Bank, 2003).

E-government. Under the impact of the Internet a new concept of government, known as electronic government (e-Government), became more and more popular and gained international recognition. During the last century the e-Government approach was debated in international and national circles. For example, Hudson (2002) noted that e-Government is often used to refer to electronic service delivery, which includes delivery through telephone call centers as well as on-line provision, while Fountain (2003: 6) considered e-Government as "the current potential to build government services and practices using existing technologies and applications". Basu (2004) stated that "e-government refers to the use by government agencies of information technologies … that have the ability to transform relations with citizens, businesses and other arms of government".

Generally, e-Government designates any transaction that involves the government and that is carried out, even partially, using electronic means, thereby making public administration more effective and efficient, more open and transparent, improving the quality of public services, democratizing public administration, and building a fair and just society that people can trust. In other words,

e-Government aims at reliable government that reduces administrative costs and provides effective and high quality public services, by using IT as much as possible.

The initiatives of government institutions to use ICT tools and applications, including the Internet and mobile devices, to support good governance, strengthen existing relationships and build new partnerships within civil society, are known as e-Government initiatives. These initiatives, through strategies and programs aim to be effective and "include all people" in the knowledge of computer and Internet use. The primary challenge of e-Government for development, therefore, is how to accomplish this task.

E-Government plays an important role in mediating government actions and its importance will continue to rise as ICT services become more widespread. One of the main aspects of e-Government is that citizens are being taken into account mainly as customers of public services and another major aspect is the citizens' role in governance, where they are the main actors in managing community and state affairs. Next, we point out its advantages and disadvantages of e-Government.

E-Government Advantages:

- Reducing the administrative communications costs of government by using tools like e-mails, intranets and the Internet;
- improving the general services of government institutions provided to individuals, including citizens, businesses and other government organizations;
- delivering better and faster and 24 hour service through agencies websites services;
- providing services on the basis of self-serve; finding information easier by electronic search engines;
- providing services no matter the location of the citizens, for instance, easy access for people from rural areas;

- improving government transparency by offering to the public a large amount of information on government policies, archival and historical information, and some useful statistics;
- create a stronger and closer relationship between citizens and government; empowerment of citizens.

E-Government Disadvantages:

- in most of developing countries the problem of accountability arises from the absence of monitoring agencies;
- need of specific rules and regulations to achieve more democratic and transparent transactions;
- need of highly training programs for the employees and IT specialists of government institutions for implementing and managing e-government;
- low rate of internet usage across the countries.

E-Disclosure. E-Disclosure consists of identification, preservation, retrieval, exchange and production of documents from electronic sources in electronic form. In the field of public administration, e-Disclosure represents a form of communication between public administrators, on the one hand, as information providers; and citizens, voters, taxpayers, customers, grant givers, bond holders, vendors, employees, governing boards, oversight bodies and managers, on the other hand, as information recipients. Disclosure is one of the pillars of good governance; it assures both accountability and transparency of the public institutions.

E-Services. In the context of public services, e-services represent services provided online by government to its citizens. The government's e-Services bring a series of benefits (Ionescu, 2005), both for LPA and for citizens, as the main users of information. Among these *benefits* are

the following: reduction of public expenditure, of bureaucracy and corruption at public institution level; increasing transparency regarding the use and administration of public funds; improvement of information and public service access, as per the laws regarding data protection and free access to public information; removal of the direct contact between civil servants and citizens/businesses; provision of information and high quality public services through electronic means; increasing the administrative capacity of public institutions in order to fulfill their role and their objectives and to provide information and public services in a transparent way; promoting the collaboration between public institutions to provide public services through electronic means; redefining the relationship between citizens and public administration, respectively between the business environment and public administration; and promoting the use of internet and of new technologies within public institutions.

The Internet aids good governance by increasing transparency and customer-oriented service delivery. The Internet has become a powerful instrument through which public sector entities provide citizens with regular, accurate information and services as well as increase their transparency as part of good governance practice. Technology has changed the way public organizations relate to the public. The Internet offers the possibility of increasing interaction between citizens and administration, which is what distinguishes e-Administration from traditional public administration (Chadwick, 2003). The literature points out the behavior of public managers, suggesting that agency relationships in the sector motivate such managers to provide information to enable the monitoring of their actions (Laswad, Fisher & Oyelere, 2005). E-Disclosure has the *benefits* of low cost, wider reach, frequency and speed. Despite these benefits, e-Disclosure *varies* across companies and across countries as well as across public entities.

E-Democracy. E-Democracy offers the possibility to improve the deficits of the present representative democracy including the following: incapacity of politicians to listen and discuss with citizens; citizens indifference and mistrust in politicians; increasing abstention of citizens from the political process; governments and policy makers searching for a way to re-engage the citizen through more participatory democracy (Korakas, 2008).

By participative democracy, we mean a democracy that offers plenty of opportunities to participate and in which citizens actively use different forms of participation to effect change. In other words, with this kind of democracy, citizens do more than just cast their vote at regular intervals – either to elect representatives or to help with the making of a political decision. It means they also participate in the political process in other ways, showing their preferences through advisory committees, opinion polls, petitions, parliamentary requests or numerous other forms of participation.

In order to change the way in which people interact with government and politicians, the Internet represents a basic tool for exercising political rights, generating a broad range of the e-Democracy concept. E-Democracy promotes the emergence of a more participatory and deliberative democracy, one that bridges the gap between policy makers and citizens. E-Democracy allows citizens to participate in the policy making processes at a local, national or global level, helping to build public support and legitimacy and providing access to transparent information.

Citizens participate in the political and democratic process in different ways using e-Democracy (MORI, 2005; OECD, 2001):

- Information, the citizens are informed by the government and are keeping informed about its policy;

- Consultation, the citizens are consulted by the government and asked to give feedback on government policy;
- Active participation, the citizens think and act together with the government to help create definitions of policy issues and their solutions;
- Co-decision making, the citizens can directly decide on policy matters.

In order to implement an e-Democracy process, the following objectives have to be fulfilled: involve a maximum number of citizens to discuss and understand the issues; enhance the education role in this process: reinstate a culture of democracy and participation; increase the quality and the representative ness of results. Thus e-Democracy is more about democracy than technology. It promotes active citizenship and participation in policy formation through deliberation, not just participation in elections every few years. E-Democracy is also an education tool that can help to create a "culture of democracy". E-Democracy therefore implies accountability, policy checks, participatory policy implementation, participatory policy decision, participatory policy formulation and participatory deliberations - exchange of views, access to information- transparency, civic education and eco-social security. There are various E-democracy models. These include parallel use of top-down tools or e-Consultations; bottom-up tools or e-Petitions; collaborative approach between citizens and policy makers, with iterations of agenda setting (online questionnaires), online deliberations/ dialogue (customized, moderated forums), online voting (online questionnaires & surveys), and interactive municipal council meetings. A component of e-Democracy in an early phase of development is online voting. E-voting adapts ITC to democratic procedures to meet people's need for simplicity and convenience. The benefits of e-voting compared with the traditional paper-based voting systems include increasing citizens' access to democratic processes and encouraging participation.

Advantages of e-Democracy include taking into consideration citizens' proposals; increasing the level of social cohesion for communities; include input of citizens in planning and executing different projects; improving quality of life; and increasing the quality of the debates, quality of the dialog between citizens and administration.

E-democracy disadvantages, as seen by Bozinis (2007), include the following: technological security problems with the danger to alter voting results; increased polarity of opinions and ideas; danger of political activity by hackers; the existence of the digital divide and the lack of information about the new technologies on the part of a large proportion of the population.

Principles of Good Governance

Many governmental and non governmental organisations focus on the attributes that they believe constitute "good governance". International organisations like the United Nations Public Administration Network (UNPAN) and Organization for Economic Co-Operation and Development (OECD) have excelled in providing characteristics or principles of "good governance" such as stakeholder engagements, transparency, the equalities agenda, ethical and honest behaviour, accountability and sustainability. Good governance (according to United Nations Economic and Social Commission for Asia and the Pacific) has eight major characteristics. It is: participatory, consensus oriented, accountable, transparent, responsive, effective and efficient, equitable and inclusive, and follows the rule of law. These characteristics assure that corruption is minimized, the views of minorities are taken into account and that the voices of the most vulnerable in society are heard in decision-making. They are also responsive to the present and future needs of society. The White Paper on European Governance underscores five principles of good governance:

openness, participation, accountability, effectiveness and coherence.

From the above discussion it should be clear that good governance is an ideal that is difficult to achieve in its totality. Very few countries and societies have come close to achieving good governance in its totality. Governments can borrow some ideas of good governance from their business counterparts. Corporate governance represents a process through which private organizations are directed and controlled within acceptable ethical standards and represents a trend towards greater corporate responsibility. In order to improve corporate management, accountability and transparency, the World Bank established the notion of codifying governance, which led to many states developing Corporate Governance Codes, mainly focused on companies listed on the stock exchange. This is also the case in Romania, where the companies admitted to trading on the regulated market of the Bucharest Stock Exchange (BSE) ("issuers") have to adopt and comply with the provisions of the Corporate Governance Code on a voluntary basis.

While both public and private entities are operating in a free market and, from this point of view are treated equally; however, if private companies listed on stock exchange have to comply with a Corporate Governance Code, the same requirement could also be applied to the public sector entities. Thus a "Public Corporate Governance Code" could be developed, that is geared specially to the public interest.

Thus, *within the public sector*, effective corporate governance means that public agencies and officials must demonstrate compliance with the following six characteristics:

- composed of people with the knowledge, ability and commitment to fulfill their responsibilities;
- understand their purpose and whose interests they represent;
- understand the objectives and strategies of the departments;

- understand what constitutes reasonable information for good government and do everything possible to obtain it;
- prepared to ensure that the department's objectives are met and that operational performance is never less than satisfactory;
- fulfill their accountability obligations to those whose interests they represent by regularly and adequately reporting on their department's activities and effectiveness.

The content of a public governance code has been the subject of debate in many publications. The statistics of European Corporate Governance Institute (ECGI) reveal the index of corporate governance codes in many countries. Although all the countries (72 countries) presented by ECGI adopted a code of corporate governance applicable to private sector, in terms of public sector there are only a few countries which developed best practices or codes of public governance.

First of all, in an international context, International Federation of Accountants (IFAC) Public Sector Committee published its study on Corporate Governance in the Public Sector, which showed that improving governance is high on the agenda in various countries, but only a few have issued a code of good practice or good governance for the public sector. In the case of UK there exists a *"Corporate governance in central government departments: Code of good practice (2005)"*, that guides central government departments, focusing on the role of departmental management boards and how they can support ministers and heads of departments; and *"The Good Governance Standard for Public Services (2004)"* published by Chartered Institute of Public Finance and Accountancy (CIPFA) and the Office for Public Management in the UK that sets out six core principles of good governance and their supporting principles for public service organizations.

OECD developed *"OECD Guidelines on Corporate Governance of State-Owned Enterprises September 2005"*, viewed as a complement to the OECD Principles of Corporate Governance, on which they are based and with which they are fully compatible. The Guidelines are explicitly oriented to issues that are specific to corporate governance of State-Owned Enterprises (SOE) and consequently take the perspective of the state as an owner of an enterprise and focusing on policies that would ensure good corporate governance. In order to carry out its ownership responsibilities, the state can benefit from using tools that are applicable to the private sector, including the OECD Principles of Corporate Governance. While the Guidelines are primarily intended to cover commercial enterprises under central government ownership and federal ownership, authorities could also promote their use by sub-national levels of governments that also own enterprises. They are also useful for non-commercial SOEs fulfilling essentially special public policy purposes, whether or not they are in a corporate form. It is in the government's and the public's interest that all these categories of SOEs are run professionally and to apply good governance practices.

Despite the development of codes or standards in some countries in the field of public corporate governance, at the present there is no generally applicable Public Corporate Governance Code in Romania, either in central or in local government.

One of the most important features of good governance is **transparency**. However, there is no commonly agreed upon definition of this concept. Despite this, transparency is a core principle that upholds the provision of appropriate, necessary and relevant information to stakeholders when needed and upon demand. A feature of modern corporations is information asymmetry between corporate insiders and outside stakeholders. This situation creates incentives for opportunistic actions by insiders. The incentive, however, for public companies is to become more transparent for the good of their investors. The public sector is facing the same challenge for their users: citizens, business and other government agencies.

Cotterrell (1999) defines government transparency as the availability of information on matters that are pertinent to the public; the opportunity for citizens to participate in political decisions; and the accountability of government to legal processes and to public opinion. "Openness and transparency" can be "understood as the availability and accessibility of relevant information about the functioning of the polity." (Gerring & Thacker, 2004). Some focus on basic elements of public sector transparency – for example, the public and timely availability of information about legislation, regulation and other public measures that affect business behavior. Others deal with the broader objective of transparency-that is, governments' "openness to the public gaze" or successful "communication of policymakers' intentions" (OECD, 2003).

Piotrowski and Borry (2009) explained that openness and transparency in government are widely and almost universally accepted as being a part of good government. While Florini (2004) considers transparency and openness as the bedrocks of democracy, the driver of prosperity, and even a guarantor of security, citizens around the world are demanding that their governments open their files and governments are responding. The author states that this trend toward transparency holds great promise for improving the state of the world and is indispensable for reducing corruption. Drew & Nyerges (2004), quoting different authors, consider transparency as a vehicle for democratic decisionmaking processes by enhancing participatory opportunities and making them more equitable, effective and efficient from a long-term perspective. Transparency is an issue relating to efficiency and long-term cost savings for governments. Transparency of governments toward their citizens is a necessary part of government accountability, and a necessary part of a true democracy (Grigorescu, 2003).

The Internet is a means of increasing transparency, it facilitates the delivery of more information, more quickly, and thus empowers citizens to monitor government performance more closely (Pina, Torres, & Royo, 2007). In this way, transparency aims at ensuring a wider access of citizens to information and documents in the possession of state institutions, citizen participation in decision making processes and ensuring the legitimacy, effectiveness and accountability of the administration towards the citizen.

The concept of transparency of decision-making process carried out in public institutions concerns the provision of access to documents in the management of state institutions and citizens in consultation on the adoption of regulations. Specifically, transparency entails:

- information on the part of persons on public interest issues to be discussed by local and central public administration authorities, and on draft legislation;
- consulting citizens and associations legally established on the initiative of public authorities in the preparation of normative acts;
- active participation of citizens in administrative decisions and in making normative acts.

Transparency is also a principle with high applicability in the budgetary process of the public sector. With respect to transparency, all tax payers have the possibility to know the destination of their taxes and fees paid to state.

In order to reach a high level of transparency, there are some actions that should be done. These actions take into account all the steps and stages in budgetary process; transparency, in particular, should refer to budgetary elaboration, execution and report.

A communication strategy ensures that citizens, public sector officials, and representatives of the business community and civil society feel they are active participants in public governance with a critical influence over the government process. The Internet, as a new communication technology, allows governments to achieve the goals of accountability and transparency and to rapidly disseminate vast amounts of information. On the one hand, citizens, as costumers and main stakeholders have a fundamental right in a well-functioning democracy - to know what their public officials are doing. Being well informed, citizens can actively participate in the government process. On the other hand, government has to assume the obligation of effective communications and to inform citizens about its actions to instill confidence in their citizens.

In this paper we mostly approach transparency as principle of good governance, which tries to emphasize the challenges of e-Disclosure in Romanian LPA.

GOVERNANCE OF PUBLIC SECTOR IN ROMANIA

Catalysts Towards Promoting Public Sector Governance in Romania

Being a code law country, Romania, has a legal system based on French Napoleonic Code with clearly written and accessible law. The Romanian public sector is operated using public administration and public finance laws, while a government program is promoting public sector governance in Romania. Since Romania became member of European Union in 2007, one of its objectives is legislative harmonization.

According to the OECD (2001), the greater capacity for broadcasting information over the Net has increased the pressure upon LPA to practice greater transparency. The e-Europe plans for 2002, 2005 and 2010 for the development of e-Government underscore the importance of the improvement in transparency and presentation of accounts to citizens. Entities such as the International Monetary Fund and the OECD have established codes for good practice, concerning transparency.

Recent legislative reforms encourage citizen participation in local public life and guarantee public access to information. In the case of Europe, the European Committee of Ministers Recommendation 19/2001 established the basic principles of local democratic participation policies. This recommendation has stimulated the development of various national regulations (Serrano, Mar, Pilar, 2008).

The new constitutions of Central and Eastern European countries often include rights of access to public information (Edes, 2000). These provisions come as a reaction against the secrecy practiced for decades under socialist rulers. The Romanian Government has dedicated a lot of effort in recent years to developing a legal framework favouring the development of the Information Society and e-Government. Public sector institutions have to be involved not only passively, in the process of disclosing information to the public, but they have also to actively participate in the dissemination process of information. The new ruler require the active involvement in helping citizens to fulfill their missions for registration as voters, tax payers, obtaining a birth certificate, registration of a car, obtaining and renewal of a driving license, issuing and renewal of passport could be done by making material available to the citizenry and by making it aware of laws, trends and facts that could affect their lives.

At the European level, there is a political and institutional framework on governance, well-defined since 2001, in the White Book of European Governance; and it still is in the process of implementation by creating cooperation policies in all EU and acceding countries. A first step towards regulating the political framework of European governance was made in 1998 by the Convention on Access to Information. The convention governs public participation in decision-making and access to justice in environmental matters. The Convention describes the right to public information, right to public participation, and access to justice for failure to observe the two rights.

The Convention regulates public participation in decisions on policy issues, from their inception on the formal policy agenda, by requiring state structures to manage transparent information, public participation during preparation of plans and programs related to public policy problems, and public participation during preparation of implementing regulations, including the norms and legal instruments required or as generally applicable.

In Romania the governance structures have evolved during the last twenty years from a totalitarian to a democratic system. The most important change occurred in the late 1990s when the status of public functionary was regulated; the law regarding local public administration came into effect in 2001. Starting in 2001, Romanian governance regulations are following the international trend. The law on electronic signature and the law on free access to public interest information were issued. In 2002 the law on electronic commerce was enacted, in 2003 the law regarding decisional transparency in public administration came into effect. Out of these specific laws, Romanian governance is framed in official government policy. The government program presents the governance principles but also the government targets, such as "Strategy – digital Romania", development of Romanian's national platform (e-Romania and National Electronic System (SEN)) by integrating new electronic services, while increasing public access to computerized public services, increasing the number of enterprises using the Internet as the main device of interaction with state institutions, increasing the security of communications networks and information security in order to enhance the citizens' protection in cyberspace, and providing a proper regulation framework to foster such development plans.

Some of these objectives have been already put into practice by initiatives and government actions including online services, e-forms, virtual payment desk, e-procurement, e-transportation permits.

In Romania, five principles currently govern e-Government implementation:

- transparency in providing information and public services;
- equal access, without discrimination, to public information and services, including people with disabilities;
- efficient use of public funds;
- privacy, to guarantee the secrecy of personal data;
- ensure availability of information and public services.

And the basic features, or pardigms of e-Government are considered to be:

- use of electronic communication technologies, ie, email, chat, websites, etc. or technical paradigm,
- applying new methods of information management or managerial paradigm,
- increasing the political participation of citizens and increased administrative apparatus or Functional Efficiency paradigm.

Actions and Initiatives Regarding E-Government, E-Services, E-Procurement, E-Disclosure

To achieve the e-Government objectives such as redefining the relationship between citizen or business and government for the purpose of facilitating their access to services and public information through ICT; eliminating direct contact between the public official and citizen; providing information and quality public services through electronic means; promoting cooperation between public institutions to provide public services electronically, the Romanian government has to sustain the Romanian state institutions' modernization. This requires effort to promote and implement the information society by creating a single national information system, designed to ensure alignment of our country to European standards of public services, by redefining the relationship between citizens, companies, social operators and state institutions. Creating a functional, modern state, high-performing and interactive by rethinking processes and procedures associated with the use of governance based on ICT is not possible without creating conditions for access to electronic communications infrastructure. The e-Government system increases transparency in providing information, allowing equal access to public information and services and efficient use of public funds.

At the same time, both medium- and long-term, the state will see a reduction in public spending, resulting from elimination of bureaucratic procedures and simplifying working procedures. The introduction of electronic payment systems, for instance, reduces the underground economy. For Romania the benefit of these systems is estimated to reduce by 10 to 15% of the underground economy, the equivalent to several billion Euros annually.

The most important steps made by Romania regarding e-government started after 2000:

- 2002 – implementation of Electronic System of Public Procurement (SEAP) – which is a nation-wide governmental website for procurement in Romania where government agency as clients and private sector as vendors can interact after being authenticated by the system. The system works on a reverse auction basis (http://www.e-guvernare.ro),
- 2003 - deployment of National Electronic System (SEN) is a point of access to services and information to those concerned central and local government institutions (http://www.e-guvernare.ro),
- 2003 – launching of Electronic Tender System Transport (SAET) –an electronic service for international transport licenses,

- 2009 – implementation of Virtual Payment Desk (GVP) - a website that facilitates citizens' and businesses' taxes payment and traffic fines payments.

The National Electronic System gives 24/7 access to information from central and local government institutions, official forms and interactive services. 164 official forms from 465 public institutions, and five interactive services are currently available, such as VAT declaration and submission of statistical information. To use these services, the number of which is growing progressively, citizens and businesses must register to obtain an access code and a password. So, SEN represents eloquent evidence of the benefits of adoption of electronic systems, and the development in this area has been satisfactory. In early 2009, 800 institutions were connected to this system; in October 2009 their number was over 11.500. Also, the number of auctions in Electronic System of Public Procurement has increased from under 2% in the early years to over 12% presently.

The main proposals for improving the implementation of e-Government in Romania are as follows: establish the electronic identity for citizens and companies (eID); increase the online services for businesses and citizens by local and central public institutions; define the necessary exchange of information in electronic form (e-Records Management - ERM) between systems of government at central and / or local level inclusiding the identification, security and communication protocols; Electronic Records Management System improvement - IT system for the exchange of electronic records between central and / or local government institutions through interoperability, homogeneity, standardization and electronic data transfer and information; implement a centralized management of information / data - a single source of data for all entities / systems in e-government; and creating a single point of access to data, a single grouping source of important information.

Romanian Civil Society: How it Helps Ensures Public Sector Transparency

Exposure of government decisions and information to the public, participation in decision-making via vote, and independent research accountability, and monitoring of governments by civil society are long-recognized forms of civic engagement for promoting transparency. Civil society is represented by the social and civic institutions and organizations which constitute the foundation of a functioning democracy. Beyond the institutional aspects, civil society consists of citizens, who, associated in various ways, participate in public life to influence politics and defend and promote the interests of the public.

While definitions of civil society as a concept often diverge from one another, overall agreement exists that this notion encompasses the arena of voluntary, unforced collective action around shared interests, purposes and values. Civil society commonly embraces a diversity of spaces, actors and institutional forms, varying in their degree of formality, autonomy and power.

Decentralization has played a pivotal role in engaging civil society in the governance process, the approach enabling citizens to participate more actively in governance. Citizen's needs play an important part in determining "good" governance, in helping to determine the allocation and management of resources to respond to collective problems. Civil Society involvement can help improve governance, but in and of itself, it will not be effective. A well-informed public will participate in increasing the credibility of government. To ensure transparency and accountability in the public sector is therefore essential to promote freedom of information, consultation, and participation and implementation of public policies.

In Romania, civil society has been built up differently from those countries with a strong democratic tradition. After the downfall of the communist regime, the idea of civil society was misunderstood in Romania. It was initially linked with partisan politics, because an organization named Civic Alliance had participated in government (later this organization became a political party). This had created confusion for most people who believed that civil society is subordinated to politics. Economic and political modernization are necessary conditions for the development of civil society, but they are not sufficient. The status and power of expression of civil society depend on the progress of cultural and psychosocial factors; among which individual autonomy is an important one. Due to the late attainment of *de facto* autonomy, true Romanian civil society appeared only in the late 1990s. The citizens' involvement in the socio-political life of local community and the country is still low. It is still the prevailing idea that the state must do everything for the good of its citizens. In addition, some more time is required for citizens to learn and acquire the rules of social conduct to become more politically active and responsible. Slowly this situation has changed, as Romanian citizens are still a small stakeholder in the public sector system, as transparency and the financial-related benefits have started to have an effect on the cost and execution of public services. In some countries, for instance, civil society organizations take an active role in monitoring procurement. In the case of Romanian e-Auction system, the transparency was focused on more significant sources of corruption rather than the system's high volume of low-value transactions which would not be cost-effective to monitor. There is still a lack of communication between government and civil society/citizens, even if many structures at both the national and local levels have been institutionalized to facilitate interaction between them. Administrative corruption is one of the factors that make such changes more difficult.

The Report on the state of civil society in Romania from 2005 made by World Alliance for Citizen Participation (CIVICUS) together with the Romanian non-governmental organization Civil Society Development Foundation (CSDF) have showed that the Civil Society Diamond for Romania is rather well-balanced among its four dimensions (structure, environment, values and impact) and is of moderate size (Civil Society Development Foundation, 2005). But the same report reveals low citizen participation, together with a poor level of organization and limited interrelations among civil society organizations represent obstacles for the development of a strong civil society sector. Moreover, Romanian civil society has not managed to develop a common identity. Its role in society is, for the most part, ignored by the public and its public image remains marked by negative stereotypes.

The role of Romanian civil society is thus not very significant in influencing political decisions, and working for economic and/or public interest. In this context, strengthening civil society by establishing more NGOs with clear goals to cover the whole range of social activities is one way to reinvigorate the Romanian society. There are two ways of strengthening and diversifying civil society institutions. First, through the connection to international institutions of civil society and second, creating a virtual civil society through the Internet. This second approach could increase social cohesion, facilitate access to information and public participation in various activities.

For the purpose of this chapter we argue that good governance means engaging stakeholders and making accountability real for citizens. Government is one of the actors in governance. Other actors involved in governance vary depending on the level of government that is under discussion. Governments have multiple levels of accountability. First, to the public (citizens) and to those who have the authority and responsibility to hold them to account on the public's behalf (Parliament, ministers, government departments, regulators). All actors, other than government and the military, are grouped together as part of the "civil society" in the Romanian context.

Civil society organizations are involved in decision making on social development or public decisions. Examples of Romanian civil society institutions are non-governmental organizations (NGOs); community organizations (community-based organizations); professional associations; political organizations; civic clubs; trade unions; philanthropy; social clubs and sports organizations; cultural institutions; religious organizations; environmental movements; media; etc. With regard to the citizens' information on local government reform, public policy, good governance and transparency, we present some examples of Romanian civil society institutions that are actively involved in promoting such issues and thereby contributing to decision making on social development or public interest decisions.

The Institute for Public Policy (IPP) is one of the most active Romanian non-governmental organizations that advocate for increased quality of policymaking processes in Romania, carrying out research and promotion of new ideas in areas such as public administration reform, transparency in institutions, and the integrity of elected representatives and officials. *Civil Society Development Foundation' (CSDF).* The CSDF's mission with regard to the information, financing, training, research and advocacy to build the capacity of civil society organizations, the main activities include acting in the field of civic and influencing public policies, good governance, democracy and human rights, and representing the NGOs interests. Also, the *Association for Community Partnership (ACP)* is working in the field of good governance, social services, civic affairs, combating discrimination and influencing public policy. *Pro Democracy Association Brasov Branch* has the mission to strengthen democracy in Romania by encouraging civic participation; the main activities aim at public policy and good governance, combating discrimination, and supporting democracy and human rights. *Civitas '99 Association* advancess the support and enhancement of the potential students and graduates in political science, promoting civic spirit and initiative in participatory democracy and multicultural environment.

Nowadays, in constructing their democracy, the Romanian citizens have developed high expectations in terms of public services quality. The high expectations were due to various factors including self-perception as clients (by comparison with the private sector) and high mobility (the citizens who work outside the country learn to have new standards in terms of quality of service). NGOs represent a possible source of pressure on behalf of citizens. Although initially ignored by the public administration, they have proved a valuable resource for modernizing public administration. There is also a widespread belief that the increasing number of non-governmental organizations (NGOs) helps diminish corruption. Tiut (2003), however, in his study, questions the assumption that civil society by virtue of its existence, numbers, and social activities, can be sufficient to diminish corruption and its causes. He concluded that, at least in Romania, this is not the case that the greater quantity of NGOs automatically diminishes the incidence of corruption.

In Romania, the incidence of corruption still appears strong and dynamic. Civil society appears weaker and stagnant, regardless of numbers of registered NGOs, because it often shows itself to be unable to resist the pressures of the corruption-generating system. This may be well worth considering for those who measure democracy or civil society by a number of registered, albeit suspect or useless NGOs, and prescribe more NGOs as a remedy to cure the disease of corruption. Civic engagement, especially volunteering for good causes by activists, continues to be low in the former communist countries, and particularly in Romania. Lack of money, time and skills offers a partial explanation for the difference.

The Romanian democracy is still a relatively young one and the initiatives undertaken in reforming the civil service are even more recent, most of them being imposed by the European Union in the form of legislation. In many cases, even if the legislative provisions are effective in theory, they remain merely a formality and ineffective in practice, failing to lead to a true change in reality. After 1989, participatory democracy was an idea which only took shape slowly in Romania. In the pre-revolution, Communist Romania, citizens didn't have the right to state their opinion regarding political problems. After 1989, things changed, models of good practice from western states started to appear, which have been slowly but successfully put in practice in our country.

GOVERNANCE IN ROMANIAN LOCAL PUBLIC AUTHORITIES

Overview of Local Public Administration System in Romania

Local government is defined as a governing institution which has authority over a sub-national territorially defined area (Oxford Concise Dictionary of Politics, 2009). Its structure differs from country to country, being divided on sub-states, regions, provinces or counties, respectively communes as the lower-tier basic authority.

In Romania the local government agencies are defined by the Law 215/2001 of local public administration as entities which develop activities regarding local public administration, with implications in all fields of legal, economic and social aspects of citizens, and legal persons (Local Government Law, 2001).

Romanian local government is composed of:

1. County Council;
2. Local Council;
3. Mayor;
4. Local Public Services.

The local public administration, through which is realized the local autonomy in communes and towns, are composed of communes and towns' local councils, which serve as deliberative authorities; and mayors, who act as executive authorities. Local councils and mayors are elected, as provided by law, in local elections. Local councils and mayors act as local government authorities and administer public affairs in communes and towns, under the law.

Each county has a County Council which coordinates the activities of towns and communes councils, to carry out public services of county interest. The County Council is elected in local elections. The locally elected officials are the Mayor, local councilors and county councilors. For the free exercise of their mandate, they meet a public authority function. The Local Council has initiative and acts on all matters of local interest, except those which by law represents the jurisdiction of other public authorities, local or central.

Public Governance: Accountability and Transparency in Romanian LPA

Romanian LPAs have been subject to continued reform intended to improve local accountability and engagement. Increasingly, LPAs work with and through a range of organizations and partnerships in order to deliver services and to enhance local prosperity. Even though the partnerships are important in public service provision, bringing many benefits that LPA could not achieve by other means; however, partnership brings governance challenges. Thus governance arrangements must be proportionate to the risks involved. In the future it is likely that LPA will be less concerned with direct service delivery and more with commissioning and regulation, influencing behavior and supporting their communities. Community leadership may become the most important feature of local governance.

Therefore, LPAs must be able to demonstrate that they are complying with the principles of good corporate governance, being more efficient and facing the task of reconsidering their internal governance framework and adjusting it to reflect these new circumstances. The governance framework, reflecting the responsibility of holding assets in trust, ensures public entities long

term competitiveness and the optimization of the decision-making process.

Transparency, accountability and openness in reporting and disclosure of information, both operational and financial, are internationally accepted to be vital to the practice of good corporate governance. Financial reporting obligations therefore should support good corporate governance through internal reporting and external reporting:

- Effective management and decision-making require adequate internal financial reporting systems, consisting of, timely and regular submission of comprehensive and reports on every significant matter of financial administration in a public sector institution at all levels.
- External reporting is to all LPA external stakeholders who include: voters, taxpayers, customers, grant givers, bond holders, vendors, employees, governing boards, oversight bodies and managers.

The most important stakeholders in public governance are as follows: citizens, community organizations that are loosely organized, nonprofit organizations, which are often quite tightly organized, business, media, public agencies, elected politicians and trade unions. Individual stakeholders as a group should be considered like citizens for public governance and voters, taxpayers or clients of government. In the section below, we consider what good governance means by focusing on outcomes for citizens and service users.

Accountability in Romanian LPA. Real accountability requires a relationship and a dialogue. Accountability involves an agreed upon process for both accounting for LPA actions and being held to account; a systematic approach to put that process into operation; and a focus on explicit results or outcomes. Real accountability is concerned not only with reporting on or discussing actions already completed, but also with engaging with stakeholders to understand and respond to their views as the organization plans and carries out its activities.

In the study performed by the Romanian Institute for Public Policy (IPP Study, 2009) it is indicated that a number of Romanian LPAs obstruct the free access to information of public interest, through practices that vary from ignoring requests for information and to disregarding their final judgments requiring the communication of information. With regard to the perception of Romanian citizens about the issues of public accountability, the study by IPP (2009) reveals that:

- 89% believe that corruption is quite widespread in Romania;
- 61% believe that Romania's current problems are related to the functioning of public institutions;
- 42% talk often and frequently with their neighbors about town issues where they live;
- 14% have confidence in parliament, 48% in the town hall where they live and 21% in NGOs;
- 93% are not members of any organization or association that do not afford them an income;
- 93% have never participated in signing a petition or support and 70% did not participate in this type of activity;
- 15% believe they can influence important decisions taken for their locality while 12% believe they can influence important decisions taken for the whole country;
- 48% believe their life is influenced by key decisions taken by the mayor and local council and 53% believe their life is influenced by key decisions to be taken by the government, parliament and president.

Also, accountability is linked with the issue of transparency. Accountability rests on the establishment of criteria for evaluating the performance of public sector institutions. Transparency and participation of civil society are essential ingredients in establishing accountability. For the purpose of our chapter we consider that good governance means transparent decisions. Different types of organization have different statutory requirements for the publication of their decisions. Over and above these requirements, transparent decisions are more likely to be understood by staff, the public and other stakeholders, and to be implemented effectively. It is also easier to evaluate the impact of decisions that are transparent, and therefore, to have evidence on which to draw in making future decisions.

Transparency and the Romanian citizen's access to the local public interest information. Transparency and citizen's access to public interest information has been the subject of numerous articles (e.g. Castells, 2008; Tzu-Shan & Torgashina, 2008; IPP, 2009). The study of the Institute for Public Policy (2008), emphasized the use of local public administration's websites to display some minimum data regarding the local councilor's name, their CVs, the councils they belong to, in order to inform citizens and to make their work public (information about their presence at council meetings, the project initiatives decisions that they make, or annual activity reports which they are required to present as local councilors). The study reveals several problems in the degree of transparency in the LPA's use of web sites for communication with citizens.

Local transparency means the citizens' accessibility to information regarding the work of politicians and public institutions has to be carried out effectively and uniformly. For this to happen means that some local authorities must no longer believe that local autonomy means ignoring the rules of a democratic society and that the central political leaders must show respect for citizens. The evidence of this respect consists of the application of a uniform and strong transparency law. The political class must admit that access to information of public interest is still arbitrary and based on the wishes of local leaders. In some cases, the mayor may discharge the duties of publication of public interest information by displaying the notice board or data entry into the institution or by revealing it in their local newspapers and magazines.

Romanian civil society, according to Law no. 544/2001, can use legal tools to inform local business advisors, assessing the transparency of public authority in terms of accessibility to information and accuracy. With regard to the transparency of public institutions, civil society efforts never seem to be enough, as legislative and practical malfunctions are always occurring. Most problems found in connection with the enforcement of the access to public interest information are due to local government representatives' interpretation of the laws that are inconsistent with international practices. The main issues include the following. First, counselors are required to publish an annual report of activity but there are insignificant penalties for not filling it and there is no deadline for submission. Second, the confusion of the local counselors over interpretation of the transparency law relates to the protection of personal information, which leads to excessive coverage instead of full transparency with everything that can involve the citizens.

E-Disclosure Brings LPA Closer to the Romanian Citizens

The ability of LPA to address the needs of society in a transparent way could be improved through the use of ICTs. The relation between citizens and LPA has undergone significant transformation through the role played by ICT in facilitating access to public information and the delivery of public services. The citizens, as the main stakeholders of the government, demand improvements in their interaction with local administration regarding the quality and efficiency of services, a more direct and faster response to their needs as well as increased transparency of public administra-

tion. In order to bring LPAs closer to citizens, the e-Government plays an important role. The term is used both for external applications, through the use of electronic media to support the delivery of LPA information and public services; and internal applications, through the use of ICT within LPA to improve the efficiency of operations. Starting from the previous issues, we want to emphasize e-Government in the Romanian LPA context. Thus, we investigate mainly Romanian towns regarding e-Disclosure on their LPAs websites. We divide these into e-Service and e-Financial reporting.

E-Services. Law regarding the electronic payment of local taxes, no 291/2002 sets as an obligation of all municipalities and cities in Romania the deployment of electronic systems for local tax collection. These systems provide to the citizens access to the relevant information on local taxes and offer a quick, convenient solution to pay the local debts. *E-financial reporting.* The reform of LPA financial reporting has aligned with reporting practices in the private sector. By making LPA financial information available, the citizens could continuously assess a government agency through everyday interaction. The financial accountability of LPAs and their response to citizen's demands for information and services thus contribute to government openness. It is therefore relevant to determine whether Romanian LPAs are also becoming more aware of the importance of placing financial information on their Web sites to help in decision-making processes.

The Romanian legislation requires that the LPA publish on the Internet the draft budget, approved budget, budget execution, execution of the development budget, the budget correction, as well as the Budgetary Execution Account, including updating information at least once a quarter. Therefore, the Romanian regulations offer the possibility of the financial statements' electronic publication, which public entities may do voluntarily.

E-Democracy. In order to emphasize the activities that increase citizen involvement, we

Table 1. Population sample

Sample LPA towns				
Alba Iulia	Buzau	Iasi	Ploiesti	Suceava
Alexandria	Calarasi	Lugoj	Ramnicu Sarat	Targoviste
Arad	Cluj	Medgidia	Ramnicu Valcea	Targu Jiu
Bacau	Constanta	Medias	Resita	Targu Mures
Baia Mare	Craiova	Miercurea Ciuc	Roman	Tecuci
Barlad	Deva	Onesti	Satu Mare	Timisoara
Bistrita	Dr.Turnu Severin	Oradea	Sf. Gheorghe	Tulcea
Botosani	Focsani	Pascani	Sibiu	Turda
Braila	Galati	Petrosani	Sighetu Marmatiei Slatina	Vaslui
Brasov	Giurgiu	Piatra Neamt	Slobozia	Zalau
Bucuresti	Hunedoara	Pitesti		
Total: 54 LPA, out of which:				
Listing category:	41 county seats			
	13 municipalities			

have to refer to e-Democracy. The e-Democracy initiatives on the LPA websites are useful to enhance transparency, that is, enhance financial accountability through the political dimension of web and citizen dialogue. In Romania, progress towards viable electronic governance has been marked by a series of actions absolutely necessary to support this process. The first step was the establishment of the Working Party Group Promotion of Information Technology, which has as its primary objective to create the premises of implementing a sustainable information society in Romania. Also, there was developed and approved the Government Strategy on computerization of public administration.

In 2003, the National Electronic System (NES) was established as a computer system of public utility, to ensure physical and legal access to public information and public service provision to people.

Starting from the all the above issues, in our study we want to focus on the following:

1. The Internet in Romanian LPA as a tool of transparency improvement for the citizens' use, in order to see at what level is the Romanian LPA (level of information disclosed on the internet by Romanian LPA)

upon the five stages in the development of e-government according to the literature.

2. If the Romanian LPA have a primary website, what information is disclosed to citizens, as the main stakeholders, that help them to participate in LPA decision making process. In other words, we want to examine if city revenues, citizens participation and citizens financial recommendations influence the Disclosure Index of various types of information on LPA websites.

Regarding research methodology we used content analysis to investigate the websites of the main towns of Romania according to number of inhabitants (Table 1). We chose the towns with a population over 40 thousand inhabitants, based on the hypothesis already tested in previous research for private sector, where companies' size is an important predictor of corporate disclosure behaviour (Raffournier, 1995; Graven & Marston, 1999; Stolowy & Ding, 2003).

Romania is divided into counties, towns and communes, the boundaries of which are established by law. A county has one county seat, several additional municipalities and all towns and communes within that county's territorial limits. Certain towns are classified as municipalities. In our research we included only towns, county seats and some of the biggest municipalities. County seats' councils have significantly larger voter populations and geographical boundaries than other municipalities, more particularly from the same county.

Local financial resources have a special role in local development, because they represent the basis for a prompt response, in optimal conditions, to the community financial needs. In our research we analyzed the revenues of local entities for the 2008 fiscal year. According to the Law on Local Public Finance, the following categories of revenue comprise the financial resources for territorial units: taxes, duties, other fiscal revenues, no fiscal revenues, capital revenues, special destination revenues, grants from the state budget, shares of revenues to the state budget and special destination transfers. We consider that citizens could influence the level of information disclosed on the Internet by LPAs. According to the existing regulations, Romanian LPAs should have at least one person involved with public relations and the public should have free access to the LPA open meetings. Due to these regulations we count the citizen's participation on LPA decision-making process by two variables. *Citizen's participation* is an additive variable that measures the citizen's involvement on LPA decisions. Its maximum value is 8. It measures if:

1. LPA have online forum,
2. Discussions on the forum are active dialogues between Civil Society and LPA representatives.

It also measures if citizens actively respond to the LPA initiatives regarding different projects:

1. Citizens participate in polls initiated by LPA;
2. There are requests from the interested parties to provide information on draft laws of LPA;

3. Citizens participate in public meetings of the LPA;
4. There are recommendations from the citizens;
5. Citizen's recommendations were included in the draft legislative acts;
6. LPA hold meetings at the request of the legally constituted associations.

Citizen's participation is a variable which includes situations where citizens are effective participants in LPA' meetings. None of the Romanian towns organize online meetings.

Citizen's financial recommendations. Due to the fact that the essential purpose of LPAs is to serve the citizens and they should be responsible for the public's spending, in a participatory democracy citizens must be encouraged to come up with recommendations on both the income formation and LPA cost allocations. For this purpose citizen financial recommendations are a variable that counts in the existence of citizen's participation in decision-making.

Given the inclusive nature of this analysis, we do not assume *a priori* what the direction of the relationship between citizen's involvement and Internet financial reporting practice will be. We just assume that a relation is possible between the citizen's involvement and IDI.

Sample. We included in our sample only the LPA for towns over 40 thousands inhabitants. Even though the 54 towns represents only 17% of the number of Romanian towns, their population is over 8 million people, and represents more than 70% of Romanian urban population and more than 39% of the country population.

To measure the internet disclosure index for Romanian LPA we have chosen an item-based approach, following the models of Buzby (1975) and Cooke (1989) that were the first to have developed the concept of "disclosure index." Many other authors that have used this kind of index in their research (e.g., Chavent et al., 2006; Popa, Blidisel, Farcane, 2008). We have built a composite index for each LPA using un-weighted items. All disclosed items investigated in this study, presented below, were considered equally important. We have assigned the value of "one" to every item disclosed on the LPA's website and value "zero" otherwise. The disclosure index (IDI) used to measure the level of internet disclosure is determined with the following formula:

$$ScoreIDI = \sum_{i=1}^{23} IDI_i \qquad (1)$$

The 23 items represent information that LPAs disclosed both on a mandatory and voluntary basis. We group these items in three categories:

- **General information:** contact information, website, e-mail, information about LPA managers and departments, opening hours, audience hours;
- **Financial information:** planned and approved budget, budgetary execution account, financial statements, internal audit report;
- **Services:** public relation with citizens, public interest regulations and documents, e-tax, reports in doc, pdf, xls, html format, video, audio recordings, online participations at council meetings, multilingual website.

We used a multi-linear regression model for two reasons: first, because the majority of analyzed studies from literature use this model, (methodologically problems linked by the use of linear model in this type of studies are presented by Cooke (1998)), and second. due to its simplicity.

The *dependent variable* in our model is Internet disclosure index (IDI). This characterizes the behavior of Romanian LPA concerning reporting on the Internet. The index was based on the methodology proposed by Kelton and Yang (2008). The extent of Internet financial reporting

Table 2. Internet Disclosure Index (IDI) statistics

Year	2008
Score IDI	**12,94**
IDI Standard deviation	4.406
IDI Minimum Score	1
IDI Maximum Obtained Score	23

is measured both as a dichotomous variable and by a disclosure index. The dichotomous measure reflects whether or not the LPA provides or does not provide financial/non-financial information on the web. The disclosure index reflects the type and extent of information disclosed on their websites, adopted to the Romanian situation, so that it contains 23 items related both to mandatory and voluntary information that Romanian LPA have to disclose by normal media or via their websites.

The *independent variables* in our model are the following: city revenues, citizen's participation and citizens financial recommendations. The general form of the regression model is as follows:

$$ScoreIDI = \alpha_0 + \alpha_1 \operatorname{Re}venue + \alpha_2 CitPart + \alpha_3 CitFin \operatorname{Re}com + \varepsilon$$

$$(2)$$

ScoreIDI = internet disclosure index;
Revenues = city revenues
CitPart = citizens participation to LPA' decision making process;
CitFinRec = citizens recommendation as regarding budgetary issues. It is representing by a dummy variable that take the value of "one" if citizens recommendation have been taken into consideration and "zero" otherwise;

Our hypotheses may be accepted if the parameters of the model are statistically significant, and the model itself is also significant, that is, it can reasonably explain the variability of the index, that is, the R-square indicator, or the coefficient

Table 3. Coefficients of the model (stepwise method - dependent variable: IDI)

Model	Unstandardized Coefficients		Standardized Coefficients	t	Sig.	Collinearity Statistics	
	B	Std. Error	Beta			Tolerance	VIF
(Constant)	6.984	.913		7.615	.000		
CitPart	1.721	.234	.715	7.370	.000	1.000	1.000

of determination is high enough. These aspects are discussed further below. To generate the results, we used the *enter method*, according to which all the factors above were introduced in the model. The results show a R-square (56.8%), which is statistically significant (on the level of 0,005). Unfortunately only one of the parameters of the model is statistically significant – citizens participation. We can also observe a low tolerance of some factors, which indicates possible collinearity.

In the next step we applied the *stepwise method*, which introduces variable by variable in the model and eliminates those that are either statistically not significant or create collinearity. Therefore it redefines the entire model. We obtained two new models. We can observe all variables were eliminated except for citizens' participation and financial recommendations. The first new model has less explanatory power as the R-square drops to 55.2%, the second model, which includes as independent variable only citizens participation has an explanatory power of 51.1%. In the second model the F value is also higher and the collinearity statistics show a tolerance of 1. The characteristics of this model are presented in the table below (Table 3).

It is worthwhile to analyze also the data of the excluded variables (see Table 4). The significance

level of the political influence and municipality type is quite low, these factors could be also statistically significant determinants if significance level would be set higher. On the other hand the tolerance of variables is 1; therefore no collinearity would be expected.

The results of our investigation revealed a positive association between revenues of LPA and citizens financial recommendations and internet disclosure index, which is in line with the conclusion of previous studies.

The findings are that among the analyzed variables only citizens participation are influencing the level of e-disclosure by Romanian LPA. Analyzing the selected Romanian municipalities' websites through the perspective of both e-services (public services through internet) and digital democracy (citizens' participation to the governing process through internet) we found a poor level of information dissemination on the cities websites. This opinion is in accordance with Stoica & Ilas (2009). Information content of cities' official websites is relatively meager. Even in terms of usability, cities' sites are only acceptable; in terms of security and data protection, there is practically no concern.

Regarding *e-Services* we observed a poor range of services provided via the Internet by the municipalities. For example, the local taxes

Table 4. Regression - excluded variables (stepwise method - dependent variable: IDI)

Model	Beta In	t	Sig.	Partial Correlation	Collinearity Statistics		
(stepwise)					Tolerance	VIF	Minimum Tolerance
CitFinRec	.282	2.159	.036	.289	.515	1.944	.515
Revenues	.127	1.236	.222	.171	.876	1.142	.876

could be paid online, but there is no city where the utility bills could be paid using the City Hall official webpage as a portal. Currently, in Romania, there are 60 electronic payment systems of local taxes, 44 are in Romanian towns out of which 27 are county seats. In over 60% of the Romanian municipalities' citizens and companies could pay their local taxes online. However, although in Romania over 6 million people have Internet access, and cards issued by banks are approaching 10 million citizens, citizens still prefer the cash payment of taxes. Banks have discussed with local authorities the option to expand online payment of local taxes to the all county seats in the year 2010.

Regarding *e-Democracy* we also observe a poor range of participation. Only 20% of the surveyed towns (especially large towns) have on line discussion forums for citizens and less have forums where officials are actively responding to citizens. Therefore, the online forums may be considered either a channel for receiving citizens' complaints, or a communication environment for individuals facing the same problems relating to LPA. But citizens are starting to be involved in the decision making process by participating in the LPA open meetings and making recommendations to the officials. A slow movement to participatory democracy may be observed in a few towns where citizens' recommendations were incorporated in the local regulations. Twelve years after the birth of the first city webpage in Romania, local e-Governance seems to be still making its first steps. It is hoped that the national law of free access to information, observing good governance practices and the more active involvement of civil society will contribute to improve Romanian local governance.

Switching to electronic interaction between authorities and citizens involves major changes in the way internal operations of public administration that requires adaptation and new ways of working, including adequate and stable partnerships with the private sector and civil society, but also entails changing approaches to and involvement

of citizens in solving public problems. Electronic democracy in Romania has not developed enough and there are no prerequisites for the creation and improvement of such systems (Burcea, 2006). The public sector system is still incomplete and not integrated into the mainstream of national information. Citizens Information websites (Presidential Administration, the Chamber of Deputies, Senate, Government ministries, local councils, prefectures, mayors) are mostly operational, but are not built in accordance with a common set of standards or requirements that allow integration into a single portal, as well as providing optimal conditions for access to information of public interest.

Taking into account the three components of e-Government, we can say Romania has to face the challenges imposed by the need for increased interaction between authorities, officials, citizens, business and civil society and must have the ability to exploit specific opportunities and information technologies to achieve strengthening sustainable partnerships designed to streamline the relationships between the local government stakeholders and LPAs.

E-GOVERNANCE MODEL FOR ROMANIAN LPA

E-governance initiatives are common in most countries as they promise a more citizen-centric government and reduce operational cost. Unfortunately most of these initiatives have not been able to achieve the benefits claimed. Often the reason for this failure is a techno-centric focus rather than a governance-centric focus. We propose a model of e-Governance with three components: e-Disclosure, e-Democracy and e-Government, which correspond to Romanian context. This model should help LPAs to establish their e-governance vision. The strategy should also deal with constraints regarding necessary infrastructures, telecommunications, and Internet access. We propose this e-governance model to position the overall evolution of Romanian local government within the e-governance strategy. To evaluate the Romanian LPA concerning e-governance we use an E-Governance Maturity Model (Gartner, 2000).

Gartner, an international e-business research consultancy firm, has formulated a four-phase e-government maturity model. These phases have been defined based on experiences with e-commerce and e-governance in Europe.

E-Governance Maturity Model (Gartner)

Early 90's Information → Presence
Mid 90's Interaction → Intake process
Present Transaction → Complete transaction
Future Transformation → Integration and organizational changes

Phase 1: Information

In the *first phase,* e-governance first becomes present on the web, providing the external public with relevant information. The format of the first government websites is similar to that of a brochure or leaflet. The value to the public represents the publicly accessible government information; processes are described and thus become more transparent, which improves democracy and service.

Phase 2: Interaction

In the *second phase,* the interaction between government and the public is stimulated with various applications. People can ask questions via e-mail, using search engines for information and are able to download all sorts of forms and documents. These functionalities save time. In fact the complete intake of (simple) applications can be done online 24/7. Normally this would have only been possible at a counter during open hours. Internally government organizations use Local Area Networks (LAN), intranets and e-mail to communicate and exchange data. The bottom line is that more efficiency and effectiveness is achieved because a large part of the intake process is done online. However, citizens still have to go to the office to finalize the transaction, by paying a fee, handing over evidence or signing papers. The use of electronic communications tools speeds up the internal government processes.

Phase 3: Transaction

With *phase three* the complexity of the technology is increasing, but customer value will also be higher. Complete transactions can be done without going to an office. Examples of online services are: filling income tax, filling property tax, extending/renewal of licenses, visa and passports and online voting. Phase three is mainly complex because of security and personalization issues – e.g., digital (electronic) signatures are necessary to enable legal transfer of services. On the business side the government is starting with e-procurement applications. In this phase, internal processes have to be redesigned to provide good service. Government needs to create new laws and legislation that will enable paperless transactions with legal certification. The bottom line is that the complete process is online now, including payments, digital signatures etc. This saves time, paper and money.

Phase 4: Transformation

The *fourth phase* is the transformation phase in which all information systems are integrated and the public can get services at one (virtual) counter. One single point of contact for all services is the ultimate goal. The complex aspect in reaching this goal is mainly on the internal side, e.g. the necessity to drastically change culture, processes and responsibilities within the LPA. Government employees in different departments have to work together in a smooth and seamless way. In this phase cost savings, efficiency and customer

Table 5. E-governance elements linked with the maturity model phases

	e-disclosure	e-democracy	e-government
Information	X		
Interaction	X	X	
Transaction	X	X	X
Transformation	X	X	X

satisfaction are reaching highest possible levels. In each of the four phases, the delivery of online services and use of ICTs in government operations serve one or more of the aspects of e-governance: e-government, e-democracy, e-disclosure.

According with studies of Stoica & Ilas (2009) and Tiron et al. (2009), between our model of e-governance elements and maturity model phases we suppose that are links described in the Table 5:

The items of Information phase: e-disclosure

- mission statements, organizational structure;
- budget, performance indicators, audited accounts;
- addresses, opening hours, employees, telephone numbers;
- laws, rules and regulations;
- petitions, news;
- management reports.

The items of Interaction phase: e-disclosure & e-democracy includes the items of previous phase and the follows:

- correspondence, consultation papers, white papers, policies, petitions;
- government glossary;
- downloading forms on websites;
- submitting forms;
- online help with filling in forms (permits, birth / death certificates);
- intake processes for permits etc;
- e-mail;
- newsletters;

- discussion groups (e-democracy);
- polls and questionnaires;
- personalized web pages;
- notification.

The items of Transaction phase: e-disclosure & e-democracy & e-government include the items of previous phases as well as the following:

- license applications / renewals;
- renewing car tags, vehicle registration;
- personal accounts (my-tax, my-fines, my-licenses etc.);
- payment of (property) taxes;
- payment of tickets and fines;
- paying utility bills;
- registering and voting online.

The transformation phase assumes that the LPA will have a personalized website with integrated personal account for all services.

Each LGA started with the delivery of online information. Gradually, some of them developed some e-democracy and e-government elements. I n some cases, the public demand is the driving force; in other cases cost saving aspects for the government are leading. Based on our previous studies, e.g. Tiron et al, (2009), and Stoica & Ilas, (2009) as well, we can say that presently, Romanian LPAs are at the beginning of Phase Three: Transaction, because there are incipient transactions that could be done without going to an office. Moreover, also in Romania are working 60 electronic payment systems of local taxes, but in approximately 50% of the Romanian municipalities taxes are still cash paid, with very few customers using existing e-payment options.

The Gartner Four Phases of E-Governance Model demonstrates the progression of e-government in the connected environment and identifies strategy and other factors that contribute to success in each phase. Therefore we have to find strategies for Romanian LPA to get closer to the Phase Four: Transformation. The Gartner model was chosen as a goal to which the Romanian system of government should aspire to. The objectives through the implementation of eGovernment are the following:

- efficiency improvement in working of state entities with citizen
  - ○ stimulate rapid growth of Internet access
  - ○ shortening information dissemination
  - ○ improving information quality
  - ○ significant reduction of the administrative costs for state and those generated by rules for citizens and businesses.

Challenges, Solutions and Recommendations

The main practical challenges we faced in this study were the lack of a single point of data access, just one source as well as the lack of grouping of the main information. Also, the small number of online services offered to the citizens and to the business environment, as well as the lack of the framework definition of necessary to the electronic change of information.

As in many developing countries and economies in transition, in Romania the management of public financial resources constitutes the most fundamental responsibility and challenge of LPAs. A number of incidents in local administration, whether they involved fraud, improper administration, badly informed managers or failing supervision, have created a basis for improvements

in administration. Some incidents, influenced by the focus on core activities and market ideology, involve the hiving off or outsourcing public services through decentralization and privatization. As a consequence, too little attention had been paid to LPA's responsibility for the performance of public tasks and safeguarding public interests.

In Romania, the main problem remains the lack of accountability of local elected representatives and public servants. Another problem is the distribution of funds from central government, this process being done on political grounds. This leads to a massive migration policy and to focus on national policy rather than addressing the current problems of each community. The solution proposed by us would be the rigorous application of the principle of self-government and autonomy for local authorities. The minimization of corruption is critical to reduce poverty and generating social and sustainable development, promoting good governance and public accountability and transparency in LPA. The provision of LPA services online could improve efficiency as well as eliminate access points for corrupt practices.

Fostering good governance and focusing on outcomes for the citizen, the end users of the services, can expedite the process of transparency and accountability of the elected representatives of the LPA. The LPA has to set principles of good governance, to ensure that services are delivered effectively to the service users, including the following principles:

Emphasize Organizational Purpose and Outcomes

The LPA should make sure it has a clear vision of its purpose in terms of the provision of public services, and that this is clearly communicated. It should use management control tools to measure the value for money and implement appropriate systems that emphasize the performance of LPA in order to provide high quality services.

Performing Performance in Clearly Defined Functions and Roles

The LPA should be clear about the functions they are performing and their objectives and include a process for holding the executive to account for achieving those objectives. It should be clear about the respective roles of the management team, including executives and non-executives, and for ensuring those roles are adhered to. It should also have clear strategies for the relationship between the LPA and the service users.

Promoting Values and Establishment of Good Governance Ethics

The LPA should take the lead in establishing and promoting values for the organization and theirs staff. These should reflect public expectation about the conduct and behavior of those who control public services. This should include, for example, openness in decisions, and striving to reduce inequality among service users.

Taking Informed, Transparent Decisions and Managing Risk

The LPA should take account of the public records in decision-making process. They should be explicit about the criteria on which decisions were based and the impact and consequences of those decisions. They should implement systems which provide high quality information on which decisions can be based. Also, they should have an effective system of risk management, including the monitoring of risk management and publicly reporting controls.

In Romania, achieving transparency itself is a lengthy process in which civil society must be included. Neither the integration into the European Union or other structures can fill the gap of education and public attitude. The NGOs' credibility is often dependent on information sources, and their mission is closely related to the promotion of democratic mechanisms. Civil society must go beyond this approach, being undeceived by the apparent transparency of institutions in Romania.

- The LPA Websites must be updated periodically; this task being expressly provided in the job description of the person who takes care of updating information in general and include the regular inclusion information about counselors. Citizens must be assured of up to date information by the Website.
- Endowment of rooms where board meetings take place with useful equipment

registration and promoting the practice of recording Council meetings on local television.

- Automatically display all the information about public spending in support of the work Counselors (Session daytime, mobile phone costs, travel costs in abroad, possible housing services provided to them etc).
- The provision of sanctions in case of failure to present clear statements of assets and interests, on time, with mistakes or omissions by the Counselors and review the legal framework relating to punish officials who do not care, by law, by displaying them.

Developing the Capacity and Capability of the LPA to be Effective

This involves that the leaders have the skills, knowledge and experience they need to perform their functions well. LPA should have systems to ensure that their recruitment, appraisal and development systems are focused on developing talent such that the organization can better deliver its public services.

Engaging Stakeholders and Making Accountability Real

The LPA should make clear, to themselves and to their staff, to whom they are accountable and for what. They should then take an active and planned approach to dialogue with and accountability to the citizens, its staff and the other bodies to whom they are accountable. LPA have to assess the dialogue with service users and accountability to the public, to evaluate their impact on decisions and to decide what improvements may be needed.

FURTHER RESEARCH DIRECTIONS

Our chapter contributes to the understanding of the implication level of the internet in Romanian LPA as a tool of transparency improvement for the citizens use, as well as if the Romanian LPA have a primary websites, what information are disclosed to citizens, as the main stakeholders, that help them to participate in LPA decision making process.

In our future research, having as starting point the limits of the present e-disclosure model we'll take into account other factors that may influence the level of LPA internet disclosure and we will extent our variables sample. Also, we will perform a test of the e-governance model proposal for Romanian LPA for all existing sites of urban local administration, taking into account criteria like the cities' websites components: security and personal data protection, usability, contents, type of provided services, and digital democracy.

From the perspective of the chapter focus we suggest as an insight of a future book to emphasize a comparative analysis regarding the models of e-governance, good corporate governance in nations' public sector. This approach of benchmarking will get to a better openness to the understanding and the takeover of the good practices of different countries or systems, providing a snapshot of performance through a critical analysis of one or another public organization against the compared ones. Also, this technique helps the public organizations to understand where they are in relation to a particular standard.

CONCLUSION

Within the growing pressure on governments to improve their financial responsibilities, the chapter emphasized the literature on the governance process, focusing on the information revealed by LPA in the transparency increasing process as part of their policy of good governance practice. The main focus of the chapter was on civil society and good governance within the Romanian context. The Romanian public sector has undergone many changes, especially after the socialist regime, and is presently at the gates of democracy. Therefore, we relate the development of local public government's relation with citizens, emphasizing accountability for the management and control of public resources as well as the delivery services and its transparency.

We discuss LPAs increasing their transparency as part of their good governance practice policy. If they provide clear, understandable and reliable information and increase their transparency, they could improve the image of LPA and the confidence of citizens. From our research observations we may conclude that the strategy of communication on the Internet by Romanian LPA is limited, generally, to an ornamental web presence, one that does not respond efficiently to the requirements of the digital society.

The chapter revealed some weaknesses of the present Romanian LPAs in relation to the citizens, especially in the field of e-disclosure to the citizens; limited transparency; impaired broad and long-term perspective on the good governance and limited resource utilization. For this reason, the proposals we made for Romanian LPAs could achieve good governance by harnessing information for decision-making through the use of ICT.

The future in the public sector, like in private sector, is online disclosure of information for the users; this will make LPA take advantages of the Internet's facilities (Popa, Blidisel, Pop, 2008) and will reduce their agency costs. But, first of all, the Romanian politicians have to change their attitudes and be convinced that the future of communication is digital media.

REFERENCES

Basu, S. (2004). E-government and developing countries: An overview. *International Review of Law Computers*, *18*(1), 109–132. doi:10.1080/13600860410001674779

Bellamy, C., & Taylor, J. A. (1998). *Governing in the information age*. Buckingham, UK: Open University Press.

Bovaird, T., Bovaird, A. G., & Löffler, E. (2003). *Public management and governance*. New York, NY: Routledge.

Bozinis, A. I. (2007). Governance and democratic procedures in the information society era. *Journal of the Social Sciences*, *3*(3), 123–126. doi:10.3844/jssp.2007.123.126

Burcea, S. G. (2006). Perspectives of e-democracy in European area. *Theoretical and Empirical Researches in Urban Management*, *1*(1).

Buzby, S. L. (1975). Company size, listed versus unlisted stocks, and the extent of financial disclosure. *Journal of Accounting Research*, *13*(1), 16–37. doi:10.2307/2490647

Castells, M. (2008). The new public sphere: Global civil society. *Communication Networks, and Global Governance, 616*(3).

Chadwick, A. (2003). Bringing e-democracy back in: Why it matters for future research on e-governance. *Social Science Computer Review*, *21*(4), 443–455. doi:10.1177/0894439303256372

Chavent, M., Ding, Y., Fu, L., Stolowy, H., & Wang, H. (2006). Disclosure and determinants studies: An extension using the Divisive Clustering Method (DIV). *European Accounting Review*, *15*(2), 181–218. doi:10.1080/09638180500253092

Christopher, G., & Reddick, A. (2004). Two-stage model of e-government growth: Theories and empirical evidence for U.S. cities. *Government Information Quarterly*, *21*, 51–64. doi:10.1016/j.giq.2003.11.004

Civil Society Development Foundation. (2005). *Dialogue for civil society: Report on the state of civil society in Romania, 2005.*

Cooke, T. E. (1989). Disclosure in the corporate annual reports of Swedish companies. *Accounting and Business Review*, *19*(74), 113–124.

Cooke, T. E. (1998). Regression analysis in accounting disclosure studies. *Accounting and Business Review*, *28*(3), 209–224.

Cooper, L. T. (2004). Big questions in administrative ethics: A need for focused, collaborative effort. *Public Administration Review*, *64*(4), 395–407. doi:10.1111/j.1540-6210.2004.00386.x

Cotterrell, R. (1999). Transparency, mass media, ideology and community. *Cultural Values*, *3*(4), 414–426.

Drew, C. H., & Nyerges, T. L. (2004). Transparency of environmental decision making: A case study of soil cleanup inside the Hanford 100 area. *Journal of Risk Research*, *7*(1), 33–71. doi:10.1080/1366987042000151197

Edes, B. W. (2000). The role of government information officers. *Journal of Government Information*, *27*(4), 455–469. doi:10.1016/S1352-0237(00)00179-9

Florini, A. (2004). Behind closed doors: Governmental transparency gives way to secrecy. *Harvard International Review*, *26*(1), 18–21.

Fountain, J. E. (2003). *Information, institutions and governance: Advancing a basic social science research program for digital government.* National Centre for Digital Government. USA: Harvard University.

Gerring, J., & Thacker, S. C. (2004). Political institutions and corruption: The role of unitarism and parliamentarism. *British Journal of Political Science, 34*(2), 295–330. doi:10.1017/S0007123404000067

Governance, D. org initiative. (2010). *What is digital governance?* Retrieved April 20, 2010, from http://216.197.119.113/artman/publish/index1.shtml

Grigorescu, A. (2003). International organizations and government transparency: Linking the international and domestic realms. *International Studies Quarterly, 47*, 643–667. doi:10.1046/j.0020-8833.2003.04704003.x

Grove, A. S. (1997). *Only the paranoid survive.* London, UK: Profile Books Ltd.

Hiller, J. S., & Belanger, F. (2001). *Privacy strategies for electronic government, in e-government 2001* (Abramson, M. A., & Means, G. E., Eds.). Oxford, UK: Rowman and Littlefield Publishers.

Hudson, J. (2002). Digitising the structures of government: The UK's information age government agenda. *Policy and Politics, 30*(4), 515–531. doi:10.1332/030557302760590431

Institute for Public Policy (IPP). (2009). *Barometer of public opinion.* Bucharest, Romania: IPP publishing.

Ionescu, C. (2005). Sinteza Raportului de audit Performanta Sistemului Electronic National privind implementarea tehnologiilor informatice în scopul asigurării accesului la informatii publice si furnizării de servicii publice informatizate către persoane fizice sau juridice. *Curtea de Conturi a României.* Retrieved on January 12, 2009, from http://www.rcc.ro/documente/sinteza%20sen06.pdf

Kelton, A., & Yang, Y. (2008). The impact of corporate governance on Internet financial reporting. *Journal of Accounting and Public Policy, 27*(1), 62–87. doi:10.1016/j.jaccpubpol.2007.11.001

King, M. A. (2001). The cost manager and the Internet. *Journal of Cost Management, 5*(6), 15–17.

Kooiman, J. (1993). *Modern governance: New government-society interactions.* London, UK: Saga.

Kooiman, T. (1993). *Social and political governance. Modern governance.* London, UK: Sage Publications.

Korakas, C. (2008). *E-democracy. Opportunities and problems.* Access2Democracy Foundation. Retrieved April 22, 2010, form http://www.access2democracy.org

Laswad, F., Fisher, R., & Oyelere, P. (2005). Determinants of voluntary Internet financial reporting by local government authorities. *Journal of Accounting and Public Policy, 24*(2), 101–121. doi:10.1016/j.jaccpubpol.2004.12.006

Moon, M. J. (2002). The evolution of e-government among municipalities: Rhetoric or reality? *Public Administration Review, 62*(4), 424–434. doi:10.1111/0033-3352.00196

MORI. (2005). *What works: Key lessons from recent e-democracy literature.* UK government. Retrieved November, 20, 2009, from http://www.e-Democracy.gov.uk

OECD. (2001). Citizens as partners. In *OECD handbook on information, consultation and public participation in policy-making.* Paris, France: OECD Publications Service.

OECD. (2003). *Public sector transparency and international investment policy.* Retrieved from http://www.oecd.org/dataoecd/45/22/2506884.pdf

OECD. (2005). *OECD guidelines on corporate governance of state-owned enterprises.* OECD Publishing. Retrieved October 13, 2009, from http://www.ecgi.org/codes/documents/oecd_soe_en.pdf

Pina, V., Torres, L., & Royo, S. (2007). Are ICTs improving transparency and accountability in the EU regional and local governments? An empirical study. *Public Administration, 85*(2), 449–472. doi:10.1111/j.1467-9299.2007.00654.x

Piotrowski, S. J., & Borry, E. L. (2009). Governmental transparency and websites: The case of New Jersey municipalities. In Reddick, C. G. (Ed.), *Strategies for local e-government adoption and implementation: Comparative studies.* Hershey, PA: IGI Global.

Pollitt, C., & Boukaert, G. (1994). *Public management reform. A comparative analysis.* Oxford, UK: Oxford University Press.

Popa, A., Blidisel, R., & Pop, A. (2008). Investor relations on the Internet. An empirical study of Romanian listed companies. In Fikusz (Ed.), *2008 Business sciences –Symposium for Young Researchers Proceedings,* (pp.187-197), Budapest, Hungary: Budapest Tech.

Raffournier, B. (1995). The determinants of voluntary financial disclosure by Swiss listed companies. *European Accounting Review, 4*(2), 261–280. doi:10.1080/09638189500000016

Savas, E. (2000). *Privatization and public-private partnership.* New York, NY: Chatham House Publishers.

Serrano, C., Mar, R. T., & Pilar, P. T. (2008). *Factors influencing e-disclosure in local public administrations.* (Documento de Trabajo -03). Facultad de Ciencias Económicas y Empresariales, Universidad de Zaragoza. Retrieved November 20, 2009, from http://www.dteconz.unizar.es/DT2008-03.pdf

Stoica, V., & Ilas, A. (2009). Romanian urban e-government. Digital services and digital democracy in 165 cities. *Electronic. Journal of E-Government, 7*(2), 171–182.

Stolowy, H., & Ding, Y. (2003). Les facteurs déterminants de la stratégie des groupes français en matière de communication sur leurs activités de recherché et développement. *Finance Contrôle Stratégie, 3*(1), 39–62.

Tiron Tudor, A., Blidisel, R., & Popa, A. (2009). E-financial reporting within the Romanian public sector governance. In D. Remenyi (Ed.), *9th European Conference on e-Government Westminster Business School, University of Westminster, London, UK 29-30 June 2009,* (pp. 628- 637). Dublin, Ireland: Trinity College Dublin.

Tiut, A. (2003). Corruption and civil society in Romania: Striving for an answer, or at least a clear picture. Retrieved on May 12, 2009, from http://www.eumap.org/journal/features/2003/july/ccsromania

Treasury, H. M. (2005). *Corporate governance in central government departments: Code of good practice.* London, UK: Crown Copyright.

Tzu-Shan, T., & Torgashina, N. (2008). The usage of Information-Communication Technologies in government-citizen relations: A case study of Khanty-Mansiysk autonomous Okrug-Yugra. *Journal of Informatics & Electronics, 3*(1), 63–77.

United Nations Economic Commission for Europe (UNCE). (2008). *Guidebook on promoting good governance in public-private partnerships.* New York, NY; Geneva, Switzerland: United Nations.

World Bank Workshop. (2003). Reinventing government: Innovations in public sector reform using ICT. Retrieved on May 12, 2010, from www1.worldbank.org/publicsector/edevelopment.doc

ADDITIONAL READING

Barr, T. (2000). User Perspectives of the Future of the Internet ', *ALIA 2000,* Retrieved on January 12, 2009, from http://conferences.alia.org.au/alia2000/proceedings/trevor.barr.html.

Blidisel, R., Popa, A., & Pop, A. (2008). Budgetary and Accounting Experience in Public Sector, *Fikusz 2008 Business Sciences –Symposium for Young Researchers Proceedings,* Budapest: Budapest Tech, 7-18.

Bolivar, M. P. (2007). E-Government and Public Financial Reporting-The Case of Spanish Regional Governments. *American Review of Public Administration, 37*(2), 142–177. doi:10.1177/0275074006293193

Brown, D. (2005). Electronic government and public administration. *International Review of Administrative Sciences, 71*(2), 241–254. doi:10.1177/0020852305053883

Debreceny, M. (2002). The determinants of Internet financial reporting. *Journal of Accounting and Public Policy, 21*(4-5), 371–394. doi:10.1016/S0278-4254(02)00067-4

Dreze, X., & Zufryden, F. (2004). Measurement of Online Visibility and its Impact on Internet Traffic. *Journal of Interactive Marketing, 18*(1), 20–37. doi:10.1002/dir.10072

Edmiston, K. D. (2003). State and local e-government: Prospects and challenges. *American Review of Public Administration, 33*(1), 20–45. doi:10.1177/0275074002250255

Galindo, F. (2004). Electronic government from the legal point of view: Methods. *International Review of Law Computers & Technology, 18*(1), 7. doi:10.1080/13600860410001674706

Gandia, P. (2008). Determinants of web site information by Spanish city councils. *Journal Online Information Review, 32*(1), 35–57. doi:10.1108/14684520810865976

Graven, B. N., & Marston, C. L. (1999). Financial reporting on the internet by leading UK companies. *European Accounting Review, 8*(2), 321–333. doi:10.1080/096381899336069

Hazlett, S.-A., & Hill, F. (2003). E-government: The realities of using IT to transform the public sector. *Managing Service Quality, 13*(6), 445. doi:10.1108/09604520310506504

Hodge, F., Kennedy, M., & Maines, L. (2002) Recognition versus Disclosure in Financial Statements: Does Search-facilitating Technology Improve Transparency? Retrieved on January 12, 2009 from http://ssrn.com/abstract=351440.

Holden, S. H., Norris, D. F., & Fletcher, P. D. (2003). Electronic government at the local level: Progress to date and future issues. *Public Performance & Management Review, 26*(4), 325. doi:10.1177/1530957603026004002

Horn, S. P. (2003). Taxation of e-commerce. *Journal of American Academy of Business, Cambridge, 2*(2), 329–338.

Katchanovski, I., & La Porte, T. (2005). Cyberdemocracy or Potemkin E-Villages? Electronic Governments in OECD and Post-Communist Countries. *International Journal of Public Administration, 28*(7/8), 665–681. doi:10.1081/PAD-200064228

Kim, P. S., Halligan, J., Cho, N., & Eikenberry, A. M. (2005). Toward Participatory and Transparent Governance: Report on the Sixth Global Forum on Reinventing Government. *Public Administration Review, 65*(6), 646–654. doi:10.1111/j.1540-6210.2005.00494.x

Komito, L. (2005). E-participation and governance: Widening the net. *Electronic Journal of E Government, 3*(1), 39–48.

Laswad, A. (2005). Determinants of voluntary Internet financial reporting by local government authorities. *Journal of Accounting and Public Policy, 24*(2), 101–121. doi:10.1016/j.jaccpubpol.2004.12.006

*** Law no. 215/2001, Local government law, with amendments and completions (O.G. no. 204/2001).

*** Law no. 286/2006 amending and supplementing Local public administration law. No 215/2001 (O.G. no. 621 of July 18, 2006)

*** Law no. 52/2003 regarding the decisional transparency in public administration

*** Law no. 544/ 2001 regarding the free access to public interest information (O.G. no 663/2001)

Lymer, A. (1997). The use of the Internet for corporate reporting: A discussion of the issues and survey of current usage in the UK. *Journal of Financial Information Systems,* Retrieved on May 22, 2009, from http://www.shu.ac.uk/schools/fsl/fisjnl//vol1996/pprs1997/lymer97.htm.

Lymer, A., Debreceny, R., Gray, G., & Rahman, A. (1999). Business Reporting on the Internet, Retrieved on April 17, 2009 from http://www.iasc.org.uk.

Massumi, B. (1987). *Introduction: Rhizome. A Thousand Plateaus: Capitalism and Schizophrenia*. Minneapolis, USA: University of Minnesota Press.

Perez, C., Bolívar, M. P. R., & López-Hernández, A. M. (2008). E-Government process and incentives for online public financial information, *Journal. Online Information Review, 32*(3), 379–400. doi:10.1108/14684520810889682

Perez, C., López, A., & Rodríguez, M. P. (2005). Citizens' access to on-line governmental financial information: Practices in the European Union countries. *Government Information Quarterly, 22*(4), 258–276. doi:10.1016/j.giq.2005.02.002

Perez, C., López-Hernández, A. M., & Bolívar, M. P. R. (2007). Citizens' access to on-line governmental financial information: Practices in the European Union countries. *American Review of Public Administration, 37*(2), 142–177.

Pina, V., & Torres, L. (2003). Reshaping Public Sector Accounting: An International Comparative View. *Canadian Journal of Administrative Sciences, 20*(4), 334–350. doi:10.1111/j.1936-4490.2003.tb00709.x

Popa, A., Blidisel, R., & Farcane, N. (2008). Internet Business Reporting a challenge: The case of Romanian Manufacturing Enterprises, *DAAAM International Viena*, Annals of DAAAM for 2008&Proceedings of the 19th International DAAAM Symposium Intelligent Manufacturing &Automation: Focus on next Generation of Intelligent Systems and Solutions, Trnava, Slovakia, 1101-1103.

Tiron-Tudor, A, Blidisel, R. (2007). Romanian Accrual Accounting Experience in Public Higher Education Sector, *International Journal of Business Research*, 7(6), Academy of International Business and Economics, Los Angeles, SUA, 121-131.

Wang, H, Rubin, B L. (2004). Embedding e-finance in e-government: a new e-government framework, *Electronic Government, an International Journal,* 1(4), 362-373.

Chapter 14
Making Room for E-Government through Succession Planning

Kim Loutzenhiser
Troy University, USA

ABSTRACT

Few innovations have more impact on government's work culture and the delivery of public services than e-government. E-government is a global phenomenon that is much researched, but researchers often neglect to research the demands it places on the human resources, the administrative infrastructure, and training and development. There is very little written on e-government and why it matters in succession planning. Those who design and implement well executed e-government systems need technological and culturally relevant competencies to make e-government responsive to e-citizens. In addition, there is no shortage of articles on government budget overruns tied to IT projects. The rush to have needed technologies has outpaced recruitment and training strategies to manage the technology infrastructure that makes e-government work. The infrastructure of e-government includes concepts tied to the provision of a seamless flow of services, logical one-stop-shops, efficiency, and an ability to do more with less. These concepts, however, will not support e-government indefinitely without adequate succession planning. The succession planning for this year and beyond must include training, maintaining and transitioning employees in a world where technical competencies need to be addressed and citizens clamor for more direct involvement. Succession planning can train employees to create a work culture that promotes accountability, transparency, efficiency, and build an appreciation for a competent representative bureaucracy. Succession planning, more than any other tool, can tap into the diversity pipeline, something that could narrow the digital divide. Human resources in the public sector faces fierce competition for talent. Talent is recruited nationally and internationally. Thus the public service is at risk if it persists in holding onto 20th century technology and 20th century cultural world-views.

DOI: 10.4018/978-1-60960-159-1.ch014

INTRODUCTION

Government public relations no longer happens solely through public relations professionals. It is now decentralized through blogs, social networks, text messaging, photo sharing, wikis and virtual worlds – the Web 2.0 World. Succession planning can address the benchmark strength in human resource capacity tied to e-government. The thrust of e-government requires a closer look at employees and the kind of talent needed to communicate through technology in a way that is usable, helpful and easy. E-government thus requires that management employ its talent differently. Without a tool to identify talent management needs and how to address them, e-government or any other kind of service delivery, will not meet the complex challenges currently posed by globalization, economic woes, unprecedented retirements, and existing challenges in the competition for talent. A skilled public work force and one trained for a world of globalization and increasing diversity will be needed in a twenty-first government that will have to govern with the aid of civil society (Huddleston, 2000).

E-GOVERNMENT RECRUITMENT

The practice of e-government will not achieve best practices status until it addresses systems of recruiting, maintaining, training and planning for the provision of public services. No doubt e-government is an integral part of public service delivery for many governments, particularly in the United States. Public Human resource organizations, however, have not been quick to take the lead in using Web 2.0 technologies that could benefit them including LinkedIn, Facebook and Twitter – this is not an exhaustive list. Web 2.0 technologies are interactive and important to learning the communication venues frequented by Generation X. Recruitment of this generation will not be easy without embracing the online places

they frequently visit. The Obama administration is noted for attempting to revamp the federal government and making it "cool" for young people to work for the public service. Without embracing Generation X communication venues, however, it is tough to make government a desirable place for young professionals to work.

The recruitment benefits using Web 2.0, social media and social networking are not fully known. Still there is no better time to learn relevant social media tools. The variety of communication outlets means that there are many different ways to connect with talent and people looking for jobs. There are myriad online ways to learn about what the competition is doing in terms of recruitment. There are blogs (http://www.recruitingblogs.com/), web sites (http://hrmtoday.com/), wikis (http://thehumanresource.wikispaces.com/page/diff/Home/88551151) and more. In London for example, there is a civil service live network (http://network.civilservicelive.com/). These technologies bring dramatic changes in communication, which can be static, interactive, transactional or transformational (Melitski, 2003). The transformational usages of e-government are also evident where succession planning takes center stage.

e-government cannot exist without e-Public Servants to provide services to its e-Citizens. Each of the e-Players exists in concert. They are networked in a communication system that may include an e-Manager, e-Planner, or e-Collector of revenue working from their office or their home to offer a government service. Succession planning can assess whether a government has a workforce capable of facilitating the delivery of services in a networked system. If the prediction of unprecedented number of retirements does not move succession planning to the fore, the economy and technology will be a couple of major reasons to move to take an in depth review of succession planning and e-government (Roberts 2003; Roddy 2004).

Succession planning is a tool to continuously and systematically identify, assess and develop personnel to enhance performance (Kim, 2003). Initially it focused on leadership gaps left by baby boomer retirements and developed to identify and develop leaders to replace those leaving. It has evolved into a tool for an organization-wide effort to continuously assess competencies and skills gaps throughout an organization. It also offers an opportunity to plan for the future and work toward a diverse workforce to address nontraditional working arrangements and a multigenerational workforce (Helton and Jackson 2007; Fillichio 2006). Succession planning was initiated following predictions that baby boomer retirements would lead to a knowledge gap of crisis proportions in the public service. It goes beyond the baby boomer talent retiring from the workforce. It is now about being able to compete for talent with the private sector, have a preparedness to meet technology demands, work easily with a diverse work force, and have cross training to do more with less (Fillichio 2006). Without infusing technological skill sets into succession planning, the competition for talent may be lost. This is a world that few could have envisioned a decade ago (Roddy 2004.)

Nearly ten years ago, Congress addressed the need for investing in IT to build competency and capacity in the government infrastructure and human resource pool (Seifert, 2008). The Clinger-Cohen Act created the Office of Electronic Government to manage security, build capacity and address issues of access (Government Accountability Office, December 2004). The Act addressed the need to include citizens, improve government operations, communications and public services (Government Accountability Office, March 2004). In 2007 Congress passed the eGovernment Re-Authorization Act.

Beyond these acts of Congress, it takes real leadership to make dramatic change manageable within organizations. It is important to have a leader that has the ability to change an organization to succeed in a modern world. Organizational culture does not adapt easily to change even

if needed changes represent an improvement (Hartley & Allison, 2000) Leadership is part of a clear succession plan, one that results in major organizational change. Strong and effective leadership can ameliorate the culture clashes that come with rapid change. Such leadership can provide the vision necessary to help employees experience the benefits of a diverse workforce. Dimensions of diversity include demographics such as race, culture, gender, sexual orientation, ethnic origin, body shape, disability, etc. Another dimension includes career patterns, mobility, and an ability to work any place and any time (Fillichio 2006) Within this diverse workforce, those who are most comfortable with technology are workers from Generation X. This generation has a work orientation that puts their age cohort at odds with other cohorts, such as Baby Boomers who enjoy more structured, traditional work and workplaces.

HOW MIGHT THE OBAMA ADMINISTRATION INFLUENCE E-SUCCESSION?

President Barack Obama campaigned through texting, Facebook, email and other electronic communication forms. This is evidence that mastering technology and its benefits builds an effective organization. President Obama could be dubbed the first Web 2.0 president. The White house Web site includes Facebook, YouTube, Twitter, Flickr, MySpace, iTunes, Vimeo, and LinkedIn (http://www.whitehouse.gov/2010). Clearly for this president, the time has come to embrace a more open Internet, a *connected* system of representation, technology in schools and world-wide-web (www) use to promote transparency. It seems remiss to not talk about what public management has to do with a networked system, especially when the World Wide Web is being promoted as a tool to achieve transparency. The morale of public servants has suffered after decades of Reagan like government bashing. Any study of e-government and the personnel system behind it benefits if we ask, "what does trust have to do with it?" Succession planning is important to keep the personnel system sound and can address employment gaps that would preclude transparency from becoming a best practice in government (2010 Talent Management). The training necessary to use technology in an honest, efficient and transparent way can lure talent into the public sector. Linking technology to employee recruitment and development serves as a talent management plan.

It may be unrealistic to suggest that e-government can solve issues tied to the public trust. The tension or distrust between leaders and their public is a historic one (Taylor & Burt, 2005). Divided government, checks and balances, a two chamber legislature and separate but shared powers were written into the Constitution because of distrust in government. Madison is repeatedly quoted for saying "If men were angels, no government would be necessary." Thus trust issues are an ongoing incentive to work on the government's relationship with its citizens. Succession planning is one tool and e-government is another to improve the relationship between government and the citizens. Both succession planning and e-government in tandem can serve as a vehicle to help achieve the ideals of justice, equality and freedom.

What does the availability of e-government do to the quality of the exchange between e-Citizens and e-Public Servants? It means the capacity to change the nature of the relationship between leaders and their public has to do with the ability of public servants to develop an electronic platform that enhances transparency and accountability (Roy, 2003). If public trust matters and contributes to the quality of the exchange, it is important to recruit, train and develop people to make e-government serve as a true paradigm shift toward transparency and strengthening social capital (Carter & Belanger, 2005; Farazmand, 2002).

E-government offers an opportunity to make government more transparent and accountable – variables that correlate to public trust. While it is hard to get at the precise meaning of quality for public services, in a democratic system it has something to do with being honest, trustworthy, civic minded, and be responsive to humanity in shared public and virtual spaces (Hard, 1989). Political machine run governments such as in nineteenth century New York City, Kansas City and Chicago, were able to deliver services, but not able to do so in a way that was transparent or accountable. These governments were associated with distrust and corruption. It follows that citizens are more satisfied with a service if they receive it through an exchange that is courteous, service oriented and honest. The New Public Management focused not only on services but also on civility, customer services and running government more like a business. The culture of civil service had to change with the values ushered in by the New Public Management. From the 1990s to the present, governments at all levels have focused on performance, customer service, diversity, and doing more with less. Current public servants need to provide a high level of customer service through exchanges in the online world. However, what does service with a smile look like when there is no face-to-face interaction? The answer to this goes back to leadership, training and development.

Leadership and organizational change go together. Succession planning started out with an effort to address a gap in leadership. It has expanded to include efforts to prepare for workforce changes throughout an organization. E-government involves technological and cultural changes that reconfigure the world-of-work. Today the disappearing bureaucrat might have something to do with retirement. But it can also have something to do with the fact that e-government means many bureaucrats can do their job from home. Now that public employees engage in everyday communication via the World Wide Web, it is important to assess the benchmark strength provided by knowledge workers inside government and the technology needed to provide services. Just what kind of leadership, training and personnel are needed to provide e-government that is customer service friendly? This question relates e-government to the customer-oriented values of the New Public Management.

E-government means that all types of current public employees are using e-Communication or assisting with digital service delivery to some degree. E-government utilizes information technology (IT), information sharing and access, and changes the definition of what constitutes public knowledge (Freidman, 2007). The challenge therefore is to train public servants to first address security issues and make use of technology to achieve transparency goals; then it becomes an issue of leadership to instill the change in the organizational culture. Public officials engaged in budgeting need skills to post a budget online in a user friendly way. One of these skills is the ability to communicate online. The hierarchy of communications flattens when more people engage in Web 2.0 technologies, e-government, or other technological innovations. E-government, along with new media networking, changes and strengthens pluralism as we know it. The distinction between the knower and the known is no longer distinguishable. Public managers need to manage information networks and know the implications of citizens having ready access to public information. Thomas Friedman's flat world (2009) plays out through e-government. Today more than ever, the public has come to expect a responsive government. As journalist Friedman demonstrated throughout his book *The World Is Flat*, the public is expecting more information in a faster amount of time. Being constrained by a system largely designed before the proliferation of the Internet into mainstream culture has caused the public sector to fall considerably behind the private sector in terms of responsiveness and also on many other levels. Again, this is another situation where public administration leaders will have to encourage the use of technology to increase responsiveness, while at the same time ensuring

subordinates abide by what may appear to be antiquated regulations and laws (Friedman, 2007).

How do public managers insure a process that monitors information to guarantee that e-government works to arrive at public interest? How do they receive the competencies to do this? The knower and the known become less distinguishable because citizens have blogs, as do government entities. Public servants need to not only manage service delivery but also manage information on the World Wide Web. Knowledgeable citizens are preferable but it requires that people working on the other side of the exchange also have the skills and competencies to provide an added value to the exchange. Training, leadership, and succession planning have much to contribute to bringing about these changes.

E-government also introduces a new technology, a new work culture and new environment to the public workforce. Hence it radically changes the nature of work. Without planning for the development and recruitment of talent, e-government loses its potential to provide short and long term improvements to the quality of the exchange between citizens and their government. The rise of e-government presents fundamental reasons to do succession planning. For example, instead of looking for the top three candidates who apply for a position, succession planning works to get the right persons into critical positions. At a time when there is mandate to manage diversity, a massive flood of retirements, and the perennial need for talent, the changes imposed by e-government offers one more reason for succession planning to be the vehicle for managing multiple engines of change.

E-government can enhance transparency and also offer accountability. It can keep multiple stakeholders informed. Information, communication and citizen engagement can lower public distrust in government (Marlowe, 2004). E-government needs leadership to shepherd support for investment in the proper information infrastructure and related training to prevent budget overruns and facilitate implementation (Taylor & Burt, 2005). Another important aspect of IT is that makes communication across vast distances easy and inexpensive. Networking within and between countries requires a new skill set and worthy of studying further. The United States is no longer in the lead here and can learn from developing nations who have had a long history of collaborating between states (Freidman, 2007). Early adapters in technological innovations have a resource that other countries may not have in that technological skills and resources are definitely a sought after commodity. For instance, India is a resource rich nation with a large population of technically competent citizens. There is thus a regrouping of nations that would not have been predictable without easy communication across large distances through the Internet. People are now one click away from each other. The world is a smaller stage like never before. Nations that use e-government to enhance transparency and accountability open communication with citizens and with each other. The United States may have its first Web 2.0 Presidency, but someone needs to manage the change that not only requires a regrouping within the government bureaucracy but also a skilled facilitator to address the changes that must also occur in the organizational culture within government.

WHY E-GOVERNMENT NEEDS SUCCESSION PLANNING

Employees trained in the practice of e-government can work to give it better definition. Government is still lagging when it comes to working with technology that builds relationships in new ways and forms. By viewing e-government as a process and not an outcome, it still comes down to people forging relationships within government and outside. Just like the man behind the curtain representing the Wizard of Oz, there is a person behind the computer, smart phone, or other

technology. Again, the new types of relationships formed as a result of e-government mean that someone has to manage organizational cultures that prove resistant to public service delivery modes such as e-government. Succession planning offers yet another opportunity to lead organizations through change in a way that makes government organizations more adaptable to e-government.

Succession planning has evolved to plan for diversity, train for new modes of delivery, and to create an organizational culture that works beyond today. Succession management is currently done in conjunction with a strategic plan to identify competencies that will meet with the mission and goals of the organization. Human resources capacity, for example, can be measured in terms of *bench strength.* This bench strength encompasses training, development and recruitment, which are tied to technology. Technology is thus one way for organizations to keep current. It also takes time, money and resources to be current in the field. The fast evolution of e-government parallels the retirement of Baby Boomers. This is fortuitous, particularly since the implementation of E-government meets with the resistance of the Baby Boomer organizational culture (Crumpacker 2007). The transition of old and new talent can ease the pains associated with e-government's rise (Holden, Norris & Fletcher, 2003). Almost by definition e-government conjures up an image of someone plugging-in government to illuminate it further. More research needs to be done on how e-government is more than just a technological innovation. People providing e-government services need to be brought on board to bring about improvements in the public service. Reform is another one of those elusive terms that could be applied to e-government, but any innovation that increases citizen participation is bound to be an improvement.

E-GOVERNMENT, PUBLIC TRUST AND SUCCESSION PLANNING

Without public trust, it will be harder to mobilize public support for huge investments in technological infrastructure at a time of IT project cost overruns, budget deficits and daily news accounts of states going broke across the U.S. This does not bode well for the public's support of continued funding for such projects. Succession planning could help get the right people in the right positions to make more accurate estimates of technology projects. It makes sense to call for training programs and assess staffing needs tied to IT projects (Roddy, 2004; Kim & Kim, 2003). It also makes sense to highlight the benefits of e-government. Today more than 70% of taxpayers filed taxes on line. Driver's license renewal is another example where citizens are participating in increasing numbers (Baumgarten and Chui 2009). This is a time saver and it reduces citizen's aggravation with government red tape. Trained employees at all levels are the key to being proactive and to spread the word about useful technologies that make working with government easy, time saving and effective (Davis, 1989). It is unlikely that citizens will go out of their way to promote technology, but employees can promote e-government services through their own web site, facebook, wiki's, blogs or other resource. The greatest shift in organizational culture lies in the citizen participation that is allowable in blogs, wikis and mashups. This may be where technological innovations meet the resistance of organizational culture.

Along with these technological changes, everyone across the world is adapting to the unprecedented ethnological changes. There are major benefits to training employees to stretch and build their skills in adaptability, technology and diversity (Kim & Kim, 2003). Succession planning offers a road map to government organizations today. Today it is a tool to build a future that embraces diversity, technology and shared ownership in civic and organizational culture. Succession planning is all about adaptability and therefore should address issues that minimize the digital divide (Justice, Melitski & Smith, 2004). Within this digital divide there are social justice issues present in statistics showing poorer and less educated citizens not participating in technological innovations (Justice, Melitski & Smith, 2004).

The investment in technology provides mounting justification to advocate succession planning. E-government will lose support if it does not give universal benefits to all (Holden, Norris & Fletcher, 2003). However, cost limits to implementation of technological and succession planning for e-government will present leadership challenges (Chen & Perry, 2003). Organization capacity requires constant attention to who is retiring and who needs to be hired to allow for continuity where necessary, and accommodate change when required (Helton & Jackson 2007). Human resources information systems (HRIS) offer many types of systems to assist with succession planning.

The fears over technology and technological security fit in the complicated balancing act between liberty and order. It takes training to be able to make decisions in areas that have no easy answers. Trained employees are important to effective implementation of e-government. These employees must uphold values inherent in the United States Constitution. Liberty and technological security are both important. There is no doubt that technological security is an issue. Fraud, Internet viruses, identity theft and other crimes that have been yet to be invented are all security considerations. In designing e-government service delivery it is important to allow for discussions, communications and feedback in a world that requires internal and external communications (Kim & Kim, 2003). However, adequate security must also be maintained, which requires a delicate balancing act for government,

E-GOVERNMENT IS A TOOL OF PUBLIC ADMINISTRATION

E-government can be an effective tool for public administration. At the same time, however, change does not come easy, particularly when it does not fit with an existing organizational culture. For this reason, ongoing succession planning must accommodate the ever-changing organization. Baby Boomers will retire; Generation Xers will come on board. One way to accommodate these changes is to use a *stages* approach, which offers a continuum for training through change that is static, interactive, transactional and transformational (Melitski, 2003). Subsection planning can take government employees through this continuum to incorporate and prepare for change. This same concept of *stages* can be applied to the citizens embarking on the new world of e-government. E-government has been designed to be user friendly, but many citizens will struggle with understanding and institutionalizing the technology and subsequent changes in the way they formerly dealt with their government (Marlowe, 2004). The relationship between citizen satisfaction, government performance, public trust and social capital are part of civil society. The question is what a networked society does to civic culture

The stage analysis of change suggests that transformation will not occur without thinking through the ways public servants make e-government happen. This process includes a discussion of what enhanced citizen engagement and communication would look like and how employees might play a role using e-government as a tool for building civil society. At a minimum it is necessary to know the competencies necessary for citizens to participate in e-government. In order for e-government to be successful, the IT infrastructure requires an investment to build capacity in human resources through training and development and by building a pipeline for diversity (Roddy, 2004; Siegel 2007). Public managers must work jointly with human resources to address competencies tied to succession planning in e-government. Government organizations can streamline planning efforts to build organizational capacity. Succession planning fits nicely in the effort to implement e-government infrastructures. Large-scale change of any kind requires assessment methods, scheduled evaluations and alignment (Melitski, 2003).

Succession planning addresses entire organizations in terms of innovations, retirements and diversity needs and the usual buzz words such as efficiency and effectiveness, demand adaptability as well as cultural and technical competencies. E-government adds value to an arena that already has plenty of technical competencies (Justice, Melitski & Smith, 2006). E-government can improve the relationship between the governed and those who govern, but it takes planning to have any hope that the public finds it in their interests (Marlowe, 2004). There are a lot of forces at play and without adequate planning; public officials will not be able to utilize e-government to capacity.

When governments address succession planning, they also must address globalization at the same time. Globalization makes competition for knowledgeable employees paramount (Kudo, 2008). Since the U.S. is at a juncture to re-evaluate what it means to be a strategic player in a "flatter" world and simultaneously address financial woes, the justification for human resource planning, succession planning and the investment in an e-government infrastructure matter greatly. E-government and e-services are producing other global super powers (Jreisat, 2004). In order to make e-government an asset, it is timely to hire and train talent to make digital services convenient to everyone (Holden, Norris & Fletcher, 2003). The search for new talent works to build organizational capacity and adaptability (Chen & Perry, 2003). E-government therefore adds a new dimension to what we already know about outsourcing and succession planning (Chen & Perry, 2003).

E-government technology offers HR professionals an ability to do more with each government professional and offer more services while spending less money the potential to do more with less (Eoyang, 2008). In essence, with e-government citizens are performing administrative tasks and are administrators by proxy (Brown, 2005). The distinction between routine and nonroutine, however, is where the public employee matters once more. The public employee is the professional pulling strings behind the curtain that handles matters of administrative discretion. In keeping it simple, participation and engagement must come with assurance of security and ease (Kim & Kim, 2003). Public administrators need to either be IT specialists or work closely with IT professionals to be keenly aware of the digital divide. Employees must work to broaden access at every innovation. The mantra becomes make online services accessible, convenient and user friendly to everyone (Justice, Melitski & Smith, 2006). Security measures, however, can get in the way of simplicity but this is where the public administrator exercises his or her craft (Kim & Kim, 2003). Information sharing is part of representative government. Integration and data sharing goes with the territory of technology and e-government (Melitski, 2003). Here investment in an e-government infrastructure offers opportunities for civil society.

CONCLUSION

The process of e-government is an evolving one. It requires leadership in public administration, investment in human resources and IT infrastructures and adaptability. The newer versions of succession planning require proponents to justify its need, particularly in today's economic hard times. E-government enthusiasts need to argue for the investment in technology, time and human resources to overcome barriers to implementation. Change happens in stages and requires strong leadership and organization to guide it (Kim & Kim, 2003).

Ultimately the investment in succession planning and e-government infrastructure offers promise. Not only does it allow for global networking but it also shifts the emphasis toward citizen driven service delivery, which helps civil society (Brown, 2005). The new public administration draws from private sector values to run governments more like a business. In this sense, it means treating citizens more like customers and employing user-friendly service delivery mechanisms (Brown, 2005). The emphasis on customer service requires a culture shift – a transition that can be achieved through succession planning, new technology, training and strategic planning. Business values, however, do not always work especially where participatory government is encouraged and valued. There are times where the cacophony of citizen voices can keep a citizen from ever being treated like a customer. It is an example of the ongoing need to offer the best customer service possible in a way that is tailor made to fit with competing values in the public sector.

E-government has taken over so rapidly that it is surprising to say that it is still in the early stages. It radically changes everyday life in the government work force. It changes the government and citizen relationship and plays out differently depending on the level of government size and target audience served (Holden, Norris & Fletcher, 2003). Instead of sharing usable knowledge, the government is offering usable technology to be used by the public work force and those they serve. The ease of use is related to those who use it. The theme of useable technology goes along with the need to adapt networks used by growing numbers of citizens. The Obama campaign and now the Obama administration mastered the various social networks, such as Facebook, MySpace, and YouTube. While this is far from an exhaustive list, it is exemplary of the growing number of users in both public and private sectors. The adaptation toward multiple versions of e-government services is another chapter in reinventing government. The idea that public employees are behind e-government also deserves more acknowledgements. E-government produces research questions that can keep academics busy for a long time.

REFERENCES

Baumgarten, J., & Chui, M. (2009). E-government 2.0. *McKinsey Quarterly.* Retrieved from https://www.mckinseyquarterly.com/E-government_20_2408

Brown, D. (2005). Electronic government and public administration. *International Review of Administrative Sciences*, *71*(2), 241–254. doi:10.1177/0020852305053883

Carter, L., & Belanger, F. (2005). The utilization of e-government services: Citizen trust, innovation and acceptance factors. *Information Systems Journal*, *15*, 5–25. doi:10.1111/j.1365-2575.2005.00183.x

Chen, Y., & Perry, J. (2003). Outsourcing for e-government: Managing for success. *Public Performance & Management Review*, *26*(4), 404–421. doi:10.1177/1530957603026004007

Cooper, T. L. (2005). Civic engagement in the twenty-first century: Toward a scholarly and practical agenda. *Public Administration Review*, *65*(5), 534–535. doi:10.1111/j.1540-6210.2005.00480.x

Davis, F. (1989). Perceived usefulness, perceived ease of use and user acceptance of Information Technology. *Management Information Systems Quarterly*, *13*, 319–340. doi:10.2307/249008

Farazmand, A. (2002). Administrative ethics and professional competence: Accountability and performance under globalization. *International Review of Administrative Sciences*, *68*, 127–143. doi:10.1177/0020852302681007

Fillichio, C. (2006). Getting ready for the retirement tsunami: Linda Springer, director of the U.S. Office of Personnel Management, discusses what the federal government needs to do before its retirement peak in 2008-10. *Public Management*, *35*(1), 3–6.

Freidman, T. L. (2007). *The world is flat: A brief history of the twenty-first century*. New York, NY: Picador.

Government Accountability Office. (2004). *Electronic government: Federal agencies have made progress implementing the e-government act of 2002* (GAO-05-12). Retrieved from www.gao.gov/cgi-bin/getrpt?GAO-05-12

Government Accountability Office. (2004). *Electronic government: Initiatives sponsored by the office of management and budget have made mixed progress* (GAO-04-561T). Retrieved from www.gao.gov/cgi-bin/getrpt?GAO-04-561T

Hard, D. K. (1989). A partnership in virtue among all citizens: The public service and civic humanism. *Public Administration Review*, 101–105.

Hartley, J., & Allison, M. (2000). The role of leadership in the modernization and improvement of public services. *Public Money & Management Review*, 35-40.

Helton, K., & Jackson, R. (2007). Navigating Pennsylvania's dynamic workforce: Succession planning in a complex environment. *Public Personnel Management*, *36*(4), 335–347.

Huddleston, M. W. (2000). Onto the darkling plain: Globalization and the American public service in the twenty-first century. *Journal of Public Administration: Research and Theory*, *10*(4), 665–684.

Jreisat, J. (2004). Governance in a globalizing world. *International Journal of Public Administration*, *27*(13-14), 1003–1029. doi:10.1081/PAD-200039883

Justice, J. B., Melitski, J., & Smith, D. L. (2006). E-government as an instrument of fiscal accountability and responsiveness: Do the best practitioners employ the best practices? *American Review of Public Administration, 36*, 301–322. doi:10.1177/0275074005283797

Kim, S., & Kim, D. (2003). South Korean public officials' perceptions of values, failure, and consequences of failure in e-government leadership. *Public Performance & Management Review, 26*(4), 360–375. doi:10.1177/1530957603026004004

Kudo, H. (2008). Does e-government guarantee accountability in public sector? Experiences in Italy and Japan. *Public Administration Quarterly, 32*(1), 93–120.

Marlowe, J. (2004). Part of the solution, or cogs in the system? The origins and consequences of trust in public administrators. *Public Integrity, 6*(2), 93–113.

Melitski, J. (2003). Capacity and e-government performance: An analysis based on early adopters of Internet technologies in New Jersey. *Public Performance & Management Review, 26*(4), 376–390. doi:10.1177/1530957603026004005

Roberts, A. (2003). In the eye of the storm? Societal aging and the future of public service reform. *Public Administration Review, 63*(6), 720–733. doi:10.1111/1540-6210.00335

Roddy, N. (2004). Leadership capacity building model: Developing tomorrow's leadership in science and technology–an example in succession planning and management. *Public Personnel Management, 33*(4), 487–495.

Roy, J. (2003). The relationship dynamics of e-government: A case study of the city of Ottawa. *Public Performance & Management Review, 26*(4), 391–403. doi:10.1177/1530957603026004006

Seifert, J. W. (2008). *Reauthorization of the e-government Act: A brief overview* (RL 34492).

Taylor, J., & Burt, E. (2005). Voluntary organizations as e-democratic actors: Political identity, legitimacy and accountability and the need for new research. *Policy and Politics, 33*(4), 601–616. doi:10.1332/030557305774329127

White House. (2009a). *The White House: President Barack Obama*. Retrieved from http://wwwhttp://www.whitehouse.gov/.govtrack.us/congress/bill.xpd?bill=s110-2321

White House. (2009b). *The Obama-Biden plan*. Retrieved from http://change.gov/agenda/technology_agenda/

Afterword

ABSTRACT

This book has examined the impact of virtual public spheres or the use of ICT by civil society to enhance participation in the political process and governance. The work of many scholars, including those included in this work, as well as theoretical developments, point to virtual public spheres as providing the link between e-government and e-democracy. Critical to the capability of virtual public spheres to this is their capacity to strengthen social capital offline as well as online.

AFTERWORD

The chapters in this book show that virtual public spheres can serve as the bridge connecting e-Government with e-Democracy. Virtual public spheres represent an extension of civil society and deliberative democracy into the virtual realm of ICT. Whereas e-Government is largely service-driven and emphasizes efficiencies in operations, e-Democracy takes the concept further to encompass both deliberative and participatory practices while emphasizing inclusion and equal access. The critical factor that virtual public spheres can contribute to e-Democracy, which is largely absent from e-Government, however well conceived, is social capital. Social capital is necessary to maintain strong, stable civil society (Putnam, 2000). However, as some of the chapters in this book point out, making the transition from offline to online democracy is not without its problems. Two of the most serious issues with ICT indentified in the literature are deconcentration and the flood of information online, both discussed in detail in Chapter One. Decentralization leads to fragmentation (and polarization) and too much information contributes to paralysis of decision-making, both elements that could undermine democracy. The proliferation of information sources and the absence of a central point of control results in users who, faced with a veritable flood of information (much of which is unreliable or unverifiable), choose content on the basis of whether it agrees with their opinions or not. Furthermore, Dahlberg (2005) notes that the Internet's lack of order increases the threat of corporate colonization that extends beyond corporate control of online communication to the competition for the attention of everyday users.

How can virtual public spheres meet these challenges? What lens should be used to make larger sense of these developments against the increasingly shifting backdrop of modern social movements? One needs to look to modern democratic theory in order to place e-Democracy within the broadest possible context. Fuchs (2003), for example, considers three theories, "strong democracy" (put forward by

Benjamin Barber), "discoursive democracy"(based on Habermas), and "directly-deliberative polyarchy" theory (developed by social theorists Cohen and Sabel). The three theories overlap in important aspects:

Their starting point is criticism of existing liberal democracy. It proceeds from two perspectives, normative and practical. From a normative point of view, they object that liberal democracy is now hardly in keeping with a reasonably demanding interpretation of the democracy principle. From a practical point of view they presume that liberal democracy confronts problems no longer amenable to solution within its institutional framework and by its procedures alone. The most important problem they see is the unquestioned dominance of particular interests in politics, which in the long run erode the foundations of the democratic process itself. According to these approaches, participatory democracy is thus the normatively desirable and the practically necessary form of democracy; it is: "desirable both in itself and as a problem solver." (Cohen & Sabel 1997: 314)

Fuchs considers three important points regarding e-Democracy including directness of participation (i.e., all citizens actually making political decisions), deliberation (i.e., the means by which political discourse is conducted), and institutionalism (i.e., the mediums through which participatory practices are upheld and supported). The chief participatory mechanisms emerging from ICT are: (1) Internet-facilitated referendums and (2) interactive communication where a common will of citizens can be formed as a result of online deliberation. However, given the current state of things, there are several basic issues regarding both mechanisms, which need to be better addressed before either one can inspire more confidence in their ability to transform the democratic process. Concerning Internet referenda, the chief drawbacks include: too many important policy questions to be left to large populations to decide, inability to inform citizens of important information surrounding voting referendum issues due to lack information, low motivation to participate on the part of citizens, and lack of accountability for referendum policy. Deliberation using interactive formats is equally troublesome for several reasons including the issue of fragmentation identified by several authors in this work and because e-Forums do not typically allow for complete interaction between all citizens. Groups such as AmericaSpeaks have addressed this last problem with limited success. Additionally, "partners in communication are neither physically nor visually present; they are mutually anonymous others... In Internet communication, the anonymous other is thus not identifiable as a citizen belonging to the same demos as ego himself." In other words, in situations where citizens cannot see and directly address the other (as is the case with online public spheres), there is no guarantee that the other belongs to the same community and, therefore, is a valid stakeholder in discussions involving community interests. Thus, while there exist available remedies for the negative effects of decentralization and information over-load, they are not also without some problems of their own. In this book, we make the case that mechanisms might be devised that enable the virtual public sphere's democracy-enhancing features while at the same time reducing or eliminating its negative effects. Most importantly, virtual public spheres offer the promise of extending civil society's reach into the virtual world.

The skeptical view of virtual public spheres questions whether e-Participation will produce lasting political change. Kuhlen (1998), for example, examines the role information, communication, and media all play in relation to direct democracy. More importantly though from our perspective, Kuhlen's work investigates the value of virtual public spheres to support the contention that increased discussion, interaction (between citizens, groups, and politicians) and participation can produce a more informed body politic. Kuhlen, however, casts doubts on the Internet's ability to produce radical change in democratic political systems; he argues that ICT will instead usher in a regime in which that the media will lose its monopoly on shaping public opinion. Another positive, if limited, change is the potential for ICT forums to increase interaction between geographically distant people, provide feedback to posted ideas, create banks of easily accessible knowledge, and allow for real-time reaction to statements posted on forums. Kuhlen concludes that e-Democracy probably will not replace current indirect, representative systems of democracy.

Several authors in this book concur with this limited view of the potential of virtual public spheres to effect dramatic political change, particularly in societies that do not have a long tradition of democratic politics. Nonetheless, we affirm that the true value of virtual public spheres to offline political systems seems to lie in their capacity to contribute to offline civil society through an infusion of online social capital. Several earlier researchers have investigated the capacity of ICT to help build social capital, particularly among socially marginalized groups and individuals. Law and Keltner (1995), for example, found that ICT helped the social integration of marginalized groups through enhanced access to others like themselves. By providing additional opportunities for communication among community members, one also raises the overall level of social trust, which might be transformed into collective action towards achieving common social goals (Kavanaugh and Patterson, 2001). Increased interaction might lead to civic engagement, but the social capital also leads to an improvement in the community's overall quality of life. For example, Alkalimat and Williams (2001), in a study of community technology centers, found that increasing social capital was the critical ingredient in promoting social and political change in the community.

Glogoff (2001) reinforces the point that online communication can help increase social capital, especially among disenfranchised groups. Other authors examine the effects on social capital of a resident-maintained "networked community" in Melbourne, Australia (Meredyth, Hopkins, Ewing and Thomas (2002). The authors found that as a result of the increased access to electronic communication, there has been an augmentation of bonding capital but this has not had the desired effect of increasing bridging social capital. It is possible that in groups that are more integrated into society's mainstream, the impact of virtual public spheres is even more pronounced. For example, in a study of a middle-class suburban community in Toronto, Canada, Hampton and Wellman (1999) found that Internet usage bolsters social ties, regardless of whether they were strong or weak before.

Quan-Haase and Wellman (2002) discuss the effect of the Internet in general on social capital. They point out that three approaches to the effects of the Internet on social capital can be identified. First, the Internet acts as a transformative agent. This is in keeping with the literature that asserts that ICT can bring about a dramatic increase in civic engagement. Second, the Internet diminishes bonding social capital. In other words, the Internet serves as a gigantic distraction drawing people away from family and community with its entertainment and information opportunities. Third, the Internet supplements bridging social capital. Thus, instead of taking people away from what they normally do, it simply adds an alternative means to accomplish many of the same communicative ends; in addition to talking on the telephone, people are sending each other e-mail and instant messages. As Quan-Haase and Wellman write, "Although face-to-face and telephone contact continue, they are complemented by the Internet's ease in connecting geographically dispersed people and organizations bonded by shared interests" (2002, 9).

The bulk of the cited research points to encouraging signs regarding the linkages between virtual public spheres and social capital. In general, they open up the opportunity for increasing communication among people, even if it merely complements pre-existing modes of communication. Some virtual public spheres aspire to both bridging social capital and bonding social capital, given their close connection to communities in a specific geographic location. Most of the virtual public spheres that were discussed, however, have more limited ambitions. For them, an enlargement of bridging social capital as a result of their efforts would be enough. Moreover, as Quan-Haase and Wellman and others point out, this alone may be sufficient to bring about the political change desired by the proponents of virtual public spheres.

In this book, Monnoyer-Smith, Raman, Hacker et al, and Anderson and Bishop utilize theoretical frameworks to describe the transition from offline to online deliberative democracy. Monnoyer-Smith frames the discussion of ICT and deliberation using the notion of *deliberative machines*. She reassesses the role of ICT in public deliberation and looks at the conditions surrounding discursive interactions. Her analysis shows that virtual public spheres may be unique in allowing previously excluded populations access to public discourse. Her work allows researchers to see deliberative procedures in a broader socio-political context. From this perspective, virtual public spheres are potentially transformative mechanisms that extend participation in novel ways.

Raman argues for a blended model of deliberative e-Democracy, one that does not privilege online venues and interactions but employs technologies in strategic combination with existing civic networks to improve governance in developing countries. In this work, she shows the important nexus between offline civil society and virtual public spheres, broadly defined to include non-Internet technological applications.

Hacker and Morgan argue that the partnership of e-government with new media networking can significantly increase the connections of e-government to e-democracy. They argue, "Democracy involves citizen input, deliberation, and involvement with public spheres (Hackerand Morgan, 2011)." The rise of social media, therefore, provides unique opportunities for the development of virtual public spheres. However, drawing upon the work of van Dijk (2006) they point out that the powerful in society also tend to be early ICT adopters and, in a manner that somewhat recalls the economist Douglass North's Path Dependence theory (North 2009), elites thus have a disproportionate effect on the evolution of technological change. In this way, Hacker, et al, charge that new social networks, including those that arise around new media, can perpetuate existing social inequities.

Anderson and Bishop survey a number of studies of e-government and e-democracy initiatives. They point out the difficulty in moving from e-government to e-democracy and find that many efforts fall short of the sustained deliberation needed to achieve e-democracy. Anderson and Bishop see a need for e-democracy initiatives to embrace approaches that better enhance deliberation rather than simply make government more accessible. They aim to refocus research efforts on the characteristics reinforced by the creation of deliberative forums in the virtual world. Moreover, they recognize that the move to e-democracy is incomplete without a more robust virtual public sphere.

According to Fuchs (2003), directness of participation was a major strength of e-Democracy, helping to extend civil society's reach into the virtual world. Barnes and Kaase (1979) found close correlation between individual participation and civil society. Furthermore, Foley and Edwards (1996) speculate that,

"it seems likely that specifically political associations (whether social-movement organizations, interest groups, or political parties) are more conducive to promoting civic engagement than many other sorts of association. That would certainly be in keeping with Tocqueville's argument" (p. 52). In their chapters, Backhouse, Gimeno and Freeman, Nyirenda, and Bwalya, et al. discuss attempts to employ ICT to enhance participation for the purpose of social change.

Gimeno and Freeman present a case study of human rights videoblogging on YouTube, the popular video-sharing website. According to Gimeno and Freeman, vidoeoblogging enables individuals to upload human rights videos to the Internet and possibly effect profound social change on a global level. However, this unprecdented ability to communicate wrongs also underscores the need for universal ethics standards to protect the rights of victims as a critical element of a virtual public sphere that is informed by Habermas' normative theory of communicative action.

Bwalya et al argue that in developing countries such as Botswana, concerted efforts to promote ICT usage and create an appropriate ICT infrastructure, are but the initial steps in the long process needed to reach e-Democracy. E-Democracy is a multi-dimensional phenomenon that is deeply embedded in a country's policy, culture, finances, in addition to its organizational and regulatory environments. Thus a stumbling block in developing countries that want to move towards e-Democracy is the absence of a strong civil society, a theme that is reiterated by Nyirenda. Further, Nyirenda's study corroborates the ICT paradox, in other words, "that while ICTs can be a solution to aid civil society organizations overcome their contextual bottlenecks, it is in many cases these same contextual bottlenecks that limit civil society's ability to effectively apply technology to achieve their organizational challenges…" Thus, while one of e-Democracy's strengths is political participation enhancement, the paradox—at least in developing countries—is that strong civil society and high levels of popular participation are the necessary preconditions of e-Democratic status.

Backhouse evaluates the role of e-participation in virtual public spheres. She situates e-participation within a broader discussion of the public sphere, highlighting the possibilities for robust virtual public spheres. Backhouse notes the complexities involved in creating venues for e-participation. She notes that quality participation requires significant attention to their design and support. Moreover, these venues can work in concert with more traditional forms of participation. As noted with the discussion of AmericaSpeaks, this can deepen participatory engagement in many ways.

As pointed out in the first chapter, e-Government can be a catalytic force for social capital, which could help spur the transition to e-Democracy. The chapters in the third section by Burbridge, Das and DiRienzo, Tudor, Popa and Blidsel, Loutzenhsier, and Loukis, Xenakis, and Tseperli examine the many challenges that many countries face as they try to navigate from offline to online government and eventually, it is hoped, to e-Democracy.

Burbridge et al using a cross-country study of 140 countries examines the impact of trust on the level of e-Government, showing that, even controlling for level of development and other socio-economic factors, trust was a major factor determining level of e-Government. They argue that trust has a significant impact on the use of e-government. Drawing upon survey data, they develop a rich analysis of the role trust plays in encouraging e-government iniatives

Tudor, Popa and Blidsel point out the challenges facing Romania as it moves toward e-government. Romanian civil society is still a work in progress and efforts to ensure transparency and participation are ongoing. This raises several issues for local public administration and efforts to implement e-Government.

Tudor, et al find that e-Government in local public administration is an evolving process. Transitioning from totalitarian regime to democratic government and without a well-established civil society, Romania continues to seek ways to incorporate ICT into the governance structure. E-disclosure is an important component of the successful transition to e-government in this regard. Transparency, accountability and resource allocation present significant challenges to overcome in this transition

Loutzenhiser views e-Government through the lens of succession planning in public administration. She argues that succession planning is a good tool for helping to bridge the digital divide. It can also help with global networking and in shifting the emphasis more towards citizen-driven service delivery. In the case of the latter, e-Government can be used to help strengthen civil society.

Loukis, Xenakis, and Tseperli look at the use of Computer Supported Argument Visualization (CSAV) techniques as a way to overcome barriers to e-Participation. They provide a detailed look at the process and its implications for e-participation. They use a pilot project by the Greek Parliament to evaluate how such technology can advance e-participation. They find CSAV can enhance e-participation efforts in a number of ways. This technology allows participants to see the core content of legislation in ways that make complex issues more comprehensible to lay citizens. They conclude that CSAV technology can increase the quantity and quality of participatory efforts both online and offline.

REFERENCES

Alkalimat, A., & Williams, K. (2001). Social capital and cyberpower in the African American community: A case study of a community technology center in the dual city . In Keeble, L., & Loader, B. D. (Eds.), *Community informatics: Shaping computer-mediated social networks* (pp. 177–204). London, UK: Routledge.

Barnes, S. H., & Kaase, M. (1979). *Political action: Mass participation in five Western democracies*. Beverly Hills, CA: Sage Publications.

Cohen, J., & Sabel, C. (1997). Directly-deliberative polyarchy (with Charles Sabel). *European Law Journal*, *3*(4), 313–342. doi:10.1111/1468-0386.00034

Dahlberg, L. (2001). The Internet and democratic discourse: Exploring the prospects of online deliberative forums extending the public sphere. *Information Communication and Society*, *4*(4), 615–633. doi:10.1080/13691180110097030

Foley, M. W., & Edwards, B. (1996). The paradox of civil society. *Journal of Democracy*, *7*(3), 38–52. doi:10.1353/jod.1996.0048

Fuchs, D. (2003). *Models of democracy: Participatory, liberal and electronic democracy*. Presented at the ECPR Joint Sessions of Workshops, Edinburgh, U.K. March 28th-April 2nd 2003.

Glogoff, S. (2001). Virtual connections: Community bonding on the net. *First Monday*, *6*(3–5). Retrieved from http://firstmonday.org/htbin/cgiwrap/bin/ojs/index.php/fm/article/view/840/749.

Hampton, K. N., & Wellman, B. (1999). Netville on-line and off-line: Observing and surveying a wired world. *The American Behavioral Scientist*, *43*(3), 475–492. doi:10.1177/00027649921955290

Kavanaugh, A., & Patterson, S. (2001). The impact of community computer networks on social capital and community involvement. *The American Behavioral Scientist*, *45*(3), 496–509. .doi:10.1177/00027640121957312

Kuhlen, R. (1998). *Direct democracy-the role of electronic communication forums for a new public in the information society*. Retrieved from http://www.inf-wiss.unikonstanz.de/People/RK/Texte/art98.pdf

Meredyth, D., Hopkins, L., Ewing, S., & Thomas, J. (2000). Measuring social capital in a networked housing estate. *First Monday, 7*(10). Retrieved from http://firstmonday.org/htbin/cgiwrap/bin/ojs/index. php/fm/article/view/994/915.

Putnam, R. (2000). *Bowling alone: The collapse and revival of American community.* New York, NY: Simon & Schuster.

Quan-Haase, A., & Wellman, B. (2002). How does the Internet affect social capital? In M. Huysman & V. Wulf (Eds.), *Social capital and Information Technology* (pp. 113–132). Cambridge, MA: MIT Press. Retrieved from http://www.chass.utoronto.ca/~wellman/netlab/PUBLICATIONS/_frames.html

Compilation of References

Abril, P. S. (2007). A (My)Space of one's own: On privacy and online social networks. *Northwestern Journal of Technology and Intelelctual Property, 6*(1). Retrieved June 16, 2009, from http://www.law.northwestern.edu/journals/njtip/v6/n1/4/?title=A+(My)Space+of+One's+Own:+On+Privacy+and+Online%0D%0ASocial+Networks&author=Patricia+Sanchez+Abril&pagination=&startpage=&endpage=&issueTitle=&issueDate=Fall+2007&vol=6&n=1&jTitle=Northwestern+Journal+of+Technology+and+Intellectual+Property&cite=

Adler, R. B., & Rodman, G. (2005). *Understanding human communication* (9th ed.). New York, NY: Oxford University Press, Inc.

Agamben, G. (2009). *What is an apparatus? and other essays*. Stanford, CA: Stanford University Press.

Agre, P. E. (2002). Real-time politics: The Internet and the political process. *The Information Society, 18*, 311–331. doi:10.1080/01972240290075174

Ajzen, I. (1991). The theory of planned behavior. *Organizational Behavior and Human Decision Processes, 50*, 179–211. doi:10.1016/0749-5978(91)90020-T

Akrich, M. (1992). The description of technical objects. In Bijker, W. E., & Laws, J. (Eds.), *Shaping technology/building society. Studies in sociotechnical change* (pp. 205–224). Cambridge, MA: MIT Press.

Albrecht, S. (2006). Whose voice is heard in online deliberation? A study of participation and representation in political debates on the Internet. *Information Communication and Society, 9*(1), 62–82. doi:10.1080/13691180500519548

Alesina, A., Baqir, W., & Easerly, W. (1999). Public goods and ethnic divisions. *The Quarterly Journal of Economics, 114*(4), 1243–1284. doi:10.1162/003355399556269

Alesina, A., Devleeschauwer, A., Easterly, W., Kurlat, S., & Wacziarg, R. (2003). Fractionalization. *Journal of Economic Growth, 8*, 155–194. doi:10.1023/A:1024471506938

Alesina, A., & La Ferrara, E. (2002). Who trusts others? *Journal of Public Economics, 85*, 207–234. doi:10.1016/S0047-2727(01)00084-6

Alexander, L. (2005). *Is there a right of freedom of expression?* New York, NY: Cambridge University Press. doi:10.1017/CBO9780511614668

Al-Shafi, S., & Weerakkody, V. (2009). *Understanding citizen's behavioural intention in the adoption of e-government services in the state of Qatar*. Paper presented at 17th European Conference on Information Systems, ECIS 2009.

Alterman, E. D. (2006). The social context. In Germany, J. B. (Ed.), *Person-to-person-to-person: Harnessing the political power of online social networks and user-generated content* (pp. 37–40). Washington, DC: Institute for Politics, Democracy & the Internet.

Altman, D. (2002). Prospects for e-government in Latin America. *International Review of Public Administration, 7*(2), 5–20.

Amnesty International. (2007). Egypt–systematic abuses in the name of security. Retrieved October 31, 2007, from http://www.amnesty.org/en/library/asset/MDE12/001/2007/en/dom-MDE120012007en.pdf

Anderson, L., & Bishop, P. (2005). E-government to e-democracy: Communicative mechanisms of governance. *Journal of E-Government*, *2*(1), 5–26. doi:10.1300/J399v02n01_02

Anderson, C., & Paskeviciute, A. (2006). How ethnic and linguistic heterogeneity influence the prospects for civil society: A comparative study of citizenship behavior. *The Journal of Politics*, *68*(4), 783–802. doi:10.1111/j.1468-2508.2006.00470.x

Anheier, H., Glasius, M., & Kaldor, M. (2001). Introducing global civil society. In Anheier, H., Glasius, M., & Kaldor, M. (Eds.), *Global civil society*. Oxford, UK: Oxford University Press.

Anheier, H., & Themudo, N. (2002). Organisational forms of global civil society: Implications of going public. In Glasius, M., Kaldor, M., & Anheier, H. (Eds.), *Global civil society*. New York, NY: Oxford University Press.

Annett, A. (2001). Social fractionalization, political instability, and the size of the government. *IMF Staff Papers*, *48*(3), 561–592.

Applegate, L., Neo, B.-S., & King, J. (1995). *Singapore tradeNet: Beyond tradeNet to the intelligent island*. Harvard Business School, case study.

Arefi, M. (2003). Revisiting the Los Angeles Neighborhood Initiative (LANI): Lessons for planners. *Journal of Planning Education and Research*, *22*(4), 384. doi:10.1177/0739456X03022004005

Argaez, E. D. (2009). *The Internet big picture: World Internet users and population stats*. Retrieved February 12, 2010, from http://www.internetworldstats.com/stats.htm

Aslama, M., & Erikson, I. (2009). *Public spheres, networked publics, networked public spheres? Tracking the Habermasian public sphere in recent discourse*. The Donald McGannon communication research center. Working paper.

As-Saber, S., Hossain, K., & Srivastava, A. (2007). Technology, society and e-government: In search of an eclectic framework. *Electronic Government: An International Journal*, *4*(2), 156–178. doi:10.1504/EG.2007.013981

Bächtiger, A., & Pedrini, S. (2008). *Dissecting deliberative democracy: A review of theoretical concepts and empirical findings*. Paper presented at the EPOP Conference, Manchester.

Backhouse, J. (2007). E-democracy in Australia: The challenge of evolving a successful model. *The Electronic* [from www.ejeg.com]. *Journal of E-Government*, *5*(2), 107–116. Retrieved March 16, 2010.

Baier, A. C. (1986). Trust and antitrust. *Ethics*, *96*, 231–260. doi:10.1086/292745

Baiocchi, G. (2005). *Militants and citizens: The politics of participatory democracy in Porto Alegre*. Palo Alto, CA: Stanford University Press.

Balkin, J. M. (2004). Digital speech and democratic culture: A theory of freedom of expression for the information society. *New York University Law Review*, *79*(1), 1–55.

Banerjee, A., Iyer, L., & Somanathan, R. (2005). History, social divisions, and public goods in rural India. *Journal of the European Economic Association*, *3*, 639–647.

Barber, B. (1984). *Strong democracy*. Berkeley, CA: University of California Press.

Barber, B. (1984). *Strong democracy: Participatory politics for a new age*. Berkely, CA: University of California Press.

Barber, B. (1984). *Strong democracy*. Berkeley, CA: University of California Press.

Barber, B. (2000). Which technology for which democracy? Which democracy for which technology? *International Journal of Communications Law and Policy*, *6*. Retrieved December 11, from http://www.ciaonet.org/olj/ijclp/ijclp_6/ijclp_6e.pdf

Barlow, A. (2007). *The rise of the blogosphere*. Westport, CT: Praeger.

Barney, D. (2004). *The network society*. Malden, MA: Polity Press.

Barro, R. J. (1999). Determinants of democracy. *The Journal of Political Economy*, *107*(2), 158–183. doi:10.1086/250107

Barry, A. (2001). *Political machines. Governing a technological society*. London, UK: Athlone Press.

Bartlett, D. M. C. (2000). Civil society and democracy: A Zambian case study. *Journal of Southern African Studies*, *26*(3), 429–446. doi:10.1080/030570700750019655

Basu, S. (2004). E-government and developing countries: An overview. *International Review of Law Computers & Technology*, *18*(1), 109–132. doi:10.1080/13600860 410001674779

Baumgarten, J., & Chui, M. (2009). E-government 2.0. *McKinsey Quarterly*. Retrieved from https://www.mck-inseyquarterly.com/E-government_20_2408

Bayley, C., & French, S. (2008). Designing a participatory process for stakeholder involvement in a societal decision. *Group Decision and Negotiation*, *17*(3), 195–210. doi:10.1007/s10726-007-9076-8

Bedia. (2009). *Botswana information and statistics*. Retrieved November 16, 2009, from http://www.bedia.co.bw/article.php?id_mnu=37

Beers, D. (2006). The public sphere and online, independent journalism. *Canadian Journal of Education*, *29*(1), 109–130. doi:10.2307/20054149

Behar, A., & Prakash, A. (2004). India: Expanding and contracting democratic space. In Alagappa, M. (Ed.), *Civil society and political change in Asia* (pp. 192–222). Stanford, CA: Stanford University Press.

Behrouzi, M. (2008). The idea of democracy and its distortions: From Socrates to Cornel West. *Journal of Public Deliberation*, *4*(1), 13. Retrieved from http://services.bepress.com/jpd/vol4/iss1/art13.

Bekkers, V. (2004). Virtual policy communities and responsive governance: Redesigning online debates. *Information Polity*, *9*(3-4), 193–203.

Bekkers, V., & Homburg, V. (2007). The myths of e-government: Looking beyond the assumptions of a new and better government. *The Information Society*, *23*, 373–382. doi:10.1080/01972240701572913

Bélanger, F., Hiller, J., & Smith, W. (2002). Trustworthiness in electronic commerce: The role of privacy, security, and site attributes. *The Journal of Strategic Information Systems*, *11*, 245–270. doi:10.1016/S0963-8687(02)00018-5

Bellamy, C., & Taylor, J. A. (1998). *Governing in the information age*. Buckingham, UK: Open University Press.

Benett, L. (2008). Youth and digital democracy: Intersections of practice, policy and the marketplace. In W. L. Bennett (Ed.), *Civic life online: Learning how digital media can engage youth.* (pp. 25-50). The John D. and Catherine T. MacArthur Foundation Series on Digital Media and Learning. Cambridge, MA: The MIT Press.

Benhabib, S. (Ed.). (1996). *Democracy and difference: Contesting the boundaries of the political*. Princeton, NJ: Princeton University Press.

Benhabib, S. (1996). Toward a deliberative model of democratic legitimacy. In Benhabib, S. (Ed.), *Democracy and difference: Contesting the boundaries of the political* (pp. 67–94). Princeton, NJ: Princeton University Press.

Benkler, Y. (2006). *The wealth of networks: How social production transforms markets and freedom*. New Haven, CT: Yale University Press.

Bennett, W. L., & Entman, R. M. (Eds.). (2001). *Mediated politics: Communication in the future of democracy*. Cambridge, UK: Cambridge University Press.

Berquist, L. (2008). Communication policy and technology. In Grant, A. E., & Meadows, J. H. (Eds.), *Communication technology update and fundamentals* (11th ed., pp. 66–76). Boston, MA: Focal Press, Elsevier.

Besson, S., & Marti, J. L. (Eds.). (2006). *Deliberative democracy and its discontents*. Hampshire, UK: Ashgate.

Best, M. L., & Kumar, R. (2008). Sustainability failures of rural telecenters: Challenges from the sustainable access in rural India (sari) project. *Information Technologies and International Development*, *4*(4), 31–45. doi:10.1162/itid.2008.00025

Beynon-Davies, P. (2007). Models for e-government. *Transforming Government, People. Process and Policy*, *1*(1), 7–28.

Bimber, B. (2000). Measuring the gender gap on the Internet. *Social Science Quarterly*, *81*(3), 868–876.

Bimber, B. (2003). *Information and American democracy: Technology in the evolution of political power*. Cambridge, UK: Cambridge University Press. doi:10.1017/CBO9780511615573

Bimber, B., & Davis, R. (2005). *Campaigning online.* New York, NY: Oxford University Press.

Bishop, P., & Davis, G. (2002). Mapping public participation in policy choices. *Australian Journal of Public Administration, 61*(1), 14–29. doi:10.1111/1467-8500.00255

Bishop, P., Kane, J., & Patapan, H. (2002). The theory and practice of e–democracy: Agency, trusteeship and participation on the Web. *International Review of Public Administration, 7*(2), 21–31.

Bishop, P., & Anderson, L. (2004). *E-government to e-democracy: High tech solutions to no tech problems.* Paper presented at the Australian Electronic Governance Conference, Melbourne, Australia. Retrieved from http://www.public-policy.unimelb.edu.au/egovernance/papers/05_Bishop.pdf

Black, L., Burkhalter, S., Gastil, J., & Stromer-Galley, J. (2009). Methods for analyzing and measuring group deliberation. In Bucy, E., & Holbert, R. L. (Eds.), *Sourcebook for political communication research: Methods, measures, and analytical techniques.* Mahwah, NJ: Routledge.

Bligh, A. The Hon, Premier of Queensland. (2006). *Response to petition 553-05.* Retrieved from http://www.parliament.qld.gov.au/view/EPetitions_QLD/responses/553-05.pdf

Bligh, A. The Hon, Premier of Queensland. (2007). *Response to petition 931-07.* Retrieved from http://www.parliament.qld.gov.au/view/EPetitions_QLD/responses/TP2778-2007.pdf

Blondiaux, L., & Cardon, D. (2006). Dispositif participatifs. *Politix, 75,* 3–9. doi:10.3917/pox.075.0003

Bohm, D. (2003). *The essential David Bohm.* New York, NY: Routledge.

Bohm, D., & Edwards, M. (1991). *Changing consciousness: Exploring the hidden source of the social, political, and environmental crises facing our world.* San Francisco, CA: Harper.

Bohm, D., & Hiley, B. (1993). *The undivided universe: An ontological interpretation of quantum mechanics.* London, UK: Routledge.

Bohm, D., & Peat, D. (2000). *Science, order, and creativity.* London, UK: Routledge.

Bolton, R. (2005). *Habermas's theory of communicative action and the theory of social capital.* Paper presented at the Association of American Geographers meeting. Denver, Colorado. Retrieved March 31, 2007, from http://www.williams.edu/Economics/papers/Habermas.pdf

Bordewijk, J. L., & van Kaam, B. (1986). Towards a new classification of teleinformation services. *Intermedia, 14,* 16–21.

Bourdieu, P. (1991). *Language and symbolic power.* Cambridge, MA: Harvard University Press.

Bovaird, T., Bovaird, A. G., & Löffler, E. (2003). *Public management and governance.* New York, NY: Routledge.

Bozinis, A. I. (2007). Governance and democratic procedures in the information society era. *Journal of the Social Sciences, 3*(3), 123–126. doi:10.3844/jssp.2007.123.126

Bratman, B. E. (2002). Brandeis and Warren's *The Right to Privacy* and the birth of the right to privacy. *Tennessee Law Review, 69*(623), 623–651.

Brown, D. (2005). Electronic government and public administration. *International Review of Administrative Sciences, 71*(2), 241–254. doi:10.1177/0020852305053883

Brown, D. (2008). Historical perspectives on communication technology. In Grant, A. E., & Meadows, J. H. (Eds.), *Communication technology update and fundamentals* (11th ed., pp. 10–40). Boston, MA: Focal Press, Elsevier.

Brown University. (2002). *Second annual global e-government study shows Taiwan, South Korea, and Canada overtaking United States.* Press release. Retrieved from http://www.insidepolitics.org/PressRelease02int.html

Brown, E. (2009). Plato's ethics and politics in The Republic. In. E. N. Zalta (Ed.), *The Stanford encyclopedia of philosophy (Fall 2009 edition).* Retrieved from http://plato.stanford.edu/archives/fall2009/entries/plato-ethics-politics/

Burcea, S. G. (2006). Perspectives of e-democracy in European area. *Theoretical and Empirical Researches in Urban Management, 1*(1).

Bushman, B. J., & Wessman, L. R. (2006). Short-term and long-term effects of violent media on aggression in children and adults. *Archives of Pediatrics & Adolescent Medicine, 160,* 348–352. doi:10.1001/archpedi.160.4.348

Buzby, S. L. (1975). Company size, listed versus unlisted stocks, and the extent of financial disclosure. *Journal of Accounting Research*, *13*(1), 16–37. doi:10.2307/2490647

Bwalya, K. J. (2009). IT and role/analysis of information resource in decision making in Botswana. *Conference Proceedings, IST-Africa*, May 2009, Kampala, Uganda.

Cala Carrillo, J., & de la Mata, M. L. (2004). Educational background, modes of discourses and argumentation: Comparing women and men. *Argumentation*, *18*, 403–426. doi:10.1007/s10503-004-4906-1

Calabrese, A. (2004). The promise of civil society: A global movement for communication rights. *Continuum: Journal of Media & Cultural Studies*, *18*(3), 317–329. doi:10.1080/1030431042000256081

Caldwell, G. (2005). *Witness 2005 annual report*. Retrieved April 6, 2007, from http://www.witness.org/images/stories/pdf/Annual_Report_2006h.pdf

Calenda, D. (2006, November). *Digital encounters with politics. The political use of the Internet by young people in three European countries*. Paper presented at the Open international research and postgraduate seminar Politics on the Internet: New Forms and Media for Political Action, Department of Political Science & International Relations, University of Tampere (Finland).

Calhoun, C. (1993). Civil society and the public sphere. *Public Culture*, *5*(2), 267–280. doi:10.1215/08992363-5-2-267

Callaghy, T. (1994). Civil society, democracy, and economic change in Africa: A dissenting opinion about resurgent societies. In Harbeson, J., Rothchild, D., & Chazan, N. (Eds.), *Civil society and the state in Africa*. Boulder, CO: Lynne Rienner.

Cappella, J. N., Price, V., & Nir, L. (2002). Argument repertoire as a reliable and valid measure of opinion quality: Electronic dialogue during campaign 2000. *Political Communication*, *19*, 73–93. doi:10.1080/105846002317246498

Carlsson, C., Carlsson, J., Puhakainen, J., & Walden, P. (2006). *Nice mobile services do not fly. Observations of mobile services and the Finnish consumers*. 19th Bled eConference eValues, Bled, Slovenia, June 5 - 7, 2006.

Carpini, M. X. D., Cook, F. L., & Jacobs, L. R. (2004). Public deliberations, discursive participation and citizen engagement: A review of empirical literature. *Annual Review of Political Science*, *7*(1), 325–344. doi:10.1146/annurev.polisci.7.121003.091630

Carter, L., & Bélanger, F. (2005). The utilization of e-government services: Citizen trust, innovation and acceptance factors. *Information Systems Journal*, *15*(1), 5–25. doi:10.1111/j.1365-2575.2005.00183.x

Carter, L., & Bélanger, F. (2003). Diffusion of innovation and citizen adoption of e-government services. *The Proceedings of the 1st International E-Services Workshop*, (pp. 57–63).

Castells, M. (2008). The new public sphere: Global civil society, communication networks, and global governance. *The Annals of the American Academy of Political and Social Science*, *616*(1), 78–93. doi:10.1177/0002716207311877

Castells, M. (2000). Toward a sociology of the network society. *Contemporary Sociology*, *29*, 693–699. doi:10.2307/2655234

Castells, M. (2001). *The Internet galaxy: Reflections on the Internet, business, and society*. New York, NY: Oxford University Press.

Castells, M. (2009). *Communication power*. New York, NY: Oxford University Press.

CBS News. *(2003, June4)*. Howard Dean's Internet love-in. *Retrieved from* http://www.cbsnews.com/stories/2003/06/04/politics/main557004.shtml

C-DAC. (2010). Language technology initiatives at C-DAC Noida. Retrieved December 11, 2009, from http://tdil.mit.gov.in/ cdacnoidaapril03.pdf

Cecez-Kemanovic, V., & Janson, M. (1999). *Rethinking Habermas's theory of communicative action in Information Systems*. Paper posted to University of Missouri-St. Louis. Retrieved March 30, 2007, from www.umsl.edu/~mjanson/myarticles/habermas.pdf

Centre for Civil Society. (2004). *What is civil society?* Retrieved February, 13, 2010, from http://www.lse.ac.uk/collections/CCS/what_is_civil_society.htm

Chadwick, A., & May, C. (2003). Interactions between states and citizens in the age of the Internet. 'E-government' in the United States, Britain and the European Union. *Governance, 16*(2), 271–300. doi:10.1111/1468-0491.00216

Chadwick, A. (2003). Bringing e-democracy back in: Why it matters for future research on e-governance. *Social Science Computer Review, 21*(4), 443–455. doi:10.1177/0894439303256372

Chadwick, A. (2009). Web 2.0: New challenges for the study of e-democracy in an era of informational exuberance. *I/S: A Journal of Law and Policy for the Information Society, 5*(1), 9-41.

Chaffey, D. (2006). *E-business and e-commerce management* (3rd ed.). London, UK: FT Prentice Hall.

Chan, B. (2005). Imagining the homeland: The Internet and diasporic discourse of nationalism. *The Journal of Communication Inquiry, 29*(4), 336–368. doi:10.1177/0196859905278499

Chaput, M. (2008). Analyser la discussion politique en ligne. De l'idéal délibératif à la reconstruction des pratiques argumentatives. *Reseaux, 150,* 83–106.

Chatfield, D. (1991). The information revolution and the shaping of a democratic global order. In Riemer, N. (Ed.), *New thinking and developments in international politics: Opportunities and dangers* (pp. 135–165). Lanham, MD: University Press of America.

Chavent, M., Ding, Y., Fu, L., Stolowy, H., & Wang, H. (2006). Disclosure and determinants studies: An extension using the Divisive Clustering Method (DIV). *European Accounting Review, 15*(2), 181–218. doi:10.1080/09638180500253092

Chen, Y., & Dimitrova, D. (2006). Electronic government and online engagement: Citizen interaction with government via Web portals. *International Journal of Electronic Government Research, 2*(1), 54–76. doi:10.4018/jegr.2006010104

Chen, Y., & Perry, J. (2003). Outsourcing for e-government: Managing for success. *Public Performance & Management Review, 26*(4), 404–421. doi:10.1177/1530957603026004007

Chengeta, N. N. (2003). *The technology based incubation in Botswana.* Workshop Paper on Technology-based Business Incubators in SADC Countries; Mauritius: WAIT publication.

Chevallereau, F. X. (2005). *The impact of e-government on competitiveness, growth and jobs.* IDABC eGovernment Erman Observatory Background Paper.

Christians, C. G., Fackler, M., Rotzoll, K. B., & McKee, K. B. (1997). Invasion of privacy. In *Media ethics: Cases and moral reasoning* (5th ed., pp. 109–124). USA: Longman.

Christopher, G., & Reddick, A. (2004). Two-stage model of e-government growth: Theories and empirical evidence for U.S. cities. *Government Information Quarterly, 21,* 51–64. doi:10.1016/j.giq.2003.11.004

CIA. (2009). *The world fact book–India.* Retrieved December 11, 2009, from https://www.cia.gov/library/publications /the-world-factbook/geos/in.html

CIA. (2010). *The world factbook.* Retrieved November 8, 2009, from https://www.cia.gov/library/publications/the-world-factbook/geos/bc.html

Ciborra, C., & Navarra, D. D. (2003). *Good governance and development aid: Risks and challenges of e-government in Jordan.* Paper presented at the IFIP WG 8.2 - WG 9.4, Athens, Greece.

CIVICUS: World Alliance for Citizen Participation. (2003/2004). *The CIVICUS civil society index toolkit.*

Civil Society Development Foundation. (2005). *Dialogue for civil society: Report on the state of civil society in Romania, 2005.*

Cizek, K. (2005). Safety and security. In S. Gregory, G. Caldwell, R. Avni, & T. Harding (Eds.), *Video for change: A guide for advocacy and activism* (pp. 20-73). Retrieved April 9, 2007, from http://www.witness.org/images/stories/pdf/VideoforChange_SafetyandSecurity_Titled.pdf

Clark, J., & Themudo, N. (2003). The age of protest: Internet-based dot causes and the anti-globalization movement. In Clark, J. (Ed.), *Globalizing civic engagement: Civil society and transnational action.* London, UK: Earthscan.

Clift, S. *(2002)*. E-governance to e-democracy: Progress in Australia and New Zealand toward Information-Age democracy. *Retrieved from*http://www.publicus.net/articles/aunzedem.html

Clift, S. (2003). *E-democracy, e-governance, and public net-work.* Retrieved from http://www.publicus.net/articles/edempublicnetwork.html

Clift, S. (2004). Saving democracy from the Information Age. *CIO Government Magazine, Australia.* Retrieved from http://stevenclift.com/?p=114

Cohen, J., & Arato, A. (1992). *Civil society and political theory.* Cambridge, MA: MIT Press.

Cohen, J., & Sabel, C. (1997). Directly-deliberative polyarchy with Charles Sabel. *European Law Journal, 3*(4), 313–342. doi:10.1111/1468-0386.00034

Cohen, J. E. (2006). Citizen satisfaction with contacting government on the Internet. *Information Polity, 11,* 51–65.

Cohen, J. (1989). Deliberation and democratic legitimacy. In Hamlin, A., & Pettit, P. (Eds.), *The good polity* (pp. 17–34). Oxford, UK: Basil Blackwell.

Coleman, S. (2004). Connecting parliament to the public via the Internet: Two case studies of online consultations. *Information Communication and Society, 7*(1), 1–22. doi:10.1080/1369118042000208870

Coleman, S. (2005a). New mediation and direct representation: Reconceptualizing representation in the digital age. *New Media & Society, 7*(2), 177–198. doi:10.1177/1461444805050745

Coleman, S., & Gøtze, J. (2001). *Bowling together: Online public engagement in policy deliberation.* London, UK: Hansard Society Publishing.

Coleman, S. (2001). The transformation of citizenship. In Axford, B., & Huggins, R. (Eds.), *New media and politics* (pp. 109–125). London: Sage.

Coleman, S. & Rowe C. (2005). *Remixing citizenship. Democracy and young people's use of the internet.* Research report, Carnegie Young People Initiative.

Coleman, S. (2005b). *Direct representation. Towards a conversational democracy.* London: IPPR publication.

Coleman, S. (2008). Doing IT for themselves: Management versus autonomy in youth e-citizenship. In L.W. Bennett (Ed.), *Civic life online: Learning how digital media can engage youth.* (pp. 189-206). The John D. and Catherine T. MacArthur Foundation Series on Digital Media and Learning. Cambridge, MA: The MIT Press.

Coleman, S., & Norris, D. F. (2005). *A new agenda for e-democracy.* (Forum Discussion Paper No. 4). Retrieved Nov 2009, from http://www.oii.ox.ac.uk/resources/publications/FD4.pdf

Collier, P. (1998). *The political economy of ethnicity.* Washington, DC: World Bank.

Collier, P. (2002). Social capital and poverty: A microeconomic perspective. In Van Bastelaer, T. (Ed.), *The role of social capital in development* (pp. 19–41). Melbourne, Australia: Cambridge University Press. doi:10.1017/CBO9780511492600.003

Compeau, D. R., & Higgins, C. A. (1995). Application of social cognitive theory to training for computer skills. *Information Systems Research, 6*(2), 118–143. doi:10.1287/isre.6.2.118

Comscore. (2009). *81 million Americans visited a government website in July.* Retrieved from http://comscore.com/Press_Events/Press_Releases/2009/9/81_Million_Americans_Visited_a_Go vernment_Web_Site_in_July

Conklin, J., & Begeman, M. (1989). gIBIS: A tool for all reasons. *Journal of the American Society for Information Science American Society for Information Science, 40*(3), 200–213. doi:10.1002/(SICI)1097-4571(198905)40:3<200::AID-ASI11>3.0.CO;2-U

Conklin, J. (2003). Dialog mapping: Reflections on an industrial strength case study. In Kirschner, P., Buckingham Shum, S., & Carr, C. (Eds.), *Visualizing argumentation: Software tools for collaborative and educational sense-making.* London, UK: Springer Verlag.

Contractor, N., & Monge, P. (2003). *Theories of communication networks.* New York, NY: Oxford.

Cook, K., & Cooper, R. (2003). Experimental studies of cooperation, trust, and social exchange. In Ostrom, E., & Walker, J. (Eds.), *Trust and reciprocity, interdisciplinary lessons from experimental research* (pp. 209–244). New York, NY: Russell Sage Foundation.

Cooke, T. E. (1989). Disclosure in the corporate annual reports of Swedish companies. *Accounting and Business Review, 19*(74), 113–124.

Cooke, T. E. (1998). Regression analysis in accounting disclosure studies. *Accounting and Business Review, 28*(3), 209–224.

Coombs, W. T. (1998). The Internet as potential equalizer: New leverage for confronting social irresponsibility. *Public Relations Review, 24*(3), 289–303. doi:10.1016/S0363-8111(99)80141-6

Cooper, L. T. (2004). Big questions in administrative ethics: A need for focused, collaborative effort. *Public Administration Review, 64*(4), 395–407. doi:10.1111/j.1540-6210.2004.00386.x

Cooper, T. L. (2005). Civic engagement in the twenty-first century: Toward a scholarly and practical agenda. *Public Administration Review, 65*(5), 534–535. doi:10.1111/j.1540-6210.2005.00480.x

Cotterrell, R. (1999). Transparency, mass media, ideology and community. *Cultural Values, 3*(4), 414–426.

Couldry, N. (2003). Digital divide or discursive design: On the emerging ethics of information space. *Ethics and Information Technology, 5*, 89–97. doi:10.1023/A:1024916618904

Court, J. (2003). Assessing and analyzing governance in India: Evidence from a new survey. World Governance Assessment, Overseas Development Institute, UK. Retrieved December 11, 2009, from http://www.odi.org.uk/resources/download/3145.pdf

Crabtree, J. (2002). *Is the Internet bad for democracy?* openDemocracy. Retrieved December 2009, from http://www.opendemocracy.org/media-edemocracy/article_822.jsp

Cropf, R., & Casaregola, V. (2007). Community networks. In Anttiroiko, A. V., & Malkia, M. (Eds.), *Encyclopedia of digital government*. Hershey, PA: IGI Reference.

Cropf, R., & Casaregola, V. (1998). Virtual town halls: Using computer networks to improve public discourse and facilitate service delivery. *Research and Reflection, 4*(1). Retrieved from http://www.gonzaga.edu/rr/v4n1/cropf.htm

Currall, S., & Judge, T. (1995). Measuring trust between organizational boundary role persons. *Organizational Behavior and Human Decision Processes, 64*, 151–170. doi:10.1006/obhd.1995.1097

Dahl, R. A. (1971). *Polyarchy: Participation and opposition*. New Haven, CT: Yale University Press.

Dahlberg, L. (2007). Rethinking the fragmentation of the cyberpublic: From consensus to contestation. *New Media & Society, 9*(5), 827–847. doi:10.1177/1461444807081228

Dahlberg, L. (2001a). The Internet and democratic discourse: Exploring the prospects of online deliberative forums extending the public sphere. *Information Communication and Society, 4*(4), 615–633. doi:10.1080/13691180110097030

Dahlberg, L. (2001b). Democracy via cyberspace: Examining the rhetorics and practices of three prominent camps. *New Media & Society, 3*(2), 187–207. doi:10.1177/14614440122226038

Dahlberg, L. (2007). The Internet, deliberative democracy, and power: Radicalizing the public sphere. *International Journal of Media and Cultural Politics, 3*(1), 47–64. doi:10.1386/macp.3.1.47_1

Dahlgren, P. (2006). Civic participation and practices: Beyond deliberative democracy. In Carpentier, N., Pruulmann-Wengerfeld, P., & Nordenstreng, K. (Eds.), *Researching media, democracy and participation* (pp. 23–35). Tartu, Estonia: Tartu University Press.

Dallow, P. (2007). Mediatising the Web: The new modular extensible media. *Journal of Media Practice, 8*, 341–258. doi:10.1386/jmpr.8.3.341_1

Davis, R. (1999). *The Web of politics: The Internet's impact on the American political system*. Oxford, UK: Oxford University Press.

Davis, F. D., Bagozzi, R. P., & Warshaw, P. R. (1989). User acceptance of computer technology: A comparison of two theoretical models. *Management Science, 35*(8), 982–1003. doi:10.1287/mnsc.35.8.982

Davis, F. D., Bagozzi, R. P., & Warshaw, P. R. (1992). Extrinsic and intrinsic motivation to use computers in the workplace. *Journal of Applied Social Psychology, 22*, 1111–1132. doi:10.1111/j.1559-1816.1992.tb00945.x

Davis, F. (1989). Perceived usefulness, perceived ease of use and user acceptance of Information Technology. *Management Information Systems Quarterly, 13*, 319–340. doi:10.2307/249008

de Certeau, M. (1984). *The practice of everyday life.* Berkeley, CA: University of California Press.

Dean, J. (2005). Communicative capitalism: Circulation and the foreclosure of politics. *Cultural Politics, 1*(1), 51–74. doi:10.2752/174321905778054845

Dederich, L., Hausman, T., & Maxwell, S. (2006). *Online technology for social change: From struggle to strategy.* New York, NY: dotOrganize

Deleuze, G. (1988). *Foucault.* Minneapolis, MN: University of Minnesota Press.

Deleuze, G. (1992). *The fold, Leibniz and the baroque.* Minneapolis, MN: University of Minnesota Press.

Deleuze, G. (1995). *Negotiations.* New York, NY: University Press.

Deleuze, G., & Guattari, F. (1988). A thousand plateaus: Capitalism and schizophrenia: *Vol. 2.* (*trans. Brian Massumi*). London, UK: Athlone.

Deleuze, G., & Parnet, C. (2002). *Dialogues.* New York, NY: Columbia University Press.

Delhey, J., & Newton, K. (2004). *Social trust: Global pattern or Nordic exceptionalism?* (Wissenschauftszentrum Berlin für Sozialforschung (WZB) Discussion Paper SP I 2004-202).

Dempsey, J., & Weitzner, D. (1998). *Regardless of frontiers: Protecting the human right to freedom of expression on the global Internet* (introduction & overview). Center for Democracy & Technology and the Global Liberty Internet Campaign. Retrieved April 5, 2007, from http://gilc.org/speech/report/

Denton, R. (2009). *The 2008 presidential campaign: A communication perspective.* Lanham, MD: Rownam & Littlefield.

Department of IT. BT and S&T, Government of Karnataka. (2009). *Home page.* Retrieved November 23, 2009, from http://www.bangaloreitbt.in/

Deuze, M. (2004). What is journalism? *Journalism, 6*(4), 442–464. doi:10.1177/1464884905056815

Devadoss, P. R., Pan, S. L., & Huang, J. C. (2002). Structurational analysis of e-government initiatives: A case study of SCO. *Decision Support Systems, 34*(3), 253–269. doi:10.1016/S0167-9236(02)00120-3

Diamond, L. (1989). Beyond authoritarianism and totalitarianism: Strategies for democratization. *The Washington Quarterly, 12*, 141–142. doi:10.1080/01636608909443713

Diamond, L., Linz, J. J., & Lipset, S. M. (Eds.). (1988). *Democracy in developing countries: Africa (Vol. 2).* Boulder, CO: Lynne Rienner.

Dillon, A., & Morris, M. (1996). User acceptance of Information Technology: Theories and models. In Williams, M. (Ed.), *ARIST (Vol. 31).* Medford, NJ: Information Today.

Dobransky, K., & Hargittai, E. (2006). The disability divide in Internet access and use. *Information Communication and Society, 9*(3), 313–334. doi:10.1080/13691180600751298

Drapeau, M., & Wells, L. (2009). *Social software and national security: An initial net assessment.* Center for Technology and National Security Policy, National Defense University.

Drew, C. H., & Nyerges, T. L. (2004). Transparency of environmental decision making: A case study of soil cleanup inside the Hanford 100 area. *Journal of Risk Research, 7*(1), 33–71. doi:10.1080/1366987042000151197

Dryzek, J. S. (2000). *Deliberative democracy and beyond: Liberals critics, contestations.* Oxford, UK: Oxford University Press.

Dryzek, J. S., & Niemeyer, S. (2008). Discursive representation. *The American Political Science Review, 102*(4), 481–493. doi:10.1017/S0003055408080325

Duncombe, R., & Heeks, R. (1999). *Information, ICTs and small enterprise: Findings from Botswana.* (Development Informatics Working Paper Series, Working Paper 7), Institute for Development Policy and Management, Manchester, UK, 1999. Retrieved July 23, 2009, from http://www.man.ac.uk/idpm/idpm_dp.htm

Dunne, K. (2007). *The possible use of political online forums to engage young people in local politics.* Paper presented at the Institute of Communication Studies (ICS) Postgraduate Conference, Leeds, United Kingdom.

Dutton, W. H. (2007). *Through the network (of networks)-the fifth estate.* Oxford Internet Institute. Retrieved November 2009, from http://people.oii.ox.ac.uk/dutton/wp-content/uploads/2007/10/5th-estate-lecture-text.pdf

Easterly, W., & Levine, R. (2001). What have we learned from a decade of empirical research on growth? It's not factor accumulation: Stylized facts and growth models. *The World Bank Economic Review, 15*(2), 177–219. doi:10.1093/wber/15.2.177

Economist Intelligence Unit. (2007). *e-readiness rankings.* Retrieved January 10, 2007, from http://globaltechforum.eiu.com/index.asp?layout=rich_story&doc_id=6427

Edes, B. W. (2000). The role of government information officers. *Journal of Government Information, 27*(4), 455–469. doi:10.1016/S1352-0237(00)00179-9

Edgar, A. (2006). *Habermas: The key concepts.* New York, NY: Routledge.

Edwards, A. (2006). ICT strategies of democratic intermediaries: A view on the political system in the digital age. *Information Polity, 11*(2), 163–176.

E-government handbook. (2007). *Handbook.* Retrieved March 15, 2007, from http://www.cdt.org/egov/handbook/trust.shtml

EIPA. et al. (2007). *Study on interoperability at local and regional level, final version.* Retrieved from http://www.epractice.eu/en/node/281708

Eley, G. (1992). Nations, publics, and political cultures: Placing Habermas in the nineteenth century. In Calhoun, C. (Ed.), *Habermas and the public sphere* (pp. 318–331). Cambridge, MA: MIT Press.

Elliman, T., Macintosh, A., & Irani, Z. (2007). A model building tool to support group deliberation. *International Journal of Cases on Electronic Commerce, 3*(3), 33–44.

Elliot, D. (2003). Moral responsibilities and the power of pictures. In Lester, P. M., & Ross, S. D. (Eds.), *Images that injure: Pictorial stereotypes in the media* (2nd ed., p. 7). Westport, CT: Praeger.

EP. (2009). *European social policy.* (pp. 249-336). Retrieved December 21, 2009, from http://find.galegroup.com/gtx/start.do?prodId=EAIM&userGroupName=nm_a_nmlascr

Erman, N., & Todorovski, L. (2009). Mapping the e-government research with social network analysis. *EGOV,* 13-25.

European Commission, & Capgemini. (2009). *E-government benchmarking survey. Smarter, faster, better e-government-8th benchmark measurement.* Retrieved from http://ec.europa.eu/information_society/eeurope/i2010/benchmarking/index_en.htm

European Commission. (2004). *European interoperability framework for Pan-European e-government services IDABC.* Retrieved from http://ec.europa.eu/idabc/servlets/Doc?id=19529

European Commission. (2005). *Shaping Europe's digital revolution.*

European Commission. (2006). *Riga ministerial declaration on e-inclusion.* Retrieved from http://ec.europa.eu/information_society/events/ict_riga_2006/doc/declaration_riga.pdf

European Commission. (2009a). *e-inclusion.* Retrieved from http://ec.europa.eu/information_society/activities/einclusion/index_en.htm

European Commission. (2009b). *Malmö ministerial declaration.* Retrieved from http://epractice.eu/files/Malmo%20Ministerial%20Declaration%202009.pdf

European Commission. (2009c). *Study on user satisfaction and impact in the EU27.* Retrieved from http://ec.europa.eu/information_society/activities/egovernment/studies/index_en.htm

Eurostat. (2009). *Statistics on information society.* Retrieved from http://epp.eurostat.ec.europa.eu/portal/page/portal/information_society/

Fahmy, S. (2005). U.S. photojournalists' & photo editors' attitudes & perceptions: Visual coverage of 9/11 & the Afghan War. *Visual Communication Quarterly, 12,* 146–163. doi:10.1207/s15551407vcq1203&4_4

Fahmy, S., & Wanta, W. (2007). What visual journalists think others think. *Visual Communication Quarterly*, *14*, 16–31.

Fallows, D. (2007). *Chinese online population explosion: What it may mean for the Internet globally... and for US users*. Pew Internet & American Life Project. Retrieved November 11, 2007, from http://www.pewinternet.org/pdfs/China_Internet_July_2007.pdf

Farazmand, A. (2002). Administrative ethics and professional competence: Accountability and performance under globalization. *International Review of Administrative Sciences*, *68*, 127–143. doi:10.1177/0020852302681007

Farrell, T. J. (1979). The female and male modes of rhetoric. *College English*, *40*(8), 909–921. doi:10.2307/376528

Fenton, N., & Downing, J. (2003). Counter public spheres and global modernity. *Javnost/The Public*, *10*(1), 15–32.

Fillichio, C. (2006). Getting ready for the retirement tsunami: Linda Springer, director of the U.S. Office of Personnel Management, discusses what the federal government needs to do before its retirement peak in 2008-10. *Public Management*, *35*(1), 3–6.

Fishbein, M., & Ajzen, I. (1975). *Belief, attitude, intention and behaviour: An introduction to theory and research*. Reading, MA: Addison-Wesley.

Fishkin, J. S. (1993). *Democracy and deliberation: New directions in democratic reform*. New Haven, CT: Yale University Press.

Fishkin, J. S. (2004). Consulting the public through deliberative polling. *Journal of Policy Analysis and Management*, *22*(1), 128–133. doi:10.1002/pam.10101

Fishkin, J. S. (1991). *Democracy and deliberation*. New Haven, CT: Yale University Press.

Flew, T., & Young, G. (2005). *From e-government to online deliberative democracy*. Paper presented at the International Conference on Engaging Communities, Brisbane, Australia. Retrieved from http://www.engagingcommunities2005.org/abstracts/Flew-Terry-final.pdf

Florini, A. (2004). Behind closed doors: Governmental transparency gives way to secrecy. *Harvard International Review*, *26*(1), 18–21.

Foley, M. W., & Edwards, B. (1996). The Paradox of Civil Society. *Journal of Democracy*, *7*(3), 38–52. doi:10.1353/jod.1996.0048

Foley, M. W., & Edwards, B. (1997). Escape from politics? Social theory and the social capital debate. *The American Behavioral Scientist*, *40*(5), 550–561. doi:10.1177/0002764297040005002

Foucault, M. (1977). *Discipline and punish: The birth of the prison*. New York, NY: Random House.

Foucault, M. (2008). *The birth of biopolitics: Lectures at the College de France, 1978-1979*. New York, NY: Palgrave MacMillan.

Fountain, J. E. (2003). *Information, institutions and governance: Advancing a basic social science research program for digital government*. National Centre for Digital Government. USA: Harvard University.

Fraser, N. (2007). Transnationalizing the public sphere: On the legitimacy and efficacy of public opinion in a post-Westphalian world. *Theory, Culture & Society*, *24*(4), 7–30. doi:10.1177/0263276407080090

Fraser, N. (1992). Rethinking the public sphere: A contribution to the critique of actually existing democracy. In Calhoun, C. (Ed.), *Habermas and the public sphere* (pp. 109–142). Cambridge, MA: MIT Press.

Freedom House. (2006). *Freedom of the world*. Retrieved January 10, 2007, from http://www.freedomhouse.org/

Freidman, T. L. (2007). *The world is flat: A brief history of the twenty-first century*. New York, NY: Picador.

Freschi, A. C., Medaglia, R., & Norbjerg, J. (2009). A tale of six countries: e-participation research from an administration and political perspective. In Macintosh, A., & Tambouris, E. (Eds.), *Electronic participation* (pp. 36–45). Springer. doi:10.1007/978-3-642-03781-8_4

Froomkin, A. M. (2004). Technologies for democracy. In Shane, P. (Ed.), *Democracy online: The prospects for political renewal through the Internet* (pp. 3–20). New York: Routledge.

Fuchs, D. (2003). *Models of democracy: Participatory, liberal and electronic democracy*. Presented at the ECPR Joint Sessions of Workshops, Edinburgh, U.K. March 28th-April 2nd, 2003.

Fukuyama, F. (1999). *The great disruption: Human nature and the reconstitution of social order*. New York, NY: The Free Press.

Fukuyama, F. (1995). *Trust: The social virtues and the creation of prosperity*. New York, NY: Free Press.

Fukuyama, F. (2001). Social capital, civil society and development. *Third World Quarterly*, *22*(1), 7–20. doi:10.1080/713701144

Fung, A. (2003). Recipes for public spheres: Eight institutional choices and their consequences. *Journal of Political Philosophy*, *11*(3), 338–367. doi:10.1111/1467-9760.00181

Fung, A. (2006). Varieties of participation in complex governance. *Public Administration Review*, *66*, 66–76. doi:10.1111/j.1540-6210.2006.00667.x

Fung, A., & Wright, E. O. (2001). Deepening democracy: Innovations in empowered participatory governance. *Politics & Society*, *29*(1), 5–44. doi:10.1177/0032329201029001002

Ganesh, S., & Barber, K. F. (2009). The silent community: Organizing zones in the digital divide. *Human Relations*, *62*(6), 851–874. doi:10.1177/0018726709104545

Gans, H. J. (2004). Sources and journalists. In *Deciding What's News: A study of CBS Evening News, NBC Nightly News, Newsweek, and Time* (25th ed.) (pp. 117-118). Illinois: Northwestern University Press.

Garrett, R. K., & Jensen, M. J. (2009). *E-democracy writ small: The impact of the Internet on citizen access to local elected officials*. Paper presented at the Annual Meeting of the International Communication Association, Chicago. Retrieved from http://www.allacademic.com/

Gastil, J., & William, K. M. (2005). A nation that (sometimes) likes to talk. In Gastil, J., & Levine, P. (Eds.), *The deliberative democracy handbook* (pp. 3–19). San Franciso, CA: Wiley & Sons/ Jossey-Bass.

Gefen, D., Rose, G., Warkentin, M., & Pavlou, P. A. (2005). Cultural diversity and trust in IT adoption: A comparison of potential e-voters in the USA and South Africa. *Journal of Global Information Management*, *13*(1), 54–78. doi:10.4018/jgim.2005010103

Geiselhart, G., Griffiths, M., & Fitzgerald, B. (2003). What lies beyond service delivery-an Australian perspective. *Journal of Political Marketing*, *2*(3-4), 213–233. doi:10.1300/J199v02n03_12

Gellner, E. (1994). *Conditions of liberty: Civil society and its rivals*. New York, NY: Penguin Press.

Gerring, J., & Thacker, S. C. (2004). Political institutions and corruption: The role of unitarism and parliamentarism. *British Journal of Political Science*, *34*(2), 295–330. doi:10.1017/S0007123404000067

Gerster Consulting. (2008). *ICT in Africa: Boosting economic growth and poverty reduction*. 10th meeting of the African Partnership Forum. Retrieved July 22, 2009, from http://www.gersterconsulting.ch/docs/ICT-Africa_Report_final_engl.pdf

Giddens, A. (1984). *The constitution of society: Outline of the theory of structuration*. Los Angeles, CA: University of California Press.

Gimeno, J. D. M. (2008). *YouTube and mainstream journalism: Strange bedfellows?* Paper presented at the 2008 International Communication Association (ICA) conference, Journalism Ethics Division, May 22-26, 2008, Montreal, Quebec, Canada.

Gimeno, J. D. M., & Freeman, B. C. (2009). *The ethics of videoblogging: Public journalists have their say on YouTube*. Paper presented at the University of Melbourne and the International Communication Association (ICA)'s Journalism in the 21st Century: Between Globalization and National Identity, July 16-17, 2009, University of Melbourne, Australia.

Gimmler, A. (2001). Deliberative democracy, the public sphere and the Internet. *Philosophy and Social Criticism*, *27*(4), 21–39. doi:10.1177/019145370102700402

Gitlin, T. (1998). Public sphere or public sphericules? In Liebes, T., & Curran, J. (Eds.), *Media, ritual, identity* (pp. 168–175). London: Routledge.

Glaeser, E., Laibson, D., Scheinkman, J., & Soutter, C. (2000). Measuring trust. *The Quarterly Journal of Economics*, *115*(3), 811–846. doi:10.1162/003355300554926

Gleason, S. (2010). Harnessing social media. *American Journalism Review*, *32*, 6–7.

Goodin, R. E., & Dryzek, J. S. (2006). Deliberative impacts: The macro-political uptake of min-publics. *Politics & Society, 34*(2), 219–244. doi:10.1177/0032329206288152

Gormley, K. (1992). One hundred years of privacy. *Wisconsin Law Review,* •••, 1335.

Gould, J. (2008). Subsidiary sovereignty and the constitution of political space in Zambia? In Gewald, J.-B., Hinfelaar, M., & Macola, G. (Eds.), *One Zambia, many histories: Towards a history of post-colonial Zambia.* Leiden, The Netherlands; Boston, MA: Brill Academic Publishers. doi:10.1163/ej.9789004165946.i-304.95

Governance, D. org initiative. (2010). *What is digital governance?* Retrieved April 20, 2010, from http://216.197.119.113/artman/publish/index1.shtml

Government Accountability Office. (2004). *Electronic government: Federal agencies have made progress implementing the e-government act of 2002* (GAO-05-12). Retrieved from www.gao.gov/cgi-bin/getrpt?GAO-05-12

Government Accountability Office. (2004). *Electronic government: Initiatives sponsored by the office of management and budget have made mixed progress* (GAO-04-561T). Retrieved from www.gao.gov/cgi-bin/getrpt?GAO-04-561T

Government of Karnataka. (1997). Mahiti–the millennium IT policy. Retrieved November 23, 2009, from http://www.bangaloreitbt.in/word document/pdf/IT%20policy.pdf

Granovetter, M. (1973). The strength of weak ties. *American Journal of Sociology, 78*(6), 1360–1380. doi:10.1086/225469

Grant, A., & Meadows, J. (2008). *Communication technology update and fundamentals* (11th ed.). Boston, MA: Focal Press, Elsevier.

Grant, A. (2008). The mobile revolution. In Grant, A. E., & Meadows, J. H. (Eds.), *Communication technology update and fundamentals* (11th ed., pp. 343–350). Boston, MA: Focal Press, Elsevier.

Greffet, F., & Wojcik, S. (2008). Parler politique en ligne. Une revue des travaux français et anglo-saxons. *Reseaux, 150*, 19–50.

Griffin, G. (1995). Shoot first: The ethics of Australian press photographers. *Australian Studies in Journalism, 4*, 3–29.

Grigorescu, A. (2003). International organizations and government transparency: Linking the international and domestic realms. *International Studies Quarterly, 47*, 643–667. doi:10.1046/j.0020-8833.2003.04704003.x

Gronlund, A. (2003). e-democracy: In search of tools and methods for effective participation. *Journal of Multi-Criteria Decision Analysis, 12*(2-3), 93–100. doi:10.1002/mcda.349

Gronlund, A. (2009). ICT is not participation, is not democracy – eParticipation development models. In Macintosh, A., & Tambouris, E. (Eds.), *Electronic participation* (pp. 12–23). Springer. doi:10.1007/978-3-642-03781-8_2

Gronlund, A., & Astrom, J. (2009). Do IT right: Measuring effectiveness of different e-consultation designs. In Macintosh, A., & Tambouris, E. (Eds.), *Electronic participation* (pp. 90–100). Springer. doi:10.1007/978-3-642-03781-8_9

Gronlund, A. (2002). Emerging infrastructures for e-democracy: In search of strong inscriptions. *e-Service Journal, 2*(1), 62-89.

Grönlund, Å., Gross, T., & Ives, B. (2001). *E-democracy: A panacea or Pandora's box? E-everything: E-commerce, e-government, e-household, e-democracy.* 14th Bled Electronic Commerce Conference, Bled, Slovenia, June 25 – 26.

Gross, L., Katz, J. S., & Ruby, J. (Eds.). (1988). *Image ethics: The moral rights of subjects in photographs, film, and television.* New York, NY: Oxford University Press.

Gross, L., Katz, J. S., & Ruby, J. (Eds.). (2003). *Image ethics in the digital age.* Minnesota: University of Minnesota Press.

Grove, A. S. (1997). *Only the paranoid survive.* London, UK: Profile Books Ltd.

Grugel, J. (2002). *Democratization: A critical introduction.* Houndmills, UK: Palgrave.

Guru, G. (2005). Citizenship in exile: A Dalit case. In Reifeld, H., & Bhargava, R. (Eds.), *Civil society, public sphere and citizenship: Dialogues and perceptions* (pp. 260–276). Thousand Oaks, CA: Sage.

Gutmann, A., & Thompson, D. (2004). *Why deliberative democracy?* Princeton, NJ: Princeton University Press.

Gyimah-Boadi, E. (1996). Civil society In Africa. *Journal of Democracy, 7*(2), 118–132. doi:10.1353/jod.1996.0025

Habermas, J. (1981). Theory of communicative action: *Vol. 1. (trans. Thomas McCarthy)*. Boston, MA: Beacon Press.

Habermas, J. (1996). *Between facts and norms: Contributions to a discourse theory of law and democracy.* Cambridge, MA: MIT Press.

Habermas, J. (1991). *The structural transformation of the public sphere: An inquiry into a category of bourgeois society.* Cambridge, MA: MIT Press.

Habermas, J. (2001). The public sphere: An encyclopedia article. In Durham, M. G., & Kellner, D. M. (Eds.), *Media and cultural studies: Keyworks* (pp. 102–107). Oxford, UK: Blackwell Publishers.

Habermas, J. (1984). *The theory of communicative action: Reason and the rationalisation of society* (*Vol. 1*). (McCarthy, T., Trans.). Boston, MA: Beacon Press.

Habermas, J. (1987). The uncoupling of system and lifeworld. In *The theory of communicative action: Lifeworld and system: A critique of functionalist reason* (*Vol. 2*, pp. 153–198). (McCarthy, T., Trans.). Boston, MA: Beacon Press.

Habermas, J. (in German 1962, English Translation 1989). *The structural transformation of the public sphere: An inquiry into a category of bourgeois society.* Cambridge MA: The MIT Press.

Hacker, K. (2002a). Network democracy and the fourth world. *European Journal of Communication Research, 27*, 235–260.

Hacker, K. (2002b). *Network democracy, political will and the fourth world: Theoretical and empirical issues regarding computer-mediated communication (NMN) and democracy. Keynote address to EURICOM.* The Netherlands: Nigmegan.

Hacker, K. (2004). The potential of computer-mediated communication (NMN) for political structuration. *Javnost/ The Public, 11*, 5-26.

Hacker, K., & Todino, M. (1996). Virtual democracy at the Clinton White House: An experiment in electronic democratization. *Javnost/The Public, 3*, 71-86.

Hafez, K. (2002). Journalism ethics revisited: A comparison of ethics codes in Europe, North Africa, the Middle East, and Muslim Asia. *Political Communication, 19*, 225–250. doi:10.1080/10584600252907461

Hair, J. F. Jr, Anderson, R. E., Tatham, R. L., & Black, W. C. (1992). *Multivariate data analysis*. New York, NY: Macmillian.

Hair, J. F., Black, W. C., & Babin, B. J. Anderson, R. E. & Tatham R. L. (2006). *Multivariate data analysis*, 6th ed. Upper Saddle River, NJ: Prentice-Hall, Incorporated.

Hansard Society. (2010). *Digital democracy*. Retrieved from http://hansardsociety.org.uk/blogs/eDemocracy/

Hard, D. K. (1989). A partnership in virtue among all citizens: The public service and civic humanism. *Public Administration Review*, 101–105.

Hargittai, E., & Walejko, G. (2008). The participation divide: Content creation and sharing in the digital age. *Information Communication and Society, 11*(2), 239–256. doi:10.1080/13691180801946150

Hargittai, E. (2006). Hurdles to information seeking: Spelling and typographical mistakes during users' online behavior. *Journal of the Association for Information Systems, 7*(1), 52–67.

Hargittai, E. (1999). Weaving the Western Web: Explaining differences in Internet connectivity among OECD countries. *Telecommunications Policy, 23*(10/11).

Harrison, J. (2004). *From image to icon? Ethics and taste in photographic portrayals of the death of Pym Fortuyn.* The University of Queensland Web. Retrieved March 15, 2008, from http://espace.library.uq.edu.au/view.php?pid=UQ:10515

Hartley, J., & Allison, M. (2000). The role of leadership in the modernization and improvement of public services. *Public Money & Management Review,* 35-40.

Hauser, G. (1998). Vernacular dialogue and the rhetoricality of public opinion. *Communication Monographs, 65*(2), 83–107. doi:10.1080/03637759809376439

Heim, M. (1993). *The metaphysics of virtual reality*. New York, NY: Oxford University Press.

Heitzman, J. (1999). Democratic participation in Bangalore: Implementing the Indian 74th amendment. Cited in Madon, S., & Sahay, S. (2000). Democracy and information: A case study of new local governance structures in Bangalore. *Information Communication and Society, 3*(2), 173–191.

Held, D. (1987). *Models of participation. Cambridge, UK: Polity Press. Georgiadis, A. (1997). General principles of civil law*. Athens, Greece: Sakkoulas Publications.

Helton, K., & Jackson, R. (2007). Navigating Pennsylvania's dynamic workforce: Succession planning in a complex environment. *Public Personnel Management, 36*(4), 335–347.

Henderson, L. (1998). Access and consent in public photography. In Gross, L., Katz, J. S., & Ruby, J. (Eds.), *Image ethics: The moral rights of subjects in photographs, film, and television* (pp. 91–107). New York, NY: Oxford University Press.

Hendriks, C. (2002). Institutions of deliberative democratic processes and interest groups: Roles, tensions and incentives. *Australian Journal of Public Administration, 61*(1), 64–75. doi:10.1111/1467-8500.00259

Herrscher, R. (2002). A universal code of journalism ethics: Problems, limitations, and proposals. *Journal of Mass Media Ethics, 17*(4), 277–289. doi:10.1207/S15327728JMME1704_03

Hibbing, J. R., & Theiss-Morse, E. (2002). *Stealth democracy: Americans' beliefs about how government should work*. Cambridge, UK: Cambridge University Press. doi:10.1017/CBO9780511613722

Hill, K. A., & Hughes, J. E. (1998). *Cyberpolitics: Citizen activism in the age of the Internet*. Lanham: Rowman & Little.eld.

Hiller, J. S., & Belanger, F. (2001). *Privacy strategies for electronic government, in e-government 2001* (Abramson, M. A., & Means, G. E., Eds.). Oxford, UK: Rowman and Littlefield Publishers.

Hindman, M. (2009). *The myth of digital democracy*. Princeton, NJ: Princeton University Press.

HIPSSA Project. (2008). *Support for harmonization of ICT policies in sub-Sahara Africa*. Retrieved July 20, 2009, from http://ua-ue-frontend.irislink.com:8080/alfresco/d/d/workspace/SpacesStore/f32c4370-03e2-11de-a48b-3f161803b677/HIPSSA_Project.doc

Ho, A. (2002). Reinventing local governments and the e-government initiative. *Public Administration Review, 62*(4), 434–444. doi:10.1111/0033-3352.00197

Hodges, L. W. (Ed.). (2002). Cases and commentaries. *Journal of Mass Media Ethics, 17*(4), 318–327. doi:10.1207/S15327728JMME1704_07

Holderness, M. (1998). Who are the world's information poor? In Loader, B. (Ed.), *Cyberspace divide* (pp. 35–56). London, UK: Routledge.

Horrigan, J. (2010). *Broadband adoption and use in America*. Washington, DC: Federal Communications Commission.

Huddleston, M. W. (2000). Onto the darkling plain: Globalization and the American public service in the twenty-first century. *Journal of Public Administration: Research and Theory, 10*(4), 665–684.

Hudson, J. (2002). Digitising the structures of government: The UK's information age government agenda. *Policy and Politics, 30*(4), 515–531. doi:10.1332/030557302760590431

IDA, & IMF. (2007). *Heavily Indebted Poor Countries (HIPC) Initiative and Multilateral Debt Relief Initiative (MDRI) — status of implementation*. International Development Association (IDA) and International Monetary Fund (IMF).

Inglehart, R., & Baker, W. (2000). Modernization, cultural change, and the persistence of traditional values. *American Sociological Review, 65*(1), 19–51. doi:10.2307/2657288

Institute for Public Policy (IPP). (2009). *Barometer of public opinion*. Bucharest, Romania: IPP publishing.

Institute for the Quantitative Study of Society. Stanford University. Retrieved from http://www.stanford.edu/group/siqss/Press_Release/Preliminary_Report-4-21.pdf

Insua, D. R. (2008). Introduction to the special issue on e-democracy. *Group Decision and Negotiation, 17*(3), 175–177. doi:10.1007/s10726-007-9077-7

International Commission of Jurists. (2005). *Iraq: The trial of Saddam Hussein and the rights of the victims.* Retrieved April 9, 2007, from www.icj.org/IMG/pdf/IQTrial_Saddam_R.victims_.pdf

International Council on Human Rights Policy. (2002). Human rights as a news topic. In *Journalism, media and the challenges of human rights reporting* (pp. 2–3). Vernier, Switzerland: ATAR Roto Press.

International Telecommunication Union. (2007). *World telecommunication/ICT indicators.* Retrieved 12 September, 2008, from http://www.itu.int/ITU- D/icteye/Indicators/Indicators.aspx# K. Banaian & B. Roberts (Eds.). (2008). *The design and use of political economy indicators: Challenges of definition, aggregation and application.* New York, NY: Palgrave Macmillan.

Ionescu, C. (2005). Sinteza Raportului de audit Performanta Sistemului Electronic National privind implementarea tehnologiilor informatice în scopul asigurării accesului la informatii publice si furnizării de servicii publice informatizate către persoane fizice sau juridice. *Curtea de Conturi a României.* Retrieved on January 12, 2009, from http://www.rcc.ro/documente/sinteza%20sen06.pdf

Irvin, R., & Stansbury, J. (2004). Citizen participation in decision making: Is it worth the effort? *Public Administration Review, 64*(1), 55–65. doi:10.1111/j.1540-6210.2004.00346.x

Ismail, S., & Wu, I. (2003). *Broadband Internet access in OECD countries: A comparative analysis.* (FCC Office of Strategic Planning and Policy Analysis Working Paper: Washington, DC).

Iyengar, S., & Jackman, S. (2003). *Technology and politics: Incentives for youth participation.* Paper presented for the presentation at the International Conference on Civic Education Research, New Orleans, USA.

Jankowski, N., & Van Os, R. (1998). Internet based political discourse: A case study of electronic democracy in Hoogveen. In Shane, P. M. (Ed.), *Democracy online. The prospects for political renewal through the Internet* (pp. 181–195). London, UK: Routledge.

Janoski, T. (1998). *Citizenship and civil society. A framework of rights & obligations in liberal, traditional and social democratic regime.* Cambridge, UK: Cambridge University Press.

Janssen, D., & Kies, R. (2005). Online forums and deliberative democracy. *Acta Politica, 40,* 317–335. doi:10.1057/palgrave.ap.5500115

Jenkins, H., & Thorburn, D. (2004). *Democracy and new media.* Cambridge, MA: MIT Press.

Johansson-Stenman, O., Mahmud, M., & Martinsson, P. (2006). *Trust and religion: Experimental evidence from Bangladesh.* Department of Economics, Göteborg University, Mimeo.

Jreisat, J. (2004). Governance in a globalizing world. *International Journal of Public Administration, 27*(13-14), 1003–1029. doi:10.1081/PAD-200039883

Justice, J. B., Melitski, J., & Smith, D. L. (2006). E-government as an instrument of fiscal accountability and responsiveness: Do the best practitioners employ the best practices? *American Review of Public Administration, 36,* 301–322. doi:10.1177/0275074005283797

Kahn, R., & Kellner, D. (2005). Oppositional politics and the Internet: A critical/reconstructive approach. *Cultural Politics: An International Journal, 1*(1), 75–100. doi:10.2752/174321905778054926

Kahn, R., & Kellner, D. (2004). New media and Internet activism: From the battle of Seattle to blogging. *New Media & Society, 6*(1), 87–95. doi:10.1177/1461444804039908

Kamarck, E. C., & Nye, J. S. Jr., (Eds.). (2002). *Governance.com: Democracy in an Information Age.* Washington, DC: Brookings Institution Press.

Kane, J., & Bishop, P. (2002). Consultation or contest: The danger of mixing modes. *Australian Journal of Public Administration, 61*(1), 87–94. doi:10.1111/1467-8500.00261

Kane, J., & Patapan, H. (2010). The promise of e-democracy. *Griffith Review, 1*(3).

Kanungo, S. (2004). On the emancipatory role of rural information systems. *Information Technology & People, 17,* 407–422. doi:10.1108/09593840410570267

Kaufmann, D. (2004). *Corruption, government and security: Challenges for the rich country and the world.* Global Competitiveness Report 2004/2005. Retrieved January 11, 2007, from http://siteresources.worldbank.org/INTWBIGOVANTCOR/Resources/ETHICS.xls

Kaufmann, D., & Kraay, A. (2002). *Growth without governance.* (World Bank Policy Research Working Paper No. 2928), Washington, D.C. Retrieved November 23, 2009, from http://www.worldbank.org/wbi/governance / pubs/growthgov.html.

Kaufmann, D., Kraay, A., & Mastruzzi, M. (2008). *Governance matters VII: Aggregate and individual governance indicators, 1996-2007.* (World Bank Policy Research Working Paper No. 4654), Washington, D.C. Retrieved November 23, 2009, from http://www.worldbank.org/wbi/ governance/pubs/aggindicators.html

Ke, W., & Wei, K. K. (2004). Successful e-government in Singapore. *Communications of the ACM, 47*(6), 95–99. doi:10.1145/990680.990687

Keane, J. (1998). *Civil society: Old images, new visions.* Stanford, CA: Stanford University Press.

Keane, J. (2000). Structural transformations of the public sphere. In Hacker, K., & van Dijk, J. (Eds.), *Digital democracy: Issues of theory and practice* (pp. 70–89). London, UK: Sage.

Keith, S., Schwalbe, C. B., & Silcock, B. W. (2006). Images in ethics codes in an era of violence and tragedy. *Journal of Mass Media Ethics, 21*(4), 245–264. doi:10.1207/s15327728jmme2104_3

Kellner, D. (1999). New technologies: Technocities and the prospects for democratization. In Downey, J., & McGuigan, J. (Eds.), *Technocities.* London: Sage.

Kelton, A., & Yang, Y. (2008). The impact of corporate governance on Internet financial reporting. *Journal of Accounting and Public Policy, 27*(1), 62–87. doi:10.1016/j.jaccpubpol.2007.11.001

Keniston, K., & Kumar, D. (Eds.). (2004). *IT experience in India: Bridging the digital divide.* New Delhi: Sage.

Kersten, G. E. (2003). e-democracy and participatory decision processes: Lessons from e-negotiation experiments. *Journal of Multi-Criteria Decision Analysis, 12*(2-3), 127–143. doi:10.1002/mcda.352

Kien, S. S., & Siong, N. B. (2000). Reengineering effectiveness and the redesign of organizational control: A case study of the inland revenue authority of Singapore. In *Process think: Winning perspectives for business change in the Information Age.* Hershey, PA: Idea Group Publishing.

Kim, C.-G., & Holzer, M. (2006). Public administrators' acceptance of the practice of digital democracy: A model explaining the utilization of online forums in South Korea. *International Journal of Electronic Government Research, 2*(2), 22–48. doi:10.4018/jegr.2006040102

Kim, S., & Kim, D. (2003). South Korean public officials' perceptions of values, failure, and consequences of failure in e-government leadership. *Public Performance & Management Review, 26*(4), 360–375. doi:10.1177/1530957603026004004

Kim, K., & Prabhakar, B. (2000). Initial trust, perceived risk, and the adoption of internet banking. *Proceedings of ICIS 2000,* Brisbane, Australia, Dec. 10-13, 2000.

King, J. (2006). Democracy in the information age. *Australian Journal of Public Administration, 65*(2), 16–32. doi:10.1111/j.1467-8500.2006.00479.x

King, M. A. (2001). The cost manager and the Internet. *Journal of Cost Management, 5*(6), 15–17.

King, D. C. (2002). Catching voters on the Web. In Kamarck, E. C., & Nye, J. S. Jr., (Eds.), *Governance. com: Democracy in an Information Age* (pp. 104–115). Washington, DC: Brookings Institution Press.

Kirschner, P., Buckingham Shum, S., & Carr, C. (2003). *Visualizing argumentation: Software tools for collaborative and educational sense-making.* London, UK: Springer Verlag.

Kitch, C. (2006). Useful memory in Time Inc. Magazines. *Journalism Studies, 7*(1), 94–110. doi:10.1080/14616700500450384

Klitgaard, R., Justesen, M.K., & Klemmensen R. (2005). The political economy of freedom, democracy and terrorism. Dept. of Political Science and Public Management University of Southern Denmark, mimeo.

Kooiman, J. (1993). *Modern governance: New government-society interactions.* London, UK: Saga.

Kooiman, T. (1993). *Social and political governance. Modern governance.* London, UK: Sage Publications.

Korakas, C. (2008). *E-democracy. Opportunities and problems.* Access2Democracy Foundation. Retrieved April 22, 2010, form http://www.access2democracy.org

Kovačić, Z. J. (2005). The impact of national cultures on worldwide e-government readiness. *Informing Science Journal, 8,* 143–159.

Kraut, R., Patterson, M., Lundmark, V., Kiesler, S., Mukophadhyay, T., & Scherlis, W. (1998). Internet paradox: A social technology that reduces social involvement and psychological well-being? *The American Psychologist, 53*(9), 1017–1031. doi:10.1037/0003-066X.53.9.1017

Krueger, C. (2008, August). Campaigns connect on-line, in person. *St. Petersburg Times,* 3B.

Kudo, H. (2008). Does e-government guarantee accountability in public sector? Experiences in Italy and Japan. *Public Administration Quarterly, 32*(1), 93–120.

Kuhn, M. (2007). Interactivity and prioritizing the human: A code of blogging ethics. *Journal of Mass Media Ethics, 22*(1), 18–36.

Kulezsa, J. (2009). Which legal standards should apply To Web-logs? The present legal position of Internet journals in the European *iuris prudence* in the light of the European Parliament Committee's on Culture and Education report and Polish Supreme Court decision. *Lex Electronics, 13*(3), 1–22.

Kunz, F. A. (1995). Review: Civil society in Africa. *The Journal of Modern African Studies, 33*(1), 181–187. doi:10.1017/S0022278X00020991

Kunz, W., & Rittel, H. (1979). *Issues as elements of Information Systems.* (Working Paper No. 131). Berkley, CA: University of California Press. Retrieved from http://www-iurd.ced.berkeley.edu/pub/WP-131.pdf

Kvasny, L. (2006). Cultural (re)production of digital inequality in a US community technology initiative. *Information Communication and Society, 9*(2), 160–181. doi:10.1080/13691180600630740

La Porta, R., Lopez-de-Silanes, F., Shleifer, A., & Vishny, R. (1997). Trust in large Organizations. *American Economic Review Papers and Proceedings, 87,* 333–338.

Larsen, E., & Rainie, L. (2002). *The rise of the e-citizen: How people use government agencies' websites.* Pew Internet and American Life Project. Retrieved January 13, 2007, from http://www.pewinternet.org/reports/toc.asp?Report=57

Lasprogata, G., King, N. J., & Pillay, S. (2004). Regulation of electronic employee monitoring: Identifying fundamental principles of employee privacy through a comparative study of data privacy legislation in the European Union, United States and Canada. *Stanford Technology Law Review, 4.*

Laswad, F., Fisher, R., & Oyelere, P. (2005). Determinants of voluntary Internet financial reporting by local government authorities. *Journal of Accounting and Public Policy, 24*(2), 101–121. doi:10.1016/j.jaccpubpol.2004.12.006

Latane, B., Williams, K. D., & Harkins, S. (1979). Many hands make light the work: The causes and consequences of social loafing. *Journal of Personality and Social Psychology, 37,* 822–832. doi:10.1037/0022-3514.37.6.822

Latham, M. (2001). Direct democracy in Werriwa. In Bishop, P., Kane, J. & Patapan, H. (2002) The theory and practice of e–democracy: Agency, trusteeship and participation on the Web. *International Review of Public Administration, 7*(2), 21–31.

Latour, B. (1987). *Science in action: How to follow scientists and engineers through society.* Milton Keynes, UK: Open University Press.

Latour, B. (1993). *We have never been modern.* New York, London: Harvester Wheatsheaf.

Latour, B. (1999). *Pandora's hope. Essays on the reality of science studies.* Cambridge, MA; London, UK: Harvard University Press.

Latour, B. (2005). *Reassembling the social: An introduction to actor-network theory.* Oxford, UK: Oxford University Press.

Latour, B. (2008). Pour un dialogue entre science politique et sciences studies. *Revue Francaise de Science Politique, 58*(4), 657–678. doi:10.3917/rfsp.584.0657

Latour, B. (2010). *Making law. An ethnography of the Conseil d'Etat.* Cambridge, UK: Polity Press.

LeDuc, L., Niemi, R., & Norris, P. (Eds.). (2002). *Comparing democracies* (*Vol. 2*). London, UK: Sage.

LeDuc, L. (2003). *The politics of direct democracy: Referendums in global perspective*. Ontario, Canada: Broadview Press.

Lee, M., & Turban, E. (2001). A trust model for internet shopping. *International Journal of Electronic Commerce*, *6*, 75–79.

Leib, E. J. (2004). *Deliberative democracy in America: A proposal for a popular branch of government*. University Park, PA: Pennsylvania State University Press.

Leigh, A. (2006). Trust inequality and ethnic heterogeneity. *The Economic Record*, *82*(258), 268–280. doi:10.1111/j.1475-4932.2006.00339.x

Lekorwe, M. (1999). Local government, interest groups and civil society. In *Public administration and policy in Botswana*. Kenwyn/ Cape Town, South Africa: Juta & Co. Ltd.

Lester, P. M. (2006). *Visual communication: Images with messages* (4th ed.). Belmont, CA: Wadsworth.

Lester, P. M. (1995). Photojournalism ethics timeless issues. In Emery, M., & Smythe, T. C. (Eds.), *Readings in mass communication*. Brown & Benchmark Publishers.

Levinson, S. (1990). Privacy vs. the public's right to know. *The World and I, 1990*(9).

Levy, F. (2008). *Becoming a star in the YouTube revolution*. New York, NY: Alpha.

Lim, M., & Kann, M. E. (2008). Politics: Deliberation, mobilization, and networked practices of agitation. In Varnelis, K. (Ed.), *Networked publics* (pp. 77–108). Cambridge, MA: MIT Press.

Lingeropoulos, A. (2002). *Lectures of Roman law. Classical legal library* (*Vol. 32*). Athens, Greece: Sakkoulas Publications.

London School of Economics Centre for Civil Society. (2004). *What is civil society?* Retrieved from http://www.lse.ac.uk/collections/CCS/what_is_civil_society.htm

Loukis, E., Wimmer, M., Charalabidis, Y., Triantafillou, A., & Gatautis, R. (2007). Argumentation systems and ontologies for enhancing public participation in the legislation process. In M. Wimmer, H. Scholl, & A. Grönlund (Eds.), *Proceedings of EGOV 2007 International Conference*, (LNCS 4656). Regensburg, Germany: Springer Verlag.

Lukensmeyer, C., & Brigham, S. (2002). Taking democracy to scale: Creating a town hall meeting for the twenty-first century. *National Civic Review*, *91*(4), 351–366. doi:10.1002/ncr.91406

Lyons, D., & Stone, D. (2008, December 1). President 2.0. *Newsweek*.

Macintosh, A., Gordon, T., & Renton, A. (2009). Providing argument support for e-participation. *Journal of Information Technology & Politics*, *6*(1), 43–59. doi:10.1080/19331680802662113

Macintosh, A. (2006). *Challenges and barriers of e-participation in Europe?* Macintosh, A. (2006). E-participation in policy-making: The research and the challenges. In Cunningham, P., & Cunningham, M. (Eds.), *Exploiting the knowledge economy: Issues, applications and case studies*. Amsterdam, The Netherlands; Washington, DC: IOS Press.

Macintosh, A. (2004). *Characterizing e-participation in policy-making*. Paper presented at the 37th Annual Hawaii International Conference on System Sciences. Retrieved from http://ieeexplore.ieee.org/xpls/abs_all.jsp?arnumber=1265300

Macpherson, C. B. (1977). *The life and times of liberal democracy*. London, UK; New York, NY: Oxford University Press.

Madon, S. (1997). The information-based global economy and socio-economic development: The case of Bangalore. *The Information Society*, *13*(3). doi:10.1080/019722497129115

Manin, B. (1987). On legitimacy and political deliberation. *Political Theory*, *15*(3), 338–368. doi:10.1177/0090591787015003005

Manin, B. (2002). L'idée de démocratie délibérative dans la science politique contemporaine. Introduction, généalogie et éléments critiques. *Politix*, *15*(57), 37–55.

Manin, B. (2005). Délibération et discussion. *Swiss Political Science Review, 10*(4), 34–46.

Manor, J. (1993). *Power, poverty and poison: Disaster and response in an Indian city.* New Delhi: Sage.

Mansbridge, J. (1983). *Beyond adversary democracy.* Chicago, IL: University of Chicago Press.

Mansbridge, J. (1999). Everyday talk in the deliberative system. In Macedo, S. (Ed.), *Deliberative politics* (pp. 211–242). Oxford, UK: Oxford University Press.

Mansbridge, J. (1998). The many faces of representation. Retrieved from http://www.ksg.harvard.edu/prg/mansb/faces.htm

Marcus, A., & Perez, A. (2007). m-YouTube mobile UI: Video selection based on social influence. In J. Jacko (Ed.), *Proceedings from the Human-Computer Interaction, Part III.* Heidelberg/ Berlin, Germany: Springer-Verlag.

Margolis, M., & Resnick, D. (2000). *Politics as usual: The cyberspace revolution.* London, UK: Sage.

Marlowe, J. (2004). Part of the solution, or cogs in the system? The origins and consequences of trust in public administrators. *Public Integrity, 6*(2), 93–113.

Maskell, P. (2000). Social capital, innovation, and competitiveness. In Baron, S., Field, J., & Schuller, T. (Eds.), *Critical perspectives.* New York, NY: Oxford University Press.

Mauro, P. (1995). Corruption and growth. *The Quarterly Journal of Economics, 110*(2), 681–712. doi:10.2307/2946696

McAllister, I. (2001). Elections without cues: The 1999 Australian republic referendum. *Australian Journal of Political Science, 36*(2), 247–269. doi:10.1080/10361140120078817

McCaughey, M., & Ayers, M. (Eds.). (2003). *Cyberactivism: Online activism in theory and practice* (pp. 1–21). New York, NY: Routledge.

Meadows, J. H. (2008). Conclusions. In Grant, A. E., & Meadows, J. H. (Eds.), *Communication technology update and fundamentals* (11th ed., pp. 351–354). Boston, MA: Focal Press, Elsevier.

Melitski, J. (2003). Capacity and e-government performance: An analysis based on early adopters of Internet technologies in New Jersey. *Public Performance & Management Review, 26*(4), 376–390. doi:10.1177/1530957603026004005

Menou, M. J. (2002). *Digital and social equity? Opportunities and threats on the road to empowerment.* Paper prepared for The Digital Divide from an Ethical Viewpoint, International Center for Information Ethics Symposium, Ausberg, Germany.

Metaxiotis, K., & Psarras, J. (2004). e-government: New concept, big challenge, success stories. *Electronic Government: An International Journal, 1*(2), 141–178. doi:10.1504/EG.2004.005174

Millard, J. (2006). *E-governance and e-participation: Lessons from Europe in promoting inclusion and empowerment.* Retrieved from http://citeseerx.ist.psu.edu/viewdoc/summary?doi=10.1.1.117.3155

Millard, J. (2009). e-participation. *European Journal of e-Practice, 7.*

Miller, F. (2010). Aristotle's political theory. In E. N. Zalta (Ed.), *The Stanford encyclopedia of philosophy (Spring 2010 edition).* Retrieved from http://plato.stanford.edu/archives/spr2010/entries/aristotle-politics/

Ministry of Communication and Transport. (2006). *National information and technology policy.* Lusaka, Zambia: Government Republic of Zambia.

Misuraca, G. C. (2006). E-governance in Africa: From theory to action: A practical-oriented research and case studies on ICTs for local governance. *ACM International Conference Proceeding Series, 151,* 209-218.

Monnoyer-Smith, L. (2006a). Citizen's deliberation on the Internet: An exploratory study. *International Journal of Electronic Government Research, 2*(3), 58–74. doi:10.4018/jegr.2006070103

Monnoyer-Smith, L. (2006b). How e-voting technology challenges traditional concepts of citizenship: An analysis of French voting rituals. In Krimmer, R. (Ed.), *Electronic voting 2006* (pp. 61–68). Bonn, Germany: GI Lecture Notes in Informatics.

Monnoyer-Smith, L. (2007). Citizen's deliberation on the Internet: A French case. In Norris, D. (Ed.), *E-government research: Policy and management* (pp. 230–253). Hershey, PA: IGI Publishing.

Monnoyer-Smith, L. (in press). The technological dimension of participation. A comparison between on and off-line participation. In Shane, P. M., & Coleman, S. (Eds.), *Connecting democracy: Online consultation and the future of democratic discourse*. Cambridge, MA: MIT Press.

Monnoyer-Smith, L. (2009). Deliberation and inclusion: Framing online public debate to enlarge participation. A theoretical proposal. *I/S: A Journal of Law and Policy for the Information Society, 5*(1), 87-116.

Moon, M. J. (2002). The evolution of e-government among municipalities: Rhetoric or reality. *Public Administration Review, 62*(4), 424–435. doi:10.1111/0033-3352.00196

Moon, J. M., Welch, W. E., & Wong, W. (2005). What drives global e-governance? An exploratory study at a macro level. *Proceedings of the 38th Hawaii International Conference on System Sciences*, (pp 1-10).

Moore, M. (1999). Truth, trust and market transactions: What do we know? *The Journal of Development Studies, 36*(1), 74–88. doi:10.1080/00220389908422612

Moorman, C., Deshpand, R., & Zaltman, G. (1993). Factors affecting trust in market research relationships. *Journal of Marketing, 57*, 81–101. doi:10.2307/1252059

Morgan, R. M., & Hunt, S. (1994). The commitment-trust theory of relationship marketing. *Journal of Marketing, 58*(3), 20–38. doi:10.2307/1252308

MORI. (2005). *What works: Key lessons from recent e-democracy literature*. UK government. Retrieved November, 20, 2009, from http://www.e-Democracy.gov.uk

Morris, D. (1999). *Vote.com: How big money lobbyists and the media are losing their influence and the Internet is giving power back to the people*. New York, NY: Renaissance Books.

Morrisett, L. (2003). Technologies of freedom? In Jenkins, H., & Thorburn, D. (Eds.), *Democracy and new media* (pp. 21–31). Cambridge, MA: MIT Press.

Mossberger, K., Tolbert, C. J., & McNeal, R. S. (2007). *Digital citizenship: The Internet, society, and participation*. Cambridge, MA: MIT Press.

Mossberger, K., Tolbert, C., & Stansbury, M. (2003). *Virtual inequality: Beyond the digital divide*. Washington, DC: Georgetown University Press.

Muhlberger, P. (2004). Access, skill, and motivation in online political discussion: Testing cyberrealism. In Shane, P. M. (Ed.), *Democracy online* (pp. 225–238). London, UK: Routledge.

Muhlberger, P. (2002). *Political values and attitudes in Internet political discussion: Political transformation or politics as usual?* Paper presented at the Euricom Colloquium: Electronic Networks & Democracy, Nijmegen, Netherlands.

Muhlberger, P. (2005). *Attitude change in face-to-face and online political deliberation: Conformity, information, or perspective taking?* Paper presented at the American Political Science Association, 2005 Annual Meeting. Retrieved April 24, 2010, from http://www.geocities.com/pmuhl78/AttitudeDelib.pdf

Mukerji, M. (2008). Telecentres in rural India: Emergence and a typology. *The Electronic Journal on Information Systems in Developing Countries, 35*(5), 1–13.

Mutula, S., & Van Brakel, P. (2006). An evaluation of e-readiness assessment tools with respect to information access: Towards an integrated information tools. *International Journal of Information Management, 26*, 212–223. doi:10.1016/j.ijinfomgt.2006.02.004

Myers, D. G. (1999). *Social psychology* (6th ed.). USA: The McGraw-Hill Companies, Inc.

Ndou, V. (2004). E-government for developing countries: Opportunities and challenges. *The Electronic Journal on Information Systems in Developing Countries EJISDC, 18*(1), 1–24.

Netchaeva, I. (2002). E-government and e-democracy. *The International Journal for Communication Studies, 64*(5), 467–477.

Newton, K., & Delhey, J. (2005). Predicting cross-national levels of social trust: Global pattern or Nordic exceptionalism? *European Sociological Review, 21*(4), 311–327. doi:10.1093/esr/jci022

Nichol, L. (Ed.). (1996). *On dialogue.* London, UK: Routledge.

Nichol, L. (Ed.). (2003). *The essential David Bohm.* London, UK: Routledge.

Nie, N., & Lutz, E. (2000). *Internet and society: A preliminary report.* Stanford

Nielsen Company. (2009). *Nielsen announces September U.S. online video usage data.* Retrieved December 13, 2009, from http://en-us.nielsen.com/main/news/news_releases/2009/october/nielsen_announces Nielsen/ Netratings. (2006). *YouTube U.S. Web traffic grows 75 percent week over week, according to Nielsen/Netratings.* Retrieved February 17, 2007, from http://www.nielsen-netratings.com/pr/pr_060721_2.pdf

Nigam, A. (2005). Civil society and its underground: Explorations in the notion of political society. In Reifeld, H., & Bhargava, R. (Eds.), *Civil society, public sphere and citizenship: Dialogues and perceptions* (pp. 236–259). Thousand Oaks, CA: Sage.

Norris, P. (2001). *A digital divide: Civic engagement, information poverty, and the Internet in democratic societies.* New York, NY: Cambridge University Press.

Norris, P., & Curtice, J. (2006). If you build a political website, will they come? *International Journal of Electronic Government Research, 2*(2), 1–21. doi:10.4018/jegr.2006040101

Norris, P. (2003). *Deepening democracy via e-governance.* Report for the UN World Public Sector Report. Retrieved December 11, 2009, from http://ksghome.harvard.edu/~pnorris/ ACROBAT/e-governance.pdf

Northrup, A., Kraemer, K., Dunkle, D., & King, J. (1990). Payoffs from computerization: Lessons over time. *Public Administration Review, 50*(5), 505–514. doi:10.2307/976781

Noveck, B. S. (2000). Paradoxical partners: Electronic communication and electronic democracy. *Democratization, 7*(1), 18–35.

Noveck, B. S. (2008). Wiki government. *Democracy Journal, 7.* Retrieved April 24, 2010, from http://www.democracyjournal.org/pdf/7/031-043.noveck.final.pdf

Nugent, J. (2001). If e-democracy is the answer, what's the question? *National Civic Review, 90*(3), 221–233. doi:10.1002/ncr.90303

Obi, T. (2009). The 2009 Waseda University international e-government ranking. Retrieved from http://www.giti.waseda.ac.jp/GITS/news/download/e-Government_Ranking2009_en.pdf

O'Brien, R. (1999). *The philosophical history of the idea of civil society.* Retrieved from http://www.web.net/~robrien/papers/civhist.html

OECD. (2001). Citizens as partners. In *OECD handbook on information, consultation and public participation in policy-making.* Paris, France: OECD Publications Service.

OECD. (2003). *Broadband Internet access in OECD countries: A comparative analysis.*

OECD. (2003). *Public sector transparency and international investment policy.* Retrieved from http://www.oecd.org/dataoecd/45/22/2506884.pdf

OECD. (2003). *The e-government imperative: Main findings.* March policy brief.

OECD. (2005). *OECD guidelines on corporate governance of state-owned enterprises.* OECD Publishing. Retrieved October 13, 2009, from http://www.ecgi.org/codes/documents/oecd_soe_en.pdf

OECD. (2009). *Rethinking e-government services: User-centred approaches.* OECD e-government studies.

Ogden, M. R. (2008). Teleconferencing. In Grant, A. E., & Meadows, J. H. (Eds.), *Communication technology update and fundamentals* (11th ed., pp. 321–342). Boston, MA: Focal Press, Elsevier.

Ohl, R. (2008). Computer supported argument visualisation: Modelling in consultative democracy around wicked problems. In Okada, A., Buckingham Shum, S., & Sherborne, T. (Eds.), *Knowledge cartography: Software tools and mapping techniques.* London, UK: Springer.

Omar, B. (2007). The switch to online newspapers: Could immediacy be a factor? In *Proceedings from the Australian New Zealand Communication Association 2007 Conference.* Melbourne, Australia.

Ono, H., & Zavodny, M. (2003). Gender and the Internet. *Social Science Quarterly, 84*(1), 111–121. doi:10.1111/1540-6237.t01-1-8401007

Organisation for Economic Cooperation and Development. (2003a). *Citizens as partners–information, consultation and public participation in policy-making*. Paris, France: OECD.

Organisation for Economic Cooperation and Development. (2004b). *Promise and problems of e-democracy: Challenges of online citizen engagement*. Paris, France: OECD.

Organization for Economic Co-operation and Development. (2003b). *Engaging citizens online for better policy-making: Policy brief*. Paris, France: OECD.

Organization for Economic Co-operation and Development. (2004a). *Evaluating public participation in policy making*. Paris, France: OECD.

Osimo, D. (2008). *Web 2.0 in government: Why and how?* European Commission, Joint Research Centre, Institute for Prospective Technological Studies Report.

Papacharissi, Z. (2002). The virtual sphere: The Internet as a public sphere. *New Media & Society, 4*(1), 9–27. doi:10.1177/14614440222226244

Papacharissi, Z. (2009). The virtual sphere 2.0: The Internet, the public sphere, and beyond. In Chadwick, A., & Howard, P. (Eds.), *Routledge handbook of Internet politics* (pp. 230–245). New York, NY: Routledge.

Parvez, Z. (2006). Informatization of local democracy: A structuration perspective. *Information Polity, 11*(2), 67–83.

Pateman, C. (1970). *Participation and democratic theory*. Cambridge, UK: Cambridge University Press.

Pavlik, J. V. (2005). *Journalism competencies in the digital age: Twelve core principles*. Paper presented at the III Congrès Internacional Comunicació I Realitat, Barcelona, Spain. Retrieved March 15, 2008 from http://cicr.blanquerna.url.edu/2005/Abstracts/PDFsComunicacions/vol1/01/PAVLIK_John.pdf

Peixoto, T. (2008). *E-participatory budgeting: e-democracy from theory to success?* Working paper. Retrieved April 24, 2010, from http://edc.unige.ch/edcadmin/images/Tiago.pdf

Perkins, M. (2002). International law and the search for universal principles in journalism ethics. *Journal of Mass Media Ethics, 17*(3), 193–208. doi:10.1207/S15327728JMME1703_02

Persell, C., Green, A., & Gurevich, L. (2001). Civil society, economic distress, and social tolerance. *Sociological Forum, 16*(2), 203–230. doi:10.1023/A:1011048600902

Peterson, E., & Seifert, J. (2002). Expectation and challenges of emergent electronic government: The promise of all things E? *Perspectives on Global Development and Technology, 1*(2), 193–212. doi:10.1163/156915002100419808

Pew Research Center. (2008). *The Internet's broader role in campaign 2008: Social networking and online videos take off*. Retrieved February 19, 2008, from http://people-press.org/report/384/internets-broader-role-in-campaign-2008

Pina, V., Torres, L., & Royo, S. (2007). Are ICTs improving transparency and accountability in the EU regional and local governments? An empirical study. *Public Administration, 85*(2), 449–472. doi:10.1111/j.1467-9299.2007.00654.x

Piotrowski, S. J., & Borry, E. L. (2009). Governmental transparency and websites: The case of New Jersey municipalities. In Reddick, C. G. (Ed.), *Strategies for local e-government adoption and implementation: Comparative studies*. Hershey, PA: IGI Global.

Polat, R. (2005). The Internet and political participation: Exploring the explanatory links. *European Journal of Communication, 20*, 435–459. doi:10.1177/0267323105058251

Pollitt, C., & Boukaert, G. (1994). *Public management reform. A comparative analysis*. Oxford, UK: Oxford University Press.

Poor, N. (2005). Mechanisms of an online public sphere: The website slashdot. *Journal of Computer-Mediated Communication, 10*(2).

Popa, A., Blidisel, R., & Pop, A. (2008). Investor relations on the Internet. An empirical study of Romanian listed companies. In Fikusz (Ed.), *2008 Business sciences –Symposium for Young Researchers Proceedings,* (pp.187-197), Budapest, Hungary: Budapest Tech.

Pratchett, L., Wingfield, M., & Polat, R. K. (2006). Local democracy online: An analysis of local government websites in England and Wales. *International Journal of Electronic Government Research, 2*(3), 75–92. doi:10.4018/jegr.2006070104

Pratchett, L. (1999). New fashions in public participation: Towards greater democracy? *Parliamentary Affairs, 52*(4), 617–633. doi:10.1093/pa/52.4.616

Price, V. (2006). Citizens deliberating online: Theory and some evidence. In Davies, T., & Noveck, B. S. (Eds.), *Online deliberation: Design, research, and practice* (pp. 37–58). Chicago, IL: University of Chicago Press.

Prott, L. V. (1986). Cultural rights as people's rights in international law. *Bulletin of the Australian Society of Legal Philosophy, 10*(4), 4–19.

Purcell, K., Mitchell, A., Rosentiel, T., & Olmstead, K. (2010). *Understanding the participatory news customer.* Pew Internet and American Life Project. Retrieved from http://pewinternet.org/Reports/2010/Online-News/Part-1.aspx?r=1

Putnam, R. D. (1995). Bowling alone: America's declining social capital. *Journal of Democracy, 6*(1), 65–78. doi:10.1353/jod.1995.0002

Queensland Government (2000). *Regional communities 2000 report.*

Queensland Government. (2003). *About us.* Retrieved from http://www.premiers.qld.gov.au/about/community/pdf/edemocracy.pdf

Raffournier, B. (1995). The determinants of voluntary financial disclosure by Swiss listed companies. *European Accounting Review, 4*(2), 261–280. doi:10.1080/09638189500000016

Rajagopal, A. (Ed.). (2009). *The Indian public sphere: Readings in media history.* New York, NY: Oxford University Press.

Rajchman, J. (2000). *The Deleuze connections.* Cambridge, MA: MIT Press.

Raman, V. (2008). Examining the 'e' in government and governance: A case study in alternatives from Bangalore City, India. *Journal of Community Informatics, 4*(2), 405-437. Retrieved November 23, 2009, from http://ci-journal.net/index.php/ciej/article/view/437/405

Ranerup, A. (2000). Online forums as an arena for political discussions. In Ishida, T., & Isbister, K. (Eds.), *Digital cities. Technologies, experiences, and future perspectives* (pp. 209–223). Berlin, Germany: Springer.

Rao, S. S. (2008). Social development in Indian rural communities: Adoption of telecentres. *International Journal of Information Management, 28*(6), 474–482. doi:10.1016/j.ijinfomgt.2008.01.001

Ravallion, M. (2009). *A comparative perspective on poverty reduction in Brazil, China and India.* (Policy Research Working Paper 5080). The World Bank Development Research Group. Retrieved December 11, 2009, from http://www.wds.worldbank.org/ external/default/WDSContentServer/ IW3P/IB/2009/11/30/000158349_20091130085835/Rendered/ PDF/WPS5080.pdf

Raynes-Goldie, K., & Walker, L. (2008). Our space: Online civic engagement tools for youth. In L. Bennett (Ed.), *Civic life online: Learning how digital media can engage youth.* (pp. 161-188). The John D. and Catherine T. MacArthur Foundation Series on Digital Media and Learning. Cambridge, MA: MIT Press.

Reifeld, H., & Bhargava, R. (Eds.). (2005). *Civil society, public sphere and citizenship: Dialogues and perceptions.* Thousand Oaks, CA: Sage.

Reiter, M. K., & Rubin, A. D. (1998). Crowds: Anonymity for Web transactions. *ACM Transactions on Information and System Security, 1*(1), 66–92. doi:10.1145/290163.290168

Renton, A. (2006). Seeing the point of politics: Exploring the use of CSAV techniques as aids to understanding the content of political debates in the Scottish Parliament. *Artificial Intelligence and Law, 14,* 277–304. doi:10.1007/s10506-007-9040-6

Renton, A., & Macintosh, A. (2007). Computer supported argument maps as a policy memory. *Information Society Journal, 23*(2), 125–133. doi:10.1080/01972240701209300

Renton, A., & Macintosh, A. (2005). Exploiting argument mapping techniques to support policy making. In K. V. Andersen, A. Gronlund, R. Traunmueller, & M. Wimmer (Eds.), *Electronic government: Workshop and poster proceedings of the Fourth International Conference – EGOV*. Linz, Germany: Trauner Verlag.

Rhodes, R. A. W. (1997). *Understanding governance, policy networks governance reflexivity and accountability*. Buckingham, UK: Open University Press.

Rittel, H. W. J., & Weber, M. M. (1973). Dilemmas in a general theory of planning. *Policy Sciences, 4*, 155–169. doi:10.1007/BF01405730

Ritzen, J., Easterly, W., & Woolcock, M. (2001). *On good politicians and bad policies: Social cohesion, institutions and growth*. Working Paper, Washington DC. World Bank

Robbin, A., Courtright, C., & Davis, L. (2005). Policy: ICTs and political life. *Annual Review of Information Science & Technology, 38*(1), 410–482. doi:10.1002/aris.1440380110

Roberts, P., & Webber, J. (1999). Visual truth in the Digital Age: Towards a protocol for image ethics. *Australian Computer Journal, 31*(3), 78–82.

Roberts, A. (2003). In the eye of the storm? Societal aging and the future of public service reform. *Public Administration Review, 63*(6), 720–733. doi:10.1111/1540-6210.00335

Rodan, D., & Balnaves, M. (2009). Democracy to come: Active forums as indicator suites for e-participation and e-governance. In Macintosh, A., & Tambouris, E. (Eds.), *Electronic participation* (pp. 175–185). Springer. doi:10.1007/978-3-642-03781-8_16

Roddy, N. (2004). Leadership capacity building model: Developing tomorrow's leadership in science and technology–an example in succession planning and management. *Public Personnel Management, 33*(4), 487–495.

Rodrick, D. (1999). Where did all the growth go? External shocks, social conflict, and growth collapses. *Journal of Economic Growth, 1*, 149–187.

Rose, R. (2005). A global diffusion model of e-governance. *Journal of Public Policy, 25*(1), 5–27. doi:10.1017/S0143814X05000279

Rowe, G., & Frewer, L. J. (2004). Evaluating public-participation exercises: A research agenda. *Science, Technology & Human Values, 29*(4), 512–557. doi:10.1177/0162243903259197

Roy, J. (2003). The relationship dynamics of e-government: A case study of the city of Ottawa. *Public Performance & Management Review, 26*(4), 391–403. doi:10.1177/1530957603026004006

Russell, A. (2005). Political parties as vehicles of political engagement. *Parliamentary Affairs, 58*(3), 555–569. doi:10.1093/pa/gsi051

Rycroft, A. (2007). *Young adults and virtual public spheres: Building a new political culture*. A long paper submitted as part of the requirements for Master of Arts in Professional Communication. Retrieved October 16, 2009, from http://SunshineCommunications.ca/articles/virtual_public_spheres.pdf. Victoria, Canada: Royal Roads University.

Ryder, G. (2009). The digital divide: Investigating the Isle of Man's dilemma using exploratory research to resolve the problem. In Z. Irani, A. Ghoneim, M. Ali, S. Alshawi, O. Y. Saatcioglu, & A. G. Cerit (Eds.), *European and Mediterranean Conference on Information Systems*. Izmir, Turkey. Retrieved from http://www.iseing.org/emcis/EMCIS2009/_private/Accepted%20Refereed%20papers.htm

Sabo, O., Rose, J., & Flak, L. S. (2008). The shape of e-participation: Characterizing an emerging research area. *Government Information Quarterly, 25*(3), 400–428. doi:10.1016/j.giq.2007.04.007

Sabo, O., Rose, J., & Nyvang, T. (2009). The role of social networking services in e-participation. In Macintosh, A., & Tambouris, E. (Eds.), *Electronic participation* (pp. 46–55). Berlin/Heidelberg, Germany: Springer. doi:10.1007/978-3-642-03781-8_5

Sanders, L. (1997). Against deliberation. *Political Theory, 25*, 347–375. doi:10.1177/0090591797025003002

Savas, E. (2000). *Privatization and public-private partnership*. New York, NY: Chatham House Publishers.

Scanlon, T. (1972). A theory of freedom of expression. *Philosophy & Public Affairs*, *1*(2), 204–226.

Scheuerman, W. E. (2005). Busyness and citizenship. *Social Research*, *72*(2), 447–471.

Scholl, H. J., Barzilai-Nahon, K., Ahn, J.-H., Popova, O. H., & Re, B. (2009). *E-commerce and e-government: How do they compare? What can they learn from each other?* Paper presented at the 42nd Hawaii International Conference on System Sciences.

Schudson, M. (1997). Why conversation is not the soul of democracy. *Critical Studies in Mass Communication*, *14*(4), 297–309. doi:10.1080/15295039709367020

Schuldt, B. A. (2004). MAMA on the Web: Ethical considerations for our networked world. In Quigley, M. (Ed.), *Information society and ethics: Social and organizational issues*. Hershey, PA: IRM Press.

Schwartzberg, J. E. (2008). *India*. Encyclopedia Britannica.

Seaton, J. (2005). Painful news. In *Carnage and the Media: The making and breaking of news about violence* (p. 5). London, UK: Penguin Books, Ltd.

Seifert, J. W. (2008). *Reauthorization of the e-government Act: A brief overview* (RL 34492).

Selvin, A., Shum, S. B., & Sierhuis, M. (2001). *Compendium: Making meetings into knowledge event*. Paper presented at Knowledge Technologies, Austin, Texas.

Sen, A. (1999). *Development as freedom*. New York, NY: Knopf.

Serrano, C., Mar, R. T., & Pilar, P. T. (2008). *Factors influencing e-disclosure in local public administrations*. (Documento de Trabajo -03). Facultad de Ciencias Económicas y Empresariales, Universidad de Zaragoza. Retrieved November 20, 2009, from http://www.dteconz.unizar.es/DT2008-03.pdf

Setianto, B. (2007). Somewhere in between: Conceptualizing civil society. *The International Journal of Non-Profit Law*, *10*(1), 109–118.

Seyle, D. C., McGlohen, M., Ryan, P., Durham-Fowler, J., & Skiadas, T. (2008). *Deliberative quality across time and gender: An introduction to the effectiveness of deliberation scale*. Poster presented at the annual meeting of the ISPP 31st Annual Scientific Meeting, Paris, France. Retrieved April 24, 2010, from http://www.allacademic.com/meta/p245886_index.html

Shackleton, P., Fisher, J., & Dawson, L. (2004). *Evolution of local government e-services: The applicability of e-business maturity models*. Paper presented at the 37th Annual Hawaii International Conference on System Sciences. Retrieved from http://ieeexplore.ieee.org/iel5/8934/28293/01265308.pdf?isnumber=&arnumber=1265308

Shane, P. M. (Ed.). (2004). *Democracy online. The prospect for political renewal Through the Internet*. New York, NY: Routledge.

Shappin, S., & Shaeffer, S. (1985). *Leviathan and the air pump*. Princeton University Press.

Shirky, C. (2008). *Here comes everybody: The power of organizing without organizations*. New York, NY: Penguin Press.

Shirky, C. (2008). *Here comes everybody: The power of organizing without organizations*. New York, NY: Penguin Books.

Shleifer, A., & Vishny, R. (1993). Corruption. *The Quarterly Journal of Economics*, *108*(3), 599–618. doi:10.2307/2118402

Simpson, R., & Cotè, W. (2006). Journalists and violence. In *Covering violence: A guide to ethical reporting about victims and trauma* (2nd ed., pp. 1–12). USA: Columbia University Press.

Singh, H., Das, A., & Joseph, D. (2004). *Country-level determinants of e-government maturity*. Nanyang Technological University, Working Paper.

Sintomer, Y., Herzberg, C., & Röcke, A. (2008). Participatory budgeting in Europe: Potentials and challenges. *International Journal of Urban and Regional Research*, *32*(1), 164–178. doi:10.1111/j.1468-2427.2008.00777.x

Smith, A., Schlozman, K., Verba, S., & Brady, H. (2009). *The internet and civic engagement*. Pew Internet and American Life Project.

Smith, A. (2009). *Civic engagement online: Politics as usual.* Retrieved from http://pewresearch.org/pubs/1328/online-political-civic-engagement-activity

Smith, A. (2009). *The Internet's role in campaign 2008.* Pew Internet & American Life Project. Retrieved from http://www.pewinternet.org/Reports/2009/6--The-Internets-Role-in-Campaign-2008.aspx

Smith, D., & Torres, C. (2006, February 5). Timeline: A history of free speech. *The Observer.* Retrieved April 21, 2007, from http://www.guardian.co.uk/media/2006/feb/05/religion.news

Snider, J. H. (2008). Crackpot or genius? Canada steps onto the world stage as a democratic innovator. *Journal of Public Deliberation, 4*(1), 12. Retrieved from http://services.bepress.com/jpd/vol4/iss1/art12.

Soest, V. C. (2009). *Stagnation of a miracle Botswana's governance record revisited.* (Working Paper no.99, German Institute of Global and Area Studies). Retrieved September 23, 2009, from www.giga-hamburg.de/workingpapers.

Solvang, B. K. (2009). Political participation and democracy in the digital age: Effects of ICT-based communication forms between the authorities and the citizens on traditional channels of participation and democracy In *Proceedings of the Third International Conference on Digital Society,* (pp. 46-51). Cancun: Mexico: IEEE Computer.

Srivastava, S. C., & Teo, T. S. (2007). What facilitates e-government development? A cross-country analysis. *Electronic Government, an International Journal, 4*(4), 365–378.

Stahl, B. (2005). The ethical problem of framing e-government in terms of e-commerce. *The Electronic* [from www.ejeg.com]. *Journal of E-Government, 3*(2), 77–86. Retrieved June 15, 2009.

Stahl, B. C. (2005). The paradigm of e-commerce in e-government and e-democracy. In Huang, W., Siau, K., & Wei, K. K. (Eds.), *Electronic government strategies and implementation* (pp. 1–19). Hershey, PA: Idea Group.

Stalder, F. (2006). *Manuel Castells: The theory of the network society.* Malden, MA: Polity Press.

Steiner, J., Bächtiger, A., Spörndli, M., & Steenberge, M. (2004). *Deliberative politics in action. Analysing parliamentary discourse.* Cambridge, UK: Cambridge University Press.

Steyaert, J. C. (2004). Measuring the performance of electronic government services. *Information & Management, 41,* 369–375. doi:10.1016/S0378-7206(03)00025-9

Stoica, V., & Ilas, A. (2009). Romanian urban e-government. Digital services and digital democracy in 165 cities. *Electronic. Journal of E-Government, 7*(2), 171–182.

Stolowy, H., & Ding, Y. (2003). Les facteurs déterminants de la stratégie des groupes français en matière de communication sur leurs activités de recherché et développement. *Finance Contrôle Stratégie, 3*(1), 39–62.

Stren, R., & Polese, M. (2000). *The social sustainability of cities: Diversity and the management of change.* Toronto, Canada: University of Toronto Press.

Stromer-Galley, J. (2007). Measuring deliberation's content: A coding scheme. *Journal of Public Deliberation, 3*(1), 1–37.

Sussman, L. R. (2001). *The Internet in flux.* Press Freedom Survey 2001, Freedom House. Retrieved August 3, 2007, from http://epic.org/free_speech/pfs2001.pdf

Svensson, J. (1998). Investment, property rights and political instability: Theory and evidence. *European Economic Review, 42*(7), 1317–1342. doi:10.1016/S0014-2921(97)00081-0

Takao, Y. (2004). Democratic renewal by digital local government in Japan. *Pacific Affairs, 77*(2), 237–262.

Talbot, D. (2008). How Obama really did it: The social networking strategy that took an obscure Senator to the doors of the White House. *Technology Review.*

Talpin, J. (2007). Who governs in participatory governance institutions? The impact of citizen participation in municipal decision-making processes in a comparative perspective. In Dewitt, P., Pilet, J.-B., Reynaert, H., & Steyvers, K. (Eds.), *Towards DIY-politics. Participatory and direct democracy at the local level in Europe* (pp. 103–125). Bruges, Belgium: Vanden Broele.

Talpin, J., & Monnoyer-Smith, L. (2010). *Talking with the wind? Discussion on the quality of deliberation in the Ideal-EU project*. Paper presented at the International Political Science Association International Conference, Luxemburg. Retrieved April 24, 2010, from http://www.luxembourg2010.org/sites/default/files/Lux%20paper%20Talpin.pdf

Talpin, J., & Wojcik, S. (In press). When the youth talk about climate change. A comparison of the learning potential of online and face-to-face deliberation. *Policy and the Internet, 1*(2).

Tapscott, D. (1996). *The digital economy*. New York, NY: McGraw Hill.

Taylor, J. (2005). Iraqi torture photographs and documentary realism in the press. *Journalism Studies, 6*(1), 39–49. doi:10.1080/1461670052000328195

Taylor, S., & Todd, P. (1995). Decomposition and crossover effects in the theory of planned behavior: A study of consumer adoption intentions. *International Journal of Research in Marketing, 12*(2), 137–156. doi:10.1016/0167-8116(94)00019-K

Taylor, J., & Burt, E. (2005). Voluntary organizations as e-democratic actors: Political identity, legitimacy and accountability and the need for new research. *Policy and Politics, 33*(4), 601–616. doi:10.1332/030557305774329127

Tedesco, J. C. (2007). Examing Internet interactivity effects on young adult political information efficacy. *The American Behavioral Scientist, 50*(7), 1183–1194. doi:10.1177/0002764207300041

Tettey, W. J. (2001). Information Technology and democratic participation in Africa. *Journal of Asian and African Studies, 36*(1), 133–153. doi:10.1177/002190960103600107

The e-Brain Forum of Zambia. (2004). *Report of the Information and Communication Technology (ICT) in Local Government Workshop, ICTs for sustainability: Can local councils build capacity for change?* Lusaka, Zambia.

The Heritage Foundation. (2005). *Index of economic freedom*. Retrieved Dec 20, 2006, from http://www.heritage.org/research/features/index/

The Heritage Foundation. (2005). *Index of economic freedom*. Retrieved January 15, 2007, from http://www.heritage.org/index/

The Mo Ibrahim Foundation. (2008). *2007 Ibrahim index of African governance*. Retrieved.

The World Bank Group. (2004). *Data*. Retrieved January 15, 2007, from http://www.worldbank.org/data

Thomas, J. C., & Streib, G. (2003). The new face of government: Citizen-initiated contacts in the era of e-government. *Journal of Public Administration: Research and Theory, 13*(1), 83–102. doi:10.1093/jpart/mug010

Thomas, R. G. C. (2006). Media. In Wolpert, S. (Ed.), *Encyclopedia of India* (*Vol. 3*, pp. 105–107). Farmington Hills, MI: Thomson Gale.

Thompson, D. F. (2008). Deliberative democratic theory and empirical political science. *Annual Review of Political Science, 11*, 497–520. doi:10.1146/annurev.polisci.11.081306.070555

Thompson, R. L., Higgins, C. A., & Howell, J. M. (1991). Personal computing: Toward a conceptual model of utilization. *Management Information Systems Quarterly, 15*(1), 125–143. doi:10.2307/249443

Tiamiyu, M. A., & Aina, L. O. (2008). Information and knowledge management in the digital age: An African perspective. In Aina, L. O., Mutula, S. M., & Tiamiyu, M. A. (Eds.), *Information and knowledge management in the digital age: Concepts, technologies and African perspectives* (pp. 3–27). Ibadan, Nigeria: Third World Information Services Limited.

Tibenderana, P., & Ogao, P. J. (2008). Information Communication Technologies acceptance and use among university communities in Uganda: A model for hybrid library services end-users. *International Journal of Computing and ICT Research, 1*(1).

Timmers, P. (2007). *Agenda for e-democracy–an EU perspective*. European Commission.

Tiron Tudor, A., Blidisel, R., & Popa, A. (2009). E-financial reporting within the Romanian public sector governance. In D. Remenyi (Ed.), *9th European Conference on e-Government Westminster Business School, University of Westminster, London, UK 29-30 June 2009*, (pp. 628- 637). Dublin, Ireland: Trinity College Dublin.

Tiut, A. (2003). Corruption and civil society in Romania: Striving for an answer, or at least a clear picture. Retrieved on May 12, 2009, from http://www.eumap.org/journal/features/2003/july/ccsromania

Toomey, B. (2008). Can the use of technology encourage young people to take an active part in urban regeneration consultations? A case study from East London. *Local Economy*, 23(3), 247–251. doi:10.1080/02690940802197473

Toulmin, S. (1958). *The uses of argument*. Cambridge, UK: University Press.

TRAI. (2009). The Indian telecom services performance indicators, April-June 2009. Retrieved Dec 11, 2009, from http://www.trai.gov.in/ WriteReadData/trai/upload/Reports /48/IndicatorReport1oct09.pdf

Transparency International. (2007). *2007 Transparency International corruption perceptions index*. Retrieved September 12, 2008, from http://www.transparency.org/policy_research/surveys_indices/cpi/2007

Treasury, H. M. (2005). *Corporate governance in central government departments: Code of good practice*. London, UK: Crown Copyright.

Tschannen-Moran, M., & Hoy, W. K. (2000). A multidisciplinary analysis of the nature, meaning, and measurement of trust. *Review of Educational Research*, 70(4), 547–593.

Tulloch, J. (2006). The privatising of pain: Lincoln newspapers, mediated publicness and the end of public execution. *Journalism Studies*, 7(3), 437–451. doi:10.1080/14616700600680922

Turner, V. (1974). *Dramas, fields and metaphors: Symbolic action in human society*. Ithaca, NY: Cornell University Press.

Tzu-Shan, T., & Torgashina, N. (2008). The usage of Information-Communication Technologies in government-citizen relations: A case study of Khanty-Mansiysk autonomous Okrug-Yugra. *Journal of Informatics & Electronics*, 3(1), 63–77.

Uhr, J. (1998). *Deliberative democracy in Australia: The changing place of Parliament*. Melbourne, Australia: Cambridge University Press.

Uhr, J. (2000). Testing deliberative democracy: The 1999 Australian republic referendum. *Government and Opposition*, 35(2), 189–210. doi:10.1111/1477-7053.00023

UNDP. (2002). *E-governance an impetus for the private sector the Zambian case*. Paper presented at the Asia-Pacific Development Information Programme Workshop entitled "Promoting Co-operation in Information and Communication Technologies Development", Kuala Lumpur and Penang, Malaysia.

UNDP. (2009). United Nations Development Programme, India: Democratic governance. Retrieved December 11, 2009, from http://www.undp.org.in/index.php?option =com_content&view=article &id=20&Itemid=255

United Nations. (2003). *UN global e-government survey 2003*. New York: Department of Economic and Social Affairs, Division for Public Administration and Development Management.

United Nations. (2004). *UN global e-government readiness report 2004: Towards access for opportunity*. New York: Department of Economic and Social Affairs, Division for Public Administration and Development Management.

United Nations. (2005). *UN global e-government readiness report 2005: From e-government to e-inclusion*. New York: Department of Economic and Social Affairs, Division for Public Administration and Development Management.

United Nations. (2008). *UN e-government survey 2008: From e-government to connected governance*. New York: Department of Economic and Social Affairs, Division for Public Administration and Development Management.

United Nations. (2004). *United Nations economic and social commission for Western Asia interim report. Foundations of ICT Indicators Database*. New York, NY: United Nations.

United Nations Department of Economic and Social Affairs (UNDESA). (2003). *World public sector report 2003: e-government at the Crossroads*.

United Nations Development Programme. (2004). *Human development report 2004: Cultural liberty in today's diverse world*. New York, NY: United Nations Development Programme.

United Nations Economic Commission for Europe (UNCE). (2008). *Guidebook on promoting good governance in public-private partnerships.* New York, NY; Geneva, Switzerland: United Nations.

United Nations. (2008). *UN e-government survey 2008: From e-government to connected governance.* United Nations e-Government Readiness Knowledge Base. Retrieved March 23, 2009, from http://www2.unpan.org/egovkb /global_reports/08report.htm

United Nations. (2008). *World urbanization prospects: The 2007 revision population database.* Retrieved September 12, 2008, from http://esa.un.org/unup

UNPAN. (2008). United Nations e-government survey: From e-government to connected governance. Retrieved November 2009, from http://unpan1.un.org/intradoc/groups/public/documents/UN/UNPAN028607.pdf

Uslaner, E. M. (2002). *The moral foundations of trust.* Cambridge, UK: Cambridge University Press.

van der Graft, P., & Svensson, J. (2006). Explaining e-democracy development: A quantitative empirical study. *Information Polity, 11*, 123–134.

van Dijk, J. (2004). *The deepening divide: Inequality in the information society.* London, UK: Sage.

van Dijk, J. (2006). *The network society* (2nd ed.). London, UK: Sage.

van Dijk, J., & Hacker, K. (2000). Summary. In Hacker, K., & van Dijk, J. (Eds.), *Digital democracy: Issues of theory and practice.* London, UK: Sage Publications.

van Dijk, J. (In press). E-government and democracy. In van Dijk, J., & Hacker, K. (Eds.), *Digital democracy in a network society.* Hampton Press.

Van Dijk, J., & Hindman, M. (In press). Network propeterties and demcoracy. In van Dijk, J., & Hacker, K. (Eds.), *Digital democracy in a network society.* Hampton Press.

van Dijk, J. (1996). Models of democracy-behind the design and use of new media in politics. *Javnost/The Public, 3*, 43-56.

van Dijk, J. (2002). A framework for digital divide research. *The Electronic Journal of Communication, 12*(1-2). Retrieved July 31, 2005, from http://www.cios.org/getfile/vandijk_v12n102

van Duersen, A., & van Dijk, J. (2009). Using the Internet: Skill related problems in users' online behavior. *Interacting with Computers, 21*, 333–340.

Van Parijs, P. (2004). *Cultural diversity versus economic solidarity.* Brussels, Belgium: De Boeck Universite.

Vedel, T. (2006). The idea of electronic democracy: Origins, visions, and questions. *Parliamentary Affairs, 59*(2), 226–235. doi:10.1093/pa/gsl005

Vegh, S. (2003). Classfying form of online activism: The case of the cyberprotests against the World Bank. In McCaughey, M., & Ayers, M. (Eds.), *Cyberactivism: Online activism in theory and practice* (pp. 71–93). New York, NY: Routledge.

Venkatesh, V., Morris, M. G., Davis, G. B., & Davis, F. D. (2003). User acceptance of Information Technology: Toward a unified view. *Management Information Systems Quarterly, 27*(3), 425–478.

Veraar, M. J. (2006). Identity formation in online social networking websites. In J. B. Germany (Ed.), *Person-to-person-to-person: Harnessing the political power of online social networks and user-generated content* (pp. 53-58). GW's Institute for Politics, Democracy & the Internet.

Viera, J. D. (1988). Images as property. In Gross, L., Katz, J. S., & Ruby, J. (Eds.), *Image ethics: The moral rights of subjects in photographs, film, and television.* New York, NY: Oxford University Press.

Volken, T. (2002). Elements of trust: The cultural dimensions of internet diffusion revisited. *Electronic Journal of Sociology,* Retrieved March 10, 2007, from http://epe.lac-bac.gc.ca/100/201/300/ejofsociology/2005/01/volken.html

Volkmer, I. (2003). The global network society and the global public sphere. *Development, 46*(1), 9–16. doi:10.1177/1011637003046001566

Vromen, A. (2007). Australian young people's particpatory practices and Internet use. *Information Communication and Society, 10*, 48–68. doi:10.1080/13691180701193044

Walzer, M. (1992). The civil society argument. In Mouffe, C. (Ed.), *Dimensions of radical democracy: Pluralism, citizenship, community.* London, UK: Verso.

Ward, S. J. A. (2005). Journalism ethics from the public's point of view. *Journalism Studies, 6*(3), 315–330. doi:10.1080/14616700500131901

Warkentin, M., Gefen, D., Pavlou, P., & Rose, G. (2002). Encouraging citizen adoption of e-government by building trust. *Electronic Markets, 12,* 157–162. doi:10.1080/101967802320245929

Warren, S. D., & Brandeis, L. D. (1890). The right to privacy. *Harvard Law Review, 6*(5), 1–23.

Watson, R. T., & Mundy, B. (2001). A strategic perspective of electronic democracy. *Communications of the ACM, 44*(1), 27–30. doi:10.1145/357489.357499

Weerakkody, V., & Dhillon, G. (2008). Moving from e-government to t-government: A study of process reengineering challenges in a U.K. local authority context. *International Journal of Electronic Government Research, 4*(4), 1–16. doi:10.4018/jegr.2008100101

Weimann, G. (2006). New terrorism, new media. In *Terror on the Internet: The new arena, the new challenges* (pp. 15–32). Washington, DC: United States Institute of Peace Press.

Wellman, B., & Haythornwaite, C. (2002). The Internet in everyday life: An introduction. In Wellman, B., & Haythornwaite, C. (Eds.), *The Internet in everyday life* (pp. 3–41). Oxford, UK: Blackwell Publishing.

West, D. M. (2004). E-government and the transformation of service delivery and citizen attitudes. *Public Administration Review, 64*(1), 15–27. doi:10.1111/j.1540-6210.2004.00343.x

West, D. M. (2000). *Assessing e-government: The Internet, democracy, and service delivery by state and federal governments.* Retrieved March 2, 2007, from http://www.insidepolitics.org/egovtreport00.html

West, D. M. (2002). *Global e government 2002.* Retrieved from http://www.insidepolitics.org/egovt02int.PDF

West, D. M. (2003). *Global e-government.* Retrieved March 3, 2007, from http://www.insidepolitics.org/egovt03int.pdf

West, D. M. (2008). *Global e-government 2008.* Retrieved from http://www.brookings.edu/reports/2008/0817_egovernment_west.aspx

White, H. (1980). A heteroskedasticity-consistent covariance matrix estimator and a direct test for heteroskedasticity. *Econometrica, 48*(4), 817–838. doi:10.2307/1912934

White House. (2009a). *The White House: President Barack Obama.* Retrieved from http://wwwhttp://www.whitehouse.gov/.govtrack.us/congress/bill.xpd?bill=s110-2321

White House. (2009b). *The Obama-Biden plan.* Retrieved from http://change.gov/agenda/technology_agenda/

Whitman, J. Q. (2004). The two western cultures of privacy: Dignity versus liberty. *The Yale Law Journal, 113*(1153), 1151–1221. doi:10.2307/4135723

Wilhelm, A. G. (2000). *Democracy in the digital age: Challenges to political life in cyberspace.* New York, NY: Routledge.

Wilhelm, A. G. (2000). Virtual sounding boards: How deliberative is online political discussion? In Hague, B. N., & Loader, B. (Eds.), *Digital democracy: Discourse and decision making in the information age* (pp. 154–178). London, UK: Routledge.

Wilkins, L., & Brennen, B. (2004). Conflicted interests, contested terrain: Journalism ethics codes then and now. *Journalism Studies, 5*(3), 297–309. doi:10.1080/1461670042000246061

Wilkinson, J. S. (2008). IPTV: Streaming media. In Grant, A. E., & Meadows, J. H. (Eds.), *Communication technology update and fundamentals* (11th ed.). Boston, MA: Focal Press, Elsevier.

Wilkund, H. (2005). A Habermasian analysis of the deliberative democratic potential of ICT-enabled services in Swedish municipalities. *New Media & Society, 7*(5), 701–723. doi:10.1177/1461444805056013

Williamson, A. (2006). *Disruptive spaces and transformative praxis: Reclaiming community voices through electronic democracy.* Paper presented at the Community Informatics Research Network Conference, Prato, Italy.

Wingmore, H. J. A. (1913). *The principles of judicial proof as given by logic, psychology, and general experience and illustrated in judicial trials.* Boston, MA: Little Brown.

Witschge, T. (2004). Online deliberation: Possibilities of the Internet for deliberative democracy. In Shane, P. M. (Ed.), *Democracy online. The prospects for political renewal through the Internet* (pp. 109–122). London, UK: Routledge.

Witschge, T. (2002). *Online deliberation: Possibilities of the Internet for deliberative democracy.* Paper presented at the INSITES conference: Prospects for Electronic Democracy. Pittsburgh, Carnegie Mellon University. Retrieved April 24, 2010, from http://java.cs.vt.edu/public/projects/digitalgov/papers/onlinedeliberation_Nl.pdf

Witschge, T. (2008). Examining online public discourse in context: A mixed method approach. *Javnost - The Public, 15*(2), 75-92.

Wojcik, S. (2008). Les forums électroniques municipaux: Un espace délibératif inédit. *Hermes, 45,* 177–182.

Wood, A. F., & Smith, M. J. (2005). *Online communication: Linking technology, identity, and culture* (2nd ed.). Mahwah, NJ: Lawrence Erlbaum Associates, Publishers.

Woolgar, S. (2001). Configuring the user: The case of usability trials. *Sociological Review. Mongraph, 38,* 57–102.

World Bank Workshop. (2003). Reinventing government: Innovations in public sector reform using ICT. Retrieved on May 12, 2010, from www1.worldbank.org/publicsector/edevelopment.doc

World Bank. (2009). India country overview 2009. Retrieved Dec 11, 2009, from http://www.worldbank.org.in/WBSITE/ EXTERNAL/COUNTRIES/ SOUTHASIAEXT/INDIAEXTN/0, contentMDK:20195738~menuPK:295591 ~pagePK:141137~piPK:141127~theSitePK:295584,00.html

World Bank. (2009a). Governance in India, governance and public sector management in South Asia. Retrieved Dec 11, 2009, from http://go.worldbank.org/BNHP6XVL60

World Economic Forum. (WEF). (2007). *The networked readiness index.* Retrieved March 2, 2007, from http://www.weforum.org/pdf/gitr/rankings2007.pdf

World e-democracy forum. (2009). Germany: Political parties test unsuccessfully Obama method. Retrieved December 2009, from http://www.edemocracy-forum.com/2009/09/germany-election.html

World Values Study Group. (1994). *World values survey, 1984-93.* Ann Arbor, MI: Inter-university Consortium for Political and Social Research.

Wright, S. (2006a). Electrifying democracy? 10 years of policy and practice. *Parliamentary Affairs, 59*(2), 236–249. doi:10.1093/pa/gsl002

Wright, S. (2006b). Government-run online discussion for: moderation, censorship, and the shadow of control. *British Journal of Politics and International Relations, 8*(4), 550–568. doi:10.1111/j.1467-856X.2006.00247.x

Wright, S., & Street, J. (2007). Democracy, deliberation and design: The case of online discussion forum. *New Media & Society, 9*(5), 849–869. doi:10.1177/1461444807081230

Wright, S. (2005). Design matters: The political efficacy of government-run discussion forums. In Gibson, R., Oates, S., & Owen, D. (Eds.), *Civil society, democracy and the Internet: A comparative perspective* (pp. 80–99). London, UK: Routledge.

Wright, S., & Street, J. (2007). Democracy, deliberation and design: The case of online discussion forum. *New Media and Society.*

Yankelovich, D. (1991). *Coming to judgment: Making democracy work in a complex world.* Syracuse, NY: Syracuse University Press.

Young, I. M. (1990). *Justice and the politics of difference.* Princeton, NJ: Princeton University Press.

Young, I. M. (2002). *Inclusion and democracy.* Oxford, UK: Oxford University Press. doi:10.1093/0198297556.001.0001

Young, I. M. (1996). Communication and the other: Beyond deliberative democracy. In Benhabib, S. (Ed.), *Democracy and difference: Contesting the boundaries of the political* (pp. 120–135). Princetown University Press.

Young, I. M. (1999). Difference as a resource for democratic communication. In Bohman, J., & Rehg, W. (Eds.), *Deliberative democracy* (pp. 387–398). Cambridge, MA: MIT Press.

Zak, P. J., & Knack, S. (2001). Trust and growth. *The Economic Journal, 111,* 295–321. doi:10.1111/1468-0297.00609

Zetter, K. (2009). *Nation's first open source election software released.* Retrieved December 1, 2009, from http://www.wired.com/threatlevel/2009/10/open-source/

Zinnbauer, D. (2001). Internet, civil society and global governance: The neglected political dimension of the digital divide. *Information & Security, 7,* 45–64.

About the Contributors

Robert Cropf is an associate professor and the chair of the Department of Public Policy Studies at Saint Louis University. His recent publications include "Creating an Accelerated Joint BA-MPA Degree Program for Adult Learners" in the *Journal of Public Affairs Education* (Spring/Summer 2007) coauthored with Jennifer Kohler, and E-Government in Saudi Arabia: Between Promise and Reality" in the *International Journal of Electronic Government Research* (April-June 2008), coauthored with Maher Al-Fakhri, Patrick Kelly, and Gary Higgs. His textbook *Public Administration in the 21ˢᵗ Century* was published by Pearson-Longman in 2007. His research interests include e-government and e-democracy, urban government and politics, and public administration pedagogical theory.

William S. Krummenacher is head of academic programs for the Center for Sustainability and adjunct assistant professor of Public Policy Studies at Saint Louis University. His recent works include "Déjà vu All Over Again – Charter Reform Fails" in *More Than Mayor or Manager: Campaigns to Change Form of Government in America's Large Cities* coauthored with Todd Swanstrom and Robert Cropf, and "Regional System of Greenways: If You Can Make It In St. Louis, You Can Make It Anywhere" coauthored with Todd Swanstrom and Mark Tranel in the *National Civic Review*. His research interests include sustainability, regional governance, civic engagement and e-democracy.

* * *

Lori Anderson teaches in the Management Department at Radford University in Radford Virginia in the USA. She received her PhD from Virginia Tech. Prior to joining the academy, Lori directed and led organizations in the private and public sectors. Her research investigates governance across the public and private sectors.

Sylvia Archmann (AT) is a Seconded National Expert in the Unit on Public Management and Comparative Public Administration in EIPA (European Institute for Public Organisation, the Netherlands) since 2005, providing training, consultancy and research. She has a Master's degree in economics and informatics from the University of Vienna (Austria). She joined the Austrian civil service as an IT specialist in 1980. During her professional career to date, she has worked in various fields of public administration (including e-government, change management and reform) for several ministries and the Federal Chancellery in Austria. Before joining EIPA, she was the Director of the unit in charge of running the award-winning internet platform HELP (www.help.gv.at). She is a founding member of the IPSG Group (Innovative Public Services Group under the umbrella of EUPAN), involved in and leading projects on performance indicators and benchmarking. She was the Austrian representative for several OECD-PUMA (Public Management) projects such as the Strengthening Citizen-Government Connections working group. She also was the project leader of the Modinis Study on Interoperability on Local and Regional Level in e-government (within the EU 2010-programme). Lecturing, providing keynotes and moderations at various EU and international conferences enriches her area of expertise.

Jenny Backhouse is an academic at the Australian Defence Force Academy campus of the University of New South Wales in Canberra, Australia. Jenny has built on her early career IT experience in industry and has now been teaching in a wide range of IT technologies over many years. Currently, she has a special interest in the emerging developments and social role of Information and Communication Technologies. This includes the e-government arena with particular reference to democratic processes, the digital divide and accessibility issues.

Patrick Bishop teaches political theory in the Department of Politics, Philosophy, and Religion at Lancaster University in the United Kingdom. Previously he was head of the Department of Politics and Public Policy at Griffith University and has held posts at Adelaide University, Charles Sturt University and visiting appointments at Virginia Polytechnic and State University; George Washington University and at the Centre for Public Policy, Melbourne University. His research is mainly in the area of democracy, public policy, and public management.

Rodica Gabriela Blidisel is Lecturer of Public Accounting at West University from Timisoara, Faculty of Economics and Business Administration. She earned her PhD in Public Sector Accounting at Faculty of Economics and Business Administration of West University of Timisoara. Her research activity in the field of *e-governance, public accounting, funding of public entities, International Public Sector Accounting Standards, and Public sector entities management control* is presented in 6 books, 51 research papers published in national and international journals. Rodica Blidisel is member of Chartered Certified Accountants and Authorised Accountants (CECCAR).

John J. Burbridge, Jr. is currently a professor of operations and supply chain management in the Martha and Spencer Love School of Business at Elon University. Prior to joining the faculty at Elon, he served as dean of the Business School for eleven years. He has published many articles in such journals as the International Journal of Electronic Government Research, Journal of Global Information Management, Journal of the Academy of Business Education, Human Systems Management, and Business Insights. John has also been a member of the faculty at Loyola College in Maryland, Rutgers University, and Lehigh University. While at Loyola, he was the Director of the David D. Lattanze Center for Executive Studies in Information Systems. He has a B.S., M.S, and PhD in industrial engineering from Lehigh and has worked in industry as a senior operations research analyst and a distribution executive for a global firm, the BOC Group.

Kelvin Joseph Bwalya is currently a lecturer and Researcher at the University of Botswana. He holds a Bachelors of Science and Technology in Electrical Engineering (Moscow Power Engineering Institute Technical University) and a Masters in Computer Science (Korea Advanced Institute of Science and Technology). He is also currently pursuing his PhD in Information Systems (University of Johannesburg). He has researched at Image and Video Systems lab in Daejon, South Korea. He has worked as Principal Investigator for a PEP/IDRC funded project for developing a database management system to capture poverty metrics from Mungule in Zambia to the policymakers and other co-operating partners for informed decision-making. Currently, he is a team leader at the Tertiary Education Council for accreditation team tasked with reviewing Information Technology programmes offered at tertiary institutions in Botswana. He is also a technical project manager for a project aimed at developing a prototype SADC labour market information system. Kelvin has published extensively in the field of Information Systems in reputable journals worldwide. Email: Kelvin.Bwalya@mopipi.ub.bw

Jayoti Das is a Professor of Economics in the Martha and Spencer Love School of Business at Elon University. Her research interests are international trade and economic development, global business, and industrial organization. She has recently published in the *Journal of International Business Studies*, *Applied Economics Letters, Tourism Economics,* and *Challenge,* among others. Currently her research involves issues surrounding corruption, terrorism, and diversity and how it impacts businesses and economic development. She holds a Masters and a PhD in Economics from the University of Cincinnati. Prior to joining Elon, she was a visiting faculty at Kenyon College and Marquette University.

Cassandra E. DiRienzo is an Associate Professor of Economics and the Associate Dean in the Martha and Spencer Love School of Business at Elon University. She holds an ME and PhD in Economics from North Carolina State University. Her research interests are applications of econometrics and nonparametric statistics to global economic and business issues such as corruption, terrorism, tourism, environmental protection, and diversity. She has published in *Journal of International Business Studies*, *Applied Economics Letters, Tourism Economics, Journal of Travel Research, The International Journal of Business and Finance Research, Journal of Development and Economics,* and *Challenge,* among others.

Bradley C. Freeman (PhD, Syracuse, 2004) is an Assistant Professor in the Broadcast & Cinema Studies department at the Wee Kim Wee School of Communication & Information at Nanyang Technological University (NTU) in Singapore. His research interests include community and campus radio, popular culture, political communication, international communication, media credibility, and sound design. He previously served as Editorial Assistant for the research publication *Communication Research*.

Jacques DM Gimeno is a professor at the Institute of Political Economy of the University of Asia & the Pacific and at the De La Salle University, Manila in the Philippines. She is also currently a consultant to the government of the Republic of the Philippines. Her primary research areas are in cyberculture, human rights, political communication, and sustainable development.

Kenneth L. Hacker (Ph.D., University of Oregon) is Professor of Communication Studies at New Mexico State University. He co-edited the book (with Jan van Dijk) *Digital Democracy: Issues of Theory and Practice* (Sage, 2000) and is currently editing (Jan van Dijk,co-editor) a second volume on digital democracy (*Digital Democracy in a Network Society*, Hampton Press). His research interests include national security and communication, political images in campaign communication, and the use of new media for political dialogue.

Just Castillo Iglesias joined the European Institute of Public Administration in 2007. Since then, he has been working on e-government related issues, Information and Communication Technologies in the public sphere, and the challenges of today's public administration. He has authored and co-authored a number of articles published in e-government-related journals and magazines. He holds a Bachelor's degree in Political Science and Administration from the Universitat Pompeu Fabra in Barcelona, a Master's degree in European Studies with specialization in European International Politics from Maastricht University, and a Master's degree in East Asian Studies with specialization in East Asian Societies and International Relations from the Universitat Oberta de Catalunya.

Euripidis Loukis is Assistant Professor of Information Systems and Decision Support Systems at the Department of Information and Communication Systems Engineering, University of the Aegean. He also teaches e-government at the National Academy of Public Administration. Formerly he has been Information Systems Advisor at the Ministry to the Presidency of the Government of Greece, Technical Director of the Program of Modernization of Greek Public Administration of the Second Community Support Framework and National Representative of Greece in the programs 'Telematics' and 'IDA' (Interchange of Data between Administrations) of the European Union. He has participated in many international research programs in the areas of e-government, e-participation and ICT business value.

Kristen Kim Loutzenhiser is an Assistant Professor in Public Administration. She started teaching the MPA program for Troy University in January 2010. She is based out of Troy University's Tampa site and teaches courses in Organizational Behavior, Program Evaluation, Public Finance, Foundations in Public Administration, and Organizational Theory. She has written about succession planning, diversity in public administration, representative government, and public service delivery amidst multiple local governments and special districts. Loutzenhiser currently serves on the Board of Directors for the Sun Coast chapter of the American Society of Public Administration. Loutzenhiser has been an Executive Director for various housing and community development corporations, the urban league and evaluated government and nonprofit programs. Loutzenhiser has also managed state and county-wise political campaigns, conducted survey research, exit polls, and strategic plans.

Laurence Monnoyer-Smith gives lectures on technology assessment and participatory democracy at the University of Technology of Compiègne, France. Her work is focused on the uses of ICT in politics in order to enhance political participation: electronic voting, deliberation platforms, and participatory procedures. She is currently animating a research team on an international comparison of deliberative processes on environmental issues financed by the French ministry of ecology and sustainable development. Her next book to be published is called *Communication and Deliberation: technological challenges and transformation of citizenship* (in French, Hermes Publishing).

Eric L. Morgan (PhD University of Massachusetts) is an Associate Professor of Communication Studies at New Mexico State University. His research interests include intercultural communication, international communication, and environmental communication. He has co-authored several works with Dr. Hacker on issues concerning digital democracy as well as the communication dimensions of genomics and ethnicity.

Joshua C. Nyirenda, MPA, is a doctoral candidate in public policy analysis in the Department of Public Policy Studies at St. Louis University, St. Louis MO. Nyirenda received his MPA from Southern Illinois University at Edwardsville and has a BA in Development Studies from the University of Zambia. In addition to e-governance and e-government issues, Nyirenda's research interests include among others, Geographical Information Systems, GIS applications in government, and the use of technology to increase political participation and enhance democratic processes. He has served and continues to serve as peer reviewer for a number of academic journals.

Adina Simona Popa is Lecturer in the field of Accounting, Financial Analysis and Economics at the University "Eftimie Murgu" of Reşiţa, Department of Electrical, Economical and Computer Science Engineering. She earned her PhD in Accounting from the Economics and Business Administration Faculty of West University of Timisoara. Her research topics include financial accounting and reporting, international accounting, corporate governance, e-governance and business administration. Her academic record includes articles published in national and international journals, books, conference presentations, and research grants. She is member of the European Accounting Association, the International Association for Accounting Education & Research and of Romanian Body of Chartered Certified Accountants and Authorised Accountants (CECCAR).

Veena Raman teaches at the Pennsylvania State University. Her research centers around the many ways citizens use Information Technologies to engage with governments to get access to services and information, to deliberate and to protest. She teaches courses on new media and democracy, globalization, ethical issues surrounding new technologies, the cultural implications of new media technologies, and the role of Information Technologies in facilitating civic engagement and participatory democracy.

Adriana Tiron Tudor is Professor of Public Accounting and Financial Audit at the Babes-Bolyai University. She is member of the Superior Council of the Romanian Body of Chartered Certified Accountants and Authorised Accountants (CECCAR), Chamber of Financial Auditors (CAFR) from Romania and represents CECCAR in FEE Public Sector Committee. Her research activity in field of public sector accounting, financial accounting and reporting, consolidated financial statements and audit, is presented in 9 books, 50 research papers published in national and international journals. Professor Adriana Tiron Tudor is project manager of over 7 research programs earned within national and international competition and she is member in scientific committee of some international and national conferences and journals.

Nektaria Tserpeli holds a degree from the Faculty of Law of the Kapodistrian University of Athens. She also has a specialization in media and communication industry, and her research interests comprise privacy issues and terms of use of Web 2.0 social media. During the last years she has worked on issues pertaining to the application of Web technologies in legal practices and specifically in the formalization of legal concepts to specific semantics for the argument visualization of legal debates along the legislative process lifecycle.

Alexander Xenakis belongs to the new academic interdisciplinary field that results from the applications of the information society. He is an Economist, Political Scientist and his Doctoral thesis 'Electronic voting in the United Kingdom' was supervised by Professor Ann Macintosh (Professor of E-governance) at Edinburgh Napier University. He teaches in the Postgraduate program 'Virtual Communities' of the Department of Psychology of Panteion University. He has taken part in European research projects in the area of e-participation, has been a Reviewer for FP7 in SSH Program and an expert Consultant for the Hellenic Ministry of Electronic Governance.

Index

A

academics 62
Africa West Coast Cable (AWCC) 238
Age of Reasoning 4
American journalism 123
Aristotle 3, 33

B

Baby Boomers 278, 281, 283
bench strength 281
bloggers 127, 128, 130, 131, 132, 138
blogging 116, 117, 127, 128, 131, 132, 135, 138
blogosphere 62, 66, 68
blogs 3, 7, 11, 13, 33, 75, 95, 102, 277, 280, 282
Botswana 229, 230, 231, 232, 233, 234, 235, 236, 237, 238, 239, 240, 241
Botswana Telecommunications Authority (BTA) 234, 235
Botswana Telecommunications Company (BTC) 234, 235, 237, 238
British Broadcasting Commission (BBC) 149
broadcast technologies 3
bureaucracy model 243
Business-to-Government (B2G) 146

C

car rental firms 57
cell phones 3, 93, 97, 99
Center for Democracy & Technology (CDT) 120
chat rooms 75

citizen participation model 243, 244
citizen to citizen (C2C) 148
civic engagement 144, 209, 212, 213, 216, 217, 226, 227
civic networks 72, 73, 86
civic software 40
CIVICUS 209, 227
Civil Liberties (CL) 181
civil rights 174, 181, 188
civil society 1-6, 10, 11, 12, 13, 16, 21, 25, 29-34, 76, 77, 87, 176, 188, 189, 190, 194, 207-228
classical model of public management 243
Clinger-Cohen Act 278
co-centric circles 167
collaboration 201
communication 116, 117, 120, 125, 126, 128, 130, 131, 132, 133, 136, 137, 173, 175, 176, 178, 180, 181, 189, 195, 196, 204
communication typology 52
communicative action 117, 118, 119, 120, 132, 134, 135
Community Access Centers (CAC) 237
computer-based functional literacy (CBFL) 78
computer supported arguments 156
Computer Supported Argument Visualization (CSAV) 156, 158, 159, 160, 161, 162, 167, 168, 170, 171
Corruption Perceptions Index (CPI) 234
Critical Discourse Analysis (DCA) 37, 38
cultural barriers 80
cyberactivism 120
cyber reality 56
cyberspace 60, 124

D

decision makers 73, 75
deindividuation 125
Deleuze, Gilles 35, 36, 39, 40, 41, 42, 43, 45, 47, 49, 50, 51
deliberation theorists 35
deliberative machines 35, 36, 39, 40, 42, 43, 44, 45
deliberative paradigm 35, 36
democratic decision-making structures 59
democratic engagement 148
dependent variable 263, 264
digital democracy 92, 93, 94, 95, 96, 105, 106, 110, 111, 114
Digital Divide 93, 94, 100, 109, 110, 111, 114, 212
digital networks 74

E

e-activism 144
Eastern Africa Submarine Cable System (EASSy) 235, 238
e-business 141, 144, 146, 147, 148, 149, 150, 155
e-Citizens 277, 279
e-citizenship 38, 46
e-Collector 277
e-Communication 280
economic development 173, 182, 183, 185, 186, 187, 188
e-consultation 144, 145, 153, 162, 167
e-consultation tools 145
e-deliberation 37, 39, 40
e-democracy 1-10, 13, 15-34, 52, 53, 57-75, 86, 87, 92-96, 104, 106, 109, 110, 112, 144-149, 152-155, 173, 229, 230-241, 245, 248, 260
e-Disclosure 242, 245, 247, 252, 253, 260, 265
e-engagement 144
E-financial reporting 260, 273
e-governance 207
e-governance readiness 208, 215, 216, 219, 225
e-government adoption 174, 188

e-government readiness index (EGOV) 178, 179, 182, 183, 184, 185, 187, 190
e-governments 1, 6, 13, 14, 15, 16, 17, 20, 24, 52-57, 60-70, 92-98, 101, 102, 104, 107-112, 115, 141, 144-148, 151-155, 173-206, 229, 230, 231, 233, 234, 236, 238-241, 245, 246, 252, 253, 254, 260, 265, 273, 276-286
e-government usage 173, 174, 187, 188, 189
eInclusion 196, 197, 198, 202, 204, 205
e-inclusion policies 195
e-input 145
electronic ballots 79
electronic barriers 200
electronic channels 203
electronic media 141
electronic participation (e-participation) 141, 142, 143, 144, 145, 146, 147, 148, 149, 150, 152, 153, 154, 155
e-Manager 277
empowerment 198, 206
Enlightenment period 3, 4, 5
e-participation 1, 156, 157, 158, 168, 169, 171
e-participatory initiatives 145
e-petitions 59, 62, 145
e-Planner 277
e-Players 277
e-Public Servants 277
e-Services 245, 247, 260, 264
ethical journalism 123, 127
ethics 116, 117, 122, 123, 127, 128, 131, 132, 133, 134, 135, 136, 137
e-Transactions 245
EU governments 197
European eGovernment 195, 200, 201, 204, 205

F

Facebook 1, 95, 99, 103, 106, 151, 175
face-to-face 116, 125
Feminists 38
Foucault, Michel 35, 36, 38, 41, 42, 45, 47
freedom of expression 117, 120, 121, 124, 126, 133, 134, 136
freedom of the press 124, 133
French literature 37

G

gaming 95
Generation X 277, 278
Global Internet Liberty Campaign (GILC) 120
globalization 277, 283, 285
global positioning systems (GPS) 97
governance bureaucracy model 243
government services 173, 176, 180, 189, 190, 193
grass root organizations 175
Gross Domestic Product (GDP) 182, 183
groupware 152

H

Habermasian theory 38
Highly Indebted Poor Countries (HIPC) 213, 228
hotel chains 57
human communication 116, 132, 133
human resources information systems (HRIS) 282
human rights 116, 117, 118, 119, 120, 121, 126, 127, 128, 129, 130, 131, 132, 133, 135, 140
human rights violations 117, 121, 131, 140

I

Index of Economic Freedom (EFI) 182, 183
information and communication technologies (ICT) 1-32, 36, 52, 53, 61-67, 72, 73, 74, 77-81, 84, 85, 86, 91, 141, 142, 143, 146, 148, 149, 150, 152-155, 157, 170, 173, 174, 175, 182, 188, 195-201, 204, 205, 207, 208, 211-241, 245, 246, 253, 254, 260, 273
information and communication technology (ICT) tools 142, 148
information management model 243, 244
information technology (IT) 177, 190, 276, 278, 280, 281, 282, 283, 284
information technology (IT) knowledge 77
infrastructure 201
instant messaging (IM) 97
Internet disclosure index (IDI) 262, 263, 264
interoperability 199, 200, 201, 206

issue-based information systems (IBIS) 156, 157, 158, 159, 160, 162, 168, 169, 170

J

journalists 121, 122, 123, 126, 127, 128, 131, 132, 134

K

knowledge societies 196

L

Law Association of Zambia (LAZ) 222
legislation 156, 158, 159, 160, 161, 162, 168, 169, 170, 171
less developed countries (LDCs) 213
LEX-IS project 158, 162
LinkedIn 1
lobbyists 62, 63, 69
local public authorities (LPA) 242, 243, 247, 252, 258, 259, 260, 261, 262, 263, 264, 265, 266, 267, 268, 269, 270, 271

M

macro-political systems 75
managed e-citizenship 38
mass media 96, 97, 98, 101, 103, 105, 107, 108, 110, 111, 112
media ethics 117, 127
media technologies 92
Meetup 95
mobile phones 93
Motion Pictures Association of America (MPAA) 129, 140
Multi-Party Democracy (MMD) 221, 222
MySpace 1, 40, 95, 103

N

National Electronic System (NES) 261
networking 175, 180, 188, 196, 201
network socities 98
New Economic Recovery Program (NERP) 221
new media 92, 93, 94, 95, 96, 97, 98, 99, 101, 102, 103, 104, 105, 106, 107, 108, 109, 110, 112, 115

new media networking (NMN) 92, 93, 94, 95, 96, 97, 98, 99, 100, 101, 102, 103, 104, 105, 106, 107, 108, 109, 110, 111, 112, 113

new media technologies 73

New Public Management 279, 280

new public management (NPM) model 243, 244

non-governmental organizations (NGO) 2, 149

O

Oasis Forum 222

Office of Electronic Government 278

offline worlds 80

online businesses 148, 149

online databases 53

online forums 148, 150, 151, 152, 154

online publications 53

online services 199, 201

online texts 38

Ordinary Least Squares (OLS) 184

P

panoptism 41

Parliament 157, 158, 160, 161, 162, 167, 169, 171

participatory democracy 141, 143, 147, 148

perceived ease of use (PEU) 167

perceived usefulness (PU) 167, 177

philosophers 35, 36

photography 123, 135

photo sharing 277

political communication 53, 62, 63, 67

political inefficiency 180

political parties 156, 158, 161, 162, 167, 169

Political Rights (PR) 181

privacy 117, 118, 121, 123, 124, 127, 132, 133, 134, 135, 137, 139

proxy of trust 173

public debate 35, 38, 45, 48

Public Governance model (PGM) 243, 244

public participation 156, 157, 158, 159, 170, 171

public policy 158, 159

public-private sector partnerships (PPPs) 238

public sector 55, 56, 60

public servants 59, 62

public services 197, 199, 202, 203, 244, 245, 246, 247, 253, 254, 255, 257, 258, 260, 264, 268, 269

public spaces 74, 84

public spheres 1-23, 26-34, 72, 73, 74, 75, 76, 77, 80, 83-91, 173, 174, 175, 191

R

radio 40

real life 116, 125

representative democracy 156, 157

S

Scatter Plot Analysis 217

service delivery 57, 70

smart phones 93, 95, 96, 97

social audits 79

social behavior 94

social capital 175, 176, 178, 179, 188, 189, 190, 192

social communications 141

social facilitation 125

social groups 76, 79

social loafing 125, 135

social media 1, 3, 93, 95, 98, 99, 107, 112, 113, 151

social networking 38, 40, 95, 97, 99, 103, 106, 107, 109, 114, 142, 151, 155, 175

social networking sites 151

social networking websites 40

social networks 175, 179, 277, 284

social relationships 76

societal paradigm 61

socio-economic factors 173

Southern African Development Community (SADC) 234, 240

Sub-Saharan Africa (SSA) 210, 213, 216, 217, 221, 226

Sustainable Access in Rural India (SARI) 78

synthetic visualization 161, 162, 167

T

technical infrastructure 174

technological convergence 40

Technology Acceptance Model (TAM) 157,
        158, 167, 169
television 40
Terrestrial Trunk Radio Masts (TETRA) 160
texting 95, 99
text messaging 3, 277
Twitter 1, 93, 95, 98, 99, 102, 112

U

United National Independence Party (UNIP)
        221, 222
United Nations Department of Economic and
        Social Affairs (UNDESA) 174, 193

V

value generalization 119
Very Small Aperture Terminals (VSAT) 237,
        238
videobloggers 117, 126, 127, 128, 130, 132
videoblogging 117, 119, 128, 132, 133, 134
virtual public spheres (VPS) 1, 2, 3, 6, 7, 8,
        9, 10, 13, 15, 16, 17, 18, 19, 20, 21, 22,
        23, 26, 27, 29, 30, 31, 73, 230, 231, 232,
        233, 234, 235, 236, 238
virtual reality 116
virtual spheres 79, 83, 86, 90

virtual worlds 277
visualization 156, 157, 158, 159, 160, 161,
        162, 163, 164, 165, 166, 167, 168, 169,
        170

W

Web 2.0 40, 74, 277, 278, 280, 281
web-based surveys 62
West Africa Festoon System (WAFS) 238
Wiki-government 40
wikis 277, 282
Working Party Group Promotion of Information
        Technology 261
World Wide Web (WWW) 175

Y

YouTube 116, 117, 118, 119, 121, 125, 126,
        128, 129, 130, 132, 134, 136, 151

Z

Zambia 217, 219, 221, 222, 223, 224, 225,
        226, 227, 228,
Zambia Confederation of Trade Union (ZCTU)
        221

GREYSCALE

BIN TRAVELER FORM

Cut By _Miray_ Qty _20_ Date _06.16_

Scanned By_____ Qty_____ Date_____

Scanned Batch IDs

_____ _____ _____

Notes / Exception

_____

_____

_____

_____

_____